Communications
in Computer and Information Science   **791**

Commenced Publication in 2007
Founding and Former Series Editors:
Alfredo Cuzzocrea, Xiaoyong Du, Orhun Kara, Ting Liu, Dominik Ślęzak,
and Xiaokang Yang

More information about this series at http://www.springer.com/series/7899

Cheng He · Hongwei Mo
Linqiang Pan · Yuxin Zhao (Eds.)

Bio-inspired Computing: Theories and Applications

12th International Conference, BIC-TA 2017
Harbin, China, December 1–3, 2017
Proceedings

Editors
Cheng He (ID)
School of Automation
Huazhong University of Science
and Technology
Wuhan
China

Hongwei Mo (ID)
Automation College
Harbin Engineering University
Harbin
China

Linqiang Pan (ID)
School of Automation
Huazhong University of Science
and Technology
Wuhan
China

Yuxin Zhao (ID)
Automation College
Harbin Engineering University
Harbin
China

ISSN 1865-0929   ISSN 1865-0937 (electronic)
Communications in Computer and Information Science
ISBN 978-981-10-7178-2   ISBN 978-981-10-7179-9 (eBook)
https://doi.org/10.1007/978-981-10-7179-9

Library of Congress Control Number: 2017959592

Printed on acid-free paper

This Springer imprint is published by Springer Nature
The registered company is Springer Nature Singapore Pte Ltd.
The registered company address is: 152 Beach Road, #21-01/04 Gateway East, Singapore 189721, Singapore

Preface

Bio-inspired computing is a field of study that abstracts computing ideas (data structures, operations with data, ways to control operations, computing models, etc.) from the living phenomena or biological systems such as evolution, cells, tissues, neural networks, immune system, and ant colonies. Bio-Inspired Computing: Theories and Applications (BIC-TA) is a series of conferences that aims to bring together researchers working in the main areas of natural computing inspired from biology, for presenting their recent results, exchanging ideas, and cooperating in a friendly framework.

Since 2006, the conference has taken place at Wuhan (2006), Zhengzhou (2007), Adelaide (2008), Beijing (2009), Liverpool and Changsha (2010), Penang (2011), Gwalior (2012), Anhui (2013), Wuhan (2014), Anhui (2015), and Xi'an (2016). Following the success of previous editions, the 12th International Conference on Bio-Inspired Computing: Theories and Applications (BIC-TA 2017) was organized by Harbin Engineering University, during December 1–3, 2017.

BIC-TA 2017 attracted a wide spectrum of interesting research papers on various aspects of bio-inspired computing with a diverse range of theories and applications. In all, 50 papers were selected for the volume of *Communications in Computer and Information Science*.

We gratefully thank Harbin Engineering University, Huazhong University of Science and Technology, and Heilongjiang Society of Biomedical Engineering for extensive assistance in organizing the conference. We thank Siyuan Chen, Tong Pan, Lifang Xu, Wei Xu, Jing Zhang, Taosheng Zhang, and Haiyan Zhao for their help in collecting the final files of the papers and editing the volume. We also thank all the other volunteers, whose efforts ensured the smooth running of the conference.

The editors warmly thank the Program Committee members for their prompt and efficient support in reviewing the papers, and the authors for submitting their interesting papers.

Special thanks are due to Springer for their skilled cooperation in the timely production of these volumes.

September 2017

Cheng He
Hongwei Mo
Linqiang Pan
Yuxin Zhao

Organization

Steering Committee

Guangzhao Cui	Zhengzhou University of Light Industry, China
Kalyanmoy Deb	Indian Institute of Technology Kanpur, India
Miki Hirabayashi	National Institute of Information and Communications Technology (NICT), Japan
Joshua Knowles	University of Manchester, UK
Thom LaBean	North Carolina State University, USA
Jiuyong Li	University of South Australia, Australia
Kenli Li	University of Hunan, China
Giancarlo Mauri	Università di Milano-Bicocca, Italy
Yongli Mi	Hong Kong University of Science and Technology, Hong Kong, SAR China
Atulya K. Nagar	Liverpool Hope University, UK
Linqiang Pan	Huazhong University of Science and Technology, China
Gheorghe Păun	Romanian Academy, Bucharest, Romania
Mario J. Pérez-Jiménez	University of Seville, Spain
K.G. Subramanian	Universiti Sains Malaysia, Malaysia
Robinson Thamburaj	Madras Christian College, India
Jin Xu	Peking University, China
Hao Yan	Arizona State University, USA

Program Committee

Rosni Abdullah	Universiti Sains Malaysia, Malaysia
Muhammad Abulaish	King Saud University, Saudi Arabia
Andy Adamatzky	UK
Chang Wook Ahn	Sungkyunkwan University, South Korea
Adel Al-Jumaily	Uinversity of Technology Sydney, Australia
Jose Antonio Lozano	University of the Basque Country, Spain
Bahareh Asadi	Islamic Azad University Tabriz Branch, Iran
Eduard Babulak	EU CORDIS, Europe
Mehdi Bahrami	Rafsanjan University of Medical Sciences, Iran
Soumya Banerjee	Birla Institute of Technology Mesra, India
Jagdish Chand Bansal	ABV-Indian Institute of Information Technology and Managemment, India
Debnath Bhattacharyya	Heritage Institute of Technology, India
Monowar H. Bhuyan	Tezpur University, India
Kavita Burse	Truba Institute of Engineering and Information Technology, India
Stephen C.H. Leung	City University of Hong Kong, China

Shengxiang Yang	De Montfort University, UK
Zhixiang Yin	China
Umi Kalsom Yusof	University Sains Malaysia, Malaysia
Xuncai Zhang	China
Xingyi Zhang	Anhui University, China
Gexiang Zhang	Southwest Jiaotong University, China
Zexuan Zhu	Shenzhen University, China
Sotirios Ziavras	New Jersey Institute of Technology, USA

Sponsors

Harbin Engineering University
Huazhong University of Science and Technology
Heilongjiang Society of Biomedical Engineering

Contents

Logic Operation Model of the Complementer Based on Two-Domain DNA Strand Displacement

Wendan Xie[1], Changjun Zhou[1], Hui Lv[1], and Qiang Zhang[2(✉)]

[1] Key Laboratory of Advanced Design and Intelligent Computing,
Ministry of Education, Dalian University, Dalian, China
[2] School of Computer Science and Technology, Dalian University of Technology,
Dalian, China
zhangq30@gmail.com

Abstract. DNA strand replacement technology has the advantages of simple operation which makes it becomes a common method of DNA computing. A four bit binary number Complementer based on two-domain DNA strand displacement is proposed in this paper. It implements the function of converting binary code into complement code. Simulation experiment based on Visual DSD software is carried out. The simulation results show the correctness and feasibility of the logic model of the Complementer, and it makes useful exploration for further expanding the application of molecular logic circuit.

Keywords: Two-domain · DNA strand displacement · Compelmenter · Logic circuit

1 Introduction

With the development and progress of science, the society has developed into a highly information oriented society and computer has become an indispensable part of human life. In the second half of 20th Century, the traditional computer had a vigorous development, and the main reason is that the silicon chip is continuously updated. However, more and more information is stored with the development of big data. Due to the limitations of traditional silicon chip etching technology, the processing capacity of electronic computers is close to the limit, far from being able to meet the growing demand for large-scale computing such as the Hamilton path [1], human genetic information and other issues. The traditional computer has not been able to deal with these problems at a faster rate, so scientists have focused their attention on DNA computing [2]. DNA computing, a new computational model based on biochemical reaction [3], is based on DNA molecules and related biological enzymes as materials, which provides a new way to solve the NP-complete problem [4,5]. Some computational models constructed at the molecular level and their related theories have been validated [6,7].

In the field of nanoscience, DNA strand displacement reaction is not only an important application technology, but also a hot research direction [8,9]. The application of this technique has attracted the attention of researchers to achieve the task of the computer. The success of strand replacement reaction lies in the ingenious design of small fulcrum. Generally, there are 4–6 base sequences in the small pivot region [10], and the number of bases affects the rate of reaction, which increases exponentially with the increase of the number of bases. The strand replacement technique uses paste of molecular single strand, and reacts with input signal strand to release single strand product, which has three characteristics: self-initiation, sensitivity and accuracy. Hwang demonstrated a high specificity of the use of a DNA strand displacement-based probe on a grapheme field effect transistor (FET), single-nucleotide mismatch detection [11]. Saghatelian [12] built for the first time AND gate and forbidden gate. Molecular logic gates are the basis for the realization of molecular computers, and now a variety of DNA enzymes have been used to construct the logic model [13]. The logic gates of molecular description and the logic operations at the molecular level are realized. Its realization process is called molecular logic circuit [14,15]. Song [16] proposed architectures for the systematic construction of DNA circuits for analog computation based on DNA strand displacement.

DNA strand displacement technique has been used to construct a variety of molecular logic gate models. When constructing molecular logic cell model, we usually use single strand as input signal and double strands as gate structure. DNA strand displacement is a spontaneous reaction, and the whole process is completed by driving force between molecules, which takes use of the reaction between longer DNA single strand and part of the complementary double strands structure to replace the short strand of the original double strands molecular structure. There are many kinds of single strand structure, such as Two-domain strand proposed by Cardelli [17], Three-domain strand [18]. The simulation of the DNA strand displacement depends on the chemical reaction or Petri net conversion whose function is combining input signals and cross input signals. The structure of the signal must be fixed to assure that the gate is assembled into a larger circuit arbitrarily [17]. In addition to the numerical information, computer can deal with other information including a variety of symbols, text and images. Computer only recognizes the two states of 0 and 1 to transmit, process and store the binary digital information. In order to enable computer to facilitate the conduct of other relative add, subtract, multiply and divide relatively complex operations, numeric data must be encoded. The original code runs addition and subtraction, which is difficult to computer. In order to simplify this operation, original code is needed to convert complement.

A four bit binary number Complementer logic model based on two-domain DNA strand displacement is the first proposed in this paper, whose function is to be able to change the original code into complement and the numerical range is -15–15. The remaining of this article is organized as follows. The second part introduces the gate logic unit based on the two-domain strand displacement structure. Gates structure constructed in this paper can be combined with any of the circuit, the garbage product will not interfere with the active door, and the reactants are fully reacted. The third part introduces the simulation experiment. According to the logical relationship, the truth table is got, and then the Complementer logic circuit is constructed. The implementation of the Complementer logic circuit is accomplished by two-domain DNA strand displacement reactions. The processing speed of the Complementer based on the Two-domain strand replacement structure is fast, and the simulation results are verified by Visual DSD software. The fourth part summarizes the relevant work and future work.

2 Gate Based on Two-Domain DNA Strand Displacement

In this paper, two-domain DNA strand displacement structure is used to construct the logical model structure.

Two-domain DNA strand displacement only considers the single strand of the toehold domain t and the recognition domain. The toehold domain is a specific recognition site, which is used to identify the complementary sites in the double strands and combine the single strand with double strands. The long strand is used to represent the signal. The long single strand combines with the toehold domain of the double strands, and replaces the short single strand. Otherwise, there will not be a series of strand displacement reactions. Then the branch migration is carried out and the corresponding strand is replaced.

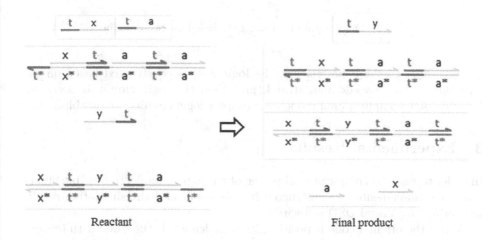

Reactant   Final product

Fig. 1. The 1 input-1 output gate based on two-domain

The most basic logic gates of the logic circuit are AND gate, NOT gate and OR gate. Some other composite doors are made up of these three basic logic gates. Based on Two-domain strand, join gate and convertor can simulate the chemical reaction process, which is similar with the logic gate of AND, OR, NOT. Therefore, they can be applied to construct 1 input-1 output gates, AND gates and other logic gates. Molecular structure as demonstrated in the Fig. 1. Single strand <t^ x> is the input signal and strand <t^ y> is the final output signal. The other single strands are the auxiliary signal strand in the whole reaction process and strand <a t^> is the medium that leads to the next strand replacement. Figure 2 is a Join gate of the 2 input-1 output, in which strand <t^ x> and <t^ y> are the input signal, strand <t^ z> is the output signal and strand <t^ a>, <z t^> are the auxiliary signal.

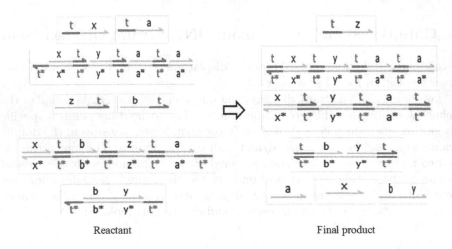

Reactant   Final product

Fig. 2. The 2 input -1 output gate based on two-domain

According to the logic relation, the logic gate is constructed based on the structure of the Two-domain strand, and then the logic circuit is designed. Finally, some computational models of complex logic circuits are established.

3   Experimental Results

In order to test the computational power of the logical model, a four bit binary number Complementer is constructed in this paper and the simulation results are verified by Visual DSD software.

When the original code is positive, its complement is the same with original code. When the original code is negative, the sign bit is immobile, the numerical bit is inverted ("1" turns into "0" or "0" becomes "1") and the lowest bit adds "1". If the original code is zero, the complement is itself [19]. The right digital of the first "1" (include the first "1") finding from the lowest bit to the highest bit are unchanged, and the left digital of the first "1" take inverse. The truth-table is shown in Table 1. A4 and S4 represent symbolic bit, A0 and S0 stand for the lowest bit, "0" represents "+", and "1" is a symbol of "-". According to the following Table 1, the logic circuit devised in this paper is illustrated in Fig. 3.

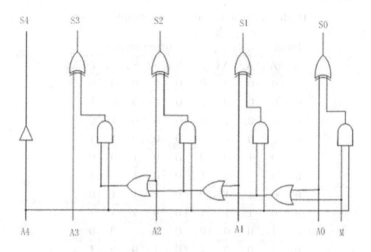

Fig. 3. Logic circuit of the Complementer

In Fig. 3, XOR gates are used to invert input data. However, the numerical inver-sion depends on whether output signal of the corresponding bit gate is "1" or not, and output signal of AND gate relies on output signal of OR gate which lower than AND gate. As can be seen from the Fig. 3, when the input signal A4 is "1", all AND gates will be open, and whether a bit is changed into "1" hinges on output signal of the previous OR gate. The input signal of M is always zero, and then output signal of the A0 remains unchanged. The higher bits are inverted or not, depending on the value of the input signal A0.

For example, when A0 = 1, output of the OR gate is "1", output signal of the A1 AND gate is "1", input signal of the A1 is reversed, output of the higher OR gates are al-ways "1", and the higher bit is inverted bit by bit. When A0 = 0, output of the OR gate is "0" and output of the A1 AND gate is "0". So that input signal of the A1 unchanged, and whether input signal of the A2 is reversed or not lies on input signal of the A1. Whether input signal of the A3 is inverted or not relies on input signal of the A2 and sign digit A4 is invariable. A4A3A2A1A0 is the input signal and S4S3S2S1S0 is the output signal.

All the operations in a computer are modulo operations [19]. The range of the positive number of the four bit binary value is 0–15. Since these numbers have a total of 16 numbers, the modulus is MOD16. Assuming that M is modular, if "a" and "b" satisfy a + b = M, then "a" and "b" complement each other. Here, a binary number is gave to verify correctness of the logic circuit molecular model of the Complementer, negative values (−10) [original] =11010, its complement (−10) = 10110. The number 6 is complement of the number 10 to modulo 16, and the sign bit is invariant. Visual DSD emulation results are shown in Fig. 4.

Figure 4 is the emulation results picture of the four bit binary code turn into complement. In this picture, the input signal is A4A3A2A1A0 = 11010 and the output signal is S4S3S2S1S0 = 10110. Here, the single strand <t^ A00> represents the "0" signal of the input signal A0, a single strand <t^ A01> stands for the "1" signal of the input signal A0, a single strand <t^ S00> delegates the

Table 1. Logic circuit of the complementer

A4	A3	A2	A1	A0	S4	S3	S2	S1	S0
0	0	0	0	0	0	0	0	0	0
0	0	0	0	1	0	0	0	0	1
0	0	0	1	0	0	0	0	1	0
0	0	0	1	1	0	0	0	1	1
0	0	1	0	0	0	0	1	0	0
0	0	1	0	1	0	0	1	0	1
0	0	1	1	0	0	0	1	1	0
0	0	1	1	1	0	0	1	1	1
0	1	0	0	0	0	1	0	0	0
0	1	0	0	1	0	1	0	0	1
0	1	0	1	0	0	1	0	1	0
0	1	0	1	1	0	1	0	1	1
0	1	1	0	0	0	1	1	0	0
0	1	1	0	1	0	1	1	0	1
0	1	1	1	0	0	1	1	1	0
0	1	1	1	1	0	1	1	1	1
1	0	0	0	1	1	1	1	1	1
1	0	0	1	0	1	1	1	1	0
1	0	0	1	1	1	1	1	0	1
1	0	1	0	0	1	1	1	0	0
1	0	1	0	1	1	1	0	1	1
1	0	1	1	0	1	1	0	1	0
1	0	1	1	1	1	1	0	0	1
1	1	0	0	0	1	1	0	0	0
1	1	0	0	1	1	0	1	1	1
1	1	0	1	0	1	0	1	1	0
1	1	0	1	1	1	0	1	0	1
1	1	1	0	0	1	0	1	0	0
1	1	1	0	1	1	0	0	1	1
1	1	1	1	0	1	0	0	1	0
1	1	1	1	1	1	0	0	0	1

"0" signal of the output signal S0, and a single strand <t^ S01> represents the "1" signal of the input signal S0. Other input and output signals are written in the same form as above. According to the simulation results in Fig. 4, it can be seen that the generation rate of the output signal strand is very fast and the input strand is fully reacted, which demonstrates the accuracy of the model.

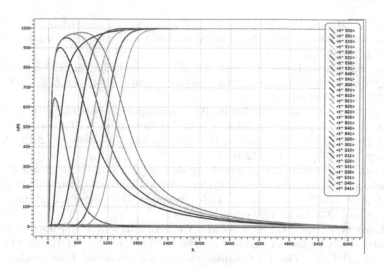

Fig. 4. Logic circuit of the complementer

4 Conclusions

Based on the Two-domain structure, the calculation model of basic gate circuit has been established and used to construct the Complementer for logic circuits. In this paper, the molecular model of the Complementer logic circuit has been verified through the simulation software Visual DSD. The results illustrate that the molecular model is feasible, and it is also shown that the whole strand substitution reaction is a completely autonomous process without any external force, which demonstrates the good computational power of strand displacement. The correctness of the model provides a basis for further research on the more complex logic structure by using the strand displacement technique.

Acknowledgments. This work is supported by the National Natural Science Foundation of China (Nos. 61772100, 61702070, 61672121, 61572093, 61402066, 61402067, 61370005, 31370778), the Program for Liaoning Innovative Research Team in University (No. LT2015002), the Basic Research Program of the Key Lab in Liaoning Province Educational Department (No. LZ2015004).

References

1. Adleman, L.M.: Molecular computation of solutions to combinatorial problems. Science **266**(5187), 1021–1024 (1994)
2. Jian, Z., Zhang, Z., Shi, Y., Li, X., Lin, H.: Linearly programmed DNA-based molecular computer operated on magnetic particle surface in test-tube. Sci. Bull. **49**(1), 17–22 (2004)
3. Zhang, D.Y., Turberfield, A.J., Yurke, B., Winfree, E.: Engineering entropy-driven reactions and networks catalyzed by DNA. Science **318**(5853), 1121 (2007)

4. Wang, Z., Huang, D., Meng, H., Tang, C.: A new fast algorithm for solving the minimum spanning tree problem based on DNA molecules computation. Biosyst. **114**(1), 1–7 (2013)

5. Wang, Z., Tan, J., Huang, D., Ren, Y., Ji, Z.: A biological algorithm to solve the assignment problem based on DNA molecules computation. Appl. Math. Comput. **244**(2), 183–190 (2014)

6. de Murieta, S.I., Rodríguez-Patón, A.: Probabilistic reasoning with a Bayesian DNA device based on strand displacement. In: Stefanovic, D., Turberfield, A. (eds.) DNA 2012. LNCS, vol. 7433, pp. 110–122. Springer, Heidelberg (2012). https://doi.org/10.1007/978-3-642-32208-2_9

7. Condon, A., Kirkpatrick, B., Maňuch, J.: Reachability bounds for chemical reaction networks and strand displacement systems. In: Stefanovic, D., Turberfield, A. (eds.) DNA 2012. LNCS, vol. 7433, pp. 43–57. Springer, Heidelberg (2012). https://doi.org/10.1007/978-3-642-32208-2_4

8. Pinheiro, A.V., Han, D., Shih, W.M., Yan, H.: Challenges and opportunities for structural DNA nanotechnology. Nat. Nanotechnol. **6**(12), 763–772 (2011)

9. Wei, B., Dai, M., Yin, P.: Complex shapes self-assembled from single-stranded DNA tiles. Nature **485**(7400), 623–626 (2012)

10. Zhang, D.Y.: Towards domain-based sequence design for DNA strand displacement reactions. In: Sakakibara, Y., Mi, Y. (eds.) DNA 2010. LNCS, vol. 6518, pp. 162–175. Springer, Heidelberg (2011). https://doi.org/10.1007/978-3-642-18305-8_15

11. Hwang, M.T., Landon, P.B., Lee, J., Choi, D., Mo, A.H., Glinsky, G., et al.: Highly specific SNP detection using 2D graphene electronics and DNA strand displacement. Proc. Natl. Acad. Sci. U.S.A. **113**(26), 7088 (2016)

12. Saghatelian, A., Volcker, N.H., Guckian, K.M., Lin, V.S., Ghadiri, M.R.: DNA-based photonic logic gates: AND, NAND, and INHIBIT. J. Am. Chem. Soc. **125**(2), 346–347 (2003)

13. Elbaz, J., Lioubashevski, O., Wang, F., Remacle, F., Levine, R.D., Willner, I.: DNA computing circuits using libraries of DNAzyme subunits. Nat. Nanotechnol. **5**(6), 417–422 (2010)

14. Kan, A., Sakai, Y., Shohda, K.I., Suyama, A.: A DNA based molecular logic gate capable of a variety of logical operations. Nat. Comput. **13**(4), 573–581 (2014)

15. Nishimura, T., Ogura, Y., Tanida, J.: Fluorescence resonance energy transfer-based mo-lecular logic circuit using a DNA scaffold. Appl. Phys. Lett. **101**(23), 233703 (2012)

16. Song, T., Garg, S., Mokhtar, R., Bui, H., Reif, J.: Analog computation by DNA strand displacement circuits. ACS Synth. Biol. **5**(8), 898 (2016)

17. Cardelli, L.: Two-domain DNA strand displacement. Math. Struct. Comput. Sci. **26**(2), 247–271 (2010)

18. Cardelli, L.: Strand algebras for DNA computing. Nat. Comput. **10**, 407–428 (2009). https://doi.org/10.1007/s11047-010-9236-7

19. Wang, M.: Principles of Computer Organization. Electronic Industry Press, South Norwalk (2001)

TS-Preemption Threshold and Priority Optimization for the Process Scheduling in Integrated Modular Avionics

Qianlin Zhou, Hui Lu$^{(\boxtimes)}$, Honglei Qin, Jinhua Shi, and Rongrong Zhou

School of Electronic and Information Engineering,
Beihang University, Beijing 100191, China
mluhui@vip.163.com

Abstract. Avionics is confronted with transitioning from a federated avionics architecture to an Integrated Modular Avionics (IMA) architecture. IMA architectures utilize shared, configurable computing, communication, and I/O resources to increase system scalability. Therefore, resources scheduling becomes a critical issue for IMA. This paper focuses on the process scheduling. We use preemption threshold scheduling strategy to improve process scheduling performance, and propose a two-stage tabu algorithm to optimize the preemption threshold and the priority respectively. Firstly, we investigate a convergence criterion to stop iteration of level-i busy period which is used to calculate the worse-case response time. Secondly, we propose the difference analysis method based on weight to evaluate the optimal schedule. Finally, we propose TS-preemption threshold and priority optimization algorithm to obtain the near-optimal assignment of the priority and the preemption threshold. The experiment results of different sizes of process scheduling problems illustrate the validity and effectivity of the algorithm.

Keywords: Integrated Modular Avionics · Process scheduling · Two-stage tabu algorithm · Evaluation method · Convergence analysis

1 Introduction

As a new generation of avionics system, IMA attracts more attentions because of the significant advantages compared with the traditional avionics [1,2]. IMA introduces the concept of partition to support one or more avionics applications and allow them execute independently to improve the stability of the system [3]. IMA dynamically dispatch system resources to partition and process. Therefore, the partition scheduling problem and process scheduling problem are critical to the performance of IMA. The partition scheduling, which is different from region division in many-objective optimization [4], aims at dispatching the time window of applications. One application in a partition can have numbers of processes. The process scheduling focuses on the better way to ensure the reliability of applications. Therefore, a high performance algorithm to schedule the process plays a critical role for IMA.

© Springer Nature Singapore Pte Ltd. 2017
C. He et al. (Eds.): BIC-TA 2017, CCIS 791, pp. 9–23, 2017.
https://doi.org/10.1007/978-981-10-7179-9_2

In fact, IMA is based on the ARINC 653 standard and inherits the characteristics of real-time operating systems. The design of the process scheduling can obtain experience from the real-time system. The process scheduling for real-time system includes fixed priority scheduling and non-fixed priority scheduling. The former has been widely used in varieties of real-time systems. It can be divided into three categories. They are fully preemptive [5,6], fully non-preemptive [5,7] and limited preemptive scheduling. There are many methods for the first two categories, like Rate-Monotonic (RM) algorithm [8,9] and Deadline-Monotonic (DM) algorithm [10]. As a kind of limited preemptive scheduling strategy, preemption threshold scheduling (PTS) [11] had been proved to have more advantages than fully preemptive and fully non-preemptive scheduling. It can improve the schedulability for a set of processes and achieve a reasonable use of the processor with reasonable preemption thresholds and priorities.

There are some discussions of PTS. Lehoczky [12] introduced the concept of the level-i busy period [13,14] to calculate the worse-case response time (WCRT) of the processes. Wang and Saksena [11] investigated some useful conclusions to guide the preemption threshold optimization, and proposed an algorithm to search a feasible assignment. Redell and Torngren [15] proposed a computational method of the exact worse-case response time for static priority scheduled tasks with offsets and jitter. Keskin et al. [16] presented a revised analysis for WCRT and extended PTS algorithm. Buttazzo et al. [17] further summarized the analysis method of WCRT.

However, there are some problems for the existing assignment algorithm. Firstly, only when $L(i)$, the length of the level-i busy period for process τ_i, is convergent can we calculate WCRT for process τ_i, Secondly, we cannot obtain the better solutions because of the lack of evaluation criteria for the performance of the assignments. Finally, the assignment obtained by the existing method [11] is not the global optimal solution, because the algorithm will terminate when a feasible assignment of the preemption threshold is obtained with given priorities.

In this paper, we use PTS to schedule processes in IMA. We focus on improving above problems and propose TS-preemption threshold and priority optimization algorithm (TPTPOA) to solve the assignment problem for preemption threshold and priority in PTS.

Firstly, we prove two conclusions of the convergence of $L(i)$ when the sum of the execution time and the blocking time meet specific conditions for process τ_i. In other conditions, we investigate a termination criterion for $L(i)$ to prevent the algorithm from getting stuck in an infinite loop.

Secondly, we propose an evaluation method to select the optimal preemption threshold with given priorities. A different weight is allocated to different process based on the difference between the deadline and WCRT. We calculate the fitness value of the arbitrary two assignments combined the weight and the quantification of the relative differences. Then we compare the better one with others and update the better one continually until all assignments are compared.

Thirdly, we propose the preemption threshold optimization algorithm with given priorities (PTOGP) to search the near-optimal assignments of the preemption threshold with given priorities by taking the assignment of the preemption threshold obtained by the existing algorithm [11] as initial minimum boundary. PTOGP uses Tabu search (TS) [18,19] or traversal search based on the size of the processes and obtains a better assignment of the preemption threshold.

Finally, we propose TPTPOA to search the global near-optimal assignments for the preemption threshold and the priority. Here, PTOGP is used as a function. As a result, the search space is decreased by one dimension. It is excellent for decreasing the computational complexity and space complexity of the scheduling algorithm.

The rest of the paper is organized as following. Section 2 gives the task model of the preemption threshold scheduling problem. Section 3 summarizes the background. In Sect. 4, we investigate a termination criterion for $L(i)$ and propose TPTPOA. Experiment results are presented in Sect. 5. Section 6 concludes the paper.

2   Optimization Model of the Preemption Threshold Scheduling Problem

On a single processor Λ, we assume a set of real-time processes $\Pi = \{\tau_1, \tau_2, \tau_3 \cdots \tau_n\}$. Each process τ_i consists of three elements C_i, D_i, T_i. They denote the execution time, the deadline and the period of process τ_i respectively. In addition, each process τ_i has a fixed priority P_i, and a threshold θ_i. There are some hypotheses.

- The switching time of the process is not considered. It means that the switch is instant whether it is caused by the preemption or the completion of a process. In addition, there is no blocking time caused by resource occupancy.
- The process will not stop unless it is preempted by other processes or it is finished.
- The priority $P_i \in [1, n]$ is unique for all processes, but the threshold $\theta_i \in [P_i, n]$ can be the same for different processes.
- The execution time is less than or equal to the deadline. At the same time, the deadline is less than or equal to the period of each process.
- The larger the value of P_i is, the higher priority the process has. Once process τ_i is being executed, it can only be preempted when the priority P_j of the new arrival process τ_j is larger than threshold θ_i.
- The necessary and sufficient condition for each process schedulability is that the WCRT of each process is not more than its deadline.

For a set of processes $\Pi = \{\tau_1, \tau_2, \tau_3 \cdots \tau_n\}$, the aim of the preemption threshold scheduling problem is to find whether there exists a feasible $\{P_i, \theta_i\}$ $(i = 1 \cdots n)$ that can make Π schedulable and give at least the near-optimal assignments if the feasible assignments are available.

3 Background

In this section, we introduce the method to calculate WCRT with a given assignment of the priority and the preemption threshold, and to obtain a feasible assignment of the preemption threshold when the priorities are given.

3.1 Analysis of the Worse-Case Response Time

The definition of the response time is shown as Fig. 1. Time 0 indicates the arrival time of a process. 'Start' and 'Finish' indicate the time when the process begins and finishes respectively. [0, Start] contains the blocking time of the lower priority processes with the higher preemption thresholds and the execution time of the higher priority processes arrived when the process is blocked. [Start, Finish] contains the execution time of the processes whose priorities are higher than the current process's preemption threshold and the current process's execution time.

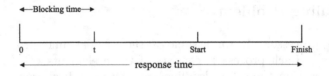

Fig. 1. The structure of the response time.

The definition of the blocking time of process τ_i is as following.

$$B(\tau_i) = max\{C_j | P_j < P_i \leq \theta_i\} \tag{1}$$

The level-i busy period is extended to calculate WCRT. It begins with the critical instant [8,11]. The process is as following [16,17].

$$\begin{cases} L^{(0)}(i) = B_i + Ci \\ L^{(s)}(i) = B_i + \sum_{\tau_j, P_j \geq P_i} \left\lceil \frac{L^{(s-1)}(i)}{T_j} \right\rceil C_j \end{cases} \tag{2}$$

We take the minimum value of $L(i)$ when $L^{(s)}(i) = L^{(s-1)}(i)$ as the length of the level-i busy period for process τ_i. Here, the number of the execution times in $L(i)$ for process τ_i can be calculated by the following formula.

$$M_i = \left\lceil \frac{L(i)}{T_i} \right\rceil \tag{3}$$

For all instances of process τ_i, the start time is as following [11,16,17].

$$\begin{cases} S^{(0)}(i,k) = B_i + \sum_{\tau_j, P_j \geq P_i} C_j & (k = 1, 2 \cdots M_i) \\ S^{(s)}(i,k) = B_i + (k-1)C_j + \sum_{\tau_j, P_j \geq P_i} (\left\lfloor \frac{S^{(s-1)}(i,k)}{T_j} \right\rfloor C_j) \end{cases} \tag{4}$$

We take $S(i, k)$ when $S^{(s)}(i, k) = S^{(s-1)}(i, k)$ as the start time for the k-th instance of process τ_i.

The completion time for all instances of process τ_i is as following.

$$\begin{cases} F^{(0)}(i, k) = S(i, k) + C_i & (k = 1, 2 \cdots M_i) \\ F^{(s)}(i, k) = S(i, k) + C_i + \sum_{\tau_j, P_j > \theta_i} \left(\left\lceil \frac{F^{(s-1)}(i,k)}{T_j} \right\rceil - \left\lfloor \frac{S^{(s-1)}(i,k)}{T_j} \right\rfloor + 1 \right) C_j \end{cases} \quad (5)$$

Similar to the start time, we take $F(i, k)$ when $F^{(s)}(i, k) = F^{(s-1)}(i, k)$ as the completion time for the k-th instance of process τ_i.

Therefore, we obtain WCRT for process τ_i using the following formula.

$$R_{imax} = max\{F(i, k) - (k - 1)T_i\} \qquad (k = 1, 2 \cdots M_i) \qquad (6)$$

3.2   The Minimum Boundary of the Preemption Threshold Assignment with Given Priorities

There are some lemmas [11] which indicate the search strategy for a feasible assignment of the preemption threshold.

Lemma 1. The worse-case response time of the processes with the lower priority will not change when processes with the higher priority change their preemption thresholds.

Lemma 2. For a set of schedulable processes, if one of the processes reduces its preemption threshold and is still schedulable, the set of the processes will also be schedulable.

Lemma 3. For a particular process, if we set its preemption threshold to n, it is still non-schedulable. It cannot be schedulable for arbitrary preemption threshold.

Based on the above lemmas, we can obtain the idea of searching the preemption thresholds minimum boundary. The assignment of the preemption threshold can start from the lowest priority process to the highest priority process. The preemption threshold should be increased from processs priority value to the maximum which denotes the number of processes until the process is schedulable. If it is still non-schedulable when the preemption threshold is the maximum, the minimum boundary of the preemption threshold is non-existent for the current assignment of the priority.

4   TS-Preemption Threshold and Priority Optimization Algorithm

In this section, we propose TPTPOA to search near-optimal assignments of the priority and the preemption threshold. The whole structure of the algorithm is shown as Fig. 2.

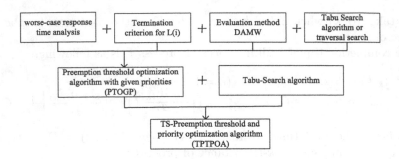

Fig. 2. The whole structure of TPTPOA.

4.1   Termination Criterion When $L(i)$ is Not Convergent

Assuming there are M processes which meet $P_j \geq P_i$ and using S_{wcet} to denote the sum of the M processes' execution time. We propose the following two theorems.

Theorem 1. If the sum of S_{wcet} and B_i is not more than the minimum period of the M processes (i.e. $S_{wcet} + B_i \leq min\{T_j \mid P_j \geq P_i\}$), $L(i)$ for process τ_i is convergent.

Proof. Assuming there are only two processes τ_s and τ_k with higher priority than process τ_i, and $T_s = 1.5T_i$, $T_k = 2T_i$. According to the computational method of $L(i)$, the three processes arrive concurrently at time 0 for their first time. $L^{(0)}(i)$ is equal to $B_i + C_i$, and $L^{(1)}(i)$ will be $B_i + C_s + C_k + C_i$. If $B_i + C_s + C_k + C_i$ is not more than T_i, the second period for all three processes are not available at the time $B_i + C_s + C_k + C_i$. Therefore, $L^{(2)}(i)$ will not increase. It means that $L^{(2)}(i) = L^{(1)}(i)$, and $L(i)$ is convergent. In addition, the number of the processes and the size of their periods have no influence on the conclusion.

Theorem 2. If S_{wcet} is more than the maximum period of the M processes (i.e. $S_{wcet} > max\{T_j \mid P_j \geq P_i\}$), $L(i)$ for process τ_i is not convergent.

Proof. Assuming there are only two processes τ_s and τ_k with higher priority than process τ_i, and $T_s = 1.5T_i$, $T_k = 2T_i$. If $C_s + C_k + C_i$ is more than $2T_i$, $B_i + C_s + C_k + C_i$ must be more than $2T_i$. Therefore, $L^{(1)}(i)$ which is equal to $B_i + C_s + C_k + C_i$ is later than the second arrival of the process τ_k with the maximum period. Therefore, the increment from $L^{(1)}(i)$ to $L^{(2)}(i)$ will be not less than $C_s + C_k + C_i$. It means that the interval of $[L^{(2)}(i), L^{(3)}(i)]$ contains at least one new arrival for all three processes. The increment from $L^{(3)}(i)$ to $L^{(4)}(i)$ will be not less than $C_s + C_k + C_i$. As a result, the iteration will be endless and $L(i)$ will be not convergent.

If the conditions of the two theorems are not satisfied, termination criterion is effective to prevent the algorithm from endless loop when $L(i)$ is not convergent.

Termination Criterion. If the difference of $L(i)$ between two consecutive iterations is more than the maximum period of all processes whose priorities are not less than P_i, the algorithm will terminate. It is as following.

$$L^{(s)}(i) - L^{(s-1)}(i) > max\{T_j | P_j \geq P_i\} \tag{7}$$

Assuming $L(i)$ is convergent, $L^{(s+1)}(i)$ is equal to $L^{(s)}(i)$ and $L^{(s)}(i)$ is equal to $L^{(s-1)}(i)$. Therefore,

$$\sum_{\tau_j, P_j \geq P_i} \left\lceil \frac{L^{(s-1)}(i)}{T_j} \right\rceil C_j = \sum_{\tau_j, P_j \geq P_i} \left\lceil \frac{L^{(s)}(i)}{T_j} \right\rceil C_j \tag{8}$$

For different processes, the execution time is different. Therefore,

$$\begin{cases} \left\lceil \frac{L^{(s)}(i)}{T_{j_i}} \right\rceil = \left\lceil \frac{L^{(s-1)}(i)}{T_{j_i}} \right\rceil \\ \vdots \quad \vdots \quad \vdots \\ \left\lceil \frac{L^{(s)}(i)}{T_{jM}} \right\rceil = \left\lceil \frac{L^{(s-1)}(i)}{T_{jM}} \right\rceil \end{cases} \Rightarrow \begin{cases} n_1 T_{jM} < L^{(s-1)}(i) \leq L^{(s)}(i) \leq (n_1 + 1)T_{jM} \\ \vdots \quad \vdots \quad \vdots \quad \vdots \\ n_M T_{jM} < L^{(s-1)}(i) \leq L^{(s)}(i) \leq (n_M + 1)T_{jM} \end{cases} \tag{9}$$

We find that $L^{(s-1)}(i)$ and $L^{(s)}(i)$ are in the same period for all processes. It means that $L^{(s)}(i)$ appears before the next arrival of all M processes.

We choose the maximum period of all processes whose priorities are not less than the current process's priority as the threshold of the increment of two adjacent iterations. If the increment is more than the maximum period, the algorithm will terminate. It means that the set of processes is non-schedulable with the current priority. It is worth mentioning that the termination criterion is only a sufficient condition.

4.2   Evaluation for Assignment of the Preemption Threshold

For a set of processes, there may exist many feasible assignments of the preemption threshold with given priorities. Therefore, rational evaluation method is essential for selecting the best assignment and optimizing the design of algorithm. We propose DAMW to solve this problem.

The difference between the deadline and WCRT can be used to judge the schedulability of a process. We define a variable V_{mi} to represent the difference and evaluate which preemption threshold has a better performance for process τ_i. The bigger value of V_{mi} means the better fault tolerance and the better performance. In addition, we also define F_{mi} to denote the superiority of V_{mi}^* which is the i-th element in the sorted V_m in ascending order compared with $V_{ni}^*(n \neq m)$. F_m is the sum of F_{mi} and denotes the fitness value of V_m. For a large number of feasible assignments, we choose two of them randomly and obtain the better one by using DAMW, and compare the better one with all other assignments. The detailed procedure of DAMW for two assignments is as following.

1. Obtain two sets $V_1 = \{V_{11}, V_{12}, \cdots V_{1n}\}$ and $V_2 = \{V_{21}, V_{22}, \cdots V_{2n}\}$ by using $V_{mi} = D_i - WCRT_i$ $(m = 1, 2; \ i = 1, 2 \cdots n)$
2. Sort elements in ascending order for each group V_m $(m = 1, 2)$
3. Assign weight as $(n - i + 1)$ for each sorted element V_{mi}^* $(m = 1, 2; \ i = 1, 2 \cdots n)$
4. Calculate F_m $(m = 1, 2)$ for each group respectively.

For each set V_{1i}^* and V_{2i}^* $(i = 1, 2 \cdots n)$, we compare the size of the two values. There are three possibilities.

- If $V_{1i}^* > V_{2i}^*$, $(n - i + 1) * (V_{1i}^* - V_{2i}^*) / V_{1i}^*$ will be added to F_1, and F_2 remains unchanged
- If $V_{1i}^* < V_{2i}^*$, $(n - i + 1) * (V_{2i}^* - V_{1i}^*) / V_{2i}^*$ will be added to F_2, and F_1 remains unchanged
- If $V_{1i}^* = V_{2i}^*$, neither F_1 not F_2 changes its value.

Compare F_1 and F_2, and the larger one corresponds to the better assignment of the preemption threshold.

4.3   The Preemption Threshold Optimization Algorithm with Given Priorities

We adopt different strategies based on the size of the processes. The traversing method is used for small scale of processes. For the large scale of processes, we propose TS-preemption threshold optimization algorithm based on TS. Here, we take 6 processes as the boundary value. The detailed processes are listed as below.

1. Use the algorithm introduced in Sect. 3 to calculate the minimum boundary of the preemption threshold with given priorities. If the minimum boundary is not exist, there is no feasible assignment of the preemption threshold with the given priorities.
2. Use the minimum boundary to initialize the current assignment and the optimal assignment, and initialize the Tabu list and put the minimum boundary into it.
3. Search all neighborhoods of the current assignment and obtain the best one with DAMW.
4. Compare the optimal assignment in the neighborhood with the assignments in the Tabu list. If it is already in the list, set it to zero and return to 3.
5. Use DAMW to compare the optimal assignment in the neighborhood with the optimal assignment. If the former one is better than the later one, use the optimal assignment in the neighborhood to update the optimal assignment.
6. Use the optimal assignment in the neighborhood to update the current assignment and put it into the Tabu list. Return to 3.
7. Terminate iteration and output the optimal preemption threshold.

4.4 TS-Preemption Threshold and Priority Optimization Algorithm

Based on the algorithm in Sect. 4.3, at least the near-optimal assignments with given priorities can be obtained. If we set up a corresponding relationship between the preemption thresholds and the given priorities, the problem will reduce one dimension. However, the solution space of the priority optimization is $O(n!)$. We propose an effective algorithm based on TS to solve this problem. The process is similar to the Sect. 4.3 and the differences between them are listed as below.

- EDF [20] has been proved to be the most effective algorithm for the preemptive scheduling problem. Although the preemption threshold scheduling is not fully preemptive and its priority is fixed, the assignment of the priority based on EDF is still a good solution and can be used as the initial assignment of the priority.
- The neighborhood solutions of the priority are obtained by exchanging the priority with each other in one step, while the neighborhood solutions of the preemption threshold only have one process with different threshold compared with the current assignment. The demonstration for it is shown as Table 1.

Table 1. The differences of the neighborhood for priority and preemption threshold

Process	Current assignment	Neighborhood of priority			Neighborhood of threshold		
		1st	2nd	3rd	1st	2nd	3rd
τ_1	1	2	3	1	2	3	1
τ_2	2	1	2	3	2	2	3
τ_3	3	3	1	2	3	3	3

4.5 The Flowchart of the TPTPOA

The flowchart is shown as Fig. 3. Switching the sequence is carried out four times. The purpose of the first two times is to guarantee that the processes' order is from the lowest priority to the highest priority, which can bring great convenience for the optimization of the preemption threshold. The third time is to ensure that the optimal neighborhood assignment of the preemption threshold corresponds to the right sequence of the processes when compared with the Tabu list. The fourth execution is to guarantee that the optimal assignments are in the original processes sequence.

5 Experiments and Results

The following experiments are implemented in Matlab R2014a, which runs in a computer with Inter(R) Core(TM) i5-4590T CPU and 4 GB RAM.

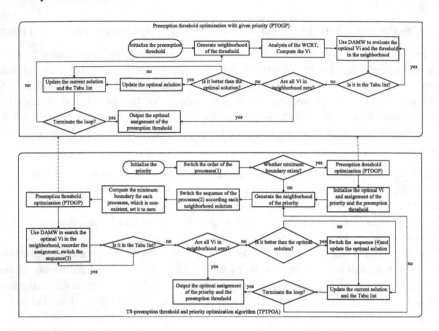

Fig. 3. The flowchart of TPTPOA

5.1   The Performance Analysis of TPTPOA

We conduct five experiments to test the validity of TPTPOA. Four, five, six, seven, eight processes are used respectively. In the algorithm, we use six as the threshold to decide which one will be used between TS and traversal search when optimizing the preemption threshold. However, we use both of them in the experiments respectively. We define TPTPOA when TS is used to optimize the preemption threshold as $TPTPOA_1$, and TPTPOA when traversal search is used to optimize the preemption threshold as $TPTPOA_2$. $Priority/Threshold_1$ and $Priority/Threshold_2$ denotes the priorities and the preemption thresholds obtained by $TPTPOA_1$ and $TPTPOA_2$ respectively. $WCRT_1$ and $WCRT_2$ denotes the worse-case response time for each process corresponding to the assignments searched by $TPTPOA_1$ and $TPTPOA_2$ respectively.

As shown in Tables 2, 3 and 5, the assignments of the priority and the preemption threshold obtained by $TPTPOA_1$ and $TPTPOA_2$ are the same. In Table 4, the assignments obtained by $TPTPOA_1$ is a part of the assignments obtained by $TPTPOA_2$. For more processes, $TPTPOA_1$ may not obtain the optimal solutions, but it can also obtain the near-optimal assignments at least. Therefore, TPTPOA with TS used to optimize the preemption threshold is an effective algorithm to optimize the assignments for the priority and the preemption threshold.

For the results in Tables 2, 3, 4, 5 and 6, the running time for $TPTPOA_1$ is 0.518199 s, 0.281927 s, 2.227995 s, 4.914453 s, 6.639471 s, respectively. The running time for $TPTPOA_2$ is 0.201472 s, 0.141070 s, 6.551539 s, 317.807542 s, none,

Table 2. The assignments of the threshold and the priority with four processes

Process	1	2	3	4
Deadline	140	180	160	90
WCET	18	40	35	30
Period	140	180	160	120
$Priority/Threshold_1$	3/3	1/4	2/4	4/4
	3/4	1/4	2/4	4/4
	3/3	2/4	1/4	4/4
	3/4	2/4	1/4	4/4
$Priority/Threshold_2$	3/3	1/4	2/4	4/4
	3/4	1/4	2/4	4/4
	3/3	2/4	1/4	4/4
	3/4	2/4	1/4	4/4
$WCRT_1$	88	123	123	70
$WCRT_2$	88	123	123	70

Table 3. The assignments of the threshold and the priority with five processes

Process	1	2	3	4	5
Deadline	120	160	180	140	100
WCET	25	35	40	30	20
Period	140	180	200	160	120
$Priority/Threshold_1$	4/4	2/5	1/5	3/3	5/5
	4/5	2/5	1/5	3/3	5/5
	4/4	2/5	1/5	3/4	5/5
	...	...	...	...	...
$Priority/Threshold_2$	4/4	2/5	1/5	3/3	5/5
	4/5	2/5	1/5	3/3	5/5
	4/4	2/5	1/5	3/4	5/5
	...	...	...	...	...
$WCRT_1$	85	150	150	115	60
$WCRT_2$	85	150	150	115	60

respectively. None denotes we cannot obtain the results in a short and tolerable time. When the number of the processes is less than six, $TPTPOA_2$ have less computational cost than $TPTPOA_1$, and it also obtains all the assignments with the same optimal WCRT. However, the computational cost will increase sharply if the number of the processes is not less than six. It cannot obtain the effective assignments in a short time with only eight processes in Table 6. Compared with $TPTPOA_2$, the computational cost of $TPTPOA_1$ increases slowly, and it will

Table 4. The assignments of the threshold and the priority with six processes

Process	1	2	3	4	5	6
Deadline	120	160	180	140	150	200
WCET	25	28	24	21	22	30
Period	140	180	200	160	160	240
$Priority/Threshold_1$	6/6	3/3	2/6	5/5	4/4	1/6
	6/6	3/4	2/6	5/5	4/4	1/6
	...	...	...	...	...	...
$Priority/Threshold_2$	6/6	3/3	2/6	5/6	4/4	1/6
	6/6	3/3	2/6	5/5	4/4	1/6
	6/6	3/3	2/6	5/6	4/5	1/6
	...	...	...	...	...	...
$WCRT_1$	55	126	150	76	98	150
$WCRT_2$	55	126	150	76	98	150

Table 5. The assignments of the threshold and the priority with seven processes

Process	1	2	3	4	5	6	7
Deadline	140	170	160	160	170	150	180
WCET	20	23	21	25	26	25	20
Period	150	180	175	180	190	180	195
$Priority/Threshold_1$	7/7	2/7	5/5	4/4	3/3	6/6	1/7
	7/7	2/7	5/6	4/4	3/3	6/6	1/7
	7/7	2/7	5/7	4/4	3/3	6/6	1/7
$Priority/Threshold_2$	7/7	2/7	5/5	4/4	3/3	6/6	1/7
	7/7	2/7	5/6	4/4	3/3	6/6	1/7
	7/7	2/7	5/7	4/4	3/3	6/6	1/7
$WCRT_1$	43	160	89	114	140	68	160
$WCRT_2$	43	160	89	114	140	68	160

significantly lower than that of $TPTPOA_2$ when the number of the processes is not less than six. Therefore, we select six as the threshold to decide which strategy will be used to optimize the preemption threshold in TPTPOA. In addition, though the running time increases slowly for TPTPOA when the number of the processes is not less than six, it may also take much time when the number of the processes is very large. We can reduce the number of the neighborhood solutions involved in updating the optimal solution in each iteration to control the increasing time cost effectively.

Table 6. The assignments of the threshold and the priority with eight processes

Process	1	2	3	4	5	6	7	8
Deadline	140	170	160	160	170	150	180	250
WCET	20	23	21	21	24	23	20	18
Period	150	180	175	180	190	180	195	280
$Priority/Threshold_1$	8/8	2/8	5/5	6/6	4/4	7/7	3/8	1/7
	8/8	2/8	5/5	6/6	4/4	7/7	3/8	1/8
	8/8	2/8	5/6	6/6	4/4	7/7	3/8	1/8
	8/8	2/8	5/6	6/6	4/4	7/7	3/8	1/7
	8/8	2/8	5/7	6/6	4/4	7/7	3/8	1/7
	8/8	2/8	5/7	6/6	4/4	7/7	3/8	1/8
	8/8	2/8	5/8	6/6	4/4	7/7	3/8	1/8
	8/8	2/8	5/8	6/6	4/4	7/7	3/8	1/7
	8/8	2/8	5/8	6/7	4/4	7/7	3/8	1/7
$WCRT_1$	43	170	108	87	132	66	152	190

5.2   Summary

We have following conclusions based on the experiment results.

Firstly, TPTPOA can obtain the assignments for both preemption threshold and priority, but the existing algorithm can only have the preemption threshold. As shown in Table 5, TPTPOA has 18 assignments of the priority and the preemption threshold with the same WCRT. We can select arbitrary one as the final assignment.

Secondly, the initial assignment of the processes' priority based on the main idea of EDF is not necessarily the optimal solution. It can be seen from Table 6. Process 2 have the less deadline than process 7, while the priority of process 2 is also less than that of process 7 in the optimal assignments. However, the assignment of the processes' priority based on EDF is still an effective initial assignment and it even could be the optimal assignment of the priority occasionally.

Finally, the better assignment does not necessarily have the larger preemption threshold. If the execution time of the process with the lowest priority is the largest one, every increase by one of its preemption threshold will make the number of the affected processes increase one. For each affected process, its blocking time will have a significant increase. It means that the performance of the new assignment becomes worse and the processes could even be non-schedulable. There is an example with the given priorities in Table 7. For process 1, all feasible preemption thresholds are 2, 3 and 4. However, the optimal preemption threshold is 2 instead of 4.

Table 7. The assignments of threshold with given priorities

Process	1	2	3	4
Deadline	200	140	100	90
WCET	40	35	30	25
Period	250	160	140	120
Minimum boundary	2	4	3	4
All feasible thresholds	2	4	3	4
	2	4	4	4
	3	4	3	4
	3	4	4	4
	4	4	3	4
	4	4	4	4
Optimal threshold	2	4	3	4
	2	4	4	4

6   Conclusion

This paper focuses on the process scheduling problem for IMA. Compared with the fully preemptive and fully non-preemptive scheduling, PTS is a more comprehensive scheduling strategy. Aiming at the problem of assigning preemption threshold and priority, we propose TPTPOA. The experiments show that algorithm has more extensive global searching ability than the existing algorithm. At least near-optimal solutions can be obtained within the acceptable time. Though the running time will increase when the number of the processes is too large, the effective assignments can still be obtained by decreasing the number of the neighborhood solutions in each iteration. Therefore, TPTPOA can be used in IMA for processes' scheduling and other real-time systems meeting the hypotheses to improve their schedulability.

The future work focuses on applying the algorithm to the model considering the sequential relationship of the process, and improving the efficiency of the algorithm.

Acknowledgments. This research is supported by the National Natural Science Foundation of China under Grant No. 61671041.

References

1. Miller, S.P., Cofer, D.D., Sha, L., Meseguer, J., Al-Nayeem, A.: Implementing logical synchrony in integrated modular avionics. In: 2009 IEEE/AIAA 28th Digital Avionics Systems Conference, Orlando, FL, pp. 1.A.3-1–1.A.3-12 (2009)
2. Ju, H., Wang, S., Zhao, T.: A modeling method of IMA dynamic reconfiguration based on AADL. In: 2015 First International Conference on Reliability Systems Engineering (ICRSE), Beijing, pp. 1–5 (2015)

3. Aeronautical Radio, Inc.: ARINC653 P1-2, Avionics application software standard interface part 1-required services, pp. 2–45 (2006)
4. Pan, L.Q., He, C., Tian, Y., Su, Y.S., Zhang, X.Y.: A region division based diversity main-taining approach for many-objective optimization. Integr. Comput. Aided Eng. **24**(3), 1–18 (2017)
5. George, L., Rivierre, N., Spuri, M.: Preemptive and non-preemptive real-time uni-processor scheduling. Technical report N2966, INRIA, pp. 1–55 (1996)
6. Baruah, S.K., Rosier, L.E., Howell, R.R.: Algorithms and complexity concerning the preemptive scheduling of periodic, real-time tasks on one processor. Real Time Syst. **2**, 301–324 (1990)
7. Marouf, M., Sorel, Y.: Scheduling non-preemptive hard real-time tasks with strict periods. In: ETFA 2011, Toulouse, pp. 1–8 (2011)
8. Liu, C.L., Layland, J.W.: Scheduling algorithms for multiprogramming in a hard real-time environment. J. Assoc. Comput. Mach. **20**, 40–61 (1973)
9. Lehoczky, J., Sha, L., Ding, Y.: The rate monotonic scheduling algorithm: exact characterization and average case behavior. In: Proceedings of Real-Time Systems Symposium, Santa Monica, CA, pp. 166–171 (1989)
10. Bertossi, A.A., Fusiello, A., Mancini, L.V.: Fault-tolerant deadline-monotonic algorithm for scheduling hard-real-time tasks. In: Proceedings of the 11th International Parallel Processing Symposium, Geneva, pp. 133–138 (1997)
11. Wang, Y., Saksena, M.: Scheduling fixed-priority tasks with preemption threshold. In: Sixth International Conference on Real-Time Computing Systems and Applications, RTCSA 1999, Hong Kong, pp. 328–335 (1999)
12. Lehoczky, J.P.: Fixed priority scheduling of periodic task sets with arbitrary deadlines. In: Proceedings of the 11th Real-Time Systems Symposium, Lake Buena Vista, FL, pp. 201–209 (1990)
13. Bril, R.J., Lukkien, J.J., Verhaegh, W.F.J.: Worst-case response time analysis of real-time tasks under fixed-priority scheduling with deferred preemption revisited. In: 19th Euromicro Conference on Real-Time Systems (ECRTS 2007), Pisa, pp. 269–279 (2007)
14. Joseph, M., Pandya, P.: Finding response times in a real-time system. Comput. J. **29**, 390–395 (1986)
15. Redell, O., Torngren, M.: Calculating exact worst case response times for static priority scheduled tasks with offsets and jitter. In: Proceedings of the Eighth IEEE Real-Time and Embedded Technology and Applications Symposium, pp. 164–172 (2002)
16. Keskin, U., Bril, R.J., Lukkien, J.J.: Exact response-time analysis for fixed-priority preemption-threshold scheduling. In: 2010 IEEE 15th Conference on Emerging Technologies and Factory Automation (ETFA 2010), Bilbao, pp. 1–4 (2010)
17. Buttazzo, G.C., Bertogna, M., Yao, G.: Limited preemptive scheduling for real-time systems. A survey. IEEE Trans. Industr. Inf. **9**(1), 3–15 (2013)
18. He, L., Yabo, L., Hong, L.: Schedule optimization for NC resource sharing based-on greed algorithm and Tabu search. In: 2009 Second International Conference on Intelligent Computation Technology and Automation, Changsha, Hunan, pp. 282–285 (2009)
19. Darmawan, I., Kuspriyanto, Priyana, Y., Joseph, M.I.: Grid computing process improvement through computing resource scheduling using genetic algorithm and Tabu Search integration. In: 2012 7th International Conference on Telecommunication Systems, Services, and Applications (TSSA), Bali, pp. 330–334 (2012)
20. Lee, J., Shin, K.G.: Preempt a job or not in EDF scheduling of uniprocessor systems. IEEE Trans. Comput. **63**(5), 1197–1206 (2014)

An Approach to the Bio-Inspired Control of Self-reconfigurable Robots

Dongyang Bie[1], Miguel A. Gutiérrez-Naranjo[2], Jie Zhao[1], and Yanhe Zhu[1(✉)]

[1] State Key Laboratory of Robotics and System, Harbin Institute of Technology,
Harbin, Heilongjiang, China
`yhzhu@hit.edu.cn`
[2] Department of Computer Science and Artificial Intelligence,
University of Seville, Seville, Spain
`magutier@us.es`

Abstract. Self-reconfigurable robots are robots built by modules which can move in relationship to each other. This ability of changing its physical form provides the robots a high level of adaptability and robustness. Given an initial configuration and a goal configuration of the robot, the problem of self-regulation consists on finding a sequence of module moves that will reconfigure the robot from the initial configuration to the goal configuration. In this paper, we use a bio-inspired method for studying this problem which combines a cluster-flow locomotion based on cellular automata together with a decentralized local representation of the spatial geometry based on membrane computing ideas. A promising 3D software simulation and a 2D hardware experiment are also presented.

1 Introduction

Modular Self-reconfigurable (MSR) robots [12] are robots built by modules which can move in relationship to each other. This ability can change its physical form and provide MSR robots a high level of adaptability and robustness [32]. The modularity allows the robot to optimize their shape for different tasks and the control of the movement of the modules represents a big challenge for the development of new research ideas [26]. In fact, such control of the modules and the locomotion planning is a complex non-linear problem and there is no analytic solution for it. According to the existence of center controller or not, current approaches can be generally divided into two categories: centralized control and decentralized control. The problem of obtaining a centralized control is a NP problem [14], so decentralized approaches are currently on the focus of many research approaches in order to achieve effective solutions.

The decentralized control of self-reconfiguration has been studied from different points of view. One of the most interesting is to consider nature as a source of inspiration. In the literature, several bio-inspired methods have been applied for the distributed control of self-reconfigurable robots, among them, methods based on cellular automata (CA) [9,35] or particle swarm optimization [34] can be cited. They all have the distributed nature for emergent systems from bottom interaction to global regular phenomenon. This match of decentralized character can contribute to the scalability of module numbers by focusing on local agents, but the convergence problem still stands out in the emergent process of swarm systems.

Recently, a bio-inspired approach based on ideas taken from membrane computing and CA has been presented [5]. In this paper, we go on with the idea of combining a cluster-flow locomotion based on CA together with a decentralized local representation of the spatial geometry based on membrane computing ideas. The used method represents a novelty in the framework of self-configurable robots in a double sense, from a theoretical and practical point of view. From a theoretical side, an abstract representation of the robot beyond its physical representation is considered. From a practical point of view, the solution is based on two of the basic features of one of the most studied membrane computing devices, the so-called cell-like P systems: On the one hand, the tree-like graph structure which can be abstracted from the hierarchical arrangement of vesicles in an alive eucaryotic cell. On the second hand, in membrane computing the information is encapsulated in vesicles and encoded by multisets of simple objects. The key point for the use of such multisets in the framework of self-configurable robots is the *interpretation* of the objects. As it will be pointed out below, such objects can represent the length, the relative angle of a module of the robot or any other feature chosen by the designer.

Next, we briefly recall some ideas about the bio-inspired computational research areas used in this paper, namely, membrane computing and CA. Membrane computing [20] is inspired by the structure and functioning of cells as living organisms able to process and generate information. In particular, it focuses on membranes, which are involved in many reactions taking place inside the cell. The basic idea is inspired in the flow of metabolites between cells of a living tissue or between the organelles in an eucaryotic cell. This flow of metabolites can be interpreted as a flow of information for computational purposes. Membrane computing devices are called P systems. They are distributed and have a high degree of parallelism. Such degree of autonomy and the possibility of locally encapsulate the local information needed for the next step of computation make these devices suitable for modelling the geometry of modular self-reconfigurable robots. The second bio-inspired tool used in this paper, CA [30], has been widely used in the literature for the control of self-reconfigurable robots. CA were introduced to decentralized control of MSR robots by Butler *et al.* [9]. Since then, many other approaches can be found in the literature (e.g., [7,10]). In this paper, CA are used to handle the distributed and parallel motion of decentralized modules in MSR robots.

The paper is organized as follows: Firstly, we recall some basics on MSR robots and membrane computing. We present how the cell-like structure of a P system can be interpreted as a configuration of a MSR. Next, we show how the configuration of a tree-like structure can be geometrically represented by a self-reconfigurable robot. Such representation is performed by a cluster-flow locomotion of spare modules inspired on the well-known turtle graphics methods. This is illustrated with a 3D software simulation and a 2D hardware experiment. Finally, the paper finishes with some conclusions and open research lines.

2   MSR Robots

There are several categories of hardware architecture for MSR robotic modules, such as lattice architecture (see, e.g., [22,28]), mobile architecture (e.g., [17,27,33]), chain architecture (e.g., [2,29]) and hybrid architecture (e.g., [6,31,35]). For the regular geometric organization, lattice architecture is the most convenient for computer modeling among all those architectures. As illustrated in Fig. 1, each module in a lattice architecture has a cubic structure with local coordinate. This module is also called sliding cube model (SCM) module, which has been used as a common module for rapid verification of control methods. Each module is a completely independent working robot with three kinds of basic motion ability: convex motion, linear motion and concave motion. A MSR robot with multi SCM modules changes its global topology by adjusting relative relationships of inner modules through a self-organizing process.

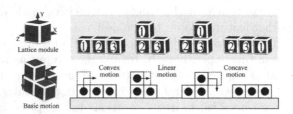

Fig. 1. A 3D structure made with blocks.

The configuration of the whole robot is determined by the relative position of inner modules. Since the independent modules have various possible motion plans, choosing an appropriate mechanism for controlling the movement of each module is a hard task [15,32]. Bearing in mind that each lattice module has six connecting faces and directly connected modules has four relative connecting

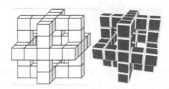

Fig. 2. A schematic representation of a 3D structure made with 42 blocks and its associated robotic structure made with modules.

orientations, a robot system with n modules has $n^{6 \times 4}$ kinds of connecting ways. Such amount of possibilities makes difficult the control of the robot even for robots with a low amount of modules, as the structure shown in Fig. 2, where a robotic structure with 42 modules is presented.

3 Membrane Computing

According to their topology[1], there are three basic sets of P system models, although other approaches are possible [20]: cell-like P systems, where membranes have a tree-like structure; tissue-like P systems, where membranes are placed in the nodes of a general graph; and spiking neural P systems, which are inspired by the structure of living neurons in a brain. In this paper we use cell-like P systems in order to represent the spatial geometry of MSR.

The basic cell-like P system model consists of a hierarchical structure composed by several membranes, embedded into a main membrane called the *skin*. Membranes divide the Euclidean space into regions, that contain multisets of objects (represented by symbols of an alphabet) and/or other membranes. The intuition behind this membrane structure is taken from biology. A membrane can be seen as a three-dimensional vesicle which is a separator of the region *inside* and the region *outside*. Biological metabolites inside the regions are modelled by object-symbols. Each region, which is defined by a membrane, can contain other symbols or other membranes, so that a P system has exactly one outer membrane, called the skin membrane, and a hierarchical relationship governing all its membranes under the skin membrane. The *information* encapsulated inside each region is encoded in the type of symbols, but also in its multiplicity. In this paper, the structure of cell-like P systems is used to construct branching structures of self-reconfigurable robots. The rooted tree nature of membranes is a perfect frame to encode the branching structure. In this paper, we use the formal framework of membrane computing in order to describe the geometry and the topology of MSR robots whose modules can be represented with a tree-like structure. The key points of the representation are the following:

1. Firstly, the geometrical structure of each segment (concerning to length, thickness, color or whatever other features) is represented by a multiset of objects placed in the corresponding membrane.
2. Secondly, the topological relations among the segments are represented by the tree-like membrane structure of the P system. If two segments are joint in the robot, the corresponding membranes are joint in the tree-like structure of the P system, i.e., one of them is contained in the other one.
3. Thirdly, the relative position of a module with respect to its father in the segment will be also encoded with a multiset of objects placed inside the corresponding membrane.

---

[1] Since there are an extensive literature on the use of CA for the control of self-reconfigurable robots, we focus on the membrane computing ideas used in this paper.

The encapsulation of the information in P systems makes possible a natural translation of the idea of module from a physical robot to the formal computational model. One of the main advantages of this formalism is that no global position is needed in order to describe the topology or geometry of the robot.

3.1   An Example

As an initial example, let us consider the figure composed by six Greek crosses as shown in Fig. 2. Each of the crosses is composed by two bars of five cubic modules. The modules at the end of the bars are shared by two crosses and the whole figure has cubical symmetry. Such figure can be thought as the composition of 42 cubical modules which can be distributed into 24 solid segments of length units 1, 2 or 3. By keeping the topological connection of (at least) one of ends of each bar, the 24 solid segments of the figure can be *unrolled* in a like-tree planar figure shown in Fig. 3(left). Let us remark that the relative position between adjacent segments in the planar representation is the same than in the original 3D figure in the following sense: *If two segments are adjacent in the planar representation, they are also adjacent in the 3D figure.*

In Fig. 3(left), a label from in $a, b, \ldots, x$ is associated to each segment and a dual representation of this tree-like structure is depicted in Fig. 3(right). In this new representation, segments of the planar structure are represented by nodes in the graph and there is an edge between the nodes x and y if and only if the segments x and y are joint in the planar representation of the figure. This dual representation will be used for representing the topology of the robot as a cell-like P system membrane structure. The correspondence is immediate since such membrane structure is also a tree-like arrangement of membranes. Figure 4(left)

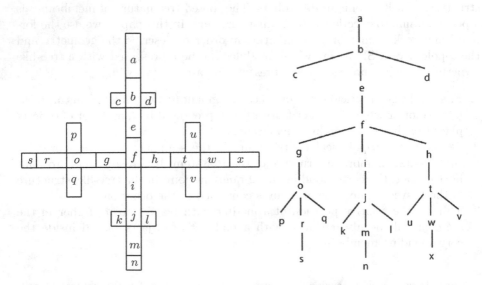

Fig. 3. Tree structure for inner relationships of the structure in Fig. 2.

shows a cell-like P system structure associated to the structure in Fig. 3. Let us remark that this cell-like P system structure takes the vertex a as the root of the tree and hence, the corresponding membrane in the P system structure is the *skin* of the P system, but any other terminal node could be taken as root.

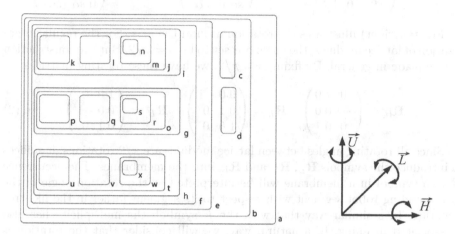

Fig. 4. Membrane structure of a P systems representing the topological structure of the tree in Fig. 3(Left). Rotation around axis (Right).

The tree-like graph in Fig. 3(right) can be immediately obtained from the P system membrane structure in Fig. 4(left), but if we want to represent the original structure from Fig. 2, several symbols must be placed in the membrane structure which encode the geometric features. Such combination of membrane structure plus the symbols associated to each membrane is called a *configuration* in membrane computing. In this example, we choose the symbol F for representing a length unit. For the sake of simplicity, in this example the unique feature of the segment of the robot described by symbols is the length. Nonetheless, other features (width, color, ...) can also been described by multisets of symbols. According to the membrane computing theory, several copies of a symbol can appear in a membrane. The number of copies of F in a membrane will represent the length of the segment associated to the number of copies of F. Instead of a global position of each segment, a representation of the *relative position* of a segment with respect to its father in the tree-like representation is proposed. In this way, some ideas are borrowed from [1, 19].

Let us consider the set of vectors $(\boldsymbol{H}, \boldsymbol{L}, \boldsymbol{U})$, with unit length, perpendicular to each other and satisfying $\boldsymbol{H} \times \boldsymbol{L} = \boldsymbol{U}$. A new vector $(\boldsymbol{H}', \boldsymbol{L}', \boldsymbol{U}')$ can be obtained from the vector $(\boldsymbol{H}, \boldsymbol{L}, \boldsymbol{U})$ by using a rotation matrix $\mathbf{R}$ with the composition $(\boldsymbol{H'}, \boldsymbol{L'}, \boldsymbol{U'}) = (\boldsymbol{H}, \boldsymbol{L}, \boldsymbol{U})\mathbf{R}$. Rotations by angle α about vectors $\boldsymbol{U}$, $\boldsymbol{L}$ and $\boldsymbol{H}$ are represented by Eq. 1 ($c\alpha = \cos\alpha$, $s\alpha = \sin\alpha$).

$$\mathbf{R}_U(\alpha) = \begin{pmatrix} c\alpha & s\alpha & 0 \\ -s\alpha & c\alpha & 0 \\ 0 & 0 & 1 \end{pmatrix} \quad \mathbf{R}_L(\alpha) = \begin{pmatrix} c\alpha & 0 & -s\alpha \\ 0 & 1 & 0 \\ s\alpha & 0 & c\alpha \end{pmatrix} \quad \mathbf{R}_H(\alpha) = \begin{pmatrix} 1 & 0 & 0 \\ 0 & c\alpha & -s\alpha \\ 0 & s\alpha & c\alpha \end{pmatrix} \quad (1)$$

Figure 4(right) illustrates the rotation around the axis. For the regular organization of lattice modules, the angle α is set to be $\alpha = \pi/2$. But the construction can be made in general. By fixing $\alpha = \pi/2$, we have these rotating matrices:

$$\mathbf{R}_U = \begin{pmatrix} 0 & 1 & 0 \\ -1 & 0 & 0 \\ 0 & 0 & 1 \end{pmatrix} \quad \mathbf{R}_L = \begin{pmatrix} 0 & 0 & -1 \\ 0 & 1 & 0 \\ 1 & 0 & 0 \end{pmatrix} \quad \mathbf{R}_H = \begin{pmatrix} 1 & 0 & 0 \\ 0 & 0 & -1 \\ 0 & 1 & 0 \end{pmatrix} \quad (2)$$

Since all rotating angles between lattice modules are $\pi/2$ rotations, it suffices to introduce the symbols $\mathbf{R}_L$, $\mathbf{R}_U$ and $\mathbf{R}_H$ into the membranes. The occurrence of such symbol in a membrane will be interpreted as the rotation angle of the corresponding robot segment with respect to its segment father in the like-tree structure. In a similar way that with the F symbol, the multiplicity has also a associated meaning. In a natural way, we will consider that the rotation is applied as many times as the number of copies. In such way, we can represent rotations of $\pi/2$, π or $-\pi/2$ by considering one, two or three copies of the symbol.

In this way, the general position of the 3D structure of Fig. 2 can be encoded in a P system configuration by considering the membrane structure shown in Fig. 4(left) and adding to the membrane i the following multiset of symbols w_i (symbol w_i describes the multiset of objects in the membrane associated to the segment i in Fig. 3, and relative orientations are organized respect to the parent membrane, the superscripts [20] denote the multiplicity):

$$
\begin{array}{llll}
w_a = F^3 & w_g = F^2\,\mathbf{R}_H & w_m = F^2 & w_s = F\,\mathbf{R}_U \\
w_b = F^2\,\mathbf{R}_U & w_h = F^2\,\mathbf{R}_H^3 & w_n = F\,\mathbf{R}_U & w_t = F^2\,\mathbf{R}_U \\
w_c = F\,\mathbf{R}_H & w_i = F^2 & w_o = F^2\,\mathbf{R}_U & w_u = F^2\,\mathbf{R}_H^3 \\
w_d = F\,\mathbf{R}_H^3 & w_j = F^2\,\mathbf{R}_U & w_p = F^2\,\mathbf{R}_H & w_v = F^2\,\mathbf{R}_H \\
w_e = F^2 & w_k = F\,\mathbf{R}_H & w_q = F^2\,\mathbf{R}_H^3 & w_w = F^2 \\
w_f = F^2\,\mathbf{R}_U & w_l = F\,\mathbf{R}_H^3 & w_r = F^2 & w_x = F\,\mathbf{R}_U
\end{array}
$$

3.2 Geometrical Interpretation of a P System Configuration

The structure of membranes in a cell-like P system is a tree-like graph. Such graph does not have an intrinsic geometric interpretation, but we can add such interpretation by giving a geometric meaning to the objects placed inside the membranes[2]. Given a P system configuration, the membrane structure and the

---

[2] These ideas has been previously used in membrane computing, see [13,21,23]. Different approaches bridging membrane computing with other geometric problems can be found in [3,4] or [16].

multisets placed in the membranes encoded all the needed information for settling the features of the modules in the robot and their relative position. Nonetheless, for a methodological point of view, such information must be interpreted in order to have a 3D model of the robot. A simple way for graphically representing a membrane structure is to make a depth-first search of it and, for each membrane containing the object F, drawing a segment of length $m \times l$, where m is the multiplicity of F and l is a length unit. This segment is drawn rotated with respect to the segment corresponding to the parent membrane with an angle of $n \times \delta$, where n is the multiplicity of objects $\mathbf{R}_i$, $i \in \{H, L, U\}$ and δ is a fixed angle ($\pi/2$ in our example). Obtaining a 3D model from a P system configuration can be made by using different methods. In this paper, the well-known turtle interpretation [1,18] is considered: A turtle is placed on an N-dimensional space (usually, $N \in \{2, 3\}$) facing in a certain direction. The turtle can move and its movements are determined by a simple object language. In its basic version the symbols only control the number of straightforward steps and the angle and direction of turns. In this way, turtle interpretation is an appropriate tool for obtaining a 3D model of a P system configuration.

4   Cluster-Flow Locomotion of Spare Modules

In this paper, the final configuration is obtained by a cluster-flow locomotion of the modules of the robot[3]. These modules move from the initial configuration to the final one determined by a P system configuration. A segment of the robot determined by a membrane containing n objects F will be built by n modules in a row. Modules have three kinds of states during the interpretation.

- **Turtle Module:** Modules which do the search work for moving as the turtle.
- **Spare Module:** Modules that can move to other areas to continue the growth of structures.
- **Finalized Module:** Modules which have reached the final position will and do not move any more.

Turtle modules do the turtle search work according to inner objects in membrane configuration, as shown in Fig. 5. Connected modules at the moving direction receive a multiset of objects in membrane configuration from former turtle modules and become new turtle modules. New turtle modules receive P system objects by reducing one F. When all neighbouring lattices meet the membrane configuration description, the turtle module changes to finalized module as a fixed part of the reconfiguration result. This locomotion allows the robot to reach the final configuration for totally connected robots. A local localization strategy is used in this decentralized control mechanism. In decentralized robotic system, there is no compass direction for turtle moving as the graphic interpretation. Instead of global map for each module, the relative orientation

---

[3] A detailed description of the cluster-flow locomotion is out of the scope of this paper. A good introduction can be found, e.g., in [8] or [11].

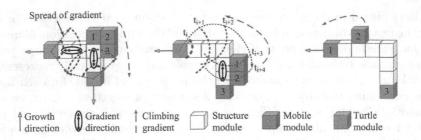

Fig. 5. Robotic segments develop by attaching new modules at neighboring lattice position in develop direction.

to connected neighbours is used. New attached modules get their global state from connected father module, which is the former turtle module. Directly connected modules can determine relative orientation through local communication on connecting surface. The regular organization of lattice-based module contributes to the computation of moving direction. The forward direction for F starts from the connecting surface receiving turtle state to the opposite surface. Turtles move by attaching a module in the neighboring lattice at the moving direction. If the neighboring lattice is not filled, spare modules in the system can move on the surface of other modules to fill it. Such modules can move on the surface of other modules, including finalized modules. Segments develop through constantly attaching new modules. CA is used for the cluster-flow locomotion of spare modules as shown in [35]. In order to get a computational model for controlling the movement of the modules, a set of CA rules has been designed, which only contains two rules. This set of rules is obviously simpler in numbers than the presented in [8]. Figure 6 show a scheme of both rules. The scheme on the left will be used for representing the convex and concave motion of one modules. The scheme on the right represents a one length movement of a module in linear motion. The gradient attraction strategy [24, 35] is used to provide moving directions for local modules[4].

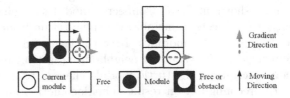

Fig. 6. A simplified set of CA rules for SCM

---

[4] See [35] for the technical details on the strategy for the maintenance of the global connection during the locomotion.

5 Simulation and Experimental Results

5.1 Convergence and Parallelism

Some multi-simulations have been performed in order to illustrate the used method. The membrane structure in Fig. 4(left) has been used in order to guide the self-reconfiguration process. Figure 7 shows multi simulations with increasing number of modules. All simulations start from a lattice structure and reconfigure to the predefined branching topology shown in Fig. 2. In order to verify the convergence of self-reconfiguration process, the number of modules is fixed according to the target configuration. Let us remark that decentralized modules are replaceable with each other, and there is no planning for particular position for each module. The whole structure is determined by the relative position of inner modules. Video attachments [36] record the corresponding self-reconfiguration process. The convergence of decentralized method is defined as the emergence of target structure, and has long been an open problem [14,24]. It is computed as the ratio of modules in the structure state and total modules that the target configuration. Since the robotic systems contain exactly the number of modules for target configuration, the convergence ratio increases to 100% when all modules change state to structure module. The used method is convergent in from the theoretical side, as the serial movement of turtle state between directly connected modules, but the convergence has also been verified in simulations, as shown in Fig. 8. Simulations in Fig. 7 are repeated 100 times, and simulation results are statistically analyzed. Statistical analysis shows

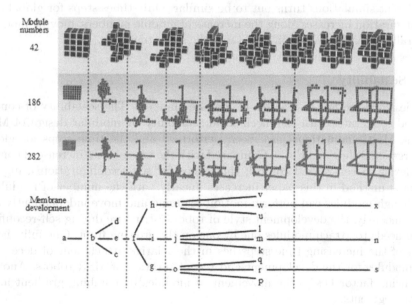

Fig. 7. Simulations with increasing number of modules by the membrane structure in Fig. 4(left).

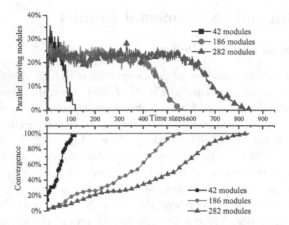

Fig. 8. Results analysis of convergent process and parallel character in decentralized modules.

the convergence of self-reconfiguration by the proposed method in Fig. 8. Compared with those emergent process [25], self-reconfigurations by the proposed method is convergent and has no unpractical assumptions. Some advantages of the physical application on real robots, and experiments are provided below. Self-reconfiguration by the proposed method is parallel in the level of independent modules. The introduction of membrane computing cooperates with the parallel nature of distributed modules. Figure 8 shows that the variation tendency in different simulations turns out to be similar. Only times steps for global self-reconfiguration increases along the increase of module numbers, moving modules in parallel in each simulation maintains the same tendency.

5.2   Scalability

The designed method is scalable to module numbers. The scalability of control method cooperates with the mechanical scalability by modular design of MSR robots. Multi simulations have been performed and the time steps for global convergence is shown in Fig. 9. Compared with the exponential increase of control complexity in centralized control, time steps for self-reconfiguration using the proposed method in this paper increases linearly with the number of modules.

Though modules can perform motion planning and move independently and simultaneously, the development style of robotic structure during self-reconfiguration needs to attach modules one by one on the growing front. One influencing factor of the increasing time steps lies in the relative attachment of decentralized modules for the development and reconfiguration of MSR robots. Another influencing factor lies in the movement of modules by climbing gradient along robotic segments.

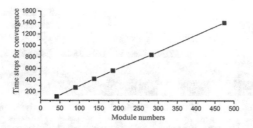

Fig. 9. Scalability to module numbers.

5.3 Experiments

The proposed method has also been verified on Modular *Self-re*configurable *Mo*bile (Seremo) robots which have been developed in the hardware laboratory at the Harbin Institute of Technology (Fig. 10(Left)). With a 80×80 (mm) lattice structure in 2D, a Seremo module is equipped with local communicating ability and local sensing ability on four connecting faces. Each module is a complete robot by itself with *onboard* sensors, actuators, processor, battery and means of communication[5]. The Seremo modules can move by rotating along the edge of neighboring modules. As shown in Fig. 10(Right), Seremo modules can achieve the convex, concave and linear motion of lattice motion in 2D. Seremo modules can autonomously connect to and disconnect from neighboring modules. Robots with Seremo modules can achieve decentralized locomotion by repeating the basic motion in Fig. 10(Right). A simple experiment with a membrane structure with two branches is shown in Fig. 11. Each branch is a segment with s modules linearly connected. All initial configurations starts from a linear structure and reconfigurations start from the first module in the right. Some experiments (with $s = 1, 2, 3, 4$) show the convergence to the topology defined by the membrane structure. Obstacles are also placed in experiments with $s = 3, 4$. With local sensing of Seremo modules, neighboring modules can sense the existing of obstacles and translate through local communication. The surface locomotion of Seremo modules can move around to the growing front according to local information. Video attachments [36] record the corresponding self-reconfiguration process.

Fig. 10. Seremo robots (Left). Lattice motion of Seremo modules (right).

---

[5] More details about the mechanical and electrical structure can be found at [6].

Fig. 11. Some experiments with Seremo robots.

6 Conclusions

The control of self-reconfigurable robots in an extremely hard task. On the one hand, it needs the development of efficient hardware modules able of performing quick and precise movements in two or three dimensions, but, on the other hand, it needs of theoretical contributions which guide the movements efficiently. Such moves depend on several changing variables. Each module processes information locally and independently from the other modules. Several modules can move simultaneously in order to reach the final configuration. Such configuration is not determined by a global position in a 3D space, but it is only determined by the relative position among the modules. In order to find an appropriate control of decentralized modules, many different ideas coming from different research areas are brought together in this paper. Among them, the partition of the Euclidean space into similar tiles where a module can be *alive* or not; a turtle interpretation for giving a *dynamic* meaning to a set of *static* symbols representing a configuration or a gradient attraction strategy for moving independent modules. The use of ideas from membrane computing can shed a new light to the local representation of the information. As pointed out above, the approach used in this paper can be considered from both theoretical and practical side, enriching each other with ideas coming from the self-configurable robots and from membrane computing. Such open research lines involve new developments in the application of the theoretical framework of membrane computing for the abstract representation of robots (and hence a deeper understanding of the theoretical possibilities) and also, from the practical side, the development of new abilities of physical robots inspired in the local encapsulation of the information. Many problems remain open. The study of how problems and techniques from both research areas can provide new solutions on the other side is matter of future research.

Acknowledgement. This work was supported by National Natural Science Foundation of China (Grant No. 61673137) and the Foundation for Innovative Research Groups of the National Natural Science Foundation of China (Grant No. 51521003).

References

1. Abelson, H., DiSessa, A.A.: Turtle Geometry: The Computer as a Medium for Exploring Mathematics. MIT Press, Cambridge (1986)
2. Baca, J., Woosley, B., Dasgupta, P., Nelson, C.A.: Configuration discovery of modular self-reconfigurable robots: real-time, distributed, Ir+XbEe communication method. Robot. Auton. Syst. **91**, 284–298 (2017)
3. Barbuti, R., Maggiolo-Schettini, A., Milazzo, P., Pardini, G.: Simulation of Spatial P System Models. Theor. Comput. Sci. **529**, 11–45 (2014)
4. Barbuti, R., Maggiolo-Schettini, A., Milazzo, P., Pardini, G., Tesei, L.: Spatial P systems. Nat. Comput. **10**(1), 3–16 (2011)
5. Bie, D., Gutiérrez-Naranjo, M.A., Zhao, J., Zhu, Y.: A Membrane Computing Framework for Self-Reconfigurable Robots (submitted)
6. Bie, D., Zhu, Y., Wang, X., Zhang, Y., Zhao, J.: L-systems driven self-reconfiguration of modular robots. Int. J. Adv. Robot. Syst. **13**(5), 1–12 (2016)
7. Bojinov, H., Casal, A., Hogg, T.: Multiagent control of self-reconfigurable robots. Artif. Intell. **142**(2), 99–120 (2002)
8. Butler, Z., Kotay, K., Rus, D., Tomita, K.: Generic decentralized control for a class of self-reconfigurable robots. In: IEEE International Conference on Robotics and Automation, ICRA 2002, vol. 1, pp. 809–816 (2002)
9. Butler, Z., Kotay, K., Rus, D., Tomita, K.: Cellular automata for decentralized control of self-reconfigurable robots. In: IEEE ICRA Workshop on Modular Robots, pp. 21–26 (2001)
10. Butler, Z.J., Kotay, K., Rus, D., Tomita, K.: Generic decentralized control for lattice-based self-reconfigurable robots. Int. J. Robot. Res. **23**(9), 919–937 (2004)
11. Fitch, R., Butler, Z.J.: Scalable locomotion for large self-reconfiguring robots. In: IEEE International Conference on Robotics and Automation, pp. 2248–2253 (2007)
12. Fukuda, T., Nakagawa, S.: Approach to the dynamically reconfigurable robotic system. J. Intell. Robot. Syst. **1**(1), 55–72 (1988)
13. Georgiou, A., Gheorghe, M., Bernardini, F.: Membrane-based devices used in computer graphics. In: Ciobanu, G., Păun, G., Pérez-Jiménez, M.J. (eds.) Applications of Membrane Computing. Natural Computing Series, pp. 253–281. Springer, Heidelberg (2006)
14. Hou, F., Shen, W.: Graph-based optimal reconfiguration planning for self-reconfigurable robots. Robot. Auton. Syst. **62**(7), 1047–1059 (2014)
15. Lakhlef, H., Bourgeois, J., Mabed, H., Goldstein, S.C.: Energy-aware parallel self-reconfiguration for chains microrobot networks. J. Parallel Distrib. Comput. **75**, 67–80 (2015)
16. Margenstern, M.: Can hyperbolic geometry be of help for P systems? In: Martín-Vide, C., Mauri, G., Păun, G., Rozenberg, G., Salomaa, A. (eds.) WMC 2003. LNCS, vol. 2933, pp. 240–249. Springer, Heidelberg (2004). https://doi.org/10.1007/978-3-540-24619-0_18
17. Perez-Diaz, F., Zillmer, R., Groß, R.: Control of synchronization regimes in networks of mobile interacting agents. Phys. Rev. Appl. **7**, 054002 (2017)
18. Prusinkiewicz, P.: Graphical applications of L-systems. In: Proceedings on Graphics Interface 1986/Vision Interface 1986, pp. 247–253. Canadian Information Processing Society, Toronto (1986)
19. Prusinkiewicz, P., Lindenmayer, A.: The Algorithmic Beauty of Plants. Virtual Laboratory. Springer, New York (1990)

20. Păun, G., Rozenberg, G., Salomaa, A. (eds.): The Oxford Handbook of Membrane Computing. Oxford University Press, Oxford (2010)

21. Rivero-Gil, E., Gutiérrez-Naranjo, M.A., Romero Jiménez, Á., Riscos-Núñez, A.: A software tool for generating graphics by means of P systems. Nat. Comput. **10**(2), 879–890 (2011)

22. Romanishin, J.W., Gilpin, K., Claici, S., Rus, D.: 3D M-blocks: self-reconfiguring robots capable of locomotion via pivoting in three dimensions. In: IEEE International Conference on Robotics and Automation, ICRA 2015, Seattle, WA, USA, 26–30 May 2015, pp. 1925–1932. IEEE (2015)

23. Romero-Jiménez, A., Gutiérrez-Naranjo, M.A., Pérez-Jiménez, M.J.: Graphical modeling of higher plants using P systems. In: Hoogeboom, H.J., Păun, G., Rozenberg, G., Salomaa, A. (eds.) WMC 2006. LNCS, vol. 4361, pp. 496–506. Springer, Heidelberg (2006). https://doi.org/10.1007/11963516_31

24. Stoy, K.: Using cellular automata and gradients to control self-reconfiguration. Robot. Auton. Syst. **54**(2), 135–141 (2006)

25. Stoy, K.: Lattice automata for control of self-reconfigurable robots. In: Sirakoulis, G.C., Adamatzky, A. (eds.) Robots and Lattice Automata. ECC, vol. 13, pp. 33–45. Springer, Cham (2015). https://doi.org/10.1007/978-3-319-10924-4_2

26. Stoy, K., Brandt, D., Christensen, D.J.: Self-Reconfigurable Robots: An Introduction. Intelligent Robotics and Autonomous Agents. MIT Press, Cambridge (2010)

27. Valentini, G., Ferrante, E., Hamann, H., Dorigo, M.: Collective decision with 100 kilobots: speed versus accuracy in binary discrimination problems. Auton. Agent. Multi-Ag. **30**(3), 553–580 (2016)

28. Vergara, A., Lau, Y.S., Mendoza-Garcia, R.F., Zagal, J.C.: Soft modular robotic cubes: toward replicating morphogenetic movements of the embryo. Plos One **12**(1), 1–17 (2017)

29. Wang, X., Jin, H., Zhu, Y., Chen, B., Bie, D., Zhang, Y., Zhao, J.: Serpenoid polygonal rolling for chain-type modular robots: a study of modeling, pattern switching and application. Robot. Cim-Int. Manuf. **39**, 56–67 (2016)

30. Wolfram, S.: Cellular Automata and Complexity: Collected Papers. Addison-Wesley, Reading (1994)

31. Yang, Z., Wu, Y., Fu, Z., Fei, J., Zheng, H.: A unit-compressible modular robotic system and its self-configuration strategy using meta-module. Robot. Cim-Int. Manuf. **49**, 39–53 (2018)

32. Yim, M., Shen, W., Salemi, B., Rus, D., Moll, M., Lipson, H., Klavins, E., Chirikjian, G.S.: Modular self-reconfigurable robot systems [grand challenges of robotics]. IEEE Robot. Autom. Mag. **14**(1), 43–52 (2007)

33. Zhang, Y., Song, G., Liu, S., Qiao, G., Zhang, J., Sun, H.: A modular self-reconfigurable robot with enhanced locomotion performances: design, modeling, simulations, and experiments. J. Intell. Robot. Syst. **81**(3–4), 377–393 (2016)

34. Zhao, J., Wang, X., Jin, H., Bie, D., Zhu, Y.: Automatic locomotion generation for a ubot modular robot-towards both high-speed and multiple patterns. Int. J. Adv. Robot. Syst. **12**, 32 (2015)

35. Zhu, Y., Bie, D., Iqbal, S., Wang, X., Gao, Y., Zhao, J.: A simplified approach to realize cellular automata for ubot modular self-reconfigurable robots. J. Intell. Robot. Syst. **79**(1), 37–54 (2015)

36. https://sites.google.com/site/modularrobots/cycling

Multi-threshold Image Segmentation Method Based on Flower Pollination Algorithm

Jingjing Xue[1]([✉]), Xingshi He[1], Xinshe Yang[1,2], Xiaoying Hao[1], and Feiyue He[1]

[1] College of Science, Xi'an Polytechnic University, Xi'an 710048, China
sara-1211@qq.com
[2] School of Science and Technology, Middlesex University London,
London NW4 4BT, UK

Abstract. Multi-threshold segmentation is a powerful technique that is used for the processing of pattern recognition and computer vision. However, traditional, exhaustive search is computationally expensive when searching for thresholds. In order to solve such challenging problems, the fitness function is designed by the maximum entropy method, the optimal threshold of segmentation is found by using the parallel optimization mechanism of Flower Pollination algorithm (FPA), then a multi-threshold image segmentation algorithm based on FPA is proposed. The experimental results show that FPA is superior to the genetic algorithm (GA) and the shuffled frog leaping algorithm (SFLA).

Keywords: Flower pollination algorithm · Image segmentation · Exhaustive search · Multi-threshold · Maximum entropy

1 Introduction

Image segmentation is very critical for the transition from image processing to image analysis. The quality of the image segmentation can directly affect the quality of the image information such as target recognition [1]. Therefore, image segmentation has been one of the hot topics in image processing. Threshold-based segmentation is a common method of image segmentation. According to the principle of separation, these methods can be classified into a few subcategories such as the Otsu's method, the maximum entropy method and the minimum error method [2], etc.

According to the number of thresholds when separating the object of interest and background, such methods can be divided into single threshold segmentation and multi-threshold segmentation. Traditional, exhaustive search algorithms have to search for the optimal combination of multiple thresholds in the gray scale of the image, therefore, calculations are complex and time-consuming. So it is difficult to meet the stringent requirements of time and speed in modern image processing and analysis. As a result, how to improve the efficiency of multi-threshold search becomes one of the hot research topics in this area.

© Springer Nature Singapore Pte Ltd. 2017
C. He et al. (Eds.): BIC-TA 2017, CCIS 791, pp. 39–51, 2017.
https://doi.org/10.1007/978-981-10-7179-9_4

Some researchers have taken into account the parallel nature and ease of implementation of optimization algorithms [3], and thus have used nature-inspired optimization algorithms to solve multiple threshold image segmentation problems. In recent years, some significant progress has been made, and algorithms such as genetic algorithm (GA) [4], particle swarm optimization (PSO) algorithm [5], artificial bee colony (ABC) algorithm and shuffled frog leaping algorithm (SFLA) have been successfully applied to parallel multi-threshold segmentation [6].

For example, in [7], Cai et al. combined GA with the maximum entropy method and studied the dual threshold segmentation method, which effectively improved the efficiency of double threshold segmentation. In 2010, Zhou and Ge combined PSO with the Otsu's method and studied the multi-threshold segmentation method [8], which effectively improved the efficiency of multi-threshold segmentation when compared with traditional Otsu's method. In addition, in [9], Horng combined ABC algorithm with the maximum entropy method, which effectively improved the efficiency of multi-threshold segmentation. In 2013 [10], in order to solve the problem of multi-threshold segmentation, Liu and Ma combined the cuckoo search algorithm with the Otsu's method, demonstrating that it outperformed both the bacterial foraging algorithm and ABC algorithm in terms of segmentation speed and segmentation thresholds. In 2011, Lu et al. combined SFLA with the 2-D Otsu's method to improve the quality of multi-threshold segmentation [11]. Therefore, it can be seen that the parallel search mechanism in swarm intelligence can improve the efficiency of image multi-thresholding.

However, the above mentioned methods have some drawbacks because they can easily fall into local optima and they cannot avoid the phenomenon of premature convergence, and consequently their scopes of application are limited. Proposed by Yang in 2012 [12], the Flower Pollination algorithm (FPA) is a new population-based optimization algorithm that simulates flower pollination behavior in nature. Although relatively new, it has been extensively researched over the past several years. For example, Yang and He used FPA to solve a multi-objective optimization problem in 2013 [13]. Rodrigues et al. applied FPA to EEG-based person identification [14]. In [15], Rodrigues et al. applied FPA to solve the problem of feature selection. In [16], Li and He used FPA to solve the travelling salesman problem. Also in 2015, Wang et al. [17] used FPA to solve the problem of multi-threshold segmentation based on Otsu's method.

In order to explore potential applications of FPA further in image multi-threshold segmentation, in this paper, we apply the FPA to maximum entropy multi-threshold segmentation. We will compare the results concerning the segmentation threshold vector, the maximum entropy values and the running time with those obtained by other methods. Therefore, the rest of this paper is organized as follows. Section 2 briefly introduces the FPA and Sect. 3 presents our proposed FPA-based multiple threshold image segmentation method. Section 4 uses experiments to validate the proposed approach and Sect. 5 concludes with discussions.

2   Flower Pollination Algorithm

The FPA is proposed by Yang in 2012, it simulates the flower pollination behavior in nature, and follows four idealized rules:

1. Biological cross-pollination is considered as global pollination process with pollen-carrying pollinators performing Lévy flights. The rule can be represented mathematically as

$$X_i^{t+1} = X_i^t + L(g^* - X_i^t), \tag{1}$$

where X_i^t is the pollen i or solution vector X_i at iteration t, and g^* is the current best solution found among all solutions at the current generation. The parameter L is a step size. Since insects may move over a long distance with various distance steps, we can use a Lévy flight to mimic this characteristic efficiently. That is L obeys Levy distribution

$$L \sim \frac{\lambda \Gamma(\lambda) \sin(\frac{\pi \lambda}{2})}{\pi} \frac{1}{s^{1+\lambda}} (s \gg s_0 > 0). \tag{2}$$

Here $\Gamma(\lambda)$ is the standard gamma function, and this distribution is valid for large steps s. In all our simulations below, we have used $\lambda = 1.5$.

2. Abiotic and self-pollination are considered as local pollination. The local pollination can be represented as

$$X_i^{t+1} = X_i^t + \epsilon(X_j^t - X_k^t), \tag{3}$$

where X_j^t and X_k^t are pollen from the different flowers of the same plant species. This essentially mimics the flower constancy in a limited neighborhood. Mathematically speaking, if X_j^t and X_k^t comes from the same species or selected from the same population, this becomes a local random walk if we draw from a uniform distribution in $[0, 1]$.

3. Flower constancy can be considered as the reproduction probability that is proportional to the similarity of two flowers involved.

4. Local pollination and global pollination can be controlled by a switch probability $p \in [0, 1]$. Due to the physical proximity and other factors such as wind, local pollination can have a significant fraction p in the overall pollination activities.

According to the above process of flower pollination, the main steps of FPA can be summarized as follows:

Step 1 Initialize all parameters of the FPA, such as population quantity n, probability $p \in [0, 1]$, the maximum number of iteration G, and generate n initial pollen population randomly.

Step 2 Calculate the quality of each pollen according to the fitness function, and find out the current optimal solution g^*.

Step 3 Generate a random real number r in $[0, 1]$, which obeys a uniform distribution.

Step 4 If $r < p$, carry out cross-pollination via Eq. (1) and then generate the next generation X_i^{t+1}.

Step 5 If $r > p$, carry out self-pollination via Eq. (3), and generate the next generation X_i^{t+1}.

Step 6 Calculate the fitness value of X_i^{t+1}, if it is superior to X_i^t, X_i^{t+1} can be selected as the next generation, or is X_i^t.

Step 7 Execute Step 2 to Step 6 until the iteration is G. Then output the best pollen.

3   Multi-threshold Segmentation Based on FPA

3.1   Maximum Entropy Multi-threshold Segmentation

In most swarm intelligence based algorithms, the selection of fitness function is important for optimization; it guides the foraging or evolution in a certain direction, and finally achieves the optimal state. In this paper, the maximum entropy method is used to implement image threshold segmentation.

The maximum entropy image segmentation method was first proposed by Kapur [18]. Suppose a gray image with L grayscale, here $L \in [0, 255]$. The corresponding pixel information entropy can be represented as:

$$H = -\sum_{i=0}^{L} p_i \ln p_i, \tag{4}$$

where $p_i = f_i/N$ is the probability that grayscale i appears, and N is the total number of pixels in the image. Suppose an image is divided into part A and part B by the threshold β, then the entropy of part A plus entropy of part B is the information entropy of all the pixels in the image [19].

$$\varphi(\beta) = H(A) + H(B)$$

$$= \ln(\sum_{i=0}^{\beta} p_i) + \ln(\sum_{i=\beta+1}^{L} p_i) - \frac{\sum_{i=0}^{\beta} p_i \ln p_i}{\sum_{i=0}^{\beta} p_i} - \frac{\sum_{i=\beta+1}^{L} p_i \ln p_i}{\sum_{i=\beta+1}^{L} p_i}. \tag{5}$$

As we know from the theory of entropy, if the threshold β can make $\varphi(\beta)$ maximum, then β is the best image segmentation threshold.

Now we expand single threshold segmentation to multi-threshold segmentation. Suppose that the number of threshold are T, then the image is divided into $T + 1$ parts. And the objective function can be represented mathematically as

$$\varphi(\beta_1, \beta_2, \cdots, \beta_T) = H(A_1) + \cdots + H(A_{T+1})$$

$$= ln(\sum_{i=0}^{\beta_1} p_i) + ln(\sum_{i=\beta_1+1}^{\beta_2} p_i) + \cdots + ln(\sum_{i=\beta_{T-1}+1}^{\beta_T} p_i)$$

$$+ ln(\sum_{i=\beta_T+1}^{L} p_i) - \frac{\sum_{i=0}^{\beta_1} p_i ln p_i}{\sum_{i=0}^{\beta_1} p_i} - \frac{\sum_{i=\beta_1+1}^{\beta_2} p_i ln p_i}{\sum_{i=\beta_1+1}^{\beta_2} p_i} \tag{6}$$

$$- \cdots - \frac{\sum_{i=\beta_{T-1}+1}^{\beta_T} p_i ln p_i}{\sum_{i=\beta_{T-1}+1}^{\beta_T} p_i} - \frac{\sum_{i=\beta_T+1}^{L} p_i ln p_i}{\sum_{i=\beta_T+1}^{L} p_i}.$$

The best threshold vector $(\beta_1^*, \beta_2^*, \cdots, \beta_T^*)$ can be represented mathematically as

$$(\beta_1^*, \beta_2^*, \cdots, \beta_T^*) = \arg \max_{(\beta_1, \beta_2, \cdots, \beta_T)} (\varphi(\beta_1, \beta_2, \cdots, \beta_T)). \tag{7}$$

Through above analyses, using FPA to maximize Eq. (6) is the key, and the solution is a multi-threshold segmentation vector.

3.2   The Process of Algorithm

In this paper, FPA is applied to maximum entropy multi-threshold segmentation to find out the optimal threshold vector. The dimension of the vector is T and its component denotes the pixel intensity whose scope is from 0 to 255. So concrete steps are as follows:

Step 1   Initialize the population and some parameters. Suppose that the number of population is n, initial pollen solutions are $X(0) = \{X1(0), X2(0), \cdots, Xn(0)\}$. Then calculate the fitness function values of every flower via Eq. (6). So $g = \max(fit(X1(0)), fit(X2(0)), \cdots, fit(Xn(0)))$ is the global optimal value, global optimal solution is g^*. Here, we use a fixed maximum number of iterations G.

Step 2   Update and get new flower species by Eq. (1) or Eq. (3), and calculate fitness. Compare them with the old solutions, if the new solution is superior to the old solution, then update the current solution and current fitness value; otherwise, keep the current solution and current fitness value. And if the fitness value of new solution is greater than g, update the global optimal solution g^* and the global optimal objective value g.

Step 3   Termination condition: If the maximum number of iterations is greater than G, turn to Step 4, else to Step 2.

Step 4   Image segmentation is performed with the point gray scale g^* corresponding to the current optimal objective value g , obtained as the optimal threshold.

4   Numerical Experiments

In order to verify the effectiveness of the FPA in the multi-threshold segmentation, we compare it with GA and SFLA in terms of optimization speed and quality, the following six open standard test images are selected: Lena, Cameraman, Boat, Airplane, Man, Rice. They are all from The University of South California SIPI Image Database (http://sipi.usc.edu/database/).

4.1   The Segmentation Results Based on FPA

Equation (6) is selected as the fitness function of FPA, the segmentation thresholds of the six standard test images are obtained by using FPA. And the segmentation results of FPA are described in Fig. 1 where the left column corresponds

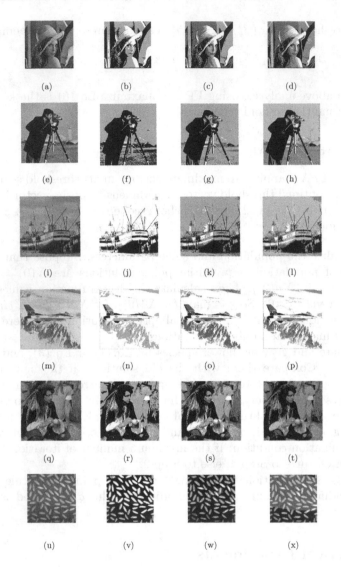

Fig. 1. The images on the first column [i.e., (a)(e)(i)(m)(q)(u)] are the standard test images. The images on the second column [i.e., (b)(f)(j)(n)(r)(v)] are the segmented images with two thresholds. The images on the third column [i.e., (c)(g)(k)(o)(s)(w)] are the segmented images with three thresholds. The fourth column corresponds to segmented images with four thresholds [i.e., (d)(h)(l)(p)(t)(x)].

to the six standard test images, and the right side corresponds to segmented images when the number of thresholds is 2, 3, and 4, respectively. These segmentation images are closer to original images as the number of segmentation thresholds increase. This is because with the increase of threshold number, the

Table 1. Optimal objective value and threshold for Image (Lena).

Method	T	Objective value	Threshold
Exhausted		12.6551	81,150
FPA	2	12.6551	81,150
GA		12.65509	82,150
SFLA		12.6463	80,154
Exhausted		15.7211	61,109,159
FPA	3	15.7207	61,108,159
GA		15.7083	64,115,163
SFLA		15.6944	68,110,162
Exhausted		18.5668	58,100,142,180
FPA	4	18.5600	61,102,143,182
GA		18.4866	57,107,146,191
SFLA		18.3768	52,110,136,178

gray scale information of the segmented image is getting rich and the features are getting clearer.

4.2   Comparison of Each Algorithm Performance

All algorithms have been programmed in MATLAB R2014a, and above six standard test images are experimental images. The control parameters of three segmentation algorithms are as follows: $n = 20$ is the size of population, $G = 100$ is the maximum number of iteration, and $p = 0.8$ is the switch probability for FPA. As for GA, $M = 0.03$ is the mutation probability, $C = 0.6$ is the crossover probability. As for SFLA, $a = 4$ is the number of group, $N_e = 8$ is the number of iteration for worst frogs in group. $S = 20$ is the biggest leap of the breaststroke. It is known in the literature that these algorithms performs relatively better when algorithm parameters are taken as above [10].

Tables 1, 2, 3, 4, 5 and 6 show the comparison of mentioned segmentation algorithms as for objective values and threshold of six images, respectively. And the comparison of mentioned segmentation algorithms for time is listed in Table 7.

Because of the random nature of heuristic search algorithms, each algorithm runs one hundred times independently. Tables 8, 9 and 10 are the comparison of three methods in terms of means and worst objective values when the threshold value is 2, 3 and 4, respectively.

In this paper, the fitness function represents the entropy between the object of interest and background, and the larger the value is, the better. The fitness values found by these three algorithms are close to those by the exhausted method, and we select a set of optimal thresholds from results. From Tables 1, 2, 3, 4, 5

Table 2. Optimal objective value and threshold for Image (Cameraman).

Method	T	Objective value	Threshold
Exhausted		12.0797	127,197
FPA	2	12.0797	127,197
GA		12.0754	129,195
SFLA		12.0746	128,198
Exhausted		15.4142	43,109,197
FPA	3	15.4142	43,109,197
GA		15.4026	40,110,198
SFLA		15.3312	56,121,197
Exhausted		18.5732	42,99,153,197
FPA	4	18.5650	44,98,153,198
GA		18.5373	37,96,156,196
SFLA		18.5194	31,95,149,199

Table 3. Optimal objective value and threshold for Image (Boat).

Method	T	Objective value	Threshold
Exhausted		11.9765	65,122
FPA	2	11.9765	65,122
GA		11.9682	62,120
SFLA		11.9603	68,125
Exhausted		15.2431	65,122,176
FPA	3	15.2431	65,122,176
GA		15.2387	63,120,176
SFLA		15.1126	82,126,179
Exhausted		18.1127	46,85,124,176
FPA	4	18.0921	48,91,127,177
GA		18.0176	60,102,142,174
SFLA		17.8650	68,120,147,176

and 6, we know for the same image, the same number of thresholds, the rank of three algorithms about threshold quality is: FPA > GA > SFLA. Because in FPA, pollinators routinely pollinate through Lévy flight, which not only can expand the search ranges and increase the diversity of the population, but also be easier to jump out of the local optima. The optimal individuals of the FPA are superior to the optimal individuals of the other two algorithms, because the internal search mechanisms of each algorithm and the updating strategies are different. Also the results of FPA are consistent with the results of the exhaustive method.

Table 4. Optimal objective value and threshold for Image (Airplane).

Method	T	Objective value	Threshold
Exhausted		12.2304	70,172
FPA	2	12.2304	70,172
GA		12.2303	70,171
SFLA		12.2242	68,172
Exhausted		15.5486	68,126,182
FPA	3	15.5486	68,126,182
GA		15.5225	71,125,185
SFLA		15.4369	74,121,172
Exhausted		18.3977	66,106,145,185
FPA	4	18.3891	64,101,144,185
GA		18.2072	62,104,162,192
SFLA		18.2834	57,96,127,181

Table 5. Optimal objective value and threshold for Image (Man).

Method	T	Objective value	Threshold
Exhausted		12.6572	90,172
FPA	2	12.6572	90,172
GA		12.6571	91,172
SFLA		12.6483	94,170
Exhausted		15.8600	61,116,174
FPA	3	15.8600	61,116,174
GA		15.8459	53,108,174
SFLA		15.7769	74,129,181
Exhausted		18.7958	61,116,174,230
FPA	4	18.7842	66,117,173,230
GA		18.6576	68,108,172,236
SFLA		18.6850	75,130,176,235

We can know from Table 7, for the same image and the same number of thresholds, intelligent algorithm is faster than the exhaustive method as for segmentation speed, and the rank of three intelligent algorithms about speed is: FPA > GA > SFLA. This is mainly attributed to the fact that FPA does not execute explicitly selection and crossover to produce the next generation of population as used in GA. As for SFLA, FPA does not classify the population, change the positions of the worst in the sub-population frogs. On the other hand, the use of the Lévy flight to achieve global optimization simplifies the operation steps of the FPA algorithm and improves the running efficiency of the algorithm.

Table 6. Optimal objective value and threshold for Image (Rice).

Method	T	Objective value	Threshold
Exhausted		11.5734	102,158
FPA	2	11.5734	102,158
GA		11.5734	102,158
SFLA		11.5472	103,148
Exhausted		14.4904	102,148,192
FPA	3	14.4859	100,148,192
GA		14.4292	101,149,197
SFLA		14.3593	100,134,196
Exhausted		17.2337	73,104,148,192
FPA	4	17.2039	77,104,148,194
GA		17.1049	73,102,136,184
SFLA		16.5429	62,117,149,169

Table 7. Comparison of time for four methods(s).

Image	T	Exhausted method	FPA	GA	SFLA
Lena (256 × 256)	2	1.6250	0.0931	0.0672	0.8730
	3	475.6170	0.1085	0.1295	0.9352
	4	2.5826e + 05	0.1264	0.1838	1.0025
Cameraman (650 × 607)	2	1.7040	0.1021	0.0540	0.9257
	3	592.6710	0.1100	0.1260	0.9867
	4	2.7031e + 05	0.1248	0.1941	1.0457
Boat (512 × 512)	2	1.6250	0.0941	0.0682	0.8260
	3	562.7440	0.1086	0.1175	0.9184
	4	2.5508e + 05	0.1274	0.1813	0.9645
Airplane (512 × 512)	2	1.5620	0.0926	0.0558	0.8076
	3	566.5990	0.1092	0.1319	0.9128
	4	2.5370e + 05	0.1315	0.1847	1.0741
Man (1024 × 1024)	2	1.7660	0.0963	0.0574	0.9081
	3	578.1240	0.1154	0.1301	0.9859
	4	2.6996e + 05	0.1255	0.2038	1.0675
Rice (256 × 256)	2	1.4690	0.0908	0.0674	0.7854
	3	441.8090	0.1046	0.1335	0.8684
	4	2.3998e + 05	0.1200	0.1833	1.0087

Table 8. Mean and worst objective value of FPA GA and SFLA for $T = 2$.

Mean				Worst		
Image	FPA	GA	SFLA	FPA	GA	SFLA
Lena	12.6551	12.5112	12.4154	12.6546	11.7398	11.6234
Cameraman	12.0794	11.8226	11.7490	12.0766	11.3918	11.1307
Boat	11.9758	11.8392	11.7495	11.9690	10.9959	11.1690
Airplane	12.2301	12.0937	11.9844	12.2290	11.4692	10.8077
Man	12.6571	12.4849	12.3957	12.6562	11.8740	11.7515
Rice	11.5726	11.4388	11.2009	11.5685	11.1566	9.0931

Table 9. Mean and worst objective value of FPA GA and SFLA for $T = 3$.

Mean				Worst		
Image	FPA	GA	SFLA	FPA	GA	SFLA
Lena	15.7121	15.3559	16.3930	15.6810	14.1510	13.3591
Cameraman	15.4009	15.0799	15.9577	15.3547	14.0689	11.2399
Boat	15.2118	14.6944	15.4171	15.0993	13.1041	11.9522
Airplane	15.5322	15.1085	16.0842	15.4558	14.0171	11.9305
Man	15.8521	15.4694	17.1148	15.8269	14.9985	13.9908
Rice	14.4405	14.0703	13.8562	14.3163	12.9330	9.1619

Table 10. Mean and worst objective value of FPA GA and SFLA for $T = 4$.

Mean				Worst		
Image	FPA	GA	SFLA	FPA	GA	SFLA
Lena	18.4291	17.8506	16.3930	16.2005	16.5763	13.3590
Cameraman	18.4657	17.8735	15.9577	18.1029	16.0294	11.2400
Boat	17.8650	16.9898	15.4171	16.2213	14.9098	11.8650
Airplane	18.2073	17.5465	16.0842	17.5032	15.4859	11.9305
Man	18.7109	18.2390	17.1148	18.4671	16.6858	13.9908
Rice	18.5244	16.4562	13.8562	16.2453	13.8171	9.1619

Thus, FPA can quickly find the optimal solutions with only a small number of population and the number of cycles with reduced computational complexity.

It is worth noting that GA is faster than FPA when the number of segmentation threshold is two, because when the dimension is not high, GA executes selection, crossover, and mutation operations to produce the next generation of population, it is easier to access to optimal solutions. While as the number of thresholds increases, the dimension of the problem is increased and the time complexity of the algorithm increases. So GA will take a long time because of the lack of global search capabilities. It is shown that the FPA is better than GA and SFLA, it is more suitable to solve the problem of multi-threshold image segmentation.

5 Conclusion

In this paper, we have proposed a multi-threshold segmentation algorithm, based on the flower pollination algorithm for the multi-threshold image segmentation. The maximum entropy method has been used to design the fitness function to guide the algorithm to find the optimal segmentation threshold. The experimental results show that for the same number of thresholds and the same set of images, the FPA is superior to the other two algorithms in terms of segmentation speed and segmentation thresholds.

It is worth pointing out that the above conclusions are based on a small number of images, and thus more tests may be needed to confirm such observations. Although the fitness of FPA is close to the exhaustive method, it has its own limitation. Its running time is slower than GA as for double threshold segmentation. Also when the number of threshold increases, the fitness value gaps between FPA and exhaustive method increase. Therefore, further studies will focus on the improvement of the proposed method for multi-threshold image segmentation. For example, the accuracy seems to be reduced as the number of thresholds increases. Further work will investigate this issue further so as to improve the accuracy. Another improvement can be the use of different performance measures to compare the quality of segmented images so as to see which performance measures are most suitable for such a comparison purpose.

Acknowledgments. This work is supported by Soft Science Research Program of Shaanxi Province in China (Grant No. 2014KRM2801), the Major program of Xi'an in China (Grant No. 2015ZB-ZY04) and the Scientific Research Fundation of the Education Department of Shaanxi Province, China (Grant No. 16JK1326).

References

1. Zhang, Y.J.: Image engineering in China 2010. J. Image Graphic. **12**(5), 753–775 (2011)
2. Yang, H.: Research on thresholding methods for image segmentation. J. Liaoning Univ. **33**(2), 135–137 (2006)
3. Pal, N.R., Pal, S.K.: A review on image segmentation techniques. Pattern Recogn. **38**(9), 1277–1294 (1993)
4. Goldberg, D.E.: Genetic Algorithm in Search, Optimization, and Machine Learning. Addison-Wesley, Reading (1989)
5. Kennedy, J., Eberhart, R.: Particle swarm optimization. In: IEEE International Conference on Neural Networks, vol. 4, pp. 1942–1948. IEEE (1995)
6. Eusuff, M., Lansey, K., Pasha, F.: Shuffled frog-leaping algorithm: a memetic meta-heuristic for discrete optimization. Eng. Optimiz. **38**(2), 129–154 (2006)

7. Cai, J.J., He, J., Guo, Q.K., Lin, F.S.: Maximum entropy double threshold image segmentation based on genetic algorithm. Comput. Program. Skills Mainten., 69–71 (2016)
8. Zhou, X.W., Ge, Y.H.: Multilevel threshold method for image segmentation based on particle swarm optimization and maximal variance. Sci. Surv. Mapp. (2010)
9. Horng, M.H.: Multilevel thresholding selection based on the artificial bee colony algorithm for image segmentation. Expert. Syst. Appl. **38**(11), 13785–13791 (2011)
10. Liu, X.N., Ma, M.: Application of cuckoo search algorithm in multi-threshold image segmentation. Comput. Eng. **39**(7), 274–278 (2013)
11. Lu, B.B., Jia, Z.H., He, D., Yang, J., Pang, S.N.: Romte-sensing image segmentation method based on improved OTSU and shuffled frog-leaping algorithm. Comput. Appl. Softw. **28**(9), 77–79 (2011)
12. Yang, X.S.: Flower pollination algorithm for global optimization. In: Durand-Lose, J., Jonoska, N. (eds.) UCNC 2012. LNCS, vol. 7445, pp. 240–249. Springer, Heidelberg (2012). https://doi.org/10.1007/978-3-642-32894-7_27
13. Yang, X.S., Karamanoglu, M., He, X.S.: Multi-objective flower algorithm for optimization. Procedia Comput. Sci. **18**(1), 861–868 (2013)
14. Rodrigues, D., Silva, G.F.A., Papa, J.P., et al.: EEG-based person identification through binary flower pollination algorithm. Expert. Syst. Appl. **62**, 81–90 (2016)
15. Rodrigues, D., Yang, X.S., Souza, A.N.D., Papa, J.P.: Binary flower pollination algorithm and its application to feature selection. In: Yang, X.-S. (ed.) Recent Advances in Swarm Intelligence and Evolutionary Computation. SCI, vol. 585, pp. 85–100. Springer, Cham (2015). https://doi.org/10.1007/978-3-319-13826-8_5
16. Li, Q., He, X.S., Yang, X.S.: A discrete flower pollination algorithm for travelling salesman problem. Comput. Modernizat. **251**(7), 37–43 (2016)
17. Wang, R., Zhou, Y., Zhao, C., Wu, H.: A hybrid flower pollination algorithm based modified randomized location for multi-threshold medical image segmentation. Bio-Med. Mater. Eng. **26**(s1), S1345–S1351 (2015)
18. Kapur, J.N., Sahoo, P.K., Wong, A.K.C.: A new method for gray-level picture thresholding using the entropy of the histogram. Comput. Vis. Graph. Image Process. **29**(3), 273–285 (1985)
19. Wang, X.H., Xu, W.B.: Study on maximum entropy multilevel threshold segmentation based on genetic algorithm. J. Guizhou Univ. **24**(4), 401–403 (2007)

An Elitist Non-dominated Sorting Hybrid Evolutionary Algorithm for Multi-objective Constrained Ship Arrangements Optimization Problem

Hao Wang[✉], Shunhuai Chen, and Liang Luo

Wuhan University of Technology, Wuhan, China
hao_wang@whut.edu.cn

Abstract. As the complexity of ship arrangements increases, general arrangements optimization technology based on evolutionary algorithms has emerged, giving enormous potential to assist designers in enhancing the range of alternative arrangements and in expediting the design process. This paper presents a hybrid evolutionary algorithm to handle the multi-objective constrained arrangements optimization problem based on elitist non-dominated sorting strategy. To enhance the efficiency of optimization, a hybrid evolutionary algorithm that couples an NSGA-II with a stochastic local search technique is used to find feasible solutions rapidly and facilitate local optimization. However, the algorithm that can rapidly find feasible solutions is also expected to contribute to better optimization. It has also been observed that lack of diversity of potential solutions leads to a local optimal solution which means the coherent arrangements could not be discovered. Hence, a modified replacement strategy is proposed to overcome this drawback. The final experimental results illustrate that the algorithm is capable of generating coherent arrangements.

Keywords: Ship arrangements · Multi-objective optimization · NSGA-II · Stochastic local search

1 Introduction

The arrangements optimization problem consists of determining the best size and position for shipboard elements on several ship decks. The optimal goals and constraints can be divided into two aspects, those of topology and geometry. The arrangements optimization problem is one of the classical Non-deterministic Polynomial Complete problems [1]. Moreover, the large number of variables and constraints are the most significant features of arrangements optimization. The large number of variables results in very high-dimensional and vast search spaces. On the other hand, the large number of constraints makes the feasible solution spaces become discrete and tiny relative to the search space. The ability to find quick solutions is a challenging task in the arrangements optimization problem.

C. He et al. (Eds.): BIC-TA 2017, CCIS 791, pp. 52–67, 2017.
https://doi.org/10.1007/978-981-10-7179-9_5

Generating general arrangements is a crucial part of ship design. The traditional general arrangements design method is a repetitive trial-and-error procedure, where different dimensions and positions of elements are adjusted until a feasible arrangement, satisfying design requirements, emerges. During the past 30 years, the attention to ship arrangements optimization has been steadily increasing. Cort and Hills [2] developed a manual iterative process for ship arrangements optimization. The opportunities and challenges within the optimization depend on the experience and inspiration of designers. Andrews [3–5] proposed a function building block approach that is still a manual optimization. As the complexity of ship arrangements increases, the design process may become tedious and time consuming for humans.

The use of computers and evolutionary techniques that are capable of generating and contrasting enormous layout schemes have become an effective and practical way for handling complicated arrangements design. Lee [6–8] used a GA to derive solutions for ship compartment layout problems. Inner walls and passages were considered during the optimization. Kim [9] proposed an expert system and a multistage optimization for submarine arrangement design. Ölçer [10,11] used an integrated multi-objective algorithm and decision-making techniques to determine the subdivisions arrangement of a ro-ro passenger ship. Parsons [12], Nick [13] and Daniels [14,15] proposed a semi-automated approach—Intelligent Ship Arrangements (ISA) that generates arrangements in an agent-genetic process driven by constraints and a single objective. The shipboard elements are firstly allocated to pre-defined zone-decks; subsequently, the assigned elements are arranged in each zone-deck. Gillespie [16,17] used a network partitioning method to identify the interaction among ship elements that have a fixed area and developed a non-spatial, network theory-based approach to assign shipboard items to structural zones. Oers [18–22] developed a packing approach combined with NSGA-II to generate three-dimensional ship configurations. Each shipboard element was assumed as a cubic unit. It is noted that a packing density objective and a constant objective were used by NSGA-II to enable the search process to proceed successfully. The NSGA-II is not necessary to generate a set of Pareto-optimal solutions in this study, but generates a large and diverse set of feasible arrangements where designers could subsequently choose an optimal solution based on their own judgment.

However, the problem of arrangements optimization was studied beyond the field of ship design. Pan [23] proposed a region division based diversity maintaining approach for crashworthiness design of vehicles. Within the field of architecture, Rodrigues et al. [24–26] used an evolutionary approach to multi-level space allocation problems. In this case, seven different evaluators were mentioned and aggregated in a single objective function subject to minimization. In other applications, such as the Facility Layout Problem, a new adaptive algorithm was proposed for a facility layout [27]. In this case, the departments' sizes are not predetermined.

The reviewed literature related to ship arrangements optimization indicates that most previous studies considered arrangements optimization as deterministic optimization, in which the size of shipboard elements is assumed to be constant. In addition, the majority of researchers formulated the arrangements optimization as a single objective optimization problem.

This paper presents an elitist non-dominated sorting hybrid evolutionary technique to the ship arrangements optimization problem, in which size and position of shipboard elements are considered as optimal variables. Three objectives representing the separation relationships, circulation efficiency and compactness are introduced to search a set of competitive design solutions.

The rest of this paper is organized as follows: Sect. 2 presents the problem formulation and how objectives and constraints are computed within the mathematical model. Section 3 describes the enhancement that couples an NSGA-II with a stochastic local search technique and the modified replacement strategy in detail. The simulation results are presented in Sect. 4. The stochastic local search technique and modified replacement strategy are discussed in Sect. 5. And, finally, the paper is concluded in Sect. 6.

2   Mathematical Model

In this section, the formulation of the arrangements optimization problem is described, and the basic nomenclature and definitions used are listed in Table 1.

Table 1. Basic nomenclature

Nomenclature			
E_i	Shipboard element i	S_i	Deck Space i
v_i	Chromosome (individual) i	c_i	New individual generated by parent individual v_i
P_i	Population of the ith generation	Q_i	Population combined P_i and P_i''
P_i'	Offspring of population P_i	P_i''	Offspring of population P_i'
x_i^k	x-coordinate of element E_k or space S_k in the individual v_i	l_i^k	Length of element E_k or space S_k in the individual v_i
y_i^k	y-coordinate of element E_k or space S_k in the individual v_i	w_i^k	Width of element E_k or space S_k in the individual v_i
z_i^k	z-coordinate of element E_k or space S_k in the individual v_i	h_i^k	Height of element E_k in the individual v_i
o_i^k	Orientation of element E_k in the individual v_i	s_i^k	Area of element E_k in the individual v_i
r_i^k	Aspect ratio of element E_k in the individual v_i	D_{ij}	Maximum separation between elements E_i and E_j
DX_{ij}	Longitudinal separation between elements E_i and E_j	DY_{ij}	Transverse separation between elements E_i and E_j
pl_{ij}	Length of longitudinal common boundary between elements E_i and E_j	pw_{ij}	Width of transverse common boundary between elements E_i and E_j
dp_{ij}	Path distance between elements E_i and E_j	d_{ij}	Arrangement difference of two individuals v_i and v_j
a_{ij}	Area of overlaps between elements E_i and E_j	cd_i	Crowding distance of solution i
U	Separation relationship satisfaction matrix	Mf	Frequency matrix of material flow
Mc	Cost matrix of material flow	R	Separation relationship matrix

2.1   Problem Formulation

The ship arrangements optimization problem can be defined as an allocation of a set of predetermined shipboard elements $\boldsymbol{E} = \{E_1, E_2 \ldots E_N\}$ on multi two-dimensional deck spaces $\boldsymbol{S} = \{S_1, S_2 \ldots S_N\}$, which satisfy the topological relations and geometric requirements.

The shipboard elements are assumed to be rectangular. Each element $E_i(x^i, y^i, z^i, s^i, r^i, h^i, o^i)$ is determined by seven variables. The x^i, y^i, z^i are the left bottom vertex point coordinate. It is noted that the area s^i and aspect ratio r^i may be intuitive to define the boundary conditions of optimization for the user, but increase the computational complexity. Hence, the length l^i and width w^i calculated by Eqs. (1) and (2) would be used during the search process.

$$l^i = \begin{cases} \sqrt{s^i \cdot r^i}, o^i = 1 \\ \sqrt{s^i / r^i}, o^i = 2 \, . \end{cases} \tag{1}$$

$$w^i = \begin{cases} \sqrt{s^i / r^i}, o^i = 1 \\ \sqrt{s^i \cdot r^i}, o^i = 2 \, . \end{cases} \tag{2}$$

Each deck space $S_i(x^i, y^i, z^i, l^i, w^i)$ is a rectangle controlled by five variables, and all elements must be inside the deck space. The main deck space S_1 is dependent on the ship's hull and is predetermined before optimization. The upper deck spaces S_i such as bridge deck space, would be decided upon during optimization according to the arrangements on the lower decks.

Different topological attributes would be assigned to each element according to their category and function before optimization. The separation attributes matrix R, material flow cost matrix Mc and material flow frequency matrix Mf would be involved in this study.

2.2   Objective Functions and Constraints

The optimization is an evolving process of a population consisting of individuals. Each individual considered in the optimization contains the size and position of all shipboard elements. And the evolving process is the transformation of those individuals with the purpose of improving their performances and satisfying their requirements. In this paper, three objective functions named Separation, Adjacency and Compactness are introduced to evaluate the topological and geometrical performance of each individual.

The Separation Function expressed by Eq. (3) is used to assess the area utilization efficiency of main deck space and the separation relationship satisfaction among shipboard elements.

$$minf_1 = \sqrt[3]{|\sum_{i=1}^{N}(s^i \cdot \varphi^i)/(l^1 \cdot w^1) - \theta| \cdot min(U) \cdot \sum_{i=1}^{N-1} \sum_{j=i+1}^{N} U_{ij}/(N! / 2)}. \tag{3}$$

where l^1 and w^1 are the length and width of the main deck space, and θ is the most efficient use of deck area. In this study, $\theta = 0.65$. φ^i is used to determine whether element E_i is on the main deck. If element E_i is on the main deck, φ^i would be equal to 1. Otherwise, φ^i would be equal to 0. U is the separation relationship satisfaction matrix and U_{ij} determined by Eqs. (4)–(9) represents the separation relationship satisfaction between element E_i and element E_j.

$$U_{ij} = \begin{cases} R_{ij}, & D_{ij} \leq t_{low} \\ R_{ij} \cdot [1 + (D_{ij} - t_{low})/(t_{low} - t_{up})], & t_{low} < D_{ij} \leq t_{up} \\ 0, & t_{up} < D_{ij}. \end{cases} \tag{4}$$

$$D_{ij} = max(DX_{ij}, DY_{ij}). \tag{5}$$

$$DX_{ij} = \begin{cases} fl_{ij}, & fl_{ij} > 0 \\ 0, & fl_{ij} \leq 0. \end{cases} \tag{6}$$

$$DY_{ij} = \begin{cases} fw_{ij}, & fw_{ij} > 0 \\ 0, & fw_{ij} \leq 0. \end{cases} \tag{7}$$

$$fl_{ij} = max(x^i + l^i, x^j + l^j) - min(x^i, x^j) - (l^i + l^j). \tag{8}$$

$$fw_{ij} = max(y^i + w^i, y^j + w^j) - min(y^i, y^j) - (w^i + w^j). \tag{9}$$

The Adjacency Function expressed by Eq. (10) is used to assess adjacency relationship satisfaction based on the total cost of material flow. If there is logistical flow between two elements E_i and E_j, the path distance dp_{ij} of E_i and E_j would be calculated as rectilinear distance by Eq. (11). δ is a coefficient which is used to calculated the distance increment due to both elements in different ship decks.

$$minf_2 = \sum_{i=1}^{N-1} \sum_{j=i+1}^{N} (dp_{ij} \cdot Mc_{ij} \cdot Mf_{ij}). \tag{10}$$

$$dp_{ij} = \begin{cases} fl_{ij} + fw_{ij} + |z^i - z^j| \cdot \delta, & fl_{ij} > 0 \quad and \quad fw_{ij} > 0 \\ fl_{ij} + |z^i - z^j| \cdot \delta, & fl_{ij} > 0 \quad and \quad fw_{ij} \leq 0 \\ fw_{ij} + |z^i - z^j| \cdot \delta, & fl_{ij} \leq 0 \quad and \quad fw_{ij} > 0 \\ |z^i - z^j| \cdot \delta, & fl_{ij} \leq 0 \quad and \quad fw_{ij} \leq 0. \end{cases} \tag{11}$$

The Compactness Function expressed by Eqs. (12)–(14) is used to assess the compactness of the arrangements. When the arrangement is neat and compact, partial boundaries of the elements would be the common boundaries. This means that the total elements' perimeters of the compact arrangement plan would be smaller.

$$minf_3 = \sum_{i=1}^{N} [2 \times (l^i + w^i)] - \sum_{i=1}^{N-1} \sum_{j=i+1}^{N} (pl_{ij} + pw_{ij}). \tag{12}$$

$$pl_{ij} = \begin{cases} -fl_{ij}, & fl_{ij} < 0 \quad and \quad fw_{ij} = 0 \\ 0, & otherwise. \end{cases} \tag{13}$$

$$pw_{ij} = \begin{cases} -fw_{ij}, & fw_{ij} < 0 \quad and \quad fl_{ij} = 0 \\ 0, & otherwise. \end{cases} \qquad (14)$$

The Constraint Functions expressed by Eqs. (15)–(17) are used to guarantee that there is no overlap among elements. The overlap is decomposed into a sub-overlap in x-coordinate and a sub-overlap in y-coordinate. Only if both sub-overlaps are merged, would there be overlaps in the deck spaces.

$$(xol_{ij} - |xol_{ij}|) \cdot (yol_{ij} - |yol_{ij}|) = 0. \qquad (15)$$

$$xol_{ij} = (x^i + l^i - x^j) \cdot (x^i - x^j - l^j). \qquad (16)$$

$$yol_{ij} = (y^i + w^i - y^j) \cdot (y^i - y^j - w^j). \qquad (17)$$

3   A Hybrid Evolutionary Algorithm

Determining arrangements optimization can be difficult due to the large size of the search space and the complexity of constraints. The Elitist Non-Dominated Sorting Genetic Algorithm (NSGA-II) has proven to be an effective method to determine multi-objective constrained optimization. However, such heuristic methods only handle a reduced set of design variables and constraints. In order to better address large-scale design variables and constraints, a hybrid evolutionary algorithm based on the NSGA-II method is used to achieve a faster convergence of search towards Pareto-optimal front and obtain a diversified solution set. In this section, the details of the elitist non-dominated sorting hybrid evolutionary algorithm are described.

3.1   Chromosome Encoding

Chromosome encoding is an important component of evolutionary algorithms. In the arrangements optimization problem, each chromosome represents a general arrangement scheme. For an arrangements optimization problem that involves N shipboard elements, each chromosome is composed of $7N$ genes. The first $3N$ genes of the chromosome represent the bottom vertices x-, y-, z-coordinates of N elements, respectively. The next $3N$ genes represent the length l^i, width w^i and height h^i of each element. The last N gene represents the orientation. It is noted that the length l^i and width w^i of elements are used for convenience in the chromosome encoding rather than area s^i and aspect ratio r^i. The z-coordinates z^i and height h^i of elements are assumed as constant in this study. The real coding is adopted, and a solution and its corresponding chromosome v can be formulated as follow:

$$v = [x^1 \dots x^N, y^1 \dots y^N, z^1 \dots z^N, l^1 \dots l^N, w^1 \dots w^N, h^1 \dots h^N, o^1 \dots o^N] \qquad (18)$$

3.2   Genetic and Stochastic Local Search Operators

As mentioned earlier, the proposed algorithm couples the NSGA-II with a stochastic local search technique to facilitate local optimization. During both search processes, the individuals are subject to a series of adaptive stochastic operators that perform positional and dimensional transformation of elements. The genetic operators that include both crossover and mutation operators are used to generate new offspring P_i' from the parent P_i. And the stochastic local search operators containing both geometric and topological operators are applied to the individuals in offspring P_i' for generating the new population P_i''. After genetic and stochastic local search operations have been carried out, the individual's objective function values and constraint violation are calculated. Then a combined population $Q_i = P_i'' \cup P_i$ is formed and sorted. Finally, the modified replacement strategy is used to generate the next population P_{i+1}.

There are two kinds of genetic operators. One kind of genetic operator will be invoked to generate new individuals at a time. In this study, if the generated random number is bigger than the crossover probability p_c, the crossover operation will be carried out; otherwise, the mutation operation will be carried out. When the crossover operator is invoked, two different individuals who have never been selected are chosen as parents. Each gene of both parents v_i and v_j is randomly crossed to produce two new individuals c_i and c_j. The crossover operation is expressed by Eqs. (19) and (20).

$$c_i(k) = 0.5 \times \{[1 + 2 \times (r_k - 0.5)] \cdot v_i(k) + [1 - 2 \times (r_k - 0.5)] \cdot v_j(k)\}. \quad (19)$$

$$c_j(k) = 0.5 \times \{[1 - 2 \times (r_k - 0.5)] \cdot v_i(k) + [1 + 2 \times (r_k - 0.5)] \cdot v_j(k)\}. \quad (20)$$

where the random number r_k is randomly generated for each gene $v(k)$ of parents. If the mutation operator is applied, just one individual, having never been selected, is chosen as a parent. And each gene of parent v_i plus a random value Δ_k is required to generate the new individual c_i. The random value Δ_k and the mutation operation are expressed by Eqs. (21) and (22) respectively.

$$\Delta_k = 2 \cdot (r_k - 0.5) \cdot (ub_k - lb_k). \quad (21)$$

$$c_i(k) = v_i(k) + \Delta_k. \quad (22)$$

where the ub_k is the upper boundary of the gene k and the lb_k is the lower boundary of the gene k.

The stochastic local search operators are applied after the offspring P_i' has been generated by genetic operation. In this search process, both kind of stochastic local search operators work by repositioning the shipboard elements to better satisfy the topological and geometric requirements. Except for the x- and y-coordinates of elements, the remaining five variables are constant during this search process. The stochastic local search operation would not be applied to the individuals with the lowest rank in the population P_i'. Since all individuals on the first front of the parent population P_i and offspring population P_i' are included in population Q_i, elitism is ensured. The topological operator is used to improve the fitness of individuals. When there is a separation relationship between the two elements E_i and E_j, and their spacing D_{ij} is less than the threshold t_{low}, the topological operator is invoked. The geometric operator is used to search for arrangements without any overlaps. Hence, the geometric operator would just be invoked if there are overlaps, and in contrast, the topological operator would be used only when there are no overlaps. If either stochastic local search operator is carried out, the elements would be translated to one of eight position, $(x + \mu, y + \mu), (x + \mu, y), (x + \mu, y - \mu), (x, y + \mu), (x, y - \mu), (x - \mu, y + \mu), (x - \mu, y), (x - \mu, y - \mu)$. The magnitude μ of the translation on x-coordinate direction is randomly calculated between 0 and the length of element, likewise, the magnitude μ of the translation on y-coordinate direction is randomly calculated between 0 and the width of element. The geometric operator is aimed to reduce the area a_i of overlap and the perimeter p_i reduced the overlap side, expressed by Eqs. (23)–(26). fl_{ij} and fw_{ij} are calculated by Eqs. (8) and (9). pl_{ij} and pw_{ij} are calculated by Eqs. (13) and (14). The topological operator is used to reduce the value of the Separation Function and Adjacency Function. The element will continue to translate until fitness cannot be further reduced.

$$a_i = \sum_{j=1}^{N, i \neq j} a_{ij}. \tag{23}$$

$$a_{ij} = \begin{cases} fl_{ij} \cdot fw_{ij}, & fl_{ij} > 0 \quad and \quad fw_{ij} > 0 \\ 0, & otherwise. \end{cases} \tag{24}$$

$$p_i = \sum_{j=1}^{N, i \neq j} p_{ij}. \tag{25}$$

$$p_{ij} = 2 \times (l_i + w_i) - \sum_{j=1}^{N, i \neq j} (pl_{ij} + pw_{ij}). \tag{26}$$

The pseudocode for stochastic local search operators is outlined as follows. In this procedure, in order to generate better individuals, the main body (Calculate μ) of this procedure is executed at most 50 times for each individual. When the process is continue to calculate all individuals of population, the total complexity is $O(50N)$.

The pseudocode for stochastic local search operators

```
for j=1:N
  Calculate the number of constraint violations n of element Ei;
  if n>0
    Geometrical operator is invoked;
  elseif n=0 and Dij<tlow
    Topological operator is invoked;
  Set k=1;
  while fitness(k)<fitness(k-1) and k<50 and u!=0
    k=k+1;
```

```
    Calculate u=random(li-u) or u=random(wi-u);
    Calculate the fitness ai, pi or f1, f2 of eight positions;
    Select the position with minimum fitness(k) as the new position of Ei;
    end while
end for
Output: the individual in population Pi.
```

3.3   Modified Replacement Strategy

Non-domination rank and crowding distance are two significant attributes of each individual in the NSGA-II. The solution with the lower rank would be retained. If both solutions have the same rank, the solution that is located in a less crowded region would be retained [28]. The crowding distance computation for objectives is used to measure the extent of proximity with other solutions. This guarantees diversity of the population and a uniformly spread out Pareto-optimal front, but the crowding distance computation for objectives is not suitable to maintain the diversity of population for arrangements optimization. In the arrangements optimization problem, two completely different arrangement schemes may have similar values of the objective functions. This means the discrepancy in solution space does not guarantee the differentiability in objective space. The failure to keep diversity of population indicates that the original replacement strategy in the NSGA-II is not sufficient to deal with such problems.

In this paper, a modified replacement strategy is used for the arrangements optimization problem. The position differences of elements are calculated to estimate the diversity of the solution. The quantity d_{ij} serves as a computation of the position difference of all elements between solution i and solution j, determined by Eq. (27).

$$d_{ij} = \sum_{k=1}^{N}(|x_k^i - x_k^j| + |y_k^i - y_k^j|).$$ (27)

The crowding distance cd_i of the solution i is expressed by Eq. (28), which minimizes the position difference of all elements with other solutions. Hence, the solution with larger crowding distance will be retained in the population if the two solution are on the same non-dominate front. Since each solution must be compared with all other solution in the population, the overall complexity of the crowding distance calculation is $O(N^2)$.

$$cd_i = min(d_{i1}, d_{i1} \ldots d_{iN}), \quad i \neq j.$$ (28)

The pseudocode of the hybrid evolutionary algorithm is outlined as follows. The fast non-dominated sorting approach with $O(MN^2)$ computational complexity is presented in [28]. The complexity of this modified replacement strategy is governed by the sorting algorithm. Since K independent sortings of at most N solutions (when all individuals are in one front F) are involved, the modified replacement strategy has $O(KNlogN)$ computational complexity.

The pseudocode of the hybrid evolutionary algorithm

```
Initialization
  Randomly generate P0;
  Set Q0=null and t=0;
While i< max generation number
  Generate offspring Pi' using genetic operators;
  Update offspring Pi' to Pi'' using stochastic local search operators;
  Qi=[pi'' pi];
  Sort Qi;
  Calculate crowding distance cdi of different front in Qi;
  Delete the duplicate individuals (cdi<threshold) in Qi;
  Add new random individuals in the population;
  Sort Qi where front={F1,F2...};
  Set Pi+1=null and j=1;
  While |Pi+1|+|Fj|<pop
    Calculate crowding distance of Fj;
    Add the jth non-dominated front Fj to Pi+1;
    j=j+1;
  end While
  Sort Fj according to crowding distance;
  Fill Pi+1 with first pop-|Pi+1| individuals of Fj;
end While
Output: non-dominated solution in Pi.
```

4   A Case Study of a Survey Ship

In this section, a survey ship arrangement optimization was carried out to test whether the proposed algorithm is capable of generating several coherent general arrangements. The shipboard elements involved in the optimization are listed in Fig. 1. Three ship deck spaces considered in the optimization are main deck space S_1, accommodation deck space S_2 and bridge deck space S_3. The z-coordinate z^i and height h^i of elements are constants during the optimization. It is noted that each stair is arranged in the same position on both decks to which it is connected. Also, the submersible decompression chamber is a fixed element during the optimization. The bridge must be arranged in the forefront of bridge deck space. The sizes of the initial population and the offspring are both set as 100. The crossover probability is set as 0.8, and the stopping criterion is set to 500 generations. Finally, four coherent arrangements with some differences were generated as shown in Figs. 2, 3, 4 and 5.

To account for the effectiveness of the stochastic local search operators, the proposed algorithm is run 10 times with and without the stochastic local search operators on each instance. The speed of the two algorithms to find the individuals without any overlaps is shown in Fig. 6. The comparison of the Pareto-optimal fronts with two different replacement strategies is shown in Fig. 7.

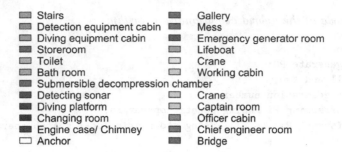

▨	Stairs	▨	Gallery
▨	Detection equipment cabin	■	Mess
▨	Diving equipment cabin	■	Emergency generator room
■	Storeroom	▨	Lifeboat
▨	Toilet	▢	Crane
▨	Bath room	▢	Working cabin
■	Submersible decompression chamber		
■	Detecting sonar	▨	Crane
■	Diving platform	▨	Captain room
■	Changing room	▨	Officer cabin
■	Engine case/ Chimney	■	Chief engineer room
▢	Anchor	■	Bridge

Fig. 1. The color-map of shipboard elements arranged on multi-decks.

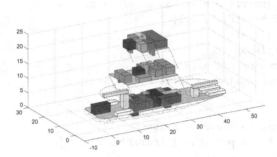

Fig. 2. The arrangement of survey ship (a).

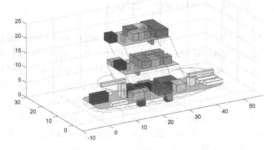

Fig. 3. The arrangement of survey ship (b).

The proposed algorithm is run 10 times with original replacement strategy and modified replacement strategy respectively. The number and similarity of solutions in two Pareto-optimal fronts using different replacement strategies is illustrated in Table 2.

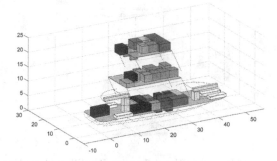

Fig. 4. The arrangement of survey ship (c).

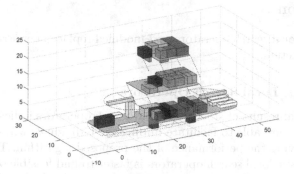

Fig. 5. The arrangement of survey ship (d).

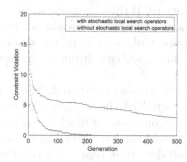

Fig. 6. The speed of the two algorithms to find the individuals without any overlaps.

Table 2. The number and similarity of solutions in two Pareto-optimal fronts using different replacement strategies.

Parameters	Original replacement strategy		Modified replacement strategy	
	Number	Similarity	Number	Similarity
Mean	85.8	91.3%	7.7	32.1%
Max	91	94.5%	11	42.9%
Min	77	87.2%	4	16.7%

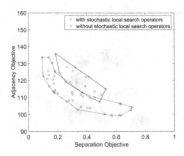

Fig. 7. The comparison of Pareto-optimal fronts with different replacement strategies.

5 Discussion

The stochastic local search operators and modified replacement strategy are discussed in this section.

5.1 Stochastic Local Search Operators

The experimental results of stochastic local search operators indicate that these kind of operators are able to facilitate finding the individuals without any overlaps, and improving the performance of the proposed algorithm. The algorithm with the stochastic local search operators is faster to find feasible solutions than the algorithm without the stochastic local search operators. When the stochastic local search operation is carried out, the solutions without any overlaps emerge between 180 and 220 generations. If the stochastic local search operators are not invoked, the solutions without any overlaps would not be able to be discovered, and the number of constraint violations is finally stable at 2–3. However, an algorithm that can rapidly find feasible solutions is expected to result in better optimization.

The Pareto-optimal fronts are also compared. The Adjacency Function and Separation Function are selected as the objective of comparison as shown in Fig. 7. The dashed line zone is composed of black dots that represents the Pareto-optimal solutions generated using the stochastic local search operators. The solid line zone is composed of red dots that represents the Pareto-optimal solutions that does not use the stochastic local search. It can be observed that the dashed line zone is at the bottom left of the solid line zone which means the solution in the dashed line zone is better than in the solid line zone. Thus, it can be concluded that the proposed coupling of the NSGA-II with a stochastic local search technique is able to improve the fitness of solutions, and enhance the performance of searching for a feasible solution.

5.2 Modified Replacement Strategy

The proposed modified replacement strategy is compared with the original replacement strategy in the NSGA-II. The comparison focuses on the number and the similarity of solutions in different Pareto-optimal fronts using the two replacement strategies. As shown in Table 2, the number of solutions in Pareto-optimal fronts using the original replacement strategy is much greater than using the modified replacement strategy. The similarity of solutions using original replacement strategy is 91.3%, and the similarity of solutions using modified replacement strategy is 32.1%. The results indicate that the diversity of population is rapidly lost when the original replacement strategy is used. The original replacement strategy would result in dozens of solutions, but all solutions represent similar arrangements. Furthermore, these solutions are just local optimal solutions. The modified replacement strategy may result in fewer solutions within the Pareto-optimal front, but the Pareto-optimal front contains several different arrangement plans. For instance, there are four different arrangements in the Pareto-optimal front as shown in Sect. 4.

6 Conclusion

This paper investigates the arrangements optimization problems where the size and position of elements are simultaneously considered as optimization variables. The main purpose of this study is to assist ship designers in enhancing the range of alternative arrangements and expediting the design process.

A multi-objective constrained optimization mathematical model of arrangements problem has been established according to the topological and geometrical requirements. The objective functions consist of three evaluators. A series of nonlinear equality constraints is used to determine whether there is overlap between two elements resulting from the constraints of optimization. A survey ship arrangements optimization is applied, and four different general arrangements of the survey ship have been generated.

In order to quickly solve arrangements optimization problems, this paper describes an elitist non-dominated sorting hybrid evolutionary algorithm, in which the NSGA-II is enriched with a stochastic local search technique to tackle the topological and geometrical requirements. It combines the advantages of using an evolutionary algorithm to search a large solution space with a stochastic local search technique to deal with geometrical constraints and locally improve each individual. The modification of the replacement is used to maintain the diversity of population. The effectiveness of both enhancements has been tested. The simulation results indicate that the proposed approach is able to generate a set of coherent arrangements.

References

1. Bénabès, J., Bennis, F., Poirson, E., Ravaut, Y.: An interactive-based approach to the layout design optimization. In: Proceedings of the 20th CIRP Design Conference, Nantes, France, pp. 511–520 (2010)
2. Cort, A., Hills, W.: Space layout design using computer assisted methods. Nav. Eng. J. 12(1), 55–68 (1987)

3. Andrews, D., Dicks, C.: The building block design methodology applied to advanced naval ship design. In: Proceedings of the 6th International Marine Design Conference, Newcastle, pp. 3–19 (1997)
4. Andrews, D.J., Pawling, R.J.: SURFCON - a 21st century ship design tool. In: Proceedings of the 8th International Marine Design Conference, Athens, Greece, pp. 150–166 (2003)
5. Andrews, D.J., Pawling, R.J.: A case study in preliminary ship design. Int. J. Marit. Eng. **150**(3), 45–68 (2008)
6. Lee, K., Han, S.: Optimal compartment layout design for a naval ship using an improved genetic algorithm. Mar. Technol. **39**(3), 159–169 (2002)
7. Lee, K.Y., Han, S.N., Roh, M.I.: An improved genetic algorithm for facility layout prob-lems having inner structure walls and passages. Comput. Oper. Res. **30**(1), 117–138 (2003)
8. Lee, K., Roh, M., Jeong, H.: An improved genetic algorithm for multi-floor facility layout problems having inner structure walls and passages. Comput. Oper. Res. **32**(4), 879–899 (2005)
9. Kim, K., Roh, M.: A submarine arrangement design program based on the expert system and the multistage optimization. Adv. Eng. Softw. **98**, 97–111 (2016)
10. Ölçer, A.: A hybrid approach for multi-objective combinatorial optimization problems in ship design and shipping. Comput. Oper. Res. **35**(9), 2760–2775 (2008)
11. Ölçer, A.: An integrated multi-objective optimization and fuzzy multi-attributive group deci-sion-making technique for subdivision arrangement of Ro-Ro vessels. Appl. Soft. Comput. **6**(3), 221–243 (2006)
12. Parsons, M., Chung, H., Nick, E.: Intelligent ship arrangements: a new approach to general arrangement. Nav. Eng. J. **120**(3), 51–65 (2008)
13. Nick, E.: Fuzzy optimal allocation and arrangement of spaces in naval surface ship design. Ph.D. thesis. University of Michigan (2008)
14. Daniels, A.S., Tahmasbi, F., Singer, D.: Intelligent ship arrangement passage variable lattice network studies and results. Nav. Eng. J. **122**(2), 107–119 (2010)
15. Daniels, A., Parsons, M.: An agent-based approach to space allocation in general arrangements. In: Proceedings of the 9th International Marine Design Conference (2006)
16. Gillespie, J., Daniels, A., Singer, D.: Generating functional complex-based ship arrange-ments using network partitioning and community preferences. Ocean Eng. **72**(7), 107–115 (2013)
17. Gillespie, J., Singer, D.: Identifying drivers of general arrangements through the use of net-work measures of centrality and hierarchy. Ocean Eng. **57**(1), 230–239 (2013)
18. Oers, B., Stapersma, D., Hopman, H.: Development and implementation of an optimization-based space allocation routine for the generation of feasible concept designs. In: 6th International Conference on Computer and IT Applications in the Maritime Industries, Cortona, pp. 171–185 (2007)
19. Oers, B., Stapersma, D., Hopman, H.: Issues when selecting naval ship configurations from a pareto-optimal set. In: Proceedings of the 12th AIAA/ISSMO Multidisciplinary Analysis and Optimization Conference, Victoria (2007)
20. Oers, B., Stapersma, D., Hopman, H.: An optimization-based space allocation routine for the generation of feasible ship designs. Ship Technol. Res. **55**(2), 51–59 (2009)
21. Oers, B., Stapersma, D., Hopman, H.: A 3D packing approach for the early stage configuration design of ships. In: Proceedings of the 10th International Naval Engineering Conference, Cortona, pp. 367–381 (2010)

22. Oers, B.: A packing approach for the early stage design of service vessels. Ph.D. thesis. Delft University of Technology (2011)
23. Pan, L., He, C., Tian, Y., et al.: A region division based diversity maintaining approach for many-objective optimization. Integr. Comput. Aided Eng. **24**, 279–296 (2017)
24. Rodrigues, E., Gaspar, A.R., Gomes, A.: An approach to the multi-level space allocation problem in architecture using a hybrid evolutionary technique. Autom. Constr. **35**(14), 482–498 (2013)
25. Rodrigues, E., Gaspar, A.R., Gomes, A.: An evolutionary strategy enhanced with a local search technique for the space allocation problem in architecture, Part 1: methodology. Comput. Aided Des. **45**, 887–897 (2013)
26. Rodrigues, E., Gaspar, A.R., Gomes, A.: An evolutionary strategy enhanced with a local search technique for the space allocation problem in architecture, Part 2: validation and performance tests. Comput. Aided Des. **45**, 898–910 (2013)
27. Neghabi, H., Eshghi, K., Salmani, M.: A new model for robust facility layout problem. Inf. Sci. **278**, 498–509 (2014)
28. Deb, K.: A fast elitist multi-objective genetic algorithm: NSGA-II. IEEE Trans. Evol. Comput. **6**(2), 182–197 (2000)

Evolutionary Algorithms' Feature Selection Stability Improvement System

Yi Liu[1(✉)], Xingchun Diao[1], Jianjun Cao[2], and Lei Zhang[1]

[1] College of Command Information Systems,
PLA University of Science and Technology, Nanjing 210007, China
`albertliu20th@163.com`, `diaoxch640222@163.com`, `2318903646@qq.com`
[2] Nanjing Telecommunication Technology Institute, Nanjing 210007, China
`jianjuncao@yeah.net`

Abstract. In order to improve the feature selection stability based on evolutionary algorithms, an evolutionary algorithms' feature selection stability improvement system is proposed. Three Filter methods' results are aggregated to provide the stability information, and feature selection stability and classification accuracy are adopted as two optimization objectives. Weighted sum, weighted product and biobjective optimization methods together are applied as the system's optimization models. Ant colony optimization, particle swarm optimization and genetic algorithm are used as testing algorithms, and experiments are taken on two benchmark datasets. The results show that the proposed system can improve the stability of evolutionary algorithms' feature selection efficiently and their classification performance simultaneously.

Keywords: Feature selection stability · Evolutionary algorithms · Feature selection · High dimensional data

1 Introduction

It is becoming a hot point of scientific researches that using machine learning and artificial intelligence technologies to mine the potential value of industry data for decision makers and enterprises with the development of big data and the improvement of information processing abilities [1]. And high dimensional data is turning into the main processing data type which contains gene, text, face data, social network data, stream data and remote sensing data etc. [2].

It is necessary that make a pre-processing for high dimensional data before putting them into applications, i.e. dimensionality reduction. There are two ways to implement data dimension reduction, feature selection and feature extraction [3]. As feature selection can hold primal information, compress data storage space, reduce the complexity of obtaining original data and have a high quality of interpretation, it is widely used to realize dimension reduction [4].

© Springer Nature Singapore Pte Ltd. 2017
C. He et al. (Eds.): BIC-TA 2017, CCIS 791, pp. 68–81, 2017.
https://doi.org/10.1007/978-981-10-7179-9_6

Traditionally, the researches of feature selection focus on improving the algorithms' accuracy and reducing their complexity, but they neglect the importance of feature selection stability. The stability of feature selection is the robustness of results with respect to small changes in the dataset composition [5]. Improving the stability of feature selection can find out relevant features, increase experts' confidence to the results, and further reduce the complexity of getting original data and time costs. The researches and applications of feature selection stability are becoming more and more fascinating with the development of high dimensional data during the past ten years [6–9].

According to the way that approaches deal with features, methods for improving the stability of feature selection can be classified as perturbation way and feature way. Perturbation way contains function perturbation strategy, data perturbation approach and hybrid way. Function perturbation strategy means that different feature selection methods are employed on the same dataset, and ensemble ways are used to combine those feature ranking lists into single one to get a stable feature subset [10, 11]. Data perturbation approach applies Bootstrap, over resampling, under resampling and data split etc. to add samples and groups of training data, and employs ensemble learning methods to combine the feature ranking results generated by the same feature selection approach [12]. Hybrid method applies data perturbation ways firstly, and employs function perturbation approaches to improve the probability of getting stable feature subset [13, 14]. Feature way develops a new feature selection method or modifies the existing methods based on the inherent information of features to improve the stability of feature selection approaches. It includes feature groups strategy and feature information approach. Feature groups strategy clusters high correlation features into groups based on some principles, and feature selection methods select stable features from those groups [15, 16]. Feature information way measure the degree of importance of features based on some evaluation rules and give higher value for important features, and selects stable feature subset from those crucial features [17, 18]. From previous statements, we can conclude that the stability of feature selection methods has become a hot point in scientific research field.

The methods of feature selection can be divided into three types, i.e. Filter, Wrapper and Hybrid. Feature selection approaches based on evolutionary algorithms (EAs) are one kind of Wrapper methods, and they have been used in many real world applications [19–21]. But they only try to improve the algorithms' accuracy and reduce the number of selected features. The feature selection stability of evolutionary algorithms is still an open issue [22].

In this paper, we propose an Evolutionary Algorithms' Feature Selection Stability Improvement System (EAFSSIS) to improve the stability of EAs. It adopts three Filter methods results to provide stability information for EAs. It uses stability and classification accuracy of EAs as two optimization objectives. It includes three optimization models which are two single objective models called Weighted Sum and Weight Product and a biobjective model. Ant Colony Optimization (ACO), Particle Swarm Optimization (PSO) and Genetic

Algorithm (GA) are employed in two benchmark datasets to validate the effectiveness of our system.

The rest of this paper is organized as follows. Section 2 is an introduction of EAFSSIS. Section 3 uses some experiments to evaluate the system's effectiveness. Section 4 comes to a conclusion.

2 EAFSSIS

In this section, we describe the detailed components of EAFSSIS and how it works. The framework of EAFSSIS is depicted in Fig. 1.

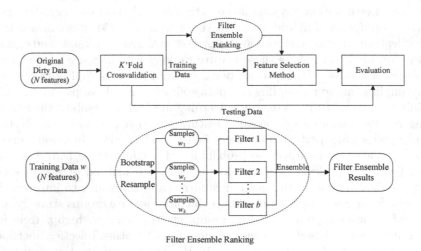

Fig. 1. The framework of EAFSSIS

As shown in Fig. 1, EAFSSIS is made up of two components, i.e. Filter Ensemble Ranking and Feature Selection Method. Original data is sampled by K'-fold cross validation to generate training data and testing data. The training data putting into Filter Ensemble Ranking component is sampled through bootstrap approach to generate k groups of samples, b Filter methods are employed to rank features, and ensemble learning way is applied to combine them as a final output. At last, the ranking results which are the stability guidance information and training data are employed as input of Feature Selection Method component to select feature subset.

There are two key issues we must resolve in EASFFIS, i.e. how to realize Filter Ensemble Ranking component and how to optimize objectives.

2.1 Filter Ensemble Ranking

Many existing researches have demonstrated that ensemble learning can improve the stability of feature selection significantly, and it is also a common way used widely in real world problems [23,24]. The Filter methods can be further categorized into two types, i.e. univariate and multivariate approach: in the first case, each single feature is evaluated from others independently; in the second one, the inter-dependencies among features are taken into account. Univariate method includes Information Gain (IG), Symmetrical Uncertainty, Gain Ratio, Chi Squared (χ^2), and One Rule etc. Multivariate method involves ReliefF, ReliefW, Support Vector Machine One, and Support Vector Machine Recursive Feature Elimination etc. Univariate method has a better stability but a worse classification performance, and multivariate method is the opposite. We develop a new approach which combines the results of univariate and multivariate methods to provide a higher quality feature ranking which makes use of both advantages. Some previous researches have showed that IG, χ^2 and ReliefF have a good comprehensive performance, so we adopt those three approaches to rank features in datasets sampled by bootstrap, and we will have $3 * k$ feature ranking lists [13]. Then we use ensemble method to aggregate those lists into one feature ranking list. Besides, different aggregation strategies have no obvious distinction between each other, so we employ median way to combine the feature rankings, i.e. assigning the median rank value to the corresponding feature across all the original lists to generate one list [13]. At last, we choose the top n features by their descending values from the list to make up of feature subset as the final output.

2.2 Models of Optimizing Objectives

EAFSSIS has two objectives needed to be maximized, i.e. the feature selection stability and classification accuracy. We use classification success rate and extension of Kuncheva index [25] as classification and stability measuring indicator.

The calculation of classification success rate is shown in Eq. 1.

$$P = \frac{P\_num + N\_num}{Num} \tag{1}$$

where Num is the number of instances, P_num is the number of positive instances classified correctly, and N_num is the number of negative instances classified correctly.

We employed extension of Kuncheva index to measure the similarity degree between feature subset generated by Filter Ensemble Ranking and feature subset of EAs as the stability value to guide the evolution of EAs. Supposing there are two feature subsets s and s', and their similarity degree can be calculated by Eq. 2.

$$EK(s, s') = \frac{|s \cap s'| - \frac{|s| \cdot |s'|}{c}}{max[-max(0, |s| + |s'| - c) + \frac{|s| \cdot |s'|}{c}; min(|s|, |s'|) - \frac{|s| \cdot |s'|}{c}]} \tag{2}$$

Its value is between $[-1, 1]$, and the larger the value, the more similar the two subsets, which means the method has a better stability.

It is important to combine those two objectives into EAs, and we proposed three models to convert them into the objectives optimized by EAs, i.e. weighted Sum, weighted Product and biobjective model.

Weighted Sum converts the two objectives into a new single objective by summation, which is shown in Eq. 3.

$$f_{ws} = \lambda P + (1 - \lambda)EK \tag{3}$$

where λ is an aggregation parameter.

Weighted Product transforms two objectives into a new single objective by product, which is shown in Eq. 4.

$$f_{wp} = P^\gamma \cdot EK^{1-\gamma} \tag{4}$$

where γ is an aggregation parameter.

Biobjective model treats the two objectives as a multiobjective optimization problem which optimizes them simultaneously, and it is shown in Eq. 5.

$$\boldsymbol{f_{bi} = MAX(P, EK)} \tag{5}$$

Equation 5 shows that we want the values of two objectives come to maximization at the same time.

3   Experiments and Discussions

In this section, we will make some experiments to evaluate the effectiveness of EAFSSIS. We adopt three classical EAs in our experiments, i.e. ACO, PSO and GA. We use four binary classification datasets[1] to implement experiments, and the characteristics of them are shown in Table 1.

Table 1. Characteristics of benchmark datasets

Benchmark datasets	Number of instances	Number of features
BASEHOCK	1993	4862
PCMAC	1943	3289
RELATHE	1427	4322
MADELON	2600	500

Besides, we apply the single objective optimization versions of the three EAs to make a comparison to evaluate the performance of EAFSSIS. After some tests, we obtain the best values of models parameters in each algorithm. The compared algorithms, their detailed information and parameters values of models are shown in Table 2.

---

[1] http://featureselection.asu.edu/datasets.php.

Table 2. Compared algorithms in EAFSSIS

EAs	Objectives	Model	Parameter value	Name
ACO	P	Single objective	/	O-ACOFS
	EK, P	Weighted sum	0.3	S-ACOFS
	EK, P	Weighted product	0.2	P-ACOFS
	EK, P	Biobjective	/	M-ACOFS
PSO	P	Single objective	/	O-PSOFS
	EK, P	Weighted sum	0.5	S-PSOFS
	EK, P	Weighted product	0.3	P-PSOFS
	EK, P	Biobjective	/	M-PSOFS
GA	P	Single objective	/	O-GAFS
	EK, P	Weighted sum	0.5	S-GAFS
	EK, P	Weighted product	0.6	P-GAFS
	EK, P	Biobjective	/	M-GAFS

Figures 2, 3 and 4 show the stability of EAFSSIS under different percentages of selected features in two testing datasets, and experiments apply five-fold cross validation and extension of Kuncheva index to measure algorithms stability.

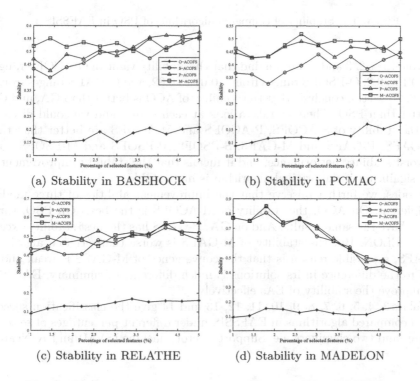

(a) Stability in BASEHOCK   (b) Stability in PCMAC

(c) Stability in RELATHE   (d) Stability in MADELON

Fig. 2. The Stability of compared algorithms of ACO in EAFSSIS.

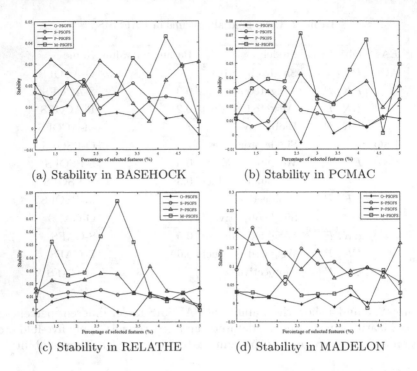

(a) Stability in BASEHOCK   (b) Stability in PCMAC

(c) Stability in RELATHE   (d) Stability in MADELON

Fig. 3. The Stability of compared algorithms of PSO in EAFSSIS.

From Figs. 2, 3 and 4, we can find that the stability value of O-ACOFS ranges from 0.1 to 0.2, O-PSOFS ranges from −0.01 to 0.02, and O-GAFS ranges from 0 to 0.06. So we can conclude that the stability of ACO is better than GA, and GA is better than PSO. Then we take a look at each figure, and we could discover that the stability of S-ACOFS, P-ACOFS and M-ACOFS are better than that of S-GAFS, P-GAFS and M-GAFS, S-PSOFS, P-PSOFS and M-PSOFS have the worst stability performance, and it means that the stability improvement is more significant if the original algorithm is more stable.

Besides, we further observe that the improvement abilities of three models are different. On ACO, the stability of M-ACOFS is the best. On PSO, three models have the same results. And on GA, P-GAFS has the best stability except in MADELON. But the stability of M-GAFS is worse than original algorithm O-GAFS, a possible reason is that the convergence of M-GAFS is weak and it leads to the difference in its solutions is much different. In summary, EAFSSIS can improve the stability of EAs effectively.

Tables 3, 4, 5, 6, 7, 8, 9, 10, 11, 12, 13 and 14 give the classification success rate of compared algorithms in EAFSSIS under different percentages of selected features and two classifiers, i.e. Support Vector Machine (SVM) and K Nearest

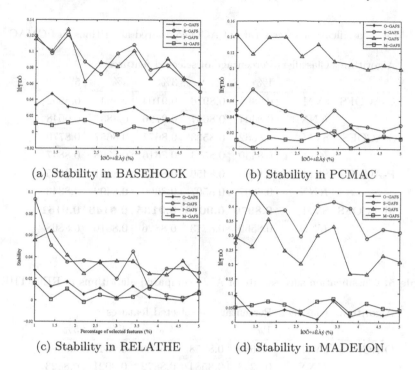

(a) Stability in BASEHOCK   (b) Stability in PCMAC

(c) Stability in RELATHE   (d) Stability in MADELON

Fig. 4. The Stability of compared algorithms of GA in EAFSSIS.

Neighbor (KNN). The kernel function of SVM is linear and the K value of KNN is five. And we still use five-fold cross validation

From those tables, we can find that EAFSSIS could improve not only the stability of EAs but also their classification performance. Tables 3 and 6 show that M-ACOFS gets the best classification success rate under SVM except

Table 3. Classification success rate of ACO compared algorithms in BASEHOCK

Algorithm	Classifier	Percentage of selected features				
		1%	2%	3%	4%	5%
O-ACOFS	SVM	0.9393	**0.9594**	0.9674	0.9694	0.9774
	KNN	0.9473	0.9579	0.9604	0.9649	0.9589
S-ACOFS	SVM	0.9373	0.9328	0.9448	0.9468	0.9533
	KNN	0.9232	0.9338	0.9418	0.9373	0.9287
P-ACOFS	SVM	0.9157	0.9388	0.9393	0.9453	0.9413
	KNN	0.9162	0.9378	0.9127	0.9222	0.9162
M-ACOFS	SVM	**0.9513**	0.9578	**0.9704**	**0.9739**	**0.9804**
	KNN	0.9453	0.9478	0.9569	0.9523	0.9443

Table 4. Classification success rate of ACO compared algorithms in PCMAC

Algorithm	Classifier	Percentage of selected features				
		1%	2%	3%	4%	5%
O-ACOFS	SVM	0.8898	0.8976	0.9104	0.894	0.8852
	KNN	0.8404	0.8667	0.8796	0.8837	0.9048
S-ACOFS	SVM	0.8662	0.8533	0.8677	0.8657	0.8770
	KNN	0.8430	0.8554	0.8616	0.8708	0.8847
P-ACOFS	SVM	0.8466	0.8450	0.8461	0.8461	0.8615
	KNN	0.8307	0.8507	0.8600	0.8492	0.8343
M-ACOFS	SVM	**0.8970**	**0.9079**	**0.9135**	**0.9146**	**0.9151**
	KNN	0.8569	0.8713	0.8826	0.8816	0.8868

Table 5. Classification success rate of ACO compared algorithms in RELATHE

Algorithm	Classifier	Percentage of selected features				
		1%	2%	3%	4%	5%
O-ACOFS	SVM	0.8669	0.8858	0.9180	0.9348	0.9320
	KNN	0.8248	0.8584	0.8872	0.8921	0.8823
S-ACOFS	SVM	0.8066	0.8487	0.8648	0.8886	0.9005
	KNN	0.7884	0.8241	0.8563	0.8669	0.8788
P-ACOFS	SVM	0.8108	0.8304	0.8459	0.8613	0.8689
	KNN	0.7702	0.8206	0.8374	0.8542	0.8746
M-ACOFS	SVM	**0.8893**	**0.9068**	**0.9215**	**0.9355**	**0.9404**
	KNN	0.8227	0.8402	0.8745	0.8872	0.8914

Table 6. Classification success rate of ACO compared algorithms in MADELON

Algorithm	Classifier	Percentage of selected features				
		1%	2%	3%	4%	5%
O-ACOFS	SVM	0.8792	0.8985	0.9031	0.9038	0.9046
	KNN	0.6638	0.6727	0.6754	0.6723	0.6700
S-ACOFS	SVM	0.7138	0.8469	0.8788	0.8919	0.8804
	KNN	0.6081	0.6073	0.5962	0.6077	0.6150
P-ACOFS	SVM	0.7138	0.8346	0.8819	0.8896	0.8812
	KNN	0.6081	0.6073	0.5969	0.6065	0.6135
M-ACOFS	SVM	**0.8972**	**0.9019**	**0.9085**	**0.905**	**0.9073**
	KNN	0.6465	0.6465	0.6458	0.6454	0.6442

Table 7. Classification success rate of PSO compared algorithms in BASEHOCK

Algorithm	Classifier	Percentage of selected features				
		1%	2%	3%	4%	5%
O-PSOFS	SVM	0.8660	0.8746	0.9182	0.9167	0.9448
	KNN	0.8419	0.8856	0.8811	0.8836	0.8982
S-PSOFS	SVM	**0.8796**	0.9021	**0.9278**	**0.9503**	**0.9508**
	KNN	0.8349	0.8570	0.8982	0.8976	0.9112
P-PSOFS	SVM	0.8555	**0.9092**	0.9212	0.9257	0.9403
	KNN	0.7983	0.8721	0.8846	0.9042	0.8986
M-PSOFS	SVM	0.6945	0.7552	0.7923	0.7571	0.8183
	KNN	0.6704	0.7336	0.7978	0.7892	0.7998

Table 8. Classification success rate of PSO compared algorithms in PCMAC

Algorithm	Classifier	Percentage of selected features				
		1%	2%	3%	4%	5%
O-PSOFS	SVM	0.7602	0.7854	0.8029	0.8132	0.8240
	KNN	0.7354	0.7745	0.8327	0.8450	0.8440
S-PSOFS	SVM	0.7385	0.7787	0.8178	0.8204	0.8338
	KNN	0.7504	0.8111	0.8307	0.8312	0.8394
P-PSOFS	SVM	**0.7900**	**0.8096**	**0.8662**	**0.859**	**0.8667**
	KNN	0.7406	0.7648	0.8008	0.827	0.8343
M-PSOFS	SVM	0.6341	0.6855	0.7149	0.7082	0.7395
	KNN	0.6301	0.7139	0.6979	0.7555	0.7601

Table 9. Classification success rate of PSO compared algorithms in RELATHE

Algorithm	Classifier	Percentage of selected features				
		1%	2%	3%	4%	5%
O-PSOFS	SVM	0.8143	0.85	0.8599	0.8914	0.9082
	KNN	0.7631	0.7764	0.8227	0.8297	0.8458
S-PSOFS	SVM	**0.8297**	**0.8521**	**0.8928**	**0.9012**	0.9131
	KNN	0.7533	0.8045	0.8402	0.8423	0.8725
P-PSOFS	SVM	0.7975	0.8339	0.8767	0.8942	**0.9229**
	KNN	0.7694	0.7982	0.8080	0.8290	0.8570
M-PSOFS	SVM	0.7113	0.7456	0.7953	0.8164	0.8331
	KNN	0.6461	0.6839	0.7288	0.7379	0.7414

Table 10. Classification success rate of PSO compared algorithms in MADELON

Algorithm	Classifier	Percentage of selected features				
		1%	2%	3%	4%	5%
O-PSOFS	SVM	0.7000	**0.7869**	0.7796	0.8338	0.8227
	*K*NN	0.6365	0.6527	0.6673	0.6719	0.6704
S-PSOFS	SVM	0.6969	0.7673	0.7667	0.8404	**0.8558**
	*K*NN	0.6473	0.6388	0.6404	0.6631	0.6504
P-PSOFS	SVM	**0.7088**	0.7581	**0.8577**	**0.8623**	0.8077
	*K*NN	0.6365	0.6288	0.6300	0.6446	0.6292
M-PSOFS	SVM	0.5823	0.5988	0.6669	0.6962	0.7362
	*K*NN	0.6058	0.6058	0.6254	0.6369	0.6288

Table 11. Classification success rate of GA compared algorithms in BASEHOCK

Algorithm	Classifier	Percentage of selected features				
		1%	2%	3%	4%	5%
O-GAFS	SVM	0.9147	0.9453	0.9639	0.9719	0.9769
	*K*NN	0.8766	0.9142	0.9373	0.9533	0.9498
S-GAFS	SVM	0.9172	0.9573	**0.9699**	0.9764	**0.9819**
	*K*NN	0.8992	0.9338	0.9619	0.9468	0.9488
P-GAFS	SVM	**0.9303**	**0.9604**	**0.9699**	**0.9794**	**0.9819**
	*K*NN	0.8866	0.9303	0.9508	0.9513	0.9584
M-GAFS	SVM	0.7737	0.8018	0.8154	0.8379	0.8495
	*K*NN	0.7597	0.8108	0.8299	0.8299	0.8404

Table 12. Classification success rate of GA compared algorithms in PCMAC

Algorithm	Classifier	Percentage of selected features				
		1%	2%	3%	4%	5%
O-GAFS	SVM	0.7792	0.8425	0.8765	0.8785	0.9022
	*K*NN	0.8173	0.8657	0.8842	0.8744	0.8862
S-GAFS	SVM	0.8132	0.8430	0.8513	0.8641	0.8893
	*K*NN	0.8106	0.8780	0.8873	0.9007	0.8981
P-GAFS	SVM	**0.8518**	**0.897**	**0.9202**	**0.9331**	**0.9310**
	*K*NN	0.8147	0.8775	0.8939	0.8996	0.8991
M-GAFS	SVM	0.7334	0.7777	0.8116	0.8132	0.8276
	*K*NN	0.7154	0.7277	0.7540	0.7725	0.7879

Table 13. Classification success rate of GA compared algorithms in RELATHE

Algorithm	Classifier	Percentage of selected features				
		1%	2%	3%	4%	5%
O-GAFS	SVM	0.8087	0.8458	0.904	0.9089	0.9384
	KNN	0.7806	0.8129	0.8248	0.8402	0.8563
S-GAFS	SVM	0.8248	**0.8732**	0.8893	0.9187	**0.9488**
	KNN	0.8073	0.8381	0.8493	0.8605	0.8795
P-GAFS	SVM	**0.8276**	0.8725	**0.9201**	**0.9271**	0.9334
	KNN	0.8066	0.8388	0.8494	0.8549	0.8738
M-GAFS	SVM	0.7246	0.7785	0.8234	0.8353	0.8514
	KNN	0.6875	0.7155	0.7505	0.7603	0.7981

Table 14. Classification success rate of GA compared algorithms in MADELON

Algorithm	Classifier	Percentage of selected features				
		1%	2%	3%	4%	5%
O-GAFS	SVM	0.8192	**0.8669**	0.8742	0.9069	0.9108
	KNN	0.6446	0.6635	0.6773	0.6715	0.6885
S-GAFS	SVM	**0.8273**	0.8446	**0.8965**	**0.9104**	**0.9138**
	KNN	0.6150	0.6288	0.6238	0.6323	0.6435
P-GAFS	SVM	0.7750	0.8615	0.8958	0.8996	0.8962
	KNN	0.6204	0.6127	0.6342	0.6577	0.6500
M-GAFS	SVM	0.6285	0.6650	0.7762	0.7338	0.7946
	KNN	0.6258	0.6400	0.6454	0.6515	0.6592

one exception. S-PSOFS obtains the best results in BASEHOCK and RELATHE, and P-PSOFS has strong classification ability in PCMAC and MADELON. P-GAFS is the best in the opinion of classification performance except in MDELON where S-GAFS gets the best result. Besides, we can also conclude that the classification ability of SVM is better than KNN as most good results are gotten on SVM.

4 Conclusions

In this paper, we propose a system called EAFSSIS to improve the feature selection stability of EAs. After experiments, we can make some conclusions.

(1) The stability of original algorithms is different. The stability of ACO is better than GA, and that of PSO is the worst.
(2) If an algorithm has a better stability, its improvement is more significant by EAFSSIS.

(3) Different optimization models have different results in EAFSSIS, biobjective model has the best result on ACO, weighted Sum and weighted Product are almost the same on PSO, and weighted Product is good on GA.
(4) EAFSSIS can improve an algorithms stability and classification performance at the same time.
(5) SVM is better than KNN in the point of classification performance.

In the future, we will further improve the performance of EAFSSIS and modify it to fit for more EAs.

Acknowledgments. This work was supported by the Natural Science Foundation of China under Grant 61371196.

References

1. Emani, C.K., Cullot, N., Nicolle, C.: Understandable big data: a survey. Comput. Sci. Rev. **17**, 70–81 (2015)
2. OSullivan, B., Wooldridge, M.: Feature Selection for High Dimensional Data. Springer, Heidelberg (2015)
3. Guo, H.X., Li, Y.J., Shang, J., Gu, M.Y., Huang, Y.Y., Gong, B.: Learning from class imbalanced data: review of methods and applications. Expert. Syst. Appl. **73**, 220–239 (2017)
4. Fan, M., Chou, C.A.: Exploring stability based voxel selection methods in mvpa using cognitive neuroimaging data: a comprehensive study. Brain Inform. **3**, 193–203 (2016)
5. Kalousis, A., Prados, J., Hilario, M.: Stability of feature selection algorithms: a study on high-dimensional spaces. Knowl. Inf. Syst. **12**, 95–116 (2007)
6. Garcia-Torres, M., Gomez-Vela, F., Melian-Batista, B., Moreno-Vega, J.M.: High-dimensional feature selection via feature grouping: a variable neighborhood search approach. Inf. Sci. **326**, 102–118 (2016)
7. Li, Y., Si, J., Zhou, G.J., Huang, S.S., Chen, S.C.: FREL: a stable feature selection algorithm. IEEE Trans. Neural Netw. Learn. Syst. **26**, 1388–1402 (2015)
8. Somol, P., Novovicovaa, J.: Evaluating stability and comparing output of feature selectors that optimize feature subset cardinality. IEEE Trans. Pattern Anal. **32**, 1921–1939 (2010)
9. Tohka, J., Moradi, E., Huttunen, H.: Comparison of feature selection techniques in machine learning for anatomical brain MRI in dementia. Neuroinformatics **14**, 1–18 (2016)
10. Zhou, Q.F., Ding, J.C., Ning, Y.P., Luo, L.K., Li, T.: Stable feature selection with ensembles of multi-reliefF. In: 10th International Conference on Natural, pp. 742–747. IEEE Press, New York (2014)
11. Fahad, A., Tari, Z., Khalil, I., Almalawi, A.Y., Zomaya, A.: An optimal and stable feature selection approach for traffic classification based on multi-criterion fusion. Future Gener. Comput. Syst. **36**, 156–169 (2014)
12. Kim, H.J., Choi, B.S., Huh, M.Y.: Booster in high dimensional data classification. IEEE Trans. Knowl. Data Eng. **28**, 29–40 (2016)
13. Pes, B., Dessi, N., Angioni, M.: Exploiting the ensemble paradigm for stable feature selection: a case study on high-dimensional genomic data. Inf. Fusion **35**, 132–147 (2017)

14. Wang, H., Khoshgoftaar, T.M., Seliya, N.: On the stability of feature selection methods in software quality prediction: an empirical investigation. Int. J. Softw. Eng. Know. **25**, 1467–1490 (2015)
15. Yu, L., Ding, C., Loscalzo, S.: Stable feature selection via dense feature groups. In: 14th ACM SIGKDD International Conference on Knowledge Discovery and Data Mining, pp. 803–811. ACM, New York (2008)
16. Kamker, I., Gupta, S.K., Phung, D., Venkatesh, S.: Stabilizing l_1-norm prediction models by supervised feature grouping. J. Biomed. Inform. **59**, 149–168 (2016)
17. Shu, L., Ma, T.Y., Latecki, L.J.: Stable feature selection with minimal independent dominating sets. In: ACM International Conference on Bioinformatics, pp. 450–457. ACM, New York (2013)
18. Beinrucker, A., Dogan, U., Blanchard, G.: Extensions of stability selection using subsamples of observations and covariates. Stat. Comput. **5**, 1–19 (2016)
19. Erguzel, T.T., Ozekes, S., Gultekin, S., Tarhan, N.: Ant colony optimization based feature selection method for QEEG data classification. Psychiatr. Invest. **11**, 243–250 (2014)
20. Singh, S., Selvakumar, S.: A hybrid feature subset selection by combining filters and genetic algorithm. In: International Conference on Computing. Communication and Automation, pp. 283–289. IEEE Press, New York (2015)
21. Dudek, G.: Artificial immune system with local feature selection for short term load forecasting. IEEE Trans. Evol. Comput. **21**, 116–130 (2017)
22. Xue, B., Zhang, M.J., Brownw, W.N., Yao, X.: A survey on evolutionary computation approaches to feature selection. IEEE Trans. Evol. Comput. **20**, 606–626 (2016)
23. Zhang, Y., Gong, D.W., Cheng, J.: Multiobjective particle swarm optimization approach for cost based feature selection in classification. IEEE ACM Trans. Comput. Bioinform. **14**, 64–75 (2017)
24. Aldehim, G., Wang, W.J.: Weighted heuristic ensemble of filters. In: SAI Intelligent Systems Conference, pp. 609–615. IEEE Press, New York (2015)
25. Nogueira, S., Brown, G.: Measuring the stability of feature selection with applications to ensemble methods. In: Schwenker, F., Roli, F., Kittler, J. (eds.) MCS 2015. LNCS, vol. 9132, pp. 135–146. Springer, Cham (2015). doi:10.1007/978-3-319-20248-8_12

Global Path Planning of Unmanned Surface Vessel Based on Multi-objective Hybrid Particle Swarm Algorithm

Hao Zhou, Dongming Zhao[✉], and Xuan Guo

School of Automation, Wuhan University of Technology, Wuhan 430070, China
zhzmq@whut.edu.cn

Abstract. A multi-objective hybrid particle swarm algorithm is proposed to solve the problem that the current unmanned surface vessel (USV) global routing algorithm is easy to fall into the local optimal solution and the optimization target is single. The snap jump feature of simulated annealing algorithm is used to improve global search capability of particle swarm algorithm, and the three objective functions of path length, path smoothness and path security are used to optimize the path. The simulation result shows that the algorithm can improve the smoothness of the inflection point and the security of the path on the shortest path.

Keywords: Path planning · Simulated annealing · Mixed particle swarm · Multi-objective optimization · USV

1 Introduction

Unmanned Surface Vehicle [1,2] (USV) has the characteristics of good maneuverability, high speed, autonomy, etc. The main function of USV is to replace people to perform some special, dangerous tasks.

Global path planning is a prerequisite security for USV navigation safety. Now the mainstream global path planning algorithms are Dijkstra algorithm [3], A* algorithm [4], simulated annealing algorithm [5–8], genetic algorithm [9–12], ant colony algorithm [13,14], particle swarm algorithm [15] and some algorithm based on them. Dijkstra algorithm searches for the shortest path with a high success rate, but the algorithm is less efficient. A* algorithm is a heuristic algorithm with more efficient, easy to implement, but its heuristic function is not easy to choose. The process of simulated annealing algorithm is simple, the operation efficiency is also high, but the algorithm is slow to converge, and the search target is not strong. Genetic algorithm is a parallel search algorithm, the global search ability is strong, but the local search ability is poor. Ant colony algorithm is also a parallel search algorithm, the global search ability is strong, but its calculation is generally large, the search time is longer, and it is easy to fall into the local optimal solution. Particle swarm algorithm is also a kind

© Springer Nature Singapore Pte Ltd. 2017
C. He et al. (Eds.): BIC-TA 2017, CCIS 791, pp. 82–91, 2017.
https://doi.org/10.1007/978-981-10-7179-9_7

of parallel search algorithm, the global search ability is strong, and it has the advantages of low parameter setting, fast convergence speed and high precision, but there is also a problem that it is easy to fall into the local optimal solution.

Aiming at the above problem, a global path planning algorithm based on multi-objective mixed particle swarm (MOMPSO) is proposed. The snap jump feature of simulated annealing algorithm is used to improve global search capability of particle swarm algorithm, and three optimal functions of path length, path smoothness and path security is used to improve the practicality of the path.

2   Background

The global path planning problem of USV can be described as: in a complex marine environment with obstacles, set a starting point and an end point, through the corresponding algorithm to solve a two-point optimal path. The theory of traditional particle swarm based path planning algorithm and the problems encountered in its practical use is as follows.

The basic particle swarm algorithm has two key properties: velocity and position, where velocity represents the direction and distance at which the particle can move, and the next position is determined by the current position and velocity. Assuming that the target search space is D-dimensional, the particle swarm consists of N particles, where the i-th particle can be expressed as a D-dimensional vector, the velocity of the particle is also a D-dimensional vector. p_{best} is now the optimal position of individual particle, and g_{best} is the global optimal position of the particle group to the current search. According to the above definition, the formula for particle update speed and position is as follows:

$$v_{id} = \omega * v_{id} + c_1 r_1 (p_{id} - x_{id}) + c_2 r_2 (p_{gd} - x_{id}). \tag{1}$$

$$x_{id} = x_{id} + v_{id}. \tag{2}$$

where c_1 and c_2 are the learning factors, and r_1 are r_2 the uniform random numbers in the range of $[0,1]$, ω is the inertia weight.

As the algorithm has a certain randomness, when the value of ω is set improperly, the basic particle swarm algorithm tends to prematurely converge, resulting in the rapid decrease of the particle velocity. In this situation, the algorithm may fail to search for an optimal path.

3   Particle Swarm Optimization Based on Simulated Annealing

3.1   Improved Particle Swarm Optimization

In order to solve the problem that the basic particle swarm algorithm is too fast to get into the local optimum. The initial temperature, the annealing method and the ability to accept a poor solution with a certain probability are added in the particle swarm algorithm based on simulated annealing to optimize basic algorithm. The improvement is mainly reflected in the following five aspects:

(1) Add t_0 as "initial temperature":

$$t_0 = Fit(p_g)/\ln 5. \qquad (3)$$

where $Fit(x)$ is the fitness function and p_g is the global extreme value;

(2) Add λ as "Annealing coefficient":

$$t_{k+1} = \lambda t_k. \qquad (4)$$

(3) Increasing the probability of the particle being chosen as the global optimum at the current temperature:

$$TFit(p_i) = e^{-(Fit(p_i)-Fit(p_g))/t} / \sum_{i-1}^{N} e^{-(Fit(p_i)-Fit(p_g))/t}. \qquad (5)$$

where t is the current temperature and N is the number of particles in the particle group;

(4) By simulating the snap jump feature of the simulated annealing algorithm, p_i is chosen from all particles as global optimal p'_g to replace p_g, which is the true global optimal. In other words, to accept a poor solution with a certain probability. Roulette method is used to select p'_g, where the probability of each particle is chosen as the global optimal is calculated by the formula (5).

(5) The velocity and position of each particle are updated according to the following formulas:

$$\nu_{i,j}(t+1) = \varphi\{\nu_{i,j}(t) + c_1 r_1[p_{i,j} - x_{i,j}(t)] + c_2 r_2[p_{g,j} - x_{i,j}(t)]\}. \qquad (6)$$

$$x_{i,j}(t+1) = x_{i,j}(t) + \nu_{i,j}(t+1), j = 1, 2, \cdots, d. \qquad (7)$$

$$\varphi = 2/(2 - (c_1 + c_2) - \sqrt{(c_1 + c_2)^2 - 4(c_1 + c_2)}). \qquad (8)$$

where φ is the compression factor and d is the dimension of the solution.

3.2   Algorithm Steps and Processes

The process of particle swarm optimization based on simulated annealing is shown in Fig. 1, and the concrete steps are as follows.

(1) Parameter initialization, and randomly set the speed and location of each particle.

(2) Evaluation of fitness of each particle, the position and adaptive value are stored in p_{best}, which is individual extreme value of each particle, and the best fitted p_{best} is saved in g_{best}, the global extreme value.

(3) Determine t_0, which is the initial temperature.

(4) The fitness values of the particles at the current temperature are determined according to the formula (5).

(5) p_{best} is determined by Roulette method from all p_i.

(6) The speed and position of each particle are updated according to Eqs. (6) and (7).

(7) Calculate the fitness value of each particle, and update p_{best} and g_{best}, and then do annealing operation according to formula (4).

(8) If the outcome satisfies the termination condition, the algorithm terminates and outputs the result, otherwise returns to step (4).

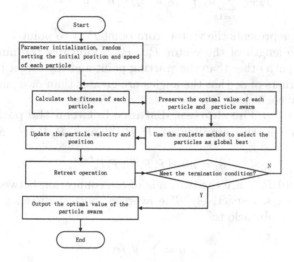

Fig. 1. Algorithm process of particle swarm algorithm based on simulated annealing

4 Hybrid Particle Swarm Optimization for Multi-objective Optimization

4.1 Target Function Setting

Global path planning of USV requires three optimization goals: the path length is as short as possible, the path is as smooth as possible and the security is optimal. Assuming there are n path points in a path, the path corresponds to n-1 lines. The form of each path is $L = [P_0, P_1, P_2, \cdots, P_n, P_{n+1}]$, where P_0 is the starting point S and P_{n+1} is the target point T. The three goals that need to be implemented are defined as follows.

(1) Path Length f_1: calculated by calculating the sum of the lengths of the segments in the path. The length of each path is calculated as follows:

$$d_1 = |P_i + P_{i+1}| = \sqrt{(x_{i+1} - x_i)^2 + (y_{i+1} - y_i)^2} \qquad (9)$$

$$f_1 = \sum_{i=0}^{n} d_i. \qquad (10)$$

where (x_i, y_i) is the coordinates of path point p_i and d_i is the distance between two points.

(2) Path smoothness f_2: corner of path point P_i shown in Fig. 2, the formula is as follows:

$$\alpha_i = \cos^{-1} \times \neg P_{i-1} P_i / (| P_{i-1} P_i \parallel P_i P_{i+1} |) \tag{11}$$

$$f_2 = (\sum_{i=1}^{n} \alpha_i + k \times \pi/2)/n, n > 0 \tag{12}$$

where $\overline{P_{i-1}P_i}$ represents the vector from point P_{i-1} to point P_i, and $|P_{i-1}P_i|$ represents the length of the vector $\overline{P_{i-1}P_i}$. n indicates the number of path points in the path other than the starting point and the target point. k is the number of corners of α_i that the angles are greater than or equal to $\pi/2$, also called penalty coefficient.

(3) Path safety f_3: The shortest distance between the path point and the obstacles is the smaller of $P_i P_i^{(0)}$ and $P_i P_i^{(1)}$, as shown in Fig. 3.

$$d_i = min\{P_i P_i^{(0)}, P_i P_i^{(1)}\}. \tag{13}$$

where $P_i^{(0)}$ and $P_i^{(1)}$ are the two ends of the connection between path point and the obstacles, respectively. The average shortest distance d of all path points from the obstacle is:

$$d = \sum_{i=1}^{n} d_i/n. \tag{14}$$

Where n represents the number of path points in the path other than the starting point and the target point. The path security formula is defined as follows:

$$f_3 = \lambda * k/d. \tag{15}$$

where d is the average of the shortest distance of the path point from the obstacle. λ for the weight adjustment factor, used to solve the problem of average distance is too small after the countdown. k is the number of the path points that the minimum distance between the path point and the obstacles is zero.

4.2   The Objective Function Maps to the Fitness Function

This paper uses the weighting coefficient method to solve the problem of the problem of multi-objective function mapping to fitness function of algorithm. By assigning a weight value to each objective function, then obtain the new fitness function by doing weighted summation of each objective function. The representation is as follows:

$$FitV = \omega_1 * f_1 + \omega_2 * f_2 + \omega_3 * f_3. \tag{16}$$

where $\omega_1 \omega_2 \omega_3$ are the weighting coefficient of the objective function $f_1 f_2 f_3$, respectively. And $\omega_1 + \omega_2 + \omega_3 = 1$.

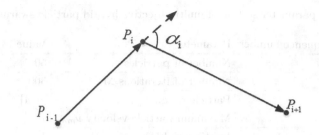

Fig. 2. Sketch map of corner

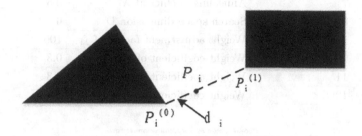

Fig. 3. The shortest distance between path point and obstacles

5 Simulation Test

5.1 Parameter Settings

In the quad-core 2.2 GHZ, 8G memory PC machine using Matlab 2014a software for simulation test. In the test, the environmental model is a 200 × 200 two-dimensional space, the coordinates of the starting point and the target point are (20, 180) and (160, 110) respectively, and four polygonal obstacles are designed in the model. The initial setting of each parameter in the multi-objective hybrid particle swarm algorithm is shown in Table 1.

5.2 Simulation Results

Simulation of single-target ant colony algorithm, single-objective hybrid particle swarm optimization algorithm and multi-objective hybrid particle swarm optimization algorithm. The simulation path is shown in Fig. 4, the total length of the path varies with the number of iterations of the algorithm is shown in Fig. 5, the corner of the path points and its average value is shown in Fig. 6, the shortest distance and the mean distance of the path points from the obstacles is shown in Fig. 7.

5.3 Results Analysis

In order to evaluate the merits of path planning performance of various intelligent algorithms, this paper proposes a self-path planning performance evaluation

Table 1. Initial parameter setting of multi-objective hybrid particle swarm algorithm

Sequence number	Parameter	Value
1	Number of particles N	50
2	Number of iterations M	500
3	Particle range	[0, 1]
4	Maximum particle velocity ν_{max}	1
5	Inertia weight ω	1
6	Acceleration constant c_1, c_2	2
7	Annealing coefficient λ	0.5
8	Search space dimension D	6
9	Weight adjustment factor of f_1	100
10	Weight coefficient of f_1	0.3
11	Weight coefficient of f_2	0.3
12	Weight coefficient of f_3	0.4

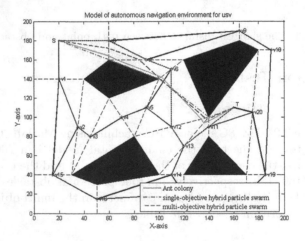

Fig. 4. Simulation paths of each algorithm

method, using the three indicators of the optimal path planned by each intelligent algorithm, length L, average corner α, average shortest distance d from obstacles, to evaluate the path planning performance of the algorithm.

First of all, the three indicators were normalized by the following min-max standardized formula:

$$X^* = (X - X_{min})/(X_{max} - X_{min}). \tag{17}$$

where X can be used to represent L, α or d, X_{min} represents the minimum value, and X_{max} represents the maximum value. After normalizing the three indicators of the algorithm, the normalized values of the three indicators are obtained: L_i^*,

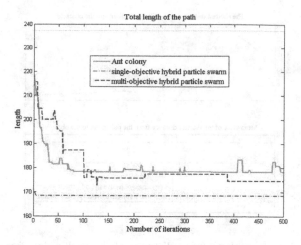

Fig. 5. Total length of the path varies with the number of iterations of each algorithm

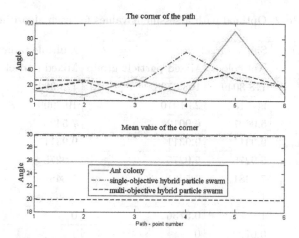

Fig. 6. Corner of the path points and its average value of each algorithm

α_i^*, d_i^*. Then the weighting coefficient method is used to calculate the evaluation value of path planning performance of each algorithm.

$$S_i = 100 * \{k_1 * (1 - L_i^*) + k_2 * (1 - \alpha_i^*) + k_3 * d_i^*\}. \tag{18}$$

where k_i represents the weight of the three indicators. The evaluation values of each algorithm are calculated according to the parameters in Table 1. The results are shown in Table 2.

From the evaluation values of the algorithms calculated in Table 2, it can be seen that the evaluation value 80.04 of the multi-objective hybrid particle swarm

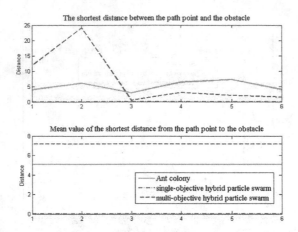

Fig. 7. Shortest distance and the mean distance of the path points from the obstacles of each algorithm

Table 2. Optimal path assessment values for each algorithm

Parameter	Single target		Multiple target
	Ant colony	Mixed particle group	Mixed particle group
L	178.3049	168.3738	174.9821
α	25.7184	23.1910	19.7909
d	5.0607	0.0012	7.5493
$L_{max} - L_{min}$	9.9311	9.9311	9.9311
$\alpha_{max} - \alpha_{min}$	5.9275	5.9275	5.9275
$d_{max} - d_{min}$	7.5481	7.5481	7.5481
L_*	1	0	0.6654
α_*	1	0.5736	0
d_*	0.6702	0	1
S	26.81	42.79	80.04

algorithm is significantly higher than that of the single-objective ant colony algorithm (26.81) and the single-objective mixed particle swarm algorithm (42.79), which indicates that the multi-objective mixed particle swarm optimization The planned path is optimal on the comprehensive evaluation of the three indicators with the shortest path, smoothness and safety.

6 Conclusion

Aiming at the problem that the traditional particle swarm algorithm is easy to fall into the local optimal solution, an improved algorithm is proposed by using the hysteresis of the simulated annealing algorithm. By adding the multi-objective optimization, the practicability of the algorithm is improved. The simulation results show that the improved algorithm can optimize the path smoothness of unmanned navigation and improve the security of the path and meet the requirements of the global path planning of unmanned ships.

References

1. Liu, Z.X., Zhang, Y.M., Yu, X., et al.: Unmanned surface vehicles: an overview of developments and challenges. Ann. Rev. Control **41**, 71–93 (2016)
2. Zhuang, J.Y., Su, Y.M., Liao, Y.L., et al.: Unmanned surface vehicle local path planning based on marine radar. J. Shanghai Jiaotong Univ. **46**(9), 1371–1375 (2012)
3. Ferariu, L., Cîmpanu, C.: Pareto genetic path planning hybridized with multi-objective Dijkstra's algorithm. In: 18th International Conference on System Theory, Control and Computing (ICSTCC), pp. 341–346. IEEE (2014)
4. Chabini, I., Lan, S.: Adaptations of the A* algorithm for the computation of the fast paths in deterministic discrete-time dynamic network. IEEE Trans. Intell. Transp. Syst. **3**(1), 134–136 (2002)
5. Wang, Z.P., Gao, G.C., Yang, W.P.: An improved fast simulated annealing combinatorial optimization. Syst. Eng. Theory Pract. (S1000-6788) **5**(2), 73–76 (1999)
6. Liang, Y., Xu, L.: Global path planning for mobile robot based genetic algorithm and modified simulated annealing algorithm. In: Genetic and Evolutionary Computation Conference, pp. 303–308 (2009)
7. Romeijn, H.E., Smith, R.L.: Simulated annealing for constrained global optimization. J. Global Optim. **5**(2), 101–126 (1994)
8. Chen, L., Aihara, K.: Chaotic simulated annealing by a neural network model with transient chaos. Neural Netw. **8**(6), 915–930 (1995)
9. Gao, Y.F., Sun, Y., Zheng, W.J.: Genetic algorithm for optimizing the layout of logistics park based on shortest path and elitist strategy. J. Inf. Comput. Sci. **12**(10), 3765–3774 (2015)
10. Tu, J., Yang, S.X.: Genetic algorithm based path planning for a mobile robot. In: IEEE International Conference on Robotics and Automation, pp. 1221–1226 (2003)
11. Han, W.G., Baek, S.M., Kuc, T.Y.: Genetic algorithm based path planning and dynamic obstacle avoidance of mobile robots. In: IEEE International Conference on Systems, Man, and Cybernetics, pp. 2747–2751. IEEE (1997)
12. Kala, R., Shukla, A., Tiwari, R., Shafahi, Y.: Robotic Path Planning using Hybrid Genetic Algorithm Particle Swarm Optimisation. Inderscience Publishers, Geneva (2012)
13. Dorigo, M., Gambardella, L.M.: Ant colony system: a cooperative learning approach to the traveling sales-man problem. IEEE Trans. Evol. Comput. **1**(1), 53–66 (1997)
14. Hasany, R.M., Shafahi, Y.: Ant colony optimisation for finding the optimal railroad path. Inst. Civil Eng. Transp. **170**(4), 218–230 (2017)
15. Kennedy, J., Eberhart, R.: Particle swarm optimization. In: The 1995 IEEE International Conference on Neural Networks, pp. 1942–1948. IEEE (1995)

Predicting Essential Proteins Based on Gene Expression Data, Subcellular Localization and PPI Data

Xiujuan Lei[1(✉)], Siguo Wang[1], and Linqiang Pan[2,3]

[1] School of Computer Science, Shaanxi Normal University,
Xi'an 710119, Shaanxi, China
{xjlei,wangsiguo}@snnu.edu.cn
[2] Key Laboratory of Image Information Processing and Intelligent Control,
School of Automation, Huazhong University of Science and Technology,
Wuhan 430074, Hubei, China
lqpan@mail.hust.edu.cn
[3] School of Electric and Information Engineering,
Zhengzhou University of Light Industry, Zhengzhou 450002, Henan, China

Abstract. Predicting essential proteins is indispensable for understanding the minimal requirements of cellular survival and development. In recent years, many methods combined with the topological features of PPI networks have been proposed. However, most of these approaches ignored the intrinsic characteristics of biological attributes. This paper integrates Gene expression data, Subcellular localization and PPI networks to identify essential proteins, named GSP. We use local average connectivity and edge clustering coefficient unite with gene expression data to measure centralities of nodes. Compared with non-essential proteins, essential proteins appear more frequently in some subcellular localizations such as Nucleus and considering that different compartments play different roles, thus we integrate subcellular localization information to identify essential proteins. The computational experiment results on the yeast PPI networks show that the proposed method GSP outperforms other state-of-art methods including DC, EC, IC, SC, NC, LAC, PeC, WDC and UDoNC.

Keywords: Essential proteins · Gene expression data · Subcellular localization information · PPI networks

1 Introduction

Proteins are important macromolecules that sustain life activities [1]. Essential proteins are those proteins that can result in lethality or infertility of a cell if one of them has been deleted [2]. Identifying essential proteins is necessary not only for understanding the molecular mechanisms of cellular life but also for disease diagnosis, medical treatments and drug design [3,4].

© Springer Nature Singapore Pte Ltd. 2017
C. He et al. (Eds.): BIC-TA 2017, CCIS 791, pp. 92–105, 2017.
https://doi.org/10.1007/978-981-10-7179-9_8

In the previous studies, there were many traditional experimental methods, such as gene knockouts [5], RNA interference [6] and conditional knockouts [7]. These biological methods are time consuming and expensive, hence many computational approaches as complementary and alternative methods have been proposed to predict essential proteins. With the development of high-throughput technologies [8], such as yeast two-hybrid [9], tandem affinity purification and mass spectrometry [10], many high-quality and large-scale PPI datasets have been published to provide fundamental and abundant data for computational approaches to predict essential proteins [11].

One group of researchers focus on detecting essential proteins based on their topological features in protein-protein interaction (PPI) networks, since previous studies have shown that the removal of those proteins with a larger number of neighbors in PPI networks is more likely to cause the organism to die [12]. Therefore, many centrality methods have been come up with such as Eigenvector Centrality (EC) [13], Information Centrality (IC) [14], Degree Centrality (DC) [15], Betweenness Centrality (BC) [16], Subgraph Centrality (SC) [17], Sum of Edge Clustering Coefficient Centrality (NC) [18]. In addition, Local Average Connectivity (LAC) [19] and a Topology Potential-Based method (TP) [20] are also common topology based methods. These methods based on the centrality of proteins in the PPI networks and determined whether proteins are essential in terms of their sorting scores. However, these centrality methods have their own limits. For example, a significant proportion of PPI networks obtained from high-throughput biological experiments have been found to contain false positives and they highly depend on the accuracy of PPI networks and ignore the useful biological features [21–24]. To overcome these limitations, some researchers have proposed methods to predict essential proteins by integrating their topological properties with their biological properties.

Considering the interaction data and Gene Ontology (GO) annotations, Hsing et al. [25] developed a method for predicting highly-interacting proteins. By using supervised machine learning-based methods, Acencio et al. [26] combined network topological properties with genomic features, such as cellular localization and biological process information to identify essential proteins. Li et al. [27] proposed a new prediction method called PeC and Tang et al. [28] proposed another one, WDC, which integrated network topology with gene expression profiles. Localization-Specificity for Essential protein Detection (LSED) [29] introduced subcellular localization information to predict essential proteins. Recently, Peng et al. [30] proposed a new prediction method, named UDoNC, by combining the domain features of proteins with their topological properties in PPI networks. These methods, which integrated network topologies and biological information, improved the accuracy of predicting essential proteins compared with the centrality measures based on the network topological features. Besides some researches consider protein complexes into predicting essential proteins. Qin et al. [31] identified essential proteins based on network topology properties and protein complexes, named LBCC, which based on the combination of local density, betweenness centrality and in-degree centrality of complex.

What's more, some researchers constructed dynamic networks to reduce the effect of noise in the PPI networks. Luo *et al.* [32] introduced a new method named CDLC to predict essential proteins by integrating dynamic *LAC* and in-degree of proteins in complexes.

In this paper, we present a new method to predict essential proteins by integrating gene expression, subcellular localization and PPI networks. We use the edge clustering coefficient (*ECC*) and *LAC* in the PPI networks to determine the topological properties of a protein node. Gene expression information is used to evaluate how strongly two interacting proteins are co-expressed. According to subcellular localization data, we can know the distribution of proteins in each compartment, hence we assume that the proteins are more likely to be essential proteins with the wider range of distribution in Nucleus. Furthermore, we synthetically consider the role of each part in predicting essential proteins. The computational experiment results show that the GSP method outperforms other existing methods: DC [15], EC [14], IC [15], SC [17], NC [18], LAC [19], PeC [27], WDC [28], and UDoNC [30]. In the following subsections, we will introduce how to use these information and integrate them to calculate a protein's essentiality.

2 Method

In this study, we propose a new method based on Gene expression, Subcellular localization and PPI networks, named GSP. The basic ideas behind GSP are as follows: (1) highly linked proteins are more likely to be essential proteins than low-linked ones; (2) the essential proteins in the same cluster have more opportunities for co-expression; (3) in the Nucleus, the wider the distribution of the proteins is, the more likely the essential proteins are. In GSP, a protein's essentiality is determined by the connectivity level, the probability that a protein is co-clustered and co-expressed with its neighbors and the size of the distribution in the Nucleus. In order to describe GSP more clearly, we provide the following definitions and descriptions. Figure 1 is a general frame of GSP.

2.1 Network Topology

From the perspective of network topology, we firstly consider the local variable *ECC*, which is used to evaluate the degree of tightness between two protein nodes. Then we consider that *ECC* cannot fully reflect the characteristics of the network topologies, hence we take proteins modular nature that is *LAC* into account, which mainly reflects the connectivity of protein neighbors and neighbors. *ECC* and *LAC* are defined as follows.

Given an edge $e(u, v)$ in the undirected graph G, the *ECC* of an edge (u, v) is defined as [33]:

$$ECC(u, v) = \frac{Z_{u,v} + 1}{min\{d_u, d_v\}} \tag{1}$$

where $Z_{u,v}$ represents the number of triangles built on edge (u, v), d_u and d_v represent the degree of nodes u and node v, respectively.

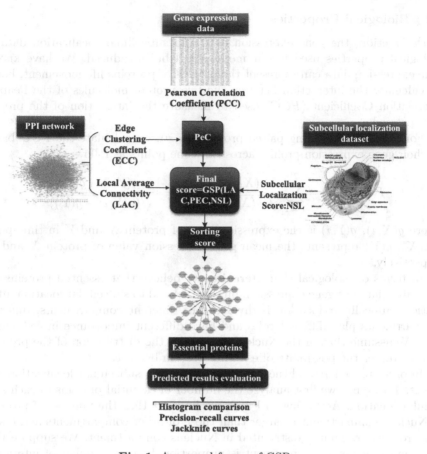

Fig. 1. A general frame of GSP.

The *LAC* of a node [15] describes the closeness of its neighbors. The *LAC* of a node v is defined as:

$$LAC(v) = \frac{\sum_{u \in N_v} deg^{C_v}(u)}{|N_v|} \qquad (2)$$

where N_v represents the neighbors of node v, and $|N_v|$ represents the number of nodes in N_v. C_v is the subgraph induced by N_v. For a node u in C_v, its local connectivity in C_v is represented as $deg^{C_v}(u)$. Here, for each protein v we use the normalized *LAC* value $NLAC(v)$ calculated by the following formula:

$$NLAC(v) = \frac{LAC(v) - minLAC(v)}{maxLAC(v) - minLAC(v)} \qquad (3)$$

where $maxLAC(v)$ and $minLAC(v)$ denote the maximum value and minimum value of *LAC* for all nodes in graph G, respectively.

2.2   Biological Properties

In this section, the gene expression data and subcellular localization data as biological properties used in our method will be introduced. We have known gene expression data can represent the process of proteins life movement, hence we calculate the interaction between the two protein molecules of the Pearson Correlation Coefficient (PCC) used to measure the interaction of the protein co-expressed.

For each corresponding paired proteins (u, v), we calculate the PCC based on their gene expression profiles across all time points as follow:

$$PCC(u,v) = \sum_{i=1}^{T} \frac{g(X,i) - \overline{g}(X)}{\sqrt{(g(X,i) - \overline{g}(X))^2}} \cdot \frac{g(Y,i) - \overline{g}(Y)}{\sqrt{(g(Y,i) - \overline{g}(Y))^2}} \qquad (4)$$

where $g(X,i)$, $g(Y,i)$ is the expression level of protein X and Y in time point i. $\overline{g}(X)$, $\overline{g}(Y)$ represents the mean gene expression value of protein X and Y, respectively.

In terms of biological characteristics, we believe that essential proteins are not only related to gene expression, but also related to subcellular location information. Subcellular location is divided into different compartments, different compartments play different roles and have different importance in cell activities. We assume that in the Nucleus, the wider the distribution of the proteins is, the greater the possibility of essential protein becomes.

In order to understand the relationship between subcellular localization and essential proteins, we first analyze the number of essential proteins in each subcellular location. According to Fig. 2, we find out that the number of proteins in Nucleus compartment is larger than those of other compartments and essential proteins are mainly distributed in Nucleus compartment. We suppose that the importance of a compartment is proportional to the number of interacted proteins in this compartment.

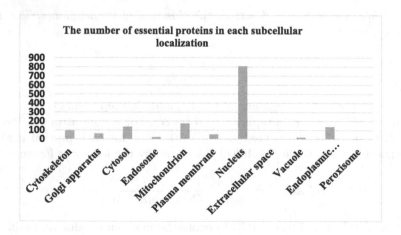

Fig. 2. The number of essential proteins in each subcellular location.

Let C_{max} denote the protein with the largest number of times appears in subcellular localization of the Nucleus, $|i|$ represents the number of times of the protein i appears in the nucleus. The importance of protein i, denoted as $NSL(i)$ in Eq. (5), is calculated by the ratio of its size to the largest size of the Nucleus as Eq. (1). From the definition, the value of $NSL(i)$ is in the range of $(0, 1]$.

$$NSL(i) = \frac{|i|}{|C_{max}|} \qquad (5)$$

2.3   The Ranking Score and GSP Algorithm

Network topologies and biological properties are of equal importance, how to effectively evaluate their contribution to identify essential proteins is the focus of our method. The GSP method consists of two steps. The first step is integrating PPI networks with gene expression data, and the second step is computing the ranking score.

Based on the definitions of ECC and PCC, Li et $al.$ [23] proposed a new centrality measure which is named as PeC. It combined the PPI network topology with gene expression data. Thus, the probability of paired proteins (u, v) is defined as the following:

$$Pc(u,v) = ECC(u,v) \times PCC(u,v) \qquad (6)$$

For a protein v, its $PeC(v)$ is defined as the sum of the probabilities that the protein and its neighbors belong to a same cluster:

$$PeC(v) = \sum_{u \in N_v} P_c(u,v) \qquad (7)$$

where N_v denotes the set of all neighbors of node v.

The ranking score of our algorithm GSP is a linear combination of the three scores: a centrality score is derived from the combination of gene expression data with ECC named as $PeC(i)$, LAC of a node marked as $NLAC(i)$, subcellular localization score $NSL(i)$. We believe that subcellular localization score $NSL(i)$ play a more significant role in ranking score to identify essential proteins. Also, we consider that the combination of $PeC(i)$ and $NLAC(i)$ represent the centrality score of a node. Therefore, for a protein i, its sorting score is calculated as follows:

$$H(i) = (1 - \alpha) \times NSL(i) + \alpha \times [(1 - \beta) \times NLAC(i) + \beta \times PeC(i)] \qquad (8)$$

where $\alpha \in [0, 1]$ and $\beta \in [0, 1]$ are used to adjust the proportion of these three scores. We can also analyze which part among gene expression data, subcellular localization and PPI networks is more important in our method to identify essential proteins by adjusting the values of α and β. In the process of constantly modifying α and β, we can determine optimal values of them to predict essential proteins.

3 Results and Discussion

In this section, we first introduce the data used in the experiment. Then we analyze the parameters α and β towards the performance of GSP algorithm. Next, GSP is compared with the other existing methods, such as DC [15], EC [14], IC [15], SC [17], NC [18], LAC [19], PeC [27], WDC [28] and UDoNC [30]. We adopt three types of popular comparison method: (1) Histogram comparison methodology. Firstly, the score of each protein is calculated according to Eq. (8) are in descending order. Next, the top 1, 5, 10, 15, 20 and 25% proteins are selected as candidate essential proteins. Then, we compare prediction results with the set of known essential proteins. Finally, the performance is presented in the form of histograms of the number of essential proteins predicted by each algorithm. (2) Precision-recall curves. (3) Jack-knife curves.

3.1 Experimental Data

In order to verify our proposed method GSP, we perform a group of experiments on the following datasets. The yeast PPI network consists of 5,093 proteins and 24,743 interactions that download from DIP database [34] on Oct.10, 2010. The yeast gene expression data download from GEO database [35] on Oct.27, 2005 contains 7074 gene expression profiles at 36 time points from three consecutive metabolic cycles, each cycle contains 12 time points. Subcellular localization dataset of yeast is downloaded from COMPARTMENTS database [36] on Aug.30, 2014 includes 5095 yeast proteins and 206,831 subcellular localization records. The known essential proteins data are collected from four different databases: MIPS [37], SGD [38], DEG [2], and SGDP (http://www-sequence. stanford.edu/group). Among the 1285 essential proteins, 1167 essential proteins present in the DIP network.

3.2 The Effect of Parameter on Performance

In our method GSP, the protein score is related to parameters α and β, which are used to adjust the weight of gene expression data, subcellular localization and PPI networks in the final ranking score. The scope of two parameters is in the interval [0, 1]. To investigate the effect of parameter α and β of our method, we evaluate the prediction accuracy by setting different values of α and β. Figure 3 shows the comparative results with different values of parameters α and β. Here, we select top 1, 5, 10, 15, 20 and 25% proteins identified by GSP, respectively. The prediction accuracy is measured in terms of a number of true essential proteins in top candidates. Figure 1 shows that GSP achieves the highest predicted accuracy when α and β are assigned as 0.1, 0.7, respectively. In particular, when $\alpha = 0$, namely only subcellular localization information is used, parameter β has no effect, all the results are the same.

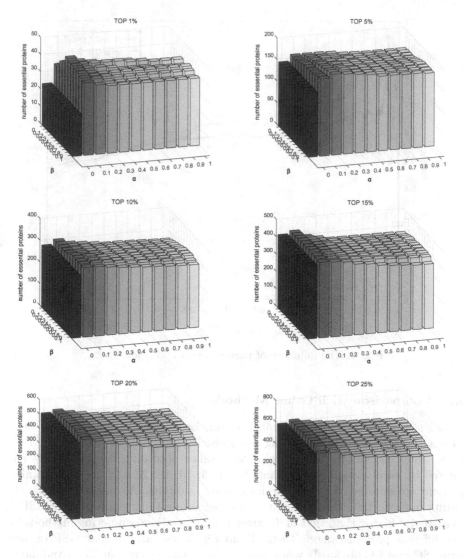

Fig. 3. The influence of parameters α and β. (a) Top 1% (Top 51) (b) Top 5% (Top 255) (c) Top 10% (Top 510) (d) Top 15% (Top 764) (e) Top 20% (Top 1019) (f) Top 25% (Top 1274)

In order to further analyze the influence of the parameters α and β, we utilize the precision-recall curves with five sets of parameters α and β, such as $\alpha = 0.1$ and $\beta = 0.7$, $\alpha = 0.1$ and $\beta = 1$, $\alpha = 0.1$ and $\beta = 0$, $\alpha = 0$ and $\beta = 0.7$, $\alpha = 1$ and $\beta = 0.7$. The results are shown in Fig. 4. According to Fig. 4, when $\alpha = 0.1$ and $\beta = 0.7$, the result is the best. In this paper, we consider the optimal values to be $\alpha = 0.1$ and $\beta = 0.7$.

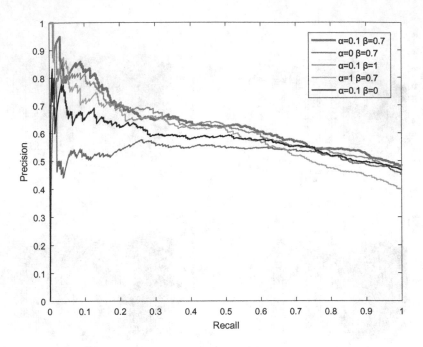

Fig. 4. The influence of parameters α and β for GSP.

3.3   Comparison with Other Methods

In order to evaluate the performance of our proposed method GSP, we compare our approach to the following methods: DC, EC, IC, SC, NC, LAC, PeC, WDC and UDoNC. Firstly, proteins are ranked according to their scores calculated by each method. After that, top 1, 5, 10, 15, 20 and 25 of the ranked proteins are selected as candidates for essential proteins. As shown in Fig. 5, the results indicate that the percentage of essential proteins predicted by GSP is consistently higher than that of discovered by nine other competing methods for the different proteins among them. From Fig. 5, we can see that GSP outperforms SC and EC obviously when predicting no more than top 25% candidates. Taking top 1%(51) predicted essential proteins for example, 44 essential proteins are correctly identified by the GSP while SC and EC correctly predicted both are 24. For predicting TOP 25% essential candidates, GSP achieves more than 30% improvements compared with DC, IC, SC, EC, and more than 10% improvements compared with UdoNC.

3.4   Comparison the Experimental Results Based on Precision-Recall Curves

To validate the performance of GSP, we study the *Precision − Recall(PR)* of GSP on the PPI networks and compared with nine other methods.

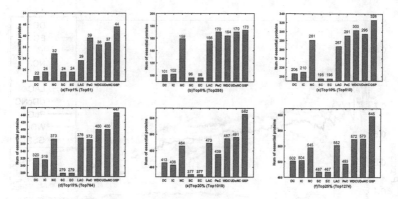

Fig. 5. GSP compared with several existing methods. (a) Top 1% (Top 51) (b) Top 5% (Top 255) (c) Top 10% (Top 510) (d) Top 15% (Top 764) (e) Top 20% (Top 1019) (f) Top 25% (Top 1274)

Precision represents the proportion of essential proteins in the predicted results, which can be calculated as:

$$Precision = \frac{TP}{TP + FP} \tag{9}$$

where TP indicates the number of true positives and FP means the number of false positives. *Recall* means the proportion of essential proteins in all essential proteins, which can be calculated as:

$$Recall = \frac{TP}{TP + FN} \tag{10}$$

where FN is the number of false negatives. Figure 6 shows the PR curves of GSP and nine other methods on the PPI networks, we can see that compared with nine other methods, the PR curve of the new method shows an improvement for predicting essential proteins.

3.5 Comparison the Experimental Results Based on Jackknife Curves

To further verify the performance of GSP and other nine methods for predicting essential proteins, we use jackknife curves. The experimental results validated by Jackknife curves are shown in Fig. 7. In Fig. 7, the X-axis represents the proteins ranked from the highest score to the lowest score for each method, while Y-axis is the cumulative count of essential proteins with respect to ranked proteins. The Area Under Curve (AUC) corresponding to each method is used to measure their performance. The bigger the area is, the better performance the method has. As shown in Fig. 5, our proposed method GSP performs better than the other nine methods.

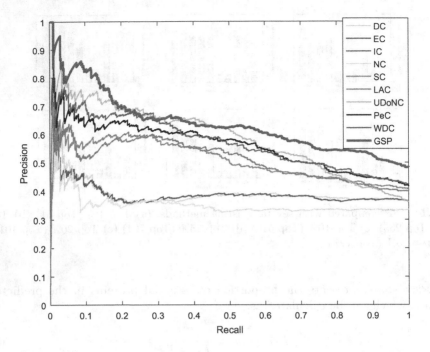

Fig. 6. The PR curves of GSP and that of other methods

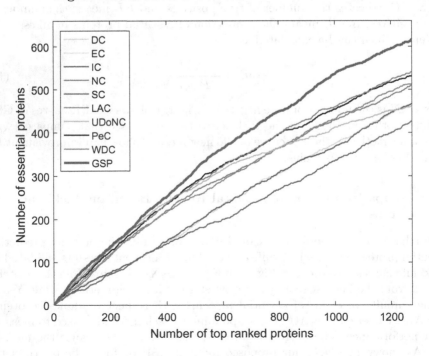

Fig. 7. The jackknife curves of GSP and that of other nine methods

4   Conclusion

It is believed that predicting essential proteins is very useful for disease study and drug design. At present, the prediction of essential proteins is still a hot topic in the era of post-genome. However, many centrality measures were proposed at the network level and generally ignored the relationship between the network topologies and biological features. In this research, we have proposed a new essential protein discovery method that integrate Gene expression data, Subcellular localization and PPI networks, named GSP. We use the ECC and LAC in the PPI network to determine the topological properties of a protein node. Gene expression information is used to evaluate how strongly two interacting proteins are co-expressed. Subcellular localization data are used to determine the distribution of proteins in the Nucleus, and we assume that the proteins are more likely to be essential proteins with the wider range of distribution. At the same time, we take into account the weightiness of each part in predicting essential proteins. Experimental results show that the GSP method outperforms other previous centrality methods: DC, EC, IC, SC, NC, LAC, and three other methods by integrating topological features and protein complex data sources: PeC, WDC, UDoNC. Our experimental results also show that our proposed GSP method that integrate network topological features and biological attributes is effective for identifying essential proteins.

Acknowledgments. This paper is supported by the National Natural Science Foundation of China (61672334, 61502290, 91530320, and 61401263), Industrial Research Project of Science and Technology in Shaanxi Province (2015GY016), and the Innovation Scientists and Technicians Troop Construction Projects of Henan Province (154200510012).

References

1. Glass, J.I., Hutchison, C.A., Smith, H.O., Venter, J.C.: A systems biology tour de force for a near-minimal bacterium. Mol. Syst. Biol. **5**, 330 (2009)
2. Zhang, R., Lin, Y.: DEG 5.0, a database of essential genes in both prokaryotes and eukaryotes. Nucleic Acids Res. **37**, 455–458 (2009)
3. Li, M., Zheng, R.Q., Li, Q., Wang, J.X., Wu, F.X., Zhang, Z.H.: Prioritizing disease genes by using search engine algorithm. Curr. Bioinform. **11**, 195–202 (2016)
4. Lan, W., Wang, J.X., Li, M., Peng, W., Wu, F.X.: Computational approaches for prioritizing candidate disease genes based on PPI networks. Tsinghua Sci. Technol. **20**, 500–512 (2015)
5. Giaever, G., Chu, A.M., Ni, L., Connelly, C., Riles, L., Vronneau, S., Dow, S., Lucaudanila, A., Anderson, K., Andr, B.: Functional profiling of the Saccharomyces cerevisiae genome. Nature **418**, 387 (2002)
6. Cullen, L.M., Arndt, G.M.: Genome-wide screening for gene function using RNAi in mammalian cells. Immunol. Cell Biol. **83**, 217–223 (2005)
7. Roemer, T., Jiang, B., Davison, J., Ketela, T., Veillette, K., Breton, A., Tandia, F., Linteau, A., Sillaots, S., Marta, C.: Large-scale essential gene identification in candida albicans and applications to antifungal drug discovery. Mol. Microbiol. **50**, 167–181 (2003)

8. Uetz, P., Giot, L., Cagney, G., Mansfield, T.A., Judson, R.S., Knight, J.R., Lockshon, D., Narayan, V., Srinivasan, M., Pochart, P., Qureshi-Emili, A., Li, Y., Godwin, B., Conover, D., Kalbfleisch, T., Vijayadamodar, G., Yang, M., Johnston, M., Fields, S., Rothberg, J.M.: A comprehensive analysis of protein-protein interactions in Saccharomyces cerevisiae. Nature **403**, 623–627 (2000)

9. Ito, T., Chiba, T., Ozawa, R., Yoshida, M., Hattori, M., Sakaki, Y.: A comprehensive two-hybrid analysis to explore the yeast protein interactome. Natl. Acad. Sci. U. S. A. **98**, 4569–4574 (2001)

10. Ho, Y., Gruhler, A., Heilbut, A., Bader, G.D., Moore, L., Adams, S.L., Millar, A., Taylor, P., Bennett, K., Boutilier, K.: Systematic identification of protein complexes in Saccharomyces cerevisiae by mass spectrometry. Nature **415**, 180 (2002)

11. Mering, C.V., Krause, R., Snel, B., Cornell, M., Oliver, S.G., Fields, S., Bork, P.: Comparative assessment of large-scale data sets of protein—[Ndash]—-protein interactions. Nature **417**, 399–403 (2002)

12. Jeong, H., Mason, S.P., Barabsi, A.L., Oltvai, Z.N.: Lethality and centrality in protein networks. Nature **411**, 41–42 (2001)

13. Bonacich, P.: Power and centrality: a family of measures. Am. J. Soc. **92**, 1170–1182 (1987)

14. Snee, R.D.: Validation of regression models: methods and examples. Technometrics **19**, 415–428 (1977)

15. Hahn, M.W., Kern, A.D.: Comparative genomics of centrality and essentiality in three eukaryotic protein-interaction networks. Mol. Biol. Evol. **22**, 803–806 (2005)

16. Joy, M.P., Brock, A., Ingber, D.E., Huang, S.: High-betweenness proteins in the yeast protein interaction network. Biomed. Res. Int. **2005**, 96 (2005)

17. Estrada, E., Rodrguez-Velzquez, J.A.: Subgraph centrality in complex networks. Phys. Rev. E **71**, 056103–056103 (2005)

18. Li, M., Wang, J., Wang, H., Pan, Y.: Identification of essential proteins based on edge clustering coefficient. IEEE/ACM Trans. Comput. Biol. Bioinform. **9**, 1070 (2012)

19. Li, M., Wang, J., Chen, X., Wang, H., Pan, Y.: A local average connectivity-based method for identifying essential proteins from the network level. Comput. Biol. Chem. **35**, 143 (2011)

20. Li, M., Lu, Y., Wang, J., Wu, F.X., Pan, Y.: A topology potential-based method for identifying essential proteins from PPI networks. IEEE/ACM Trans. Comput. Biol. Bioinform. **12**, 372 (2015)

21. Wang, J., Li, M., Chen, J., Pan, Y.: A fast hierarchical clustering algorithm for functional modules discovery in protein interaction networks. IEEE/ACM Trans. Comput. Biol. Bioinform. **8**, 607–620 (2011)

22. Wang, J.X., Chen, J.E., Min, L., Hu, B., Gang, C.: Modifying the DPClus algorithm for identifying protein complexes based on new topological structures. BMC Bioinform. **9**, 1–16 (2008)

23. Zhao, B., Wang, J., Li, M., Wu, F.X., Pan, Y.: Detecting protein complexes basedon uncertain graph model. IEEE/ACM Trans. Comput. Biol. Bioinform. **11**, 486–497 (2014)

24. Peng, W., Wang, J., Zhao, B., Wang, L.: Identification of protein complexes using weighted PageRank-Nibble algorithm and core-attachment structure. IEEE/ACM T. Comput. Biol. Bioinform. **12**, 179–192 (2015)

25. Michael, H., Grant, B.K., Artem, C.: The use of gene ontology terms for predicting highly-connected 'hub' nodes in protein-protein interaction networks. BMC Syst. Biol. **2**, 1–14 (2008)

26. Acencio, M.L., Lemke, N.: Towards the prediction of essential genes by integration of network topology, cellular localization and biological process information. BMC Bioinform. **10**, 290 (2009)

27. Li, M., Zhang, H., Wang, J.X., Pan, Y.: A new essential protein discovery method based on the integration of protein-protein interaction and gene expression data. BMC Syst. Biol. **6**, 15 (2012)

28. Tang, X., Wang, J., Zhong, J., Pan, Y.: Predicting essential proteins based on weighted degree centrality. IEEE/ACM Trans. Comput. Biol. Bioinform. **11**, 407 (2014)

29. Peng, X., Wang, J., Wang, J., Wu, F.X., Pan, Y.: Rechecking the centrality-lethality rule in the scope of protein subcellular localization interaction networks. Plos One **10**, e0130743 (2015)

30. Peng, W., Wang, J., Cheng, Y., Lu, Y., Wu, F., Pan, Y.: UDoNC: an algorithm for identifying essential proteins based on protein domains and protein-protein interaction networks. IEEE/ACM Trans. Comput. Biol. Bioinform. **12**, 276–288 (2015)

31. Chao, Q., Sun, Y., Dong, Y.: A new method for identifying essential proteins based on network topology properties and protein complexes. Plos One **11**, e0161042 (2016)

32. Luo, J., Kuang, L.: A new method for predicting essential proteins based on dynamic network topology and complex information. Comput. Biol. Chem. **52**, 34–42 (2014)

33. Radicchi, F., Castellano, C., Cecconi, F., Loreto, V., Parisi, D.: Defining and identifying communities in networks. Natl. Acad. Sci. U. S. A. **101**, 2658–2663 (2004)

34. Xenarios, I., Salwnski, L., Duan, X.J., Higney, P., Kim, S.M., Eisenberg, D.: DIP, the database of interacting proteins: a research tool for studying cellular networks of protein interactions. Nucleic Acids Res. **30**, 303 (2002)

35. Tu, B.P., Mcknight, S.L.: Logic of the yeast metabolic cycle: temporal compartmentalization of cellular processes. Science **310**, 1152 (2005)

36. Binder, J.X., Pletscher-Frankild, S., Tsafou, K., Stolte, C., ODonoghue, S.I., Schneider, R., Jensen, L.J.: Compartments: Unification and Visualization Of Protein Subcellular Localization Evidence. Database, (2014–01-01) 2014, bau012 (2014)

37. Mewes, H.W., Amid, C., Arnold, R., Frishman, D., Güldener, U., Mannhaupt, G., Münsterkötter, M., Pagel, P., Strack, N., Stümpflen, V., Warfsmann, J.: MIPS: analysis and annotation of proteins from whole genomes. Nucleic Acids Res. **34**, D169 (2006)

38. Isseltarver, L., Christie, K.R., Dolinski, K., Andrada, R., Balakrishnan, R., Ball, C.A., Binkley, G., Dong, S., Dwight, S.S., Fisk, D.G.: Saccharomyces genome database. Methods Enzymol. **350**, 329 (2002)

Semi-Supervised Classification Based on SAGA for PolSAR Images

Hongying Liu[1(✉)], Zhi Wang[1], Feixiang Wang[1], Haisheng Deng[2], and Licheng Jiao[1]

[1] Key Laboratory of Intelligent Perception and Image Understanding of Ministry of Education, Xidian University, Xi'an 710071, China
hyliu@xidian.edu.cn
[2] Xijing University, Xi'an 710199, China

Abstract. Polarimetric Synthetic Aperture Radar (PolSAR) has been meeting the requirements in acquiring images for all-day, free of light, weather and other reasons, so it is widely applied in military and civilian life. PolSAR images contain abundant information. Its processing and interpretation have played more and more important role in national defense construction and economic development. However, the classification accuracy for PolSAR images using conventional clustering-based methods is quite limited. In this paper, a novel semi-supervised classification method is proposed. The Simulated Annealing-Genetic Algorithm (SAGA) is designed to optimize the iterative mechanism for finding the optimal centers of Fuzzy C-means (FCM) clustering, which avoids the local optimum. This leads to more accurate divisions on each category. Experimental results on synthesized and real PolSAR images confirm the superior performance of the proposed algorithm compared with conventional methods.

Keywords: Polarimetric SAR (PolSAR) · Fuzzy C-means (FCM) clustering · Simulated Annealing-Genetic Algorithm (SAGA)

1 Introduction

As polarimetric synthetic aperture radar (PolSAR) provides more detailed scattering information of the ground object, it has been widely used in terrain classifications. In general, the PolSAR features used in polarimetric SAR image classification methods mainly include two categories: the supervised classification and unsupervised one.

In the supervised classification, the training set for each category is selected by the ground truth of the polarimetric SAR images. For each pixel of the polarimetric SAR image, the 3×3 covariance/coherency matrix has three real parameters and three complex parameters of a total of nine parameters, indicating the polarized information of the pixel. However, for the real PolSAR

© Springer Nature Singapore Pte Ltd. 2017
C. He et al. (Eds.): BIC-TA 2017, CCIS 791, pp. 106–116, 2017.
https://doi.org/10.1007/978-981-10-7179-9_9

data, it is challenging to select the training set for each category in the high-dimensional polarimetric SAR data when there is no ground truth. On the other hand, the unsupervised classification can automatically discriminate and finish the classification through the inherent attributes of the data. The unsupervised classification of polarimetric SAR image based on scattering features (the Colude decomposition [1], tee Huynen decomposition [2], tic Pauli decomposition [2], the Barmers-Holm decomposition [3,4], the Yang decomposition [5], the van Zyl decomposition [6], the Freeman decomposition [7], the Yamaguchi four compinent decomposition [8]), color features or other features, has the characteristics of independent of data, which makes it widely applied in polarimetric SAR image classification.

Among the unsupervised classification methods, Fuzzy clustering is one of the important in the field of knowledge discovery and pattern recognition. And one of the most widely used fuzzy clustering algorithms is the Fuzzy C-means clustering (FCM) [9] algorithm. To reach the purpose of clustering, it determines the similarity by the geometry distance among the data points in Euclidean space. Therefore, FCM algorithm has laid the foundation for other fuzzy clustering analysis methods in both theory and practical applications. The algorithm is simple in design and wide in application, but there are still some problems such as it easy to fall into the local optimum, so the further research is needed. Considering the cost of post-processing and iterative time, the FCM algorithm is designed as a semi-supervised method in this paper.

Simulated Annealing (SA) algorithm [10] was proposed by Metropolis, which is inspired by heat balance in statistical thermodynamics. Specifically, it is a mathematical simulation of the solid annealing process. So the SA is regarded as a probabilistic technique for approximating the global optimum of a given function. Specifically, it is a heuristic to approximate global optimization in a large search space. It is often used when the search space is discrete. For problems where finding an approximate global optimum is more important than finding a precise local optimum in a fixed amount of time, SA may be preferable to alternatives such as gradient descent [11]. Besides, Genetic Algorithm (GA) [12] is also a heuristic algorithm inspired by the process of natural selection that belongs to the larger class of evolutionary algorithms (EA). GA are commonly used to generate high-quality solutions to optimization and search problems by relying on bio-inspired operators such as selection, crossover, and mutation.

In this paper, the SAGA-FCM is proposed for semi-supervised classification of the PolSAR images. SA and GA are combined together to take place of iterative mechanism in FCM which may easily fall into the local optimum. Because both the SA and the GA are the algorithms to approximate the global optimum of the objective function, so this clustering algorithm may reach the global optimization. And it is the SA that overcomes the premature phenomena of GA. Notably, the genetic encoding and fitness function in our design is tailor to PolSAR images. FCM reaches the optimum by minimizing the objective function, however, selection in GA is usually depend on the fitness values which are sorted in descending order. And features extracted from PoSAR data are always in the form of float vectors or matrices. For achieving the simple operation for selection, crossover and mutation and the low complexity in choosing and computing the fitness values, floating point encoding is chosen as genetic encoding method, and the fitness function is the reciprocal of the objective function in the paper.

The remainder of this paper is organized as follows. Section 2 presents the proposed SAGA-FCM algorithm in details. Section 3 shows the experimental results. Section 4 gives conclusions.

2   The Proposed Method

The key idea of the proposed SAGA-FCM is described in this section, and the flowchart is given in Fig. 1. The SAGA is utilized to search the optimal clustering centers of FCM implemented on PolSAR data, which will overcomes the weakness that it is easy to fall into the local optimum and produce the approximate global optimization.

The classical FCM is designed as a semi-supervised algorithm based on the following three concerns: (1) In order to avoid the random initialization of the cluster centers, there is not too much cost for the post-processing to get the ideal classification result; (2) To reduce the number of iterations to reach the optimal clustering centers; (3) Only small number of labeled sample and large number of unlabeled ones are utilized to improve the classification accuracy.

2.1   Semi-supervised Clustering on PolSAR Data

In this paper, FCM clustering is designed as a semi-supervised algorithm by utilized very small amount of labeled sample to initialize the centers of FCM, and the color features of PolSAR data is chosen as the features to run the algorithm. The steps of Semi-FCM is briefly stated as below.

The Semi-FCM algorithm attempts to partition a finite collection of N elements $X = x_1, x_2, \cdot, x_N$, where $x_i \in R^{1 \times 3}, i = 1, 2, \cdots, N$ into a collection of n fuzzy clusters.

Given a finite set of data and the initial centers initialized by small amount of labeled data, then the algorithm returns a list of n fuzzy cluster centers $C = c_1, c_2, \cdot, c_n$ and a membership value matrix W. $W = w_{i,j}, i = 1, 2, \cdot, N, j = 1, 2, \cdot, n$, where each element, $w_{i,j}$, tells the degree of element, x_i, belongs to cluster c_j.

The FCM aims to minimize an objective function:

$$J = \sum_{j}^{n} \sum_{i}^{N} w_{i,j}^{b} \parallel x_i - c_j \parallel^2 \tag{1}$$

where:

$$w_{i,j} = \frac{1}{\sum_{k=1}^{n}(\frac{\|x_i - c_j\|}{\|x_i - c_k\|})^{\frac{2}{b-1}}} \tag{2}$$

$$c_j = \frac{\sum_{i=1}^{N} w_{i,j}^b x_i}{\sum_{i=1}^{N} w_{i,j}^b} \tag{3}$$

The fuzzier b determines the level of cluster fuzziness. A larger b results in smaller membership values, $w_{i,j}$, and hence, fuzzier clusters.

2.2 Simulated Annealing and Genetic Algorithm

The idea of Simulated Annealing (SA) is based on the principle of solid annealing. When the temperature of the solid is high, the solid internal energy is relatively large. And when the temperature is slowly decreasing, the internal energy decreases. Finally, when the solid is at normal temperature, the internal energy can reach the minimum, at that time, the particles in the solid are the most stable. Simulated annealing algorithm is based on this principle, and basic steps are given as below:

Step 1: Initializing the initial temperature T_0, the temperature cooling coefficient k, the termination temperature T_{end}, the initial state s_0 the maximum number of iteration N.

Step 2: Let $s = s_0, i = 1$, pick a random state s'.

Step 3: If the energy function meet the inequality $E(s') > E(s)$, then $s = s'$; Otherwise, if $P = exp((E(s) - E(s'))/T) \geq random(0,1)$, then $s = s'$.

Step 4: If $i < N$, $T = kT$, $i = i + 1$, go to Step 2, otherwise the iteration is terminated.

Genetic Algorithm (GA) is a stochastic search method which is derived from the evolution in biology (genetic mechanism of survival of the fittest). It was first proposed by Professor J. Holland. And it is the probabilistic optimization method which can automatically obtain the optimum of the search space, adaptively adjust the search direction, do not need to determine the rules. Steps of GA are given as below:

Step 1: Initializing parameters of GA: Population size pop_size, the maximum number of evolution Max_Gen; Crossover probability P_c; Mutation probability P_m.

Step 2: Assume the evolution number $Gen = 0$, initialize 0th population pop whose population size is pop_size.

Step 3: Compute the fitness values f_i of the ith individual in 0th population pop_0, where $i = 1, 2, \cdot, pop\_size$.

Step: Let $pop = pop_0$.

Step 4: Conduct the operation of selection, crossover, and mutation on the pop according to the fitness values f, the crossover probability P_c, and the mutation probability P_m and the new population pop' is produced.

Step 5: Compute the fitness values f_i of the ith individual in Gen^{th} population pop', where $i = 1, 2, \cdot, pop\_size$.

Step 6: If $Gen < Max\_Gen$, let $Gen = Gen + 1, pop = pop'$ and go to Step 4. Otherwise the iteration is over and return the optimal population pop^1.

2.3   SAGA-FCM on PolSAR Data

Since Semi-FCM discussed may also fall into the local optimum, and combination of SA and GA (SAGA) can help the local optimum reach the global optimum. In this paper, SAGA is used to optimize Semi-FCM to achieve better performance of the clustering algorithm. Also, the color features of PolSAR data is chosen as the features to run the algorithm. Based on the SAGA and Semi-FCM, Fig. 1 shows the flowchart of SAGA-FCM, the details are shown as below:

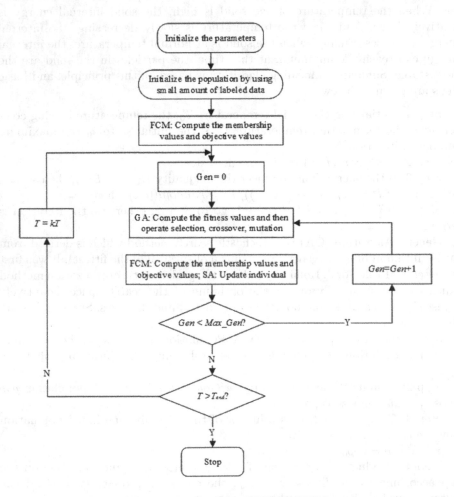

Fig. 1. The flowchart of SAGA-FCM

Step 1: PolSAR data $X = x_1, x_2, \cdot, x_N$, where $xi \in R^{13}, i = 1, 2, \cdot, N$. Parameters of FCM: The number of clustering centers n; the fuzzier b. Parameters of GA: Population size pop_size; The maximum number of evolution Max_Gen; Crossover probability P_c; Mutation probability P_m; Parameters of SA: The initial temperature of annealing T_0; The temperature cooling coefficient k; Termination temperature T_{end}.

Step 2: Initialize $T = T_0$ temperature. Assume the initial number of evolution $Gen = 0$. Initialize 0th population pop, each individual in the population pop is the centers for clustering.

Step 3: For the jth center of the ith individual in pop, compute the membership value matrix W, the FCMs objective function J^i, so the fitness values of the ith individual is $f_i = 1/J_i$, where $i = 1, 2, \cdot, pop\_size, j = 1, 2, \cdot, n$; Partition all the sample into the n cluster according the membership value.

Step 4: Conduct the operation of selection, crossover, and mutation for the pop according to fitness value f, crossover probability P_c, mutation probability P_m; Compute the membership values and fitness values f_i' for new population; if $f_i' > f_i$, the new individual must replace the old individual; if not, probability $P = exp((f_i - f_i')/T)$ should be used to accept the new individual, and discard the old individual.

Step 5: If $Gen < Max\_Gen$, $Gen = Gen + 1$, go to Step3. Otherwise, go to Step6.

Step 6: If $T < T_{end}$, stop to conduct the algorithm, return the global optimal individual; Otherwise, perform cooling operation $T = kT$, then go to Step 2.

3   Experimental Results

In order to evaluate the effectiveness of SAGA-FCM, the synthesized data and real PolSAR datasets from different SAR systems are used in the experiments. The synthesize data consist of relatively simple terrains with regular shapes, more homogeneous regions, and controllable number of looks or speckle noises. It is ideal experimental data for assessing the robustness of the proposed algorithm. Besides, the real PolSAR datasets contain complex types of terrains, heterogeneous regions, and diversified imaging conditions, which are more appropriate for evaluating the applicability of the algorithms under study. The Semi-FCM algorithms are implemented for comparison.

On a PC with 3.2 GHz Intel Core i3 processor with 4GB memory, all the experiments are conducted under MATLAB 2016b environment, and the color feature of each pixel from these dataset are chosen to evaluate our algorithm. Also, 1% labeled sample are selected to initialize the centers for clustering. All the experiment are repeated 10 times to compute the ratio between the number of correctly classified pixels and the total number of pixels for testing, which is called the average overall accuracy (OA) for short.

3.1   A. Results on Synthesized Data

A 12-look fully polarimetric dataset with 120×150 pixels and nine classes of land-covers denoted as $Q_1, Q_2, \cdot, Q_9$ is synthesized by the Monte Carlo method adopted in [13]. The classes are from nine covariance matrices calculated from the real data of NASA/JPL AIRSAR in 1989.

The classification accuracies using different algorithms with 1% labeled samples are compared. The visual results are shown in Fig. 2, and the quantitative results are listed in Fig. 2.

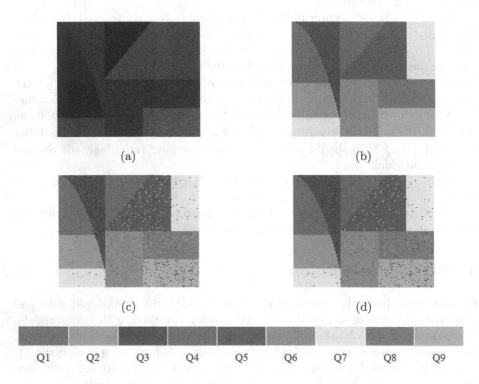

Fig. 2. Synthesized data and the classification results with different methods. (a) Pauli pseudocolored image (b) Ground truth (c) Results with Semi-FCM (d) Results with SAGA-FCM

It can be seen that the SAGA-FCM has higher OA. It is superior to Semi-FCM in classifying class Q_2, Q_3, Q_6, Q_8. These results explain the effectiveness SAGA in the SAGA-FCM. Fig. 2 shows that the accuracies on Q_1 and Q_4 are the same, and the accuracies on Q_5, Q_7 and Q_9 are very close. It is probably because these classes are from very homogeneous regions of real PolSAR dataset.

3.2   Results on Flevoland(in the Netherlands) from AIRSAR

In this experiment, the sub-image of the PolSAR image from Flevoland region of the Netherlands with 300×270 pixels and six classes is chosen to evaluate our method. This experimental data is L-band 4-look polarimetric dataset with a resolution of 12×6, obtained by NASA/ JPL AIRSAR in 1989. The classification accuracies using different algorithms with 1% labeled samples are compared. The visual results are shown in Fig. 3, and the quantitative results are listed in Fig. 3.

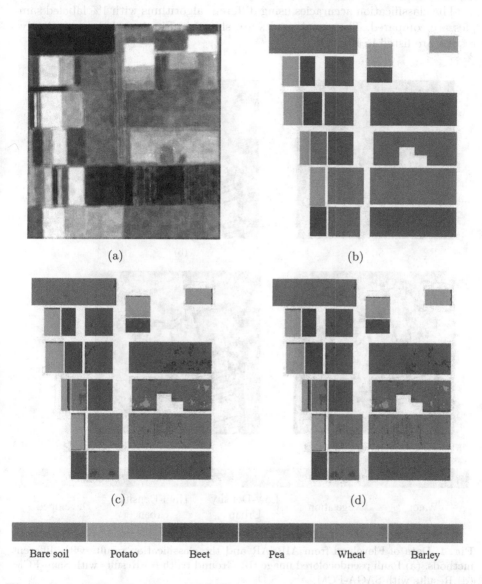

(a)

(b)

(c)

(d)

| Bare soil | Potato | Beet | Pea | Wheat | Barley |

Fig. 3. Data of Flevoland from AIRSAR and the classification results with different methods. (a) Pauli pseudocolored image (b) Ground truth (c) Results with Semi-FCM (d) Results with SAGA-FCM.

3.3   Results on San Francisco from RADARSAT-2

The L-band 4-look fully polarimetric dataset from the San Francisco Bay by RADARSAT-2 in 2008 with 1300×1300 pixels and five classes is chosen for this experiment.

The classification accuracies using different algorithms with 1% labeled samples are compared. The visual results are shown in Fig. 4, and the quantitative results are listed in Fig. 4.

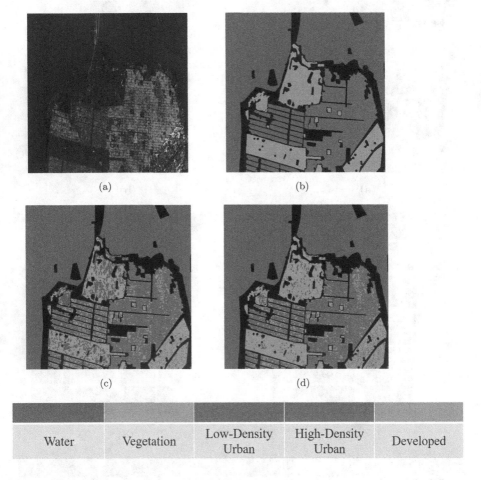

Fig. 4. Data of Flevoland from AIRSAR and the classification results with different methods. (a) Pauli pseudocolored image (b) Ground truth (c) Results with Semi-FCM (d) Results with SAGA-FCM.

For these terrains, although they are relatively homogeneous, it is not easy to be classified due to the different density of the terrains. For example, neither of SAGA-FCM and Semi-FCM has high accuracy on developed area and high-density urban area. It is probably because these area contains hetero-geneous regions, and diversified imaging conditions. While, the proposed SAGA-FCM still shows better performance than Semi-FCM. Figure 4 demonstrates that the SAGA-FCM has much better classification? effect on the vegetation area. And Fig. 4 indicates that on the vegetation area the accuracy of SAGA-FCM reaches 84.28%, however, the accuracy of Semi-FCM is only 59.93%. Thus, the OA of SAGA-FCM is higher than that of Semi-FCM. Therefore, the proposed SAGA-FCM still has good performance on datasets containing complex types of terrains.

4 Conclusions

In this paper, a new polarimetric SAR image classification algorithm named as SAGA-FCM is proposed. The semi-supervised implementation of FCM can avoid the random initialization of the cluster centers so that the number of iteration is reduced. And to overcome the weakness that Semi-FCM may also fall into the local optimum, the Simulated Annealing (SA) and Genetic Algorithm (GA) are combined together to optimize Semi-FCM to reach the global optimum which shows good performance on polarimetric SAR image classification. The experiments on the synthesized data and real PolSAR datasets indicates that high performance can be obtained by the proposed SAGA-FCM. In the future, the proposed algorithm will be evaluated on more PolSAR datasets.

References

1. Cloude, S.R., Pottier, E.: An entropy based classification scheme for land applications of polarimetric SAR. IEEE T. Geosci. Remote **35**(1), 68–78 (1997)
2. Cloude, S.R., Pottier, E.: A review of target decomposition theorems in radar polarimetry. IEEE T. Geosci. Remote. **34**(2), 498–518 (1996)
3. Barnes, R.M.: Roll-invariant decompositions for the polarization covariance matrix. In: Polarimetry Technology Workshop. Redstone Arsenal, AL (1988)
4. Holm, W.A., Barnes, R.M.: On radar polarization mixed target state decomposition techniques. In: 1988 IEEE National Radar Conference, pp. 249–254. IEEE (1988)
5. Yang, J., Yamaguchi, Y., Yamada, H., Sengoku, M., Lin, S.M.: Stable decomposition of a Kennaugh matrix. IEICE Trans. Commun. **E81–B**(6), 1261–1268 (1998)
6. Van Zyl, J.J.: Unsupervised classification of scattering behavior using radar polarimetry data. IEEE T. Geosci. Remote. **27**(1), 36–45 (1989)
7. Freeman, A., Durden, S.L.: A three-component scattering model for polarimetric SAR data. IEEE T. Geosci. Remote. **36**(3), 963–973 (1998)
8. Yamaguchi, Y., Moriyama, T., Ishido, M., et al.: Four-component scattering model for polarimetric SAR image decomposition. IEEE T. Geosci. Remote. **43**(8), 1699–1706 (2005)
9. Bezdek, J.C.: Pattern Recognition with Fuzzy Objective Function Algorithms. Springer Science & Business Media, Boston (2013)
10. Metropolis, N., Rosenbluth, A.W., Rosenbluth, M.N., et al.: Equation of state calculations by fast computing machines. J. Chem. Phys. **21**(6), 1087–1092 (1953)

11. Seiler, M.C., Seiler, F.A.: Numerical recipes in C: the art of scientific computing. Risk Anal. **9**(3), 415–416 (1989)
12. Holland, J.H.: Adaptation in Natural and Artificial Systems: An Introductory Analysis with Applications to Biology, Control, and Artificial Intelligence. MIT press, Cambridge (1992)
13. Liu, B., Hu, H., Wang, H., et al.: Superpixel-based classification with an adaptive number of classes for polarimetric SAR images. IEEE T. Geosci. Remote. **51**(2), 907–924 (2013)

Spiking Neural P Systems with Minimal Parallelism

Yun Jiang[1,2(✉)], Fen Luo[1], and Yueguo Luo[3]

[1] Detection and Control of Integrated Systems Engineering Laboratory,
Chongqing Technology and Business University, Chongqing 400067, China
[2] School of Computer Science and Information Engineering,
Chongqing Technology and Business University, Chongqing 400067, China
jiangyun@email.ctbu.edu.cn
[3] College of Computer Engineering, Yangtze Normal University,
Chongqing 408100, China

Abstract. This paper is an attempt to relax the condition of using the rules in a maximally parallel manner in the framework of spiking neural P systems with exhaustive use of rules. To this aim, we consider the minimal parallelism of using rules: if one rule associated with a neuron can be used, then the rule must be used at least once (but we do not care how many times). In this framework, we study the computational power of our systems as number generating devices. Weak as it might look, this minimal parallelism still leads to universality, even when we eliminate the delay between firing and spiking and the forgetting rules at the same time.

Keywords: Membrane computing · Spiking neural P system · Minimal parallelism · Computing universality

1 Introduction

Through millions of years human brain has evolved into a complex and enormous information processing system, where more than a trillion neurons work in a cooperation manner to perform various tasks. Therefore, brain is a rich source of inspiration for informatics. Specifically, it has provided plenty of ideas to construct high performance computing models, as well as to design efficient algorithm. Inspired from the biological phenomenon that neurons cooperate in the brain by exchanging spikes via synapses, various neural-like computing models have been proposed, such as artificial neural networks [1] and spiking neural networks [2]. These neural-like computing models have performed significantly well in solving real life problems.

In the framework of membrane computing, a kind of distributed and parallel neural-like computing model were proposed in 2006 [3], which is called spiking neural P systems (SN P systems for short). Briefly, an SN P system consists of a set of neurons placed in the nodes of a directed graph that are linked by synapses.

© Springer Nature Singapore Pte Ltd. 2017
C. He et al. (Eds.): BIC-TA 2017, CCIS 791, pp. 117–130, 2017.
https://doi.org/10.1007/978-981-10-7179-9_10

These neurons send signals (spikes) along synapses (edges of the graph). This is done by means of firing rules, which are of the form $E/a^c \rightarrow a^p; t$: if the number of spikes contained in the neuron is described by the regular expression E (over the alphabet $\{a\}$), then c spikes are consumed and p spikes are produced after a delay of t steps; the produced spikes are sent to all neurons to which there exist synapse leaving the neuron where the rule is applied. The second type of rules are forgetting rules, of the form $a^s \rightarrow \lambda$. The meaning is that $s \geq 1$ spikes are just removed from the neuron, provided that the neuron contains exactly s spikes. The system evolves synchronously: a global clock is assumed and in each time unit each neuron which can use a rule should do it. But the work of the system is sequential locally: only (at most) one rule is used in each neuron. When the computation halts, no further rule can be applied, and a result is obtained, which can be defined in different ways, e.g., in the form of the time elapsed between the first two consecutive spikes sent into the environment.

For the past decade, there have been quite a few research efforts put forward to SN P systems. Many variants of SN P systems have been considered [4–18]. Most of the obtained classes of SN P systems are computationally universal, equivalent in power to Turing machines [19–28]. An interesting topic is to find small universal SN P systems [29–35]. In certain cases, polynomial solutions to computationally hard problems can also be obtained in this framework [36, 37]. Moreover, SN P systems have been applied to solve real-life problems, for example, to design logic gates, logic circuits [38] and databases [39], to perform basic arithmetic operations [40, 41], to represent knowledge [42], to diagnose fault [43–45], to approximately solve combinatorial optimization problems [46].

Besides using the rules of a neuron in the sequential mode introduced above, it is also possible to use the rules in a parallel way. An exhaustive manner of rule application is considered in [47]: whenever a rule is enabled in a neuron, it is used as many times as possible for the number of spikes from that neuron, thus exhausting the spikes it can consume in that neuron. Also in [47], SN P systems with exhaustive use of rules are proved to be universal, both in the accepting and the generative cases.

In this paper we propose a minimal parallelism [48] which, as far as we know, have not yet been considered in the framework of SN P systems: from each set of rules associated with a neuron, if a rule can be used, then the rule must be used at least once (maybe more times, without any restriction). Here we consider SN P systems with minimal parallelism function as generator of numbers, which is encoded in the distance between the first two steps when spikes leave the system. Weak as it might look, we prove the equivalence of our systems with Turing machines in the generative mode, even in the case of eliminating two of its key features – delays and forgetting rules – simultaneously. In the proof of this result, we play a trick (also useful in other similar cases, like [47]) of representing a natural number n (the content of a register) by means of $2n + 2$ spikes (in a neuron).

This work is started by the mathematical definition of SN P systems with minimal parallelism, and then the computational power of SN P systems with minimal parallelism is investigated as number generator, in the case of eliminating delays and forgetting rules at the same time. It is proved in a constructive way that SN P systems with minimal parallelism can compute the family of sets of Turing computable natural numbers. At last, the paper is ended with some comments.

2   SN P Systems with Minimal Parallelism

Before introducing SN P systems with minimal parallelism, we recall some prerequisites, including basic elements of formal language theory [49] and basic notions in SN P systems [3, 50].

For a singleton alphabet $\Sigma = \{a\}$, $\Sigma^* = \{a\}^*$ denotes the set of all finite strings of symbol a; the empty string is denoted by λ, and the set of all nonempty strings over $\Sigma = \{a\}$ is denoted by Σ^+. We can simply write a^* and a^+ instead of $\{a\}^*$, $\{a\}^+$. A regular expression over a singleton alphabet Σ is defined as follows: (i) λ and a is a regular expression, (ii) if E_1, E_2 are regular expressions over Σ, then $(E_1)(E_2)$, $(E_1) \cup (E_2)$, and $(E_1)^+$ are regular expressions over Σ, and (iii) nothing else is a regular expression over Σ. Each regular expression E is associated with a language $L(E)$, which is defined in the following way: (i) $L(\lambda) = \{\lambda\}$ and $L(a) = \{a\}$, (ii) $L((E_1) \cup (E_2)) = L(E_1) \cup L(E_2)$, $L((E_1)(E_2)) = L(E_1)L(E_2)$, and $L((E_1)^+) = L(E_1)^+$, for all regular expressions E_1, E_2 over Σ.

In what follows, we give the formal definition of SN P systems with minimal parallelism.

An SN P system with minimal parallelism of degree $m \geq 1$ is a construct of the form

$$\Pi = (O, \sigma_1, \sigma_2, \ldots, \sigma_m, syn, out),$$

where:

1. $O = \{a\}$ is a singleton alphabet (a is called spike);
2. $\sigma_1, \sigma_2, \ldots, \sigma_m$ are neurons of the form

$$\sigma_i = (n_i, R_i), 1 \leq i \leq m,$$

   where:
   (1) $n_i \geq 0$ is the initial number of spikes placed in the neuron σ_i;
   (2) R_i is a finite set of rules of the following two forms:
      - Firing rule: $E/a^c \rightarrow a^p; d$, where E is a a regular expression over $\{a\}$, $c \geq 1$, $d \geq 0$, with the restriction $c \geq p$. Specifically, when $d = 0$, it can be omitted;
      - Forgetting rule: $a^s \rightarrow \lambda$, for some $s \geq 1$, with the restriction that for each rule $E/a^c \rightarrow a^p; d$ of type (1) from R_i, we have $a^s \notin L(E)$;
3. $syn \subseteq \{1, 2, \ldots, m\} \times \{1, 2, \ldots, m\}$ is the set of synapses between neurons, with restriction $(i, i) \notin syn$ for $1 \leq i \leq m$ (no self-loop synapse);
4. $out \in \{1, 2, \ldots, m\}$ indicates the output neuron, which can emit spikes to the environment.

The firing rule of the form $E/a^c \rightarrow a^p; d$ with $c \geq p \geq 1$ is called an *extended rule*; if $p = 1$, the rule is called a *standard rule*. If $L(E) = \{a^c\}$, the rule can be simply written as $a^c \rightarrow a^p; d$. Specifically, if $d = 0$, it can be omitted and the rule can be simply written as $a^c \rightarrow a^p$.

The firing rule $E/a^c \rightarrow a^p; d \in R_i$ can be applied if the neuron σ_i contains k spikes, $a^k \in L(E)$ and $k \geq c$. However, the essential we consider here is not the form of the rules, but the way they are used. Using the rule in a minimal parallel manner, as suggested in the Introduction, means the following. Assume that $k = sc + r$, for some $s \geq 1$ (this means that we must have $k \geq c$) and $0 \leq r < c$ (the remainder of dividing k by c). Then nc, $1 \leq n \leq s$ spikes are consumed, $k - nc$ spikes remain in the neuron σ_i, and np spikes are produced after d time units (a global clock is assumed, marking the time for the whole system, hence the functioning of the system is synchronized). If $d = 0$, then the produced spikes are emitted immediately, if $d = 1$, then the spikes are emitted in the next step, and so on. In the case $d \geq 1$, if the rule is applied at step t, then in steps $t, t + 1, \ldots, t + d - 1$ the neuron is closed, and it cannot receive new spikes (if a neuron has a synapse to a closed neuron and sends a spike along it, then the spike is lost). In step $t + d$, the neuron fires and becomes open again, hence it can receive spikes (which can be used in step $t + d + 1$). The spikes emitted by a neuron are replicated and are sent to all neurons σ_j such that $(i, j) \in syn$.

The forgetting rules are applied as follows: if the neuron contains exactly s spikes, then the rule $a^s \rightarrow \lambda$ can be used, and this means that all s spikes are removed from the neuron.

In each time unit, in each neuron which can use a rule we have to use a rule, either a firing or a forgetting one. Since two firing rules $E_1/a^{c_1} \rightarrow a^p; d_1$ and $E_2/a^{c_2} \rightarrow a^p; d_2$ can have $L(E_1) \cap L(E_2) \neq \emptyset$, it is possible that several rules can be applied in a neuron. This leads to a non-deterministic way of using the rules (but a firing rule cannot be interchanged with a forgetting rule, in the sense that $a^s \notin L(E)$).

The configuration of the system is described both by the numbers of spikes present in each neuron and by the number of steps to wait until it becomes open (if the neuron is already open this number is zero). Thus, the initial configuration is $\langle n_1/0, n_2/0, \ldots, n_m/0 \rangle$. Using the rules as described above, we can define *transitions* among configurations. Any sequence of transitions starting from the initial configuration is called a *computation*. The computation proceeds and a spike train, a sequence of digits 0 and 1, is associated with each computation by marking with 0 for the steps when no spike is emitted by the output neuron and marking with 1 when one or more spikes exit the system. A computation halts if it reaches a configuration where no rule in the neuron can be used.

The result of a computation can be defined in several ways. In this work, we consider SN P systems with minimal parallelism as number generators: assuming the first time and the second time spike(s) emitted from the output neuron is at step t_1 and t_2, the computation result is defined as the number $t_2 - t_1$. For an SN P system Π, the set of all numbers computed in this way is denoted by $N_2^{min}(\Pi)$, with the subscript 2 reminding that only the distance between the first two spikes of any computation is considered. Then, we denote by $Spik_2N^{min}P_m(rule_k, cons_r, forg_q)$ the family of all sets $N_2^{min}(\Pi)$ computed as above by SN P systems with at most $m \geq 1$ neurons, using at most $k \geq 1$ rules in each neuron, with all spiking rules $E/a^c \rightarrow a^p; d$ having $c \leq r$, and all forgetting rules $a^s \rightarrow \lambda$ having $s \leq q$. When one of the parameters m, k, r, q is not bounded, then it is replaced with $*$.

In order to clarify the definitions, we here discuss an example. In this way, we also introduce a standard way to pictorially represent a configuration of an SN P system, in particular, the initial configuration. Specifically, each neuron is represented by a "membrane" (a circle or an oval), marked with a label and having inside both the current number of spikes (written explicitly, in the form a^n for n spikes present in a neuron) and the evolution rules; the synapses linking the neurons are represented by arrows; besides the fact that the output neuron will be identified by its label, i_0, it is also suggestive to draw a short arrow which exits from it, pointing to the environment.

In the system Π_1 (Fig. 1) we have two neurons, labeled with 1 and 2 (with neuron σ_2 being the output one), which have 5 and 2 spikes, respectively, in the initial configuration. Both of the two neurons fire at the first step of the computation.

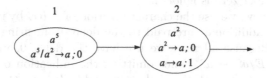

Fig. 1. A simple example of an SN P system with minimal parallel

In the output neuron σ_2, the rule $a^2 \rightarrow a; 0$ is used at the first step, a spike is sent out to the environment and no spike remains in σ_2. In neuron σ_1, one can notice that $5 = 2 \times 2 + 1$, hence we can non-deterministically choose the rule $a^5/a^2 \rightarrow a$ to be applied once or twice at the same time. If σ_1 uses the rule twice at the first step, it sends two spikes to neuron σ_2 immediately (one for each use of the rule) and neuron σ_2 spikes again, using the rule $a^2 \rightarrow a; 0$ at the second step of the computation. Thus, the result of the computation in this case is $2 - 1 = 1$.

If the rule $a^5/a^2 \rightarrow a$ is used only once at the first step by neuron σ_1, it sends one spike to neuron σ_2. At the second step, neuron σ_2 fires again, using the rule $a \rightarrow a; 1$ at the second step. At the third step the spike generated emits the system and the result of the computation is $3 - 1 = 2$.

Hence, Π_1 generates the finite set $\{1, 2\}$.

3   Universality Result

In this section we prove that SN P systems with minimal parallelism are still universal when eliminating both delays and forgetting rules at the same time.

Nevertheless, the elimination has a price in terms of the number of neurons in the modules. Our universality proof will use the characterization of NRE by means of register machine.

A register machine is a construct $M = (m, H, l_0, l_h, I)$, where m is the number of registers, H is the set of instruction labels, l_0 is the start label (labeling an ADD instruction), l_h is the halt label (assigned to instruction HALT), and I is the set of instructions; each label from H labels only one instruction from I, thus precisely identifying it. The labeled instructions are of the following forms:

- $l_i : (ADD(r), l_j)$ (add 1 to register r and then go to the instruction with label l_j),
- $l_i : (SUB(r), l_j, l_k)$ (if register r is non-empty, then subtract 1 from it and go to the instruction with label l_j, otherwise go to the instruction with label l_k),
- $l_h : HALT$ (the halt instruction).

It is known that the register machine can compute all sets of numbers which are Turing computable, even with only three registers [51]. Hence, it characterizes NRE, i.e., $N(M) = NRE$ (NRE is the family of length sets of recursively enumerable languages – the family of languages recognized by Turing machines). We have the convention that when comparing the power of two number generating devices, number zero is ignored.

In the proof below, we use the characterization of NRE by means of register machine, with an additional care paid to the delay from firing to spiking, and forgetting rules. Because all rules we use have the delay 0, we write them in the simpler form $E/a^c \rightarrow a^p$, hence omitting the indication of the delay. Also a change is made in the notation below: we add $dley_t$ to the list of features mentioned between parentheses, meaning that we use SN P systems whose rules $E/a^c \rightarrow a^p; d$ have $d \leq t$ (the delay is at most t).

Theorem 1.

$$Spik_2 N^{min} P_*(rule_3, cons_4, forg_0, dley_0) = NRE.$$

Proof. In view of the Turing-Church thesis, the inclusion in NRE can be proved directly, so we only have to prove the inclusion $NRE \subseteq Spik_2 N^{min} P_*(rule_3, cons_4, forg_0, dley_0)$. The proof is achieved in a constructive way, that is, an SN P system with minimal parallelism is constructed to simulate the universal register machine.

Let $M = (m, H, l_0, l_h, I)$ be a universal register machine. Without lose of generality, we assume that the result of a computation is the number from register 1 and this register is never decremented during the computation.

We construct an SN P system Π as follows, simulating the register machine M and spiking only twice, at an interval of time which corresponds to the number computed by the register machine.

For each register r of M we consider a neuron σ_r in Π whose contents correspond to the contents of the register. Specifically, if the register r holds the number $n \geq 0$, then the neuron σ_r will contain $2n + 2$ spikes; therefore, any register with the value 0 will contain two spikes.

Increasing by 1 the contents of a register r which holds the number n means increasing by 2 the number of spikes from the neuron σ_r; decreasing by 1 the contents of a non-empty register means to decrease by 2 the number of spikes; checking whether the register is empty amounts at checking whether σ_r has two spikes inside.

With each label l of an instruction in M we also associate a neuron σ_l. Initially, all these neurons are empty, except for the neuron σ_{l_0} associated with the start label of M, which contains 2 spikes. This means that this neuron is "activated". During the computation, the neuron σ_l which receives 2 spikes will become active. Thus, simulating an instruction $l_i : (op(r), l_j, l_k)$ of M means starting with neuron σ_{l_i} activated, operating the register r as requested by op, then introducing 2 spikes in one of the neuron $\sigma_{l_j}, \sigma_{l_k}$, which becomes active in this way. When the neuron σ_{l_h}, associated with the halting label of M, is activated, the computation in M is completely simulated in Π, and we have to output the result in the form of a spike train with the distance between the first two spikes equals to the number stored in the first register of M. Additional neurons will be associated with the registers and the labels of M, in a way which will be described immediately.

In what follows, the work of system Π is described (that is how system Π simulates the ADD, SUB instructions of register machine M and outputs the computation result).

Simulating an ADD instruction $l_i : (ADD(r), l_j, l_k)$

This instruction adds one to the register r and switches non-deterministically to label l_j or l_k. As seen in Fig. 2, this module is initiated when two spikes enter neuron σ_{l_i}. Then the neuron σ_{l_i} sends two spikes to neuron $\sigma_{i,1}$, $\sigma_{i,2}$ and σ_r, adding one to the content of the register. In the next step, the spikes emitted by $\sigma_{i,1}$ arrive in $\sigma_{i,3}$ (which will in turn be sent to $\sigma_{i,6}$ in the following step) and $\sigma_{i,4}$, while the spikes of $\sigma_{i,2}$ reaches $\sigma_{i,4}$ and $\sigma_{i,5}$. Neuron $\sigma_{i,4}$ will allow us to switch non-deterministically to either σ_{l_j} or σ_{l_k}. If $\sigma_{i,4}$ uses the rule $a^4/a^2 \to a$ only once, then two spikes will be blocked in $\sigma_{i,8}$ (those coming from $\sigma_{i,4}$ and $\sigma_{i,5}$), while just one will arrive in neuron $\sigma_{i,7}$, waiting for other spikes to come. In the next step, the neuron $\sigma_{i,4}$ fires again (this time applying the rule $a^2 \to a^2$), sending two spikes to $\sigma_{i,7}$ and $\sigma_{i,8}$. The two spikes are blocked in $\sigma_{i,8}$ again, while the two spikes from $\sigma_{i,4}$ and the spike from $\sigma_{i,6}$ reaches $\sigma_{i,7}$. Together with the one spike await, the neuron $\sigma_{i,7}$ can get fired, activating neuron σ_{l_j} one step later.

On the other hand, if $\sigma_{i,4}$ uses the rule $a^4/a^2 \to a$ twice, it consumes all of the four spikes inside, and produces two spikes, having no spike left. This means that, in the following step, $\sigma_{i,7}$ receives two spikes and $\sigma_{i,8}$ gets three (two from $\sigma_{i,4}$ and one from $\sigma_{i,5}$). Now $\sigma_{i,8}$ contains three spikes and fires, activating σ_{l_k} in the following step. One step later, $\sigma_{i,7}$ receives another spike from $\sigma_{i,6}$ and the three spikes together get blocked here.

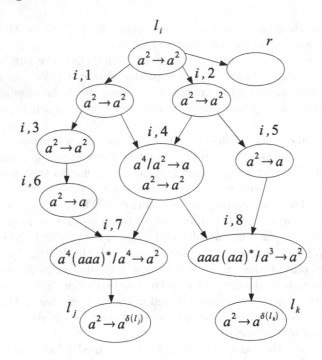

Fig. 2. Module ADD (simulating $l_i : (ADD(r), l_j, l_k)$)

It is clear that, after each ADD instruction, neuron $\sigma_{i,7}$ and $\sigma_{i,8}$ will hold three or two spikes, respectively, depending on the times of application of rule $a^4/a^2 \rightarrow a$ chosen non-deterministically in the neuron $\sigma_{i,4}$. Thanks to the regular expressions used in the rules of $\sigma_{i,7}$ and $\sigma_{i,8}$, this does not disturb further computations using this instruction.

Simulating a SUB instruction $l_i : (SUB(r), l_j, l_k)$
The SUB module (shown in Fig. 3) is initiated when two spikes are sent to neuron σ_{l_i}. This neuron fires and its spike reaches neurons $\sigma_{r,1}$, $\sigma_{r,2}$ and σ_r. The three rules of neuron σ_r allow us to differentiate whether the register is empty or not. As we have explained, a register containing the value n means the corresponding neuron holds $2n + 2$ spikes. If register r stores number $n > 0$, that is to say σ_r contains at least 4 spikes, the spike coming from σ_{l_i} makes the neuron fire (by the rule $aaa(aa)^+/a^3 \rightarrow a$) and send a spike to $\sigma_{r,6}$, which makes sure that the rule is used only once. In the next step, $\sigma_{r,6}$ gets fired and send a spike to $\sigma_{r,8}$, and another spike passing from $\sigma_{r,2}$ to $\sigma_{r,4}$ reaches $\sigma_{r,8}$ at the same time. These two spikes make $\sigma_{r,8}$ can not be fired. In parallel, two spikes will arrive in neuron $\sigma_{r,7}$, one along $\sigma_{r,1}$-$\sigma_{r,3}$-$\sigma_{r,5}$-$\sigma_{r,7}$, and the other σ_r-$\sigma_{r,6}$-$\sigma_{r,7}$. These two spikes make $\sigma_{r,7}$ get fire, then $\sigma_{r,9}$, and as we will explain later, eventually allow us to reach σ_{l_j}.

On the other hand, when register r stores number zero (σ_r contains 2 spikes), the spike received from σ_{l_i} fires the rule $a^3/a^2 \rightarrow a$. The neuron σ_r spikes,

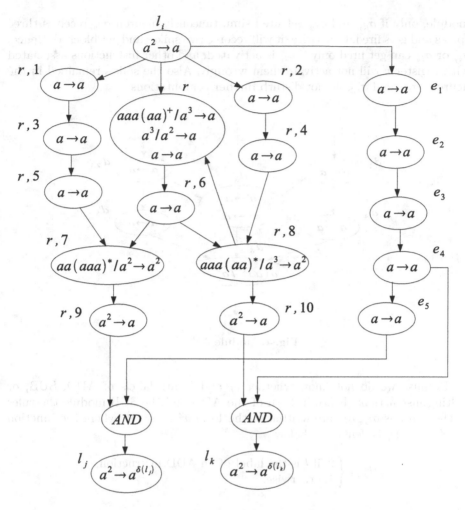

Fig. 3. Module SUB (simulating $l_i : (SUB(r), l_j, l_k)$)

consuming two of the three spikes it contains. This spike is sent to neuron $\sigma_{r,6}$, then to neurons $\sigma_{r,7}$ and $\sigma_{r,8}$. In the following step, σ_r fires again (using the rule $a \to a$), consuming its last spike and sending a new spike to $\sigma_{r,7}$ and $\sigma_{r,8}$ (the value of register r is now degraded and needs to be reconstituted). This spike reaches neuron $\sigma_{r,7}$ at the same time that the one coming from $\sigma_{r,5}$. Then $\sigma_{r,7}$ cannot get fired because it contains now three spikes. Meanwhile, $\sigma_{r,8}$ also contains now three spikes. It gets fired and spikes, allowing $\sigma_{r,10}$ to fire in the following step. It also emits two spikes to σ_r which reconstitute the value 0 in the register r before reaching σ_{l_k}.

The reader can check that two AND modules (the AND module is shown in Fig. 4) are embedded in the SUB module, making sure that further instructions associated with register r will not wrongly switches to l_i and l_j here. In this module, only if σ_{d_1} and σ_{d_2} get fired simultaneously, neuron σ_{d_6} receives three spikes and gets fired. Otherwise, it will receive two spikes and get blocked. Hence, σ_{l_j} or σ_{l_k} can get fired only if σ_{l_i} is activated, and other instructions associated with register r will not activate them wrongly. Also the spikes remained in the neurons $\sigma_{r,7}$ and $\sigma_{r,8}$ do not disturb further computations.

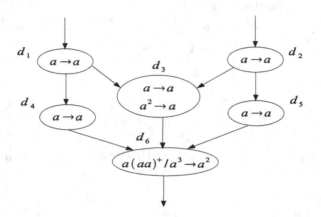

Fig. 4. Module AND

Because we do not know whether l_j and l_k are labels of ADD, SUB, or halting instructions, hence in both of the ADD and the SUB module the rules in the neurons σ_{l_j}, σ_{l_k} are written in the form $a^2 \rightarrow a^{\delta(l_s)}$, where the function $\delta : H \rightarrow \{1, 2\}$ is defined as below:

$$\delta(l) = \begin{cases} 2, & \text{if } l \text{ is the label of an ADD instruction,} \\ 1, & \text{otherwise.} \end{cases}$$

Outputting a computation

As shown in Fig. 5, when the computation in M halts, two spikes reach the neuron σ_{l_h} of Π_1. In that moment, register 1 of M stores value n and neuron σ_1 of Π_1 contains $2n + 2$ spikes. The spike emitted by l_h reaches neuron 1 (hence containing an odd number of spikes). Thanks to the neuron $\sigma_{h,2}$, it leads neuron σ_1 to fire continuously, consuming two spikes at each step. One step after receiving the spike from σ_{l_h}, neuron σ_1 fires and two spikes reach neuron $\sigma_{h,2}$. Next, neuron $\sigma_{h,4}$ simultaneously receives a spike from $\sigma_{h,3}$, gets fired and sends a spike to neuron σ_{out}, which spikes for the first time one step later. From then on, neuron $\sigma_{h,4}$ receives a couple of spikes from $\sigma_{h,2}$ that do not let it fire again, until two steps after neuron σ_1 fires for the last time (using the rule $a^3 \rightarrow a$). When neuron σ_1 stops spiking, neuron $\sigma_{h,4}$ will receive one spike, making σ_{out} fire again and emitting its second and last spike (exactly n steps after the first one).

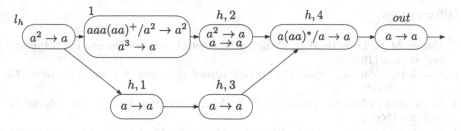

Fig. 5. Module FIN (ending the computation)

From the above description of the work of system Π, it is clear that the system Π_1 correctly simulates the register machine M and outputs exactly the value n computed by M, i.e., $N(M) = N_2^{min}(\Pi)$. This concludes the proof. $\square$

4   Conclusions and Discussions

In this work, we investigated the computational power of SN P systems with minimal parallelism using as number generator. Specifically, an SN P system with minimal parallelism is constructed to compute any set of Turing computable natural numbers. Many issues remain to be investigated for this new class of SN P systems.

It remains to consider the SN P systems with minimal parallelism as language generator. Moreover, it is worth investigating the acceptive case for SN P systems with minimal parallelism.

In the proof of Theorem 1, there are 10 auxiliary neurons in each ADD module, and 27 in each SUB module. So compared to the results in [29–35], the SN P system with minimal parallelism seems to have no advantage in the aspect of small universal SN P system. It is highly possible that this disadvantage can be made up by constructing the modules differently. This task is left as an open problem to the readers.

Also in the proof of Theorem 1, the feature of delay and forgetting rule are not used. It is of interests to check if the number of neurons in universal SN P systems with minimal parallelism can be reduced with using delay or forgetting rule. Moreover, from a point of view of computation power, the boundary between the universality and non-universality of SN P systems with minimal parallelism is still open.

Acknowledgments. This work was supported by National Natural Science Foundation of China (61502063).

References

1. Hagan, M.T., Demuth, H.B., Beale, M.H.: Neural Network Design. PWS Publishing, Boston (1996)
2. Ghosh-Dastidar, S., Adeli, H.: Spiking neural networks. Int. J. Neur. Syst. **19**, 295–308 (2009)
3. Ionescu, M., Păun, G., Yokomori, T.: Spiking neural P systems. Fund. Inform. **71**, 279–308 (2006)
4. Cavaliere, M., Ibarra, O.H., Păun, G., Egecioglu, O., Ionescu, M., Woodworth, S.: Asynchronous spiking neural P systems. Theor. Comput. Sci. **410**, 2352–2364 (2009)
5. Pan, L., Păun, G.: Spiking neural P systems with anti-spikes. Int. J. Comput. Commun. **4**, 273–282 (2009)
6. Ionescu, M., Păun, G., Pérez-Jiménez, M.J., Yokomori, T.: Spiking neural dP systems. Fund. Inform. **111**, 423–436 (2011)
7. Pan, L., Wang, J., Hoogeboom, H.J.: Spiking neural P systems with astrocytes. Neural Comput. **24**, 805–825 (2012)
8. Pan, L., Zeng, X., Zhang, X., Jiang, Y.: Spiking neural P systems with weighted synapses. Neural Process. Lett. **35**, 13–27 (2012)
9. Song, T., Pan, L., Păun, G.: Spiking neural P systems with rules on synapses. Theor. Comput. Sci. **529**, 82–95 (2014)
10. Wang, J., Hoogeboom, H.J., Pan, L., Păun, G., Pérez-Jiménez, M.J.: Spiking neural P systems with weights. Neural Comput. **22**, 2615–2646 (2014)
11. Song, T., Liu, X., Zeng, X.: Asynchronous spiking neural P systems with anti-spikes. Neural Process. Lett. **42**, 633–647 (2015)
12. Song, T., Pan, L.: Spiking neural P systems with rules on synapses working in maximum spiking strategy. IEEE Trans. Nanobiosci. **14**, 465–477 (2015)
13. Song, T., Pan, L.: Spiking neural P systems with rules on synapses working in maximum spikes consumption strategy. IEEE Trans. Nanobiosci. **14**, 38–44 (2015)
14. Song, T., Gong, F., Liu, X., Zhao, Y., Zhang, X.: Spiking neural P systems with white hole neurons. IEEE Trans. Nanobiosci. **15**, 666–673 (2016)
15. Zhao, Y., Liu, X., Wang, W., Adamatzky, A.: Spiking neural P systems with neuron division and dissolution. PLoS ONE **11**, e0162882 (2016)
16. Wu, T., Zhang, Z., Păun, G., Pan, L.: Cell-like spiking neural P systems. Theor. Comput. Sci. **623**, 180–189 (2016)
17. Jiang, K., Chen, W., Zhang, Y., Pan, L.: Spiking neural P systems with homogeneous neurons and synapses. Neurocomputing **171**, 1548–1555 (2016)
18. Song, T., Pan, L.: Spiking neural P systems with request rules. Neurocomputing **193**, 193–200 (2016)
19. Ibarra, O.H., Păun, A., Rodríguez-Patón, A.: Sequential SNP systems based on min/max spike number. Theor. Comput. Sci. **410**, 2982–2991 (2009)
20. Neary, T.: A boundary between universality and non-universality in extended spiking neural P systems. In: Dediu, A.-H., Fernau, H., Martín-Vide, C. (eds.) LATA 2010. LNCS, vol. 6031, pp. 475–487. Springer, Heidelberg (2010). https://doi.org/10.1007/978-3-642-13089-2_40
21. Song, T., Pan, L., Jiang, K., Song, B., Chen, W.: Normal forms for some classes of sequential spiking neural P systems. IEEE Trans. Nanobiosci. **12**, 255–264 (2013)
22. Zhang, X., Zeng, X., Luo, B., Pan, L.: On some classes of sequential spiking neural P systems. Neural Comput. **26**, 974–997 (2014)

23. Wang, X., Song, T., Gong, F., Zheng, P.: On the computational power of spiking neural P systems with self-organization. Sci. Rep. **6**, 27624 (2016)
24. Chen, H., Freund, R., Ionescu, M.: On string languages generated by spiking neural P systems. Fund. Inform. **75**, 141–162 (2007)
25. Krithivasan, K., Metta, V.P., Garg, D.: On string languages generated by spiking neural P systems with anti-spikes. Int. J. Found. Comput. Sci. **22**, 15–27 (2011)
26. Zeng, X., Xu, L., Liu, X.: On string languages generated by spiking neural P systems with weights. Inform. Sci. **278**, 423–433 (2014)
27. Song, T., Xu, J., Pan, L.: On the universality and non-universality of spiking neural P systems with rules on synapses. IEEE Trans. Nanobiosci. **14**, 960–966 (2015)
28. Wu, T., Zhang, Z., Pan, L.: On languages generated by cell-like spiking neural P systems. IEEE Trans. Nanobiosci. **15**, 455–467 (2016)
29. Păun, G., Păun, A.: Small universal spiking neural P systems. Biosystems **90**, 48–60 (2007)
30. Zhang, X., Zeng, X., Pan, L.: Smaller universal spiking neural P systems. Fund. Inform. **87**, 117–136 (2008)
31. Pan, L., Zeng, X.: A note on small universal spiking neural P systems. In: Păun, G., Pérez-Jiménez, M.J., Riscos-Núñez, A., Rozenberg, G., Salomaa, A. (eds.) WMC 2009. LNCS, vol. 5957, pp. 436–447. Springer, Heidelberg (2010). https://doi.org/10.1007/978-3-642-11467-0_29
32. Song, T., Jiang, Y., Shi, X., Zeng, X.: Small universal spiking neural P systems with anti-spikes. J. Comput. Theor. Nanosci. **10**, 999–1006 (2013)
33. Zeng, X., Pan, L., Pérez-Jiménez, M.J.: Small universal simple spiking neural P systems with weights. Sci. China. Inform. Sci. **57**, 1–11 (2014)
34. Metta, V.P., Raghuraman, S., Krithivasan, K.: Small universal spiking neural P systems with cooperating rules as function computing devices. In: Gheorghe, M., Rozenberg, G., Salomaa, A., Sosík, P., Zandron, C. (eds.) CMC 2014. LNCS, vol. 8961, pp. 300–313. Springer, Cham (2014). https://doi.org/10.1007/978-3-319-14370-5_19
35. Song, T., Pan, L.: A small universal spiking neural P systems with cooperating rules. Rom. J. Inf. Sci. Technol. **17**, 177–189 (2014)
36. Ishdorj, T.-O., Leporati, A., Pan, L., Zeng, X., Zhang, X.: Deterministic solutions to QSAT and Q3SAT by spiking neural P systems with pre-computed resources. Theor. Comput. Sci. **411**, 2345–2358 (2010)
37. Pan, L., Păun, G., Pérez-Jiménez, M.J.: Spiking neural P systems with neuron division and budding. Sci. China Inform. Sci. **54**, 1596–1607 (2011)
38. Song, T., Zheng, P., Wong, M.L., Wang, X.: Design of logic gates using spiking neural P systems with homogeneous neurons and astrocytes-like control. Inform. Sci. **372**, 380–391 (2016)
39. Díaz-Pernil, D., Gutiérrez-Naranjo, M.J.: Semantics of deductive databases with spiking neural P systems. Neurocomputing (2017). doi:https://doi.org/10.1016/j.neucom.2017.07.007
40. Zeng, X., Song, T., Zhang, X., Pan, L.: Performing four basic arithmetic operations with spiking neural P systems. IEEE Trans. Nanobiosci. **11**, 366–374 (2012)
41. Liu, X., Li, Z., Liu, J., Liu, L., Zeng, X.: Implementation of arithmetic operations with time-free spiking neural P systems. IEEE Trans. Nanobiosci. **14**, 617–624 (2015)
42. Wang, J., Shi, P., Peng, H., Pérez-Jiménez, M.J., Wang, T.: Weighted fuzzy spiking neural P systems. IEEE Trans. Fuzzy Syst. **21**, 209–220 (2013)

43. Peng, H., Wang, J., Pérez-Jiménez, M.J., Wang, H., Shao, J., Wang, T.: Fuzzy reasoning spiking neural P systems for fault diagnosis. Inform. Sci. **235**, 106–116 (2013)
44. Wang, J., Peng, H.: Adaptive fuzzy spiking neural P systems for fuzzy inference and learning. Int. J. Comput. Math. **90**, 857–868 (2013)
45. Wang, T., Zhang, G., Zhao, J., He, Z., Wang, J., Pérez-Jiménez, M.J.: Fault diagnosis of electric power systems based on fuzzy reasoning spiking neural P systems. IEEE Trans. Power Syst. **30**, 1182–1194 (2015)
46. Zhang, G., Rong, H., Neri, F., Pérez-Jiménez, M.J.: An optimization spiking neural P system for approximately solving combinatorial optimization problems. Int. J. Neur. Syst. **24**, 1440006 (2014)
47. Ionescu, M., Păun, G., Yokomori, T.: Spiking neural P systems with exhaustive use of rules. Int. J. Unconv. Comput. **3**, 135–154 (2007)
48. Ciobanu, G., Pan, L., Păun, G., Pérez-Jiménez, M.J.: P systems with minimal parallelism. Theor. Comput. Sci. **378**, 117–130 (2007)
49. Rozenberg, G., Salomaa, A. (eds.): Handbook of Formal Language: Volume 3 Beyond Words. Springer, Heidelberg (1997). https://doi.org/10.1007/978-3-642-59126-6
50. Păun, G., Rozenberg, G., Salomaa, A. (eds.): The Oxford Handbook of Membrane Computing. Oxford University Press, New York (2010)
51. Minsky, M.: Computation - Finite and Infinite Machines. Prentice Hall, Englewood Cliffs (1967)

Model Checking for Computation Tree Logic with Past Based on DNA Computing

Yingjie Han, Qinglei Zhou, Linfeng Jiao, Kai Nie, Chunyan Zhang, and Weijun Zhu$^{(\boxtimes)}$

School of Information Engineering, Zhengzhou University, Zhengzhou 450001, China
zhuweijuntougao@163.com

Abstract. Deoxyribonucleic acid (DNA) computing provides a novel way of breaking through the limitations of traditional computation framework. Some complicated computational problems on small-scale have been solved. Model checking is a notable verification technique which is important to security-critical system. We employ DNA computing models and propose DNA algorithms for checking four elementary formulas of computation tree logic with past-time constructs in this paper. The model checking algorithms based on DNA computing are proved to be practicable and valid by simulations. The time complexity of the algorithms is reduced to linearity while the classical algorithm is PSPACE-complete. It indicates that a complexity computational problem is solved on DNA-computing based and the problems which can be solved by DNA computing are enriched. Meanwhile, it could be a benefit to diagnosis and treatment of genetic diseases at molecular level.

Keywords: CTL · Past-time constructs · Model checking · DNA computing · Memory-less filtering model

1 Introduction

DNA computing is one of the most popular research hotspots to find the new computing paradigms that exploit the specific characteristics of the molecules [1]. There are two kinds of DNA computing model in processing different problems. One is laboratory scale human-operated DNA computing models for solving complex computational problems [2–4]. The other is molecular-scale, autonomous, and partially programmable. The computations are essentially driven by the self-assembly of DNA molecules and are modulated by DNA-manipulating enzymes. DNA self-assembly based applications involve DNA strand displacement [5,6], DNA nanotechnology [7], nanomaterials [8,9] and so on.

Model checking is a technology that can answer such questions as whether a system satisfies a given property automatically or not. If the answer is no, it can provide counter-examples showing under which circumstances the error can be generated [10]. Temporal logics, which are modal logics that enable the description of occurrence of events, serve as a classical tool for specifying behaviors of concurrent and reactive systems. It supports model checking technology that allows

© Springer Nature Singapore Pte Ltd. 2017
C. He et al. (Eds.): BIC-TA 2017, CCIS 791, pp. 131–147, 2017.
https://doi.org/10.1007/978-981-10-7179-9_11

large and complex (finite) systems to be verified automatically. Computation tree logic (CTL) is one of the most commonly-used temporal logics to describe the branch temporal properties of systems [11]. In computer science, most theoretical studies of temporal logics only use the future-time constructs and ignore the past-time constructs. Actually, the past-time constructs can be very useful when it comes to express certain properties. It is well known that allowing both past-time and future-time constructs makes temporal specification easier to write and more natural to understand. The past-time constructs make it more expressive to specify the property of reactive and concurrent systems. Moreover, adding past-time constructs does not increase the complexity of model checking problems [12]. In a word, past-time constructs appear to play an important role in compositional specification somewhat analogous to that of history variables [13]. The parallelism of DNA computing and the vast storage of DNA molecules provide us the opportunity to break the state space limitation of model checking. In 2006, Ernest Allen Emerson, who was the Turing Award winner, applied DNA computing in model checking for the first time. He proposed a DNA-computing-based method and designed a checking algorithm for CTL formula EFp (EFp means the atomic proposition p holds eventually along some system paths) [14]. In his work, the Kripke structure was employed in modeling the system, and states and transitions of the system model were encoded by DNA molecules. The model checking problem, whether the system satisfies the property specified by the CTL formula EFp, was transformed into DNA molecule chain reaction process. The use of DNA restriction enzymes results in reduced reliability and efficiency of the solution. In addition, the counter-examples cant be provided to guide the modification if the system doesnt satisfy EFp. In 2016, model checking for propositional linear temporal logic (PLTL) with pure-future based on sticker automata DNA computing has been implemented by Dr. Zhu et al. [15]. He designed the model checking algorithms for four elementary PLTL formulas and five commonly-used properties. Han et al. [16] proposed the model checking algorithm for PLTL formula Xp (Xp means the property p is valid in the next state). Furthermore, model checking algorithms for the CTL formulas EXp (EXp means that the property p is valid in the next state of some paths) and AXp (AXp means that the property p is valid in the next state of all paths) are also implemented on the basis of Xp model checking. Up to now, there are no DNA algorithms for CTL_p model checking. The model checking problem for CTL_p within the DNA computing remains unsolved. We deliberate on the problem of model checking for an extension of computation tree logic by past-time constructs (CTL_p). It is a PSPACE-complete problem [17] and is hard to be solved on traditional computers. We propose the model checking algorithms for CTL_p on DNA-computing based. The model checking algorithms for AHp (AHp means p held on all states for every path in the past), EHp (EHp means there exists some paths such that for each state on these paths p held in the past), AOp (AOp means p held along all system paths in the past) and EOp (EOp means p held eventually along some system paths in the past) are deliberated, where p is an atomic propositions.

The rest part of the paper is organized as follows. We give a brief introduction of CTL_p and the DNA computing model employed in this paper in Sect. 2. We elaborate the method of model checking for CTL_p based on memory-less filtering model in Sect. 3 and show the simulation results in Sect. 4. In Sect. 5, there is the conclusion and future work.

2 Preliminary

2.1 The Syntax of CTL_p

Two possible views regarding the nature of past induce two different extensions [17]. In the first view, past is branching and each moment may have several possible futures and several possible pasts. In the second view, past is linear. Both views assume that past is finite. In this paper, we assume that past is determined (means that at any time along any computation there is a completely fixed linear history of all events which already took place), finite (means a run of a system always has a starting point), and cumulative (means whenever the system performs some steps and advances with the time, its history becomes richer and longer) [17].

We assume a given nonempty finite set $AP = \{p, q, \ldots\}$ of atomic propositions. CTL_p formulas are given by [17, 18]. Let AP be a set of atomic proposition names. A CTL_p formula is

$$\varphi, \Psi :: = p \mid q \mid \neg\varphi \mid \varphi \vee \Psi \mid EX\varphi \mid EY\varphi \mid E[\varphi U\Psi] \mid A[\varphi U\Psi] \mid E[\varphi S\Psi] \mid A[\varphi S\Psi]$$

Standard abbreviations include true, false, $\varphi \wedge \Psi$, $\varphi \rightarrow \Psi$, as well as

$$AHp = \neg EO\neg p, \ EHp = \neg AO\neg p, \ AOp = A(trueSp), \ EOp = E(trueSp)$$

$$AGp = \neg EF\neg p, \ EGp = \neg AF\neg p, \ AFp = A(trueUp), \ EFp = E(trueUp)$$

$$AYp = \neg EY\neg p, \ AXp = \neg EX\neg p$$

H (historically), O (once), S (since) and Y (yesterday) are the constructs of CTL_p where G (globally), F (future), U (until) and X (next) are the constructs of CTL. H is the temporal dual of G and O is the temporal dual of F. S is the temporal dual of U and Y is the temporal dual of X. The well-known future-only CTL is enriched with past-time constructs H, O, S and Y.

2.2 The Semantics of CTL_p

A CTL-model is a triple $M = (S, R, Label)$, where S is a non-empty set of states, $R \subseteq S \times S$ is a total relation on S, which relates to $s \in S$ its possible successor states, and $label : S \rightarrow 2^{AP}$ assigns to each state $s \in S$ the atomic propositions $Label(s)$ that are valid in s. A path $\delta \in S^\omega$ is an infinite sequence of states $s_0 s_1 s_2 \ldots$ such that $(s_i, s_{i+1}) \in R$ for all $i \geqslant 0$. The set of paths starting in state s of the model M is defined by $P_M(s) = \{\delta \in S^\omega \mid \delta[i] = s,\ i > 0\}$. Suppose that φ and Ψ are CTL$_p$ formulas. The satisfaction relation $\models$ is defined by:

$s \models p$, iff $p \in Label(s)$

$s \models \neg\varphi$, iff $\neg(s \models \varphi)$

$s = \varphi \vee \Psi$, iff $(s \models \varphi) \vee (s \models \Psi)$

$s \models AH\varphi$, iff $\forall\ \delta \in P_M(s)$, for all $j < i$, $\delta[i - j] = \varphi$

$s \models EH\varphi$, iff $\exists\ \delta \in P_M(s)$, for all $j < i$, $\delta[i - j] = \varphi$

$s \models AO\varphi$, iff $\forall\ \delta \in P_M(s)$, for some $j < i$, $\delta[i - j] = \varphi$

$s \models EO\varphi$, iff $\exists\ \delta \in P_M(s)$, for some $j < i$, $\delta[i - j] = \varphi$

$s \models A[\varphi S\Psi]$, iff $\forall\ \delta \in P_M(s)$, $\exists\ 0 \leqslant j \leqslant i$, $\delta[j] = \Psi \wedge (\forall\ j < k \leqslant i)$, $\delta[k] = \varphi$

$s \models E[\varphi S\Psi]$, iff $\exists\ \delta \in P_M(s)$, $\exists\ 0 \leqslant j \leqslant i$, $\delta[j] = \Psi \wedge (\forall\ j < k \leqslant i)$, $\delta[k] = \varphi$

$s \models AY\varphi$, iff $\forall\ \delta \in P_M(s)$, $i > 0$, $\delta[i - 1] = \varphi$

$s \models EY\varphi$, iff $\exists\ \delta \in P_M(s)$, $i > 0$, $\delta[i - 1] = \varphi$

$s \models AG\varphi$, iff $\forall\ \delta \in P_M(s)$, $\forall\ j \geqslant 0$, $\delta[i + j] = \varphi$

$s \models EG\varphi$, iff $\exists\ \delta \in P_M(s)$, $\forall\ j \geqslant 0$, $\delta[i + j] = \varphi$

$s \models AF\varphi$, iff $\forall\ \delta \in P_M(s)$, $\exists\ j \geqslant 0$, $\delta[i + j] = \varphi$

$s \models EF\varphi$, iff $\exists\ \delta \in P_M(s)$, $\exists\ j \geqslant 0$, $\delta[i + j] = \varphi$

$s \models A[\varphi U\Psi]$, iff $\forall\ \delta \in P_M(s)$, $\exists\ j \geqslant i$, $\delta[j] \models \Psi \wedge (\forall\ 0 \leqslant k \leqslant j)$, $\delta[k] \models \varphi$

$s \models E[\varphi U\Psi]$, iff $\exists\ \delta \in P_M(s)$, $\exists\ j \geqslant i$, $\delta[j] \models \Psi \wedge (\forall\ 0 \leqslant k \leqslant j)$, $\delta[k] \models \varphi$

$s \models AX\varphi$, iff $\forall\ \delta \in P_M(s)$, $\delta[i + 1] = \varphi$

$s \models EX\varphi$, iff $\exists\ \delta \in P_M(s)$, $\delta[i + 1] = \varphi$

We have the following inferences about the CTL$_p$ according to the semantics.

(a) $AHp \rightarrow EHp$. The system model satisfies the property specified by EHp if the system model satisfies the property specified by AHp.

(b) $AHp \rightarrow AOp$. The system model satisfies the property specified by AOp if the system model satisfies the property specified by AHp.

(c) $AHp \rightarrow EOp$. The system model satisfies the property specified by EOp if the system model satisfies the property specified by AHp.

(d) $AOp \rightarrow EOp$. The system model satisfies the property specified by EOp if the system model satisfies the property specified by AOp.

(e) $EHp \rightarrow EOp$. The system model satisfies the property specified by EOp if the system model satisfies the property specified by EHp.

2.3   The Memory-Less Filtering Model

We employ Adlemans memory-less filtering model [1] in order to implement the CTL$_p$ model checking on DNA-computing based. The operations which are all achievable for manipulating single-stranded DNA molecules biologically are as follows [1,19,20].

(a) anneal(T): By a drop in temperature, the single-stranded DNA molecules which are complementary with each other according to the Watson-Crick law are paired with each other automatically in tube T.

(b) ligate(T, ligase): DNA ligase repairs the DNA strand skeleton in (a), and forms complete double-stranded DNA molecules.

(c) melt(T): Double-stranded DNA molecules are forced to be separated into single-strand molecules by rising temperature in T.

(d) merge(T_1, T_1, T_2): Pour the solution of test tube T_2 into T_1.

(e) substring-extract(T, x): Pick a test tube T and a string x, and provide a test tube that holds all strings in T that have the string x as a substring.

(f) separate(T, T_x, T_r, x): Consider a test tube T and a string x, and produce two new tubes, T_x and T_r, where T_x consists of all strings in T which contain the string x as a subsequence, while T_r holds all strings in T which do not have the string x as a subsequence.

(g) length-separate(T, T_m, m): Start with a test tube T and a positive integer m, and produce a test tube T_m that contains all strings in T which have length less than or equal to m.

(h) prefix-extract(T, T_x, x): Extract all the DNA single-strands that begin with x from the tube T and put them into tube T_x.

(i) postfix-extract(T, T_x, x): Extract all the DNA single-strands that end with x from the tube T and put them into tube T_x.

(j) detect(T): Pick a test tube T and output "yes" if T contains at least one DNA molecule; otherwise, output "no".

3   Model Checking for CTL$_p$ based on DNA computing

3.1   The Generation of the System Paths

Firstly, we construct the CTL-model $M = (S, R, Label)$ of the system to be checked, Secondly, we generate the running paths of the system model. The algorithm is shown below.

Algorithm 1. Getruns()

Input: Tube T_s, containing the single-stranded DNA molecules of states of the system model. Tube T_e, containing the Watson-Crick complementary molecules of transitions of the system model. Empty tube T_m(m stands for the states number of the system model).

Output: Tube T_m, containing system paths from the initial state to the terminal state.

Begin

1: T_s=merge(T_s, T_s, T_e);
2: T_s=anneal(T_s);
3: T_s=ligate(T_s, ligase);
4: T_s=melt(T_s);
5: T_s=prefix-extract(T_s, sini);
6: T_s=postfix-extract(T_s, ster);
7: length-separate(T_s, T_m, m);
8: **return** T_m;

End

Merging the two tubes into T_s means pouring the solution of tube T_e into tube T_s. The DNA molecules anneal and pair with each other sufficiently, and short double strands ligate to form long double strands. After melting, the double DNA strands split into single-stranded DNA molecules. Those single-stranded DNA molecules encoding the paths that begin with s_{ini} and end with s_{ter} are amplified by polymerase chain reaction (PCR). Length separation of DNA molecules is implemented by gel electrophoresis. Paths whose length are less than or equal to m are extracted into the tube T_m. At last, T_m contains the system paths which begin with s_{ini} and end with s_{ter}.

3.2   The Model Checking Algorithms for CTL$_p$

We propose the model checking algorithms to verify whether the system model satisfies AHp, EHp, AOp and EOp respectively. The following DNA algorithms are suitable for both CTL and CTL$_p$ model checking.

The Model Checking Algorithm for AHp. AHp is valid if and only if for all the states on every path p held in past time. The key to model checking for AHp is to check the existence of non-p. The model checking algorithm is shown in algorithm $CheckAH()$.

Algorithm 2. CheckAH()

Input: The DNA molecules of a system model and an empty tube T_m. Empty tube T_r and T_p.
Output: Yes or No (provide counter-examples)
Begin
1: T_s=Getruns();
2: separate (T_s, T_r, T_p, r);
3: **if** ((detect(T_r)==NULL)&(detect(T_p)≠ NULL)) **then**
4:     **return** Yes;
5: **else**
6:     **return** No;
7: **end if**
End

The paths of the system model are obtained by using algorithm $Getruns()$ and put them into the tube T_m. The biotin-avidin magnetic system is utilized to separate strands in tube T_m into tube T_p and T_r according to the Watson-Click complementary of r (represented by r). After the separating, DNA molecules which contain r are extracted into tube T_r and the rest molecules are extracted into tube T_p. The detection is implemented by graduated PCR. The model checking result is "yes" and the system model satisfies AHp if there are not any

DNA molecules in T_r but there are some DNA molecules in T_p; Otherwise, the model checking result is "no" and the system model doesnt satisfy AHp. The DNA molecules in T_r are the counter-examples.

Model Checking Algorithm for EHp. EHp is valid if and only if there exists some path such that for each state on this path p held. Whether the tube T_p is empty is the key to model checking for EHp. The model checking algorithm is shown in algorithm $CheckEH()$.

Algorithm 3. CheckEH()

Input: The DNA molecules of a system model and an empty tube T_m.
Output: Yes or No (provide counter-examples)
Begin
  1: T_m=Getruns();
  2: separate (T_m, T_r, T_p, r);
  3: **if** (detect(T_p)$\neq$ NULL) **then**
  4:   **return** Yes;
  5: **else**
  6:   **return** No;
  7: **end if**
End

The paths of the system model are obtained by using algorithm $Getruns()$ and are put into the tube T_m. After separating, DNA molecules which contain DNA fragment of r are extracted and then put into tube T_r and the rest molecules are extracted and then put into tube T_p. It indicates that p held on each state of each path if there are some DNA molecules in T_p. The model checking result is yes and the system model satisfies EHp accordingly; Otherwise, the model checking result is no and the system model doesnt satisfy EHp. The DNA molecules in tube T_r are the counter-examples.

Whether the system model satisfies EHp or not can be easily checked according to the Inference (a). That is AHp→EHp. The system model satisfies AHp means that p held on all states of each path. Therefore, p held on some states of each path is a matter of course.

Model Checking Algorithm for AOp. AOp is valid if and only if p held for all paths in the past. The key to model checking for AOp is to check the existence of non-p. The model checking algorithm is shown in algorithm $CheckAO()$.

Algorithm 4. CheckAO()

Input: The DNA molecules of a system model and an empty tube T_m.
Output: Yes or No (provide counter-examples)
Begin

1: T_m=Getruns();
2: separate (T_m, T_p, T_r, r);
3: **if** $((\text{detect}(T_r)==\text{NULL})\&\&(\text{detect}(T_p)\neq\text{NULL}))$ **then**
4:     **return** Yes;
5: **else**
6:     **return** No;
7: **end if**

End

The paths of the system model are obtained by using algorithm Getruns() and put them into the tube T_m. The biotin-avidin magnetic system is utilized to separate strands in tube T_m into tube T_p and T_r according to the Watson-Click complementary of p (represented by p̱). After the separation, DNA molecules which contain p are extracted into tube Tp and the rest molecules are extracted into tube T_r. The detection is implemented by graduated PCR. The model checking result is yes and the system model satisfies AOp if there are not any DNA molecules in T_r but there are some DNA molecules in T_p; Otherwise, the model checking result is no and the system model doesnt satisfy AOp and the molecules in T_r are the counter-examples. There is another simple way to check whether the system model satisfies AOp. The system model satisfies AOp if the system model satisfies AHp according to Inference (b).

The Model Checking Algorithm for EOp. EOp is valid if and only if p held on some paths eventually in the past. Whether the tube T_p is empty is the key to model checking for EOp. The model checking algorithm for EOp is shown in algorithm *CheckEO()*.

Algorithm 5. CheckEO()

Input: The DNA molecules of a system model and an empty tube T_m.
Output: Yes or No (provide counter-examples)
Begin

1: T_m=Getruns();
2: separate $(T_m, T_p, T_r, \underline{p})$;
3: **if** $\text{detect}(T_p)\neq\text{NULL}$ **then**
4:     **return** Yes;
5: **else**
6:     **return** No;
7: **end if**

End

The paths of the system model are obtained by using algorithm *Getruns()* and are put into the tube T_m. After the separate, DNA molecules which contain DNA fragments of p are extracted and then put into tube T_p and the rest molecules are extracted and then put into tube T_r. It indicates that p held on some states of some paths if there are some DNA molecules in T_p. The model checking result is yes and the system model satisfies EOp accordingly; Otherwise, the model checking result is no and the system model doesnt satisfy EOp. The DNA molecules in T_r are the counter-examples. There are simple ways to check whether the system model satisfies EOp. The system model satisfies EOp according to Inference (c), (d), and (e).

3.3   The Time Complexity Analysis of the Model Checking Algorithms

The time complexity is defined by the number of the steps of the bio-operations. Here what we mean is the total number of biological operations in the process of the algorithm. We don't distinguish between the different operations here, even though the time that each of them needs may be very different. Algorithm *Getruns()* generates paths of the system model in $O(n)$ bio-steps. The time complexity of algorithm Getruns() is $O(n)$. The verification algorithms employ the output of algorithm Getruns() and executes some bio-operations such as separation and detection. Each bio-operation is executed only once. Therefore, the time complexity of our approach is $O(n)$. It indicates that our algorithm can complete its mission in linear time, whereas the existing classical model checking algorithm for CTL with past is in need of exponential time. This benefits from the parallel computing originated from DNA computing.

4   Simulations and Results

Since the molecular manipulations we employed are all achievable biologically [1,12,13], we employ simulation experiments instead of biological experiments. On the one hand, we utilize Nucleic Acid Package (NUPACK) [21] for the analysis and design of nucleic acid sequences. On the other hand, we develop a simulation platform to verify the feasibility of our approach. The single-stranded DNA molecules can be regarded as strings consisting of A, T, G, C. Some basic biochemical reactions can be simulated on a computer according to their principles. For example, hybridization and ligation can be simulated by concatenating the designated strings, gel electrophoresis can be simulated by arranging strings by their length, and affinity purification can be simulated by searching for the particular strings and so on. We simplify the complexity of algorithm design by introducing the following constraints: constant temperature and perfect complementarity.

4.1   The Design of DNA Encoding

Each state s_i is encoded by a single-stranded DNA molecule of 16nt. Each relation (s_i, s_j) connecting state s_i with state s_j is encoded by a single-stranded

DNA molecule that consists of the complement of the second 3 half-mer of the DNA strand of s_i and the complement of the first 5 half-mer of the DNA strand of s_j. Assume that the formal part of the DNA molecule of s_i is 5H(si)3, and the latter part is 5T(si)3. Each transition (si,sj) is encoded by a single-stranded DNA molecule 3H(e)T(e)5. If s_i is the initial state, $H(e) = 3'\overline{H(s_i)T(s_i)}5'$; Otherwise $H(e) = 3'\overline{T(s_i)}5'$. If s_j is the terminal state, $T(e) = 3'\overline{C(s_i)}5'$; Otherwise $T(e) = 3'\overline{H(s_j)T(s_j)}5'$. The encoding rule is shown in Fig. 1.

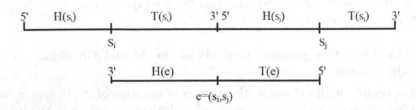

Fig. 1. DNA encoding rule of system model

Suppose that the CTL model of the system to be checked is shown in Fig. 2. Here the states are depicted by circles, and the relation R is denoted by arrows. The labeling Label(s_i) is indicated beside the state s_i.

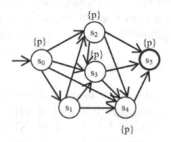

Fig. 2. The CTL model of a system to be checked

There are 14 paths in Fig. 1. The paths represented by the state sequence and the atomic proposition held on the each state respectively are shown in Table 1.

In order to provide the counter-examples, the DNA fragment of the atomic propositions which holds on the state are encoded into the DNA molecule of the state. The DNA encoding of the system model is shown in Table 2. The encoding of relations is omitted because they can be derived from the encoding of the states.

The reliability and validity of DNA encoding are analyzed and verified by NUPACK to ensure specific hybridization between DNA sequences. Hybridization mismatches may lead to computational errors and reduce stability and reliability

Table 1. Paths of the system model

No	Path	No	Path
1	$s_0 s_2 s_5$ (ppp)	8	$s_0 s_2 s_4 s_5$ (pppp)
2	$s_0 s_3 s_5$ (ppp)	9	$s_0 s_3 s_4 s_5$ (pppp)
3	$s_0 s_4 s_5$ (ppp)	10	$s_0 s_1 s_3 s_4 s_5$ (prppp)
4	$s_0 s_1 s_2 s_5$ (prpp)	11	$s_0 s_1 s_2 s_4 s_5$ (prppp)
5	$s_0 s_1 s_3 s_5$ (prpp)	12	$s_0 s_1 s_2 s_3 s_5$ (prppp)
6	$s_0 s_1 s_4 s_5$ (prpp)	13	$s_0 s_2 s_3 s_4 s_5$ (ppppp)
7	$s_0 s_2 s_3 s_5$ (pppp)	14	$s_0 s_1 s_2 s_3 s_4 s_5$ (prpppp)

Table 2. Encoding of states of the system model

Object	DNA sequence
p	5'GGCC3'
r	5'CGCG3'
s0	5' GCTGACGGCCGACAGC 3'
s1	5' CGTGCACGCGTGAACG 3'
s2	5' GCCGATGGCCTACGGC 3'
s3	5' GCTGATGGCCTACGGC 3'
s4	5' GCTGATGGCCTACTGC 3'
s5	5' CGTGCAGGCCTGAACG 3'

of DNA computing. On the one hand, the reliability and validity of the DNA encoding of each state are verified by NUPACK and on the other hand, the reliability and validity of all the paths of the system model composed of state sequences are verified by NUPACK. Lets take the 14th path $s_0 s_1 s_2 s_3 s_4 s_5$ for example. The DNA sequence and its complementary sequence are shown in Fig. 3. As is shown in Fig. 4, the dark red line indicates that DNA molecules pair with each other with the probability of nearly 100%. It suggests that the free energy close to the minimum free energy (MFE). As is shown in Fig. 5, the position of the red line indicates that all bases of two single strands are completely complementary to each other, and the color of the red line indicate that the probability of all the pairs are approximately equal to 1. On the basis of the above analysis, The DNA sequences satisfy the minimum free energy constraint, and the DNA molecules share the same melting temperature. Therefore, the experimental results are biologically reliable and valid. Limited to the space, we don't show the result of all the states and paths.

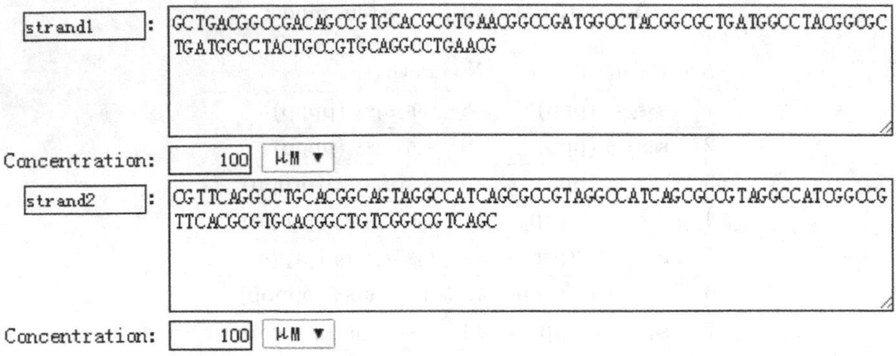

strand1
GCTGACGGCCGACAGCCGTGCACGCGTGAACGGCCGATGGCCTACGGCGCTGATGGCCTACGGCGC
TGATGGCCTACTGCCGTGCAGGCCTGAACG
Concentration:
100
μM
strand2
CGTTCAGGCCTGCACGGCAGTAGGCCATCAGCGCCGTAGGCCATCAGCGCCGTAGGCCATCGGCCG
TTCACGCGTGCACGGCTGTCGGCCGTCAGC
Concentration:
100
μM

Fig. 3. The DNA sequence of path $s_0s_1s_2s_3s_4s_5$

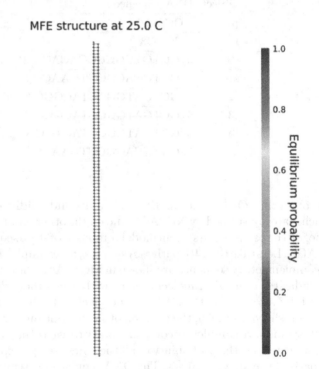

MFE structure at 25.0 C
1.0
0.8
0.6
0.4
0.2
0.0
Equilibrium probability
Free energy of secondary structure: -186.53 kcal/mol

Fig. 4. The MFE of the DNA sequence of path $s_0s_1s_2s_3s_4s_5$ (Color figure online)

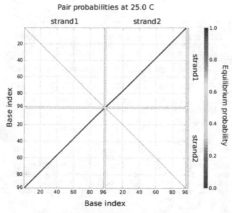

Fig. 5. The pairing probability of the DNA sequence of path $s_0s_1s_2s_3s_4s_5$ in equilibrium (Color figure online)

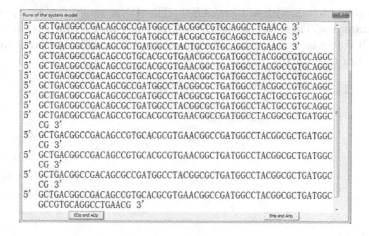

Fig. 6. The running paths of the system model which are shown in Fig. 2.

4.2 Simulation Results

The simulation results of the system model (see Fig. 2) are shown in Figs. 6, 7 and 8. The running paths which are shown in Fig. 6 are generated by algorithm *Getruns()*. Here, we don't need to do four experiments, because *AHp* and *EHp* can be determined by whether T_r is empty and T_p is not empty after the separation according to r, and AOp and EOp can be determined by whether T_r is empty and T_p is not empty after the separation according to p.

The simulation result of model checking for *AHp* and *EHp* is shown in Fig. 7. After separation and detection, there are some DNA strands in T_r. It indicates that p didn't hold for all states in the full path. The system model doesnt satisfy

Fig. 7. The simulation result of model checking for AHp and EHp.

AHp according to algorithm *CheckAH()*. The DNA molecules in T_p are the counter-examples. There are some DNA molecules in T_p which means that p held for all states in some paths. The system model satisfies *EHp* according to the algorithm *CheckEH()*.

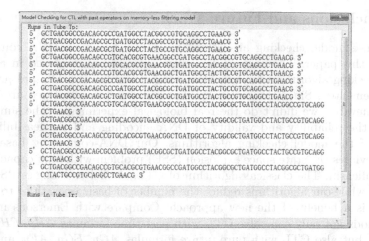

Fig. 8. The simulation result of model checking for AOp and EOp.

The simulation result of AOp and EOp is shown in Fig. 8. After separation and detection, there are some DNA molecules in T_p but there are no DNA molecules in T_r. It indicates that p held for some states in the full path. The system model satisfies AOp according to algorithm $CheckAO()$. Logically, p held for some states eventually in some paths is a matter of course. The system model satisfies EOp according to algorithm $CheckEO()$. The same conclusion can be deduced from Inference (d) and (e).

5   Conclusions and Future Work

We propose model checking algorithms for CTL_p based on DNA computing model in this paper. The memory-less filtering model is employed in and the model checking algorithms for four elementary formulas of CTL_p are proposed and implemented. Since the molecular manipulations we employed are biologically achievable, we didn't do the real biological experiments. The simulation confirms the reliability and validity of DNA encoding and the feasibility and validity of the model checking algorithms. Our DNA-computing based approach alleviates the state space explosion (SSE) problem with high capacity and high parallelism. The classical algorithm of CTL_p model checking is PSPACE-complete while our algorithms reduce the number of basic operations to linearity. This is a benefit of the new approach. Compare with Emersons method, our methods not only can solve CTL with past-time formulas AHp, EHp, AOp and EOp but also CTL with pure-future formulas AGp, EGp, AFp, and EFp. Searching the paths forward from the current state is the way to implement CTL model checking. Searching the paths backward from the current state is the way to implement CTL_p model checking. When the system model doesn't satisfy the desired properties, our methods can provide counter-examples. DNA restriction endonuclease isnt necessary, and the requirements for reaction environment (temperature, PH, ion concentration, reaction time, amount of enzyme used) is relatively low. We will continue studying the computational completeness of our approach in the future. We have to exploit other solution to $A[pSq]$, $E[pSq]$, AYp and EYp model checking because they cant be solved by memory-less filtering model. In view of the limitations of the memeory-less filtering models, such as exponential spatial complexity, we will attempt to use some state-space reduction strateges and employ DNA self-assembly model to achieve temporal logic model checking. DNA computing is achieved through the specific reaction between DNA molecules. The use of DNA computing may in turn contribute to the study of the field of human life, such as diagnosis and treatment of human genetic diseases. We will explore the practical application of our approach in diagnosis and treatment of human genetic diseases.

Acknowledgments. This work was supported by the National Natural Science Foundation of China under Grant 61572444, U1204608, and China Postdoctoral Science Foundation under Grant 2015M572120, as well as Basic and Cutting-edge technology research projects of Henan Province Science and Technology Department under Grant 152300410055.

References

1. Zimmermann, K.H., Martínez-Pérez, I., Ignatova, Z.: DNA computing models. Springer, New York (2008)
2. Adleman, L.M.: Molecular computation of solutions to combinatorial problems. Science **266**(5187), 1021–1023 (1994)
3. Lipton, R.J.: DNA solution of hard computational problems. Science **268**(5210), 542–545 (1995)

4. Fan, Y.K., Qiang, X.L., Xu, J.: Sticker model for maximum clique problem and maximum in-dependent set. Chin. J. Comput. **33**(2), 305–310 (2010)
5. Shi, X.L., Wang, Z.Y., Deng, C.Y., et al.: A novel bio-sensor based on DNA strand displacement. PLoS ONE **9**(10), e108856 (2014)
6. Li, X., Song, T., Shi, X.L., et al.: A universal fast colorimetric method for DNA signal de-tection with DNA strand displacement and gold nanoparticles. J. Nano-mater. **2015**, 1–9 (2015)
7. Li, X., Li, H., Song, T., et al.: Highly biocompatible drug-delivery systems based on DNA nanotechnology. J. Biomed. Nanotechnol. (2017)
8. Shi, X.L., Chen, C.Z., Li, X., et al.: Size controllable DNA nanoribbons assembled from three types of reusable brick single-strand DNA tiles. Soft Matter **11**(43), 8484–8492 (2015)
9. Shi, X.L., Wu, X.X., Song, T., et al.: Construction of DNA nanotubes with controllable diameters and patterns by using hierarchical DNA sub-tiles. Nanoscale **8**(31), 14785–14792 (2016)
10. Clarke, E.M., Grumberg, O., Peled, D.A.: Model Checking. MIT Press, Cambridge (1999)
11. Emerson, E.A.: Using branching time temporal logic to synthesize synchronization skele-tons. Sci. Comput. Program. **2**(3), 241–266 (1982)
12. Lichtenstein, O., Pnueli, A., Zuck, L.: The Glory of the Past. Logics of Programs. Springer, Heidelberg (1985)
13. Emerson, E.A.: Temporal and modal logic. In: Handbook of Theoretical Computer Science, vol. B, pp. 995–1072 (1990)
14. Emerson, E.A., Hager, K.D., Konieczka, J.H.: Molecular model checking. Int. J. Found. Comput. Sci. **17**(04), 733–741 (2006)
15. Zhu, W.-J., Zhou, Q.-L., Li, Y.-L.: LTL model checking based on DNA computing. Acta Electron. Sin. **44**(6), 1265–1271 (2016)
16. Han, Y.-J., Zhu, W.-J., Jiao, L.-F., et al.: DNA computing methods of LTL model checking on Xp. Mini-Micro Syst. **38**(3), 553–558 (2017)
17. Kupferman, O., Pnueli, A.: Once and for all. In: IEEE Symposium on Logic in Computer Science, vol. 78, pp. 25–35 (1995)
18. Laroussinie, F., Schnoebelen, P.: A hierarchy of temporal logics with past. Theoret. Comput. Sci. **148**(2), 303–324 (1995)
19. Adleman, L.M.: Molecular computation of solutions to combinatorial problems. Science **266**(5187), 1021–1024 (1994)
20. Adleman, L.M.: On constructing a molecular computer. In: DIMACS, vol. 27, pp. 1–21 (2007)
21. NUPACK (2017). http://www.nupack.org/partition/new

A Hybrid Parameter Adaptation Based GA and Its Application for Data Clustering

Kangfei Ye[1] and Weiguo Sheng[2($\boxtimes$)]

[1] College of Computer Science, Zhejiang University of Technology,
Hangzhou 310023, Zhejiang, People's Republic of China
[2] Department of Computer Science, Hangzhou Normal University,
Hangzhou 311121, Zhejiang, People's Republic of China
`w.sheng@ieee.org`

Abstract. The performance of genetic algorithm (GA) critically depends on the rates of variation operation. In this paper, we propose a hybrid parameter adaptation scheme, which integrates the traditional adaptive and self-adaptive method, to dynamically control the crossover and mutation rate of GA during evolution. Such a scheme can take advantage of both adaptive and self-adaptive mechanisms, thus effectively setting the parameters of GA. The resulting GA has been applied for data clustering. Our results show that the proposed scheme is beneficial and the resulting GA outperforms the adaptive GA or self-adaptive GA for data clustering.

Keywords: Genetic Algorithm · Adaptive · Self-adaptive · Clustering

1 Introduction

Genetic Algorithms (GAs), inspired by natural evolution [1,2], have been widely used as global optimization techniques. Although GAs have been successfully applied in various science and engineering problems, their performances are sensitive to the setting of parameters of variation operation. It is now well established that the proper setting of parameter values are problem-specific [3]. Further, different values of parameters are typically optimal at different stages of the search process [4]. Therefore, setting the parameters properly is a difficult and challenging task, which remains an open issue in GA literature [5]. To deal with such a task, many different methods have been suggested in literature. A systematic review can be found in [6].

Generally, based on how the parameters are changed, existing methods can be broadly classified as adaptive and self-adaptive approaches. In adaptive control schemes, parameter values are adjusted based on certain feedback from GA's evolution. While in the self-adaptive approach, parameter values are encoded in the solutions and subjected to evolution [7]. For adaptive methods, with proper measure of the fitness landscape during the search, they usually can achieve an appropriate balance between exploration and exploitation. There methods

© Springer Nature Singapore Pte Ltd. 2017
C. He et al. (Eds.): BIC-TA 2017, CCIS 791, pp. 148–160, 2017.
https://doi.org/10.1007/978-981-10-7179-9_12

can alleviate the risk of poor performance arising from inappropriate settings when extensive parameter tuning is not practical. However, the characteristics of fitness landscape are often complex and difficult to predict, especially for complex multimodal fitness landscapes, thus limiting their performances. Self-adaptive methods, on the other hand, is an individual level based parameter adaptation and have been successfully applied in various problems [8,9]. Such methods can save GA users a considerable amount time by removing the need of setting the rates of variation operation. However, it has been shown that leaving everything in the hands of the algorithm like this manner is not viable as the evolutionary may quickly stuck in local optimums with zero or very low parameter values attached to the solution in the population [10].

To overcome the drawbacks of traditional adaptive and self-adaptive methods, in this paper we propose a hybrid parameter adaptation scheme to dynamically control probabilities of crossover and mutation of GA during evolution. Further, to test the feasibility of the proposed scheme, it is applied for solving clustering problems.

The rest of this paper is organized as follows. We first review related work in Sect. 2. Then the clustering problem is described in Sect. 3. This is followed by describing our proposed scheme in Sect. 4 and its application for data clustering in Sect. 5. Section 6 presents our experiments. Finally, we conclude the paper with a summary in Sect. 7.

2 Related Work

Various mechanisms have been proposed for dynamic parameter setting in literature [6], and they can be divided into three categories: deterministic, adaptive or self-adaptive approach. Deterministic methods generally set the parameter values based on predetermined time-varying rules. For example, Fogarty [11] proposed to employ a rule to vary mutation rate in GAs, where the mutation rate decreases exponentially over the number of generations.

Self-adaptation inspired from Evolutionary Strategies was first extended to GA to set its mutation rate by Bäck [8,12]. In [9], Hinterding employed a self-adaptation scheme to dynamically vary the strength of Gaussian mutation in GA. In [7,12,13], a self-adaptive parameter control method was proposed to control both mutation and crossover rates simultaneously. These early works have shown promising results comparing to traditional GAs. However, such schemes can make the mutation/crossover rates quickly decline to zero, causing undesirable results. To overcome such an issue, in [12], a fixed lower boundary of $1/n$ (n is the length of chromosome) is introduced. In [14], Kruisselbrink studied the dynamics of a fixed lower boundary approach and proposed an alternative rule to update the boundary of mutation. In [10], Glickman and Sycara identified multiple conditions that lead to the above issue, such as the learning rate, the relationship between mutation rate and selection pressure. In [15], Rijn applied a self-adaptive GA to the container loading problem. In this method, the self-adaptive scheme is coupled with a strategy, which regularly performs a reset of mutation rate p to 0.2. In [16], Kivijärvi et al. introduced a GA-based cluster-ing method, in which the crossover and mutation probability are self-adapted. The experimental results show the method is able to deliver better or comparable results than a carefully fine-tuned static GA.

In adaptive methods, certain feedback from the GA's evolution is used to guide the adjustment of parameters. Srinivas and Patnaik [17] varied the prob-abilities of crossover and mutation depending on the fitness of each selected individual and population diversity. Kenny [18] presented an adaptive GA to solve the vehicle routing problem with time windows (VRPTW) based on a population diversity measure and achieved promising results. Ginley et al. [19] introduced a population diversity measure called standard population diversity (SPD) to adapt the crossover and mutation rate. In [20], the parent fitness is used in determining mutation probability, a parent with high fitness will be assigned with low mutation rate and vice viva. As a result, highly fit individuals are protected while the individuals with low fitness are subjected to high crossover probabilities. While in [21], Liu et al. varied the probabilities of crossover and mutation depending on the rank of individuals instead of their fitness. These methods have shown promising results, however, their effectiveness depends on the user-defined feedback rules. Since GA's run is an intrinsically dynamic, adap-tive process, it is quite difficult to define feedback rules, which can appropriately reflect such a process.

3   Clustering Problem

The task of clustering is to partition a data set D into k partitions, denoted as $C(C_1 \dots C_k)$, such that data objects are similar with each other from the same cluster and dissimilar from different clusters. The similarity is generally measured based on the Euclidean distance as

$$d(x_1, x_2) = \sqrt{\sum_{m=1}^{M}(x_1^m - x_2^m)^2} \qquad (1)$$

where x_i is a data object with M attributes x_i^m $(m = 1, 2 \dots M)$.

In order to evaluate the quality of clustering solutions, the Sum of Squared Error (SSE) is typically employed. The SSE is computed as

$$SSE = \sum_{i=1}^{n} \sum_{j=1, x_i \in C_j}^{k} |x_i - \mu_j|^2 \qquad (2)$$

Here, μ_j denotes the centroid of cluster C_j. The clustering problem is therefore to optimize SSE, which is known to be NP hard.

4   Proposed Hybrid Scheme

As discussed above, adaptive and self-adaptive parameter control approaches have different pros and cons, which may complement with each other. Here,

Algorithm 1. Adaptive GA

1: Randomly initialize P individuals using real-value representation;
2: Calculate fitness value for each individual in the initial population;
3: **while** termination condition is not met **do**
4:     Select parent pairs;
5:     Apply crossover with the probability calculated according to equation (3);
6:     Perform mutation on each offspring after crossover with the probability calculated according to equation (4);
7:     Calculate fitness value of the offspring;
8: **end while**
9: Output the final solutions;

---

we investigate such a potential by proposing a hybrid scheme to dynamically control the crossover and mutation rate simultaneously. In this section, before presenting our proposed scheme, we first describe two methods, an adaptive GA (AGA) and a self-adaptive GA (SAGA), which will be used as the base of our scheme.

4.1 AGA Method

By considering the fitness of individuals as the feedback from GA's evolution process, Srinivas and Patnaik [17] proposed an adaptive method to vary mutation and crossover rates as

$$p_c = \begin{cases} k_1 \cdot \frac{f_{max}-f'}{f_{max}-f_{ave}}, & \text{if } f' \geq f_{ave} \\ k_2, & \text{if } f' < f_{ave} \end{cases} \qquad (3)$$

$$p_m = \begin{cases} k_3 \cdot \frac{f_{max}-f}{f_{max}-f_{ave}}, & \text{if } f \geq f_{ave} \\ k_4, & \text{if } f < f_{ave} \end{cases} \qquad (4)$$

where f' is the larger fitness value of parent solutions, f_{ave} is the average fitness of population, and f_{max} is the maximum fitness value of the population. Here, k_1, k_2, k_3 and k_4 are constant values within the range of $[0.0, 1.0]$. A value of 1 is assigned to k_1 and k_2, while k_3 and k_4 choose a value of 0.5, which is recommended in [17]. The outline of the method is shown in Algorithm 1.

In the above method, individuals with high fitness values will be protected by assigning them a low value of p_c and p_m. Such a method has shown to perform well on a wide range of problems. However, the rules used in this method may not appropriate capture the intrinsically dynamic, adaptive process of GA's evolution, thus limiting its performance.

4.2 SAGA Method

The self-adaptive method, as considered in this work, is proposed by Bäck [12]. In this method, a real number representation is used to encode the crossover and

---

Algorithm 2. Self-Adaptive GA

1: Randomly initialize P individuals using real value representation;
2: Calculate fitness value for each individual in the initial population;
3: **while** termination condition is not met **do**
4:       Select parent pairs;
5:       Determine the crossover and mutation rate for offspring by recombining the
            rates encoded in parents;
6:       Calculate the crossover rate according to equation (5) and then cross the parents
            with the calculated rate;
7:       Calculate the mutation rate according to equation (5) and then perform muta-
            tion on each offspring with the calculated rate;
8:       Calculate fitness value of the offspring;
9: **end while**
10: Output the final solutions;

---

mutation rate, which is added at the tail of each individual. The rate associated with each individual is then subjected to evolution using a logistic transformation model as

$$p' = (1 + \frac{1-p}{p} \cdot \exp(-\gamma \cdot N(0,1)))^{-1} \tag{5}$$

such that mutation probability p' is distributed according to a logistic normal distribution with probability density function

$$f_{p'}(x) = \frac{1}{\sqrt{2\pi}\gamma x(1-x)} \exp(\frac{-(\ln \frac{x}{1-x} - \zeta)^2}{2\gamma^2}) \tag{6}$$

where $\zeta = \ln \frac{p}{1-p}$.

The proposed model follows the principles from the continuous domain and fulfills the requirement that the expected change of p should be zero and small changes should occur with a higher probability than large ones. The parameter γ in the equation is used to control the speed of adaptation and a large (small) value of γ causes a high (low) speed of adaptation. It is empirically defined as 0.22 in [12]. The outline of the method is shown in Algorithm 2.

The working principle of SAGA is that the better values of encoded parameters are more likely to produce better offspring, which in turn get a higher change of surviving and hence lead to better parameter values. Although it works well on many practical applications, an inherent problem faced in this method is that the search strategy of the parameter values itself is subjected to premature convergence, i.e. causing the mutation rate quickly decline to zero.

4.3   Hybrid Scheme

To overcome issues of the above methods, here we propose a hybrid method, in which the AGA method is incorporated into the SAGA method to periodically reset the crossover and mutation rates. Since the AGA is capable of detecting convergence by observing fitness value and preventing the population to get stuck

---

Algorithm 3. Proposed Scheme

1: Randomly initialize P individuals using real value representation;
2: Calculate fitness value for each individual in the initial population;
3: Calculate the value of G according to equation (7) and assign it to variable target-
   Gen;
4: **while** termination condition is not met **do**
5:    Select parent pairs;
6:    Decode the crossover and mutation rate in the parents, denoted as $P_c(t)$, $P_m(t)$;
7:    **if** (currentGen = targetGen) **then**
8:       Calculate the value of G according to equation (7), and set value of target-
         Gen as targetGen = currentGen + G;
9:       Calculate $P_c^1(t)$ and $P_m^1(t)$ according to equations (3) and (4);
10:      Reset $P_c(t)$ and $P_m(t)$ with the calculated rates in all individuals;
11:   **else**
12:      Calculate $P_c^1(t)$ and $P_m^1(t)$ according to equation (5);
13:   **end if**
14:   Perform the crossover on the parent with probability $P_c^1(t)$;
15:   Perform mutation on each offspring with $P_m^1(t)$;
16: **end while**
17: Output the final solutions;

---

at local optima, the resulting values can therefore be used to guide the setting of crossover and mutation rates in SAGA. Specifically, we initially restrict the mutation rate to the range of $[0.005, 0.5]$. Then, during the evolution, the reset operation is performed at every G generations, which is define as

$$G = \frac{\xi \cdot f_{max}}{f_{ave}} \tag{7}$$

where $\xi > 0$, f_{ave} is the average fitness value of the population, and f_{max} is the maximum fitness value of the population.

According to the equation, the closer f_{ave} to f_{max} the smaller G should be. So, the reset operation will be performed more frequent along with the decline of population diversity. This operation aims to adjust the parameter values to a reasonable value when they tend to stuck at very low values and thus preventing the population from stagnation. For the experiments performed in this work, we set the value of ξ to be 20, which is experimentally determined and not supposed to be the best.

5 Application for Data Clustering

5.1 Representation

We encode the cluster centers using a real value presentation. To encode k clusters in a M dimensional space, the length of the individual is $M \times k$. The initial centers of clusters are randomly generated and only valid values are considered to be included in the initial population. The crossover rate p_c and mutation rate

Table 1. Real data sets used in the experiments

Datasets	Attributes	Objects	Clusters
Iris	4	150	3
Seeds	7	210	3
Wine	13	178	3
yeast2945	15	2945	5

p_m are attached at the tail of each individual. The initial crossover and mutation rates are also randomly generated such that $p_c \in [0, 1.0], p_m \in [0.005, 0.5]$.

5.2   Selection

Considering the characteristics of self-adaptation, with proper selection pressure, SAGA can reduce the probability of premature convergence. Therefore, tournament selection [22] is used in this paper. This selection operation selects the best individual as the parent from the candidate pool with size of s. In this selection operation, the selection pressure can be easily adjusted by changing the tournament size. The larger tournament size, the higher the resulting selection pressure will be. Here, a tournament size of 2 is used.

5.3   Crossover and Mutation

For recombination, the arithmetic crossover [23] and Gaussian mutation have been considered. The arithmetic crossover works as

$$offspring1 = a * parent1 + (1 - a) * parent2 \qquad (8)$$

$$offspring2 = (1 - a) * parent1 + a * parent2 \qquad (9)$$

where $a \in [0,1]$ and the value of constant a is assigned to be 0.5 here.

Following crossover, Gaussian mutation is performed to maintain sufficient diversity in the population. This operator adds a unit Gaussian distributed random value to the chosen gene.

5.4   Fitness Function

In the clustering analysis, minimizing the Sum of Squared Error implies minimizing the intra-cluster variance and maximizing the inter-cluster variance. The smaller SSE is, the better of cluster division. Therefore, we define $f = 1/SSE$, thus trying to maximizing the fitness.

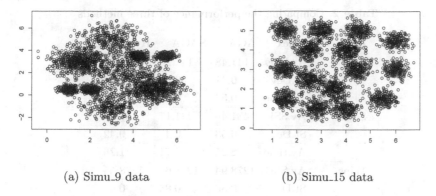

(a) Simu_9 data   (b) Simu_15 data

Fig. 1. Distribution of simulated data sets

6 Experiments

In this section, experiments are carried out to evaluate the feasibility of the proposed method. We first describe several data sets used in the experiment along with the parameter configuration. This is followed by describing the analyzing results. All results reported in this section are obtained on a PC with $i5$-2400 Processor running *Windows* 10 operation system.

6.1 Fitness Function

Both real and simulated data sets have been used for experiments. Specifically, four real data sets (Iris, Seeds, Wine and yeast2945) and two artificial data sets (Simu_9 and Simu_15) are considered. Table 1 shows the properties of data sets, including the number of attributes, number of clusters and number of the instances.

Simulated Data. The dataset Simu_9 has 3300 two-dimensional data points with 9 clusters. The 9 clusters are generated according to a spherical bivariate normal distribution as shown in Fig. 1(a). While, the Simu_15 data set has 3200 two-dimensional data points with 15 clusters as shown in Fig. 1(b). Note some noisy data objects scattering between clusters are introduced into both data sets.

Real Data. The Iris data contains 150 objects in four dimensions and it has three physical clusters. The Seeds data set is collected in three different varieties of wheat, 70 objects each, with 210 objects in total with 7 attributes. The Wine has 178 examples labeled into 3 types and each example has 13 continuous attributes, which are the results of chemical analysis of three different varieties of wine grown in the same region of Italy. The above three data sets are available at the UCI Repository [24]. The yeast2945 is a gene expression data set, and it is a subset of the yeast data [25]. In this subset, the data for the time points 90

Table 2. Comparing the performance of three methods

Datasets	Index	AGA	SAGA	Hybrid GA
Iris	Av.SSE	141.48	141.26	141.47
	St.Dev	0.31	0.39	0.42
	Av.time	0.54	0.98	0.43
Seeds	Av.SSE	431.46	431.17	431.29
	St.Dev	0.53	0.4	0.49
	Av.time	2.25	4.71	1.76
Wine	Av.SSE	1278.94	1278.67	1278.55
	St.Dev	0.86	0.85	0.6
	Av.time	8.23	15.28	6.99
yeast2945	Av.SSE	31140.3	31226.3	31175.7
	St.Dev	206.86	258.65	253.04
	Av.time	845.97	886.63	683.97
Simu_9	Av.SSE	544.72	544.46	543.58
	St.Dev	16.14	17.18	17.03
	Av.time	23.57	51.13	18.33
Simu_15	Av.SSE	205.65	208.87	204.56
	St.Dev	10.59	17.46	7.91
	Av.time	80.27	114.46	52.91

and 100 min are excluded and 2945 genes remain out of 6200 yeast genes. Here we set the number of clusters of yeast2945 to 5.

All data sets are normalized such that each attribute has an average value of 0 and a standard deviation of 1.

6.2   Results and Discussion

We performed experiments to evaluate our proposed method and compared it with AGA and SAGA based clustering methods. All results reported are the mean of best solutions obtained from 50 independent runs unless otherwise stated. To compare performance of three algorithms in terms of efficiency and solution quality, we recorded SSE values and average run rime. To make the comparison among the three algorithms more meaningful, the population size of the algorithms is set to be identical of 50. Further, the same termination condition, i.e., the fitness value of the best individual has not changed for n ($n = 50$) generations, is used for all algorithms to be compared. The results are reported in Table 2.

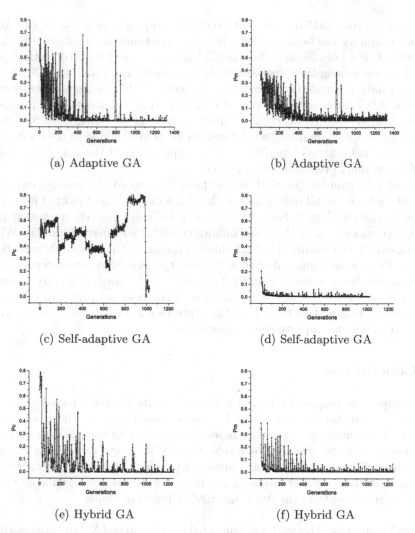

(a) Adaptive GA

(b) Adaptive GA

(c) Self-adaptive GA

(d) Self-adaptive GA

(e) Hybrid GA

(f) Hybrid GA

Fig. 2. The change of crossover and mutation rate during evolution in three different GAs

From the results, it can be seen that our proposed method can generally achieve comparable or better clustering solutions than AGA and SAGA based clustering methods. This indicates that the adaptive and self-adaptive mechanisms can complement with each other to improve the solutions. Considering the time cost, our proposed method is superior to the other two methods. Specifically, Table 2 shows, for iris and seeds datasets, which is relatively easy to solve, the three methods have comparable results in terms of SSE values while our proposed method is much efficient. On the wine data, our proposed method can deliver the best result in term of both the SSE values and time efficiency.

While, on the yeast2945 dataset (with relative complex search space), the AGA is able to produce the best solutions, however, consume much longer time than our method. For both Simu_9 and Simu_15 datasets, our proposed method performs the best among three methods to be compared. In overall, the SAGA and AGA can have comparable performance on some of the data sets to be tested. However, it is time consuming even on relatively simple datasets. Our proposed method can save up to nearly 20% time comparing to AGA, 50%–60% time comparing to SAGA on most test datasets. This is mainly due to the reset operation, which helps the GA perform further exploration of the search space and therefore prevents premature convergence.

In order to gain insight of three methods, we record the average crossover and mutation rate of all individuals of the three methods and plotted it against the generations in Fig. 2. For SAGA, it can be seen that the mutation rate quickly decreases to near the lower boundary and start hovering over it. While the crossover rate remains at a high value throughout the process of evolution, thus results in a large amount of time to converge. For AGA, crossover rate and mutation rate become small as individuals with high fitness gradually accumulated. For our proposed method, it shows that the reset operation can decrease the crossover rate and increase mutation rate in a reasonable and appropriate manor, thus helping improve the performance.

7   Conclusions

In this paper, we proposed a hybrid parameter control scheme for adapting the crossover and mutation probability. In the proposed scheme, the reset operation based on an adaptive strategy is implemented to adjust the crossover and mutation probability produced by a self-adaptive strategy. To evaluate the proposed method, we apply it for data clustering problem. Our experimental results indicate that the proposed method can efficiently deliver comparable or better clustering solutions than the AGA and SAGA based methods.

Acknowledgments. This work was supported by the National Natural Science Foundation of China (Grant No. 61573316).

References

1. Holland, J.H.: Adaptation in Natural and Artificial Systems: An Introductory Analysis with Applications to Biology, Control, and Artificial Intelligence. MIT press, Cambridge (1992)
2. Burke, E.K., Kendall, G., et al.: Search Methodologies. Springer, Heidelberg (2005)
3. Pabico, J.P., Albacea, E.A.: The interactive effects of operators and parameters to GA performance under different problem sizes. arXiv preprint arXiv:1508.00097 (2015)
4. Eiben, A.E., Smith, J.E., et al.: Introduction to Evolutionary Computing, vol. 53. Springer, Heidelberg (2003)

5. Mills, K., Filliben, J.J., Haines, A.: Determining relative importance and effective settings for genetic algorithm control parameters. Evol. Comput. **23**(2), 309–342 (2015)
6. Karafotias, G., Hoogendoorn, M., Eiben, Á.E.: Parameter control in evolutionary algorithms: trends and challenges. IEEE Trans. Evol. Comput. **19**(2), 167–187 (2015)
7. Bäck, T., Eiben, A.E., van der Vaart, N.A.L.: An emperical study on GAs "Without Parameters". In: Schoenauer, M., Deb, K., Rudolph, G., Yao, X., Lutton, E., Merelo, J.J., Schwefel, H.-P. (eds.) PPSN 2000. LNCS, vol. 1917, pp. 315–324. Springer, Heidelberg (2000). https://doi.org/10.1007/3-540-45356-3_31
8. Bäck, T.: Self-adaptation in genetic algorithms. In: Proceedings of The First European Conference on Artificial Life, pp. 263–271. MIT Press, Cambridge (1992)
9. Hinterding, R.: Gaussian mutation and self-adaption for numeric genetic algorithms. In: IEEE International Conference on Evolutionary Computation, vol. 1, p. 384. IEEE (1995)
10. Glickman, M.R., Sycara, K.: Reasons for premature convergence of self-adapting mutation rates. In: Proceedings of the 2000 Congress on Evolutionary Computation, vol. 1, pp. 62–69. IEEE (2000)
11. Fogarty, T.C.: Varying the probability of mutation in the genetic algorithm. In: Proceedings of the Third International Conference on Genetic Algorithms, pp. 104–109. Morgan Kaufmann Publishers Inc., San Francisco (1989)
12. Bäck, T., Schütz, M.: Intelligent mutation rate control in canonical genetic algorithms. In: Raś, Z.W., Michalewicz, M. (eds.) ISMIS 1996. LNCS, vol. 1079, pp. 158–167. Springer, Heidelberg (1996). https://doi.org/10.1007/3-540-61286-6_141
13. Smith, J.E., Fogarty, T.C.: Adaptively parameterised evolutionary systems: self adaptive recombination and mutation in a genetic algorithm. In: Voigt, H.-M., Ebeling, W., Rechenberg, I., Schwefel, H.-P. (eds.) PPSN 1996. LNCS, vol. 1141, pp. 441–450. Springer, Heidelberg (1996). https://doi.org/10.1007/3-540-61723-X_1008
14. Kruisselbrink, J.W., Li, R., Reehuis, E., Eggermont, J., Bäck, T.: On the lognormal self-adaptation of the mutation rate in binary search spaces. In: Proceedings of the 13th Annual Conference on Genetic and Evolutionary Computation, pp. 893–900. ACM (2011)
15. van Rijn, S., Emmerich, M., Reehuis, E., Bäck, T.: Optimizing highly constrained truck loadings using a self-adaptive genetic algorithm. In: 2015 IEEE Congress on Evolutionary Computation (CEC), pp. 227–234. IEEE (2015)
16. Kivijärvi, J., Fränti, P., Nevalainen, O.: Self-adaptive genetic algorithm for clustering. J. Heuristics **9**(2), 113–129 (2003)
17. Srinivas, M., Patnaik, L.M.: Adaptive probabilities of crossover and mutation in genetic algorithms. IEEE Trans. Syst. Man Cybern. B **24**(4), 656–667 (1994)
18. Zhu, K.Q.: A diversity-controlling adaptive genetic algorithm for the vehicle routing problem with time windows. In: Proceedings of the 15th IEEE International Conference on Tools with Artificial Intelligence, pp. 176–183. IEEE (2003)
19. Mc Ginley, B., Maher, J., O'Riordan, C., Morgan, F.: Maintaining healthy population diversity using adaptive crossover, mutation, and selection. IEEE Trans. Evol. Comput. **15**(5), 692–714 (2011)
20. Thierens, D.: Adaptive mutation rate control schemes in genetic algorithms. In: Proceedings of the 2002 Congress on Evolutionary Computation, CEC 2002, vol. 1, pp. 980–985. IEEE (2002)

21. Liu, Z., Zhou, J., Lai, S.: New adaptive genetic algorithm based on ranking. In: 2003 International Conference on Machine Learning and Cybernetics, vol. 3, pp. 1841–1844. IEEE (2003)
22. Deb, K.: An introduction to genetic algorithms. Sadhana **24**, 293–315 (1999)
23. Michalewicz, Z.: Genetic Algorithms + Data Structures = Evolution Programs. Springer, Heidelberg (1996)
24. Lichman, M.: UCI machine learning repository (2013). http://archive.ics.uci.edu/ml
25. Cho, R.J., Campbell, M.J., Winzeler, E.A., Steinmetz, L., Conway, A., Wodicka, L., Wolfsberg, T.G., Gabrielian, A.E., Landsman, D., Lockhart, D.J., et al.: A genome-wide transcriptional analysis of the mitotic cell cycle. Mol. Cell **2**(1), 65–73 (1998)

Population Control in Evolutionary Algorithms: Review and Comparison

Yuyang Guan[1], Ling Yang[1], and Weiguo Sheng[2(✉)]

[1] College of Computer Science, Zhejiang University of Technology,
Hangzhou 310023, Zhejiang, People's Republic of China
[2] Department of Computer Science, Hangzhou Normal University,
Hangzhou 311121, Zhejiang, People's Republic of China
w.sheng@ieee.org

Abstract. Population size in evolutionary algorithms (EAs) is critical
for their performance. In this paper, we first give a comprehensive review
of existing population control methods. Then, a few representative methods are selected and empirically compared on a range of well-known
benchmark functions to show their pros and cons.

Keywords: Evolutionary algorithms · Population control · Parameter
control

1 Introduction

Evolutionary algorithms (EAs) are a broad class of stochastic search heuristics
that perform optimization or learning tasks. While they have been successfully
applied to various science and engineering problems, the performance of EAs
depends critically on the setting of various parameters [1], among which the
population size is perhaps the most important one. Generally, a too small population size will lead to the premature convergence of EAs, while a too large
size will reduce the EAs' efficiency. In traditional EAs, the population size is
typically specified by the user to a fixed value and remains constant during the
entire evolution. However, it has been well recognized that the optimal size of
population is problem-specific [2–6]. Further, it has been demonstrated that different population sizes may be required at different stages of evolution [7–10].
To specify the population size in such a manner therefore may significantly limit
the performance of EAs.

To deal with the above issue, dynamic population control has become an
active yet important research topic and many different schemes have been proposed in literature [9,11–14]. Several works of reviewing or comparing existing
methods have been presented. In 1999, Costa [2] gave a comparative study of
population control methods, in which five dynamic population control schemes
are reviewed and compared. More than a decade later, Karafotias [15] provided
a survey regarding to the parameter control in EAs. Although a few dynamic

© Springer Nature Singapore Pte Ltd. 2017
C. He et al. (Eds.): BIC-TA 2017, CCIS 791, pp. 161–174, 2017.
https://doi.org/10.1007/978-981-10-7179-9_13

population control methods have been reviewed, this work focuses mainly on parameter setting schemes for variation operators of EAs. Recently, Piotrowski [16] presented another review along with comparison results of several dynamic population control schemes. The scope of this work, however, is limited to the differential evolution (DE).

In this paper, we give a comprehensive review of the population control methods proposed in EA literature. Further, several representative methods have been selected and compared to gain deep understanding of their pros and cons.

2   Population Control in Evolutionary Algorithms

Much work has been carried out regarding to the control of population size in EAs. In this section, we first provide an overview of theoretical studies in the field and then review exiting methods, which are divided in three categories, i.e., deterministic, adaptive and self-adaptive methods.

2.1   Theoretical Studies

In [17], Holdener recognized that the optimal allocation of trials in genetic algorithm (GA) characterized by the conjunction of substantial complexity and initial uncertainty as well as a requirement of employing new information in the population to rapidly reduce this uncertainty. This area remains untouched for many years until Goldberg studied the population size as a parameter from a theoretical point of view based on the decomposition for designing competent GAs. In this work, Goldberg [18] considers the evolution of GA as the growth of building blocks (BBs) and points out that a successful GA should ensure an adequate supply of BBs in the initial population. In [19], Reeves calculated the minimum population size required for at least one instance of every allele being presented at each locus in binary string as well as n-nary representation. While having all alleles present in the initial population is important, this work suggests that the present of desired building blocks in the initial population is crucial for the GAs' performance. Later, in [20], Goldberg determined the probability of actual building blocks presented in a population and developed models to calculate population size required for the success probability of GA asymptotically reaching 100%. Apart from the building block theory, the population size has also been studied under the statistical decision. In [21], De Jong presented several equations to determine the population size based on the noise theory in statistical decision. In [7], Goldberg extended the equations to calculate the size of population based on the permissible errors between building blocks, variation and complexity of the problem. While, in [22], Harik developed an alternative equation to predict the quality of solution found in a given population size based on the theory of random walks and gamblers ruin. Unfortunately, the above theoretical studies are generally not practical for real applications. However, they do reveal that the population size is crucial for the performance of EAs.

2.2   Deterministic Methods

To deal with the issue of population size, many methods seek to dynamically change it during evolution based on deterministic rules. In [12,23–25], Fernández et al. presented a method based on the phenomena of plague [12], in which a fixed number of individuals (i.e., the worst ones) are removed at every generation of evolution. Instead of removing individuals at each generation, Brest [13] proposed a method, which gradually reduces the population size by half each time when a specific condition is met during the evolution. This reduction mechanism has been successfully used in EAs for solving various optimization problems [26–32]. Extending the above mechanism, in [33], Brest et al. designed a method, which starts with a small population size at the beginning. Then, during the evolution, the population is first increased with a specific size determined by a constant value and then reduced by half. Although it has shown to be promising [33], Neri [34] pointed out that such a method is not working well in DE. Rather than increasing or decreasing a specific number of individual after each specific number of generations during evolution, a few methods have been proposed to automatically adjust the size of population based on predefined functions. For example, Koumousis et al. introduced functions with saw-tooth shape [35] and sinusoidal oscillating [36] for adjusting the population size. Other functions, such as linear functions [30,37,38] have also been used for population control and applied in various optimization problems [39–42].

2.3   Adaptive Methods

Adaptive methods utilize feedback from the search to determine the direction and magnitude of change of population size. Based on the feedback information used, we divide the existing methods into three categories and review them accordingly.

Fitness Based Methods. The methods falling into this category adaptively change the population size based on the fitness of individuals. In [43–47], the size of a population is modified if the fitness of the best individual does not change for a period of time. Specifically, Montiel [43] et al. calculated the amounts of individuals should be inserted or deleted from the population based on two variables, "Cycling" and "Variance". The "Cycling" is used to account the number of times that the fitness of the best individual does not have a significant change and the "Variance" is used to calculate the variance of the fitness of the best individuals during the "Cycling" period. In [44], new individuals are inserted into the population when the fitness of the best individual does not improve in m generations. In [45,48], the population is first ordered based on the fitness of individuals and a predefined percent of individuals is inserted or deleted from the population. In [46], a predefined number of individuals are added if the best individual does not change for m generations while the population is resized to its initial size if the best individual improves its fitness. In [47], a new population is created by selecting good individuals from an extinguished population when extinction occurs, and at every generation, individuals will be eliminated when they reach their lifetime. In [49–53], subpopulations are used for competitive evolution and are resized based their fitness. Typically, when the average fitness of a subpopulation falls below a predefined significance level, it will be removed. Specifically, in [50], Smorodkina provided a competition scheme between two parallel subpopulations, while Hinterding [51] and Harik [52] do not restrict the number of subpopulations. Schlierkamp-Voosen [49] employs a migration scheme, in which the best individual is migrated to all other subpopulations. While, Zhan [53] suggested that all the poor subpopulations randomly migrate one individual to the good subpopulations.

Apart from the above methods, some methods employ lifetime and survival probability, which is derived from the fitness, to control the population size. The classical method is the Genetic Algorithm with Varying Population Size (GAVaPS) proposed by Arabas et al. [11], which introduced the concept of age for the individual. In this method, population size is dictated by birth and death of individuals, controlled by their lifetime and measured by fitness. Proceeding in a generational manner, each individual's age is increased at each time step and removed when it exceeds its lifetime. The lifetime mechanism is extended using non-random mating to prevent incest by Fernándes et al. [54,55], and applied to multimodal optimization [56], vehicle detection [57] and distribution network reconfiguration [10]. The main drawback of GAVaPS is that, in the worst case, the population size will be doubled in the successive generations thus may lead to population explosion. To address such an issue, Bäck [58] proposed to preserve all the fittest individuals and only two new individuals will be generated and inserted into the population at each generation. This scheme has been applied to co-operative co-evolution by Lorio and Li [59]. In [47], Zhang developed an extinction scheme for population control. In this scheme, individuals will be eliminated if there are no improvements made during the evolution. While, in [60], Vellev introduced the concept of survival probability, which defines a collective probability used to control the size of the population. Along this line, Cook [61] described another formula to calculate the survival probability for population size control.

Distribution Based Methods. This kind of methods control the population size based on the distribution information of population. In [7], Goldberg first proposed a micro GA in which the population is reinitialized when a nominal convergence (e.g., when all the individuals have either identical or very similar genotypes) is detected. In [62], a similar re-initialization scheme is introduced with an elitist strategy along with a competition scheme, which chooses the winner individuals to be included into the population. The micro GA has been successfully applied in various applications [63–65], which show a better performance compared to the standard GA. Another way to measure the distribution of population is to calculate the distance between individuals. In [66,67], Khor and Tan suggested the desired population size should be bounded within a limit, measured by the maximum distance between each other in the population.

Liang [68] combined the relative ascending directions and the distance between two individuals to determine whether they are located in the same peak. This information is then used for population control. In [69], Yang calculated the sum Euclidean distances and generated a new population if it does not change for a period of time. While in [70], the individual with the smallest Euclidean distance will be removed at every generation as a mechanism for population control. In [71], Auge introduced a dispersion degree for population control. A population initialization is launched when the calculated dispersion degree meets the stopping criterion and the population size is increased by a factor of 2. In addition, Shi [72] assumed the center of the population moved slowly when the variance of population is large. In this case, the population size is decreased to accelerate the speed of convergence and vice versa.

Fitness and Distribution Based Methods. The methods in this category are based on both the fitness and distribution information for population control. Smith [73] presented such a method, in which the mean fitness and variance of population is calculated and compared to a predefined desired value to decide whether assign more (or less) individuals to a population. This method was extended by Harik [22], in which the distance between the best and second best BBs is also considered. In [74], Tirronen provided a method based on fitness diversity measured by the distance between pairs of individuals along with their fitness values to control population size.

Population Status Based Methods. These methods change the population size when the current population status meets a certain condition. They have been used in genetic programming (GP), where solutions are represented as trees of variable size and depth, for population control. In [75], Wagner proposed to employ the node information for population control. Two kinds of nodes (i.e., soft and hard) are used and the soft node is employed to control the addition of new individuals to a population while the hard node is used to control which individuals might be added. This method has been used in GP to address forecasting problem in [76,77]. In [70], Ding presented an artificial bee colony algorithm where the colony size is used to control the reproduction and death rate of the population. If the colony size is larger than the initial size, the reproduction rate threshold will be increased while the death threshold is decreased.

2.4   Self-adaptive Methods

This approach encodes the population size to be adapted into the individuals and undergo mutation and recombination. Such a method was first proposed by Teo [78] to adapt the population size in different evolution (DE). The method, however, shows no significant advantages over the DE with fixed population sizes. In [79], Eiben discussed such an approach and proposed a hybrid variant of self-adaptive method for GA. The work shows that it is possible to define the population size at individual level. The results show that the proposed method has better performance than GAs with fixed population sizes.

Table 1. Parameter setting of the six algorithms

Methods	Parameter	Values
dynNP-DE	Number of different population sizes (P_{max})	4
	Crossover operator	2-point
SAMDE	The sign of trigger (P)	P = 0: increase
		P = 4: decrease
	Crossover operator	2-point
GAVaPS	MaxLifeTime/MinLifeTime	7/1
	The rate of choosing individuals to reproduce	40%
APAGA	MaxLifeTime/MinLifeTime	11/1
	The rate of choosing individuals to reproduce	Fixed 2
PL-GA	Crossover operator	Uniform
GPS-GA	Crossover operator	Uniform

3 Experimental Comparison

In this section, we shall experimentally compare several representative methods for dynamically population control to show their advantages and disadvantages. In the following subsections, after describing the data sets in Subsect. 3.1 and the parameter settings of the algorithms in Subsect. 3.2, we report the comparison results in Subsect. 3.3.

3.1 Test Suit

To access the performance of different population control strategies, a range of well-known benchmark test functions have been considered. For the unimodal case, we select four functions presented in [21] with minimum value zero, the Sphere Model, Griewangk's Function, Step Function and Quartic Function. For the multi-model case, the Rastrigin's function [29], Six-Hump Camel Back Function, Branin Function and Goldstein-Price's Function have been considered. In addition, the Schwefel's Function [71], which is a deceptive function, and the Rosenbrock's Valley Function [16], which has a very complex search space, has also been considered.

3.2 Algorithms and Parameter Settings

The following six population control algorithms have been selected for comparison. The GAVaPS [11], in which each newly born individual is allocated with a lifetime measured by fitness. Proceeding in a generational manner, individual's age is increased at each generation and removed when it exceeded its lifetime. The APAGA [58], which is similar as the GAVaPS with an exception that the fittest member will always kept in the population. In addition, only two new

Table 2. Comparison results of six methods on 10 benchmark functions

Fun.	No. of Calls	Methods					
		GAVaPS	APAGA	PL-GA	GPS-GA	dynNP-DE	SAMDE
f_1	100000	5.02E−05	**5.01E−05**	5.02E−05	5.04E−05	5.02E−05	5.02E−05
f_2	250000	4.94E−02	5.14E−02	5.74E−02	4.91E−02	5.08E−02	**3.87E−02**
f_3	200000	0.11E+00	0.11E+00	**0.00E+00**	**0.00E+00**	**0.00E+00**	**0.00E+00**
f_4	300000	7.43E−03	**3.52E−03**	1.05E−02	1.56E−02	1.59E−02	1.23E−02
f_5	100000	−1.02E+01	−1.02E+00	**−1.03E+00**	−1.02E+00	**−1.03E+00**	**−1.03E+00**
f_6	200000	0.40E+00	0.45E+00	**0.39E+00**	**0.39E+00**	0.40E+00	0.40E+00
f_7	200000	0.31E+01	0.31E+01	0.31E+01	0.39E+01	**0.30E+01**	0.31E+01
f_8	300000	2.86E−02	3.25E−01	2.42E−02	5.73E−02	**1.76E−02**	2.64E−02
f_9	100000	−8.38E+02	−8.38E+02	**−8.37E+02**	−8.36E+02	**−8.37E+02**	−8.36E+02
f_{10}	300000	3.89E+04	3.89E+04	3.88E+04	3.89E+04	**3.90E+04**	**3.90E+04**

individuals will be generated and inserted into the population at each generation. The PL-GA [17], which starts with a small population size and doubling the population size when the GA converges. The GPS-GA [50], in which two subpopulations are evolved in parallel. The dynNP-DE [13], in which the population size is periodically descending during the evolution, and the new population size is equal to half the previous population size. The SAMDE [45], in which the population diversity is considered to increase or decrease the population sizes. These algorithms are based on different rationales for population control and have been widely applied for various applications.

The parameter setting for the six algorithms are taken from the original papers. However, to make the comparison fair, a few parameters, which are common for these algorithms, are set as the same values. Specifically, the initial population size N of 20, crossover rate of 0.65 and bit mutation operator rate 0.015 are used. All algorithms to be compared adopt the tournament operator for selection. The other parameter settings for the six algorithms are shown in Table 1.

3.3 Results and Discussion

The comparison results of the six algorithms are shown in Table 2 in terms of solution quality. Each algorithm is run on each function 10 times. The best results over the ten trials are then averaged. From the results, it can be seen that the dynNP-DE and SAMDE algorithms outperform other four algorithms on f_1, f_3, f_5, f_7, f_9 functions. Between the dynNP-DE and SAMDE, the dynNP-DE shows better performances on multi-model functions, while SAMDE is good at searching the unimodal functions. From the function point of view, for the function f_3, dynNP-DE, SAMDE, PL-GA and GPS-GA can identify the global optimum, while the GAVaPS and APAGA fail to do so. This result could suggest that frequently removing individuals from the population will decrease the robustness of the algorithm. For the functions f_6, only PL-GA and GPS-GA is

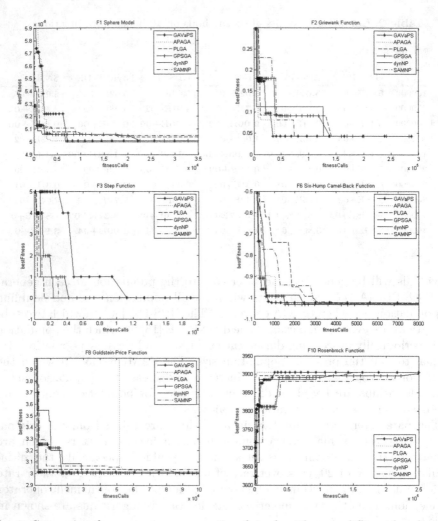

Fig. 1. Comparing the convergence properties of six algorithms on different benchmark

able to find promising solutions. For the function f_8, which is the most difficult to solve among the ten functions, it can be noticed that all algorithms can be trapped in local optimum. In overall, dynNP-DE performs the best as it could deliver the best results on most of test functions. This is followed by the SAMDE, PL-GA and GPS-GA.

Figure 1 shows the convergence properties of the six strategies, in which the average of best fitness values are plotted versus the actual function evaluations of the six algorithms. It can be observed that GAVaPS and APAGA can converge much faster than the dynNP-DE, SAMDE, PL-GA and GPS-GA. For example, on the test function f_{10}, GAVaPS and APAGA are able to identify the optimal solution with around $4 * 10^3$ function evaluations. Specifically, on unimodal functions, for instance, f_1, f_2, PL-GA and GPS-GA perform the worst in terms of convergence and can take more than $1 * 10^4$ function evaluations to converge than other four algorithms. Generally, PL-GA is the slowest method among the six methods, while the GPS-GA is the fastest strategy.

From both the quality and convergence property, it can be generally concluded that the GAVaPS and APAGA perform well on unimodal functions and its extended version APAGA has even better performance. The main fault of GAVaPS is excessive growth of individuals and results in an expensive evolution while APAGA slows down the increasing rate of population and improves its efficiency. The PL-GA and GPS-GA have good performance for multi-model functions especially in terms of convergence speed. While, the dynNP-DE and SAMDE algorithms can perform the best in most of the test functions by average.

4 Conclusions

In this paper, we first present an extensive review of population control methods in evolutionary algorithms. Then, we experimentally examine and analyze a few representative methods on a set of well-known benchmark functions. The results show that the dynNP-DE perform the best in most of the test functions by average. This mainly due to the dynNP-DE is able to maintain a proper balance of exploration and exploitation thus achieving a good performance.

Acknowledgments. This work was supported by the National Natural Science Foundation of China (Grant No. 61573316).

References

1. De Jong, K.: Parameter setting in EAs: a 30 year perspective. In: Lobo, F.G., Lima, C.F., Michalewicz, Z. (eds.) Parameter Setting in Evolutionary Algorithms. SCI, vol. 54, pp. 1–18. Springer, Heidelberg (2007). https://doi.org/10.1007/978-3-540-69432-8_1
2. Costa, J.C., Tavares, R., Rosa, A.: An experimental study on dynamic random variation of population size. In: 1999 IEEE International Conference on Systems, Man, and Cybernetics, IEEE SMC 1999 Conference Proceedings, vol. 1, pp. 607–612. IEEE (1999)
3. Eiben, Á.E., Hinterding, R., Michalewicz, Z.: Parameter control in evolutionary algorithms. IEEE Trans. Evol. Comput. **3**(2), 124–141 (1999)
4. Eiben, A.E., Marchiori, E., Valkó, V.A.: Evolutionary algorithms with on-the-fly population size adjustment. In: Yao, X., et al. (eds.) PPSN 2004. LNCS, vol. 3242, pp. 41–50. Springer, Heidelberg (2004). https://doi.org/10.1007/978-3-540-30217-9_5
5. Hu, T., Banzhaf, W.: The role of population size in rate of evolution in genetic programming. In: Vanneschi, L., Gustafson, S., Moraglio, A., De Falco, I., Ebner, M. (eds.) EuroGP 2009. LNCS, vol. 5481, pp. 85–96. Springer, Heidelberg (2009). https://doi.org/10.1007/978-3-642-01181-8_8

6. Romero, G., Mora, A.M., Fernandes, C.: Studying the effect of population size in distributed evolutionary algorithms on heterogeneous clusters. Appl. Soft. Comput. **38**(C), 530–547 (2016)
7. Goldberg, D.E.: Sizing populations for serial and parallel genetic algorithms. In: Proceedings of the 3rd International Conference on Genetic Algorithms, pp. 70–79 (1989)
8. Schaffer, J.: A study of control parameters affecting online performance of genetic algorithms for function optimization, San Meteo, California (1989)
9. Smith, R.E., Smuda, E.: Adaptively resizing populations: algorithm, analysis, and first results. Complex Syst. **9**, 47–72 (1995)
10. Weise, T., Wu, Y., Chiong, R.J.: Global versus local search: the impact of population sizes on evolutionary algorithm performance. J. Global. Optim. **66**(3), 511–534 (2016)
11. Arabas, J., Michalewicz, Z., Mulawka, J.: GAVaPS-a genetic algorithm with varying population size. In: Proceedings of the First IEEE Conference on Evolutionary Computation, IEEE World Congress on Computational Intelligence, pp. 73–78. IEEE (1994)
12. Fernández, F., Tomassini, M., Vanneschi, L.: An empirical study of multipopulation genetic programming. Genetic Program. Evol. Mach. **4**(1), 21–51 (2003)
13. Brest, J., Maučec, M.S.: Population size reduction for the differential evolution algorithm. Appl. Intell. **29**(3), 228–247 (2008)
14. Ahrari, A., Shariat-Panahi, M.: An improved evolution strategy with adaptive population size. Optimization **64**(12), 2567–2586 (2015)
15. Karafotias, G., Hoogendoorn, M., Eiben, Á.E.: Parameter control in evolutionary algorithms: trends and challenges. IEEE Trans. Evol. Comput. **19**(2), 167–187 (2015)
16. Piotrowski, A.P.: Review of differential evolution population size. Swarm Evol. Comput. **32**, 1–24 (2017)
17. Holdener, E.A.: The art of parameterless evolutionary algorithms. Ph.D. thesis, Missouri University of Science and Technology (2008)
18. Goldberg, D.E., Deb, K., Clark, J.H.: Genetic algorithms, noise, and the sizing of populations. Urbana **51**, 61801 (1991)
19. Reeves, C.R.: Using genetic algorithms with small populations. In: ICGA, vol. 590, p. 92 (1993)
20. Goldberg, D.E., Sastry, K., Latoza, T.: On the supply of building blocks. In: Proceedings of the 3rd Annual Conference on Genetic and Evolutionary Computation, pp. 336–342. Morgan Kaufmann Publishers Inc. (2001)
21. De Jong, K.A.: Analysis of the behavior of a class of genetic adaptive systems (1975)
22. Harik, G., Cantú-Paz, E., Goldberg, D.E., Miller, B.L.: The Gambler's ruin problem, genetic algorithms, and the sizing of populations. Evol. Comput. **7**(3), 231–253 (1999)
23. Fernandez, F., Vanneschi, L., Tomassini, M.: The effect of plagues in genetic programming: a study of variable-size populations. In: Ryan, C., Soule, T., Keijzer, M., Tsang, E., Poli, R., Costa, E. (eds.) EuroGP 2003. LNCS, vol. 2610, pp. 317–326. Springer, Heidelberg (2003). https://doi.org/10.1007/3-540-36599-0_29
24. Fernandez, F., Tomassini, M., Vanneschi, L.: Saving computational effort in genetic programming by means of plagues. In: The 2003 Congress on Evolutionary Computation, CEC 2003, vol. 3, pp. 2042–2049. IEEE (2003)

25. de Vega, F.F., Cantú-Paz, E., López, J.I., Manzano, T.: Saving resources with plagues in genetic algorithms. In: Yao, X., et al. (eds.) PPSN 2004. LNCS, vol. 3242, pp. 272–281. Springer, Heidelberg (2004). https://doi.org/10.1007/978-3-540-30217-9_28

26. Brest, J., Zamuda, A., Fister, I., Maučec, M.S.: Large scale global optimization using self-adaptive differential evolution algorithm. In: 2010 IEEE Congress on Evolutionary Computation (CEC), pp. 1–8. IEEE (2010)

27. Brest, J., Maučec, M.S.: Self-adaptive differential evolution algorithm using population size reduction and three strategies. Soft Comput. 15(11), 2157–2174 (2011)

28. Zamuda, A., Brest, J., Mezura-Montes, E.: Structured population size reduction differential evolution with multiple mutation strategies on CEC 2013 real parameter optimization. In: 2013 IEEE Congress on Evolutionary Computation (CEC), pp. 1925–1931. IEEE (2013)

29. Yang, M., Cai, Z., Guan, J., Gong, W.: Differential evolution with improved population reduction. In: Proceedings of the 13th Annual Conference Companion on Genetic and Evolutionary Computation, pp. 143–144. ACM (2011)

30. Ali, M.Z., Awad, N.H., Suganthan, P.N., Reynolds, R.G.: An adaptive multipopulation differential evolution with dynamic population reduction. IEEE Trans. Cybern. 47(9), 2768–2779 (2017)

31. Iacca, G., Mallipeddi, R., Mininno, E., Neri, F.: Super-fit and population size reduction in compact differential evolution. In: Memetic Computing, pp. 1–8 (2011)

32. Zamuda, A., Brest, J.: Population reduction differential evolution with multiple mutation strategies in real world industry challenges. In: Rutkowski, L., Korytkowski, M., Scherer, R., Tadeusiewicz, R., Zadeh, L.A., Zurada, J.M. (eds.) EC/SIDE -2012. LNCS, vol. 7269, pp. 154–161. Springer, Heidelberg (2012). https://doi.org/10.1007/978-3-642-29353-5_18

33. Brest, J., Zamuda, A., Fister, I., Maučec, M.S., et al.: Self-adaptive differential evolution algorithm with a small and varying population size. In: 2012 IEEE Congress on Evolutionary Computation (CEC), pp. 1–8. IEEE (2012)

34. Neri, F., Tirronen, V.: Recent advances in differential evolution: a survey and experimental analysis. Artif. Intell. Rev. 33(1–2), 61–106 (2010)

35. Koumousis, V.K., Katsaras, C.P.: A saw-tooth genetic algorithm combining the effects of variable population size and reinitialization to enhance performance. IEEE Trans. Evol. Comput. 10(1), 19–28 (2006)

36. Koumousis, V., Dimou, C.: The effect of oscillating population size on the performance of genetic algorithms. In: Proceedings of the 4th GRACM Congress on Computational Mechanics (2002)

37. Tanabe, R., Fukunaga, A.S.: Improving the search performance of shade using linear population size reduction. In: 2014 IEEE Congress on Evolutionary Computation (CEC), pp. 1658–1665. IEEE (2014)

38. Yuan, X., Zhang, B., Wang, P., Liang, J., Yuan, Y., Huang, Y., Lei, X.: Multiobjective optimal power flow based on improved strength pareto evolutionary algorithm. Energy 122, 70–82 (2017)

39. Polakova, R., Tvrdik, J., Bujok, P.: Evaluating the performance of l-shade with competing strategies on CEC 2014 single parameter-operator test suite. In: IEEE Congress on Evolutionary Computation, pp. 1181–1187 (2016)

40. Viktorin, A., Pluhacek, M., Senkerik, R.: Network based linear population size reduction in shade. In: International Conference on Intelligent Networking and Collaborative Systems, pp. 86–93 (2016)

41. Guo, S.M., Tsai, S.H., Yang, C.C., Hsu, P.H.: A self-optimization approach for l-shade incorporated with eigenvector-based crossover and successful-parent-selecting framework on CEC 2015 benchmark set. In: Evolutionary Computation, pp. 1003–1010 (2015)
42. Zheng, Y.J., Zhang, B.: A simplified water wave optimization algorithm. In: Evolutionary Computation, pp. 807–813 (2015)
43. Montiel, O., Castillo, O., Melin, P., Sepúlveda, R.: Intelligent control of dynamic population size for evolutionary algorithms. In: IC-AI, pp. 551–557 (2006)
44. Wang, H., Rahnamayan, S., Wu, Z.: Adaptive differential evolution with variable population size for solving high-dimensional problems. In: 2011 IEEE Congress on Evolutionary Computation (CEC), pp. 2626–2632. IEEE (2011)
45. Wang, X., Zhao, S., Jin, Y., Zhang, L.: Differential evolution algorithm based on self-adaptive adjustment mechanism. In: 2013 25th Chinese Control and Decision Conference (CCDC), pp. 577–581. IEEE (2013)
46. Elsayed, S.M., Sarker, R.A.: Differential evolution with automatic population injection scheme for constrained problems. In: 2013 IEEE Symposium on Differential Evolution (SDE), pp. 112–118. IEEE (2013)
47. Zhang, C., Chen, J., Xin, B., Cai, T., Chen, C.: Differential evolution with adaptive population size combining lifetime and extinction mechanisms. In: 2011 8th Asian Control Conference (ASCC), pp. 1221–1226. IEEE (2011)
48. Zhao, S., Wang, X., Chen, L., Zhu, W.: A novel self-adaptive differential evolution algorithm with population size adjustment scheme. Arab. J. Sci. Eng. **39**(8), 6149–6174 (2014)
49. Schlierkamp-Voosen, D., Muhlenbein, H.: Adaptation of population sizes by competing subpopulations. In: Proceedings of IEEE International Conference on Evolutionary Computation, pp. 330–335. IEEE (1996)
50. Smorodkina, E., Tauritz, D.: Greedy population sizing for evolutionary algorithms. In: IEEE Congress on Evolutionary Computation, CEC 2007, pp. 2181–2187. IEEE (2007)
51. Hinterding, R., Michalewicz, Z., Peachey, T.C.: Self-adaptive genetic algorithm for numeric functions. In: Voigt, H.-M., Ebeling, W., Rechenberg, I., Schwefel, H.-P. (eds.) PPSN 1996. LNCS, vol. 1141, pp. 420–429. Springer, Heidelberg (1996). https://doi.org/10.1007/3-540-61723-X_1006
52. Harik, G.R., Lobo, F.G.: A parameter-less genetic algorithm. In: Proceedings of the 1st Annual Conference on Genetic and Evolutionary Computation, vol. 1, pp. 258–265. Morgan Kaufmann Publishers Inc. (1999)
53. Zhan, Z.H., Zhang, J.: Co-evolutionary differential evolution with dynamic population size and adaptive migration strategy. In: Proceedings of the 13th Annual Conference Companion on Genetic and Evolutionary Computation, pp. 211–212. ACM (2011)
54. Fernándes, C., Rosa, A.C., Rosa, A.C.: NiGaVaPS - a outbreeding in genetic algorithms. In: ACM Symposium on Applied Computing, pp. 477–482 (2000)
55. Fernándes, C., Rosa, A.: Self-regulated population size in evolutionary algorithms. In: International Conference on Parallel Problem Solving from Nature, pp. 920–929 (2006)
56. Fernándes, C., Rosa, A., Pais, A.R., Norte, T.: A study on non-random mating and varying population size in genetic algorithms using a royal road function. In: Proceedings of the 2001 Congress on Evolutionary Computation, vol. 1, pp. 60–66 (2001)
57. Lee, H.S., Lee, J.H., Kim, E.T.: Optimal classifier ensemble design for vehicle detection using GAVaPS. J. Inst. Control Robot. Syst. **16**(1), 96–100 (2010)

58. Bäck, T., Eiben, A.E., Van Der Vaart, N.A.L.: An empirical study on gas "Without Parameters". In: International Conference on Parallel Problem Solving from Nature, pp. 315–324 (2000)
59. Iorio, A., Li, X.: Parameter control within a co-operative co-evolutionary genetic algorithm. In: Guervós, J.J.M., Adamidis, P., Beyer, H.-G., Schwefel, H.-P., Fernández-Villacañas, J.-L. (eds.) PPSN 2002. LNCS, vol. 2439, pp. 247–256. Springer, Heidelberg (2002). https://doi.org/10.1007/3-540-45712-7_24
60. Vellev, S.: An adaptive genetic algorithm with dynamic population size for optimizing join queries. Adv. Res. Artif. Int. **82**, 82–88 (2008)
61. Cook, J.E., Tauritz, D.R.: An exploration into dynamic population sizing. In: Conference on Genetic and Evolutionary Computation, pp. 807–814 (2010)
62. Krishnakumar, K.: Micro-genetic algorithms for stationary and non-stationary function optimization. In: 1989 Symposium on Visual Communications, Image Processing, and Intelligent Robotics Systems, pp. 289–296. International Society for Optics and Photonics (1990)
63. Coello, C.A., Pulido, G.T.: Multiobjective optimization using a micro-genetic algorithm. In: Proceedings of the 3rd Annual Conference on Genetic and Evolutionary Computation, pp. 274–282. Morgan Kaufmann Publishers Inc. (2001)
64. Xu, Y., Liu, G.: Detection of flaws in composites from scattered elastic-wave field using an improved μGA and a local optimizer. Comput. Methods Appl. Mech. **191**(36), 3929–3946 (2002)
65. Ryoo, J., Hajela, P.: Handling variable string lengths in GA-based structural topology optimization. Struct. Multidiscip. Optim. **26**(5), 318–325 (2004)
66. Khor, E.F., Tan, K.C., Wang, M.L., Lee, T.H.: Evolutionary algorithm with dynamic population size for multi-objective optimization. In: Conference of the IEEE Industrial Electronics Society, IECON 2000, vol. 4, pp. 2768–2773 (2000)
67. Tan, K.C., Lee, T.H., Khor, E.F.: Evolutionary algorithms with dynamic population size and local exploration for multiobjective optimization. IEEE Trans. Evol. Comput. **5**(6), 565–588 (2001)
68. Liang, Y., Leung, K.S.: Genetic algorithm with adaptive elitist-population strategies for multimodal function optimization. Appl. Soft. Comput. **11**(2), 2017–2034 (2011)
69. Yang, M., Cai, Z., Guan, J., Guan, J.: An improved adaptive differential evolution algorithm with population adaptation. In: Conference on Genetic and Evolutionary Computation, pp. 145–152 (2013)
70. Ding, M., Chen, H., Lin, N., Jing, S., Liu, F., Liang, X., Liu, W.: Dynamic population artificial bee colony algorithm for multi-objective optimal power flow. Saudi. J. Biol. Sci. **24**(3), 703–710 (2017)
71. Auger, A., Hansen, N.: A restart CMA evolution strategy with increasing population size. In: The 2005 IEEE Congress on Evolutionary Computation, vol. 2, pp. 1769–1776 (2005)
72. Shi, E.C., Leung, F.H.F., Law, B.N.F.: Differential evolution with adaptive population size. In: International Conference on Digital Signal Processing, pp. 876–881 (2014)
73. Smith, R.E., Smuda, E.: Adaptively resizing populations: algorithm, analysis, and first results. Complex Syst. (1993)
74. Tirronen, V., Neri, F.: Differential evolution with fitness diversity self-adaptation. In: Chiong, R. (ed.) Nature-Inspired Algorithms for Optimisation. SCI, vol. 193, pp. 199–234. Springer, Heidelberg (2009). https://doi.org/10.1007/978-3-642-00267-0_7

75. Wagner, N., Michalewicz, Z.: Genetic Programming with Efficient Population Control for Financial Time Series Prediction (2001)
76. Wagner, N., Michalewicz, Z.: Parameter Adaptation for GP Forecasting Applications (2007)
77. Wagner, N., Michalewicz, Z., Khouja, M., Mcgregor, R.R.: Time series forecasting for dynamic environments: the DyFor genetic program model. IEEE Trans. Evol. Comput. 11(4), 433–452 (2007)
78. Teo, J.: Exploring dynamic self-adaptive populations in differential evolution. Soft Comput. 10(8), 673–686 (2006)
79. Eiben, A.E., Schut, M.C., Wilde, A.R.D.: Is self-adaptation of selection pressure and population size possible?: a case study. In: International Conference on Parallel Problem Solving from Nature, pp. 900–909 (2006)

A Family of Ant Colony P Systems

Ping Guo[1,3](✉), Mingzhe Zhang[1], and Jing Chen[2]

[1] College of Computer Science, Chongqing University, Chongqing, China
guoping@cqu.edu.cn
[2] School of Software Engineering, Chongqing University, Chongqing, China
[3] Chongqing Key Laboratory of Software Theory and Technology, Chongqing, China

Abstract. Ant colony algorithm is a kind of bionic evolutionary algorithm, which is widely used in the field of optimization. Membrane computing is a new computing model, which has the characteristics of distributed, maximal parallelism and non-deterministic. Different with the most current researches that use ant colony algorithm as the sub-algorithm in the framework of the membrane algorithm, this paper considers the realizing ant colony algorithm completely by evolution rules, and we design new ant colony P system Π_{ACS}, which includes the membrane structure and evolutionary rules. This paper not only provides a new way to realize the ant colony algorithm, but also lays a foundation for building a general framework for solving optimization problems in membrane computing.

Keywords: Evolutionary rules · Cell-like P system · Membrane computing · Ant colony algorithm

1 Introduction

Ant colony algorithm is a bionic evolutionary algorithm based on population. The initial ant colony algorithm, also known as ant system (AS), is an optimization algorithm proposed by Dorigo to simulate the foraging behavior of ants in nature [1]. However, in order to break though the limitation of AS, Dorigo proposed an improved ant colony algorithm in 1997, as known as ant colony system (ACS) [2,3], which greatly improved the performance of the ant colony algorithm. Recently, with the improvement of ant colony algorithm, it has been widely used in many fields, such as solving TSP problem [2,3,22,23], vehicle routing [4], project scheduling [5], data mining [6], image processing [7], network routing [8,21] and so on. At present, ant colony algorithm has become a hot topic in intelligent computing [9].

Membrane computing is a distributed, great parallel and non-deterministic computing model, which is proposed by Paun in 1998 [10]. And it is a new subject in the field of biological computing, and it is also a hot research topic in the fields of computer science, mathematics, economics, biology, artificial intelligence, automatic control and so on in recent years. Many studies show

© Springer Nature Singapore Pte Ltd. 2017
C. He et al. (Eds.): BIC-TA 2017, CCIS 791, pp. 175–193, 2017.
https://doi.org/10.1007/978-981-10-7179-9_14

that the membrane computing model has the same computing capacity as Turing machine [11–13]. Because of the maximal parallelism of membrane computing, theoretically, the combination of membrane computing and ant colony algorithm not only can expand the distributed characteristics and parallel of the ant colony search, but also can greatly improve the search efficiency of the ant colony algorithm.

Currently, the main idea of ant colony algorithm based on membrane computing is using the ant colony algorithm as a sub-algorithm in P systems [14–20]. These researches used the electronic computer model to realize the ant colony algorithm, and utilized the evolution rules to integrate the calculation results. Therefore, these P systems not only include the evolution rules of the membrane computing model, but also include the calculation formula of the electronic computer model. That is to say, they do not have a unified computing model under the framework of membrane computing, which makes it difficult to be realized. However, in this paper, we try to design a family of P systems which are different from previous works by following works.

- Realize the process of simplified ant colony algorithm in cell-like P systems completely by using evolution rules.
- Build a computational framework to solve problems by using ant colony algorithm in cell-like P systems.

In this paper, we propose a P system which realizes the ant colony algorithm called ant colony P system Π_{ACS}. In Sect. 2, we introduce the foundations about ant colony algorithm and membrane computing. In Sect. 3, we propose the definition and the calculation process of Π_{ACS}. In Sect. 4, we give a detailed description about the rule sets in Π_{ACS}. In Sect. 5, we give an instance of Π_{ACS} to prove its validity and feasibility. Finally, in the last section we present the summary and the prospect of our research.

2   Foundations

2.1   Ant Colony Algorithm

The earliest ant colony algorithm is proposed by Dorigo in 1992, which is called ant system (AS). And it was first applied to the TSP. Although AS is useful for discovering good or optimal solutions for small TSP problem, the time required to find such results made it infeasible for lager problems. To break through the limitation of AS, Dorigo proposed an improved ant colony algorithm in 1997, which is called ant colony system (ACS) [2].

The ACS works as follows: m ants are initially positioned on n cities chosen according to some initialization rule (e.g. randomly). Each ant builds a tour by repeatedly applying a stochastic greedy rule (the state transition rule). While constructing its tour, the ant also modifies the amount of pheromone on the visited edges by applying the local updating rule. Once all ants have terminated their tour, the amount of pheromone on edges is modified again (by applying the global updating rule). In ACS, ants are guided, in building their tours, by both heuristic information (they prefer to choose short edges) and by pheromone information. An edge with a high amount of pheromone is a very desirable choice.

ALGORITHM 1. The ACS Algorithm

Initiallization;
while *End-Condition is not satisfied* **do**
    Each ant is put on a starting node;
    while *There are some ants have not built a complete solution* **do**
        Each ant applies state transition rules to incrementally build a solution;
        Local pheromone updating rule is applied;
    end
    A global pheromone updating rule is applied;
end

In ACS, *the state transition rule* is shown as follows: an ant positioned on node r chooses the city s to move to by applying the rule given by Eq. 1, where $J_k(r)$ is the set of cities that remain to be visited by ant k positioned on city r, $\tau(r, u)$ is the amount of pheromone on edge (r, u), $\eta(r, u)$ is the heuristic information on edge (r, u), both β and q_0 $(0 \leq q_0 \leq 1)$ are parameters, q is a random number uniformly distributed in $[0, 1]$, and S is random variable selected according to the probability distribution given in Eq. 2. The state transition rule makes it easier for the ants to choose the edges with shorter length and more pheromone.

$$s = \begin{cases} \arg\max_{u \in J_k(r)}\{[\tau(u, s)][\eta(u, s)]^{\beta}\} & q \leq q_0 \\ S & otherwise \end{cases} \tag{1}$$

$$P_k(r, s) = \begin{cases} \dfrac{[\tau(r,s)][\eta(r,s)]^{\beta}}{\sum\limits_{u \in J_k(r)} [\tau(u, s)][\eta(u, s)]^{\beta}} & s \in J_k(r) \\ 0 & otherwise \end{cases} \tag{2}$$

While building a tour, ants visit edges and change their pheromone levels by applying the local updating rule of Eq. 3, where ρ and τ_0 are parameters.

$$\tau(r, s) = (1 - \rho)\tau(r, s) + \rho\Delta\tau(r, s) \tag{3}$$

Where ρ is a parameter, and $\Delta\tau(r, s)$ is a constant which is decided by a parameter $\tau_0(\Delta\tau(r, s) = \tau_0)$.

And after all the ants finish building the tours, only the globally best ant (i.e. the ant which constructed the shortest tour from the beginning of the trail) is allowed to deposit pheromone using the global updating rule of Eq. 4, where α is a parameter.

$$\tau(r, s) = (1 - \alpha)\tau(r, s) + \alpha\Delta\tau(r, s) \tag{4}$$

Where α is a parameter, and the value of $\Delta\tau(r,s)$ is calculated by Eq. 5.

$$\Delta\tau(r,s) = \begin{cases} L_{gb}^{-1} & (r,s) \in global\ best\ tour \\ 0 & otherwise \end{cases} \tag{5}$$

Where L_{gb} is the length of the global best tour.

Ant colony algorithm, on the one hand, has been widely used because of its distributed computing and strong robustness. On the other hand, has been widely studied because of its surface convergence and global optimization problems.

2.2 Membrane Computing

The design of Ant Colony P System is based on cell-like P systems. Formally, a cell-like P system (of degree $m \geq 1$) can be defined as the form:

$$\Pi = (O, \mu, \omega_1, \ldots, \omega_m, R_1, \ldots, R_m, \rho_1, \ldots, \rho_m, i_o) \tag{6}$$

where,

(1) O is the alphabet. Each symbol represents one kind of objects in the systems. O^* is the finite and non-empty multiset over O where λ is empty string, and $O^+ = O^* - \{\lambda\}$;
(2) μ is a membrane structure with m membrane, labeled by 1, 2, ..., m;
(3) $\omega_i (1 \leq i \leq m)$ is a string over O and represents the multiset of objects placed in membrane i. For example, there are 5 copies of object a and 3 copies of object b in membrane i, then we have $\omega_i = a^5 b^3$. $\omega_i = \lambda$ means that there is no object in the membrane i.
(4) $R_1, \ldots, R_m$ are finite sets of possible evolution rules over O associated with the regions 1, 2, ..., m of μ. The rules in $R_i (1 \leq i \leq m)$ are of the form $U \rightarrow V|_a$, with $a \in O$, $U \in O^+$, $V = V'$ or $V = V'\delta$, $V' \in (O \times Tar)^*$, and $Tar = \{here; out; in_j | 1 \leq j \leq m\}$. "here" means V is remained in the same region, "out" means V goes out of the region, and in_j means V goes to inner membrane j. δ is a special symbol not in O, and it means that the membrane which includes it will be dissolved and the contents of this membrane will be left in the outer one. Object a is a promoter in rule $U \rightarrow V|_a$, this rule can only be applied in the presence of object a.
(5) $\rho_i (1 \leq i \leq m)$ represents the precedence relation between the rules. If $\rho_i = \{a \rightarrow b > c \rightarrow d\}$, both object a and c are available, the rule $a \rightarrow b$ will be preferred according to their precedence relation.
(6) i_o is output region of the system and it saves the final result.

In each membrane, the execution of evolutionary rules will follow the following two principles.

– **Non-determinism:** Suppose n rules compete for the reactants which can only support $m(m < n)$ rules to be applied, then the m rules are chosen non-deterministically.
– **Maximal parallelism:** All of the rules that can be applied must be applied simultaneously.

3   Design of Ant Colony P System Π_{ACS}

In this paper, we design an ant colony P system to search complete graphs by ACS. We assume that the undirected complete graph $G = (V, E)$, where V contains n nodes, E is the set of edges in the graph and the initial amount of the pheromone in each edge is 1. In Π_{ACS}, there are m ants search the graph G randomly, and output the optimal path which consist of the edges with the largest amount of pheromone. In the process of searching, we ignore the length of the edges (the heuristic information). That is to say, the ant chooses the next node only depend on the amount of the pheromone in the edges.

3.1   Definition of Π_{ACS}

Based on Eq. 6, the Ant Colony P system Π_{ACS} can be defined as:

$$\Pi_{ACS} = (O, \mu, \omega, R, i_o) \tag{7}$$

where,

(1) O is the set of objects, it includes the set of objects in the main membrane and sub-membranes, and the set of objects related to the evolution rules in the main membrane and sub-membranes. Table 1 shows the main objects as well as its meaning in Π_{ACS}.

(2) μ represents the initial membrane structure of Π_{ACS}. As shown in Fig. 1, there are n sub-membranes in the main membrane. Each sub-membrane will build a solution for the problem, and generate objects to record the solution.

(3) ω is the multiset of objects in all the membranes of the initial structure. In the main membrane, $\omega_0 = \{t, q_{i_o}, x^g, y^m\} \cup \{e_{ij}|1 \leq i \leq n, 1 \leq j \leq n, i \neq j\} \cup \{c_{ij}|1 \leq i \leq n, 1 \leq j \leq, i \neq j\} \cup \{p_i|1 \leq i \leq n\} \cup \{a_i|1 \leq i \leq n\}$, where n is the number of nodes in the graph, q_{i_o} means the output path will start with node $i_o(i_o \in \{1, 2, \ldots, n\})$, x^g represents the system will run g iterations, and y^m represents there are m ants in the system. In sub-membranes, $\omega_i = \{v_i\}$, $1 \leq i \leq n$, where v_i is the identification of the sub-membrane i. The detail meaning of the objects are shown in Table 1.

(4) R is the set of rules of all the membranes, we will give a detailed description about the rules in the Sect. 4. $R = R_1 \cup R_2 \cup R_3$, where R_1 includes the rules for searching path (SP), R_2 includes the rules for updating pheromone (UP), R_3 includes the rules for output the optimal path (OOP). The rules in Π_{ACS} mainly include the following three forms:

(a) $u \rightarrow v_1(v_2, in_i/out), k$
(b) $u \rightarrow v_1(v_2, in_i/out)|_w, k$
(c) $u \rightarrow v_1[v_2], k$

where u, v_1, v_2 and w are multisets of the objects, in/out is the target identification, k represents the priority of the rule, and the higher the value of k, the higher the priority. The rules like (a) represent consume the multiset u, and generate multisets v_1 and v_2 that v_1 will stay in the current membrane (*here*, which is usually omitted), and v_2 will be output to the parent

Fig. 1. The initial membrane structure of Π_{ACS}

membrane of the current membrane (out) or input to the sub-membrane i (in_i). The rules like (b) is similar to (a), but they will be executed only if there is object w. The rules like (c) represent consume the multiset u, generate multiset v_1 in the current membrane and generate a new sub-membrane that containing multiset v_2.

(5) i_o is output region of P system. In this paper, the output membrane is decided by the object q_{i_o} in the main membrane.

The following table shows us the meaning of the main objects in Π_{ACS}. In the table, $|x|$ represents the amount of the object x.

Table 1. The meaning of the main objects in Π_{ACS}

Object	Description
e_{ij}	$\|e_{ij}\|$ represents the amount of the pheromone on edge (i,j), $1 \leq i \leq n, 1 \leq j \leq n, i \neq j$
c_{ij}	There is no ant that walked by edge (i,j), $1 \leq i \leq n, 1 \leq j \leq n, 1 \neq j$
d_{ij}	$\|d_{ij}\|$ represents how many times the ants walk by edge (i,j), $1 \leq i \leq n, 1 \leq j \leq n, i \neq j$
r_{ij}, h_{ij}	Request the main membrane to input the $ejk(k \in 1,2,\ldots,n)$ into the sub-membrane i
p_i	Deciding the start nodes of the ants randomly
v_i	The target of sub-membrane $i, 1 \leq i \leq n$
a_i	They are used to avoid the conflict of inputing the same e_{ij} to the different sub-membranes, $1 \leq i \leq n$
q_{i_o}	Decide the output membrane
x	$\|x\|$ represents the number of iterations of ant colony searching
y	$\|y\|$ represents the amount of the ants in Π_{ACS}
t	It is used to start the computing of Π_{ACS}

3.2   Calculation Process of Π_{ACS}

The calculation process of Π_{ACS} includes three parts. Firstly, each ant will search the path. Then the amount of the pheromone on the edges will be updated. Finally, after all the iterations are finished, the optimal path will be outputted.

Searching Path (SP). SP is the process for each to build a solution. In the beginning, m ants will be put on different nodes randomly (Rule r_1: input different objects $q_i(1 \leq i \leq n)$ into m sub-membranes). Then, each ant chooses the next node by taking the roulette wheel. And it is worth to noting that the m ants build solutions in parallel.

As shown in Eq. 8, in the roulette wheel, $P_k(r, s)$ is the probability of ant k move from node r, $\tau(r, s)$ is the amount of the pheromone on edge $(r, s)(\tau(r, s) = |e_{rs}|)$, and $J_k(r)$ is the set of cities that remain to be visited by ant k positioned on city r.

$$P_k(r, s) = \begin{cases} \dfrac{\tau(r,s)}{\displaystyle\sum_{u \in J_k(r)} \tau(u, s)} & s \in J_k(r) \\ 0 & otherwise \end{cases} \tag{8}$$

In Π_{ACS}, it will choose one e_{ij} randomly from all the copies of $e_{ij}(i = r, j \in J_k(r))$ to decide the next node. This choice is consistent with the Eq. 8 according to the non-determinacy of the evolution rules.

Updating Pheromone (UP). In Π_{ACS}, there is just global update for the pheromone. When all the ants finish searching the path (there are m objects t_0 in the main membrane), the global update will be executed. As shown in the Eq. 9, if there are $|d_{ij}|$ ants walked by the edge $(i, j)(|d_{ij}| > 0)$, it will add $|d_{ij}|$ to the amount of the pheromone on the edge (by r_19). Else if there are no ant walked by the edge $(i, j)(|d_{ij}| = 0)$, and the amount of the pheromone is greater than 1 ($|e_{ij}| > 1$), it will minus 1 from the amount of the pheromone (by r_20). In the other cases, the amount of the pheromone on the edges is not changed.

$$|e_{ij}| = \begin{cases} |e_{ij}| + |d_{ij}| & |d_{ij}| > 0 \\ |e_{ij}| - 1 & |d_{ij}| = 0 \ \&\& \ |e_{ij}| > 1 \\ |e_{ij}| & otherwise \end{cases} \tag{9}$$

Output the Optimal Path (OOP). After Π_{ACS} has finished all the iterations (there is no object x in the main membrane, $|x| = 0$), it will output the optimal path which starts with node i_o. The following OOP algorithm shows us the process of the output. And Fig. 3 shows the parallel execution of the rules in Π_{ACS}, where r_i is the id of rules. We will give a detailed description about the rules in Sect. 4.

ALGORITHM 2. The algorithm for output the optimal path

Data: The start node i_o
Result: The optimal path
// Build the output membrane (BOM);
$Path \leftarrow \{\}$;
$i \leftarrow i_o$ (node i is the current node where the ant is positioned) (r_{24});
Build the output membrane (r_{25});
// Transfer the neighbor edges pheromone (TNEP);
$Path \leftarrow Path \cup \{i\}$, and request the main membrane to input the pheromone information (r_3);
Transfer the pheromone information from the main membrane to the sub-membrane (r_4-r_6);
In the sub-membrane, delete the e_{ij} whose $j \in Path$ (r_8);
Start searching the next node (r_{26});
// Search the next node (SNN);
if *Path has not included all the nodes (there is object e_{ij}) (r_{27})* **then**
  // Output the next node (ONN);
  Find the neighbor edge with the maximum amount of the pheromone (r_{30}-r_{35});
  Output the next node j to the inner layer membrane (r_{36}, r_{39}, r_{40});
  $i \leftarrow j$, go to step 4 (r_{36});
else
  // End the calculation (End);
  Delete the useless objects (r_{14}, r_{15}) and end the calculation (r_{29});
end

As shown in Fig. 2, there is the calculation process of Π_{ACS}. We proposed the label number of the rules in the figure, and in Sect. 4, we will give a detailed description of all the rules.

4   Rule Sets in Ant Colony P System Π_{ACS}

In this section, we will give a detailed description about the evolution rules in Π_{ACS}. There are three parts of the rules: rule set for searching path (SP), rule set for updating pheromone (UP), and rule set for outputting the optimal path (OOP). We assume that there are m ants and n nodes in Π_{ACS}.

4.1   Rule Set for SP

This rule set includes the rules in the main membrane and sub-membranes. These rules simulate the ants to choose the next node by roulette.

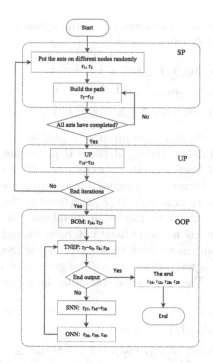

Fig. 2. The calculation process of Π_{ACS}

(1) Put the ants on different nodes randomly

In the main membrane, r_1 will be executed if there is object t. In order to choose m sub-membranes randomly, the objects $\{y, p_i\}$ will be consumed, and generate $\{y, p_i\}$ in the main membrane and object q_i in the sub-membrane i. At the same time, r_2 will be executed to delete the object t. In sub-membranes, object q_i represents the current node where the ant is, and the sub-membrane will record the nodes that the ant has walked by. r_1 and r_2 are given as follows.

$$r_1 : yp_i \rightarrow yp_i(q_i, in_i)|_t 1; 1 \leq i \leq n$$
$$r_2 : t \rightarrow \lambda, 2$$

(2) Build the path

In the sub-membrane $k (1 \leq k \leq n)$, if there is object q_i, r_3 will be executed to generate objects $\{p_i, u_i\}$ and output object r_{ki} to the main membrane. Object p_i is used to record the nodes that the ant has walked by. Object r_{ki} is used to request the main membrane to input the pheromone the neighbor edge of node i to the sub-membrane k. r_3 is given as follows.

$$r_3 : v_k q_i \rightarrow p_i u_i v_k(r_{ki}, out), 1; 1 \leq i \leq n, 1 \leq k \leq n$$

In the main membrane, if there is the object r_{ki}, r_4 and r_5 will be executed to input the required e_{ij} to the sub-membrane k. Then r_6 will be executed to transfer object t_1 to the sub-membrane k as the signal to be completed. These rules are shown in the following.

$$r_4 : r_{ki}a_i \to a_i h_{ki}, 1; 1 \leq i \leq n, 1 \leq k \leq n$$
$$r_5 : e_{ij} \to e_{ij}(e_{ij}, in_k)|_{h_{ki}}, 1; 1 \leq i \leq n, 1 \leq j \leq n, 1 \leq k \leq n$$
$$r_6 : h_{ki} \to (t_1, in_k), 2; 1 \leq i \leq n, 1 \leq k \leq n$$

In the sub-membranes, after the input of e_{ij}, r_7 and r_8 will be executed to generate object t_2 and delete the e_{ij} if there is p_i exiting. After that, if there are nodes that have not been visited (e_{ij} exits), r_9 will be executed to make the roulette. Object t_3 is generated as a signal. Object q_j is used to record the node (r_3 can be executed again). And objects $d_{ij}d_{ji}$ (because the graph is undirected) will be generated and output to the main membrane in order to update the pheromone. Else if there is no node have not been visited (no e_{ij}), r_{10} will be executed to make the ant move back to the start node (recorded by object u_i). Object t_4 is used as a signal. Object t_0 will be generated and output the main membrane to start UP. These rules are shown in the following.

$$r_7 : t_1 \to t_2, 2$$
$$r_8 : e_{ij} \to \lambda|_{p_j}, 1; 1 \leq i \leq n, 1 \leq j \leq n$$
$$r_9 : t_2 e_{ij} \to t_3 q_j(d_{ij}d_{ji}, out), 1; 1 \leq i \leq n, 1 \leq j \leq n$$
$$r_{10} : t_2 v_k u_i \to t_4 v_k(d_{ik}d_{ki}t_0, out), 2; 1 \leq i \leq n, 1 \leq k \leq n$$

In the sub-membranes, at the end of SP, r_{11} r_{15} will be executed to delete the useless objects.

$$r_{11} : e_{ij} \to \lambda|_{t_3}, 1; 1 \leq i \leq n, 1 \leq j \leq n$$
$$r_{12} : u_i \to \lambda|_{t_3}, 1; 1 \leq i \leq n; \qquad r_{13} : t_3 \to \lambda, 2$$
$$r_{14} : p_i \to \lambda|_{t_4}, 1; 1 \leq i \leq n; \qquad r_{15} : t_4 \to \lambda, 2$$

4.2   Rule Set for up

All the rules in the rule set for UP is executed in the main membrane. Each ant will transfer a signal after SP (r_{10}), so if there are m objects t_0, all the ants have completed SP. At this time, r_{16} will be executed to start UP.

$$r_{16} : t_0^m \to t_1, 1$$

If there is object t_1 in the main membrane, Π_{ACS} will mark the edges that have been visited by the ants. r_{17} will be executed to transfer cij to b_{ij}, if there is object d_{ij}, it will mark that edge (i, j) has been visited once. r_17 will be executed many times (the amount of object d_{ij}) at the same time. r_{18} will be also executed to generate t_2 as a signal of completing the marking work.

$$r_{17} : d_{ij}c_{ij} \to d_{ij}b_{ij}|_{t_1}, 1; 1 \leq i \leq n, 1 \leq j \leq n$$
$$r_{18} : t_1 \to t_2, 2$$

Then, it will update the amount the pheromone on the edges according to Eq. 8. r_{19} is executed to add the amount of the pheromone on the edges that have been visited by the ants. r_{20} is executed to minus 1 from the edges that no ants visited (marked by c_{ij}) if its amount is larger than 1. r_{21} is executed to transfer b_{ij} back to c_{ij}.

$$r_{19} : d_{ij} \rightarrow e_{ij}|_{t_2}, 1; 1 \leq i \leq n, 1 \leq j \leq n$$
$$r_{20} : e_{ij}^2 c_{ij} \rightarrow e_{ij} c_{ij}|_{t_2}, 1; 1 \leq i \leq n, 1 \leq j \leq n$$
$$r_{21} : b_{ij} \rightarrow c_{ij}|_{t_2}, 1; 1 \leq i \leq n, 1 \leq j \leq n$$

After the generation of object t_2, if there is more iterations should be done (object x exits), r_{22} will be executed to consume $\{x, t_2\}$ and generate object t to start next iteration (r_1 can be executed). Else if all the iterations have been done (no object x), r_{23} will be executed to start OOP.

$$r_{22} : xt_2 \rightarrow t, 2; \qquad r_{23} : t_2 \rightarrow t_3, 3$$

4.3 Rule Set for OOP

If there is object t_3 in the main membrane, Π_{ACS} will begin to output the optimal path in accordance with the OOP algorithm in Sect. 3.2.

(1) Build the output membrane (BOM)

The output membrane in Π_{ACS} is decided by object $q_{i_o} (i_o \in \{1, 2, \ldots, n\})$ in the main membrane. It will generate multi-layer membranes in the sub-membrane i_o, and each layer in the membrane will record a node by object $p_i (i \in \{1, 2, \ldots, n\})$. The outside layer record the node that be visited firstly.

In the main membrane, if there is objects $\{q_{i_o} t_3\}$, r_{24} will be executed to generate objects $\{cex_i q_{i_o}\}$ and input them to the sub-membrane i_o. Then in the sub-membrane i_o, r_{25} will be executed be generate the next layer membrane.

$$r_{24} : q_i t_3 \rightarrow (cex_i q_i, in_i), 1; 1 \leq i \leq n$$
$$r_{25} : ce \rightarrow e[c], 1$$

(2) Transfer the neighbor edge pheromone (TNEP)

Because of the execution of r_{24}, there is object q_i in the sub-membrane i_o. So as same as the process in SP, r_3 will be executed in the sub-membrane to generate object r_{ki} and output it to the main membrane. Then, r_4 r_6 will be executed in the main membrane to transfer the required e_{ij} back to the sub-membrane i_o.

In the sub-membrane i_o, after the input of object t_1, r_8 will be executed to delete the e_{ij} if there is p_i exiting (which means edge (i, j) has been visited). And at the same time, r_{26} will be executed (r_7 will not be executed because it has a lower priority) to generate a signal t_5.

$$r_{26} : et_1 \rightarrow t_5, 1$$

If there are some nodes that have not been recorded into the output membrane (e_{ij} exit), r_{27} will be executed to start searching the next node (SNN). Else if all the nodes have been record to the output membrane (no e_{ij}) which means the OOP has been done, r_{28} will be executed to generate object t_4 and f. Object t_4 will make r_{14} and r_{15} to be executed to delete the useless objects in the sub-membrane. Object f will make r_{29} to be executed to record the start node of the optimal path. Then, the calculation process of Π_{ACS} is end.

$$r_{27} : t_5 e_{ij} \rightarrow t_6 e_{ij}, 1; 1 \leq i \leq n, 1 \leq j \leq n$$
$$r_{28} : t_5 \rightarrow t_4 f, 2$$
$$r_{29} : v_i f \rightarrow v_i p_i, 1; 1 \leq i \leq n$$

(3) Search the next node (SNN)

If there is object t_6 in the sub-membrane i_o, r_{30} r_{35} will be executed as follows. Firstly, we make the next node to be zero (the amount of the pheromone on the edge between the current node and the next node is 0). Then it will choose a node that has not been visited randomly, and mark it by object z_j (r_{30}). Next, it will compare the amount of the pheromone on the two edges, and update the next node to the larger one (r_{31} r_{35}). The process will be iterated until all the nodes have been compared, which means it has found the next node with the maximum amount of the pheromone. After that, r_{36} will be executed to record the next node, and transfer object q_i to the inner layer of the membrane to output (ONN). Finally, it will execute r_{37}, r_{38} to delete the useless objects.

$$r_{30} : t_6 e_{ij} \rightarrow t_7 z_j e_{ij}, 1; \qquad r_{31} : e_{ij} s \rightarrow s|_{z_j}, 1$$
$$r_{32} : t_7 e_{ij} \rightarrow t_8 s|_{z_j}, 2; \qquad r_{33} : e_{ij} \rightarrow s|_{z_j}, 3$$
$$r_{34} : t_7 z_j \rightarrow t_6, 4; \qquad r_{35} : t_8 x_i z_j \rightarrow t_6 x_j, 1$$
$$r_{36} : t_6 x_i \rightarrow et_9 q_i(q_i, in), 2; \quad r_{37} : s \rightarrow \lambda|_{t_9}, 1$$
$$r_{38} : t_9 \rightarrow \lambda, 2$$

(4) Output the next node (ONN)

In the inner layers (above 2 layers) of the output membrane, if there is object q_i, r_{39} and r_{40} will be executed to record the nodes in the optimal path. It will record the start node in the outermost layer, and the end node in the innermost layer.

$$r_{40} : q_i c \rightarrow p_i[c], 1; \quad r_{41} : q_i \rightarrow (q_i, in), 2$$

(5) END

After all the nodes have been record to the output membrane, the Π_{ACS} will enter the process of END. In this process, Π_{ACS} will do three jobs. The first one is to clear the useless objects in the sub-membrane (r_{14}, r_{15}). The second one is to generate the object in the output membrane which represents the starting node (r_{29}). The final one is to complete the output work in the output membrane (r_{39}, r_{40}).

If all the nodes have been record to the output membrane (no e_{ij}) which means the OOP has been done, r_{28} will be executed to generate object t_4 and f. Object t_4 will make r_{14} and r_{15} to be executed to delete the useless objects in the sub-membrane. Object f will make r_{29} to be executed to record the start node of the optimal path. Then, the calculation process of Π_{ACS} is end.

4.4   Parallelism Analysis for Π_{ACS}

In order to explain the parallelism of Π_{ACS} in theory, we will make a detailed analysis of the running process of Π_{ACS} in this section.

According to the maximum parallelism of P systems, the rules that meet their requirements will be executed at the same time. As shown in Fig. 3, it is the process of the execution of the rules in Π_{ACS}. We assume that the time cost for executing a rule is a slice. In the figure, rules like $[r_i]$ means r_i may be executed or not.

(1) Cost of SP

The process of SP includes put the ants into different nodes (1 slice) and each ant build the path in parallel ($5n + 1$ slice).

(2) Cost of UP

The process of UP will cost 2 slices.

We assume that there are g iterations in Π_{ACS}, which means the SP and UP will loop g times. So it will cost $g \times (5n + 4)$ slices in total.

(3) Cost of OOP

The process of OOP includes 5 parts: DOM, TNEP, SNN, ONN and END. The cost of DOM is 2 slices. The cost of TNEP is 3 slices. The cost of SNN is $1 + 3 \times (n - i + 1)$ if it has output i-1 nodes. The cost of ONN is 2 slices. The cost of END is $2 + (n - 8) + 1 = n - 5$ if $n > 7$, or 2 if $n \leq 7$. It will search n nodes in total, so the process of TNEP, SNN and ONN will be done for n times. After that, it will do the process of TNEP and END. In summary, the cost of OOP can be computed as follows (assume $n > 7$).

$$
\begin{aligned}
T_{OOP} &= T_{DOM} + n \times (T_{TNEP} + T_{SNN} + T_{ONN}) \\
&\quad + (T_{TNEP} + T_{END}) \\
&= 2 + \sum_{i=2}^{n} 3 + 1 + 3(n - i + 1) + 2 + 3 + 1 + 1 \\
&\quad + \max(0, n - 8 + 1) \\
&= 10n - 9 + \frac{3}{2}(n - 1)(n - 2) \, slices
\end{aligned}
$$

In summary, the total cost of Π_{ACS} is

$$
T = g(5n + 4) + 10n - 9 + \frac{3}{2}(n - 1)(n - 2) \sim O(n^2)
$$

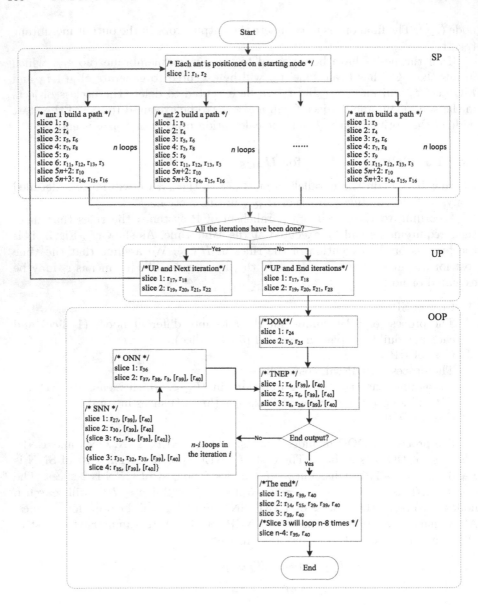

Fig. 3. The process of rules executing in Π_{ACS}

5   Instance

In this section, we will give an instance of Π_{ACS}. In the instance, we assume there are 3 ($m = 3$) ants to search the undirected complete graph which has 5 ($n = 5$) nodes. There are 3 ($g = 3$) iterations and it will output the optimal path with the start node 1 ($i_o = 1$). Figure 4 shows the initial structure of the instance.

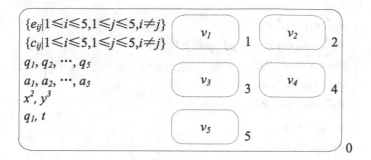

Fig. 4. The initial structure of the instance

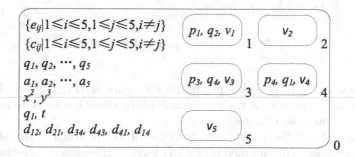

Fig. 5. The structure of the instance after searching the first node

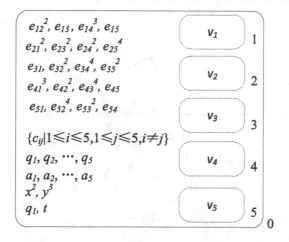

Fig. 6. The structure of the instance after UP of the first iteration

As shown in Fig. 5, it is the membrane structure of Π_{ACS} after the ants searched the first next node. The three ants are put into the start nodes, node 1, node 3, node4, and choose node 2, node 4 and node 1 as their next node. The objects like d_{ij} in the main membrane record the edges visited by the ants.

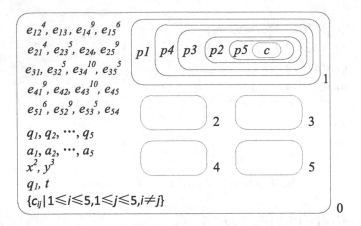

Fig. 7. The final structure of the instance

As shown in Fig. 6, it is the membrane structure of Π_{ACS} after UP of the first iteration. The amount of the pheromone of the edges has been updated (the amount of e_{ij} has been changed).

The Fig. 7 shows the membrane structure of Π_{ACS} when it has ended its calculation process. The sub-membrane 1 is used as the output membrane. The final optimal path is $1 \rightarrow 4 \rightarrow 3 \rightarrow 2 \rightarrow 5 \rightarrow 1$. And Fig. 8 shows us the final amount of the pheromone on the edges in the graph.

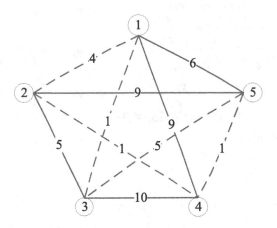

Fig. 8. The final state of the graph

In order to further illustrate the feasibility of Π_{ACS}, we also simulated the Ant Colony P System in a computer. As shown in Fig. 9, we simulated an Ant Colony P System with 100 ants, and it would run for 100 times of iteration. The data in the figure shows that with the increase of the quantity of nodes in

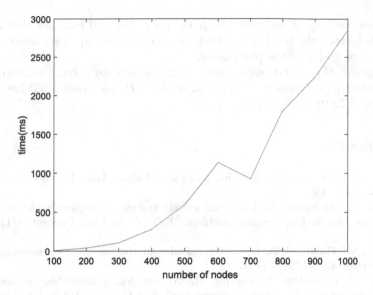

Fig. 9. The time cost (ms) of simulated Π_{ACS} with 100 ants and 100 iterations

the graph, the running time of Π_{ACS} is approximately linear increasing trend. However, in general, the time cost of Π_{ACS} is acceptable.

6 Conclusion

Ant colony system has the characteristics of strong robustness, global search, parallel and distributed computing, and being easy to be combined with other algorithms. And it has provided an effective solution for some NP-hard combinatorial optimization problems. Different from some P systems that utilize electronic computer model in sub-membranes to realize the ant colony algorithm, this paper proposes a way to realize the ant colony algorithm completely depend on the evolution rules in the P system. The ant colony P system Π_{ACS} not only has the characteristics of the ant colony system, but also has the advantage of maximum parallelism in P systems. We also proved that Π_{ACS} is feasible by the instance in Sect. 5.

Π_{ACS} is an exploration of the realization of the ant colony system by using evolutionary rules completely. In the future, researchers can improve Π_{ACS} by the following ways.

- Improve the state transition rule. In this paper, we choose an easy way (roulette) to search the path. The elements that affect the choice of the ants are only pheromone. In the following research, we can use a more complex way and add the heuristic information into it, in order to improve the convergence of the system.

- Improve the way of updating the pheromone. We will consider that adding volatile factors, the heuristic information, and the local update rule to improve the way of updating the pheromone.
- To improve Π_{ACS} and build a general framework for solving combinational optimization problems, we will try to improve Π_{ACS} to solve NP-hard problems (e.g. TSP) in the future.

References

1. Dorigo, M.: Optimization, learning and natural algorithms. Thesis Politecnico Di Milano Italy (1992)
2. Dorigo, M., Gambardella, L.M.: Ant colony system: a cooperative learning approach to the traveling salesman problem. IEEE Trans. Evol. Comput. **1**(1), 53–66 (1997)
3. Dorigo, M., Gambardella, L.M.: Ant colonies for the travelling salesman problem. Biosystems **43**(2), 73–81 (1997)
4. Reed, M., Yiannakou, A., Evering, R.: An ant colony algorithm for the multi-compartment vehicle routing problem. Appl. Soft Comput. **15**(2), 169–176 (2014)
5. Merkle, D., Middendorf, M., Schmeck, H.: Ant colony optimization for resource-constrained project scheduling. IEEE Trans. Evol. Comput. **6**(4), 333–346 (2010)
6. Parpinelli, R.S., Lopes, H.S., Freitas, A.A.: Classification-rule discovery with an ant colony algorithm. In: Khosrow-Pour, M. (ed.) Encyclopedia of Information Science and Technology, 1st edn., pp. 420–424. Idea Group, Hershey (2005). ISBN 1-59140-553-X
7. Tian, J., Yu, W., Xie, S.: An ant colony optimization algorithm for image edge detection. In: 2010 International Conference on Artificial Intelligence and Computational Intelligence, vol. 2, no. 5, pp. 751–756. IEEE Computer Society (2010)
8. Fajjari, I., Aitsaadi, N., Pujolle, G., et al.: VNE-AC: virtual network embedding algorithm based on ant colony metaheuristic. In: IEEE International Conference on Communications, vol. 34, no. 17, pp. 1–6 (2011)
9. Chinese Academy of Sciences, Thomson Reuters: 2015 World's Most Highly Cited Researchers [EB/OL]. http://thomsonreuters.com/en/articles/2015/research-elite-2015-highly-cited-researchers.html
10. Rozenberg, G., Bck, T., Kok, J.N. (eds.): Handbook of Natural Computing. Springer, Heidelberg (2012). https://doi.org/10.1007/978-3-540-92910-9
11. Păun, G., Suzuki, Y., Tanaka, H.: On the power of membrane division in P systems. Theor. Comput. Sci. **324**(1), 61–85 (2004)
12. Bernardini, F., Gheorghe, M.: Cell communication in tissue P systems: universality results. Soft Comput. **9**(9), 640–649 (2005)
13. Kishan, S.N.: Universality results for P systems based on brane calculi operation. Theor. Comput. Sci. **371**(1–2), 83–105 (2007)
14. Nishida, T.Y.: Membrane algorithm with brownian subalgorithm and genetic subalgorithm. Int. J. Found. Comput. S. **18**(6), 1353–1360 (2007)
15. Zhao, J., Wang, N.: Hybrid optimization method based on membrane computing. Ind. Eng. Chem. Res. **50**(3), 1691–1704 (2011)
16. Wang, X., Zhang, G., Zhao, J., et al.: A modified membrane-inspired algorithm based on particle swarm optimization for mobile robot path planning. Int. J. Comput. Commun. Control **10**(6), 732–745 (2015)

17. Xiao, J., Huang, Y., Cheng, Z., et al.: A hybrid membrane evolutionary algorithm for solving constrained optimization problems. Int. J. Light Electron. Opt. **125**(2), 897–902 (2014)

18. Zhang, G., Cheng, J., Gheorghe, M., et al.: A hybrid approach based on differential evolution and tissue membrane systems for solving constrained manufacturing parameter optimization problems. Appl. Soft Comput. **13**(3), 1528–1542 (2013)

19. Du, Q., Xiang, L., Liu, X.: P system based particle swarm optimization algorithm. In: Li, S., Jin, Q., Jiang, X., Park, J.J.J.H. (eds.) ITME 2013. LNEE, vol. 269, pp. 553–563. Springer, Dordrecht (2014). https://doi.org/10.1007/978-94-007-7618-0_54

20. Singh, G., Deep, K.: Hybridization of P systems and particle swarm optimization for function optimization. In: Pant, M., Deep, K., Nagar, A., Bansal, J.C. (eds.) SocProS 2013. AISC, vol. 258, pp. 395–401. Springer, New Delhi (2014). https://doi.org/10.1007/978-81-322-1771-8_34

21. Yang, J., Zhuang, Y.: An improved ant colony optimization algorithm for solving a complex combinatorial optimization problem. Appl. Soft Comput. **10**(2), 653–660 (2010)

22. Tuba, M., Jovanovic, R., Jovanovic, R.: Improved ACO algorithm with pheromone correction strategy for the traveling salesman problem. Int. J. Comput. Commun. Control **8**(3), 477–485 (2013)

23. Guo, P., Liu, Z.J.: An ant system based on moderate search for TSP. Comput. Sci. Inf. Syst. **9**(4), 1533–1551 (2012)

Using an SN P System to Compute the Product of Any Two Decimal Natural Numbers

Fangxiu Wang[1], Kang Zhou[1(✉)], and Huaqing Qi[2]

[1] School of Math and Computer, Wuhan Polytechnic University, Wuhan, China
wfx323@126.com, zhoukang65@whpu.edu.cn
[2] Department of Economics and Management, Wuhan Polytechnic University,
Wuhan, China
qihuaqing@sohu.com

Abstract. In this paper, a new SN P system is investigated in order to compute the product of any two decimal natural numbers. Firstly, an SN P system with two input neurons is constructed, which can be used to compute the product of any two binary natural numbers which have specified lengths. Secondly, the correctness of the SN P system is proved theoretically. However, the system can only be used to compute the product of any two binary natural numbers, but the product of any two decimal natural numbers often need to be computed in practical application. Therefore, it is necessary to construct a coding SN P system which converts a decimal number into a binary number and to construct a decoding SN P system which converts a binary number to a decimal number. In the end, an new SN P system is constructed to compute the product of any two decimal natural numbers. An example test shows that the SN P system can be used to compute the product of any two decimal natural numbers. Therefore, this paper provides a new method for constructing the SN P system which can compute the product of any two natural numbers.

Keywords: SN P system · Coding SN P system · Decoding SN P system · Decimal system

1 Introduction

It has been a hot issue in the research field to perform the addition of any two natural numbers by using the spiking neural P system. The paper [1] solves the problem of the product of an arbitrary binary natural number and a fixed binary natural number, but does not solve the problem of the product of any two binary natural numbers. Although the paper [2] solves the problem of the product of any two natural binary numbers, it is not applicable to the product of any two decimal natural numbers. However, people are more accustomed to calculate the product of any two decimal numbers in practical application. Therefore, in this paper we need to construct a spiking neural P system which can perform the product of any two decimal natural numbers.

ⓒ Springer Nature Singapore Pte Ltd. 2017
C. He et al. (Eds.): BIC-TA 2017, CCIS 791, pp. 194–206, 2017.
https://doi.org/10.1007/978-981-10-7179-9_15

2   Construction of a Binary Multiply SN P System with Two Input Neurons

In this section an SN P system is constructed to perform the addition of two binary natural numbers. It is composed of $k(k + 11)/2 + 4$ neurons (see Fig. 1).

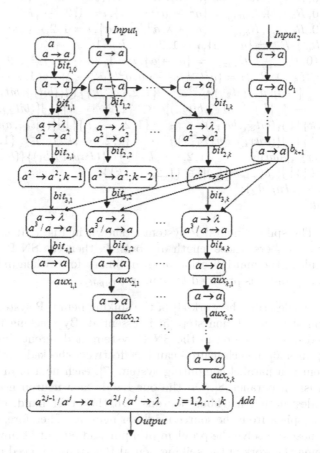

Fig. 1. A SN P system that compute the product of arbitrary two binary natural numbers whose lengths are both k

For any two binary natural numbers m and n whose length are k, where m, $n \geq 0$ and $k \geq 1$, a spiking neural P system is constructed as Fig. 1 in order to compute the product of m and n. As can be seen from the Fig. 1, to compute $m \cdot n$, the spiking neural P system [3] is constructed as follows:

$$\prod_{Mult}(k) = (O, \sigma_{Input_1}, \sigma_{Input_2}, \sigma_{bit_{1,0}}, \sigma_{bit_{1,1}}, \cdots, \sigma_{bit_{1,k}}, \sigma_{bit_{2,1}}, \cdots, \sigma_{bit_{2,k}},$$
$$\sigma_{bit_{3,1}}, \cdots, \sigma_{bit_{3,k}}, \sigma_{bit_{4,1}}, \cdots, \sigma_{bit_{4,k}}, \sigma_{aux_{1,1}}, \sigma_{aux_{2,1}}, \sigma_{aux_{2,2}}, \cdots, \sigma_{aux_{k,1}}, \sigma_{aux_{k,2}},$$
$$\cdots, \sigma_{aux_{k,k}}, \sigma_{Add}, syn, in, out), \text{ where:}$$

(1) $O = \{a\}$;

(2) $\sigma_{Input_1} = (0, R_{Input_1}), R_{Input_1} = \{a \to a\}$;

(3) $\sigma_{Input_2} = (0, R_{Input_2}), R_{Input_2} = \{a \to a\}$;

(4) $\sigma_{bit_{1,0}} = (1, R_{bit_{1,0}}), R_{bit_{1,0}} = \{a \to a\}$;

(5) $\sigma_{bit_{1,i}} = (0, R_{bit_{1,i}}), R_{bit_{1,i}} = \{a \to a\}, i = 1, 2, \cdots, k$;

(6) $\sigma_{bit_{2,i}} = (0, R_{bit_{2,i}}), R_{bit_{2,i}} = \{a \to \lambda, a^2 \to a^2\}, i = 1, 2, \cdots, k$;

(7) $\sigma_{bit_{3,i}} = (0, R_{bit_{3,i}}), R_{bit_{3,i}} = \{a^2 \to a^2; k - i\}, i = 1, 2, \cdots, k$;

(8) $\sigma_{bit_{4,i}} = (0, R_{bit_{4,i}}), R_{bit_{4,i}} = \{a \to \lambda, a^3/a \to a\}, i = 1, 2, \cdots, k$;

(9) $\sigma_{b_i} = (0, R_{b_i}), R_{b_i} = \{a \to a\}, i = 1, 2, \cdots, k + 1$;

(10) $\sigma_{aux_{i,j}} = (0, R_{aux_{i,j}}), R_{aux_{i,j}} = \{a \to a\}, i = 1, 2, \cdots, k, j = 1, 2, \cdots, i$;

(11) $\sigma_{Add} = (0, R_{Add}), R_{Add} = \{a^{2j-1}/a^j \to a, a^{2j}/a^j \to \lambda, j = 1, 2, \cdots, k\}$;

(12) $syn = \{(Input_1, bit_{2,i})|i \in \{1, 2, \cdots, k\}\} \bigcup \{(bit_{1,i}, bit_{1,i+1})|i \in \{0, 1, \cdots, k - 1\}\} \bigcup \{(bit_{1,i}, bit_{2,i})|i \in \{1, 2, \cdots, k\}\} \bigcup \{(bit_{2,i}, bit_{3,i})|i \in \{1, 2, \cdots, k\}\} \bigcup \{(bit_{3,i}, bit_{4,i})|i \in \{1, 2, \cdots, k\}\} \bigcup \{(bit_{4,i}, aux_{i,1})|i \in \{1, 2, \cdots, k\}\} \bigcup \{(aux_{i,j}, aux_{i,j+1})|i \in \{1, 2, \cdots, k, j \in \{1, 2, \cdots, i - 1\}\} \bigcup \{(aux_{i,i}, Add)|i \in \{1, 2, \cdots, k\}\} \bigcup \{(Input_2, b_1)\}\{(b_i, b_{i+1})|i \in \{1, 2, \cdots, k\}\} \bigcup \{(b_{k+1}, bit_{4,i})|i \in \{1, 2, \cdots, k\}\}$;

(13) $in = \{Input_1, Input_2\}$;

(14) $out = Add$;

Theorem 1. The spiking neural P system is shown in Fig. 1. If m and n are any two binary numbers whose length are both k, then the SN P system can output the result of the multiplication $m \cdot n$ in binary form when m is provided to neuron σ_{Input_1} and n is provided to neuron σ_{Input_2}.

Proof. In order to describe the work [4] of the spiking neural P system as shown in Fig. 1, a complete calculation step [5] is essential. By tracking the number of spikes stored in each neuron in the SN P system at different time step, the use of spiking rules [6] in each neuron can be effectively checked. As the spiking neural P system is a parallel computing system [7], each neuron in the system performs its task in parallel [8]. On the one hand, each neuron needs to send spikes to the destination neighbor neurons. On the other hand, each neuron needs to receive spikes from the source neighbor neurons. Therefore, any neuron in the system needs to solve the problem of input and output at any time step. Before describing the work of the spiking neural P system, we need to make the following conventions:

(1) If there is a neuron σ_{aux} in the system, then the variable aux is used to store the number of spikes contained in the neuron.

(2) If neuron σ_{aux} needs to send spikes to the destination neighbor neurons or the environment, then the number of spikes output by the neuron is represented by aux_out.

(3) If neuron σ_{aux} need delay spiking, then the delay time is stored in aux_t.

(4) To distinguish whether neuron σ_{aux} is open or close, a variable aux_switch is required. If $aux\_switch = 1$, it means that neuron is open to the destination neighbor neurons or the environment; otherwise, it indicates that the neuron is turned off.

Therefore, according to the work principle of the spiking neural membrane system, the process of computing the product of any two binary natural numbers with their length are both k is as follows:

(1) Using $t = 0$ to represent the initial time step of the system. $bit_{1,0} = 1$ indicates that there is one spike in neuron $\sigma_{bit_{1,0}}$ in the current pattern [9].

(2) It is shown that the number of spikes present in all the neurons in the time t in the system and the spikes sent by the system to the environment.

(3) The number of spikes which is sent by the input neurons σ_{Input_1} and σ_{Input_2} is calculated in the following formula.

$$\begin{cases} Input_1 = Input_1 - 1 \ and \ Input_1\_out = 1 \ if \ Input_1 = 1 \\ Input_1\_out = 0 \ otherwise \end{cases} \quad (1)$$

and

$$\begin{cases} Input_2 = Input_2 - 1 \ and \ Input_2\_out = 1 \ if \ Input_2 = 1 \\ Input_2\_out = 0 \ otherwise \end{cases} \quad (2)$$

(4) The number of spikes sent to the neuron $\sigma_{b_{i+1}}$ by neuron σ_{b_i} $(1 \le i \le k-1)$ is calculated as follows.

$$\begin{cases} b_i = b_i - 1 \ and \ b_i\_out = 1 \ if \ b_i = 1 \\ b_i\_out = 0 \ otherwise \end{cases} \quad (3)$$

(5) The number of spikes sent to neuron $\sigma_{bit_{2,i}}$ by neuron $\sigma_{bit_{1,i}}$ $(0 \le i \le k)$ is as follows.

$$\begin{cases} bit_{1,i} = bit_{1,i} - 1 \ and \ bit_{1,i}\_out = 1 \ if \ bit_{1,i} = 1 \\ bit_{1,i}\_out = 0 \ otherwise \end{cases} \quad (4)$$

(6) The number of spikes sent to neuron $\sigma_{bit_{3,i}}$ by neuron $\sigma_{bit_{2,i}}$ $(1 \le i \le k)$ is as follows

$$\begin{cases} bit_{2,i} = bit_{2,i} - 2 \ and \ bit_{2,i}\_out = 2 \ if \ bit_{1,i} = 2 \\ bit_{2,i} = bit_{2,i} - 1 \ and \ bit_{2,i}\_out = 0 \ if \ bit_{1,i} = 1 \\ bit_{2,i}\_out = 0 \ otherwise \end{cases} \quad (5)$$

(7) The number of spikes sent to neuron $\sigma_{bit_{4,i}}$ by neuron $\sigma_{bit_{3,i}}$ $(1 \le i \le k)$ is as follows.
If $bit_{3,i} = 2$ and $bit_{3,i}\_t = k - i$,then the following spiking rules are performed.

$$\begin{cases} bit_{3,i} = bit_{3,i} - 2 \\ bit_{3,i}\_out = 2 \\ bit_{3,i}\_t = bit_{3,i}\_t - k + i \\ bit_{3,i}\_switch = 1 \end{cases} \quad (6)$$

If $bit_{3,i} = 2$ and $bit_{3,i}\_t < k - i$,then the following spiking rules are performed.

$$\begin{cases} bit_{3,i}\_out = 0 \\ bit_{3,i}\_t = bit_{3,i}\_t + 1 \\ bit_{3,i}\_switch = 0 \end{cases} \quad (7)$$

If $bit_{3,i} \neq 2$, then

$$bit_{3,i}\_out = 0 \tag{8}$$

(8) The number of spikes sent to neuron $\sigma_{aux_{i,1}}$ by neuron $\sigma_{bit_{4,i}}(1 \leq i \leq k)$ is as follows.

$$\begin{cases} bit_{4,i} = bit_{4,i} - 1 \ and \ bit_{4,i}\_out = 1 \ if \ bit_{4,i} = 3 \\ bit_{4,i} = bit_{4,i} - 1 \ and \ bit_{4,i}\_out = 0 \ if \ bit_{4,i} = 1 \\ bit_{4,i}\_out = 0 \ otherwise \end{cases} \tag{9}$$

(9) The number of spikes sent to neuron $\sigma_{aux_{i,j+1}}$ or σ_{Add} by neuron $\sigma_{aux_{i,j}}(1 \leq i \leq k, i \leq j \leq k)$ is as follows.

$$\begin{cases} aux_{i,j} = aux_{i,j} - 1 \ and \ aux_{i,j}\_out = 1 \ if \ aux_{i,j} = 1 \\ aux_{i,j}\_out = 0 \ otherwise \end{cases} \tag{10}$$

(10) The number of spikes sent to the environment by σ_{Add} is as follows.

$$\begin{cases} Add = Add - j \ and \ Output = 1 \ if \ Add = 2j - 1 \\ Add = Add - j \ and \ Output = 0 \ if \ Add = 2j \\ Output = 0 \ otherwise \end{cases} \tag{11}$$

(11) After receiving spikes from neuron $\sigma_{aux_{i,j}}(1 \leq i \leq k)$, σ_{Add} has the following spikes.

$$Add = Add + \sum_{i=1}^{k} aux_{i,i}\_out \tag{12}$$

(12) After receiving spikes from neuron $\sigma_{aux_{i-1,j}}$, $\sigma_{aux_{i,j}}$ has the following spikes.

$$aux_{i,j} = aux_{i,j} + aux_{i-1,j}\_out, i = 2, 3, \cdots, k; j = i, i + 1, \cdots, k \tag{13}$$

(13) After receiving spikes from neuron $\sigma_{bit_{4,i}}$, $\sigma_{aux_{1,i}}$ has the following spikes.

$$aux_{1,i} = aux_{1,i} + bit_{4,i}\_out, i = 1, 2, \cdots, k \tag{14}$$

(14) If $bit_{3,i}\_switch = 1$ then the number of spikes in neurons $\sigma_{bit_{4,i}}$ and $\sigma_{bit_{3,i}}$ is calculated as follows.

$$\begin{cases} bit_{4,i} = bit_{4,i} + bit_{3,i}\_out \\ bit_{3,i} = bit_{3,i} + bit_{2,i}\_out \end{cases} \tag{15}$$

where $i = 1, 2, \cdots, k$.

(15) After receiving spikes from neuron $\sigma_{b_{k+1}}$, neuron $\sigma_{aux_{4,i}}$ has the following spikes.

$$bit_{4,i} = bit_{4,i} + b_{k+1}\_out, i = 1, 2, \cdots, k \tag{16}$$

(16) After receiving spikes from neuron σ_{Input_1}, neuron $\sigma_{bit_{2,i}}$ has the following spikes.

$$bit_{2,i} = bit_{2,i} + Input_1\_out, i = 1, 2, \cdots, k \tag{17}$$

(17) After receiving spikes from neuron $\sigma_{bit_{1,i}}$, neuron $\sigma_{bit_{2,i}}$ has the following spikes.

$$bit_{2,i} = bit_{2,i} + bit_{1,i\_}out, i = 1, 2, \cdots, k \tag{18}$$

(18) After receiving spikes from neuron $\sigma_{bit_{1,i-1}}$, neuron $\sigma_{bit_{1,i}}$ has the following spikes.

$$bit_{1,i} = bit_{1,i} + bit_{1,i-1\_}out, i = 1, 2, \cdots, k \tag{19}$$

(19) If $t + 1 \leq k$, then the number of spikes in neurons σ_{Input_1} and σ_{Input_2} are updated as follows.

$$\begin{cases} Input_1 = Input_1 + x_{t+1} \\ Input_2 = Input_2 + y_{t+1} \end{cases} \tag{20}$$

(20) The number of spikes in neuron $\sigma_{b_i}(i = 1, 2, \cdots, k)$ is updated as follows.

$$\begin{cases} b_1 = b_1 + Input_2\_out \\ b_2 = b_2 + b_{i-1}\_Out \end{cases} \tag{21}$$

(21) Let $t = t + 1$. If $t \leq 3k + 5$, then repeat step (2) to step (20). Otherwise, the computation is ended.

Through the above process, one can get the product of any two binary natural numbers whose length are both k.

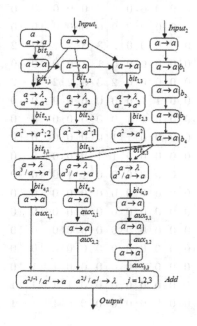

Fig. 2. An SN P system that performs the multiplication between two binary natural numbers whose lengths are both 3

For example, in order to compute the product $5 \cdot 6 = 30$, a binary representation $101_2 \cdot 110_2 = 11110_2$ is required. Therefore, $m = 101_2, n = 110_2, k = 3$. The spiking neural P System $\prod_{Mult}(3)$, which is used to compute the product, is shown in Fig. 2. Table 1 gives the number of spikes contained in each neuron in each step.

Table 1. Number of spikes in each neuron of $\prod_{Mult}(2)$ (the system illustrated in Fig. 2) and number of spikes sent to the environment, at each time step during the computation of the multiplication $101_2 \cdot 110_2 = 11110_2$

Step	0	1	2	3	4	5	6	7	8	9	10	11	12	13	14
$Input_1$	0	1	0	1	0	0	0	0	0	0	0	0	0	0	0
$Input_2$	0	0	1	1	0	0	0	0	0	0	0	0	0	0	0
$bit_{1,0}$	1	0	0	0	0	0	0	0	0	0	0	0	0	0	0
$bit_{1,1}$	0	1	0	0	0	0	0	0	0	0	0	0	0	0	0
$bit_{1,2}$	0	0	1	0	0	0	0	0	0	0	0	0	0	0	0
$bit_{1,3}$	0	0	0	1	0	0	0	0	0	0	0	0	0	0	0
$bit_{2,1}$	0	0	2	0	1	0	0	0	0	0	0	0	0	0	0
$bit_{2,2}$	0	0	1	1	1	0	0	0	0	0	0	0	0	0	0
$bit_{2,3}$	0	0	1	0	2	0	0	0	0	0	0	0	0	0	0
$bit_{3,1}$	0	0	0	2	2	2	0	0	0	0	0	0	0	0	0
$bit_{3,2}$	0	0	0	0	0	0	0	0	0	0	0	0	0	0	0
$bit_{3,2}$	0	0	0	0	0	2	0	0	0	0	0	0	0	0	0
$bit_{4,1}$	0	0	0	0	0	0	2	3	3	2	2	2	2	2	2
$bit_{4,2}$	0	0	0	0	0	0	0	1	1	0	0	0	0	0	04
$bit_{4,3}$	0	0	0	0	0	0	2	3	3	2	2	2	2	2	2
b_1	0	0	0	1	1	0	0	0	0	0	0	0	0	0	0
b_2	0	0	0	0	1	1	0	0	0	0	0	0	0	0	0
b_3	0	0	0	0	0	1	1	0	0	0	0	0	0	0	0
b_4	0	0	0	0	0	0	1	1	0	0	0	0	0	0	0
$aux_{1,1}$	0	0	0	0	0	0	0	0	1	1	0	0	0	0	0
$aux_{2,1}$	0	0	0	0	0	0	0	0	0	0	0	0	0	0	0
$aux_{2,2}$	0	0	0	0	0	0	0	0	0	0	0	0	0	0	0
$aux_{3,1}$	0	0	0	0	0	0	0	0	0	0	0	0	0	0	0
$aux_{3,2}$	0	0	0	0	0	0	0	0	0	0	0	0	0	0	0
$aux_{3,3}$	0	0	0	0	0	0	0	0	0	0	1	1	0	0	0
Add	0	0	0	0	0	0	0	0	0	1	1	1	1	0	0
$Output$	0	0	0	0	0	0	0	0	0	0	1	1	1	1	0

3   Construction of a Decimal Multiplication Spiking Neural System with Two Input Neurons

3.1   Construction of a Coding Spiking Neural System Based on the Conversion of Decimal Numbers into Binary Numbers

Figure 3 is a coding spike neural P system [10] that converts a decimal number into a binary number. It can be seen that x must be a natural number in a certain range from spiking rules of and forgetting rules. It can be correctly encoded only when $x \in \{0, 1, \cdots, 2^k - 1\}$. In other words, the use range of different encoders is not the same. The larger the value of k, the wider the scope of its application. Table 2 shows the specific encoding process of $49_{10} = 110001_2$.

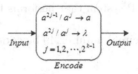

Fig. 3. An SN P system that performs the coding

In the system there is one neuron with label $Encode$; neuron σ_{Encode} is also the output one. In the initial configuration there are x spikes in neuron σ_{Encode}, and the neuron fires already in the first step. If number of spikes in neuron σ_{Encode} is an odd number, then the spiking rule $a^{2j-1}/a^j \rightarrow a$ is used. On the contrary, if number of spikes in neuron σ_{Encode} is an even number, then the forgetting rule $a^{2j}/a^j \rightarrow \lambda$ is used. Assume that this happens in step t. This means that at step $t + 1$ neuron σ_{Encode} emits its spike. The spiking or forgetting rule in neuron σ_{Encode} is used repeatedly until there is no spike in neuron σ_{Encode}. Note that x and k must satisfy a certain relationship: if $2^{p-1} \leq x \leq 2^p$, then k is at least p.

Table 2 In the encoding process of $49_{10} = 110001_2$, the number of spikes in the neurons and sent to the environment [11].

Table 2. Number of spikes in each neuron of the coding SN P system(illustrated in Fig. 3) and number of spikes sent to the environment, at each time step during the computation of the coding $49_{10} = 110001_2$

t	Encode	Output
0	49	0
1	24	1
2	12	0
3	6	0
4	3	0
5	1	1
6	0	1

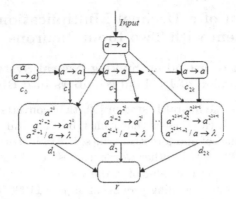

Fig. 4. An SN P system that performs the decoding

Obviously, to make the decimal number 49 be coded correctly, the value must be at least 6.

3.2   Constructing a Decoding Spiking Neural System for Converting Binary Numbers to Decimal Numbers

In order to convert a binary number to a decimal number, it is necessary to construct the decoding spiking neural P system [12] as shown in Fig. 4. If the binary number is not greater than $2^{2k} - 1$, then the system can convert it to the corresponding decimal number.

In the system there are $4k + 3$ neurons, where σ_{Input} is the input neuron and σ_{Ir} is the output one. In the initial configuration there are spikes in neurons c_0 and $d_i (1 \leq i \leq 2k)$.

Table 3 shows the spike number of every neuron in each step in the conversion process of $111111_2 = 63_{10}$.

Table 3. Number of spikes in each neuron of the decoding SN P system (illustrated in Fig. 4) and number of spikes sent to the environment, at each time step during the computation of the decoding $111111_2 = 63_{10}$

t	Input	c_0	c_1	c_2	c_3	c_4	c_5	c_6	d_1	d_2	d_3	d_4	d_5	d_6	Decode
0	0	1	0	0	0	0	0	0	1	2	4	8	16	32	0
1	1	0	1	0	0	0	0	0	1	2	4	8	16	32	0
2	1	0	0	1	0	0	0	0	3	3	5	9	17	33	0
3	1	0	0	0	1	0	0	0	1	4	5	9	17	33	1
4	1	0	0	0	0	1	0	0	2	1	6	9	17	33	3
5	1	0	0	0	0	0	1	0	2	2	1	10	17	33	7
6	1	0	0	0	0	0	0	1	2	3	2	1	18	33	15
7	0	0	0	0	0	0	0	0	2	3	3	2	1	34	31
8	0	0	0	0	0	0	0	0	1	2	3	2	1	0	63

3.3   Construction of Decimal Multiplication SN P System

If the input of a multiplier has an encoding function and its output has a decoding function, a decimal multiplier can be designed. Through the previous analysis, a decimal multiplication SN P system is designed such as Fig. 5.

The system consists of three parts. The function of the first part is to convert two decimal natural numbers into two binary natural numbers. The function of the middle part is to calculate the product of two binary natural numbers. The function of the third part is to convert the binary natural number into a decimal

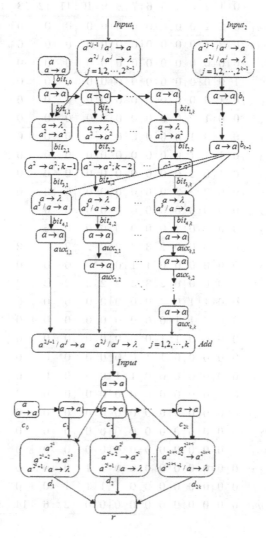

Fig. 5. An SN P system that performs the multiplication between two decimal natural numbers

natural number. $Input_1$ and $Input_2$ are two input neurons and r is the output neuron.

For example, in order to compute the product $5 \cdot 6 = 30$, so $k = 3$. Table 4 gives the number of spikes in each neuron at each time step.

Table 4. Number of spikes in each neuron of the SN P system(illustrated in Fig. 4)and number of spikes sent to the environment, at each time step during the computation of the multiplication $5 \cdot 6 = 30$

Step	0	1	2	3	4	5	6	7	8	9	10	11	12	13	14
$Input_1$	5	2	1	0	0	0	0	0	0	0	0	0	0	0	0
$Input_2$	6	3	1	0	0	0	0	0	0	0	0	0	0	0	0
$bit1_0$	0	0	0	0	0	0	0	0	0	0	0	0	0	0	0
$bit1_1$	1	0	0	0	0	0	0	0	0	0	0	0	0	0	0
$bit1_2$	0	1	0	0	0	0	0	0	0	0	0	0	0	0	0
$bit1_3$	0	0	1	0	0	0	0	0	0	0	0	0	0	0	0
$bit_{2,1}$	0	2	0	1	0	0	0	0	0	0	0	0	0	0	0
$bit_{2,2}$	0	1	1	1	0	0	0	0	0	0	0	0	0	0	0
$bit_{2,3}$	0	1	0	2	0	0	0	0	0	0	0	0	0	0	0
$bit_{3,1}$	0	0	2	2	2	0	0	0	0	0	0	0	0	0	0
$bit_{3,2}$	0	0	0	0	0	0	0	0	0	0	0	0	0	0	0
$bit_{3,3}$	0	0	0	0	2	0	0	0	0	0	0	0	0	0	0
$bit_{4,1}$	0	0	0	0	0	2	3	3	2	2	2	2	2	2	2
$bit_{4,2}$	0	0	0	0	0	0	0	1	1	0	0	0	0	0	0
$bit_{4,3}$	0	0	0	0	0	2	3	3	2	2	2	2	2	2	2
b_1	0	0	1	1	0	0	0	0	0	0	0	0	0	0	0
b_2	0	0	0	1	1	0	0	0	0	0	0	0	0	0	0
b_3	0	0	0	0	1	1	0	0	0	0	0	0	0	0	0
b_4	0	0	0	0	0	1	1	0	0	0	0	0	0	0	0
$aux_{1,1}$	0	0	0	0	0	0	0	0	1	1	0	0	0	0	0
$aux_{2,1}$	0	0	0	0	0	0	0	0	0	0	0	0	0	0	0
$aux_{2,2}$	0	0	0	0	0	0	0	0	0	0	0	0	0	0	0
$aux_{3,1}$	0	0	0	0	0	0	0	0	0	0	0	0	0	0	0
$aux_{3,2}$	0	0	0	0	0	0	0	0	0	0	0	0	0	0	0
$aux_{3,3}$	0	0	0	0	0	0	0	0	0	1	1	0	0	0	0
Add	0	0	0	0	0	0	0	0	1	1	1	1	0	0	0
$Output$	0	0	0	0	0	0	0	0	0	0	0	2	6	14	30

4   Conclusions

In this paper, it is investigated to compute the product of any two decimal natural numbers by using a new spiking neural P system. No matter in theory or in practice, it is effective to use the system to compute any two natural products. Therefore, this paper provides a new method for the CPU design of the spiking neural P system. It should be noted that the hardware structure designed here can only compute the product of any two unsigned decimal integers, but it is invalid to the product of the signed integers. Therefore, in the near future the existing spiking neural P system need to be improved so that it can be used to compute the product of any two signed decimal integers.

Acknowledgments. This project was supported by the Special Scientific Research Fund of Food Public Welfare Profession of China (Grant No. 201513004-3), the Hubei Province Natural Science Fund Project (2016CFB273), the Humanities and Social Sciences Fund Project of Hubei Provincial Education Department (17Y071), and the Guiding Scientific Research Project of Hubei Provincial Education Department (B2017072, B2017078).

References

1. Gutrrez-Naranjo, M.A., Leporati., A.: First steps towards a CPU made of spiking neural P systems. Int. J. Comput. Comm. Contr. **4**(3), 244–252 (2009)
2. Zhang, X., Zeng, X., Pan, L.: A spiking neural P system for performing multiplication of two arbitrary natural numbers. Chin. J. Comput., 2362–2372 (2009)
3. Song, T., Pan, L.: Asynchronous spiking neural P systems with local synchronization. Inf. Sci. **219**, 197–207 (2012)
4. Song, B., Pan, L., Pérez-Jiménez, M.J.: Tissue P systems with protein on cells. Fundam. Inform. **144**, 77–107 (2016)
5. Wu, T., Zhang, Z., Pan, L.: Cell-like spiking neural P systems. Theor. Comput. Sci. **623**, 180–189 (2016). doi:10.1016/j.tcs.2015.12.038
6. Pan, L., Wang, J., Hoogeboom, H.J.: Asynchronous Extended Spiking Neural P Systems with Astrocytes. In: Gheorghe, M., Păun, G., Rozenberg, G., Salomaa, A., Verlan, S. (eds.) CMC 2011. LNCS, vol. 7184, pp. 243–256. Springer, Heidelberg (2012). doi:10.1007/978-3-642-28024-5_17
7. Zeng, X., Zhang, X., Song, T., Pan, L.: Spiking neural P systems with thresholds. Neural Comput. **26**, 1340–1361 (2014)
8. Zhang, G., Rong, H., Neri, F., Prez-Jimnez, M.J.: An optimization spiking neural P system for approximately solving combinatorial optimization problems. Int. J. Neural Syst. **24**(5), 1–16 (2014)
9. Pan, L., Zeng, X., Zhang, X.: Time-free spiking neural P systems. Neural. Comput. **23**(5), 1320–1342 (2011)
10. Ramanujan, A., Krithivasan, K.: Control words of transition P systems. In: Bansal, J., Singh, P., Deep, K., Pant, M., Nagar, A. (eds.) Proceedings of Seventh International Conference on Bio-Inspired Computing: Theories and Applications (BIC-TA 2012). AISC, vol. 201, pp. 145–155. Springer, India (2013). doi:10.1007/978-81-322-1038-2_13

11. Verlan, S., Quiros, J.: Fast Hardware Implementations of P Systems. In: Csuhaj-Varjú, E., Gheorghe, M., Rozenberg, G., Salomaa, A., Vaszil, G. (eds.) CMC 2012. LNCS, vol. 7762, pp. 404–423. Springer, Heidelberg (2013). doi:10. 1007/978-3-642-36751-9_27

12. Pan, L., Pèrez-Jimènez, M.J.: Spiking neural P systems with neuron division and budding. Sci. China Inf. Sci. **54**(8), 1596–1607 (2011)

13. Song, B., Pan, L.: Computational efficiency and universality of timed P systems with active membranes. Theoret. Comput. Sci. **567**, 74–86 (2015)

14. Song, B., Pérez-Jiménez, M.J., Pan, L.: Computational efficiency and universality of timed P systems with membrane creation. Soft Comput. **19**(11), 3043–3053 (2015)

A Modified Standard PSO-2011 with Robust Search Ability

Hongguan Liu[✉] and Fei Han

School of Computer Science and Communication Engineering, Jiangsu University,
Zhenjiang 212013, Jiangsu, China
{2211508015,hanfei}@ujs.edu.cn

Abstract. Standard particle swarm optimization 2011(SPSO2011, takes SPSO for short) was proposed to overcome problems that there is bias of the search area existing in the conventional PSO depending on rotational invariant property. The performance of SPSO is affected by the distribution of the center of the search range and the global search ability fades away during the iteration process. In this paper, in order to reinforce diversity-maintain ability as well as improve local search ability, a modified diversity-guided SPSO (DGAP-MSPSO) algorithm is proposed. A modified SPSO variant with average point method is first applied till the swarm loses its diversity thus to improve local search ability. Then, the search process turns to another new SPSO variant in which an enhanced diversity-maintain operator is used for global search. The DGAP-MSPSO switches alternately between two SPSO variants according to swarm diversity, thus its search ability is improved. Experimental results shows that our proposed algorithm, the DGAP-MSPSO algorithm, gets better performance on most test functions compared with other SPSO variants.

Keywords: Particle swarm optimization · Swarm diversity · Global search ability · Local search ability · Average point method

1 Introduction

Since the particle swarm optimization algorithm was proposed in 1995 [1], the algorithm has been successfully applied to many problems such as artificial neural network training, function optimization and pattern classification etc. The search performance of conventional PSO variants is affected by many factors, such as the number of local optima, the design variables, the topology structure, the ill-conditioned and non-separable problems [2,3] etc.

The SPSO algorithm [4] was proposed to overcome non-separable problems [5,6]. The two important factors of SPSO are the center of the search range and the search radius. The center of the search range is determined by the center of gravity of current position, the local best position and personal best position. The update rule of the center of gravity guarantees rotation invariant

© Springer Nature Singapore Pte Ltd. 2017
C. He et al. (Eds.): BIC-TA 2017, CCIS 791, pp. 207–222, 2017.
https://doi.org/10.1007/978-981-10-7179-9_16

property of SPSO. It has been discussed in [7] that rotation invariance properties have predictive effects on non-separable problems. However, the most common versions of PSO are rotation variant, thus performances of conventional PSO are easily affected by rotation of the coordinate system [8]. A modified SPSO (MSPSO) was proposed to maintain center diversity by utilizing a diversity-maintain operator and thus to improve global search ability [9]. Two random diagonal matrices was introduced in MSPSO to improve swarm diversity which shows less purposeful due to the randomness of this scheme.

Although PSO have been applied successfully on many optimization problems, it still suffers from premature convergence when it is applied on multimodal functions. Many papers solved premature convergence problems by introducing diversity-maintain operator. In [10], a spatial extension PSO(SEPSO) was proposed. In SEPSO, every particle is enclosed in a sphere with some radius. These spheres bounce off when they collide with each other by the way diversity is maintained. Later, the adaptive radius and bounce parameters were added to improve the performance of SEPSO in [11]. In [12], the author added swarm diversity by extending the particles with self-organized criticality. In [13], a diversity-guided PSO, the ARPSO was proposed to prevent premature convergence which alternates between phases of attraction and repulsion according to swarm diversity. The ARPSO consumes more time than basic PSO variants for attracting and repulsing particles during search process. Moreover, the mechanism of attraction and repulsion has never been applied to SPSO variants. Based on [13], a hybrid PSO variant, the DGHPSOGS, which takes advantages of random search and semi-deterministic search was developed to improve search performance as well as maintain swarm diversity [14]. Although the DGHPSOGS improved convergence performance to a great extent, it required derivative information of object function and it was not convenient for promotion e.g. when DGHPSOGS was applied on benchmark functions which consists of a large amount of object functions, all derivatives of object functions should be calculated which resulted in a large time consumption. Moreover, for some complex functions, a large number of flat areas exist in search domain where derivative value approach 0. Under the circumstance, derivative information did not work effectively to achieve solution, oppositely, it slowed down convergence speed.

However, the core idea of these diversity-guided algorithms that conventional PSO variant adopts different search behaviors according to swarm diversity has never been applied to SPSO variants. Moreover, although MSPSO has improved the global search ability, it emphasized global search through whole iteration process which may have bad influence when particles need local search.

In this paper, a modified diversity-guided SPSO algorithm was proposed to improve the search ability. The direction parameter dir is used to represent different phases of the algorithm. When the swarm diversity declines below predetermined threshold d_{low} , the algorithm switches to repeal each other as well as increases swarm diversity by using an enhanced diversity-maintain operator until the threshold d_{high} is met. When the swarm diversity is greater than the threshold d_{high}, we guarantee the algorithm with proper local search ability by utilizing the update rule of SPSO combining with average point method thus to decrease swarm diversity. Therefore, the modified SPSO variant is obtained which is called DGAP-MSPSO: the modified diversity-guided combining with enhanced diversity-maintain operator and average point method SPSO algorithm.

2 Particle Swarm Optimization

2.1 Basic Particle Swarm Optimization

PSO algorithm searches for the best solution by simulating the movement of birds. The population of the birds is called swarm, and the members of the population are particles. During each iteration, each particle flies in its own direction which is guided by its own previous best position and the global best position of all particles. PSO algorithm with inertia weight called basic PSO was proposed in [16]. Each particle of basic PSO algorithm three vectors, position x_i^t, velocity v_i^t and previous best position $p_i^t . i = 1, 2, .., N, t = 0, 1, ..T$, with N equals to swarm size and T equals to maximum number of iterations. The basic PSO algorithm is described as follows:

$$v_i^{t+1} = wv_i^t + c_1 R_{1,i}^t (p_i^t - x_i^t) + c_2 R_{2,i}^t (g^t - x_i^t) \tag{1}$$

$$x_i^{t+1} = x_i^t + v_i^{t+1} \tag{2}$$

g^t is the global best position of all particles for it adopts star topology. w is the inertia weight coefficient introduced by Shi and Eberhart. R is a randomly generated diagonal matrix consists of uniform random number in [0,1].

Traditional topologies for conventional PSO includes the gbest(star), lbest(circles), and von Neumann. Basic PSO adopts gbest(star) topology because this topology is the simplest topology.

2.2 Standard Particle Swarm Optimization 2011

Due to the factor that the performance of basic PSO algorithm is affected by rotation of the coordinate system [5,6,8,17–19], and is deteriorated in non-separable problems, Clerc proposed the original SPSO [4] with rotation invariant property. Figure 1 shows the performance of SPSO, basic PSO on the two dimensional Ellipse function that is rotated from 0 to 180°. The performance of SPSO is not significantly changed by rotating the search space while the performance of basic PSO is sensitive to rotation angle.

As shown in Fig. 2, for each particle and at each time step, a center of gravity G_i^t is defined around three points: the current position x_i^t, a point a little beyond the best previous personal position, P_i^t, and a point a little beyond the best previous position in the neighborhood, L_i^t, as follows:

$$\begin{cases} P_i^t = x_i^t + c_1 R_{1,i}^t (p_i^t - x_i^t) \\ L_i^t = x_i^t + c_2 R_{2,i}^t (l_i^t - x_i^t) \end{cases} \tag{3}$$

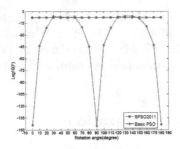

Fig. 1. Performance of two PSO variants on two dimensional rotated ellipse function.

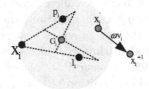

Fig. 2. Distribution of all the next possible positions (DNPP) in SPSO.

$$G_i^t = \frac{(x_i^t + P_i^t + L_i^t)}{3} \tag{4}$$

$H_i(G_i^t, \|G_i^t - x_i^t\|)$ is a hypersphere with the center G_i^t and the radius $\|G_i^t - x_i^t\|$, a random point $x^{'}$ is then defined in the hypersphere. In SPSO, velocity is updated as follows:

$$v_i^{t+1} = wv_i^t + x^{'} - x_i^t \tag{5}$$

The position update rule is the same as conventional PSO algorithm, which means the new position update rule is simply:

$$x_i^{t+1} = x_i^t + v_i^{t+1} = wv_i^t + x^{'} \tag{6}$$

The inertia weight coefficient and acceleration coefficients shown in Eq. (7) are recommended parameters in [4, 15].

$$\begin{cases} w = \frac{1}{2ln(2)} \approx 0.721 \\ c_1 = c_2 = 0.5 + ln2 \approx 1.193 \end{cases} \tag{7}$$

SPSO employs an adaptive random topology [7, 15], in which each particle randomly informs at most $K + 1$ particles (include itself), with K usually set to 3. The topology may randomly change when the global optimum shows no improvement during the last iteration.

3   The Proposed Algorithm

Although SPSO has better performance than conventional PSO variants on rotated functions, it still suffers from premature convergence when it is applied on multimodal functions. The premature convergence occurs with the loss of swarm diversity, however, it can be eased by introducing diversity into population to guide particles search behavior. The proposed algorithm adopts attraction and repulsion mechanism as well as specified search behavior according to swarm diversity to not only improve premature convergence but also increase search efficiency. The global search behavior including enhanced diversity-maintain operator and local search behavior utilizing average point method are discussed in this section.

On one hand, when the swarm is trapped into the local minimum, the swarm will lose diversity. To make the swarm jump out of the local minimum, the enhanced diversity-maintain operator is used to enlarge search radius thus to improve swarm diversity. The swarm diversity is derived by Eq. (8).

$$diversity = \frac{1}{N^p \cdot |L|} \cdot \sum_{i=1}^{N^p} \sqrt{\sum_{j=1}^{D}(p_{ij} - \overline{p_j})^2} \qquad (8)$$

where $|L|$ is the length of the maximum radius of the search space; p_{ij} is the jth component of the ith particle and $\overline{p_j}$ is the jth component of the average over all particles. It has been discussed that this diversity measure is robust with respect to the population size, the dimensionality of the problem and the search range of each of the variables.

In order to adjust search behavior to accommodate swarm diversity, when the swarm is trapped into local optimum, the algorithm switches to repulsion phase: the enhanced diversity-maintain operator is applied in the hope of strengthening the global search ability as shown in Eq. (9). In Eq. (9), the matrix M_i^t is a little different from that in MSPSO, the matrix M_i^t is also a random diagonal matrix but its element is in $[1,2]$. Under this circumstance, P_i^t and L_i^t are in an enhanced relationship rather than the complementary relationship in MSPSO.

$$\begin{cases} P_i^t = x_i^t + c_1 M_{i,t}^t (p_i^t - x_i^t) \\ L_i^t = x_i^t + c_2 M_{i,t}^t (l_i^t - x_i^t) \end{cases} \qquad (9)$$

On the other hand, when the algorithm switches to attraction phase: particles are dispersive, the update rule of SPSO combining with the average point method is used in the hope of gathering particles and converging to optimum quickly.

In both SPSO and MSPSO, the center G_i^t is decided around three points: the current position x_i^t , a point a little beyond the best previous personal position, P_i^t , and a point a little beyond the best previous position in the neighborhood, L_i^t. Meanwhile, the personal previous best position p_i^t contributes to the construction of P_i^t. For the purpose of improving local search ability of our algorithm, the personal previous best position p_i^t is replaced with a new point defined by the equation as follows:

$$p_{modified} = \frac{\sum_{j(F_i > F_{pbest_j})} pbest_j (F_i - F_{pbest_j})/\|x_i - pbest_j\|^2}{\sum_{j(F_i > F_{pbest_j})} (F_i - F_{pbest_j})/\|x_i - pbest_j\|^2} \qquad (10)$$

where F_i is the fitness of ith particle; $pbest_j$ is the previous best position of jth particle; F_{pbest_j} is the fitness corresponding to $pbest_j$; $\|x_i - pbest_j\|^2$ is the square of the Euclidean distance between target particle i and the previous best position of particle j which satisfied $F_i > F_{pbest_j}$.

The point $p_{modified}$ is the average point of particles (not include the target particle i) previous best position. Since this new generated point represents a swarm-level conformity, the movement to $p_{modified}$ enables particles search an area which consists of particle j satisfying the above condition. In this way, particles exploit the local optima area more effectively which in turn provides the algorithm a good local search ability. Under the circumstance, the update rule of our method is shown as follows:

$$\begin{cases} P_i^t = x_i^t + c_1 R_{1,i}^t (p_{modified} - x_i^t) \\ L_i^t = x_i^t + c_2 R_{2,i}^t (l_i^t - x_i^t) \end{cases} \qquad (11)$$

The proposed DGAP-MSPSO algorithm adopts the mechanism of attraction and repulsion, at the same time, enhanced diversity-maintain operator and average point method are used to improve search ability. The flowchart of the proposed algorithm is shown in Fig. 3.

Figure 3 depicts the process of proposed algorithm. Firstly, after initializing particles, swarm diversity is above a certain threshold d_{low} which means the algorithm begins with attraction phase and the direction parameter dir is set to 1. The SPSO variant combining with average point method is first used till the diversity value of the swarm is less than d_{low}. Secondly, when the swarm diversity drops down d_{low}, the algorithm turns to repulsion phase by the way the direction parameter dir is set to -1. Another SPSO variant whose update rule includes an enhanced diversity-maintain operator is used to sequentially search the solution as well as increase swarm diversity until the threshold d_{high} is met, at last, the proposed algorithm switches back to attraction phase. The mechanism of attraction and repulsion enables the algorithm switch between phases of exploitation and exploration according to swarm diversity.

In the proposed method, which SPSO variant is used to perform search is decided by swarm diversity. On one hand, the SPSO variant combining with average point method may cause the swarm to lose its diversity by the way the swarm is trapped into local minima with high likelihood. On the other hand, the enhanced diversity-maintain operator can keep swarm diversity as well as strengthen global search ability which may increase the likelihood of finding the global minima.

Let T be the max iteration number; N, the particle number; D, the dimension of particles. So the time complexity of SPSO is $T_1 = O(N \times D \times T)$, the

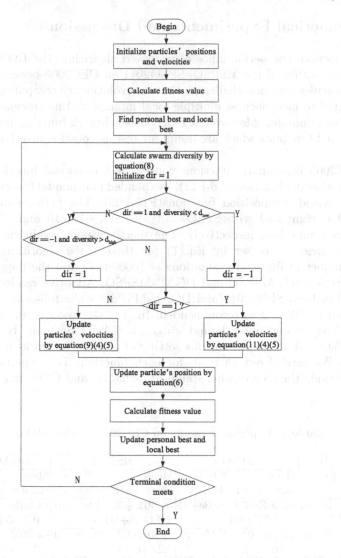

Fig. 3. The follow chart of DGAP-MSPSO

time complexity of average point method is $T_2 = O(N \times D)$. Therefore, time complexity of our proposed DGAP-MSPSO is $T = T_1 + T_2 \approx O(N \times D \times T)$, the proposed algorithm has the same order of magnitudes of time complexity as SPSO but it still consumes more CPU time than SPSO due to the additional scheme.

4   Numerical Experiments and Discussion

In this section, the performance of proposed algorithm, the DGAP-MSPSO is compared to that of the MSPSO, SPSO2011 on CEC2005 benchmark function which provides common challenges that an evolutionary computation algorithm is expected to face, such as multiple local minima and flat regions surrounding the global minimum. Moreover, CEC2005 benchmark function includes shifted and rotated functions which are useful for testing rotation invariant property of PSOs.

CEC2005 benchmark functions consist of 5 unimodal functions(F1-F5), 7 basic multimodal functions(F6-F12), 2 expanded multimodal functions(F13-F14) and 11 hybrid composition functions(F15-F25). The performance of DGAP-MSPSO is compared with SPSO and MSPSO, with 10 and 30 dimensional benchmark functions respectively. The inertia weight coefficient and acceleration coefficients are set by Eq. (7) for these three algorithms. The maximum number of function evaluations is $10000 \times D$ and the population size is 40 for SPSO2011, MSPSO and DGAP-MSPSO. Adaptive random topology is adopted in both SPSO2011 and DGAP-MSPSO while full-connected topology is applied in MSPSO as recommended. In [13], the lower bound of diversity is $d_{low} = 5.0e - 6$ and upper bound is $d_{high} = 0.25$. After many trials, we decide $d_{low} = 5.0e - 3$, $d_{high} = 0.25$, this setting of parameters works better with our scheme. We carried out 25 trials for each function. The experimental results which include the mean value, standard deviation and CPU time are shown in Table 1.

Table 1. Experiment results on CEC2005 benchmark functions

Functions	f (x^*)	Dim	SPSO Mean value ± std	SPSO CPU Time(s)	MSPSO Mean value ± std	MSPSO CPU Time(s)	DGAP-MSPSO Mean value ± std	DGAP-MSPSO CPU Time(s)
F1	-450	n=10	**-4.50E+02 ±0.00E+00**	2.03e+01	**-4.50E+02 ±0.00E+00**	1.94e+01	**-4.50E+02 ±0.00E+00**	4.41e+01
		n=30	-3.87E+02 ±9.00E+01	9.15e+01	-4.50E+02 ±2.01E-14	9.15e+01	**-4.50E+02 ±7.47E-15**	1.62e+02
F2	-450	n=10	-4.09E+02 ±8.46E+01	2.33e+01	-4.50E+02 ±1.64E-14	2.25e+01	**-4.50E+02 ±0.00E+00**	5.07e+01
		n=30	1.01E+04 ±3.86E+03	1.08e+02	-4.50E+02 ±1.45E-13	1.09e+02	**-4.50E+02 ±3.47E-14**	1.86e+02
F3	-450	n=10	2.00E+06 ±2.00E+06	2.16e+01	1.13E+05 ±2.20E+05	2.51e+01	**4.15E+04 ±3.21E+04**	4.67e+01
		n=30	3.13E+07 ±1.49E+07	9.51e+01	5.72E+05 ±4.10E+05	9.59e+01	**3.32E+05 ±1.96E+05**	1.53e+02

(*Continued*)

Table 1. (*Continued*)

F4	-450	n=10	1.41E+03 ±1.57E+03	2.76e+01	-4.50E+02 ±3.48E-14	2.71e+01	**-4.50E+02** **±0.00E+00**	5.63e+01
		n=30	3.78E+04 ±9.58E+03	1.16e+02	-1.43E+02 ±1.04E+03	1.15e+02	**-1.96E+02** **±4.82E+03**	2.03e+02
F5	-310	n=10	2.80E+02 ±9.94E+02	1.85e+01	-2.96E+02 ±3.32E+01	1.93e+01	-3.10E+02 ±0.00E+00	5.57e+01
		n=30	1.20E+04 ±3.33E+03	8.63e+01	6.97E+03 ±2.40E+03	8.57e+01	**4.12E+03** **±8.13E+02**	1.66e+02
F6	390	n=10	1.79E+04 4.14E+04	2.26e+01	4.59E+02 1.94E+02	2.10e+01	**4.40E+02** **±8.56E+01**	5.12e+01
		n=30	1.18E+06 ±3.05E+06	9.69e+01	6.30E+02 ±4.27E+02	9.51e+01	**5.71E+02** **±2.88E+02**	1.56e+02
F7	-180	n=10	-1.79E+02 1.37E+00	2.22e+01	**-1.80E+02** **±1.57E-01**	2.15e+01	-1.67E+02 ±4.76E-01	4.93e+01
		n=30	1.45E+02 ±2.34E+01	9.58e+01	**-1.80E+02** **± 1.29E-02**	9.50e+01	4.64E+03 5.32E+01	1.62e+02
F8	-140	n=10	-1.20E+02 ±8.14E-02	2.49e+01	-1.20E+02 ±8.63E-02	2.31e+01	**-1.20E+02** **± 1.83E-02**	5.83e+01
		n=30	-1.19E+02 ±9.61E-02	9.69e+01	-1.19E+02 ±5.68E-02	9.51e+01	**-1.20E+02** **±4.00E-01**	1.75e+02
F9	-330	n=10	-3.08E+02 1.03E+01	2.12e+01	-3.15E+02 6.20E+00	2.09e+01	**-3.25E+02** **±2.33E+00**	5.23e+01
		n=30	-1.88E+02 ±4.29E+01	9.19e+01	-2.18E+02 ±2.92E+01	9.16e+01	**-2.86E+02** **±9.45E+00**	1.80e+02
F10	-330	n=10	-3.03E+02 1.46E+01	2.19e+01	-3.12E+02 7.28E+00	2.13e+01	**-3.24E+02** **±2.33E+00**	5.17e+01
		n=30	-1.20E+02 ±5.48E+01	9.49e+01	-2.04E+02 ±4.35E+01	1.03e+02	**-2.80E+02** **±1.31E+01**	1.70e+02
F11	90	n=10	9.61E+01 1.65E+00	5.04e+01	9.39E+01 1.61E+00	5.00e+01	**9.25E+01** **±1.22E+00**	8.53e+01
		n=30	1.20E+02 ±2.86E+00	2.36e+02	1.17E+02 ±3.60E+00	2.36e+02	**1.07E+02** **±3.33E+00**	3.23e+02
F12	-460	n=10	1.87E+03 ±3.70E+03	2.83e+01	**5.94E+02** **±1.58E+03**	2.51e+01	5.74E+03 ±1.23E+04	5.24e+01
		n=30	9.07E+04 ±3.60E+04	1.06e+02	**3.28E+04** **±3.46E+04**	1.08e+02	2.17E+05 ±4.41E+05	1.66e+02
F13	-130	n=10	-1.29E+02 ±6.30E-01	2.61e+01	-1.29E+02 ±3.48E-01	2.62e+01	**-1.29E+02** **±3.26E-01**	5.10e+01
		n=30	-1.19E+02 ±2.80E+00	1.20e+02	-1.24E+02 ±2.00E+00	1.22e+02	**-1.27E+02** **±1.18E+00**	1.84e+02
F14	-300	n=10	-2.97E+02 ±4.82E-01	3.34e+01	-2.97E+02 ±6.39E-01	3.26e+01	**-2.98E+02** **±4.34E-01**	5.88e+01
		n=30	-2.87E+02 ±2.86E-01	1.35e+02	-2.88E+02 ±5.82E-01	1.34e+02	**-2.88E+02** **±5.73E-01**	2.02e+02

(*Continued*)

Table 1. (*Continued*)

F15	120	n=10	4.67E+02 ±1.80E+02	8.81e+02	4.41E+02 ±1.37E+02	8.50e+02	**3.90E+02 ±1.56E+02**	8.73e+02
		n=30	7.31E+02 ±1.80E+02	1.31e+04	6.28E+02 ±1.58E+02	2.44e+03	5.20E+02 ±5.38E+01	4.21e+03
F16	120	n=10	2.78E+02 ±3.16E+01	8.51e+02	2.70E+02 ±6.03E+01	8.10e+02	**2.22E+02 ±5.55E+00**	8.43e+02
		n=30	5.25E+02 ±1.43E+02	3.91e+03	3.48E+02 ±1.29E+02	3.74e+03	**3.17E+02 ±1.48E+02**	4.83e+03
F17	120	n=10	2.79E+02 ±2.78E+01	8.16e+02	2.63E+02 ±2.29E+01	8.20e+02	**2.23E+02 ±9.83E+00**	8.48e+02
		n=30	6.09E+02 ±1.62E+02	2.76e+03	3.89E+02 ±1.37E+02	4.27e+04	**3.30E+02 ±1.94E+02**	2.50e+03
F18	10	n=10	9.84E+02 ±8.26E+01	8.19e+02	8.77E+02 ±2.12E+02	8.12e+02	**8.13E+02 ±1.60E+02**	8.37e+02
		n=30	9.82E+02 ±3.57E+01	2.44e+03	9.42E+02 ±1.76E+01	2.44e+03	**9.32E+02 ±2.76E+01**	2.53e+03
F19	10	n=10	9.86E+02 ±8.34E+01	8.42e+02	8.81E+02 ±1.96E+02	8.38e+02	**6.94E+02 ±2.48E+02**	8.69e+02
		n=30	9.83E+02 ±3.13E+01	2.44e+03	9.41E+02 ±1.76E+01	2.44e+03	**9.37E+02 ±7.94E+00**	2.52e+03
F20	10	n=10	9.86E+02 ±8.36E+01	8.36e+02	**8.78E+02 ±1.93E+02**	8.40e+02	8.96E+02 ±7.35E+01	8.65e+02
		n=30	9.83E+02 ±3.13E+01	2.44e+03	9.41E+02 ±1.76E+01	2.44e+03	**9.32E+02 ±2.74E+01**	2.53e+03
F21	360	n=10	1.42E+03 ±2.10E+02	1.07e+03	**1.12E+03 ±3.26E+02**	1.07e+03	1.25E+03 ±2.54E+02	1.23e+03
		n=30	1.47E+03 ±2.37E+02	2.72e+03	1.06E+03 ±2.76E+02	2.71e+03	**9.74E+02 ±2.26E+02**	2.80e+03
F22	360	n=10	1.23E+03 ±6.60E+01	1.84e+03	1.18E+03 ±6.84E+01	8.66e+02	**1.14E+03 ±4.71E+01**	8.99e+02
		n=30	1.53E+03 ±8.14E+01	9.96e+03	1.37E+03 ±5.60E+01	2.81e+03	**1.31E+03 ±4.08E+01**	2.90e+03
F23	360	n=10	1.44E+03 ±2.28E+02	8.68e+02	1.39E+03 ±1.43E+02	1.16e+03	**1.37E+03 ±2.17E+01**	1.05e+03
		n=30	1.56E+03 ±9.49E+01	2.70e+03	1.19E+03 ±2.91E+02	2.70e+03	**9.88E+02 ±2.02E+02**	2.80e+03
F24	260	n=10	1.02E+03 ±4.43E+02	8.16e+02	5.56E+02 ±1.43E+02	8.16e+02	**5.28E+02 ±1.83E+02**	9.80e+02
		n=30	1.19E+03 ±4.29E+02	2.42e+03	6.69E+02 ±3.82E+02	2.42e+03	**4.60E+02 ±0.00E+00**	3.41e+04
F25	260	n=10	9.98E+02 ±3.69E+02	9.49e+02	**8.06E+02 ±3.07E+02**	9.21e+02	1.27E+03 ±2.40E+02	9.02e+02
		n=30	1.02E+03 ±4.19E+02	2.45e+03	**5.26E+02 ±2.17E+02**	2.44e+03	1.48E+03 ±4.96E+01	2.53e+03

The numerical experiments indicate that our proposed DGAP-MSPSO algorithm shows better performance than compared algorithms on most benchmark functions. When the dimension of problem is 10, our algorithm gets the best performance in 5 unimodal functions compared with MSPSO and SPSO. However, on F3, all the three algorithms fail in getting the global optimum, but our algorithm still gets the best result. For multimodal functions (F6-F12), DGAP-MSPSO gets better results on F6, F8, F9, F10, F11. On expanded multimodal functions (F13, F14), our algorithm gets results with the least fitness value and standard deviation. At last, for hybrid composition problems, our algorithm gets a common performance but still better than MSPSO and SPSO. In the case of 30 dimensional problem, our algorithm still shows better performance in general. Especially on 11 hybrid composition functions (F15-F25), our algorithm gets better results than SPSO and MSPSO, except the last one F25, which is still a better result compared with that of 10 dimension. As shown in Table 1, on most test functions, SPSO and MSPSO need similar CPU time. For DGAP-MSPSO algorithm, it usually takes more CPU time than compared algorithms because DGAP-MSPSO adopts an enhanced diversity-maintain operator and average point method.

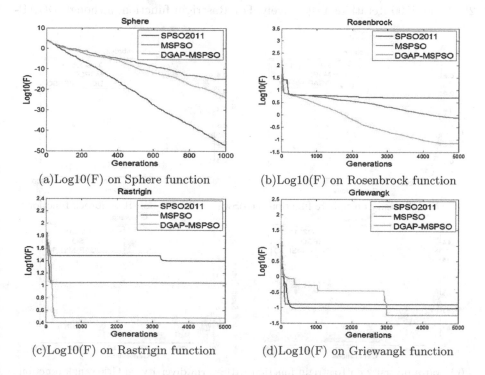

(a)Log10(F) on Sphere function

(b)Log10(F) on Rosenbrock function

(c)Log10(F) on Rastrigin function

(d)Log10(F) on Griewangk function

Fig. 4. Mean best solution versus iteration number for four test functions (n = 10) using three PSOs.

To illustrate convergence ability and specified search ability of our proposed algorithm, we carried out experiments on four representative test functions including the Sphere, Rosenbrock, Rastrigin and Griewangk functions. The Sphere function is a unimodal and convex function; the Rosenbrock function is a multimodal and non-convex function, and its global optimum is inside a long, narrow, parabolic shaped flat valley; the Rastrigin function is a multimodal and non-convex function, and it has large number of local minima; the Griewangk function is a multimodal function, and it has many widespread local minima. Without loss of generality, the following experiments are conducted on the test functions with 10 dimensions.

Figure 4 depicts the mean convergence curve of different PSOs on all four functions with dimensions. Figure 4(b), (c) and (d) shows that DGAP-MSPSO algorithm performs better than SPSO and MSPSO on three multimodal functions. For Sphere function, SPSO performs better than MSPSO and DGAP-MSPSO. SPSO algorithm descends sharply because Sphere function is unimodal and convex. The diversity-maintain operators in MSPSO and DGAP-MSPSO prevent algorithm converging sharply to some degree. For Rosenbrock function, DGAP-MSPSO converges to global optimum after 4500 iterations while SPSO and MSPSO converges to local optimum far from global optimum after 2500 and 4500 iterations respectively. For Rastrigin function, although DGAP-

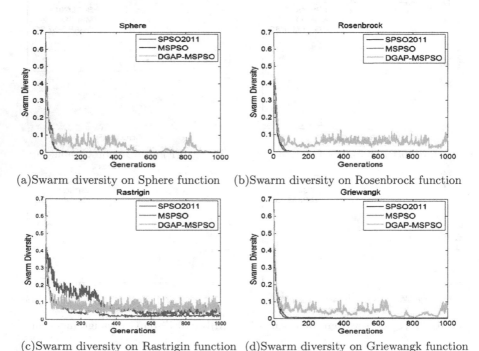

(a)Swarm diversity on Sphere function   (b)Swarm diversity on Rosenbrock function

(c)Swarm diversity on Rastrigin function   (d)Swarm diversity on Griewangk function

Fig. 5. Swarm diversity versus iteration number for four test functions (n = 10) using three PSOs.

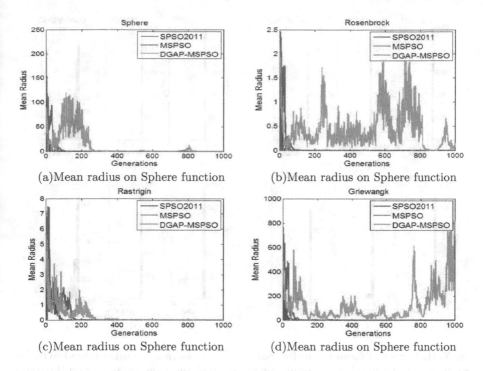

(a)Mean radius on Sphere function

(b)Mean radius on Sphere function

(c)Mean radius on Sphere function

(d)Mean radius on Sphere function

Fig. 6. Mean radius versus iteration number for four test functions ($n = 10$) using three PSOs.

MSPSO does not achieve satisfying convergence accuracy, it still converges near the global optimum which is better than SPSO and MSPSO. For Griewangk function, both SPSO and MSPSO converges to local optimum at an early stage. Though DGAP-MSPSO does not performs such convergence speed, it converges more accurately than SPSO and MSPSO. These experimental results demonstrate that our DGAP-MSPSO achieves better global and local search ability.

Figure 5 depicts swarm diversity of 3 PSOs on the four test functions. Obviously, the SPSO and MSPSO lose its swarm diversity quickly while DGAP-MSPSO keeps diversity in the whole search process. Since MSPSO adopts diversity-maintain operator and SPSO employs adaptively random topology, both these two algorithms can maintain swarm diversity to some degree. For Sphere, Rosenbrock and Griewangk functions, DGAP-MSPSO can maintain swarm diversity in the whole search process; SPSO and MSPSO shows similar performance but MSPSO performs a little better than SPSO. For Rastrigin function, SPSO loses swarm diversity quickly while MSPSO maintain high value of swarm diversity at early stage. However, DGAP-MSPSO keeps a stable swarm diversity during iteration process which in turn demonstrates the robustness of our scheme.

Figure 6 shows the mean radius of 3 PSOs on four test functions. During each iteration, we calculate the mean value of particles search radius. As discussed

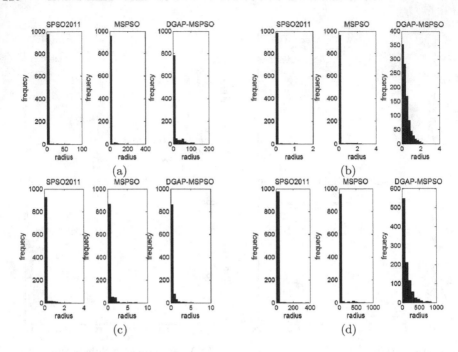

Fig. 7. Histogram of mean radius for four test functions (n = 10) using three PSOs: (a) results on Sphere function, (b) results on Rosenbrock function, (c) results on Rastrigin function, (d) results on Griewangk function.

in [9], the search radius is desirable to be larger which guarantees better global search ability. For Rosenbrock and Griewangk function, DGAP-MSPSO keeps search radius a high value during whole iteration process; Both MSPSO and SPSO can not maintain search radius, but MSPSO shows better performance than SPSO. For Sphere function, these three algorithms lose their search radius at early stage, but MSPSO achieves higher initial value and DGAP-MSPSO keeps search radius until almost 220 iteration numbers. These experimental results demonstrate a robust global search ability of DGAP-MSPSO.

Figure 7 shows histogram of mean radius on four test functions. Both SPSO and MSPSO have high frequency of search radius on small values due to their update schemes of search center while DGAP-MSPSO improves a lot. Only for Rastrigin function, DGAP-MSPSO and MSPSO have similar performance. For Sphere, Rosenbrock and Griewangk function, MSPSO shows a little better than SPSO but DGAP-MSPSO does improve a lot due to our scheme.

Below, we discuss the effects of the parameters in the DGAP-MSPSO. In adaptive random topology, each particle informs at random K particles and K = 3 is recommended parameter in [4,15] for SPSO. For our DGAP-MSPSO algorithm, we carried out experiments on the same four test functions: Sphere, Rosenbrock, Rastrigin, Griewangk functions. The swarm size is 40 and the dimension of problem is 10. We set the range of K as 1, 3, 5, 7, 9, 11, 13, 17. For Sphere

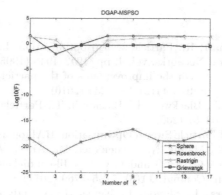

Fig. 8. The number of K for DGAP-MSPSO versus best solutions for four test functions.

function, we conduct 1000 iterations and for the other three functions we adopt 5000 iterations. We calculate mean values of 10 trials and the experiment results are shown in Fig. 8. The results show that Griewangk function is not sensitive to the changes of K while Sphere function , Rosenbrock function and Rastrigin function achieve best solutions at $K = 3$, 3, 5 respectively. Therefore, for DGAP-MSPSO, we also adopt $K = 3$ in our experiment settings.

5 Conclusion

To improve the balance between global and local search at the same time strengthen the search ability, DGAP-MSPSO was proposed in this paper. Based on MSPSO proposed before, we investigated the fact that although MSPSO improves global search ability, it cannot guarantee proper search behavior at specified time. At the same time, attraction and repulsion mechanism was introduced to guide specified search behavior. From this point of view, an enhanced diversity-maintain operator was developed in our algorithm. Moreover, a new point-generated method named average point method is introduced to take place of personal previous best, the new point contributes to the reinforcement of local search ability. The experimental results were provided to verify that the proposed algorithm performs better than MSPSO and SPSO. At last, we discuss the effects of the parameters in DGAP-MSPSO. Although our algorithm gets better results than SPSO and MSPSO, on some functions, our algorithm still failed in getting global optimum. On some complex functions, we will continue to modify our algorithm to get satisfying results.

Acknowledgments. This work was supported by the National Natural Science Foundation of China (Nos. 61572241 and 61271385), the Foundation of the Peak of Six Talents of Jiangsu Province (No. 2015-DZXX-024), and the Fifth 333 High Level Talented Person Cultivating Project of Jiangsu Province.

References

1. Kennedy, J., Eberhart, R.: Particle swarm optimization. In: IEEE International Conference on Neural Networks, vol. 4, pp. 1942–1948 (1995)
2. Chen, T.Y., Chi, T.M.: On the improvements of the particle swarm optimization algorithm. Adv. Eng. Softw. **41**(2), 229–239 (2010)
3. Poli, R., Kennedy, J., Blackwell, T., Blackwell, T.: Particle swarm optimization. Swarm Intell. **1**(1), 33–57 (2007)
4. Clerc, M.: Standard Particle Swarm Optimisation. HAL open access archive (2012)
5. Hansen, N., Ros, R., Mauny, N., Schoenauer, M., Auger, A.: Impacts of invariance in search: when CMA-ES and PSO face Ill-conditioned and non-separable problems. Appl. Soft. Comput. **11**(8), 5755–5769 (2011)
6. Hariya, Y., Kurihara, T., Shindo, T., Kenya, J.: A study of robustness of PSO for non-separable evaluation functions. In: International Symposium on Nonlinear Theory and Its Applications, vol. 1, no. 2 (2015)
7. Bonyadi, M.R., Michalewicz, Z.: A locally convergent rotationally invariant particle swarm optimization algorithm. Swarm. Intell. **3**, 159–198 (2014)
8. Spears, W.M., Green, D.T., Spears, D.F.: Biases in particle swarm optimization. Int. J. Swarm Intell. Res. **1**(2), 34–57 (2010)
9. Hariya, Y., Shindo, T., Jin'no, K.: An improved rotationally invariant PSO: a modified standard PSO-2011. In: IEEE Congress on Evolutionary Computation. IEEE (2016)
10. Krink, T., Vesterstrom, J.S., Riget, J.: Particle swarm optimisation with spatial particle extension. In: 2002 IEEE Congress on Evolutionary Computation, pp. 1474–1479 (2002)
11. Monson, C.K., Seppi, K.D.: Adaptive diversity in PSO. In: Conference on Genetic and Evolutionary Computation, pp. 59–66. New York (2006)
12. Lovbjerg, M., Krink, T.: Extending particle swarm optimizers with self-organized criticality. In: 2002 IEEE Congress on Evolutionary Computation, pp. 1588–1593 (2002)
13. Riget, J., Vesterstrom, J.S.: A diversity-guided particle swarm optimizer. In: ARPSO, p. 2 (2002)
14. Han, F., Liu, Q.: A diversity-guided hybrid particle swarm optimization. Neurocomputing **137**(4), 234–240 (2014)
15. Zambrano-Bigiarini, M., Clerc, M., Rojas, R.: Standard particle swarm optimisation 2011 at CEC-2013: a baseline for future PSO improvements. In: 2013 IEEE Congress on Evolutionary Computation, pp. 2337–2344 (2013)
16. Shi, Y., Eberhart, R.: Modified particle swarm optimizer. In: IEEE International Conference on Evolutionary Computation, IEEE World Congress on Computational Intelligence, vol. 6, pp. 69–73. IEEE Xplore (1998)
17. Hansen, N., et al.: PSO Facing Non-Separable and Ill-Conditioned Problems. HAL-INRIA (2008)
18. Clerc, M.: Particle Swarm Optimization, pp. 129–132. ISTE. Democratization in South Asia: Ashgate (2006)
19. Cheng, R., Jin, Y.: A social learning particle swarm optimization algorithm for scalable optimization. Inf. Sci. **291**(6), 43–60 (2015)

A Lexicon LDA Model Based Solution to Theme Extraction of Chinese Short Text on the Internet

Xu Wang[✉] and Jing Zhou

Communication University of China, Beijing, China
yiyunshiguang@gmail.com, zhoujing@cuc.edu.cn

Abstract. Chinese short text has become the main content of the Internet. Accurately extracting thematic terms is the basis of content analysis, query suggestions, document classification, and text clustering and other tasks for Chinese short text on the Internet. Since Chinese short text is short on the Internet, unbalanced and less of context information, the traditional text clustering model is not immediately appropriate. This paper presents a simple and generic theme model named Lexicon LDA for Chinese short text on the Internet, by using the sentence structure within the document, to enrich the context of the common Chinese word semantics. Words of each sentence which is divided by punctuation marks compose a word set. Unlike the previous method, the model distributes the theme for each word set, rather than for each document. When the data set presents a strong theme distribution, it can significantly improve the effect of the theme model through experiments. The conclusion is that extracting thematic terms of Chinese short text on the Internet is related both to the word itself and to the sentence where the word is located.

Keywords: Topic model · Short text · LDA

1 Introduction

With the speedy growth of the Internet and the extensive use of diverse social networks, people use more fragmented time to read and access information. Micro-blogging (tweet), forum news, news clips and other Chinese short text on the Internet has been becoming the main content of the Internet. The ability to accurately extract thematic terms is the basis of the content analysis, query suggestions, document classification and text clustering and other tasks for Chinese short text on the Internet [1].

Nevertheless, by reason of Chinese short text on the Internet owns less context of the information, traditional theme clustering model can not get very good results. In addition, Chinese short text on the Internet is clearly unbalanced. For instance, on social media, the number of amusement tweets is often more fantastic than the number of other classes. Therefore, the traditional theme clustering model may not be able to do theme extraction of Chinese short text on the Internet [18].

© Springer Nature Singapore Pte Ltd. 2017
C. He et al. (Eds.): BIC-TA 2017, CCIS 791, pp. 223–232, 2017.
https://doi.org/10.1007/978-981-10-7179-9_17

The idea of Lexicon LDA is inspired by the following reasons: (1) While the text is short and the document-word space is thin, the sentence-word space is still very intensive; (2) Intuitively, each sentence of Chinese short text on the Internet on the theme contribution rate is greater; and (3) The new model ought to be uncomplicated enough to ensure that it can be applied to real scenarios. Lexicon LDA uses standard Gibbs sampling, which makes it very easy to be applied within various scenes.

By comparing the results of Lexicon LDA with other methods in terms of topic coherence and document classification, it is shown that Lexicon LDA has better showing in extracting thematic of Chinese short text on the Internet than LDA.

The rest of this paper is organized as follows. Firstly we review the relevant work in Sect. 2. A detailed introduction to Lexicon LDA is presented in Sect. 3. Experimental results are shown in Sect. 4. Finally, we briefly summarize our work in Sect. 5.

2   Related Work

As stated by the necessity to mark the practice language off, the text theme extraction method can fall into two categories: unsupervised text theme extraction and supervised text theme extraction.

A representative supervised extraction approach treats the text's theme as a question of whether it is a two-category issue for keywords [21, 22]. More existent information be used by this method, the outcome is relatively good. But because of the necessity to mark high-quality training data in advance, it has the more unusual the artificial cost of pre-processing.

The existing text theme extraction study therefore concentrates on the unsupervised text theme extraction primarily, the mainstream method can be summed up into two types: based on TF-IDF statistical aspects and based on theme model.

It is easy to extract the text theme that is based on the TF-IDF statistical feature. But the semantic qualities and the significant low-frequency words of the topic distribution are ignored by this method within the document. The lexical extraction method that was based on the LDA [2] in recent years has been attention of the people [23–25].

LDA, a thematic model proposed by Blei in 2003 [2], has be a normative shape of the text clustering model. It can give each document's theme in the shape of a possibility distribution. Through analyzing some of the documents it can extract their theme out, for thematic clustering or text classification.

LDA uses the word pocket model to treat each document as a word frequency vector. LDA forecasts the distribution of the word distribution and the theme distribution. The prior distribution uses the Dirichlet distribution which is given in advance. The entire generation process is done by the Gibbs sampling formula.

$$P\left(z_i = k | z_{\neg i}, w\right) \propto \frac{n_m^{(k)} + \alpha_k}{\sum\limits_{k=1}^{K} \left(n_m^{(k)} + \alpha_k\right) \sum\limits_{t=1}^{V} \left(n_k^{(t)} + \beta_t\right)} \tag{1}$$

$z_{\neg i}$ represents a collection of all themes except i. And $n_m^{(k)}$ indicates the number of occurrences of the k-th theme in the m-th document. $n_k^{(t)}$ represents the number of times the t-th word appears under the k-th theme. And w represents the word vector of the whole word. The LDA model outputs the results for the document - the subject probability distribution θ and the topic-lexical probability distribution ϑ, as follows:

$$\theta_{m,k} = \frac{n_m^{(k)} + \alpha_k}{\sum_{k=1}^{K} \left(n_m^{(k)} + \alpha_k \right)} \tag{2}$$

$$\vartheta_{k,t} = \frac{n_k^{(t)} + \beta_t}{\sum_{t=1}^{V} \left(n_k^{(t)} + \beta_t \right)} \tag{3}$$

Generally, document-level word co-occurrence information [3] is utilized by the LDA model to category semantic-related words into individual topics, which makes the LDA model exceedingly delicate to document length and the number of documents that are associated with each topic. Because Chinese short text on the Internet carries fewer words, these models will not be able to accurately describe how the words are interrelated.

Many efforts have in fact been committed to solving the inefficiency of LDA. For instance, the relevant short text can be aggregated into a lengthy pseudo-document in a practice subject model [4] or a model of training from extraneous information can be used to help the subject matter to in short text [5]. In addition, the operation of many arbitrary LDA is also introduced to meet the specific needs of short text analysis [6–8].

In order to solve the problem of document imbalance, some of the improvement LDA use a priori information to guide the subject modeling process [9,10]. Some use asymmetric Dirichlet [11]. Note that in practice, knowledge about the given corpus is often undetected, so a priori information is not readily available.

All in all, the above method is neither applying in special context nor difficult expanding. To deal with less context of the information and unbalanced problems of Chinese short text on the Internet at the same time, we propose Lexicon LDA model.

3   The Lexicon LDA Model

Since Chinese short text on the Internet lacks sufficient contextual information, applying a traditional text clustering model directly does not work very well. To solve the above problem, we propose the Lexicon LDA model.

To enrich the context of the common Chinese word semantics, words part of each sentence which is divided by punctuation compose a word set named lexicon. In a lexicon, a node is a word that belongs to the same sentence, since a word is usually related to the adjacent words belonged to the same sentence, especially in Chinese short text on the Internets.

To convert a given set of documents into a lexicon, firstlyLexicon LDA model filters out the stop word and the low frequency word. Then scanning through a document verbatim, sentences are divided when a period, question mark, exclamation mark and ellipsis are encountered. Different words that appear in the same sentence will be considered to be a common lexicon.

To preserve the standard Gibbs sampling, Lexicon LDA model must first express the lexicons as a pseudo-document set. The statistical relationship between words, lexicons and themes is studied by assuming that the common lexicon for each word is generated by a specific probability model. It is assumed that there is a fixed potential theme in the lexicons and that each potential theme tis related to a polynomial distribution on the word φ_t drawn from Dirichlet a priori $Dir(\beta)$. The generation of the entire set of pseudo-documents converted from lexicons is explained as follows:

1. For every potential theme t, plot $\varphi_t \sim Dir(\beta)$.
2. Plot the $\theta_i \sim Dir(\alpha)$, the potential distribution of the word s_i belongs to lexicon L_i.
3. For each word $s_j \in L_i$:
   (a) Choose a potential topic $t_j \sim \theta_i$.
   (b) Select the other words in the lexicon $s_j \sim \varphi_{t_j}$.

The θ distribution represents the probability that the potential theme appears in lexicon in which each word appears, and the φ distribution represents the probability of each potential subject for every word in lexicon.

In Lexicon LDA, each Chinese short text is expressed as a mixed distribution of T implicit themes, and each topic is a multiple distribution over L lexicons. The probability graph is shown in Fig. 1:

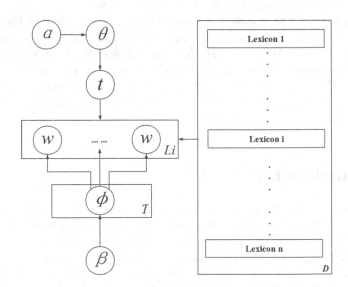

Fig. 1. Lexicon LDA probability graph

Given Chinese short text on the Internet, firstly Lexicon LDA converts it into lexicons. Then generating a pseudo-document set. Finally using standard Gibbs sampling to infer the values of latent variables in φ and θ.

Since Lexicon LDA generates lexicons, we can use the theme proportion of the θ as the theme proportion in document. Given the proportion of the theme of all the words, it can get the theme of each document accordingly.

Specifically, in order to infer the theme in the Chinese short text on the Internet, assuming the proportion of topics is equal to the expectation for lexicon of the theme proportion:

$$P(t|d) = \sum_{L_i} P(t|L_i)P(L_i|d) \qquad (4)$$

where $P(t|L_i)$ is equal to $\theta_{i,t}$, which has been studied in the lexicon LDA. For $P(L_i|d)$, using the sum of the empirical distribution for the lexicons in Chinese short text on the Internet as an estimate:

$$P(L_i|d) = \sum_s \frac{tfidf(s_i)}{Length(d)} \qquad (5)$$

where $tfidf(s_i)$ is the word frequency of s_i in lexicon L_i, and $Length(d)$ is the length of lexicon.

4   Experiments

According to the micro-blogging data collection, we design experiments to evaluate the performance of extracting thematic terms by Lexicon LDA in Chinese short text on the Internet based on topic coherence and document classification.

4.1   Experimental Setup

1) Hardware environment: Mac Book Air, Intel Core5, 1.6 GHz, 8 GB.

2) Data Sets: We use simulated login micro-blogging to capture any 500 active users of micro-blogging as experimental data. Then the marketing number and zombie number have been removed. Through artificial annotation, and ultimately get 21 topics related to a total of 30651 micro-blogging items.

3) Baseline Methods: We select two baseline methods for comparative studies.

    a) Latent Dirichlet Allocation:

        Latent Dirichlet Allocation (LDA) is a classical thematic models. Using the jgibbLDA2 package [12].

    b) Biterm Topic Model:

        Biterm Topic Model (BTM) is a thematic model dedicated to short text [13], and its main idea is to train the subject of common word pairs [14].

4) Evaluation of indicators: We apply topic coherence [15] and document classification [20] to evaluate subject quality to assess the performance of our model.

a) Topic Coherence: Topic coherence [14] can be used to evaluate quality of extracting thematic terms.

Considering a theme t, $T^{(t)} = \left(w_1^{(t)}, \cdots, w_M^{(t)} \right)$ is a set of the M most probable words belonging to the theme t *sorted by probability* $P(w|t)$. The theme t of the topic coherence score is defined as [19]:

$$C\left(t; T^{(t)}\right) = \sum_{m=2}^{M} \sum_{n=1}^{m} \log \frac{\left(w_m^{(t)}, w_n^{(t)}\right) + \varepsilon}{D\left(w_n^{(t)}\right)} \tag{6}$$

In the document, the number of times w appeared is $D(w)$, the number of times w and w_0 appear together is $D(w, w_0)$. There is no co-occurrence of two words in the case, in order to avoid the calculation of zero logarithm, we set $\varepsilon = 10^{-12}$ [16]. The final score is the average score for all theme.

b) Document Classification: The quality of extracting thematic terms is also typically evaluated on external tasks. Selected document classification as the evaluation method. The specific evaluation criteria are the average F after classification [17].

By carrying out multiple tests we set the Lexicon LDA model parameters $\alpha = 0.1$, $\beta = 0.01$. For BTM, we set $\alpha = 0.5$, $\beta = 0.005$ [12]. For LDA, we manually set $\alpha = 0.1$ and $\beta = 0.01$.

4.2   Experimental Results

1) Topic coherence: Results on micro-blogging data are shown in Fig. 2.

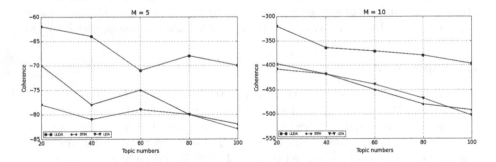

Fig. 2. Topic coherence

From the results, we can find that LDA has a poor topic coherence of the theme. We find that the average topic coherence of Lexicon LDA is obviously higher than other two models, which indicates that Lexicon LDA outperforms LDA and BTM in learning high quality topics from short texts. The outperformance of Lexicon LDA as compared to LDA is in accordance with our understanding that learning topics from dense word-word space can guarantee the topic quality even in short texts. BTM also outperforms LDA since it directly model word pairs rather than documents to solve data sparsity in short texts. It shows that the classic theme model on Chinese short text on the Internet of the theme extraction effect is not good. Because of the analysis of word pairs, BTM performance is better than that of LDA, and Lexicon LDA in micro-blogging data achieves a better topic coherence score than BTM and LDA. Compared with the other two methods, Lexicon LDA achieved the best topic coherence scores. This shows that the word-sentence space in Chinese short text on the Internet on extracting the thematic terms has some certain advantages (Table 1).

Table 1. The statistics of data sets

Data set topics	# Documents	Data set topic	#Documents
Entertainment	7442	Financial	418
IT	3295	Media	705
Life	2789	Anime	960
Education	2006	Estate	451
Sports	1452	Advertising	147
Health	1553	Tourism	756
Food	1598	Women	992
Car	878	Art	329
Fashion	1108	Literature	797
Campus	265	Games	2265
Parenting	445		

2) Document classification: The theme model can be used as a document classification method, and the document classification results show the performance of the model to learn the theme of the document.

Since Lexicon LDA and BTM do not directly simulate the subject matter of a document, it is indirectly represented by some post-reasoning strategy. Therefore, for an equitable comparison, an indirect representation of the LDA document is required. Apply a post-reasoning method to represent document d.

$$p(z|d) = \sum_w p(z|w)p(w|d) \tag{7}$$

where $p(z|w)$ is estimated by $\frac{p(z)p(w|z)}{\sum_z p(z)p(w|z)}$ and the number of times w appeared is $p(w|d)$ in document d.

In each theme, the data sets was divided into training and test subsets by random, with a ratio of 4: 1, and we used them in documents classification. All the results are shown in Fig. 3.

From the above results we can find that Lexicon LDA and BTM outperforms LDA in classifying Chinese short texts. BTM is better than LDA under the circumstance of short text. It is because that BTM directly models the word

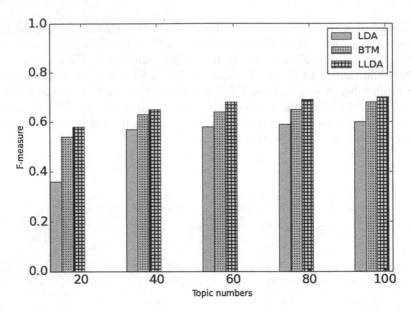

Fig. 3. Document classification

pair, avoiding the sparseness of short text. The divergence in the performance of classifying short texts suggests that the data sparsity problem seriously affects LDA, while less variation is found in Lexicon and BTM. And Lexicon LDA in the micro-blogging data set theme extraction test, the performance is always better than other methods. In general, this result illustrates the advantages of Lexicon LDA over other baseline approaches.

5   Conclusions

This paper presents a simple and generic theme model named Lexicon LDA for Chinese short text on the Internet, by using the sentence structure within the document, to enrich the context of the common Chinese word semantics. In this way, it can improve the quality of extracting thematic terms for Chinese short text on the Internet. To investigate Lexicon LDA?s ability of learning high quality topics from real-world short texts, we compare Lexicon LDA with LDA and BTM on micro-blogging data collection. Extensive experiments demonstrate that Lexicon LDA has the advantages of other extracting theme methods. Lexicon LDA is based on the framework of LDA and BTM is special form mixture of unigram, which might be the reason why Lexicon LDA works better than BTM on short texts. This suggests that the study of word-sentence space has the advantage in the extraction thematic terms.

Acknowledgments. This work was funded by the Engineering Disciplines Planning Project of the Communication University of China (No. 3132015XNG1515) and the Open Project Program of Jiangsu Engineering Center of Network Monitoring and Nanjing University of Information Science and Technology Project (PAPD and CICAEET). The authors would also like to acknowledge the input of the National Key Technology R & D Program (No. 2015BAK25B03).

References

1. Yu, L.L., Asur, S., Huberman, B.A.: Dynamics of Trends and Attention in Chinese Social Media. arXivpreprint arXiv:1312.0649 (2013)
2. Blei, D.M., Ng, A.Y., Jordan, M.I.: Latent Dirichlet allocation. J. Mach. Learn. Res. **3**(1), 993–1022 (2003)
3. Wang, X., Mc Callum, A.: Topics over time: a non-markov continuous-time model of topical trends. In: KDD, 424–433 (2006)
4. Weng, J., Lim, E.P., Jiang, J., He, Q.: Twitterrank: finding topic-sensitive influential twitterers. In: WSDM, pp. 261–270 (2010)
5. Phan, X.H., Nguyen, L.M., Horiguchi, S.: Learning to classify short and sparse text & web with hidden topics from large-scale data collections. In: WWW, pp. 91–100 (2008)
6. Zhao, W.X., Jiang, J., Weng, J., He, J., Lim, E.-P., Yan, H., Li, X.: Comparing twitter and traditional media using topic models. In: Clough, P., Foley, C., Gurrin, C., Jones, G.J.F., Kraaij, W., Lee, H., Mudoch, V. (eds.) ECIR 2011. LNCS, vol. 6611, pp. 338–349. Springer, Heidelberg (2011). https://doi.org/10.1007/978-3-642-20161-5_34
7. Chua, F.C.T., Asur, S.: Automatic summarization of events from social media. In: ICWSM (2013)
8. Chen, Y., Amiri, H., Li, Z., Chua, T.S.: Emerging topic detection for organizations from microblogs. In: SIGIR, pp. 43–52 (2013)
9. Jagarlamudi, J., Daumé III, H., Udupa, R.: Incorporating lexical priors into topic models. In: EACL, pp. 204–213 (2012)
10. Andrzejewski, D., Zhu, X., Craven, M.: Incorporating domain knowledge into topic modeling via Dirichlet forest priors. In: ICML, pp. 25–32 (2009)
11. Mc Callum, A., Mimno, D.M., Wallach, H.M.: Rethinking lda: why priors matter. In: Bengio, Y., Schuurmans, D., Lafferty, J., Williams, C., Culotta, A. (eds.) NIPS, pp. 1973–1981. Curran Associates, Inc. (2009)
12. http://jgibblda.sourceforge.net/
13. Yan, X., Guo, J., Lan, Y., Cheng, X.: A Biterm topic model for short texts. In: 22nd International Conference on World Wide Web, pp. 1445–1456. International World Wide Web Conferences Steering Committee (2013)
14. http://code.google.com/p/btm
15. Mimno, D., Wallach, H.M., Talley, E., Leenders, M., and Mc Callum, A.: Optimizing semantic coherence in topic models. In: Conference on Empirical Methods in Natural Language Processing, pp. 262–272. Association for Computational Linguistics (2011)
16. Stevens, K., Kegelmeyer, P., Andrzejewski, D., Buttler, D.: Exploring topic coherence over many models and many topics. In: 2012 Joint Conference on Empirical Methods in Natural Language Processing and Computational Natural Language Learning, ser, EMNLP-Co NLL 2012, pp. 952–961 (2012)

17. Zhou, T., Lyu, M.T., King, I., Lou, J.: Learning to suggest questions in social media. Knowl. Inf. Syst. 1–28 (2014)
18. Zuo, Y., Zhao, J., Xu, K.: Word network topic model: a simple but general solution for short and imbalanced texts. Knowl. Inf. Syst. **48**(2), 379–398 (2016)
19. Stevens, K., Kegelmeyer, P., Andrzejewski, D., Buttler, D.: Exploring topic coherence over many models and many topics. In: 2012 Joint Conference on Empirical Methods in Natural Language Processing and Computational Natural Language Learning, EMNLP-Co NLL 2012, pp. 952–961 (2012)
20. Nigam, K., Mc Callum, A.K., Thrun, S., Mitchell, T.: Text classification from labeled and unlabeled documents using EM. Mach. Learn. **39**(2—-3), 103–134 (2000)
21. Frank, E., Paynter G.W., Witten, I.H., et. al.: Domain-specific key phrase extraction. In: 16th International Joint Conference on Artificial Intelligence, Stockholm, Sweden, pp. 668–673. Morgan Kaufmann Publishers Inc., San Francisco (1999)
22. Turney, P.D.: Learning algorithms for key phrase extraction. Inform. Retrieval **2**(4), 303–336 (2000)
23. Jing, S., Wanlong, L.: Topic words extraction method based on LDA model. Comput. Eng. **36**(19), 81–83 (2010)
24. Jun, L., Dongsheng, Z., Xinlai, X., et al.: Key phrase extraction based on topic feature. Appl. Res. Comput. **29**(11), 4224–4227 (2012)
25. Zhiyuan, L.: Research on Keyword Extraction Using Document Topical Structure. Tsinghua University, Beijing (2011)

The Decoder Based on DNA Strand Displacement with Improved "AND" Gate and "OR" Gate

Weixuan Han, Changjun Zhou, Xiaojun Wang, and Qiang Zhang[✉]

Key Laboratory of Advanced Design and Intelligent Computing,
Ministry of Education, Dalian University, Dalian 116622, China
zhangq30@gmail.com

Abstract. In the computational biology, DNA strand displacement technique is used to construct the logic gate model and molecular circuits. But with the increase of number of the reaction strands, the basic logic gates cannot meet the accuracy in the reaction process. This paper improved the logical unit OR gate, AND gate to solve this problem on the basic of the seesaw model and the mechanism of DNA strand displacement reaction. Since the basic circuit of the decoder is an array of AND gates, the improvement module is applied to the decoder. The molecular circuit of decoder is constructed to realize the dynamic link between the input signal and the output signal. It is concluded that the sensitivity and accuracy of the improved decoder in the molecular circuit is improved by the Visual DSD software. The improvement module laid the foundation for the development of molecular circuits.

Keywords: DNA strand displacement · AND gate · OR gate · Decoder

1 Introduction

In recent years, the rapid development of bio-information has become a frontier research field with widely application prospect. In particular, it is a new method to become a powerful computing device in the construction of bio-materials. So far, many biological computing models that based on a variety of theoretical research have been designed in the field of scientific research. Various devices, including circuits [1–3], catalytic amplifiers [4,5], autonomous molecular motors [6–8], reconfigurable nanostructures and neural network [9–11], have recently been rationally designed to use DNA strand displacement reactions, in which two strands with partial or full complementarily hybridize, displacing in the process one or more pre-hybridized strands. Based on the natural characteristics of DNA molecules, DNA nanotechnology is a leading factor of the construction of biological computing models, and DNA strand displacement is a distinct advantage as a new self-assembly method.

The specificity and predictability of Watson and Crick base pairing make DNA a powerful and versatile material for engineering at the nanoscale. This has

© Springer Nature Singapore Pte Ltd. 2017
C. He et al. (Eds.): BIC-TA 2017, CCIS 791, pp. 233–247, 2017.
https://doi.org/10.1007/978-981-10-7179-9_18

enabled the construction of a diverse and rapidly growing set of DNA nanostructures and nanodevices through the programmed hybridization of complementary strands. In 2011, Qian [12,13], designed of a simple Seesaw logic gate, simulated the 94LS85 standard 4-bit numerical comparator and detected the 4-bit binary number square root of the logic circuit. Then, Zhang [14], realized a logical AND gate through the strand of two-stage reaction. In 2013, Zhang [15], proposed and verified the logical AND gate and OR gate. In 2014, Wang [16], realized the simple logic computation based on the DNA strand displacement. In 2015, Wang [17], used strand displacement to achieve the multi-bit adder design.

In this paper, for the improved logic model, we use the garbage collector strands to absorb the waste complex, which produced by the reaction of input strands with a partial double-stranded gate, and then to inhibit the occurrence of reversible reactions. The improved logical model includes AND logic and OR logic. Compared with the Seesaw gate, there is no threshold logic model, which avoids the errors in logic synthesis. The AND gate is constructed by two partial double-stranded cascade, and the OR gate is constructed by partial double-stranded composite gate cascade. We designed a binary-decimal decoder circuit based on the improved logic gate, which can perform the function of translating four binary numbers into 10 output signals. The simulation results of Visual DSD are consistent with the logical relationship.

2   Backgrounds

2.1   DNA Strand Displacement

It is a new method to construct the logic gate and logic circuit to realize the dynamic link between the input signal and the output signal by the DNA strand displacement cascade reaction. DNA strand displacement reaction refers to the input of single-stranded DNA molecules and its complementary partial double-stranded DNA structures biochemical reactions, and ultimately generates new double-stranded, and the release of the original double-stranded structure of single-stranded DNA molecules in the process. The DNA strand displacement branch migration process is shown in Fig. 1. The rise of DNA strand displacement is due to the absence of enzymes and other substances in the reaction process, just need to put a signal and a gate mixed together, and the calculation process takes place automatically. In recent years, theoretical work has shown that DNA

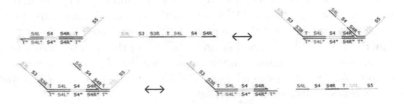

Fig. 1. The branch migration process of DNA strand displacement

strand substitution can achieve a series of complex calculations, including any representations that can be performed with chemical reactions.

2.2 Decoder

In general, the process of representing a particular object of words, symbols, or numbers can be called encoding [18]. In daily life, we often encounter the problem of coding. The Chinese character, the decimal circuit is difficult to achieve, so in the circuit of binary instead of coding, using n-bit binary code to encode the $N = 2^n$ signal of a binary circuit.

The decoder is the inverse process of encoding, each of which is given a specific meaning in the binary code state. The process of translating the specific meaning of the code state is called decoding, and the circuit of decoding operation is called the decoder.

The binary code of the decimal number, that is, BCD code. The circuit that translates into the corresponding 10 output signals is called a two-decimal decoder. The BCD code consists of 4 bits of binary code, forming into 4 input signals $A_0 \sim A_0$ and 10 output signals $Y_0 \sim Y_9$. The logical expression is as follows:

$$Y_0 = \overline{A_3 A_2 A_1 A_0}; Y_1 = \overline{A_3 A_2 A_1} A_0; Y_2 = \overline{A_2 A_1 A_0};$$
$$Y_3 = \overline{A_2 A_1} A_0; Y_4 = A_2 \overline{A_1 A_0}; Y_5 = A_2 \overline{A_1} A_0;$$
$$Y_6 = A_2 A_1 \overline{A_0}; Y_7 = A_2 A_1 A_0; Y_8 = A_3 \overline{A_0}; Y_9 = A_3 A_0.$$

2.3 Seesaw Module

Digital logic gates are usually transformed into the corresponding biological gates, so as to carry out the study of biological computation. The logic gates used in the Seesaw biochemical reaction mainly include 4 kinds, amplifier gate, integrated gate, threshold and reporter. The amplifier gate contains a threshold and a fuel that is added to the reaction. The output signal is generated only the total concentration of the input signal is greater than the initial concentration of the threshold, otherwise, the logic value of the output concentration is 0. The function of the amplifier gate is to obtain a plurality of output signals, which has the following characteristics, when a small fulcrum is a boundary point, the output signal contains the same left identification area and different right identification regions. The reason for this is that the output signal is generated by the threshold selection of the same gate complex and needs to act on the different lower gate complexes. In order to facilitate the full release of the output signal, the initial concentration of the fuel is typically set to twice the total concentration of the given output signal. The role of the integrated gate is opposite to that of the amplifier gate, which can receive multiple input signals and integrate it into an output signal after the reaction. These input signals have the following characteristics, when a small fulcrum as a demarcation point, the input signal contains the same right side of the identification area and the different left recognition area. The reason for this is that the output signal is generated by the threshold selection of the different gate complex and needs to act on the different next gate complexes. The function of the threshold gate is to filter the input signal by the size of the concentration. If the total concentration is greater than the threshold concentration, an output signal is generated, and vice versa, no output is obtained.

An integrated gate behind an amplifier gate can be realized with AND logic and OR logic, according to the experience, the threshold of the OR gate and the AND gate are respectively set as 0.6 and 1.2 in this design. Some of the logic gates in the molecular circuit are shown in Fig. 2.

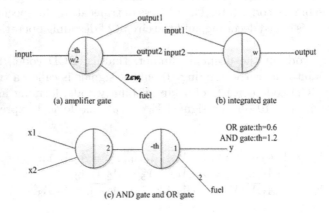

Fig. 2. The Seesaw motif of basic logic gates

In the Seesaw module designed by Winfree, when the concentration of the molecule is located in $0\ x \sim 0.2\ x$, it indicates the low level (a logic value of 0); when the concentration of the molecule is located in $0.8\ x \sim 1\ x$, it indicates the high level (a logic value of 1), otherwise, at other concentrations, the logic is error. The model can be used to perform AND gate and OR gate operation, and can be used to form a larger scale biochemical circuit.

2.4   Dual-Rail Logic Circuit

The dual-rail logic is that each variable value is represented by a pair of complementary variable values, for example, the variable A is represented by the variable A^0 and A^1, when the A^0 is in active state, the logical value of the A is 0, while the A^1 is in active state, it represents the logical value of the A is 1, when A^0 and A^0 are in active state at the same time, the circuit logic is error. Finally, each logic gate can be replaced by OR gate and AND gate. In this way, the electronic circuit becomes a dual-rail logic circuit.

3   Improved Basic Module

3.1   Redesign AND Gate and OR Gate

For the seesaw module, the molecules concentration between 0 x and 0.2 x is OFF, while the molecules concentration between 0.8 x and 1 x is ON. The molecules concentration beyond these two conditions is considered a logical error. In the large-scale biochemical circuit, with the increasing of the molecule signal fan-out, these fan out molecules participate in the downstream biochemical reaction, it will exceed the upper limit of 0.2 x in a low concentration, which will cause the subsequent reaction error occurred and the molecular output at a low concentration to be completely higher than the standard values 0.2 x. In this way, the logic relation of the whole circuit will be wrong, which is not conducive to the next circuit connection.

In other words, as the number of a Seesaw gate fan-out increases, the molecules concentration of output signal will also increase in the low concentration, thus it will amplify its low concentration, and the amplification of low concentration is particularly evident.

In order to solve the above problems, this paper design gate, gate1 and gate2 three gates logic model. The logic gate consists of three composite gates, including AND gates and OR gates. AND gate consists of gate2 and gate cascade is as shown Fig. 3(a). The OR gate consists of a gate1 and a gate cascade is as shown Fig. 3(b).

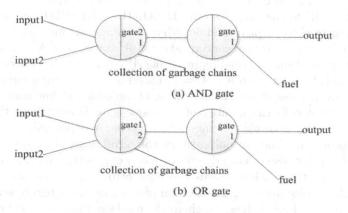

(a) AND gate

(b) OR gate

Fig. 3. The Seesaw motif of basic logic gates

Taking two inputs as an example, the input module is $A(A_0^0, A_0^1, A_1^0, A_1^1)$ and the output module is Y(AND0, AND1, OR0, OR1). When input $A(A_1^1 A_0^1)$ the output of AND gate is AND1, When input $(A_1^1 A_0^1)$, the output of OR gate is OR1. The strand displacement process of the improved base model is as shown Fig. 4.

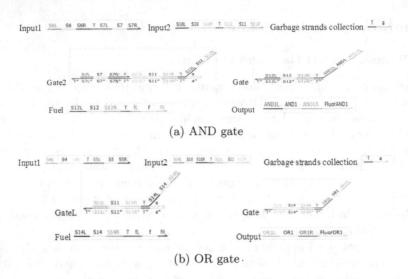

(a) AND gate

(b) OR gate.

Fig. 4. The partial strands of the improved base model

As can be seen from Fig. 4, the improved module implements the function of AND gate and OR gate. In Fig. 4(a), the input strands are <S6L^ S6 S6R^ T^ S7L^ S7 S7R^> and <S10L^ S10 S10R^ T^ S11L^ S11 S11R^>, the output strand is <AND1L^ AND1 AND1R^ FlourAND1>. In Fig. 4(b), if the input strands are <S4L^ S4 S4R^ T^ S5L^ S5 S5R^> and <S10L^ S10 S10R^ T^ S11L^ S11 S11R^>, the output strand is <OR1L^ OR1 OR1R^ FlourOR1>.

According to the designed module, when the single strand concentration of A^0 is 1 x, and the single strand concentration of A^1 is 0 x, then $A = A^0 = 1$, when the concentration of single strand representing A^1 is 1 x, and the concentration of a single strand A^0 is 0 x, then $A = A^1 = 1$. Therefore, in molecular circuits, there will not be an increase in the concentration of molecules at low concentrations due to the increase in the number of a Seesaw gate fan-out, and the logical relationships in the molecular circuits will be correctly expressed.

The improved module not only utilizes the advantages of seesaw's own biochemical circuit, but also can clearly and correctly express the logical relationship in molecular reactions, which solves the logic errors that may exist in large-scale cascaded molecular circuits. Because of the module is highly sensitive to the recognition of logic values, biochemical reaction time and accuracy have improved.

3.2   DNA Strand Displacement Process of Improved Decoder

In the binary-decimal decoder circuit, there are 4 inputs 10 outputs, respectively. The input is $A_0 \sim A_0$. The output is $Y_0 \sim Y_9$. The input strand is shown in Table 1. The output strand is shown in Table 2. For example, the input A_0^0 is represented by the strand <S4L^ S4 S4R^ T^ S5L^ S5 S5R^> (briefly called S5),

Fig. 5. The partial input and output strands structure

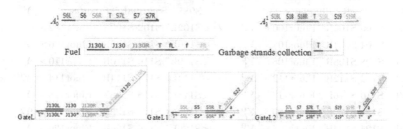

Fig. 6. The partial strands of the decoder of

and the output Y_9^1 is represented by the strand <130L^ 130 130R^ Flour 130> (briefly called Fluor130). The structure is shown in Fig. 5. Parts of the DNA strands displacement process are shown in Fig. 6.

As can be seen from Fig. 5, input strands have three domains. The first domain is a historical field of generated by the past interaction, which is not important for the next step of the reaction. The second domain is a foothold of generated by the interaction between the start signal and the gate. The third domain is the correct recognition domain (Fluor130). The recognition domain of the strand <130L^ 130 130R^ Flour 130> is used as a fluorescent marker molecule. In Fig. 6, it depicts the partial reaction strands of $A_3^1 A_2^1 A_1^1 A_0^1 = 1001$. The decoder finally output Y_9^1 when input strands of $A_3^1, A_2^1, A_1^1, A_0^1$. The gate L, gate L1 and gate L2 are the concrete manifestations of the improved module.

As can be seen from the Tables 1 and 2, this paper makes the 4 inputs and 10 outputs become 8 inputs and 20 outputs on the base of the dual logic in the circuit. DNA input strands S5, S7, S9, S11, S13, S15, S17, S19 correspond to $A_0^0, A_0^1, A_1^0, A_1^1, A_2^0, A_2^0, A_3^0, A_3^1$ respectively. DNA output strands include Fluor92 $\sim$ Fluor130.

Table 1. Input bits represented by input strands

DNA strand	Input	DNA strand	Input
<S4L^ S4 S4R^ T^ S5L^ S5 S5R^>	A_0^0	<S6L^ S6 S6R^ T^ S7L^ S7 S7R^>	A_0^1
<S8L^ S8S8R^ T^ S9L^ S9 S9R^>	A_1^0	<S10L^ S10 S10R^ T^ S11L^ S11 S11R^>	A_1^1
<S12L^ S12 S12R^ T^ S13L^ S13 S13R^>	A_2^0	<S14L^ S14 S14R^ T^ S15L^ S15 S15R^>	A_2^1
<S16L^ S16 S16R^ T^ S17L^ S17 S17R^>	A_3^0	<S18L^ S18 S18R^ T^ S19L^ S19 S19R^>	A_3^1

Table 2. Output bits represented by output strands

DNA strand	Output	DNA strand	Output
<S92L^ S92 S92R^ Fluor92>	Y_0^0	<S94L^ S94 S94R^ Fluor94>	Y_0^0
<S96L^ S96 S96R^ Fluor96>	Y_1^0	<S98L^ S98 S98R^ Fluor98>	Y_1^0
<S100L^ S100 S100R^ Fluor100>	Y_2^0	<S102L^ S102 S102R^ Fluor102>	Y_2^0
<S104L^ S104 S104R^ Fluor104>	Y_3^0	<S106L^ S106 S106R^ Fluor106>	Y_3^0
<S108L^ S108 S108R^ Fluor108>	Y_4^0	<S110L^ S110 S110R^ Fluor110>	Y_4^0
<S112L^ S112 S112R^ Fluor112>	Y_5^0	<S114L^ S114 S114R^ Fluor114>	Y_5^0
<S116L^ S116 S116R^ Fluor116>	Y_6^0	<S118L^ S118 S118R^ Fluor118>	Y_6^0
<S120L^ S120 S120R^ Fluor120>	Y_7^0	<S122L^ S122 S122R^ Fluor122>	Y_7^0
<S124L^ S124 S124R^ Fluor124>	Y_8^0	<S126L^ S126 S126R^ Fluor126>	Y_8^0
<S128L^ S128 S128R^ Fluor128>	Y_9^0	<S130L^ S130 S130R^ Fluor130>	Y_9^0

4 Simulation

4.1 The Simulation Results of Improved Model

Based on the Chap. 3, the basic module simulation of 2 inputs and 1 output in Visual DSD are as shown in Figs. 7 and 8.

In Fig. 7, <ANDL^ AND ANDR^ Flour AND> indicates output of AND logic. In Fig. 7(a), if the input strands are <S6L^ S6 S6R^ T^ S7L^ S7 S7R^> and <S10L^ S10 S10R^ T^ S11L^ S11 S11R^>, the output strand is <AND1L^ AND1 AND1R^ Flour AND1>, which marked as input (11), output 1. In Fig. 7(b), if the input strands are <S4L^ S4 S4R^ T^ S5L^ S5 S5R^> and <S8L^ S8S8R^ T^ S9L^ S9 S9R^>, the output strand is <AND0L^ AND0 AND0R^ Flour AND0>, which marked as input (00), output 0. In summary, the output is <AND1L^ AND1 AND1R^ Flour AND1> when the input module is 11, otherwise, the output is <AND0L^ AND0 AND0R^ Flour AND0>.

In Fig. 8, <ORL^ OR ORR^ Flour OR> indicates output of OR logic. In Fig. 8(a), if the input strands are <S6L^ S6S6R^ T^ S7L^ S7 S7R^> and <S10L^ S10 S10R^ T^ S11L^ S11 S11R^>, the output strand is <OR1L^ OR1 OR1R^ FlourOR1>, which marked as input (11), output 1. In Fig. 8(b), if the input strands are <S4L^ S4 S4R^ T^ S5L^ S5 S5R^> and <S8L^ S8 S8R^ T^ S9L^ S9 S9R^>, the output strand is <OR0L^ OR0 OR0R^ FlourOR0>, which marked as input (00), output 0. In summary, the output is <OR0L^ OR0 OR0R^ FlourOR0> when the input module is 00, otherwise, the output is <OR1L^ OR1 OR1R^ FlourOR1>.

4.2 The Simulation of Decoder

The basic circuit of binary-decoder is composed of the AND gates array, the binary-decimal decoder are taken as the example to construct the logic circuit in the paper. The improved modules are applied to the decoder, and parts of the simulations are shown in Fig. 9.

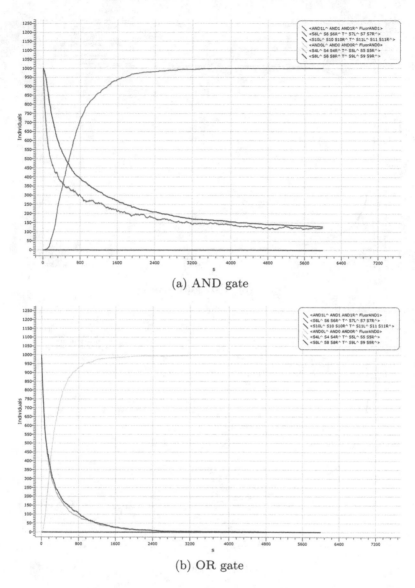

(a) AND gate

(b) OR gate

Fig. 7. The partial strands of the improved base model

In Fig. 9(a), the function of decoder $Y_0 = \overline{A_3}\ \overline{A_2}\ \overline{A_1}\ \overline{A_0}$ is realized, in the input 4-bit binary code, the meaning of 0000 is 0. That is, input $\overline{A_3}\ \overline{A_2}\ \overline{A_1}\ \overline{A_0}$ will output Y_0, input $A_3^0 A_2^1 A_1^0 A_0^0$ will output Y_0^1 in dual-rail logic. If input strands <S4L^ S4 S4R^ T^ S5L^ S5 S5R^> <S8L^ S8 S8R^ T^ S9L^ S9 S9R^> <S12L^ S12 S12R^ T^ S13L^ S13 S13R^> and <S16L^ S16 S16R^ T^ S17L^ S17 S17R^>. The output strand is <S94L^ S94 S94R^ Flour94>. In Fig. 9(b), the function of decoder $Y_1 = \overline{A_3}\ \overline{A_2}\ \overline{A_1}\ A_0$ is realized, in the input 4-bit binary

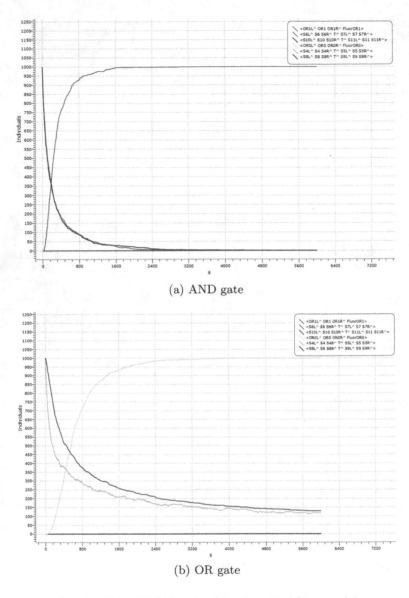

(a) AND gate

(b) OR gate

Fig. 8. The partial strands of the improved base model

code, the meaning of 0001 is 1. That is, input $\overline{A_3}\,\overline{A_2}\,\overline{A_1}\,A_0$ will output Y_1. Input $A_3^0 A_2^1 A_1^0 A_0^1$ will output Y_1^1 in dual-rail logic. If input strands <S6L^ S6 S6R^ T^ S7L^ S7 S7R^> <S8L^ S8 S8R^ T^ S9L^ S9 S9R^> <S12L^ S12 S12R^ T^ S13L^ S13 S13R^> and <S16L^ S16 S16R^ T^ S17L^ S17 S17R^>. The output strand is <S96L^ S96 S96R^ Flour96>.

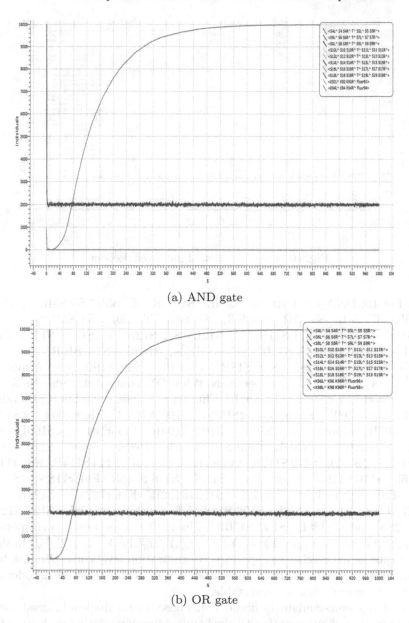

(a) AND gate

(b) OR gate

Fig. 9. The partial strands of the improved base model

And so on, the meaning of 1001 is 9. That is, input A_3A_0 will output Y_9, input $A_3^1A_0^1$ will output Y_9^1 in dual-rail logic. If input strands <S6Lˆ S6 S6Rˆ Tˆ S7Lˆ S7 S7Rˆ> and <S18Lˆ S18 S18Rˆ Tˆ S19Lˆ S19 S19Rˆ>. The output strand is <S130Lˆ S130 S130Rˆ Flour130>. The overall simulation of the output $Y_0 \sim Y_9$. The logical is shown in Fig. 10.

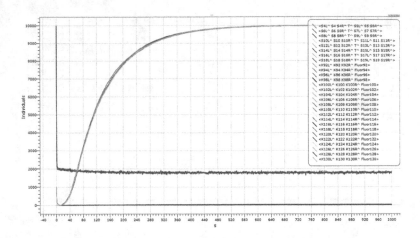

Fig. 10. The simulation of improved decoder

In Fig. 10: DNA input strands <S4L^ S4 S4R^ T^ S5L^ S5 S5R^>, <S6L^ S6 S6R^ T^ S7L^ S7 S7R^>, <S8L^ S8 S8R^ T^ S9L^ S9 S9R^>, <S10L^ S10 S10R^ T^ S11L^ S11 S11R^>, <S12L^ S12 S12R^ T^ S13L^ S13 S13R^>, <S14L^ S14 S14R^ T^ S15L^ S15 S15R^>, <S16L^ S16 S16R^ T^ S17L^ S17 S17R^> and <S18L^ S18 S18R^ T^ S19L^ S19 S19R^> correspond to $A_0^0, A_1^1, A_1^0, A_1^1, A2^0, A_2^1, A_3^0, A_3^1$ respectively. While DNA output strands <S92L^ S92 S92R^ Fluor92>, <S94L^ S94 S94R^ Fluor94>, <S96L^ S96 S96R^ Fluor96>, <S98L^ S98 S98R^ Fluor98>, <S100L^ S100 S100R^ Fluor100>, <S102L^ S102 S102R^ Fluor102>, <S104L^ S104 S104R^ Fluor104>, <S106L^ S106 S106R^ Fluor106>, <S108L^ S108 S108R^ Fluor108>, <S110L^ S110 S110R^ Fluor110>, <S112L^ S112 S112R^ Fluor112>, <S114L^ S114 S114R^ Fluor114>, <S116L^ S116 S116R^ Fluor116>, <S118L^ S118 S118R^ Fluor118>, <S120L^ S120 S120R^ Fluor120>, <S122L^ S122 S122R^ Fluor122>, <S124L^ S124 S124R^ Fluor124>, <S126L^ S126 S126R^ Fluor126>, <S128L^ S128 S128R^ Fluor128> and <S130L^ S130 S130R^ Fluor130> respectively correspond to $Y_0^0, Y_0^1, Y_1^0, Y_1^1, Y_2^0, Y_2^1, Y_3^0, Y_3^1, Y_4^0, Y_4^1, Y_5^0, Y_5^1, Y_6^0, Y_6^1, Y_7^0, Y_7^1, Y_8^0, Y_8^1, Y_9^0, Y_9^1$. In short, each output signal reaches the specified concentration level corresponding to all the input signals combinations. The simulation results prove that the decoder logic circuit is structurally correct and stable.

If we design and simulate the decoder only based on the dual-rail cascade circuit and the corresponding seesaw model biochemical circuit model, which has not been improved. The state of the molecular logic value is OFF or ON is defined by the concentration of the original Seesaw model, in other words, the molecules concentration between $0\ x$ and $0.2\ x$ is OFF, while the molecules concentration between $0.8\ x$ and $1\ x$ is ON, the simulation shown in Fig. 11.

As can be seen from the Figs. 10 and 11: The abscissa indicates the time of the biochemical reaction, the ordinate indicates the concentration of the solution. Firstly, the unimproved decoder approached the equilibrium state using

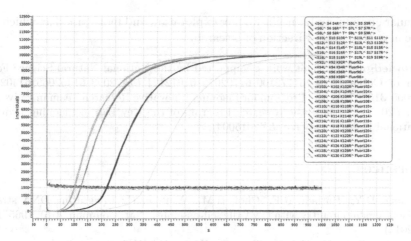

Fig. 11. The simulation of unimproved decoder

approximately 800 s, while the improved decoder approached the equilibrium state using approximately 500 s. The reaction speed of the improved decoder is faster approximately 300 s than the unimproved decoders. Secondly, In Fig. 10, the molecular concentration is 1 in the ON state (1 unit concentration of 10,000 nM in this paper), and the state of the highest concentration of the OFF state is close to and converges to 0.2, the logical relationship is correct and clear. In Fig. 11, the molecular concentration is 0.9 in the ON state, and the state of the highest concentration of the OFF state is lower than 0.2 and does not converges to 0.2, the logical relationship is correct but the upper limit of the concentration convergence is not significant. Thirdly, cascade 4–10 decoder can be applied to more complex large-scale biological logic circuit which can solve more complex DNA computing problems due to the stability and encapsulation of decoder, and it is better to choose an improved decoder from time and accuracy. Therefore, when the circuit scale is expanded, the improved module does provide a new entry point for the molecular circuit both from the agility and the correctness.

5   Conclusions

This paper redesigns the logic unit based on the DNA strand displacement and the seesaw model. To avoid logic error in the molecular circuit by adding gate L1, gate L2, the garbage collector of DNA reaction strands and removing the threshold. The improved module clarifies the upper limit of the minimum concentration and ensures that the highest concentration of the OFF state will only converge to the upper limit and never exceeded if the number of fan-out gate is increased, which avoids the error of logic output relationship. The improvement module is applied to the decoder, and it achieves the corresponding logic function of decoder. However, due to the limitations of the current research platform and technology, biochemical experiments are not perfect, the improved module cannot popularize all the molecular circuits, and it needs further exploration and more practice, which will be the next step in the direction of research.

Acknowledgments. This work is supported by the National Natural Science Foundation of China (*Nos.* 61772100, 61702070, 61672121, 61572093, 61402066, 61402067, 61370005, 31370778), the Program for Liaoning Innovative Research Team in University (*No. LT*2015002), the Basic Research Program of the Key Lab in Liaoning Province Educational Department (*No. LZ*2015004).

References

1. Zhang, D.Y., Hariadi, R.F., Choi, H.M., Winfree, E.: Integrating DNA strand-displacement circuitry with DNA tile self-assembly. Nat. Commun. **4**(6), 1965–1987 (2013)
2. Cui, G., Zhang, J., Cui, Y., Zhao, T., Wang, Y.: DNA strand-displacement digital logic circuit with fluorescence resonance energy transfer detection. J. Comput. Theor. Nanosci. **12**(9), 2095–2100 (2015)
3. Wang, Y., Zhang, W., Li, X., Cui, G.: Molecular logic gates based on localized DNA strand displacement. J. Comput. Theor. Nanosci. **13**(6), 3948–3952 (2016)
4. Feng, L., Lyu, Z., Mayer, D.: Multi-level logic gate operation based on amplified apta-sensor performance. Angewandte Chemie **54**(26), 7693–7712 (2015)
5. Allen, P.B., Arshad, S.A., Li, B., Chen, X., Ellington, A.D.: DNA circuits as amplifiers for the detection of nucleic acids on a paper fluidic platform. Lab Chip **12**(16), 2951–2958 (2012)
6. Lund, K., Manzo, A.J., Dabby, N., Michelotti, N., Johnsonbuck, A., Nangreave, J.: Molecular robots guided by prescriptive landscapes. Nature **465**(7295), 206–210 (2010)
7. Dannenberg, F., Kwiatkowska, M., Thachuk, C., Turberfield, A.J.: DNA walker circuits: computational potential, design, and verification. In: Soloveichik, D., Yurke, B. (eds.) DNA 2013. LNCS, vol. 8141, pp. 31–45. Springer, Cham (2013). https://doi.org/10.1007/978-3-319-01928-4_3
8. Yang, X., Tang, Y., Mason, S.D., Chen, J., Li, F.: Enzyme-powered three-dimensional DNA nanomachine for DNA walking, payload release, and biosensing. ACS Nano **10**(2), 2324–2329 (2016)
9. Sawlekar, R., Montefusco, F., Kulkarni, V.V., Bates, D.G.: Implementing nonlinear feedback controllers using DNA strand displacement reactions. IEEE Trans. Nanobiosci. **15**(5), 443–454 (2016)
10. Eguchi, Y., Kato, T., Tanaka, T., Maruyama, T.: A DNA-gold nanoparticle hybrid hy-drogel network prepared by enzymatic reaction. Chem. Comm. **53**(43), 5802–5814 (2017)
11. Song, T., Zheng, P., Wong, M.L.D., Wang, X.: Design of logic gates using spiking neural P systems with homogeneous neurons and astrocytes-like control. Inform. Sci. **372**, 380–391 (2016)
12. Qian, L., Winfree, E.: A simple DNA gate motif for synthesizing large-scale circuits. In: Goel, A., Simmel, F.C., Sosík, P. (eds.) DNA 2008. LNCS, vol. 5347, pp. 70–89. Springer, Heidelberg (2009). https://doi.org/10.1007/978-3-642-03076-5_7
13. Qian, L., Winfree, E.: Scaling up digital circuit computation with DNA strand displacement cascades. Science **332**(6034), 1196–1200 (2011)

14. Zhang, D.Y., Seelig, G.: Dynamic DNA nanotechnology using strand-displacement reactions. Nat. Chem. **3**(2), 103–113 (2011)
15. Zhang, C., Ma, L.N., Dong, Y.F., Yang, J., Xu, J.: Molecular logic computing model based on DNA self-assembly strand branch migration. Chinese Sci. Bull. **58**(1), 32–38 (2013)
16. Wang, Y., Tian, G., Hou, H., Ye, M., Cui, G.: Simple logic computation based on the DNA strand displacement. J. Comput. Theor. Nanosci. **11**(9), 1975–1982 (2014)
17. Wang, Z., Wu, Y., Tian, G., Wang, Y., Cui, G.: The application research on multi-digit logic operation based on DNA strand displacement. J. Comput. Theor. Nanosci. **12**(7), 1252–1257 (2015)
18. Cho, K., Merrienboer, B. V., Bahdanau, D., Bengio, Y.: On the properties of neural machine translation: encoder-decoder approaches. In: The Eighth Workshop on Syntax, Semantics and Structure in Statistical Translation, pp. 103–111 (2014)

Multi-objective Optimization for Ladle Tracking of Aluminium Tapping Based on NSGA-II

Kaibo Zhou[1,2], Yutao Zou[1,2], Hongting Wang[1,2], Gaofeng Xu[1,2],
and Sihai Guo[3(✉)]

[1] School of Automation, Huazhong University of Science and Technology,
Wuhan 430074, China
{zhoukb,M201572433,whting,xugf}@hust.edu.cn
[2] MOE Key Laboratory of Image Processing and Intelligence Control,
Wuhan 430074, China
[3] School of Automation, Wuhan University of Technology, Wuhan 430070, China
Guosihai@whut.edu.cn

Abstract. In order to realize the optimization of ladle tracking of aluminium tapping, a mathematical model, which takes the grade of aluminium, the energy required for transportation and the optimum ratio of aluminium liquid into account, is established. The traditional method optimizes the impurity content and the transport distance based on a single objective optimization, but it requires the empirical values of the weight coefficients. The paper proposes a modified multi-objective optimization model with the elitist non-dominated sorting genetic algorithm (NSGA-II). In the crossover operator process and the mutation operator process, the separately improved methods are introduced based on the ladle tracking problem of aluminium tapping, which replaces the Simulated Binary Crossover (SBX) in the original NSGA-II algorithm into Partially Matched Crossover (PMX) based on natural number coding and uses exchange mutation (EM) operator. Finally, the practical production data of the aluminium factory is used to verify the validity and practicability of the method, and the results show that this method can obtain a feasible solution for the user to choose suitable solutions, and avoid the defects of selecting empirical weighting coefficient.

Keywords: Ladle tracking of aluminium tapping · Multi-objective optimization · NSGA-II

1 Introduction

Due to the influence of high temperature ($\geq$900 °C), strong current ($\geq$200 kA) and strong magnetic field ($\geq$200 G), the internal reaction of the aluminium electrolytic cell is very complicated in the aluminium electrolysis process, as a result, the process conditions of each cell are different, and finally, the compositions of the aluminium liquid are different. The production of aluminium liquid mainly consists of primary aluminium and impurities such as iron, silicon, magnesium,

C. He et al. (Eds.): BIC-TA 2017, CCIS 791, pp. 248–262, 2017.
https://doi.org/10.1007/978-981-10-7179-9_19

copper and other elements [30,31]. Ladle tracking of aluminium tapping includes the process of aluminium blending and the overhead traveling crane scheduling, which is one of the process of aluminium ingot casting. Before ladle tracking of aluminium tapping, the plan for produced aluminium should be made firstly according to the compositions of the aluminium liquid in each cell, then the ladle is carried to electrolytic cells by the crane in the basis of produced aluminium plan, and the aluminum liquid in the cell is sucked into the ladle, generally, a ladle can hold three cells of aluminium liquid. Aluminum liquid with different compositions in 3 electrolytic cells is mixed into a new aluminum liquid in the ladle. The full load ladle will be sent to the foundry by the special delivery car and ready for the next produced aluminium. In the proportioning aluminum process, it is required that the aluminium liquid of the multiple aluminium electrolytic cells before merged in a ladle is up to a certain process standard. The running distance of crane should be considered to improve the production efficiency of aluminium and save energy. Therefore, ladle tracking of aluminium tapping is actually a combinatorial optimization problem. Because of the time constraints or the lack of constraint conditions, it is very difficult to obtain exact solutions by mathematical programming for practical engineering problems [1,17], so most of these problems are chosen to get the approximate solutions, and meta-heuristic algorithms are widely used in solving approximate solutions. By improving these algorithms properly, solutions which meet the actual needs can be obtained [5,22–24].

At present, the ladle tracking programmes of aluminium tapping are obtained by manual calculation in many aluminium factory, but this method is low efficiency, low accuracy and strong intensity of labour. Therefore, in the literature [20], a model is built with the minimum impurity content as the goal, but the enumeration method is used to solve the problem without considering the overhead traveling crane scheduling. In the literature [28], two electrolytic cells are taken as one carrying ladle, and the weight sum method is used to deal with the two targets of impurity content and crane running distance, and finally the problem is solved by the genetic algorithm, but the aluminium grades are not taken into consideration. Knowledge reasoning is used in the management of the aluminium blending problem, but the rules in the knowledge base are too few to meet the variable needs of the cells in time, and it is needed that expert guidance on the processing [21]. By the comprehensive analysis of the proportioning aluminum process, the produced aluminium program is obtained by the hybrid genetic algorithm, and the objective function is established based on the running distance of overhead travelling crane, but the solution is only for the single standard of aluminium ingot [12].

The practical process often involves multiple objective variables, which need to be optimized simultaneously [21]. The traditional methods of multi-objective optimization are weighted method and constraint method, but there are many problems such as strong subjectivity in coefficient selection, slow optimization speed and complicated calculation [10,24]. The NSGA algorithm proposed by Srinivas and Deb not only sorts the population hierarchically, but also uses the virtual fitness value to sort the solutions at each level, which can get better solution [18]. The improved NSGA, that is, the non-dominated sorting genetic algorithm with elitist strategy (NSGA-II) has higher computing efficiency than NSGA [7,23].

In this paper, a multi-objective mathematical model based on ladle tracking of aluminium tapping is established, and the optimal proportion of aluminium liquid and the energy consumption of crane are taken into account. According to the data of aluminium factories, the results obtained by using NSGA-II with good convergence are compared with the weighted sum method [8,19,26,29], it is shown that the results obtained by NSGA-II are more practical.

2   Multi Objective Mathematical Model for Ladle Tracking of Aluminium Tapping

If the standard for the aluminium liquid in each ladle is higher before blending, the aluminium liquid that fails to meet the standard can be cast into the sub-optimal standard aluminium ingot. Therefore, two objective variables of ladle tracking of aluminium tapping are put forward. One is the impurity content, when the impurity content in the aluminum liquid exceeds the standard, if the impurity content reaches the minimum, the sub standard aluminum ingots can be produced. The other is the number of the ladles, the more the number of the ladles that meet the standard, the better the aluminum liquid ratio can be achieved. In a work area, the cells are placed in a single row, and it is required that the crane running time is shorter to save energy. So the traveling distances of the overhead travelling crane are taken as the target variable, and the total traveling distances of the crane are the sum of the relative distances between the three cells while carrying a ladle. The shorter the running distances of the crane are, the less the energy consumption of the crane will be.

2.1   Decision Variables of Ladle Tracking of Aluminium Tapping

The variables that appear in the ladle tracking of aluminium tapping are defined as follows:

(1) N_i: The cell No. of the aluminium electrolytic cells, where the maximum of i is n, that is, there are n aluminium electrolytic cells in a work area.
(2) S_{jk}: The impurity content that meets the process requirements, where j is the element in the aluminium liquid, S_{jk} is the k-th standard of j element, here j mainly refers to Al, Fe and Si, k is the grade of the standard, there are 8 national standards for the aluminium ingots used by remelting, the highest standard is Al99.90, the second standard is Al99.85, and so on.
(3) P_{ij}: The test data for the elements in the cells, where i is the cell No. and is an element of N_i set, here j mainly refers to Al, Fe and Si.
(4) T_l: Ladle group No., a ladle needs to be loaded with aluminium liquid from three aluminium electrolytic cells, so the maximum value of the integer l is $\frac{n}{3}$, and the mathematical expression is $\lceil n/3 \rceil$ (Fig. 1).

Fig. 1. Aluminium production process in work area.

(5) C_{lm}: The aluminium electrolytic cell No. in the $l-th$ ladle, the desirable values of m are 1, 2, 3, where $C_{l1} < C_{l2} < C_{l3}$.

(6) M_{kl}: Whether the aluminium liquid in the $l-th$ ladle is satisfied with the standard k, if it is 1, otherwise 0.

(7) L_l: The running path of $l-th$ ladle, where

$$L_l = |N_{C_{l3}} - N_{C_{l2}}| + |N_{C_{l2}} - N_{C_{l1}}|. \tag{1}$$

(8) B_{Fel}: The percentage of Fe in the $l-th$ ladle, where

$$B_{Fel} = \frac{P_{FeC_{l3}} + P_{FeC_{l2}} + P_{FeC_{l1}}}{P_{AlC_{l3}} + P_{AlC_{l2}} + P_{AlC_{l1}}}. \tag{2}$$

(9) B_{Sil}: The percentage of Si in the $l-th$ ladle, where

$$B_{Sil} = \frac{P_{SiC_{l3}} + P_{SiC_{l2}} + P_{SiC_{l1}}}{P_{AlC_{l3}} + P_{AlC_{l2}} + P_{AlC_{l1}}}. \tag{3}$$

2.2 Objective Function of Ladle Tracking of Aluminium Tapping

(1) The impurity content of the original aluminium is the lowest, and the impurity content of the aluminium liquid should be calculated when the process standard is not met, otherwise it will be 0,

$$min f_1 = \sum_{l=1}^{\lceil \frac{n}{3} \rceil} (|B_{Fel} - S_{Fek}| + |B_{Sil} - S_{Sik}|). \tag{4}$$

(2) The traveling distance of overhead travelling crane is the shortest,

$$min f_2 = \sum_{l=1}^{\lceil \frac{n}{3} \rceil} L_l. \tag{5}$$

(3) The number of ladles to meet the process standards is the most, which meets the process standards is 1, otherwise 0,

$$max f_3 = \sum_{l=1}^{\lceil \frac{n}{3} \rceil} M_{kl}. \tag{6}$$

2.3 Constraint Conditions of Ladle Tracking of Aluminium Tapping

(1) The content of aluminium liquid in the ladle can not exceed the full load of the ladle itself, that is 10t,

$$\sum_{m=1}^{3} P_{AlC_{lm}} \leq 10t. \tag{7}$$

(2) The content of iron and silicon in each ladle shall not be higher than the standard value of the process,

$$\sum_{m=1}^{3} P_{FeC_{lm}} \leq \sum_{m=1}^{3} S_{Fek} * P_{AlC_{lm}}, \tag{8}$$

$$\sum_{m=1}^{3} P_{SiC_{lm}} \leq \sum_{m=1}^{3} S_{Sik} * P_{AlC_{lm}}, \tag{9}$$

where

$$\begin{cases} l \in [1, \lceil \frac{n}{3} \rceil] \\ k \in [1, 8]. \end{cases} \tag{10}$$

3 Design of NSGA-II for Ladle Tracking of Aluminium Tapping

The flow chart of the problem of ladle tracking of aluminium tapping based on NSGA-II is shown in Fig. 2.

3.1 Coding Design of Ladle Tracking of Aluminium Tapping

The coding is mainly designed according to the solution of the problem, and the solution of the ladle tracking of aluminium tapping is the aluminium electrolytic cell No. after the permutation and combination. As the No. of the aluminium electrolytic cells is expressed in natural numbers, the coding mode adopted is

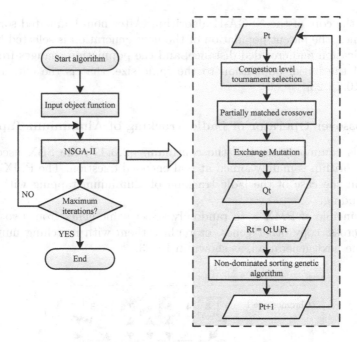

Fig. 2. An algorithm for ladle tracking of aluminium tapping based on NSGA-II.

the natural number coding. In this paper, the data of a work area are tested. There are 36 aluminium electrolytic cells in a work area, in which each of three cells consists of a ladle with a total of 12 ladles. Table 1 is a chromosome for ladle tracking of aluminium tapping, in which $(32, 22, 34)$ is the first ladle, $(35, 6, 3)$ is the second ladle, and so on, $(20, 10, 12)$ is the last ladle, and there is $C_{l1} < C_{l2} < C_{l3}$ in a ladle.

Table 1. A chromosome for ladle tracking of aluminium tapping problem.

32	22	34	35	6	3	16	11	30	33	7	28	17	14	8	5	29	21
25	31	27	26	19	15	1	36	23	2	4	18	24	13	9	20	10	12

3.2 Selection Operator of Ladle Tracking of Aluminium Tapping

When using the NSGA-II algorithm, two selection processes are required for the population. The first is the crowded championship selection while the parent population generates the progeny population, parent population needs to be chosen, crossed, and mutated to get offspring of the same size as the parent population, and the used selection operator is crowded championship selection, which two parents are generally selected from individuals based on degree of congestion that are selected randomly from population. The second selection process is the core of the NSGA-II algorithm. After non-dominated sorting the chromosomes, the parent population of the next generation is selected based on the stratification and crowded distance, and the population changes from twice the size of the initial population to the same size, that is the elite retention strategy [10,18,23].

3.3   Crossover Operator of Ladle Tracking of Aluminium Tapping

NSGA-II is commonly used in the continuum [2,5,17], the SBX used in the original algorithm is mainly aimed at real encoded question. The PMX replaces the SBX in the case of the ladle tracking of aluminium tapping with natural numbers coding.

The principle of PMX is to randomly select some genes from two chromosomes to cross, copy other genes, or replace them with matching numbers to produce the next generation, as shown in Fig. 3.

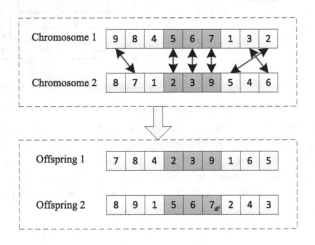

Fig. 3. Sketch map of EMX.

The Partially Matched Crossover is consisted of three steps.

Step 1. The two chromosomes are randomly selected as the parent to cross. For example, in Fig. 3, the 4th, 5th and 6th bit are selected for chromosome 1 $(9, 8, 4, 5, 6, 7, 1, 3, 2)$ and chromosome 2 $(8, 7, 1, 2, 3, 9, 5, 4, 6)$ as intersections.

Step 2. Exchange alleles between intersections on two chromosomes, and keep other genes unchanged. Aluminium tapping can not be repeated, that is, a chromosome can not have the same gene bits, therefore, it is necessary to find the corresponding matching points in the crossover gene. In Fig. 3, it can be seen that 5 and 2, 6 and 3, 7 and 9 match each other.

Step 3. Check the exchanged chromosomes and replace the duplicated data with the matching data obtained in step 2, and get a new chromosome.

In the ladle tracking problem of aluminium tapping, if there are aluminium ingots that do not meet the standard, cross again. While crossing, first, select a number from 0−1 randomly, if the number is less than the crossover probability, make Partially Matched Crossover, otherwise, do not cross.

3.4 Mutation Operator of Ladle Tracking of Aluminium Tapping

The mutation operator used in ladle problem which is based on NSGA-II is EM (Exchange Mutation). By interchanging the two randomly selected gene locations of a chromosome [9,11,14,15], it is formed that a new chromosome, as shown in Fig. 4.

The aluminium liquid is carried by ladles, and in the chromosome, a single cell No. is used as a unit, so in order to make the selected gene position not be in the same ladle, it is necessary to add a constraint here, then re-select the gene location while do not meet the condition. In Fig. 4, the gene positions selected are the 3rd and 6th, which are not in the same ladle, so mutation can be carried out.

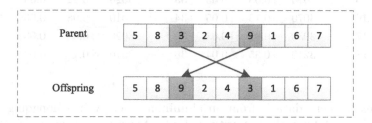

Fig. 4. Sketch map of EM.

4 Case Analysis

4.1 Experimental Data

In this paper, the aluminium ingot grade Al99.85 is used as the produced aluminium standard [13], and the process parameters of each impurity are shown in Table 2.

Table 2. The quality standard table of aluminium ingot grade Al99.85.

Grade	Chemical constituents of impurities (Mass fraction) (%) (not more than)								
	Fe	Si	Cu	Ga	Mg	Zn	Mn	Other	Sum
Al99.85	0.12	0.08	0.005	0.03	0.02	0.03	-	0.015	0.15

Table 3. Raw aluminium datasheet.

Cell No.	Al (kg)	Fe (%)	Si (%)	Cell No.	Al (kg)	Fe (%)	Si (%)
1	3170	0.12	0.03	19	3200	0.08	0.03
2	3170	0.17	0.03	20	3200	0.11	0.03
3	3120	0.37	0.13	21	3220	0.14	0.05
4	3120	0.08	0.03	22	3220	0.07	0.03
5	3100	0.85	0.18	23	3220	0.09	0.03
6	3130	0.13	0.04	24	3020	0.08	0.03
7	3100	0.12	0.05	25	3020	0.4	0.12
8	3090	0.08	0.03	26	3020	0.08	0.03
9	3170	0.11	0.04	27	3020	0.08	0.03
10	3090	0.08	0.03	28	3010	0.08	0.03
11	3090	0.09	0.03	29	3020	0.08	0.03
12	3090	0.08	0.03	30	3010	0.08	0.03
13	3080	0.08	0.03	31	3020	0.22	0.05
14	3080	0.08	0.03	32	3010	0.24	0.09
15	3070	0.08	0.03	33	3020	0.22	0.05
16	3070	0.13	0.05	34	3010	0.08	0.03
17	3080	0.07	0.03	35	3020	0.08	0.03
18	3210	0.35	0.04	36	3010	0.1	0.03

The experiment data is from an aluminium factory in Chongqing city, as shown in Table 3. Only the impurity contents of iron and silicon are selected for experiment as the two main impurity contents in aluminium liquid.

There are 36 cells selected for produced aluminium in a work area, if the aluminium liquid from three electrolytic cells is merged into one ladle, and the mass percent of impurity iron and impurity silicon does not exceed the standard content of Table 2. At most, 12 ladles can be matched to meet the standard in a work area.

4.2   Analysis of Results

In the experiment, the traditional genetic algorithm is compared with NSGA-II. The points in the NSGA-II are presented by the mean of the Pareto set of each generation, since the final solutions are the points selected from the Pareto set (Pareto optimal solution set is shown in Fig. 5), that is, the set of the first layer F_1 of the population stratification, are presented by the red rectangles. The points in GA are the mean of each target in each generation, represented by a black triangles. The experimental results are shown in Figs. 6, 7 and 8.

Simulation parameter settings: the number of genetic iteration is 150, the population size is 100, the crossover probability of GA is 0.8, the mutation

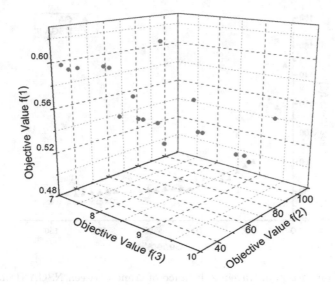

Fig. 5. Pareto optimal solution set

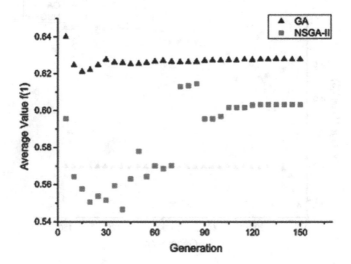

Fig. 6. Comparison of impurity content between NSGA-II and GA.

probability is 0.02, the crossover probability of NSGA-II is 0.9, and the mutation probability is 0.1.

It can be seen from the above three graphs that the solutions obtained by using NSGA-II in the same initial population are superior to that obtained by GA on the three targets. Figure 6 shows the impurity content, it is required that the impurity content should be closer to the standard, so that the remaining aluminium liquid can be mixed to achieve better mix proportions, and meet the standards except for the Al99.85 standard. Figure 7 shows the distance traveled

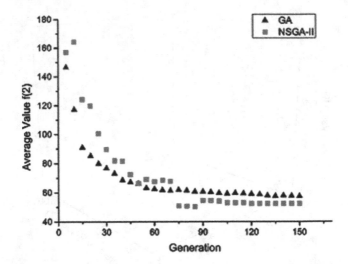

Fig. 7. Comparison of traveling distance of crane between NSGA-II and GA.

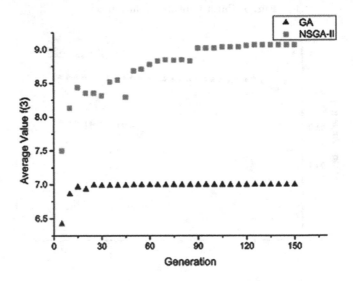

Fig. 8. Comparison of the number of ladles that meet the standard between NSGA-II and GA.

by the crane, the solutions of NSGA-II and GA are not very different, so NSGA-II has no obvious advantage over this target. In Fig. 8, the number of the ladles that meet the standard the more the better, it shows that the NSGA-II is apparently better than GA for the solution.

The part of the solutions of NSGA-II is displayed in Table 4.

Table 4. Part of the solutions of NSGA-II.

Order number of solutions	The order of the crane running to the aluminium electrolytic cell
1	2-5-1, 4-3-8, 7-6-9, 11-10-12, 16-14-13, 15-17-18, 25-27-26, 28-23-24, 21-19-20, 31-29-30, 34-35-36, 32-33-22
2	2-3-1, 5-4-8, 7-6-9, 11-12-10, 16-14-13, 15-17-18, 25-33-32, 22-23-24, 21-19-20, 31-29-30, 34-35-36, 26-27-28
3	3-1-5, 4-2-8, 7-6-9, 11-12-10, 16-14-13, 15-17-18, 25-33-32, 22-23-24, 21-19-20, 31-29-30, 34-35-36, 26-27-28
4	3-5-12, 4-2-8, 7-6-9, 11-1-10, 16-14-13, 22-17-33, 25-18-32, 15-23-24, 21-19-20, 26-27-28, 31-29-30, 34-35-36
5	1-2-5, 4-3-8, 7-6-9, 11-12-10, 16-14-13, 22-17-33, 25-18-32, 15-23-24, 21-19-20, 31-29-30, 34-35-36, 26-27-28

While the number of ladles is as large as possible, the traveling distance of crane for aluminium tapping and the impurity content should be appropriate. In this paper, the third objective solution is the optimum solution of the aluminium tapping scheme, and the content of each ladle is shown in Table 5.

Table 5. The optimal values of the objective variables for NSGA-II (The number of ladles that meet the aluminium standard is most).

Objective	Optimal value
Objective function value	[0.6261, 39, 9]
Order of aluminium tapping	3-1-5, 4-2-8, 7-6-9, 11-12-10, 16-14-13, 15-17-18, 25-33-32, 22-23-24, 21-19-20, 31-29-30, 34-35-36, 26-27-28
Standards that ladles meet	0-1-1-1-1-0-0-1-1-1-1-1
Impurity contents (Fe-Si)	0.44–0.11, 0.11–0.03, 0.12–0.04, 0.08–0.03, 0.10–0.04, 0.17–0.09, 0.29–0.03, 0.08–0.04, 0.11–0.03, 0.10–0.03, 0.09–0.03, 0.10–0.03
Traveling distance of crane	4-6-3-2-3-3-8-2-2-2-2-2

As can be seen from Table 5, the aluminium electrolytic cells that do not meet the standards are (1-3-5, 15-17-18, 25-33-32). Compared with the original aluminium, it can be found that the impurity content of the electrolytic aluminium liquid in these cells is higher and can not meet the requirements of the grade

Al99.85. Therefore, the aluminium liquid can only be matched to the second aluminium ingot grade. In industry, it is required to match a higher standard aluminium ingot as much as possible, and the solution should meet the industrial demand, reduce the running time of the crane and save energy.

5 Conclusion

Based on the optimization analysis of the path of aluminium tapping and the aluminium blending scheme, the paper puts forward three objective variables that affect the ladle tracking of aluminium tapping, and establishes the corresponding mathematical model. In view of the characteristics of the model, the NSGA-II algorithm is used to solve the problem iteratively by choosing the appropriate selection operator, crossover operator and mutation operator.

The production data of the aluminium factory is taken as the experimental data, which is used to get the solution of the multi-objective mathematical model of ladle tracking of aluminium tapping and verifies the practicability of the model. The experimental results show that the solutions obtained by the NSGA-II algorithm are optimized on the three targets of the impurity content, the number of standard ladle and the running distance of the overhead travelling crane. It is found that all the objective values are more valuable, and a number of schemes of ladle tracking of aluminium tapping that satisfy the industrial requirements can be obtained by comparing the solution with those of the current genetic algorithms. But in the engineering application, economic factors can also be taken into account, then establish the corresponding model according to the cost of aluminium ingots production and energy consumption, and is solved by the algorithm, which will be the next step of research.

Acknowledgments. The work is supported by the National High Technology Research and Development Program of China (863 Program) (No. 2013AA040705 and No. 2013AA041002) and the Fundamental Research Funds for the central Universities (WUT: 2014-IV-142).

References

1. Asadollahi-Yazdi, E., Hassan, A., Siadat, A., et al.: Multi-objective optimization for inspection planning using NSGA-II. In: 2015 IEEE International Conference on Industrial Engineering and Engineering Management (IEEM), Singapore, pp. 1422–1426 (2015)
2. Colanzi, T.E., Vergilio, S.R.: A feature-driven crossover operator for multi-objective and evolutionary optimization of product line architectures. J. Syst. Softw. **121**(1), 126–143 (2016)
3. Deb, K., Pratap, A., Aggarwal, S., et al.: A fast and elitist multiobjective genetic algorithm: NSGA-II. IEEE Trans. Evol. Comput. **6**(2), 182–197 (2002)
4. Fonseca, C., Fleming, P.: An overview of evolutionary algorithms in multiobjective optimization. Evol. Comput. **3**(1), 1–16 (1999)

5. Gui, W.H., Yang, C.H., Chen, X.F., et al.: Modeling and optimization problems and challenges arising in nonferrous metallurgical processes. Acta Autom. Sin. **39**(3), 197–207 (2013). (in Chinese)
6. Guo, S.H., Zhou, K.B., Cao, B., Yang, C.H.: Combination weights and TOPSIS method for performance evaluation of aluminum electrolysis. In: 2015 Chinese Automation Congress (CAC), Wuhan, Hubei, China, pp. 1–6, 27–29 November 2015
7. He, C., Tian, Y., Jin, Y.C., Zhang, X.Y., Pan, L.Q.: A radial space division based evolutionary algorithm for many-objective optimization. Appl. Soft. Comput. **61**, 603–621 (2017)
8. Huang, R.F., Luo, X.W., Ji, B., et al.: Multi-objective optimization of a mixed-flow pump impeller using modified NSGA-II algorithm. Sci. China Technol. Sci. **58**(12), 2122–2130 (2015). (in Chinese)
9. Karamlou, A., Bocchini, P.: Sequencing algorithm with multiple-input genetic operators: application to disaster resilience. Eng. Struct. **117**(1), 591–602 (2016)
10. Konak, A., Coit, D.W., Smith, A.E.: Multi-objective optimization using genetic algorithms: a tutorial. Reliab. Eng. Syst. Saf. **91**(9), 992–1007 (2006)
11. Kuang, H.Y., Jin, J., Su, Y.: Improving crossover and mutation for adaptive genetic algorithm. Comput. Eng. Appl. **42**(12), 93–96 (2006). (in Chinese)
12. Li, J.H., Wei, X., Rui, Z.Y., et al.: Blending and loading problem of molten aluminium and hybrid genetic algorithm optimization. Control Decis. **29**(5), 933–936 (2014). (in Chinese)
13. Liang, X.M., Zhang, S.J.: Production Technology and Management of Modern Aluminium Electrolysis. Central South University Press, Changsha (2011). (in Chinese)
14. Ma, L.X., Wang, J.Q.: Application of genetic algorithms in solving the optimal combination problem. Comput. Eng. Sci. **7**(27), 72–73 (2005). (in Chinese)
15. Moon, C., Seo, Y.: Evolutionary algorithm for advanced process planning and scheduling in a multi-plant. Comput. Ind. Eng. **48**(2), 311–325 (2005)
16. Pan, L.Q., He, C., Tian, Y., Su, Y.S., Zhang, X.Y.: A region division based diversity maintaining approach for many-objective optimization. Integr. Comput. Aided Eng. **24**(3), 1–18 (2017)
17. Ripon, K.S.N., Glette, K., Hovin, M., et al.: A Multi-objective evolutionary algorithm for solving integrated scheduling and layout planning problems in manufacturing systems. In: 2012 IEEE Conference on Evolving and Adaptive Intelligent Systems, Madrid, Spain, pp. 157–163, 17–18 May 2012
18. Srinivas, N., Deb, K.: Muiltiobjective optimization using nondominated sorting in genetic algorithms. Evol. Comput. **2**(3), 221–248 (1994)
19. Vanucci, S.C., Carrano, E.G., Bicalho, R., et al.: A modified NSGA-II for the multi-objective multi-mode resource-constrained project scheduling problem. In: IEEE Congress on Evolutionary Computation, Brisbane, Australia, pp. 1–7, 10–15 June 2012
20. Xia, Y.M.: Calculation analysis and software development of primary aluminium casting optimized proportioning aluminium method. Light Metals **42**(7), 38–41 (2005). (in Chinese)
21. Xie, W.H.: Research on Several Key Problems About the Aluminium Production Resource Management System. Central South University Library, Changsha (2012). (in Chinese)
22. Yang, C.H., Shen, D.Y., Wu, M., et al.: Synthesis of qualitative and quantitative methods in a coal blending expert system for coke oven. Acta Autom. Sin. **26**(2), 222–232 (2000). (in Chinese)

23. Yang, C.H., Wang, X.L., Tao, J., et al.: Modeling and intelligent optimization algorithm for burden process of copper flash smelting. J. Syst. Simul. **20**(8), 2152–2155 (2008). (in Chinese)
24. Yang, C.H., Wen, L.M., Zhu, H.Q.: Satisfactory optimization of raw slurry arrangement for process of alumina production. Control Decis. **23**(10), 1168–1172 (2008). (in Chinese)
25. Yusoff, Y., Ngadiman, M.S., Zain, A.M.: Overview of NSGA-II for optimizing machining process parameters. Procedia Eng. **15**(4), 3978–3983 (2011)
26. Zhang, H., Zhu, Y.L., Chang, C.G.: Burdening optimization problem of high-precision copper strips based on NSGA-II algorithm. Control Decis. **27**(7), 1071–1076 (2012). (in Chinese)
27. Zhang, J.X., Wang, G.P.: Feed formula optimization method based on multi-objective particle swarm optimization algorithm. In: 2010 2nd International Workshop on Intelligent Systems and Applications, Wuhan, Hubei, China, pp. 1–3, 22–23 May 2010
28. Zhang, Y.L.: Research and development of arranging packing of aluminium electrolysis cells intelligently. North China Univ. Technol. Libr. **42**(7), 38–41 (2005). Beijing. (in Chinese)
29. Zhang, Z.Y.: Multi-objective optimization of steelmaking continuous casting scheduling based on NSGA-II. Digit. Technol. Appl. **34**(8), 61–62 (2016). (in Chinese)
30. Zhou, K., Lin, Z., Yu, D., et al.: Cell resistance slope combined with LVQ neural network for prediction of anode effect. In: Sixth International Conference on Intelligent Control and Information Processing (ICICIP), Wuhan, Hubei, China, pp. 47–51, 26–28 November 2015
31. Zhou, K., Yu, D., Lin, Z., et al.: Anode effect prediction of aluminium electrolysis using GRNN. In: Chinese Automation Congress (CAC), Wuhan, Hubei, China, pp. 853–858, 27–29 November 2015

Short Time and Contactless Virus Infection Screening System with Discriminate Function Using Doppler Radar

Xiaofeng Yang$^{(\boxtimes)}$, Koichiro Ishibashi, Toshiaki Negishi, Tetsuo Kirimoto, and Guanghao Sun

Graduate School of Informatics and Engineering, The University of Electro-Communications, 1-5-1 Chofugaoka, Chofu, Tokyo 182-8585, Japan
feng022026@gmail.com

Abstract. Recently, infectious diseases, such as Ebola fever and Middle East respiratory syndrome, have spread worldwide. To conduct a highly accurate infection screening, our group is working on the development of a non-contact and hand-held infection screening system that can detect infected individuals within 5 s. In this study, we propose a signal processing method to improve the measurement accuracy of the infection screening system. Body surface temperature, heartbeat, and respiration rates are detected by thermography and microwave radars. To evaluate the measurement accuracy, nine subjects (normal and pseudo-infection conditions) were tested with the proposed system in a laboratory. In this study, a linear discriminate function was used to detect pseudo-infection conditions. The detection accuracy was improved to 88.9%.

Keywords: Vital signs · Doppler radar · Infection · Peak-detection

1 Introduction

The world epidemic of influenza A (H1N1) in 2009 [1], the Middle East Respiratory Syndrome (MERS) in 2012 [2], the avian influenza (H7N9) virus infection in China in 2013 [3], and the Ebola hemorrhagic fever in West Africa in early 2014 have occurred, which became the biggest epidemic in recent years [4]. In recent years, infectious diseases such as dengue fever and Ebola hemorrhagic fever have spread worldwide. Quarantine is enforced within airports as a measure to prevent the spread of infectious diseases. Within the current quarantine system, the use of thermography detection on people, as well as administering questionnaires is common. However, in measuring temperature by thermography, it is not possible to eliminate the influence of alcohol and antipyretic agents on the body surface temperature. Moreover, the questionnaire is a subjective evaluation, and there is always the possibility that the respondent does not answer honestly. Therefore, it is necessary to carry out objective and accurate quarantine measures.

To meet these requirements, we proposed a non-contact infection screening system using measured vital signs to include facial temperature, heartbeat rate

© Springer Nature Singapore Pte Ltd. 2017
C. He et al. (Eds.): BIC-TA 2017, CCIS 791, pp. 263–273, 2017.
https://doi.org/10.1007/978-981-10-7179-9_20

and respiration rate. These factors were determined based upon some studies indicating that infected people not only have higher temperatures but also have a faster heartbeat rate and respiration rate [5,6]. The idea of developing an infection screening system based on vital signs comes from the fact that infections are associated with inflammation when the infected individual becomes symptomatic. As a result of inflammation, not only body temperature but also heart and respiration rates will increase. The proposed system detects infected people via a discriminate function and the detection accuracy was improved up to 88.9%. As such, the proposed system has a higher reliability than current screening methods that only use thermography.

In this work, we focused on improving the detection accuracy of heartbeats, and reducing measurement time. The body surface displacement during respiration and heartbeat is 4–12 mm and 0.2–0.5 mm, respectively. Therefore, the heartbeat signal can be influenced by respiration [7]. The reduction of the influence of respiration is cited as a problem. As a conventional method, the fast Fourier transform (FFT) was utilized to calculate the heart rate (HR) [8–10]. However, due to low FFT resolution, the accuracy of HR measurement is poor. To solve this problem, we proposed an analog printed circuit board (PCB) to amplify and extract the heartbeat and respiration components, followed by the peak detection algorithm. This method can improve the detection accuracy up to 88.9%, and reduce measurement time to a minimum of 5 s.

2   Materials and Methods

2.1   Measurement Principle

The Doppler radar transmits microwaves from the transmitting antenna (TX), which then strikes the variable object (body surface), and is then reflected and received by the receiving antenna (RX). The frequency of the received radio frequency (RF) signal varies slightly, depending on the speed of the moving object and the Doppler effect. Using a mixer, the radar compares the transmission wave and the received RF signal. It then extracts only the frequency of the difference (Doppler frequency f_d) [11].

In order to obtain f_d at the radar output, a waveform with at least one cycle is necessary. To achieve this, the target object needs to move a distance of at least half a wavelength, or more, of the transmission frequency. This minimum distance is approximately 6.2 mm for a 24-GHz radar. The IQ output type radar has two mixers with an output phase difference of /2. This type of radar can simultaneously detect the moving speed and moving direction of the target, using two outputs [11]. The output of the direct RF input ($R_I(t)$) of the mixer is defined as in-phase, and the output of the RF input delayed by $\frac{\pi}{2}$ ($R_Q(t)$) of the mixer is defined as quadra-phase.

Figure 1 shows the fundamental mechanism of the Doppler radar vital sign detection [7,13]. A continuous wave $T(t) = A_T \cos[2\pi f t + \Phi(t)]$ is transmitted from the transmitter TX to the human body surface. Furthermore, A_T is the amplitude of the received signal, f is the carrier frequency, and $\Phi(t)$ is the phase

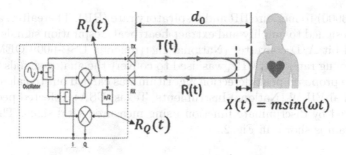

Fig. 1. Fundamental mechanism of Doppler radar vital sign detection, [12]

noise. According to the Doppler principle, the reflected wave R (t) is modulated by body surface motion X (t), such as respiration and heartbeat. Therefore, the receiver RX receives the reflected wave $R(t)$, which is expressed by (1).

$$R(t) = A_R \cos\left[2\pi ft - \frac{4\pi d_0}{\lambda} - \frac{4\pi X(t)}{\lambda} + \Phi(t)\right] \tag{1}$$

Where A_R is the amplitude of the received signal, f is the wavelength, c is the speed of light, and d_0 is the distance between the Doppler radar and the body surface. As shown in Fig. 1, when the received signal R(t) is down-converted, two baseband signals are obtained. One is the in-phase signal I(t), and the other is the quadrature phase signal Q(t).

$$I(t) = T(t) \times R_I(t)$$
$$= A_T \cos\left[2\pi ft + \Phi(t)\right]$$
$$\times A_R \cos\left[2\pi ft - \frac{4\pi d_0}{\lambda} - \frac{4\pi X(t)}{\lambda} + \Phi\left(t - \frac{2d_0}{c}\right)\right] \tag{2}$$
$$= A_I \cos\left[\frac{4\pi X(t)}{\lambda} + \frac{4\pi d_0}{\lambda} + \Phi(t) - \Phi\left(t - \frac{2d_0}{c}\right)\right] \tag{3}$$

$$Q(t) = T(t) \times R_Q(t)$$
$$= A_T \cos\left[2\pi ft + \Phi(t)\right]$$
$$\times A_R \cos\left[2\pi ft - \frac{4\pi d_0}{\lambda} - \frac{4\pi X(t)}{\lambda} + \Phi\left(t - \frac{2d_0}{c}\right) + \frac{\pi}{2}\right] \tag{4}$$
$$= A_Q \cos\left[\frac{4\pi X(t)}{\lambda} + \frac{4\pi d_0}{\lambda} + \Phi(t) - \Phi\left(t - \frac{2d_0}{c}\right) + \frac{\pi}{2}\right] \tag{5}$$

Where A_I is the amplitude of the in-phase signal, A_Q is the amplitude of quadrature phase signal.

2.2 The System Concept

The proposed infection screening system consists of a thermograph to measure facial temperature, as well as a 24 GHz microwave radar (SHARP,

DC6M4JN3000) to measure HR and respiratory rate (RR). Thereafter, an analog PCB was designed to amplify and extract heartbeat/respiration signals with low noise. A 14 bit A/D converter (National Instruments, USB-6009 OEM, USA), with a sampling rate of 1000 Hz, was used to convert the analog signals to digital signals. The proposed peak-detection algorithm was carried out to calculate vital signs with LabVIEW (National Instruments, Texas, USA). Infected people were then detected by discriminate function using measured vital signs. The system block diagram is shown in Fig. 2.

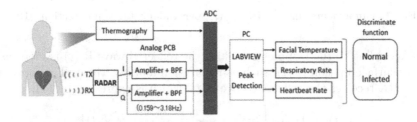

Fig. 2. System block diagram

2.3   Hardware Configuration and Software Development

Both I and Q signals include the heart beat and respiration information. We can use either the I signal or Q signal for extracting HR and RR. A required frequency component was extracted using a BPF. High-frequency noise of 3 Hz or above was eliminated by the BPF and then the heartbeat and respiration signals were extracted.

The necessary frequency component was taken out by the proposed analog BPF, reducing the influence of respiration and improving the HR detection efficiency. A part of the circuit diagram, and a graph of the PCB is shown in Fig. 3.

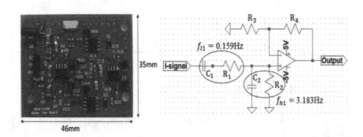

Fig. 3. Circuit diagram frequency attenuation factor of the BPF

Where I-signal is the original I signal of the Doppler radar, Output is the output of the first stage BPF which includes heartbeat/respiration signals. The cut-off low frequency and cut-off high frequency of the BPF were expressed by Eqs. (6) and (7).

$$f_{l1} = \frac{1}{2\pi R_1 C_1} = 0.159\,[\text{Hz}] \tag{6}$$

$$f_{h1} = \frac{1}{2\pi R_2 C_2} = 3.183\,[\text{Hz}] \tag{7}$$

The pass band of the first stage BPF is 0.159–3.18 Hz. An amplifier circuit and a BPF were designed on the PCB. The fabricated PCB is about the same size as the radar (46 mm × 35 mm). There are two outputs of the radar; the HR and RR were calculated from the two outputs.

The flow chart of the peak detection algorithm is shown in Fig. 4.

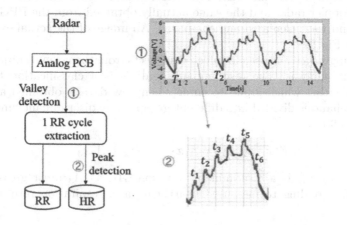

Fig. 4. Flow chart of the peak detection algorithm

Most of the previous studies have focused on the frequency-domain analysis of radar signals to detect HR using FFT [8–10]. FFT needs large computing power and takes time to achieve the calculation. Additionally, FFT needs at least some cycle-of-time domain signals to get reasonably precise frequency domain signals. As a result, FFT needs power and time in order to achieve results. We extracted the heartbeat component and respiratory component from Doppler radar using the proposed analog BPF. This filter reduced the effect of respiration and improved heartbeat detection accuracy.

From the output signals of the PCB, data for one breathing cycle was removed by valley detection. The RR was calculated by valley to valley intervals. Within one breathing cycle, the heart rate was calculated by peak detection. The advantage of the proposed peak detection algorithm is to measure HR and RR simultaneously for one respiration cycle with low calculating power.

We succeeded in the simultaneous measurement of HR and RR in a short time of 5 s with proposed peak detection, in the time domain, without using the conventional FFT.

2.4   Laboratory Test of the System

In order to evaluate the measurement accuracy, the HRs and RRs of nine subjects, with an average age of 23 years old, were measured. The test procedure consisted of two sessions: resting as the normal condition and exercising as a pseudo-infected condition. In order to achieve a pseudo-infected condition, the 9 healthy subjects performed an exercise trial of pushups 30 times. The radar and analog PCB were put behind the subject, according to the position of their chest. The distance between the radar and the subject was about 10 cm. The subjects were measured in a seated position. In order to obtain results of their HRs and RRs, they wore a pulse sensor PPG and a respiration band, contact type for measuring HR and RR. The correlation between the measured value from the Doppler radar and the value actually obtained from the PPG and respiration band was calculated and compared. An image of the actual experiment is shown in Fig. 5.

We distinguished the pseudo-infected subjects from the normal subjects using discriminant analysis. The discriminant analysis is a classification technique for discriminating which group to enter when new data is obtained after data given beforehand is divided into different groups. The discriminant function can defined as follows:

$$Z(x_1, x_2, x_3) = A_1 x_1 + A_2 x_2 + A_3 x_3 \tag{8}$$

where $Z(x_1, x_2, x_3)$ is a discriminant function, A_1, A_2, A_3 are regression coefficients corresponding to measured heartbeat rate, respiration rate and facial

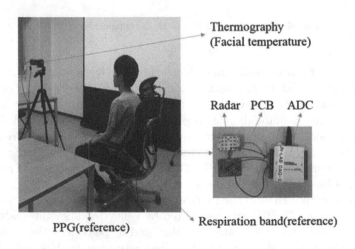

Fig. 5. Picture of experiment

temperature, respectively. And x_1, x_2, x_3 are variables of heartbeat rate, respiration rate and facial temperature, respectively.

3   Experimental Results

HR, RR, and facial temperature were measured by the proposed system, and the contact type measurement systems were used as a reference. A comparison of measured waveforms of heartbeat and respiration is shown in Fig. 6. The respiration waveform was highly correlated with the waveform measured by the respiration band. Furthermore, the heartbeat waveform showed peak-to-peak intervals similar to the waveform measured by the electrocardiogram (ECG). The results show that both heartbeat and respiration were accurately measured and this was attributed to high performance analog signal processing and proposed peak detection algorithm.

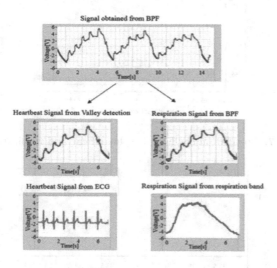

Fig. 6. Respiration and heartbeat signals

In order to evaluate measurement accuracy, the correlation coefficient was calculated. The results, outlined in Fig. 7, show that the correlation coefficient of heartbeat was 0.917, and the correlation coefficient of respiration was 0.921.

The nine normal subjects are eight males and one female, averaging 22.5 years old. In order to achieve a pseudo-infected condition, normal subjects performed pushups 30 times after the measurement of resting condition. The discriminant function was calculated using the measured vital signs of the nine normal subjects and the nine pseudo-infected subjects as shown in Eq. (9).

$$Z(x_1, x_2, x_3) = -0.09x_1 - 1.15x_2 - 6.66x_3 \qquad (9)$$

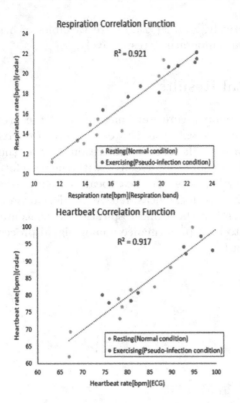

Fig. 7. Correlation coefficient of heartbeat and respiration

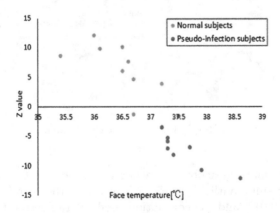

Fig. 8. Relationship between Z value and facial temperature

Where x_1 is heartbeat rate, x_2 is respiration rate, and x_3 is facial temperature. When the Z values are positive, the subjects are regarded as normal. When the Z values are negative, the subjects are regarded as infected. The discrimination results are shown in Fig. 8, by plotting the Z values versus the facial temperature of the two groups. Eight out of nine normal subjects Z values were positive, nine out of nine infected subjects Z values were negative. The detection accuracy was 88.9%.

The Z values and three viral signs are shown in Table 1.

Table 1. Z Values and three vital signs

Screening parameters			
Heartbeat rate(bpm)	Respiration rate(bpm)	Facial temperature($°C$)	Screening results $Z(x_1, x_2, x_3)$ value
Normal group			
88.3	11.2	36.5	10.1
80.0	15.5	36.7	4.7
76.8	19.8	35.4	8.6
81.6	13.3	36.6	7.6
69.4	21.4	36.7	-1.3
99.9	13.9	36.5	6.0
82.6	13.0	37.2	3.8
62.1	14.3	36	12.1
73.1	14.9	36.1	9.8
Pseudo-infected group			
97.2	20.7	37.9	-10.8
78.5	16.4	37.5	-1.7
80.8	22.1	37.3	-7.1
92.2	18.7	37.2	-3.5
77.8	20.8	37.3	-5.3
106.8	17.7	37.7	-6.9
93.1	18.1	38.6	-12.2
80.2	21.1	37.3	-5.9
94.2	21.4	37.4	-8.1

4   Discussion and Conclusion

In recent years, the epidemics of H1N1 influenza and Ebola hemorrhagic fever have been reported, and the importance of quarantine systems that detect infectious disease in patients have attracted attention. In a conventional quarantine system, measurements take time; therefore, it is not possible to examine everyone at a big airport. When returning from overseas, self-assessment of health status is mandatory, but there is a systemic lack of objectivity. Additionally, thermography is used to detect fever, but in addition to being influenced by drinking alcohol, there is an added challenge that it is impossible to identify a person temporarily suppressing fever with an antipyretic.

Therefore, an infection screening system that not only measures the surface temperature of the face by thermography, but also measures the heartbeat and RR with a small Doppler radar (24 GHz) was proposed. As a result of screening with this system, infected people were detected with an accuracy of 88.9%. The proposed system can make this determination in a short time of about 5–10 s. The system is also contactless, so it can suppress the risk of secondary infection.

In this paper, we aimed to non-contact acquisition of the HR and RR by using Doppler radar. We designed an analog BPF to extract the HR and RR. HR and RR were accurately calculated using the peak position detection algorithm in LabVIEW. The peak detection algorithm requires a relatively low calculation capability; therefore, the algorithm can be carried out by a microcomputer in the future. In the future, we will develop a hand-held and non-contact vital signs measurement system using a Doppler radar, PCB, and microcomputer. The non-contact HR/RR measurement system developed in this research is expected to be utilized in various fields, owing to its benefits that include low cost and miniaturization, which results in extremely low burdens on patients.

Our study has a few limitations. First, because of a small number of subjects in experiment, the versatility of the system cannot be verified fully. Second, the response to attitude fluctuation is still unresolved. In our future work, we will aim to solve those issues.

References

1. Nishiura, H., Kamiya, K.: Fever screening during the influenza (H1N1-2009) pandemic at Narita airport Japan. BMC Infect. Dis. **11**, 111 (2011)
2. Matsuyama, S.: Middle east respiratory syndrome (MERS) coronavirus. J. Vet. Epidemiol. **17**(2), 112–116 (2013)
3. Gao, R., Cao, B., Hu, Y.: Human Infection with a novel avian-origin influenza A(H7N9) virus. N. Engl. J. Med. **368**(20), 1888–1897 (2013)
4. Masuda, M.: Ebola hemorrhagic fever/ebola virus diseases. Dokkyo J. Med. Sci. **42**(3), 171–177 (2015)
5. Sun, G.: Design an easy-to-use infection screening system for non-contact monitoring of vital-signs to prevent the spread of pandemic diseases. In: 36th Annual International Conference of the IEEE Engineering in Medicine and Biology Society (EMBC) (2014)
6. Sun, G.: An infectious disease/fever screening radar system which stratifies higher-risk patients within ten seconds using a neural network and the fuzzy grouping method. J. Infect. **70**, 230–236 (2015)
7. Mogi, E., Ohtsuki, T.: Heartbeat Detection with Doppler Radar Based on Estimation of Average R-R Interval Using Viterbi Algorithm. IEICE Technical Report ASN2015-91, January 2016
8. Yang, X., Sun, G., Ishibashi, K.: Development of low-cost, compact noncontact heart rate/respiration measurement system using doppler radar and arduino. Jpn. Soc. Med. Biol. Eng. (2016)

9. Yokoyama, K.: Proposal of the evaluation method of the heart rate variability using the frequency information of the electrocardiogram. IEEJ Trans. Electron. Inf. Syst. **119**(1), 63–69 (1999)
10. Nakagawa, C.: Special issues no. 3: measurement technique for ergonomics, section 4 : measurements and analyses of bioelectric phenomena and others (5) measurement and analysis of autonomic indices. Ergonomics **52**(1), 6–12 (2016)
11. Nagasawa, S.: Operating principle of the mixer and characteristics of actual device. Transistor Technol. **12**, 181–182 (2004)
12. Yang, X., Ishibashi, K., Sun, G.: Non-contact acquisition of respiration and heart rates using doppler radar with time domain peak-detection algorithm. In: 39th Annual International Conference of the IEEE Engineering in Medicine and Biology Society (EMBC) (2017)
13. Huang, M., Liu, J.: A self-calibrating radar sensor system for measuring vital signs. IEEE Trans. Biomed. Circ. Syst. **10**(2), 352–363 (2016)

Fault Diagnosis in Aluminium Electrolysis Using a Joint Method Based on Kernel Principal Component Analysis and Support Vector Machines

Kaibo Zhou[1,2], Gaofeng Xu[1,2], Hongting Wang[1,2(✉)], and Sihai Guo[3]

[1] School of Automation, Huazhong University of Science and Technology,
Wuhan 430074, China
{zhoukb,xug,whting}@hust.edu.cn
[2] MOE Key Laboratory of Image Processing and Intelligence Control,
Wuhan 430074, China
[3] School of Automation, Wuhan University of Technology, Wuhan 430070, China
Guosihai@whut.edu.cn

Abstract. As a key part of aluminium smelting, the operational conditions of aluminium electrolytic cells are of great significance for the stability of the aluminium electrolysis process. As a result, developing a effective process monitoring and multiple fault diagnosis model is essential. Traditional multi-classification methods such as neural networks and multiple support vector machines (multi-SVM) have good effects. However, the connatural limitations of these methods limit the prediction accuracies. To solve this problem, a hierarchical method for multiple fault diagnosis based on kernel principal component analysis (KPCA) and support vector machines (SVM) is proposed in this paper. Firstly, test statistics, such as the comprehensive index ϕ, the squared prediction error (SPE), and Hotellings T-squared (T^2), are used for fault detection. To separate faults preliminarily, traditional K-means clustering as transition layer is applied to the principal component scores. Next, anode effect is recognized and classified by the established SVM prediction model. Compared with multi-SVM-based classification methods, the proposed hierarchical method can diagnosis different faults with a higher precision. The prediction accuracy can reach about 90%.

Keywords: Aluminium electrolysis · Fault diagnosis · Machine classification · Kernel principal component analysis · Support vector machine

1 Introduction

Due to the complex multivariable nonlinear process and extreme environment, effective fault diagnosis is still challenging in the aluminium electrolysis process. There are many types of abnormal state in the process of aluminium electrolysis [8,21]. Anode effects, for example, cause a sudden increase in the cell voltage to

20C–50 V, compared with its normal target value of 4.0C–4.5 V. The result is an increase in energy consumption. In particular these faults lead to serious harm to the stability of cell and the safe operation of aluminium electrolysis process. In fact, effective control on anode effects can reduce the emission of perfluorocarbons (PFCs) which are harmful greenhouse gases. As a result, developing an easily implemented effective system for multiple fault diagnosis is extremely necessary [12, 24, 25].

Artificial neural networks as the representative of data-driven diagnostic method can be used to establish the prediction model for fault diagnosis in aluminium electrolysis process. The power spectrum from the signal of cell resistance by means of periodogram is analyzed and Learning Vector Quantization (LVQ) neural network is introduced to predict anode effect [28]. The influence of the structure of sample and sample size to anode effect prediction accuracy is analyzed with Generalized Regression Neural Network (GRNN) [29]. The wavelet function is applied in the hidden layer of Back-Propagation Neural Network (BPNN) and the forecasting software of anode effect is established based on platform of Visual Basic 6.0 [9]. A fault diagnosis model based on modified output feedback Elman neural network with the adoption of wavelet function is proposed to avoid falling into local optimal values and improve the diagnosis rate [10]. However, artificial neural network converges on local optimal values easily and the training time is too long when it is applied for fault diagnosis. The sample size is another element with a strong influence on the reliability of fault diagnosis model.

Multivariate statistical analysis is an effective method for fault detection and diagnosis of nonlinear process. Combining with two important operations in the aluminium electrolysis process: alumina feeding and anode changing, the proposed framework is effective to detect anode spike and anode effect [14]. Aimed at keeping as much feature information as possible, optimized relative transformation matrix is proposed and statistics is used for fault detection [23]. The combination of Principal Component Analysis (PCA) and statistics is used for fault detection effectively [22]. The squared prediction error (SPE) and Hotellings T-squared (T^2) statistics are two commonly statistics. A cascade fault detection system based on two of the most important operations, alumina feeding and anode changing, is proposed in the aluminium electrolysis process [13]. In this method, Multiway Principal Component Analysis (MPCA) is used in the alumina feeding cycle and same fault detection model is applied to different cells. PCA algorithm has good application for dimensionality reduction. High dimensional data are projected onto a low dimensional model so that it is much easier to analyse, visualise and make comparisons between the historical data and the new data from a large multivariable process [13]. However, PCA is not applicable for the nonlinear structure data set of nonlinear process.

Support vector machine (SVM) as a supervised classification technique has been intensively studied and widely applied in process monitoring [18, 19, 26] and fault diagnosis [2, 11, 17]. The application of wavelet packet decomposition principal component analysis obtained the feature vector which affects estimation and classification accuracy. The SVM as an effective binary-class classification method has not been used for fault diagnosis in aluminium electrolysis process. The drawbacks of multi-SVM, such as unclassifiable region and high computational complexity, have great influence on the performance of classification results. Fault diagnosis based on many-objective optimization is also a research direction. A region division based diversity maintaining approach is proposed for many-objective optimization [1, 16].

On these arguments, a hierarchical fault diagnosis method using SVM as binary-class classifier based on subspaces of reduced dimensionality is proposed in this paper. Compared with multi-SVM classification method and neural network algorithm, the advantages of the proposed method are shown as follows.

(1) Application-oriented: A specialized method for multi-fault diagnosis in aluminium electrolysis process.
(2) Relatively efficient: The proposed method can overcome the drawbacks of multi-SVM and improve the effects of fault diagnosis.

This paper is organized as follows. In Sect. 2, a detailed mathematical description about the technical background of fault diagnosis is given and in Sect. 3, a hierarchical method for multiple fault diagnosis is introduced. It is followed by results of three statistic indexes and multiple fault diagnosis. Finally, the results are analyzed and summarized in Sect. 5.

2   Aluminium Electrolysis Fault Diagnosis Techniques

2.1   Aluminium Electrolysis Process

Figure 1 shows a schematic diagram of an aluminium reduction cell. Aluminium reduction cell is the main production equipment of aluminium smelting. It is well known that aluminium reduction cell works in the tough environment of high temperature for a long time. Under the interference of various factors, there are many abnormal phenomenas such as cathode breakage and anode effect. With the increasing attention on the state of the aluminium reduction cell, massive amounts of process data have been continuously collected and stored in databases. With data-driven approach, the historical data can be used for fault detection and fault diagnosis.

2.2   Multivariate Statistic Analysis

Hotellings T^2 test is widely applied in fault detection. Let X be a $n \times p$ data matrix in which the rows are samples and the columns are variables. T^2 statistic is given by

$$T^2 = X^T P_k \Lambda^T P_k X < T_0^2, \tag{1}$$

$$\mathrm{SPE} = X(I - P_k P_k^T)X^T < \mathrm{SPE}_0, \tag{2}$$

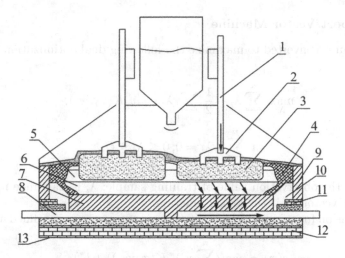

Fig. 1. Cross sectional schematic of an aluminium reduction cell: 1-Aluminium rod, 2-Steel draw, 3-Anode carbon block, 4-Side ledges, 5-Electrolyte, 6-Aluminium melt, 7-Cathodecarbon block, 8-Collector bar, 9-Side carbon block, 10-Surrounding paste draw, 11-Refractory brick, 12-Insulating brick, 13-Steel shell.

where P_k is the principal component subspace, $\Lambda = diag(\lambda_1, \lambda_2, \cdots, \lambda_3)$, k is the number of principal components, λ is the eigenvalue of the covariance matrix of X, T_0^2 shows the control limits of T^2 statistic, SPE_0 shows the control limits of SPE statistic.

The T^2 statistic follows λ distribution and SPE statistic follows a coefficient fixed χ distribution. The process is normal if Eq. (1) or Eq. (2) is true. SPE_0 can be calculated by approximate distribution. Yue and Qin [27] propose a combined index for fault detection that combines the SPE and T^2 as follows:

$$\phi = \frac{SPE}{SPE_0} + \frac{T^2}{T_0^2} < \phi_0. \tag{3}$$

The process is normal if Eq. (3) is true. The control limit ϕ_0 is defined as

$$\phi_0 = g\chi_h^2, \tag{4}$$

where the degree of freedom h for χ_h^2 distribution is

$$h = \left(\frac{k}{T_0^2} + \frac{\sum_{i=k+1}^{m} \lambda_i}{SPE_0} \right)^2 \bigg/ \left(\frac{k}{(T_0^2)^2} + \frac{\sum_{i=k+1}^{m} \lambda_i^2}{SPE_0^2} \right), \tag{5}$$

$$g = \left(\frac{k}{(T_0^2)^2} + \frac{\sum_{i=k+1}^{m} \lambda_i^2}{SPE_0^2} \right)^2 \bigg/ \left(\frac{k}{T_0^2} + \frac{\sum_{i=k+1}^{m} \lambda_i}{SPE_0} \right). \tag{6}$$

2.3 Support Vector Machine

The problem is converted to maximize the following dual optimization problem:

$$\max_{\lambda} \sum_{i=1}^{n} \lambda_i - \frac{1}{2} \sum_{i,j=1}^{n} \lambda_i \lambda_j y_i y_j K(\boldsymbol{x}_i, \boldsymbol{x}_j), \tag{7}$$

$$s.t. \sum_{i=1}^{n} y_i \lambda_i = 0, 0 \leq \lambda_i \leq C,$$

where x_i is the observation value of training sample; λ_i is Lagrange multiplier; y_i is output vector; K is the kernel function.

The decision function, which classifies the input vector $\boldsymbol{x}$, is defined as follows:

$$g(\boldsymbol{x}) = sgn((\sum_{i=1}^{n} y_i \lambda_i^* K(\boldsymbol{x}_i, \boldsymbol{x}_j)) + b^*), \tag{8}$$

$$b^* = y_j - \sum_{i=1}^{n} y_i \lambda_i^* K(\boldsymbol{x}_i, \boldsymbol{x}_j), \tag{9}$$

where sgn( ) denotes the sign function, λ^* is the optimum solution.

In this paper, one-against-all method, which is probably the earliest used implementation, is selected to construct multi-class SVM classifiers [3].

3 Hierarchical Method for Multiple Fault Diagnosis

Multivariate statistic test can detect faults effectively, but it is quite difficult to distinguish different faults. SVM is a quite efficient method of binary-class classification, but the performance for multi-class classification is not satisfactory. Combining the advantages of KPCA and SVM, a hierarchical method for multiple fault diagnosis is proposed in this paper.

Four states of electrolysis cell: normal state, anode effect (fault 1), cool cell (fault 2) and hot cell (fault 3) are selected for analysis in this paper. Taking into account different faults, seven kinds variables including amount of aluminium (x_1), aluminium liquid level (x_2), electrolyte level (x_3), electrolytic temperature (x_4), molecular ratio (x_5), cell voltage (x_6), and amount of feeding (x_7) are selected as variables. Figure 2 shows the schematic representation of the proposed approach. The joint method consists of two primary modules: (1) fault detection; (2) classification. The principal component coefficients are extracted after data process by using KPCA, which is an improved method from PCA [5,6]. The popular used kernel functions include the polynomial kernel, the Radical Basis Function (Gaussian) kernel, the sigmoid kernel. In this paper, the RBF kernel is selected for the kernel function as shown in Eq. (10).

$$K(x, x_i) = exp(-\frac{\|x - x_i\|^2}{2\sigma^2}). \tag{10}$$

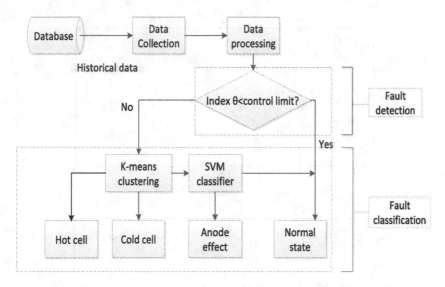

Fig. 2. Schematic representation of the proposed approach.

In the fault detection stage, statistics T^2, SPE and ϕ are calculated. The process is considered normal if Eq. (3) is true, otherwise the principal component scores will be partitioned by K-means clustering, which is the most popular clustering algorithm proposed in the literature [7,15,20]. One sample will be one of the three clusters namely cold cell, hot cell and other state.

In the fault classification stage, the principal components are used as the input variables of SVM prediction model. Other state samples composed of normal state samples and anode effect samples are classified with SVM prediction model.

4   Experimental Results and Analysis

To test the performance of the proposed method in a multiple faults experiment, 400 normal samples and 400 fault samples are extracted from the database of a $400 - kA$ series of aluminum reduction cell in Chongqing. The anode effect samples are extracted from the real-time production data in ten minutes before the occurrence of anode effect. In contrast, multi-SVM classifier is used for multiple fault diagnosis.

4.1   Fault Detection

To detect faults preliminarily, statistics T^2, SPE and ϕ are calculated. The total data samples are separated into 400 training and 120 testing samples. The results of ϕ statistic are used for fault detection. Table 1 shows the results of T^2, SPE and ϕ statistics on four different states. As can be seen, the diagnosis error of

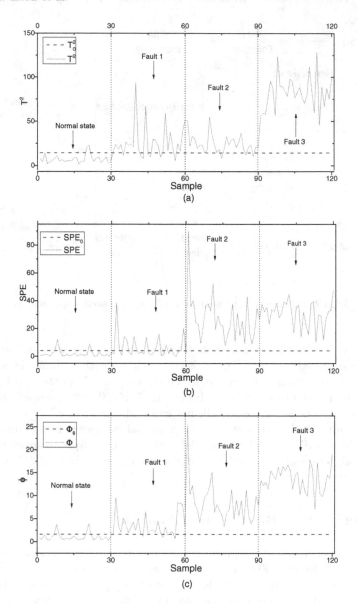

Fig. 3. Results of KPCA test on different states: (a) T^2 test, (b) SPE test, (c) ϕ test.

T^2 statistic is 6.7% on normal state, 23.3% on fault 1, 13.3% on fault 2 and all fault 3 samples are detected.

It can be observed that the diagnosis error of SPE statistic is 10% on fault 1. All fault 2 samples are diagnosed. The diagnosis error is up to 56.7% on fault 1. It illustrates that fault type is hard to be determined by SPE statistic.

Table 1. Comparison of SPE, T^2 and ϕ statistics.

State	Error (%) on T^2	Error (%) on SPE	Error (%) on ϕ
Normal	6.7	10	10
Fault 1	23.3	56.7	13.3
Fault 2	13.3	0	0
Fault 3	0	0	0

The ϕ statistic results from Table 1 have a slight advantage compared with T^2 and SPE statistics. Fault 1 and fault 2 can be diagnosed more easily by using ϕ statistic. Figure 3 shows in detail the results of T^2, SPE and ϕ statistics on four different states. It confirms that PCA can detect fault 2 and fault 3 effectively.

4.2   Classification of Multi-fault Diagnosis

Figure 4 shows the principal component scores of test samples. It can be observed that three classes, namely fault 2, fault 3 and other state consisted of normal state and fault 1, which can be isolated obviously based on the first two principal components. But other state samples cannot be distinguished intuitively.

K–means clustering was applied to these scores in order to isolate precisely between these clusters. Table 2 shows the results of K-means clustering. It can be observed that three classes are isolated effectively from all samples. Only one fault 2 sample, three fault 3 samples and three other state samples are assigned in wrong classes.

Multi-SVM model is trained by 400 normal samples and 300 anode effect samples. The principal components were used as input variables. In hierarchical method, 400 normal samples and 100 anode effect samples were selected for

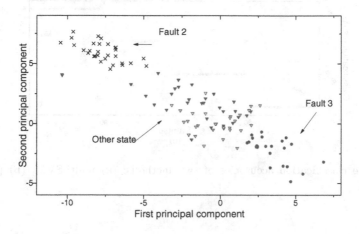

Fig. 4. The principal component scores.

training of SVM prediction model. Figure 5 shows the classification results of using multi-SVM and the hierarchical method for multiple fault diagnosis.

As can be seen from Fig. 5(a) and (b), compared with multi-SVM, hierarchical method has no obvious advantage on normal state and fault 3. However, there is obvious advantage in using hierarchical method on fault 1 and fault 2. There are only four anode effect samples and three cold cell samples are classified into wrong types in proposed method. It is very important for the prediction and treatment of anode effect. It illustrates that the classification accuracies of fault 1 and fault 2 are improved from 70% to about 90% from Fig. 6. The classification effects of normal state and fault 3 are roughly flat.

Table 2. Clustering results.

State	Results		
	Other state	Fault2	Fault 3
Other state	57	1	2
Fault 2	3	27	0
Fault 3	1	0	29

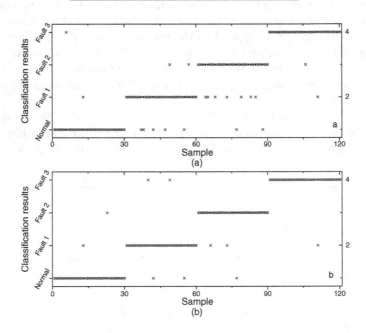

Fig. 5. The classification accuracies of two methods: (a) multi-SVM, (b) proposed method.

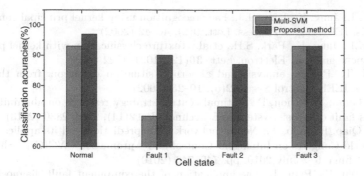

Fig. 6. Classification accuracies of two methods.

5   Conclusion and Discussion

In this paper, a hierarchical method based on KPCA and SVM is proposed for multiple fault diagnosis in aluminium electrolysis process.

Features extracted by KPCA are used as input variables. Test statistics are used to monitor the state of aluminium electrolytic cell. The principal component scores are divided into three clusters by using K-means clustering. The established SVM prediction model is used to classify anode effect and normal state.

The results indicate that the proposed hierarchical method can diagnose multiple faults effectively. In the future, the effectiveness of the proposed method will be verified in practical aluminium electrolysis process.

Acknowledgments. The work is supported by the National High Technology Research and Development Program of China (863 Program) (No. 2013AA040705 and No. 2013AA041002) and the Fundamental Research Funds for the central Universities (WUT: 2014-IV-142).

References

1. He, C., Tian, Y., Jin, Y.C., Zhang, X.Y., Pan, L.Q.: A radial space division based evolutionary algorithm for many-objective optimization. Appl. Soft. Comput. **61**, 603–621 (2017)
2. He, Y., Du, C.Y., Li, C.B., et al.: Sensor fault diagnosis of superconducting fault current limiter with saturated iron core based on SVM. IEEE Trans. Appl. Supercond. **24**(5), 5602805(5 pp.) (2014)
3. Hsu, C.W., Lin, C.J.: A comparison of methods for multiclass support vector machines. IEEE Trans. Neural Netw. **13**(2), 415–425 (2002)
4. Guo, S.H., Zhou, K.B., Cao, B., Yang, C.H.: Combination weights and TOPSIS method for performance evaluation of aluminum electrolysis. In: 2015 Chinese Automation Congress (CAC), Wuhan, Hubei, China, 27–29 November 2015, pp. 1–6 (2015)

5. Kim, K.I., Jung, K., Kim, H.J.: Face recognition using kernel principal component analysis. IEEE Signal Process. Lett. **9**(2), 40–42 (2002)
6. Kim, K.I., Jung, K., Park, S.H., et al.: Texture classification with kernel principal component analysis. Electron. Lett. **36**(12), 1021–1022 (2000)
7. Kourti, T.: Process analysis and abnormal situation detection: from theory to practice. IEEE Control Syst. **22**(5), 10–25 (2002)
8. Li, J., Guan, W., Zhou, P.: Optimal control strategy research on aluminium electrolysis fault diagnosis system. Inf. Technol. J. **12**(14), 2824–2830 (2013)
9. Li, J., Qiao, F., Guo, T.: Neural network fault prediction and its application. In: 8th World Congress on Intelligent Control and Automation (WCICA), Shandong, Jinan, China, 6–7 July 2010, pp. 740–743 (2010)
10. Li, J., Wu, H., Pian, J.: The application of the equipment fault diagnosis based on modified Elman neural network. In: International Conference on Electronic and Mechanical Engineering and Information Technology (EMEIT), Harbin, Heilongjiang, China, 12–14 August 2011, pp. 4135–4137 (2011)
11. Li, J., Zhang, Q., Wang, K., et al.: Optimal dissolved gas ratios selected by genetic algorithm for power transformer fault diagnosis based on support vector machine. IEEE Trans. Dielectr. Electr. Insul. **23**(2), 1198–1206 (2016)
12. Lin, B., Xu, L.: Energy conservation of electrolytic aluminium industry in China. Renew. Sustain. Energy Rev. **43**, 676–686 (2015)
13. Majid, N.A.A., Taylor, M.P., Chen, J.J.J., et al.: Aluminium process fault detection by multiway principal component analysis. Control Eng. Pract. **19**(4), 367–379 (2011)
14. Majid, N.A.A., Taylor, M.P., Chen, J.J.J., et al.: Multivariate statistical monitoring of the aluminium smelting process. Comput. Chem. Eng. **35**(11), 2457–2468 (2011)
15. Majid, N.A.A., Young, B.R., Taylor, M.P., et al.: K-means clustering pre-analysis for fault diagnosis in an aluminium smelting process. In: Proceedings of the 2012 4th Conference on Data Mining and Optimization (DMO), Piscataway, NJ, USA, 2–4 September 2012, pp. 43–46 (2012)
16. Pan, L., He, C., Tian, Y., et al.: A region division based diversity maintaining approach for many-objective optimization. Integr. Comput. Aided Eng. **24**(3), 1–18 (2017)
17. Ren, L., Lv, W., Jiang, S., et al.: Fault diagnosis using a joint model based on sparse representation and SVM. IEEE Trans. Instrum. Meas. **65**(10), 2313–2320 (2016)
18. Ribeiro, B.: Support vector machines for quality monitoring in a plastic injection molding process. IEEE Trans. Syst. Man Cybern. Part C **35**(3), 401–410 (2005)
19. Vapnik, V.: The Nature of Statistical Learning Theory, 2nd edn. Springer, New York (2000)
20. Venkatasubramanian, V., Rengaswamy, R., Kavuri, S.N., et al.: A review of process fault detection and diagnosis: Part III: process history based methods. Comput. Chem. Eng. **27**(3), 327–346 (2003)
21. Vogt, H., Thonstad, J.: The voltage of alumina reduction cells prior to the anode effect. J. Appl. Electrochem. **32**, 241–249 (2002)
22. Xia, M., Kong, F., Hu, F.: An approach for bearing fault diagnosis based on PCA and multiple classifier fusion. In: IEEE Information Technology and Artificial Intelligence Conference (ITAIC), Chongqing, China, 20–22 August 2011, pp. 321–325 (2011)
23. Yi, J., Huang, D., Fu, S., et al.: Optimized relative transformation matrix using bacterial foraging algorithm for process fault detection. IEEE Trans. Ind. Electron. **63**(4), 2595–2605 (2016)

24. Yin, S., Gao, H., Kaynak, O.: Data-driven control and process monitoring for industrial applications-Part I. IEEE Trans. Ind. Electron. **61**(11), 6356–6359 (2014)
25. Yin, S., Gao, H., Kaynak, O.: Data-driven control and process monitoring for industrial applications-Part II. IEEE Trans. Ind. Electron. **62**(1), 583–586 (2015)
26. You, D., Gao, X., Katayama, S.: WPD-PCA-based laser welding process monitoring and defects diagnosis by using FNN and SVM. IEEE Trans. Ind. Electron. **62**(1), 628–636 (2015)
27. Yue, H.H., Qin, S.J.: Reconstruction-based fault identification using a combined index. Ind. Eng. Chem. Res. **40**(20), 4403–4414 (2001)
28. Zhou, K., Lin, Z., Yu, D., et al.: Cell resistance slope combined with LVQ neural network for prediction of anode effect. In: Sixth International Conference on Intelligent Control and Information Processing (ICICIP), Wuhan, Hubei, China, 26–28 November 2015, pp. 47–51 (2015)
29. Zhou, K., Yu, D., Lin, Z., et al.: Anode effect prediction of aluminium electrolysis using GRNN. In: Chinese Automation Congress (CAC), Wuhan, Hubei, China, 27–29 November 2015, pp. 853–858 (2015)

A New Image Encryption Algorithm Based on DNA Dynamic Encoding and Hyper-Chaotic System

Guangzhao Cui, Yishan Liu, Xuncai Zhang$^{(\boxtimes)}$, and Zheng Zhou

College of Electrical and Electronic Engineering, Zhengzhou University of Light
Industry, Zhengzhou 450002, Henan, China
zhangxuncai@163.com, 502420227@qq.com

Abstract. Aiming at the deficiency of the low sensitivity of DNA encoding and chaotic encryption algorithms to text and key, and the limited encoding rules of DNA, etc. This paper presents a new image encryption algorithm based on DNA dynamic encoding and hyper-chaotic system. Firstly, the algorithm uses the SHA-3 algorithm to process the original image, generate a set of hash values, perform the dynamic encoding of the generated hash values and then carry out XOR operation with the original image, and then the generated hash values through Hamming distance processing to generate the initial value of the hyper-chaotic system. Secondly, the S-box is constructed by the sequence values generated by the hyper-chaotic system, and the XOR-shift manipulation is performed to the image by using the S-box. Finally, the image is scrambled by the hyper-chaotic Chen System. The simulation results and theoretical analysis show that the algorithm improves the sensitivity of key and the security of data transmission, and has better ability of anti-exhaustive attack, statistical attack and differential attack.

Keywords: Image encryption · DNA encoding · Hyper-chaotic Chen
System · S-box · SHA-3 · Hamming distance

1 Introduction

With the increasing of various media, image transmission has been widely used in different fields such as medical imaging, online teaching, communication, etc. However, the openness and sharing of the network pose a great threat to the security of image transmission. The "Prism Gate" incident of 2013 made us realize that it is imperative to solve the problem of information security transmission. Image encryption is different from text and voice encryption. Due to the strong correlation between adjacent pixels, high redundancy and special storage format in an image [1,2]. Encryption requires to use the simpler operations. If the more complex algorithm is used, then the encryption needs to pay a high price. In addition, the algorithm should be used as much as possible in parallel processing [3,4] when considering the encryption time. So the traditional

© Springer Nature Singapore Pte Ltd. 2017
C. He et al. (Eds.): BIC-TA 2017, CCIS 791, pp. 286–303, 2017.
https://doi.org/10.1007/978-981-10-7179-9_22

encryption methods, such as Data Encryption Standard (DES), Rivest-Shamir-Adleman (RSA) and Advanced Encryption Standard (AES) are not suitable for image encryption.

In recent years, a number of new image encryption algorithms have been proposed. For instance, image encryption algorithm based on chaotic system [5–8], and image encryption algorithm based on DNA encoding [9]. The chaotic system has a series of characteristics such as good pseudo random characteristics, unpredictable orbit and high sensitivity of initial state and control parameters. These properties are consistent with numerous requirements of cryptography, and because of the close relationship between chaos and cryptography, chaotic cryptography has been studied extensively and applied to image encryption [10,11]. However, the chaos produced by the low dimensional chaotic system can be predicted in a short time. The randomness of chaotic sequences is poor, the key space of encrypted images is small, the security is low, and it is easy to decipher [12,13]. Due to the complex hyper-chaos system has more than one positive Lyapunov exponents, larger key space, better sensitivity and more complex dynamical characteristics. So in order to expand the key space and increase the randomness of chaotic sequences, chaotic systems such as hyper-chaotic [14] and multilevel chaotic [15,16] are designed. Currently, hyper-chaos has been widely used in nonlinear circuits, secure communications, lasers, neural networks, biological systems and other fields. However, with the improvement of cryptanalysis technology, the hyper-chaotic encryption technology has also exposed the shortcomings of low sensitivity to the key. In order to solve these problems. The researchers suggest that DNA computing is an effective way to improve the security of chaotic image encryption technology.

Because of the large-scale parallelism, ultra-low energy consumption and high storage density inherent in DNA molecules, the image encryption algorithm based on DNA computing has the unique advantage that traditional cryptographic algorithm do not have [17,18]. In the literature [19], DNA computation was first introduced by Adleman. Because of the huge cost of biological experiments, Ning et al. proposed a pseudo DNA encryption method that utilizes the basic idea involved in DNA computing to simulate information encryption on an electronic computer, but this method can only be used for text encryption, not for image encryption. In 2010, Xue et al. proposed an encryption method based on the combination of DNA coding and chaotic sequences. The sensitivity of initial conditions and the high degree of randomness are well encrypted by using DNA encoding and hyper-chaotic systems. In the literature [20], an image encryption algorithm based on chaos and DNA dynamic encoding is proposed, which incorporates dynamic DNA encoding rules. But the rules of addition and subtraction in such codes are limited, and the security of encryption is not high by using DNA encoding alone. A color image encryption algorithm based on DNA sequence is proposed in the literature [21], which is used to encode DNA in the plane, and addition and XOR operation in encryption process, but the encoding and decoding method is single. At present, there are some other shortcomings in image encryption algorithms based on DNA manipulation and chaotic system theory. The literature [22] points out that the DNA chaotic image encryption algorithm with fixed coding and single operation rule can easily be cracked by choosing plain-text attack. In the literature [23,24], an improved image encryption algorithm based on coding and multi-chaotic mapping is proposed. Using the hyper-chaotic system to scramble the pixel position and pixel value, the pseudo DNA operation is performed by DNA encoding rules, and finally the encrypted image is obtained by DNA decoding. Özkaynak et al. found that the encryption algorithm is insecure against chosen-plain text attack and the equivalent secret key of the encryption algorithm can be obtained by four chosen plain images [25]. Liu et al. [26] re-analyzed the security of the proposed algorithm in [27], and they found out two security problems: (1) The equivalent secret key of the encryption algorithm can be reconstructed with only one pair of known plain-text or ciphertext; (2) encryption results are not sensitive with respect to change in the plain images or secret keys [7,28–30].

Aiming at the deficiency of the above DNA encoding and chaotic encryption algorithm, in this paper the image is divided into blocks, and the chaotic system, DNA dynamic encoding, hash function and Hamming distance are used to encrypt the block image, and the hash function is widely applied in the modern life, and it can be found in the aspects of integrity verification, error checking, quick searching and so on. The hash function of cryptography on the basis of guaranteeing one-way, but also have good attack resistance ability. And a fixed length hash value is generated with any length of message value as input. The original image is processed by the hash function SHA-3, and generate a set of hash values, then the XOR operation is carried out between the hash value and the original image, and the resulting hash value is processed by Hamming distance to generate the initial value of the hyper-chaotic system. And the original image and key are connected together, will effectively resist the known plain-text and chosen plain-text attacks. The dynamic coding rules adopted in the computing of DNA encryption can avoid the defect that the algorithm is easily cracked because of the fixed coding rules. Then the S-box is constructed by using the hyper-chaotic sequence value generated by hyper-chaotic system, and the S-box is used to do XOR or shift operation of the block image. The advantage of this algorithm is to improve the sensitivity of the key, the security of data transmission, the effective resistance to the attack of the known plain-text and the chosen plain-text, but also has better ability of exhaustion attack, count attack, differential attack and reduction attack.

2 Chaotic System and DNA Encoding

2.1 Hyper-chaotic Chen System

The Hyper-chaotic [31–33] Chen system is described by:

$$
\begin{cases}
\dot{x} = a(y - x), \\
\dot{y} = -xz + dx + cy - u, \\
\dot{z} = xy - bz, \\
\dot{u} = x + k,
\end{cases}
\tag{1}
$$

Where $a; b; c; d; k$ are control parameters. When $a = 36; b = 3; c = 28, d = 16$, $-0.7 \leq k \leq 0.7$, the system is in hyper-chaos status.

2.2   DNA Encoding and Computing

(1) DNA encoding

DNA is a polymer of deoxyribonucleic acid as a basic unit. The deoxynu-cleotides are made up of three parts, respectively, a molecule of phosphoric acid, a molecule of deoxyribose, and a molecule nitrogen-containing bases. There are four types of nitrogen-containing bases, namely, Adenine (A), Cytosine (C), Guanine (G) and Thymine (T). Where A and T, G and C are two mutually complementary relationships [34]. Each pixel of a gray image can be represented by 8 bit binary digits, while 0 and 1 complement each other in binary numbers, so that 00 and 11, 01 and 10 are complementary, respectively. Therefore, if four deoxynucleotides A, T, C, and G are used to represent binary numbers 00, 11, 01, and 10 respectively, each pixel value can be expressed as a DNA sequence with a length of 4. For example, the decimal value 123 is expressed as $(01\ 11\ 10\ 11)_2$, and the converted 4-bit DNA sequence is CTGT. There are eight types of coding rules that satisfy the complementary relationship between DNA bases, as shown in Table 1.

Table 1. 8 kinds DNA encoding rules

Rule1	Rule2	Rule3	Rule4	Rule5	Rule6	Rule7	Rule8
00-A	00-A	00-C	00-C	00-T	00-T	00-G	00-G
01-C	01-C	01-A	01-A	01-G	01-G	01-C	01-C
00-G	10-T	10-G	10-T	10-A	10-C	10-A	10-C
00-T	11-G	11-T	11-G	11-C	11-A	11-T	11-A

(2) XOR and NXOR operations of DNA sequences

The XOR and NXOR operations of DNA sequences are very similar to traditional algebraic calculations. There are eight kinds of DNA encoding rules, so we have eight kinds of DNA XOR and NXOR rules. When encoding

Table 2. DNA XOR and NXOR operations

XOR	A	T	C	G	NXOR	A	T	C	G
A	A	T	C	G	A	A	T	C	G
T	T	A	G	C	T	T	A	G	C
C	C	G	A	T	C	C	G	A	T
G	G	C	T	A	G	G	C	T	A

with 00-A, 11-T, 01-C, and 10-G, adding numbers with bases, the XOR operations and NXOR operations are shown in Table 2. For instance, a DNA sequence [GCAT] can be obtained by DNA sequences [GTCA] and [AGCT] with XOR operation.

3   The Design of Image Encryption Scheme

3.1   DNA Dynamic Encoded Selection Method

In the DNA encryption computing, the DNA encoding is selected as follows: We can see from Table 1, there are eight kinds different DNA encoding rules in DNA encryption computation. Each one determines the encoded value in the original image according to the formula (2) and encodes them, among them, i, j are the coordinates of each pixel value. Other matrix according to the formula (3) to determine the encoding rules, $x(i)$ is the value that needs to be encoded, which is converted into eight-bit binary sequence, and then the binary sequence is converted into a DNA sequence that consisting of four bases.

$$Rule = round(mod((i + j), 8)) + 1, \tag{2}$$

$$Rule = round(mod(x(i) * 1000, 8)) + 1, \tag{3}$$

3.2   Diagonal Extraction Method

For the convenience of presentation, for the gray image of $L * L$ (this image is a square matrix image by default. In the simulation experiment, if the encrypted image is not square, then the complement graph is made, and the complement rule is described in the encryption process), the main diagonals of the original image are first defined as $diag(0)$, and parallel to the main diagonal, the lines above are defined as $diag(-1), diag(-2), ..., diag(-L+1)$; and the following lines are defined as $diag(1), diag(2), ...,$ and $diag(L - 1)$. The definition is shown in Fig. 1.

As shown in the $L * L$ grayscale image, parallel to the diagonal, there are $L - 1$ lines above and also $L - 1$ lines below. So, when $i = 0$, $diag(-L) = 0$. The extraction formula is as follows:

$$X_i = diag(i) + diag(-L + i), \tag{4}$$

Where $i = 0, 1, 2, ..., L - 1$.

E.g: when $i = 0$, $X_0 = diag(0) + diag(-L) = diag(0)$; $X_1 = diag(1) + diag(-L + 1)$.

In this way, the extracted L elements of each time are converted into image sub-matrices, respectively, and then $L(\sqrt{L} \times \sqrt{L})$ image sub-matrices $\sqrt{L} \times \sqrt{L}$ are obtained.

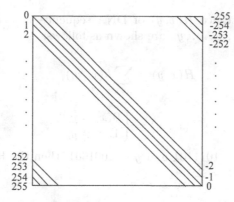

Fig. 1. The method of line definition

3.3 SHA-3 Algorithm

The HASH function is also called hash function. As a hash function, the SHA-3 algorithm is based on the sponge structure [7], which is one of the most basic modules in modern cryptography, and generates a fixed-length hash value as input for any length of message. But its compression is not a conventional compression, but an irreversible compression, once the hash operation is done, the results will not be restored to the original text. The key generated by the hash value, even if the original image has extremely small changes, the hash value produced by SHA-3 encryption will be completely different, and resulting in a completely different encryption key. So this kind of encryption method can resist brute force attack.

When the original image is converted with SHA-3-256, a set of 256-bit hash is generated: dbbf374d57de108723c923b41d768d018c8e538a2de7479962c487a03 35e1e85; The generated hash value is used as the input information for the next hash function to produce a new hash value. The loop produces eight times, and 256×8 bit hash value is obtained, and the 256×8-bit hashes is converted into 16×16 matrices.

3.4 Hamming Distance

In DNA computing, Hamming distance is used to indicate the number of different elements of the corresponding position of two equal length sequences [35]. That is to say, it is the number of characters that need to be replaced by converting a string to another string.

The Hamming distance $H(x, y)$ of DNA sequence $x = x_1, x_2, \ldots, x_n$ and DNA sequence $y = x_1, y_2, \ldots, y_n$ are shown as follows:

$$H(x, y) = \sum_{i=1}^{n} h(x_i, y_i), \tag{5}$$

$$h(x_i, y_i) = \begin{cases} 0, x_i = y_i \\ 1, x_i \neq y_i, \end{cases} \tag{6}$$

For example, if $x = 1011101$ and $y = 1001001$, then the Hamming distance of two sequences is $H_{xy} = 2$.

3.5   Key Generation

The first set of hash values produced by SHA-3 was used as key K, which was used to generate the initial value of the hyper-chaotic Chen system. The hash value produced by SHA-3, even if the original image has one bit difference, the resulting hash will be completely different, and the key will be completely different, in this way generated by the key, the anti-brute force attack is 2^{256}, and the generated key has the advantage of randomness, periodicity and long key space. Combining the original image information with the key, the algorithm will effectively resist the known plain-text and chosen plain-text attacks. Divide k by byte, which can be expressed as: k_1, k_2, k_3, ..., k_{32}. The initial value of the chaotic system is computed by formula (7)–(10):

Definition: $r_1 = k_1 \oplus k_2 \oplus k_3 \oplus k_4 \oplus k_5 \oplus k_6 \oplus k_7 \oplus k_8$, $r_2 = k_9 \oplus k_{10} \oplus k_{11} \oplus k_{12} \oplus k_{13} \oplus k_{14} \oplus k_{15} \oplus k_{16}$, $r_3 = k_{17} \oplus k_{18} \oplus k_{19} \oplus k_{20} \oplus k_{21} \oplus k_{22} \oplus k_{23} \oplus k_{24}$, $r_4 = k_{25} \oplus k_{26} \oplus k_{27} \oplus k_{28} \oplus k_{29} \oplus k_{30} \oplus k_{31} \oplus k_{32}$.

The initial value of chaotic system can be described as follows:

$$x_1 = (k_1 \oplus k_2 \oplus \ldots \oplus k_8)/4 + H(r_1, r_2), \tag{7}$$

$$y_1 = (k_9 \oplus k_{10} \oplus \ldots \oplus k_{16})/4 + H(r_2, r_3), \tag{8}$$

$$z_1 = (k_{17} \oplus k_{18} \oplus \ldots \oplus k_{24})/4 + H(r_3, r_4), \tag{9}$$

$$u_1 = (k_{25} \oplus k_{26} \oplus \ldots \oplus k_{32})/4 + H(r_4, r_1), \tag{10}$$

Where x_1, y_1, z_1 and u_1 are the given initial values.

3.6   S-Box

To bring the initial value into the Chen hyper-chaotic system to produce the hyper-chaotic sequence, and the S box is constructed by the generated chaotic sequence. Thus, the constructed S-box can effectively resist the plain-text attack.

(1) The construction of the S-box is as follows:

Step 1: Construct an empty sequence M.

Step 2: The interval $[0, 255]$ is divided into 256 sub-intervals $[(0, 1), ..., (j, j + 1), ..., (255, 256)]$ and T_j is used to denote, $j = (0, 1, 2, ..., 255)$, as shown in Fig. 2.

Step 3: Iterate hyper-chaotic Chen system model i times and get the state values x_i, y_i, z_i and u_i. The final values $f(x_i)$, $f(y_i)$, $f(z_i)$, $f(u_i)$ are obtained by the conversion of formula (11–14):

$$f(x_i) = (mod(x_i * 1000, 255), \tag{11}$$

$$f(y_i) = (mod(y_i * 1000, 255), \tag{12}$$

$$f(z_i) = (mod(z_i * 1000, 255), \tag{13}$$

$$f(u_i) = (mod(u_i * 1000, 255), \tag{14}$$

Step 4: Suppose $f(x_i)$ is in the T_j sub-interval $(j, j + 1)$. If j does not exist in sequence M, and then j is added to sequence M, and so on.

Step 5: If the number of elements in sequence M is less than 256, continue to step 3–4 until the number of elements in sequence M is 256. For example, a value of 233.6 is generated by an initial value iteration of the hyper-chaotic Chen system. This value belongs to 233–234 in T_{233}, and 233 is not in the empty sequence M, then the value 233 is added to the empty sequence M.

Step 6: Convert the elements in sequence M into 16×16 tables and get a 16×16 S-box. The $16(16 \times 16)$ S-boxes are constructed according to this method.

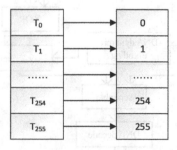

Fig. 2. The corresponding relation between the sub-interval and the integer value

3.7 Encryption Algorithm

The encryption algorithm consists of five parts. The first part of the encryption algorithm is that the original image is rearranged according to the diagonal extraction rule, the second part is the DNA dynamic encoded selection method, the third part the original image is processed by the hash function SHA-3, and generate a set of hash values, then the XOR operation is carried out between the hash value and the original image. In the forth part, the hash value generated by the SHA-3 algorithm is processed by Hamming distance and the initial value of the hyper-chaotic system is generated. The fifth part is to bring the initial value into the Chen hyper-chaotic system to produce the hyper-chaotic sequence, and then generate the S-box with the hyper-chaotic sequence value produced by it, Use S-box to replace and scramble images. The cryptographic flowchart is shown in Fig. 3. The specific encryption steps are as follows:

Step 1: Enter a 8-bit grayscale image $I(m, n)$. Fill the image with the following rules, $I = (L, L)$, here $\lfloor (\sqrt{m})^2 \rfloor$ is a ceiling operator that returns the integer part of $\lfloor (\sqrt{m})^2 \rfloor$.

$$L = max(\lfloor (\sqrt{m})^2 \rfloor, \lfloor (\sqrt{n})^2 \rfloor), \tag{15}$$

Step 2: The image is transformed into $L(\sqrt{L} * \sqrt{L})$ image sub-matrices according to the above process 3.2, and each image sub matrix is encrypted separately.

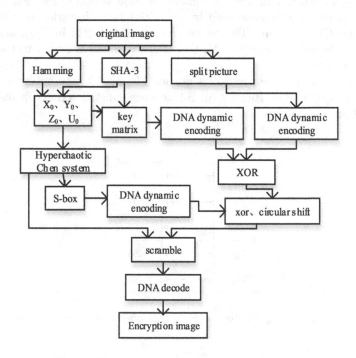

Fig. 3. Flow chart of the encryption algorithm

Step 3: Because each pixel of the grayscale image is 0–255, so each pixel value can be represented by 8-bit binary. Each element on L image sub-matrices is represented by a binary number, respectively, and a binary string with a length of $8n$ bits is obtained. The DNA coding rules of each pixel value are selected according to the formula (2) to encode the coding sequence of $4n$ bases.

Step 4: The encrypted matrix of the 16×16 obtained by the above process 3.3 is converted into a binary matrix, and then the DNA dynamic encoding rules of each element in the matrix are coded by formula (3). Finally, according to the XOR operation rule in Table 2, XOR operations are performed with the L image sub matrices obtained in step 3.

Step 5: The initial value of the formula (7–10) is x_1, y_1, z_1 and u_1, and the generation of the hyper-chaotic Chen system is mapped to four sets of chaotic sequences, and the resulting hyper-chaotic sequence is preprocessed by the formula (11–14), the final four group of hyper-chaotic sequences $f(x_i)$, $f(y_i)$, $f(z_i)$, $f(u_i)$ and then the $16(16 \times 16)$ S-boxes are generated according to Sect. 3.6, and the $16(16 \times 16)$ matrices are converted into binary matrices. The encoding rules of the DNA dynamic encoding of each element in the matrix are selected by formula (3), and get $16(16 \times 16)$ DNA encoding matrices.

Step 6: According to the XOR operation rules in Table 2, XOR operations are performed between the $16(16 \times 16)$ DNA encoding matrices obtained in Step 5 and the L image sub-matrices obtained in step 4, and encrypted according to the left cyclic shift 3 bits.

Step 7: The odd digits of the first half of the hyper-chaotic sequence $f(x_i)$ and $f(y_i)$ are extracted and added, and the even numbers of the first half of the sequence $f(z_i)$ and $f(u_i)$ are added together to form a new chaotic sequence G. And the chaotic sequence is modulo 256, and the L number of the sequence is extracted sequentially, and the L group is extracted as G_1, G_2, ... G_L, respectively, convert each group of L to a matrix of $\sqrt{L} * \sqrt{L}$, convert the L matrix to binary. The encoding rules of the DNA dynamic encoding of each element in the matrix are selected by formula (3), and get $L(\sqrt{L} * \sqrt{L})$ DNA encoding matrices and then according to the XOR operation rules in Table 2, the XOR operation is performed with the $L(\sqrt{L} * \sqrt{L})$ image sub-matrix obtained in step 6.

Step 8: The L image sub-matrices obtained in step 7 are combined into an image matrix I_1.

Step 9: According to the matrix C generated by the formula (16), the XOR operation is carried out between the matrix I_1 and the matrix C to obtain an image matrix I_2.

$$C = m * n * (x(n + j) + 0.5) * one(m, 1), \tag{16}$$

Where $j = 1, 2, 3, \ldots, 256$.

Step 10: The even digits of the first half of the hyper-chaotic sequence $f(x_i)$ and $f(y_i)$ are extracted and added, and the odd numbers of the first half of the sequence $f(z_i)$ and $f(u_i)$ are added together to form a new chaotic sequence G_0. The new sequence is obtained according to the order from small to large, and the new sequence is replaced by the value of the position of each element in the new sequence, and then obtain a new sequence. Row and column scrambling of the matrix I_2 is carried out with the new sequence, and the matrix I_3 is obtained.

Step 11: The DNA decoding of image I_3 is restored to an image matrix, and finally the encrypted image I_4 is obtained.

Decryption algorithm is the inverse process of encryption algorithm, no more details here.

4   Simulation Experiment

The simulation experiments are carried out under the environment of MATLAB 7.1. And the standard 256×256 gray image of Lena is used as the original image, and experiments are carried out under the conditions of $x_1 = 9.75, y_1 = 54, z_1 = 19, u_1 = 21$. The laboratory results of this algorithm, shown in Fig. 4, we give the encrypted and decrypted images, where (a) is the original image, and the encrypted image is shown in (b).

Fig. 4. (a) original image (b) encrypted image

5   Security Analysis

A good encryption algorithm should be able to resist different types of attacks. The security analysis of image encryption algorithm mainly includes key space, sensitivity analysis and Statistical attack analysis.

5.1   Exhaustive Attack Analysis

(1) Key space analysis

In this algorithm, the key contains 256 bytes of the SHA-3 function. If the calculation accuracy of x_1, y_1, z_1, u_1 is 10^{14}, the key space of Chen system is $10^{14} \times 10^{14} \times 10^{14} \times 10^{14} = 10^{56}$, and the key space of SHA-3(256) is 2^{128}. The total key space is: $10^{56} \times 2^{128} \approx 3.4 * 10^{94}$, which shows the algorithm has a sufficiently large key space to resist the brute force attack.

(2) Sensitivity analysis of keys

To test the sensitivity of the key, we decrypt the key with a small difference. Figure 5(a) represents the decryption diagram of $x_1 = 10$ and other key invariant. Figure 5(b), (c) and (d), respectively represent the decryption images of $y_1 = 54.3, z_1 = 20, u_1 = 21.1$ and other key invariant. Only when the decryption key is consistent with the encryption key can the image be decrypted properly. Otherwise, as long as there is a small difference between the keys, the original image can not be recovered properly, and the error decrypted image can not reflect the original image information. Therefore, we can obtain that the algorithm has key sensitivity and can effectively resist brute force attacks.

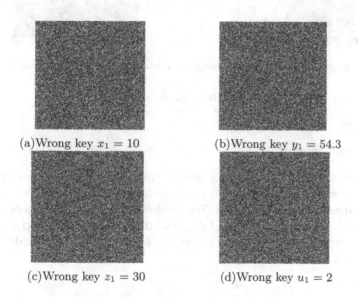

(a)Wrong key $x_1 = 10$ (b)Wrong key $y_1 = 54.3$

(c)Wrong key $z_1 = 30$ (d)Wrong key $u_1 = 2$

Fig. 5. Decryption image of error key

5.2 Statistical Attack Analysis

(1) Histogram analysis

The statistical analysis of the original image and the encrypted image is carried out. Figure 6(a) gives the original image histogram, (b) gives the encrypted image histogram, and analyze the pixel values of the original image, the image pixel is relatively concentrated before encryption, that is in interval (0, 255) at both ends of the pixel distribution is relatively small, and the middle distribution is more, but the corresponding histogram after encryption is basically uniform, and the attacker is difficult to use the statistical properties of the pixel gray value to restore the original image. It can be seen that the algorithm has good anti-statistical analysis ability.

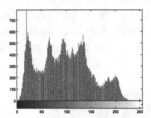 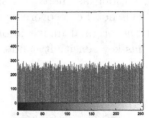

(a) Histograms of the Lena original image (b) Histograms of the Lena ciphered image

Fig. 6. Histograms analysis

(2) Correlation analysis

As we all know, in the original image, the correlation between two adjacent pixels is very high. In order to resist statistical attacks, the correlation of encrypted images must be reduced. We randomly select 2500 pairs of adjacent pixels in the horizontal, vertical and diagonal directions from the original image and the encrypted image, and then use the formula (17–20) to calculate the correlation between pixels.

$$E(x) = \frac{1}{N} \sum_{i=1}^{N} x_i. \tag{17}$$

$$D(x) = \frac{1}{N} \sum_{i=1}^{N} (x_i - E(x))^2. \tag{18}$$

$$cov(x, y) = \frac{1}{N} \sum_{i=1}^{N} (x_i - E(x))(y_i - E(x)). \tag{19}$$

$$r_{xy} = \frac{cov(x, y)}{\sqrt{D(x)} \times \sqrt{D(y)}}. \tag{20}$$

Where x and y are the gray values of the adjacent pixels in the image, $cov(x, y)$ is covariance, $D(x)$ is variance, and $E(x)$ is the average. Similarly, other results are shown in Table 3. Figure 7 shows the correlation between the original image and the horizontal, vertical, and diagonal directions of the encrypted image. The correlation coefficient of adjacent pixels of encrypted image is −0.001035. Therefore, the image encryption algorithm has a strong ability to resist statistical attacks.

Table 3. The correlation of the adjacent pixels for original and encrypted image

Correlation	Original image	Encryption image
Horizontal	0.9666	0.0140
Vertical	0.9447	0.0032
Diagonal	0.9159	−0.0195

(3) Information entropy

Information entropy is defined as the extent to which the uncertainty of a system is described. It can be used to represent the uncertainty of image information. It is well known that information entropy can test the distribution of the image gray value. The more uniform the distribution of the image gray value, the greater the entropy of the image. The formula for defining information entropy is as follows:

$$H(m) = -\sum_{t=0}^{t} P(m_i) \log_2 P(m_i). \tag{21}$$

Where M is the ith gray value on the L scale image and $P(m_i)$ is the probability of m_i. An ideal random image with information entropy value is 8, and the information entropy of the experiment is 7.9892, which illustrates the effectiveness of the proposed encryption algorithm.

5.3 Differential Attack Analysis

Differential attack refers to the attacker changes the plain-text slightly to compare the difference of the cipher-text before and after the change, and then finds the relation between the corresponding plain-text and cipher-text. NPCR (pixel change rate) and UACI (pixel average change intensity) are usually used to detect the ability of image encryption scheme to resist differential attack, and the following formulas are used to calculate NPCR and UACI:

$$C(i, j) = \begin{cases} 0, & if \quad p_1(i, j) = p_2(i, j), \\ 1, & if \quad p_1(i, j) \neq p_2(i, j). \end{cases} \tag{22}$$

$$NPCR = \frac{\sum\limits_{i=1}^{M}\sum\limits_{j=1}^{N} C(i,j)}{M \times N} \times 100\%. \tag{23}$$

$$UACI = \frac{\sum\limits_{i=1}^{M}\sum\limits_{j=1}^{N} |p_1(i,j) - p_2(i,j)|}{255 \times M \times N} \times 100\%. \tag{24}$$

Where M and N represent the length and width of the image respectively. $P_1(i, j)$ and $P_2(i, j)$ represent the corresponding cipher-text pixel values before and after the change of plain-text. The NPCR value is close to 100%, indicating that the higher the sensitivity of the image encryption scheme to the plain-text

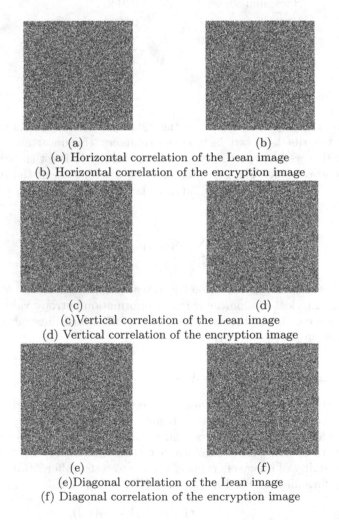

(a)   (b)
(a) Horizontal correlation of the Lean image
(b) Horizontal correlation of the encryption image

(c)   (d)
(c)Vertical correlation of the Lean image
(d) Vertical correlation of the encryption image

(e)   (f)
(e)Diagonal correlation of the Lean image
(f) Diagonal correlation of the encryption image

Fig. 7. The correlation of the adjacent pixels for original and encrypted image

image, the stronger the resistance to differential attack. The ideal value of UACI is 33%, and the closer it is to the ideal value, the stronger the ability to resist differential attacks.

Now from the experiment used in the plain-text image to change a little pixel, such as the location of pixel $(7, 8)$, change the pixel value from 128 to 30, and then according to the above formula can be calculated $NPCR = 99.5926\%$, $UACI = 33.40\%$. It can be seen that the NPCR is close to 100% and the UACI value is close to 33%, which verifies that the image encryption scheme has the ability to resist differential attacks.

6 Conclusion

In this paper, a new image encryption algorithm based on DNA dynamic encoding and hyper-chaos system is proposed. The algorithm uses DNA dynamic encoding rules to avoid the defect of encoding in DNA encryption. And uses SHA-3 algorithm and Hamming distance to improve the key space. Secondly, hyper-chaotic sequences are used to increase the complexity of the algorithm and the uncertainty of cipher-text. Finally, the encryption of the S-box provides double encryption for this algorithm. Experimental results show that the algorithm has better encryption effect, higher key space and higher sensitivity to key. In addition, the algorithm can resist exhaustive and statistical attacks and differential attacks. Therefore, the encryption scheme proposed by this algorithm can be used in secure image transmission.

Acknowledgments. The work for this paper was supported by the National Natural Science Foundation of China (Grant Nos. 61602424, 61472371, 61572446, 61472372), Plan for Scientific Innovation Talent of Henan Province (Grant No.174100510009), Program for Science and Technology Innovation Talents in Universities of Henan Province (Grant No. 15HASTIT019) and Key Scientific Research Projects of Henan High Educational Institution (18A510020).

References

1. Zhu, C.: A novel image encryption scheme based on improved hyperchaotic sequences. Opt. Commun. **285**(1), 29–37 (2012)
2. Peng, J., Jin, S., Liao, X.: A novel digital image encryption algorithm based on hyperchaos by controlling Lorenz system. In: Proceedings of the 5th International Conference on Natural Computation, pp. 395–399. IEEE Press (2009)
3. Seripeariu, L., Frunza, M.D.: A new image encryption algorithm based on inversable functions defined on Galois fields. In: International Symposium on Signals, Circuits and Systems, vol. 1, pp. 243–246. IEEE (2005)
4. Wang, X.Y., Zhang, Y.Q., Bao, X.M.: A novel chaotic image encryption scheme using DNA sequence operations. Optics Lasers Eng. **73**(1), 53–61 (2015)
5. Jiezhi, W., Zengqiang, C., Zhuzhi, Y., et al.: The generation of a hyperchaotic system based on a three-dimensional autonomous chaotic system. J. Chin. Phys. **15**(6), 1216–1225 (2006)

6. Zhu, Z.L., Zhang, W., Wong, K.W., Yu, H.: A chaos-based symmetric image encryption scheme using a bit-level permutation. Inf. Sci. **181**(6), 1171–1186 (2011)
7. Guesmi, R., Farah, M.A.B., Kachouri, A.: A novel chaos-based image encryption using DNA sequence operation and secure hash algorithm SHA-2. Nonlinear Dyn. **83**(3), 1123–1136 (2016)
8. Pareek, N.K., Patidar, V., Sud, K.K.: Image encryption using chaotic logistic map. Image Vis. Comput. **24**(9), 926–934 (2006)
9. Wei, X., Guo, L., Zhang, Q.: A novel color image encryption algorithm based on DNA sequence operation and hyper-chaotic system. J. Syst. Softw. **85**(2), 290–299 (2012)
10. Zhang, Y., Tang, Y.: A plaintext-related image encryption algorithm based on chaos. Multimedia Tools Appl. **2**, 1–23 (2017). https://doi.org/10.1007/s11042-017-4577-1
11. Akhavan, A., Samsudin, A., Akhshani, A.: Cryptanalysis of an image encryption algorithm based on DNA encoding. Opt. Laser Technol. **95**, 94–99 (2017)
12. Alvarez, G., Montoya, F., Romera, M.: Cryptanalysis of an ergodic chaotic cipher. Phys. Lett. A. **311**(2), 172–179 (2003)
13. Enayatifar, R., Sadaei, H.J., Abdullah, A.H.: A novel chaotic based image encryption using a hybrid model of deoxyribonucleic acid and cellular automata. Opt. Laser Eng. **71**, 33–41 (2015)
14. Van Droogenbroeck, M.: Partial encryption of images for real-time applications. In: Fourth IEEE Benelux Signal Processing, Hilvarenbeek, The Netherlands, pp. 11–15 (2004)
15. Gao, T., Chen, Z.: A new image encryption algorithm based on hyper-chaos. Phys. Lett. A. **372**(4), 394–400 (2008)
16. Kumar, M., Iqbal, A., Kumar, P.: A new RGB image encryption algorithm based on DNA encoding and elliptic curve Diffie-Hellman cryptography. Signal Process **125**, 187–202 (2016)
17. Zhou, C., Wei, X., Zhang, Q.: DNA sequence splicing with chaotic maps for image encryption. J. Comput. Theor. Nanosci. **7**(10), 1904–1910 (2010)
18. Wang, Q., Zhang, Q., Wei, X.: Image encryption algorithm based on dna biological properties and chaotic systems. In: IEEE Fifth International Conference on Bio-Inspired Computing: Theories and Applications (BIC-TA), pp. 132–136. IEEE (2010)
19. Adleman, L.: Molecular computation of solutions to combinatorial problems. Science **266**(5187), 1020–1024 (1994)
20. Wang, X., Zhao, J., Liu, H.: A new image encryption algorithm based on chaos. Opt. Commun. **285**(5), 562–566 (2012)
21. Xiao, G., Mingxin, L., Qin, L., Lai, X.: New field of cryptography: DNA cryptography. Chin. Sci. Bull. **51**(12), 1413–1420 (2006)
22. Özkaynak, F., Yavuz, S.: Analysis and improvement of a novel image fusion encryption algorithm based on DNA sequence operation and hyper-chaotic system. Nonlinear Dyn. **78**(2), 1311–1320 (2014)
23. Zhang, Q., Liu, L., Wei, X.: Improved algorithm for image encryption based on DNA encoding and multi-chaotic maps. AEU-Int. J. Electron. C. **68**(3), 186–192 (2014)
24. Kong, L., Li, L.: A new image encryption algorithm based on chaos. In: 35th Chinese Control Conference (CCC), pp. 4932–4937. IEEE (2016)
25. Özkaynak, F., Özer, A.B., Yavuz, S.: Security analysis of an image encryption algorithm based on chaos and DNA encoding. In: 2013 21st Signal Processing and Communications Applications Conference (SIU), pp. 1–4. IEEE (2013)

26. Liu, Y., Tang, J., Xie, T.: Crypt analyzing a RGB image encryption algorithm based on DNA encoding and chaos map. Opt. Laser Technol. **60**, 111–115 (2014)
27. Liu, L., Zhang, Q., Wei, X.: A RGB image encryption algorithm based on DNA encoding and chaos map. Comput. Electr. Eng. **38**(5), 1240–1248 (2012)
28. Shi, X., Lu, W., Wang, Z., Pan, L., Cui, G., Xu, J., LaBean, T.H.: Programmable DNA tile self-assembly using a hierarchical subtile strategy. Nanotechnology **25**(7), 075602 (2014)
29. Yang, J., Jiang, S., Liu, X., Pan, L., Zhang, C.: Aptamer-binding directed DNA origami pattern for logic gates. ACS Appl. Mater. Interacs. **8**, 34054–34060 (2016)
30. Yang, J., Chen, D., Dong, Y., Liu, S., Pan, L., Zhang, C.: Logic nanoparticle beacon triggered by the binding induced effect of multiple inputs. ACS Appl. Mater. Interfaces **6**(16), 14486–14492 (2014)
31. Sun, J., Wu, Y., Cui, G.: Finite-time real combination synchronization of three complex-variable chaotic systems with unknown parameters via sliding mode control. Nonlinear Dyn. **88**(3), 1677–1690 (2017)
32. Sun, J., Wang, Y., Wang, Y.: Finite-time synchronization between two complex-variable chaotic systems with unknown parameters via nonsingular terminal sliding mode control. Nonlinear Dyn. **85**(2), 1105–1117 (2016)
33. Sun, J., Shen, Y.: Quasi-ideal memory system. IEEE Trans. Cybern. **45**(7), 1353–1362 (2015)
34. Shiu, H., Ng, K., Fang, J.: Data hiding methods based upon DNA sequences. Inform. Sci. **180**(11), 2196–2208 (2010)
35. Gaborit, P., King, O.D.: Linear constructions for DNA codes. Theor. Comput. Sci. **334**(1–3), 99–113 (2005)

A Circuit Simplification Mechanism Based on DNA Combinatorial Strands Displacement

Xuncai Zhang[(⊠)], Feng Han, and Yanfeng Wang

College of Electrical and Electronic Engineering, Zhengzhou University of Light Industry, Zhengzhou 450002, China
zhangxuncai@163.com, 1462295227@qq.com

Abstract. Through extensive application of DNA strand displacement technology in the field of molecular computing, we know that the DNA strand of the toehold domain and the branch migration domain are covalently connected to form logical gates in traditional DNA strand displacement circuits. In this paper, we will adopt a composite strand mechanism that the toehold domain and branch migration domain in different single strand form displacing complex, and construct logical gates with combinatorial strand displacement mechanism. After that, a logic gate model is constructed, and the mechanism is verified by the design and simulation of the logical molecular model of the encoder. When the DNA signal strand is input, the signal strand molecule can be output by combination of molecular specific hybridization reaction and intermolecular strand displacement reaction. The results of Visual DSD simulation show the feasibility and accuracy of the encoder logic calculation model designed in this article.

Keywords: Strand displacement · Logic circuit · Visual DSD · Molecular computing · DNA reaction network

1 Introduction

In recent years, the application of DNA strand displacement reactions to achieve molecular computing tasks has attracted much attention. In 2000, Mao et al. constructed the XOR logic gate by using three crossed DNA Tile, and pioneered the research of nanometer logic circuit [1]. In 2005, Pencho-vsky et al. constructed a series of logic gates by using special aptamer to regulate the activity of RNA enzyme, and made a pioneering exploration for the development of this field [2]. In 2006, Seeling et al. designed and implemented the digital logic circuit based on strand displacement reaction, including AND gate, OR gate, NOT gate. These logic gates use single strands as input and output signals, which achieve signal reset, amplification, feedback and cascading [3]. In 2009, Zhang et al. proposed the amplifier circuit which has the characteristics of simplicity, fast, modularization and stable performance [4], all of these has laid a solid foundation for the implementation of large-scale cascade circuits with DNA strand displacement

ⓒ Springer Nature Singapore Pte Ltd. 2017
C. He et al. (Eds.): BIC-TA 2017, CCIS 791, pp. 304–319, 2017.
https://doi.org/10.1007/978-981-10-7179-9_23

technology [5,6]. In 2011, L.L. Qian et al. proposed a general model for constructing DNA molecular logic gates based on DNA strand displacement method, which laid a solid theoretical foundation for the construction of nanoscale biochemical logic circuits [7]. In the same year, L.L. Qian et al. published the major research achievements in Science and Nature, and the most complex biochemical logic circuits and neural networks with artificial intelligence were constructed by logical gate modules [8]. In 2012, C. Zhang et al. constructed the molecular computation model of logic AND and OR gates based on the strand displacement mechanism [9]. The formation and discovery of these theories and experiments provide a strong support for the application of strand displacement technology in logic circuit.

Based on the basic principles of DNA strand displacement reaction, a logic gate is constructed by the mechanism of combinatorial strand, and on this basis a logical molecular model of encoder circuit is constructed. When input a specific DNA molecular signal strand, through a series of specific hybridization between DNA molecules and strand displacement reaction, and the result ultimately be able to output the correct signal strand of DNA molecules. With RCN module of Visual DSD as the simulation platform, the logic calculation simulation model of 4-2 encoder is simulated. The model uses DNA single strand as input signal, through specific recognition and strand displacement reaction, and finally releases specific molecular signals as the output of logic gates. The output signal can be detected by fluorescent labeling or electrophoresis strip, but also can be combined with nanoparticles and proteins for parallel computing, cryptography, nanoelectronics, disease detection and biology and medicine [10,11].

2   The Mechanism of Combinatorial Strand Displacement

DNA intermolecular strand displacement reaction refers to strand displacement reaction between the DNA single strand and part of the complementary double-stranded structure, which can release the original double-stranded molecular structure of the single strand, thus forming a new double-strand molecular structure. The reaction is a spontaneous reaction, and its driving force is derived from the intermolecular force [4,12]. In the DNA hybridization system, the binding capacity of different single-stranded molecules is different. By replacing the weak binding single strand in the partially complementary structure with a longer single strand, DNA single strand reaction reduces the free energy of the system and puts the system in a more stable state [13]. In the analog logic device, the principle is that control the input signal strand base composition and sequence length achieve the trend of control responses [14]. Simple understanding is to replace the shorter strand with a longer DNA strand, and the replaced strand is used as the output signal to implement the molecular logic operation [15,16].

In traditional strand displacement circuits, the DNA strands are covalently connected and form logical gates in the toehold domain and branch migration regions, and in many large complex strand displacement reactions, there is often a competing interaction between the strands. In order to solve this situation, we have to create some double-strand structures which have some new functions. Based on this, we find a new mechanism called 'combinatorial displacement', and the new mechanism has a 'displacing complex' structure that is the toehold domain and the migration region in the different strands. This mechanism was proposed in 2013 by Genot A.J. et al. [17]. The specific process is shown in Fig. 1.

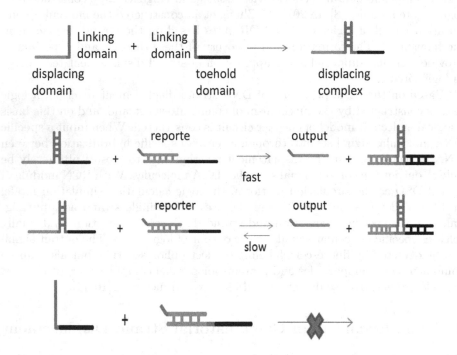

Fig. 1. The process of combinatorial strand displacement. When the two input strands have respectively displacing domain and toehold domain, the red part will be hybridized to form a structure called. And the 'displacing complex' structure will react with the reporter and get output, because the two parts are completely complementary, so the reaction speed will be faster. (Color figure online)

The first reaction construct called 'displacing complex' through hybridization of the red portion. The second reaction construct called 'displacing complex' that react rapid with a two-way reporter strand and get the output strand. Only a toehold domain (black) or displacing domain (green) cannot react. In Fig. 1, the red represent linking domain, green represent the displacing domain, and black represent the toehold domain. In the course of the reaction, the reaction rate of the positive reaction or the second reaction is rapid. And the rate of the reverse will be very slow, not enough and comparable to the forward, nor will the impact of the output of the results.

3 Construction of Logical Gate

The most basic logic circuit is the gate circuit. There are three basic forms of the gate: AND gate, OR gate and NOT gate [18]. When the gate circuit is open, certain signals are allowed to pass and are stopped in a closed state. In logic circuit, the signals that are transmitted and processed are binary digital signals, and binary digital signals are represented by logic 1 and logic 0, which represent respectively high and low levels [19,20]. The basis of constructing a molecular logic computation model is the biochemical implementation of the most basic logic gate [21,22].

The design of molecular logic gate has two main requirements: firstly, the trigger conditions must be consistent with the corresponding molecular logic gate logic, including AND logic, OR logic and NOT logic [23]; secondly, the application of molecular logic gates in cascade reactions must be taken into consideration, only molecular logic gates that can be cascaded can be assembled into complex molecular logic circuits [24].

Through the above understanding of combinatorial strand displacement, it is different from the general strand displacement reaction, and can better construct complex logic circuits. Here, the above mechanisms are used to design AND gate, OR gate and XOR gate to pave the way for constructing logical circuit.

Chemical reaction equations and mass-action kinetics provide a mathematical language for describing and analyzing chemical systems. In most cases, mass-action kinetics are used to simulate chemical experiments and to predict and explain their kinetic behavior and change [25,26]. The strand displacement reaction is a typical mass-action kinetics reaction process, so we can construct a chemical reaction network to simulate the strand displacement reaction.

3.1 Construction of Logical and Gate

The intent of AND gate can be obtained by Fig. 2. The A and B are inputs, the output is the output strand. Only the input of A and B are entered at the same time, there will be the output logic 1. When the input is A or B, there is no output strand, and output is logic 0. If the output is like this, the logic gate constructed satisfies the logic AND gate conditions, successfully simulated logic AND gate function. Only when A and B are entered, displacing complex can be constructed and participate in the subsequent reaction, because both ends of the reporter strand are both complementary complement, and the result is that will produce each part of completely complementary double-strand and produce output.

Because simple hybridization reactions cannot be cascaded, we use the more flexible strand displacement reaction as a molecular primitive. We use the principle of strand displacement and simplify the AND gate by biochemical reaction network, so that it is convenient to be used in digital logic circuit. The specific process is obtained by Fig. 3.

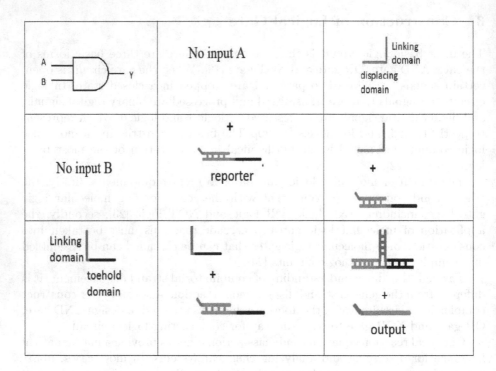

Fig. 2. A design of 'And' logic gate using combinatorial displacement. The input A is a single strand with Linking domain at one end, and B is a single strand with toehold domain at one end. In the reaction, the reaction substrate is DNA strand called reporter. Only when A and B are input simultaneously, because of the Combinatorial strand displacement reaction mechanism we know that the output strand can be rapidly output.

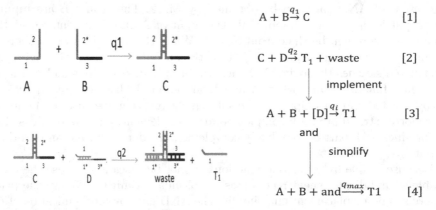

$$A + B \xrightarrow{q_1} C \qquad [1]$$

$$C + D \xrightarrow{q_2} T_1 + \text{waste} \qquad [2]$$

$$\downarrow \text{implement}$$

$$A + B + [D] \xrightarrow{q_i} T1 \qquad [3]$$

$$\text{and} \quad \downarrow \text{simplify}$$

$$A + B + \text{and} \xrightarrow{q_{max}} T1 \qquad [4]$$

Fig. 3. Unimolecular module: DNA implementation of the formal unimolecular reaction $A + B \rightarrow T_1$ with reaction index q_i. 'and' refers to AND gate, and the AND gate includes D, T_1 represents output. The whole reaction can be simplified $A + B + \text{and} \rightarrow T_1$.

3.2 Construction of Logical OR Gate

The intent of OR gate can be obtained by Fig. 4. In particular, the reaction substrate can be completely separated from the three parts, rather than the structure shown in the above Fig. 1 that has been hybridized in one piece. The most of reaction substrate is separated, and can be seen as two single-strand and an intermediate part of the double-stranded structure. It is shown in the figure for drawing convenience. As you can see from the diagram, when the input is A or B, the output is logic 0. Only when there is no output A and B at the same time, the output is logic 0. The results satisfy the principle of OR gate.

We use the principle of strand displacement and simplify the OR gate by biochemical reaction network, so that it is convenient to be used in digital logic circuit. The specific process is obtained by Fig. 5.

3.3 Construction of Logical XOR Gate

A XOR gate is a logic gate that implements logical XOR in digital logic. The XOR gate is constructed with two inputs and one output, the multi-input XOR gate can be composed with XOR gates. If the two inputs are different, the output

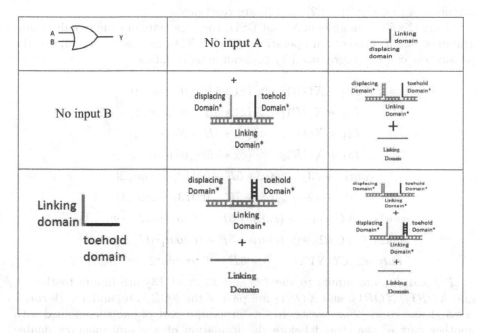

Fig. 4. The input of OR gate is A that is a single strand with displacing domain, B is a single strand with toehold domain. The reaction substrate is a complex strand that is containing 3 parts in the reaction at the same time, the output is Linking domain. A single strand is complementary to each other with the reaction substrate. When A or B with Linking domain react with reaction substrate, the output can be obtained.

is high level 1. If the two inputs are the same, the output is low level 0. It is to say that if the two inputs are different, the XOR gate outputs a high level.

It is found that during the design of logic circuit, ordinary 4-2 encoder can be optimized. Especially after the introducing of XOR gate, the circuit structure is will greatly simplified. In this case, we design exclusive XOR gate based on the mechanism of combinatorial strand displacement. And the intent of XOR gate can be obtained by Fig. 6.

When there are two different inputs, we will get the output we had defined, then the logic output is 1, when no input and two inputs, no output strand called e, then the logic output is 0. These conditions and outputs satisfy the XOR gate conditions and rules, indicating that the logical gate designed are reasonable. The logic gate designed will be demonstrated in applications of the following logic circuit.

We use the principle of strand displacement and simplify the XOR gate by biochemical reaction network, so that it is convenient to use in digital logic circuit. The specific process will be obtained by Fig. 7.

From the Fig. 7, the ideal situation is an extreme case of the requirement $q1 > q2 > q3 > qmin$ where reactions '[1]', '[2]' finish first, then reaction '[3]', '[4]' starts to produce Y_1 and Y_2, and then reactions '[5]' and '[6]' start to work. This is the only way to make the expression of XOR gate be very clear. Special attention is that the '[1]', '[2]',...'[10]' are reactions.

Using the CRN module of Visual DSD, the logic gate encode circuit is programmed, and the molecular operation model of XOR gate is simulated, and the parameters can be programmed by programming as follows:

$$I2_2 + XOR1_2 - > (c1 * 5E - 05)xor_w1|$$
$$I3_2 + XOR1_1 - > (c1 * 5E - 05)xor_w2|$$
$$I2_1 + XOR1_1 - > (c2 * 5E - 05)com1_1|$$
$$I3_1 + XOR1_2 - > (c2 * 5E - 05)com1_2|$$
$$com1_1 + I3_2 - > (c3 * 5E - 05)I2_1 + xor_w2|$$
$$com1_2 + I2_2 - > (c3 * 5E - 05)I3_1 + xor_w1|$$
$$com1_1 + XOR1_3 - > (cmin * 5E - 05)output2_+com1_w1|$$
$$com1_2 + XOR1_3 - > (cmin * 5E - 05)output2_+com1_w2|$$
$$output2_+CONV2 - > (c * 5E - 05)output2 + conv_w2|$$

$I2_2$ and $I2_1$ are inputs to the $I2$, and $I3_1$ and $I3_2$ are inputs to the $I3$, and $XOR1_3$, $XOR1_2$, and $XOR1_1$ are part of the XOR gate, and xor_w1 xor_w2 $com1_w1$ and $com1_w2$ are waste. In this process, a part of one is combined with another part of the strand before the formation of a complementary double strand. For example, in Fig. 7, before the strand X_3 is completely complementary with the X_3*, the Red areas of X_3 react with the red part of X_4, then the black part of X_3 is regarded as toehold. After that, X_3* will react with X_3 to replace the X_4, forming a stable double-strand structure. The whole reaction process ensures the reliability of the XOR gate, and it is also reflected in the program.

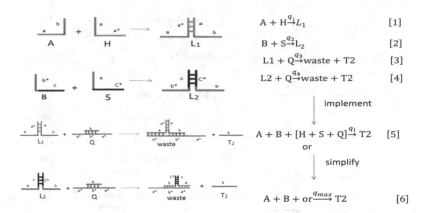

$$A + H \xrightarrow{q_1} L_1 \qquad [1]$$

$$B + S \xrightarrow{q_2} L_2 \qquad [2]$$

$$L1 + Q \xrightarrow{q_3} \text{waste} + T2 \qquad [3]$$

$$L2 + Q \xrightarrow{q_4} \text{waste} + T2 \qquad [4]$$

$$\downarrow \text{ implement}$$

$$A + B + [H + S + Q] \xrightarrow{q_i} T2 \qquad [5]$$
$$\text{or}$$

$$\downarrow \text{ simplify}$$

$$A + B + \text{or} \xrightarrow{q_{max}} T2 \qquad [6]$$

Fig. 5. Unimolecular module: DNA implementation of the formal unimolecular reaction $A + B \rightarrow T_2$ with reaction index q_i. 'or' means OR gate, and OR gate should contain '$H + S + Q$'. T_2 is output of OR gate. The whole reaction can be simplified $A + B +$ or $\rightarrow T_2$.

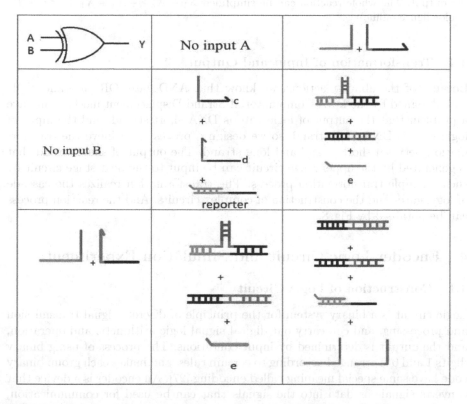

Fig. 6. The inputs of A and B are shown respectively. The reactant is reporter, c, d, and the output is e. With only one input, there will be fully complementary double-strand output and get the output e. While entering A and B at the same time, there will be two completely complementary double strand, and cannot generate output e.

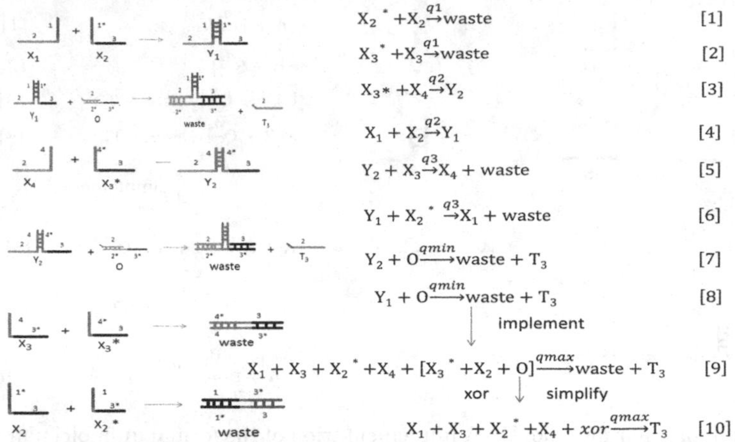

$$X_2\ ^* + X_2 \xrightarrow{q1} \text{waste} \qquad\qquad [1]$$

$$X_3\ ^* + X_3 \xrightarrow{q1} \text{waste} \qquad\qquad [2]$$

$$X_3* + X_4 \xrightarrow{q2} Y_2 \qquad\qquad [3]$$

$$X_1 + X_2 \xrightarrow{q2} Y_1 \qquad\qquad [4]$$

$$Y_2 + X_3 \xrightarrow{q3} X_4 + \text{waste} \qquad\qquad [5]$$

$$Y_1 + X_2\ ^* \xrightarrow{q3} X_1 + \text{waste} \qquad\qquad [6]$$

$$Y_2 + O \xrightarrow{qmin} \text{waste} + T_3 \qquad\qquad [7]$$

$$Y_1 + O \xrightarrow{qmin} \text{waste} + T_3 \qquad\qquad [8]$$

$$\downarrow \text{implement}$$

$$X_1 + X_3 + X_2\ ^* + X_4 + [X_3\ ^* + X_2 + O] \xrightarrow{qmax} \text{waste} + T_3 \quad [9]$$

$$\text{xor} \downarrow \text{simplify}$$

$$X_1 + X_3 + X_2\ ^* + X_4 + \text{xor} \xrightarrow{qmax} T_3 \qquad [10]$$

Fig. 7. Unimolecular module: DNA implementation of the formal unimolecular reaction $X_1 + X_2* + X_3 + X_4 \to T_3$ with reaction index q_i. 'xor' include $X_3 * + X_2 + O$, T_3 is the output. The whole reaction can be simplified $X_1 + X_2 * + X_3 + X_4 + \text{xor} \to T_3$. (Color figure online)

3.4   Transformation of Input and Output

Because of the above reactions, we know that AND gate, OR gate and XOR gate designed by the DNA Combinatorial Strand Displacement mechanism have a problem that the output of logic gate is DNA short strand, and the input of logic gate is DNA long strand, so we design a process to achieve the transformation between short strand and long strand. The output of short strand that is generated by the upper stage circuit can be input to the next stage circuit by such a simple transformation process. The transformation realizes the cascade of logic gates and the construction of complex circuits. And the reaction process can be obtained by Fig. 8.

4   Encoder Logic Circuit and Simulation Experiment

4.1   Construction of Logic Circuit

Logic circuit is a binary system for the principle of discrete signal transmission and processing, and can carry out digital signal logic arithmetic and operation, and the output is determined by input conditions. The process of using binary digits 1 and 0 is arranged according to certain rules, and makes each group binary code have some special meaning called encoding [27]. An encoder is a device that converts signals or data into the signals that can be used for communication, transmission, and storage. A logic circuit with encoding function is called an encoder [28].

In this paper, a molecular encoder is designed to encode 4 input signals into natural binary numbers. The encoder has 4 input channels, namely I_0, I_1, I_2 and

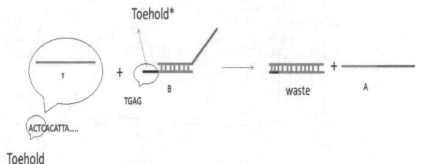

Fig. 8. T is a logic gate output short strand which the first four bases is toehold. The perfect complement to toehold is the black part called toehold* of B, with only four bases. A is the output of long strand, can be used as the next input logic gate.

Table 1. Encoder function table

Input I_0	Input I_1	Input I_2	Input I_3	Output Y_0	Output Y_1
1	0	0	0	0	0
0	1	0	0	0	1
0	0	1	0	1	0
0	0	0	1	1	1

I_3, encoding 4 channels respectively, each time only one channel input signal is logic 1, and the output is represented by 2 bit binary numbers. According to the function of the encoder, the list of functions is listed as follows. When enter input I_0, I_1, I_2 and I_3, only one is logical 1, Y_1 and Y_0 respectively represent two bit binary number output high and low. For example: when I_0 is logical 1, $Y_1 = 0$, $Y_0 = 0$; when I_1 is logic 1, Y_1Y_0 is 01. The following logical expressions can be obtained by the encoder function Table 1.

$$\begin{cases} Y_1 = \bar{I}_0\bar{I}_1I_2\bar{I}_3 + \bar{I}_0\bar{I}_1\bar{I}_2I_3 \\ Y_0 = \bar{I}_0I_1\bar{I}_2\bar{I}_3 + \bar{I}_0\bar{I}_1\bar{I}_2I_3 \end{cases} \tag{1}$$

Since the molecular logic gates designed in this paper contain two input signals, the corresponding two input logic expressions can be deformed as (2):

$$\begin{cases} Y_1 = \bar{I}_0\bar{I}_1(I_2\bar{I}_3 + \bar{I}_2I_3) \\ Y_0 = \bar{I}_0\bar{I}_2(I_1\bar{I}_3 + \bar{I}_1I_3) \end{cases} \tag{2}$$

Because of above formulas we can design 4-2 encoder logic circuit, as shown in Fig. 9.

In the logic circuit above, logic gates are replaced by molecules AND gates and molecules OR gates respectively. In the molecular model, molecular AND

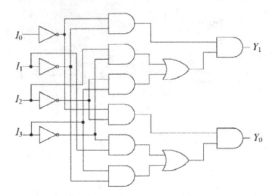

Fig. 9. Encoder logic circuit. The logic circuit is composed of 8 AND gates, 2 OR gates and 4 NOT gates. I_0 to I_3 represents 4 input signals, and Y_1 and Y_0 represent output signals. The designed molecular logic gates can be used to replace the logic gates in the encoder logic circuit diagram.

gate and molecular OR gate are replaced the logic gates in the logic circuit, the molecular NOT gate uses two kinds of different strands to represent logic 1 and logic 0, so the four NOT gates amount to the 8 DNA strands as the input signal, respectively as I_0^0, I_0^1, I_1^0, I_1^1, ...I_3^0, I_3^1. In logic circuit, the input signal $I_0 = 1$ has no effect on the output of the circuit, but in order to preserve the integrity of the logic circuit and ensure the robustness of the molecular logic circuit, the signal is still remained in the molecular logic circuit.

We know that above logic circuit is complex as shown. In order to simplify the logic circuit, here we introduce XOR gate to optimize the circuit. Simplified logic circuit is obtained by Fig. 10.

When the I_0 to I_3 is 1000, the output from top to bottom of the two AND gates and two XOR gates is 0000, so the final output Y_1Y_0 is 00 after two AND gates. When the I_0 to I_3 is 0100, the output from top to bottom of the two AND gates and two XOR gates is 0011, so the final output Y_1Y_0 is 01 after two AND gates. When the I_0 to I_3 is 0010, the output from top to bottom of the two AND gates and two XOR gates is 1100, so the final output Y_1Y_0 is 10 after two AND gates. When the I_0 to I_3 is 0001, the output from top to bottom of the two AND gates and two XOR gates is 1111, so the final output Y_1Y_0 is 11 after two AND gates.

Compared with the original logic circuit, the new logic circuit which uses the number of logic gate is less, and from the beginning of the reaction to the reaction results are expressed, only two steps reaction, and the original logic circuit is a three-stage circuit. This also greatly reduces the difficulty of the reaction.

4.2   Simulation Experiment

In the RCN module environment of Visual DSD software, the default computing reaction model and the random reaction model are selected to simulate the molecular operation model [29, 30]. After simulation, the concentration variation

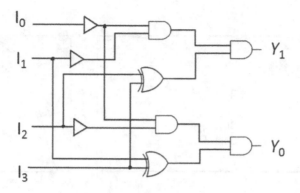

Fig. 10. Simplified encoder logic circuit. The logic circuit is composed of 4 AND gates, 2 XOR gates and 3 NOT gates. I_0 to I_3 represents 4 input signals, and Y_1 and Y_0 represent output signals. The designed molecular logic gate can be used to replace the logic gates in the encoder logic circuit diagram.

curves of 6 output strands before and after optimization are obtained. The simulation results of original logic circuit are shown in Fig. 11.

In the software platform, the molecular logic model is coded and simulated, and the simulation results of 6 outputs cases are obtained. The concentration change curves of two output strands are shown in the Fig. 11. The simulation time is 5000 s. In this period of time, changes in 3 kinds of output strand concentration are alike, and can be divided into 3 stages: in 0–400 s, the number of input strand decreased rapidly. This is because the input strand of high concentration is reactant to participate in first-stage strand reaction, and the output strand as the input of second-stage strand reaction. It can also be said that the reaction of the molecular logic model of encoder is cascade, the input signal at the next stage reaction is the output signal at the upper stage strand reaction, so the response takes a certain amount of time; after 400 s, the product of the first-stage acts as the input of the second-stage reaction, and the output of the second-stage begins to grow, so that the reaction of the third-stage begins, and the Y_0 and the Y_1 are generated. With the increase of the second-stage output, the third-stage reaction also began to react sharply, and the concentration of Y_0 and Y_1 also changed dramatically. About 1200 s later, due to the reduction of the concentration of the input strand, the inputs of two-stage and three-stage decreased, the concentration change of Y_0 and Y_1 in the growth is more and more small. When the reaction tends to steady state or input strand is consumed, the concentration fluctuation will tend to be straight. About the 4 kinds of input, when the input code is 1000, no output strand generation, so the final output Y_1Y_0 is 00; when the input code is 0100, the final output Y_1Y_0 is 01; when the input code is 0010, the final output Y_1Y_0 is 10; when the input code is 0001, Y_1 strand and Y_0 strand are output at the same time, the final output Y_1Y_0 is 11. The four output signals are in line with the expected results, indicating that the molecular model can achieve 4-2 encoder function.

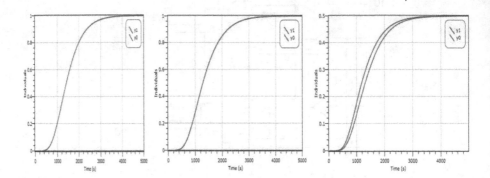

Fig. 11. The three figures are the simulation results of logic circuit which is constructed by AND gate, OR gate and NOT gate. For the first figure, the input is 0100, Y_1Y_0 is 01. You can clearly see that the green curve represents the output of the Y_0 strand that will become obvious after a period of time. The final concentration is 1, the red curve represents the output of the Y_1 strand that did not change and is 0. The second figure above, when the input is 0010, you can clearly see that the red curve represents the output of the Y_1 strand will become obvious after a period of time. The final concentration is 1, the green curve represents the output of the Y_0 strand did not change and is 0. When the input is 0001, you can clearly see after a period of time, the red curve represents the output of the Y_1 strand and the green curve represents the output of the Y_0 strand will become obvious, the final concentration is 1. In third Figure, in order to be able to clearly show that the two curves of Y_0 and Y_1 concentration in the picture, we fine tune the generation speed of the two strands of Y_0 and Y_1 in the last step of the reaction or the generation process of Y_0 and Y_1, so that there is a visible gap between the curves, which is conducive to observation. (Color figure online)

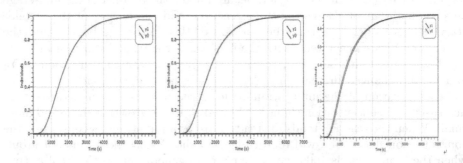

Fig. 12. The three figures are simulation results of logic circuit which is constructed by XOR gate, NOT gate, AND gate. The red curve represents the concentration of Y_1, and the green curve represents the concentration of Y_0. In the third diagram, the red curve is basically the same as the green curve. (Color figure online)

When a logical circuit is optimized by XOR gate, after the two stage reaction, the result is obtained by Fig. 12.

By comparison, it can be seen that the simulation results before and after optimization vary little, but only some changes in time, because after the optimization, XOR gate reaction may take more time. The simulation results are good, which has proved the feasibility and correctness of the logic circuit. However, due to the simplicity of the circuit structure, it can be more easily used in complex circuits.

5   Conclusion

In a word, the basic logic gates of logic circuit are constructed based on the DNA strand displacement. On this basis, through the optimization and comparison of the 4-2 encoder, the constructed logic gates are better applied in the logic circuit.

In the article, we have made some innovative work on the basis of the previous viewpoints, experimental results and a large number of literatures. Firstly, the logic gates and logic circuit are constructed by using combinatorial strand displacement mechanism which has not been applied to construct complex circuits, and the feasibility and practicability of the mechanism have been proved by simulation results. Secondly, the mechanism is different from the other mechanisms of strand displacement, the XOR gate which is constructed by this mechanism has incomparable function, and it is easier to construct more complex circuits in logic circuit. On this basis, we put the strand displacement reaction as a chemical reaction process, in this process, we use the method of chemical reaction network, simulate and analyze of the dynamic process of strand displacement, this is the first successful application through the CRN module visual DSD, and greatly expand the application of CRN in strand displacement reaction.

From the realization of the 4-2 encoder we can see that the same method can be used to achieve the same principle of 8-3 encoder, 16-4 encoder, decimal encoder and other more complex encoders and their corresponding decoding. However, there is a problem with conventional encoders that when the input signal is two or more, the output will be confused. If two or more input signal lines are true, the system must be able to respond in predetermined order, which has a priority problem. Therefore, as the future work, we will focus on according to researching priority encoders that can dispose more than two simultaneous input coded signals in a prioritized order of priority, and will try to use these components to realize data allocation, data selection, process control and other more complex circuit design.

The above results show that DNA strand displacement has broad application prospects both in theoretical research and practical operation. With the continuous progress of biological experimental technology, it will effectively promote the development of DNA computing, and provide new ideas for cryptography, computer science, and medical research. At the same time, it will make greater contribution to the research and application of nanoscale molecular logic circuit.

Acknowledgments. The work for this paper was supported by the National Natural Science Foundation of China (Grant Nos. 61602424, 61472371, 61572446, 61472372), Plan for Scientific Innovation Talent of Henan Province (Grant No. 174100510009), Program for Science and Technology Innovation Talents in Universities of Henan Province (Grant No. 15HASTIT019) and Key Scientific Research Projects of Henan High Educational Institution (18A510020).

References

1. Mao, C., Labean, T.H., Relf, J.H.: Logical computation using algorithmic self-assembly of DNA triple-crossover molecules. Nature **407**, 493–496 (2000)
2. Penchovsky, R., Breaker, R.R.: Computational design and experimental validation of oligonucleotide-sensing allosteric ribozymes. Nat. Biotechnol. **23**, 1424 (2005)
3. Seelig, G., Soloveichik, D., Zhang, D.Y.: Nucleic acid-based logic circuits. Science **314**, 1582–1588 (2006)
4. Zhang, D.Y., Winfree, E.: Control of DNA strand displacement kinetics using toehold exchange. J. Am. Chem. Soc. **131**, 17303–17314 (2009)
5. Zhang, D.Y., Seelig, G.: Dynamic DNA nanotechnology using strand-displacement reactions. Nat. Chem. **3**, 103 (2011)
6. Genot, A.J., Zhang, D.Y., Bath, J.: Remote toehold: a mechanism for flexible control of DNA hybridization kinetics. J. Am. Chem. Soc. **133**, 2177 (2011)
7. Qian, L., Winfree, E.: A simple DNA gate motif for synthesizing large-scale circuits. In: Goel, A., Simmel, F.C., Sosík, P. (eds.) DNA 2008. LNCS, vol. 5347, pp. 70–89. Springer, Heidelberg (2009). https://doi.org/10.1007/978-3-642-03076-5_7
8. Qian, L., Winfree, E., Bruck, J.: Neural network computation with DNA strand displacement cascades. Nature **475**, 368–372 (2011)
9. Zhang, C., Li, D.: Molecular logic computing model based on DNA self-assembly strand branch migration. Chin. Sci. Bull. **58**, 32–38 (2013)
10. Abels, S.G., Khisamutdinov, E.F.: Nucleic acid computing and its potentialto transform silicon-based technology. DNA RNA Nanotechnol. **2**, 13–22 (2015)
11. Song, T., Zheng, P., Wong, M.L.D.: Design of logic gates using spiking neural P systems with homogeneous neurons and astrocytes-like control. Inf. Sci. **372**, 380–391 (2016)
12. Shi, X., Wang, Z., Deng, C., Song, T., Pan, L., Chen, Z.: A novel bio-sensor based on DNA strand displacement. PLoS ONE **9**, e108856 (2014)
13. Song, T., Garg, S., Mokhtar, R.: Analog computation by DNA strand displacement circuits. ACS Synth. Biol. **5**, 898 (2016)
14. Zhang, C., Yang, J., Xu, J.: Molecular logic computing model based on self-assembly of DNA nanoparticles. Chin. Sci. Bull. **56**, 3566–3571 (2011)
15. Shi, X., Lu, W., Wang, Z., Pan, L., Cui, G., Xu, J.: Programmable DNA tile self-assembly using a hierarchical sub-tile strategy. Nanotechnology **25**, 075602 (2014)
16. Sun, J., Wu, Y., Cui, G., Wang, Y.: Finite-time real combination synchronization of three complex-variable chaotic systems with unknown parameters via sliding mode control. Nonlinear Dyn. **88**, 1677–1690 (2017)
17. Genot, A.J., Bath, J., Turberfield, A.J.: Combinatorial displacement of DNA strands: application to matrix multiplication and weighted sums. Angew. Chem. Int. Ed. Engl. **125**, 1227–1230 (2013)
18. Sun, J., Wang, Y., Wang, Y., Shen, Y.: Finite-time synchronization between two complex-variable chaotic systems with unknown parameters via nonsingular terminal sliding mode control. Nonlinear Dyn. **85**, 1105–1117 (2016)

19. Jing, Y., Song, Z., Shi, L., Zhang, Q., Zhang, C.: Dynamically arranging gold nanoparticles on DNA origami for molecular logic gates. ACS Appl. Mater. Inter. **8**, 22451 (2016)
20. Elbaz, J., Yin, P., Voigt, C.A.: Genetic encoding of DNA nanostructures and their self-assembly in living bacteria. Nat. Commun. **7**, 11179 (2016)
21. Jing, Y., Shuoxing, J., Xiangrong, L., Linqiang, P., Cheng, Z.: Aptamer-binding directed DNA origami pattern for logic gates. ACS Appl. Mater. Inter. **8**, 34054–34060 (2016)
22. Mateiu, L., Rannala, B.: Inferring complex DNA substitution processes on phylogenies using uniformization and data augmentation. Syst. Biol. **55**, 259–269 (2006)
23. Li, W., Yang, Y., Yan, H.: Three-input majority logic gate and multiple input logic circuit based on DNA strand displacement. Nano Lett. **13**, 2980 (2013)
24. Alexandru, M., Banu, V., Vellvehi, M.: Design of digital electronics for high temperature using basic logic gates made of 4H-SiC MESFETs. Mater. Sci. Forum **711**, 104–108 (2011)
25. Jing, Y., Chen, D., Dong, Y., Shi, L., Pan, L., Cheng, Z.: Logic nanoparticle beacon triggered by the binding-induced effect of multiple inputs. ACS Appl. Mater. Inter. **6**, 14486–14492 (2012)
26. Soloveichik, D., Seelig, G., Winfree, E.: DNA as a universal substrate for chemical kinetics. Nat. Acad. Sci. USA **107**, 5393–5398 (2010)
27. Nasri, A., Boubaker, A., Khaldi, W., Hafsi, B., Kalboussi, A.: Tuning negative differential resistance in a single molecule transistor: designs of logic gates and effects of various oxygen- and hydrogen-induced defects. Dig. J. Nanomater. Bios. **12**, 99–110 (2017)
28. Sun, J., Shen, Y.: Quasi-ideal memory system. IEEE Trans. Cybern. **45**, 1353–1362 (2015)
29. Wang, Y., Tian, G., Hou, H., Ye, M., Cui, G.: Simple logic computation based on the DNA strand displacement. J. Comput. Theor. Nanosci. **11**, 1975–1982 (2014)
30. Lakin, M.R., Youssef, S., Polo, F., Emmott, S., Phillips, A.: Visual DSD: a design and analysis tool for DNA strand displacement systems. Bioinformatics **27**, 3211–3213 (2011)

The Design of RNA Biosensors Based on Nano-Gold and Magnetic Nanoparticles

Jing Yang[1,2], Zhi-xiang Yin[1,2(✉)], and Jian-zhong Cui[1,2]

[1] School of Mathematics and Big Data, Anhui University of Science and Technology, Huainan, China
jyangh82@163.com, zxyin66@163.com, 983505198@qq.com
[2] School of Electronic and Information Engineering, Anhui University of Science and Technology, Huainan 232001, China
http://www.springer.com/lncs

Abstract. With the application of biosensors in environmental monitoring, these features of low sample concentrations and the need for real-time monitoring feedback in environmental monitoring, make the sensor requirements also increasing. High sensitivity, short response time and low cost are the environmental monitoring biological sensors goal. RNA has a high affinity capacity and sensitivity, and has better thermal stability after hybridization. Combined with the characteristics of nano-gold and magnetic particles in this paper, improving material and probe of electrode, propose design ideas of several biosensors with LNA, PNA for RNA viruses in water monitoring to improve biosensors in environmental monitoring of practicality.

Keywords: RNA biosensors · Magnetic nanoparticles · Gold nanoparticles · Environmental monitoring

1 Introduction

The biosensor is a new sensor technology developed in the last decades. In 1962, Clark et al. [1], have used pH or oxygen electrode by enzyme hydrolysis to detect the product of urine or glucose for the first time, which marked the birth of a biosensor. In 1967, Updike and Hicks have made glucose oxidase immobilized membrane to assemble on the oxygen electrode, and made the biosensor of glucose enzyme electrode. Since then, many scholars put the study of biosensors. Now the biosensor has been widely used in environmental monitoring. The production of biosensors in various fields of clinical medicine, food inspection, environmental monitoring, etc., caused a revolution, and its superiority attracts more researchers and promotes the rapid development of the field. The biosensor can be used in the environment, Hg^{2+}, Pb^{2+}, As^{3+}, Cd^{2+} and other heavy metal ions were detected [2–4]. PAHs, PCBs, dioxins, pentachlorophenol and other organic pollutants in the environment can also be detected [5,6], for biological oxygen demand of water bodies were real-time monitoring [7]; against

© Springer Nature Singapore Pte Ltd. 2017
C. He et al. (Eds.): BIC-TA 2017, CCIS 791, pp. 320–328, 2017.
https://doi.org/10.1007/978-981-10-7179-9_24

atmospheric pollution gases SO_2, NO_2 were analyzed [8], and bacteria, virus were detected in drinking water [9], right pesticide residues in soil and water were analyzed [10].

Generally, biosensor is three major parts from biological sensors, signal converter and signal detecting element. By the signal conversion the biosensor can be divided into electrochemical biosensors, optical biosensors and piezoelectric biosensor. RNA is the same as the detection principle of the biosensor DNA biosensor, which is different hybridization target is a piece of single-stranded RNA.

2 RNA Biosensor

Ribonucleic acid is important biological macromolecules. Each RNA molecule consists of long chains of nucleotide units; each nucleotide unit is composed of a nitrogenous base, a ribose and a phosphate group. RNA mainly includes four kinds of bases, i.e. A adenine, G guanine, C cytosine, U uracil. RNA is the genetic information intermediate carrier having the cell structure of biology, and participates in protein synthesis, also involve in regulation of gene expression. Part of the virus concerned, RNA is the only genetic material, so for virus detection we can choose RNA serves as a probe. RNA virus is a biological virus, belonging to the level of the virus. Their genetic material is composed of ribonucleic acid. Nucleic acid is usually single, also has a double chain. The virus does not like to be alone, they want as quickly as possible to find the parasitic host, so the virus is highly infectious. Virus in drinking water sources directly affects the life and health of humans and other creatures, and therefore it is particularly important for real-time monitoring of drinking water sources.

Currently research on RNA biosensor also has many. But to do real-time monitoring for the environment, it also has many disadvantages: (1) the response time is too long; (2) sensitivity to be improved; (3) reuse low; (4) detection of high costs and so on. How to solve these problems? It also is the direction of research by many scholars. Such as researchers in Polytechnic Institute of New York University of American made an ultra-sensitive biosensor capable of identifying the smallest single solution RNA viruses particles [11]. The sensitivity and response time has been greatly improved, but such sensors for real-time monitoring of the environment (considering the cost), may be enhanced and improved. This paper aims to combine nano-gold and magnetic particles to design RNA biosensors for real-time monitoring of viral in drinking water source (see Fig. 1).

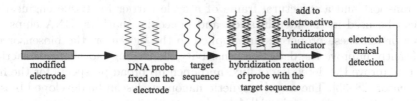

Fig. 1. The detection principle of biosensor

2.1 Gold Nanoparticle

In recent years, the application of nano materials is more and more widespread, and nano-gold was studied earlier, a wider application in nano-materials. Nanoparticles are particles in the 1–100 nm diameter. Because of its unique size structure, making nanoparticles have four basic effects, that the specific surface effect, quantum size effect, volume effect and macroscopic quantum tunneling effect. The most significant feature is a quantum size effect: when the particle size decreases, the blue shift of the absorption spectrum, the band gap increases, the valence band gradually toward low energy, and the conduction band is significantly moved to high energy, then particles is not just inert body, but is a lively giving and taking of electrons electronic objects, or is transformed into a chemically active substances. Moreover, the huge surface area of nanoparticles makes the quantum size effect is more prominent. Currently, gold nanoparticles have been widely applied to the analysis and detection of biological systems. In natan laboratory Au sol of nanoparticles were studied systematically by MPTMS (3-mereaPtoProPyl-trimethoxysilane), MEA (2-merc i.e. toethylamine), etc. to achieve the two-dimensional nano-Au sol from the surface of the gold, glass, etc. assembly [12,13], and the enhancement effect by Raman [14], SPR [15] and other means to study the interaction between Au particles and biological systems. Mirkin et al. [16] used the gold sol, the different temperature Tm of double-stranded DNA transition, based entirely complementary and mismatch, deletion and base insertion, by adjusting the temperature, observing color change in the gold sol-hybrid system to achieve a simple analysis of the DNA mismatch [17,18]. And depending on the type and concentration of the reducing agent can be prepared under laboratory conditions with different particle colloidal gold [19–27], and the method is simple, inexpensive materials. So many scholars applied it in the design of the sensor electrode.

2.2 Magnetic Nanoparticle

Magnetic nanoparticles is the recent development of a new material, the magnetic nanoparticles that has four basic effects common with nanoparticles, but also has unusual magnetic properties, such as superparamagnetic, high coercivity, low Curie temperature and high magnetic susceptibility characteristics. When it is binded to biomolecules (such as nucleic acids, proteins, peptides, etc.) on the surface of the biological species, the biological conjugate species due to dependence and dimensions of the size are similar to biological macromolecules, so it is suitable as an active magnetic resonance imaging, drug delivery and transport and a structural frame of a cycle carrier for tissue engineering, and can be used in the identification and molecular markers, DNA chips and bio-sensors. If these properties are applied to the biosensor, the biosensor can significantly improve the detection sensitivity, shortening biochemical reactions time to improve the detection of flux, and open up broad prospects for the field of biosensor [28–33]. The use of magnetic nanoparticlescan be developed biosensors DNA strand and protein [34] detection, its biggest feature is the process of overcoming the effects of pollutants on PCR test results.

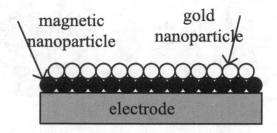

Fig. 2. The electrode is coated magnetic particles and nano-gold

The paper will be prepared using the method of magnetic particles in a homogeneous preparation method, the specific method to reference [35], and the gold nanoparticles modified electrode in the literature [36] is described (see Fig. 2).

2.3   The Design of the RNA Probe Sensor

Due to the content of virus in the monitoring of water is possible low, or is not, so when used for real-time monitoring of RNA, the design of probe will bring a huge challenge. The capture probe for RNA present mainly oligo DNA probes and two kinds of nucleic acid analogs locked nucleic acid (LNA), peptide nucleic acid (PNA) and DNA nanostructures probes. This paper will combine the advantages of magnetic nano-gold particles, using molecular self-assembly techniques to design a biosensor for the detection of RNA viruses.

LNA Probe. LNA (Locked nucleic acid) [37], include six kinds of bases: A, C, G, T, U, mC. It is a special oligonucleotide derivative, the structure comprising one or more 2'-O, 4'-C- methylene –D- furan RNA monomers. This structure is formed by reducing the shrinking effect of the rigid structure of the flexible structure of the ribose, the phosphate backbone to increase the stability of local structures. Since the LNA and DNA/RNA have the same phosphate backbone on structure, so for DNA, RNA, LNA has good ability identify and strong affinity. Compared with other oligonucleotide analogues, LNA has many advantages: (1) complementary double-stranded with the DNA or RNA has strong thermal stability (Tm = 3 8); (2) stability of anti-3'deoxynucleotide enzymatic degradation; (3) LNA-DNA hybrids can activate RNase H; (4) water-soluble, freely penetrate the cell membrane, and easily absorbed by the body; (5) without toxic effects in the body; (6) has efficient automatic oligomerization effect, and synthesis method is relatively simple, partially or fully modified LNA oligonucleotide chain amino acid used in the method were synthesized on an automated DNA synthesizer. Therefore, the LNA is fixed on the electrode of the sensor, for the detection of RNA viruses, that it will greatly increase the sensitivity of the RNA sensor (see Fig. 3).

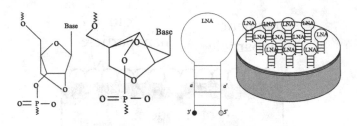

Fig. 3. The molecular structure of LNA

In structuring LNA probes, this particular form of "hairpin" structure to construct LNA probes is chose. Opposite DNA strand, LNA has better selectivity and proposed binding sequence, and the "hairpin" structure allows LNA probes labeled fluorescent substance, using reading way of molecular beacons DNA computing model to detect the content and species of RNA. Ring of "hairpin" probe is LNA chain as identify areas, and fluorescein is labeled on stem areas.

Principle: coding RNA virus with a complementary LNA measured up the chain, which was used as molecular beacons ring identification zone, and then encoded into the structure of molecular beacons. Depending on the virus to be monitored at the end of the stem of the molecular beacon fluorescein different bands is linked, and the quencher is at the end link. The use of self-assembly method to secure fixed before the design on a good electrode. Since stable hairpin structure not encountered before complementary RNA fragments, does not change its initial conditions, hairpin structure is not open, only matched sample of water containing a virus, it will open the hairpin, Since the fluorophore hairpin structure opens and the quencher away from the issue of the corresponding fluorescence, and then the fluorescence detection means for detecting the fluorescence to determine the virus-containing. The probe rapid response, high sensitivity and specificity, so high accuracy detection. And the amount of its special structure makes this probe is still in use after melting cleaning, recycling rate is high, and cost savings. Next how to determine the content of the virus according to the change in fluorescence intensity will be researched (see Fig. 4).

PNA Probe. PNA is a kind of multi-chain amide substituted ribose (or deoxyribose) phosphate backbone of nucleic acid analogues with structural stability, and is not degraded by nucleases and proteases, can be incorporated with a base complementary single-stranded nucleic acids, low cytotoxicity, electrically neutral characteristics (see Fig. 5). PNA with DNA, RNA has a strong binding force, a good sensitivity and high specificity, and because of its nature so that the electrically neutral PNA-DNA, PNA-RNA duplexes are more stable [38] and therefore the development of PNA-based probe needle biosensor to detect viral RNA is also a viable approach. Here PNA chain directly used as a probe, the detection means of the sensor, this change in the transducer changes produced by the process of hybridization recognizable electrical signals (biosensor).

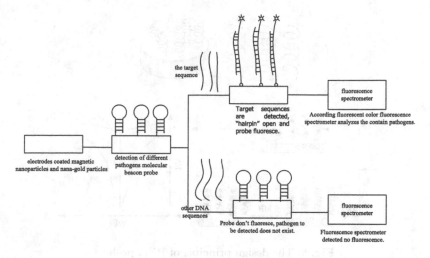

Fig. 4. The design principle of LNA probe

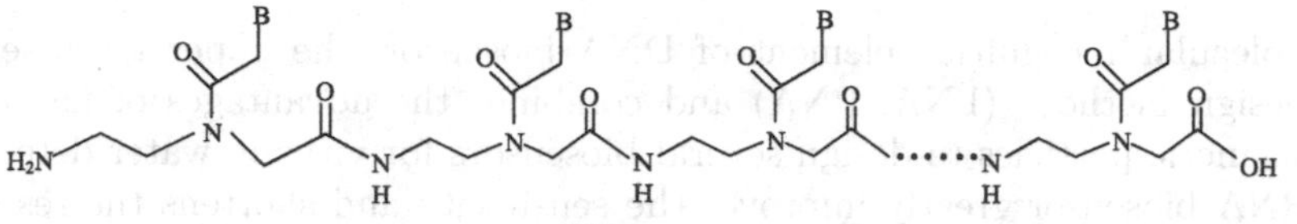

Fig. 5. The molecular structure of PNA

According to the amount of change in the signal after hybridization, PNA target can be accurately quantified. Therefore, the detection of hybridization reaction should be added to hybridization indicator. Because the gold electrode surface using nano materials, and other electrochemical activity associated with identifying agents. Enhancement of the detection signal is amplified, so that the concentration of the indirect detection of the target RNA fragments. Detection of viral species, but also the need for post-hybridization probe for melting and sequenced to determine which contained the virus.

This selection of methylene blue (Methylene blue) as an electroactive indicator, and it is a classic indicator. MB is a compound having an aromatic heterocyclic structure, which can selectively recognize a single, double-stranded DNA. In recent years, many researchers began to use it as an electrochemical indicator. Electrochemical detection is the electrochemical detection system, with micro-pulse voltammetry, detection principle in the following Fig. 6.

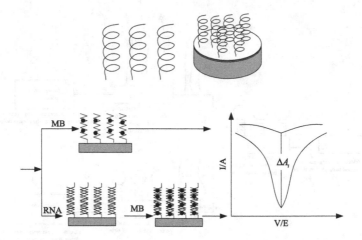

Fig. 6. The design principle of PNA probe

3   Conclution

For molecular recognition element of DNA biosensor, the paper gives several new design method- (LNA, PNA) and combines the advantages of nano-gold and magnetic particles to design several biosensors for virus in water detection. The RNA biosensor greatly improves the sensitivity and shortens the response time. And it also can be repeated use, reduce the cost. With the development of molecular biological techniques and improved experimental conditions, DNA strand in the fixation of the electrode will be increased, so that the biosensor can be designed for environments RNA real-time monitoring.

Acknowledgments. This project is supported by National Natural Science Foundation of China (No. 61702008, No. 61672001).

References

1. Clark, L.C., Lyons, C.: Electrode systems for continuous monitoring in cardiovascular surgery. Ann. Ny. Acad. Sci. **102**, 29–45 (1962)
2. Zhou, Y., Zhang, Y., Pan, F.: A competitive immunochromatographic assay based on a novel probe for the detection of Mercury (II) ions in water samples. Biosens. Bioelectro. **25**(11), 2534–2538 (2010)
3. Ghosh, S., Priyam, A., Bhattacharya, S.C.: Mechanistic aspects of quantum dot based probing of Cu (II) ions: role of dendrimer in sensor efficiency. J. Fluorescence. **19**(4), 723–731 (2009)
4. Swearingen, C.B., Wernette, D.P., Cropek, D.M., Lu, Y., Sweedler, J.V., Bohn, P.W.: Immobilization of a catalytic DNA molecular beacon on Au for Pb(II) detection. Anal. Chem. **77**(2), 442–448 (2005)
5. Yoshitsugu, A., Qian, M., Erin, E., Andrei, L., Hecht, S.M.: Identification of strong DNA binding motifs for bleomycin. J. Am. Chem. Soc. **130**(30), 9650 (2008)

6. Raz, S.R., Bremer, M.G.E.G., Giesbers, M., Norde, W.: Development of a biosensor microarray towards food screening, using imaging surface plasmon resonance. Biosens. Bioelectro. **24**(4), 552–557 (2008)
7. Soh, N., Ueda, T.: Perylene bisimide as a versatile fluorescent tool for environmental and biological analysis: a review. Talanta **85**(3), 1233–1237 (2011)
8. Sassolas, A., Blum, L.J., Lecabouvier, B.D.: Immobilization strategies to develop enzymatic biosensors. Biotechnol. Adv. **30**(3), 489–511 (2012)
9. Ceylan, K.H., Klah, H., Ozgen, C., Alp, A., Hascelik, G.: Mems biosensors for detection of methicillin resistant staphylococcus aureus. Biosens. Bioelectro. **29**(1), 1–12 (2011)
10. Chobtang, J., Boer, I.J.M.D., Hoogenboom, R.L.A.P., Haasnoot, W., Kijlstra, A., Meerburg, B.G.: The need and potential of biosensors to detect dioxins and dioxin-like polychlorinated biphenyls along the milk eggs and meat food chain. Sensors **11**(12), 11692–11716 (2011)
11. Dantham, V.R., Holler, S., Kolchenko, V., Wan, Z., Arnold, S.: Taking whispering gallery-mode single virus detection and sizing to the limit. Appl. Phys. Lett. **101**(4), 1379 (2012)
12. Grabar, K.C., Allison, K.J., Baker, B.E., Bright, R.M., Brown, K.R., Freeman, R.G., et al.: Two-dimensional arrays of colloidal gold particles: a flexible approach to macroscopic metal surfaces. Langmuir **12**(10), 2353–2361 (1996)
13. Baker, B.E., Kline, N.J., Treado, P.J., Natan, M.J.: Solution-based assembly of metal surfaces by combinatorial methods. J. Am. Chem. Soc. **118**(36), 8721–8722 (1996)
14. Koshkin, A.A., Singh, S.K., Nielsen, P., Rajwanshi, V.K., Kumar, R., Meldgaard, M.: LNA (Locked Nucleic Acids): Synthesis of the Adenine, Cytosine, Guanine, 5-Methylcytosine, Thymine and Uracil Bicyclonucleoside Monomers, Oligomerisation, and Unprecedented Nucleic AcidrRecognition. Tetrahedron **54**(14), 3607–3630 (1998)
15. Freeman, R.G., Grabar, K.C., Allison, K.J., Bright, R.M., Davis, J.A., Guthrie, A.P.: Self-assembled metal colloid monolayers: an approach to SERS substrates. Science **267**(5204), 1629–1632 (1995)
16. Lyon, L.A., Musick, M.D., Smith, P.C., Reiss, B.D., Pena, D.J., Natan, M.J.: Surface plasmon resonance of colloidal Au-modified gold films. Sensor. Actuat. B-Chem. **54**(1C2), 118–124 (1999)
17. Mirkin, C.A., Letsinger, R.L., Mucic, R.C., Storhoff, J.J.: A DNA-based method for rationally assembling nanoparticles into macroscopic materials. Nature **382**(6592), 607–609 (1996)
18. Elghanian, R., Storhoff, J.J., Mucic, R.C., Letsinger, R.L., Mirkin, C.A.: Selective colorimetric detection of polynucleotides based on the distance-dependent optical properties of gold nanoparticles. Science **277**(5329), 1078–1081 (1997)
19. Storhoff, J.J., Elghanian, R., Mucic, R.C., And, C.A.M., Letsinger, R.L.: One-pot colorimetric differentiation of polynucleotides with single base imperfections using gold nanoparticle probes. J. Am. Chem. Soc. **120**(9), 1959–1964 (1998)
20. Dykman, L.A., Lyakhov, A.A., Bogatyrev, V.A.: Synthesis of colloidal gold using high-molecular-weight reducing agents. Colloid J. Russ. Acad. Sci. **60**, 700–704 (1998)
21. Zhu, C., Yang, G., Li, H., Du, D., Lin, Y.: Electrochemical sensors and biosensors based on nanomaterials and nanostructures. Anal. Chem. **87**(1), 230 (2015)
22. Shi, H., Zhang, L., Cai, W.: Preparation and optical absorption of gold nanoparticles within pores of mesoporous silica. Mater. Res. Bull. **35**(10), 1689–1695 (2000)

23. Dai, X., Tan, Y., Xu, J.: Formation of Gold nanoparticles in the presence of O-Anisidine and the dependence of the structure of Poly (O-Anisidine) on synthetic conditions. Langmuir **18**(23), 9010–9016 (2002)
24. Lan, X., Jin, Z., Zhao, X., Gou, L.: Preparation of nanogold colloid by chemical reducing with PVP protection. Rare Metal Mat. Eng. **32**(1), 50–53 (2003)
25. Chen, W.X., Wu, W., Chen, H.X.: Preparation and Characterization of nano-colloidal precious metals Fibroin Fibrinogen bit reduction. Sci. China Series B. **33**(3), 185–191 (2003)
26. Wong, Y.T., Manimaran, M., Tay, F.E.: Synthesis and characterisation of alka-nethiolated nanogold clusters for BioMEMS applications. Int. J. Comput. Eng. Sci. **4**(3), 663–666 (2003)
27. Lee, K.M., Park, S.T., Lee, D.J.: Nanogold synthesis by inert gas condensation for immuno-chemistry probes. J. Alloy. Compd. **390**(1C2), 297–300 (2005)
28. Mandal, S., Phadtare, S., Sastry, M.: Interfacing biology with nanoparticles. Curr. Appl. Phys. **5**(2), 118–127 (2005)
29. Lu, N., Gao, A., Zhou, H., Wang, Y., Yang, X., Wang, Y.: Nterfacing biology with nanoparticles. Chin. J. Chem. **34**(3), 308C–316 (2016)
30. Nuber, S., Zabel, U., Lorenz, K., Nuber, A., Milligan, G., Tobin, A.B.: β-arrestin biosensors reveal a rapid, receptor-dependent activation/deactivation cycle. Nature **531**(7596), 661–684 (2016)
31. Safark, I., Safarkov, M.: Magnetic nanoparticles and biosciences. Monatsh. Chem. **133**, 737–759 (2002)
32. Weissleder, R., Bogdanov, A., Neuwelt, E.A., Papisov, M.: Long-circulating iron oxides for MR imaging. Adv. Drug. Deliver. Rev. **16**(2C3), 321–334 (1995)
33. Jordan, A., Scholz, R., Wust, P., Fahling, H., Felix, R.: Magnetic Fluid Hyperther-mia (MFH): cancer treatment with AC magnetic field induced excitation of bio-compatible superparamagnetic nanoparticles. J. Magn. Magn. Mater. **201**(1C3), 413–419 (1999)
34. Nam, J.M., And, S.I.S., Mirkin, C.A.: Bio-bar-code-based DNA detection with PCR-like sensitivity. J. Am. Chem. Soc. **126**(19), 5932–5933 (2004)
35. Nam, J.M., Thaxton, C.S., Mirkin, C.A.: Nanoparticle-based bio-bar codes for the ultrasensitive detection of proteins. Science **301**(5641), 1884–1886 (2003)
36. Zhen, L., Qiao, S., Gao, M.: Preparation of water-soluble magnetite nanocrystals from hydrated ferric salts in 2-pyrrolidone: mechanism leading to Fe_3O_4. Angew. Chem. **44**(1), 123–126 (2004)
37. Koshkin, A.A., Singh, S.K., Nielsen, P., Rajwanshi, V.K., Kumar, R., Meldgaard, M.: LDA (Locked Nucleic Acids): synthesis of the adenine, cytosine, guanine, 5-methylcytosine, thymine and uracil bicyclonucleoside monomers, oligomerisation, and unprecedented nucleic acid recognition. Tetrahedron **54**(14), 3607–3630 (1998)
38. Singh, R.P., Oh, B.K., Choi, J.W.: Application of peptide nucleic acid towards development of nanobiosensor arrays. Bioelectrochemistry **79**(2), 153–161 (2010)

Distributed Fuzzy P Systems with Promoters and Their Application in Power Balance of Multi-microgrids

Wenping Yu[1,2,3], Jun Wang[1,2,3]([✉]), Tao Wang[1,2,3], and Yanxiang Yang[1,2,3]

[1] School of Electrical Engineering and Electronic Information, Xihua University, Chengdu 610039, People's Republic of China
745257101@qq.com
[2] Sichuan Province Key Laboratory of Power Electronics Energy-saving Technologies and Equipment, Xihua University, Chengdu 610039, People's Republic of China
[3] Key Laboratory of Fluid and Power Machinery, Ministry of Education, Xihua University, Chengdu 610039, People's Republic of China

Abstract. This paper proposes distributed fuzzy P systems with promoters for multi-microgrids power balance, where the distributed P systems (dP systems) differ from other P systems with the ability to handle distributed input problems, which makes themselves more suitable for solving control problems. To make full use of the advantages of dP systems and provide a research idea for the power balance of multi-microgrids, promoters and fuzzy theory are introduced into dP systems to characterize a large amount of uncertain and inaccurate information. Moreover, the proposed distributed fuzzy P systems with promoters are applied to fulfill the power balance of multi-microgrids. Finally, the power balance in multi-microgrids as well as the balance between the multi-microgrids and their connecting grid is realized by three cases.

Keywords: Distributed P system · Fuzzy P system · Promoter · Multi-microgrid · Power balance

1 Introduction

Membrane computing, proposed by Păun, has received considerable attention and become a new research field in the world [1,2]. At present, there are three kinds of common membrane computing models: cell-like P systems, tissue-like P systems and neural P systems [3]. P systems are distributed parallel computing devices, but these three common models can't solve a problem in a distributed parallel way after this problem is divided into parts and these subproblems are introduced into the components of a P system which can work on these subproblems in parallel and generate the solution to the original problem by mutual communication [4]. Thus, in order to solve the problem of distributed inputs in the framework of P systems, Păun proposed a distributed structure in 2010, and the corresponding devices are called distributed P systems

© Springer Nature Singapore Pte Ltd. 2017
C. He et al. (Eds.): BIC-TA 2017, CCIS 791, pp. 329–342, 2017.
https://doi.org/10.1007/978-981-10-7179-9_25

(dP systems). P systems have a variety of characteristics (such as distributed, parallel, non-deterministic and easy to achieve communication, etc.) to make themselves suitable for solving all kinds of application problems. Furthermore, dP systems differ from other P systems with the ability to deal with distributed inputs problems, which makes themselves more suitable for control and optimization areas. Up to now, dP systems have been studied in the control and optimization fields, such as digital image processing [5], intelligent environment representation [6] and real-time optimization problem in wireless adaptive network [7], and all of them have achieved good results.

In recent years, microgrids provide a great help for the future development of smart grid, which is expected to help conventional power system to improve its performances, especially under emergency [8,9]. With the increasing importance of microgrid technology and the increasing permeability of distributed generation units (DGs), the concept of multi-microgrids made up by multiple microgrids is proposed. Multi-microgrid is the main way for DGs to access to the grid in the future, the difficulty and complexity of its power balance problem compared with a single microgrid are more prominent, so the study of its energy control and stable operation is of great significance. In addition, P systems have good application prospects in the field of microgrids control and optimization. In [10–12], the common membrane computing models are used to deal with coordinated control and economic operation of a single microgrid, and good control and optimization results are achieved. However, there is no relevant work to the application of P systems in power balance of multi-microgrids.

Due to the randomness and volatility problems when DGs are connected to the grid, the uncertain and inaccurate information contained in the multi-microgrids is more than that of a single microgrid. The promoters and fuzzy theory are integrated into the dP system so that it can better characterize a lot of uncertain and inaccurate information contained in the multi-microgrids, then distributed fuzzy P systems with promoters (PFdP systems) and cell-like fuzzy P systems with promoters (PCF P systems) are proposed. In addition, this paper attempts to apply the proposed PFdP systems and PCF P systems to multi-microgrids power balance for providing a new feasible way. Membrane computing is first used for multi-microgrids power balance in this paper. Furthermore, a simple multi-microgrid system is used as an example to demonstrate the correctness and feasibility of the proposed theory, three cases realize the internal power balance of multi-microgrids and the power balance when multi-microgrids are connected to the grid.

The rest of the paper is organized as follows. Section 2 introduces the preliminaries. Section 3 presents the definitions of PFdP systems and PCF P systems. In Sect. 4, to verify the correctness and feasibility of proposed method, reasoning computations of three cases are implemented. Finally, the paper concludes with Sect. 5.

2 Preliminaries

2.1 Fuzzy Theory

Considering the uncertainty and inaccuracy of the biological cell movement, Ref. [10] introduces the fuzzy theory into the cell-like P systems based on the traditional membrane computing framework, and proposes cell-like fuzzy P systems. The cell-like fuzzy P systems are suitable for handling fuzzy and control problems. Since information of multi-microgrids contains a lot of uncertainty and inaccuracy, the fuzzy multi-sets are used to indicate the objects in cells of fuzzy P systems in this paper. The basic definition of fuzzy multi-sets [13] is as follows.

Definition 1. *Assuming that* $U = (u_1, u_2, \ldots, u_n)$ *is on the universe of discourse, then a fuzzy multi-set* A *on* U *can be defined as* $A = \{\{f_A^1(u_1), f_A^2(u_1), \ldots, f_A^n(u_1)\}/u_1, \ldots, \{f_A^1(u_n), f_A^2(u_n), \ldots, f_A^n(u_n)\}/u_n\}$. *Where,* $\{f_A^1(u_i), f_A^2(u_i), \ldots, f_A^n(u_i)\}/u_i$ *is the membership of* u_i, *whose value is a multi-set on* $[0,1]$, *and representing the frequency of occurrence possibility of* u_i *is* $\{f_A^1(u_i), f_A^2(u_i), \ldots, f_A^n(u_i)\}$.

After the processing of the intracellular objects, there are some detailed works to be completed for fuzzy P systems, such as detailed system definition, system structure, rules and so on. Moreover, there are many apply styles of fuzzy set and fuzzy logic theory, among which fuzzy system based on fuzzy rule is widely used in control field. Thus, this paper uses a common fuzzy logic system-language fuzzy system [14] to construct the basic structure of fuzzy dP systems. The language fuzzy system describes the relationship between variables through fuzzy IF-THEN rules, and its antecedents and conclusions are fuzzy propositions. The form of this fuzzy rule is like that: If x_1 is B_{i1} and x_2 is $B_{i2}, \ldots, x_j$ is B_{ij}, Then y is $C_i, (i = 1, \ldots, k)$, where k is the number of rules in models, and input B_i and output C_i both are fuzzy quantity.

2.2 Multi-microgrids

Generally speaking, through operation control and energy management of a single microgrid, the grid-connected or autonomous operation modes can be realized and the adverse effects of intermittent DGs accessed to the grid can be reduced. At the same time, it can maximize the use of distributed generation output, reduce carbon dioxide emissions, and improve the power quality and reliability of the grid [15]. Compared with a single microgrid, multi-microgrids need to complete three key jobs to achieve system stability and ensure power supply reliability and power quality, including ensuring individual control and normal operation of the internal sub-microgrids under the grid-connected or autonomous operation modes, achieving coordinated control among the sub-microgrids, and maintaining the power balance between the multi-microgrids and the connecting grid. Moreover, due to the randomness and volatility problems of DGs accessed to the grid, the uncertain and inaccurate information contained in multi-microgrids is more than that of a single microgrid [16], so the multi-microgrids power balance problem compared with a single microgrid is more difficult and complex, the study of multi-microgrids energy control and stable operation is of great significance.

In general, a multi-microgrid consists of two or more sub-microgrids, each of which includes some DGs, loads and storage systems. Typically, the sub-microgrids are in parallel or in series to construct a multi-microgrid, then connected with the grid. This paper focuses on the parallel structure of multi-microgrids, as shown in Fig. 1, a multi-microgrid contains two sub-microgrids which consist of random micro-sources (PV and WT), non-tunable micro-source (FC) and tunable micro-source (MT), non-tunable load (L1) and tunable load (L2), and storage systems (Storage 1 and Storage 2). The multi-microgrid is connected to an external grid via a transformer (T1).

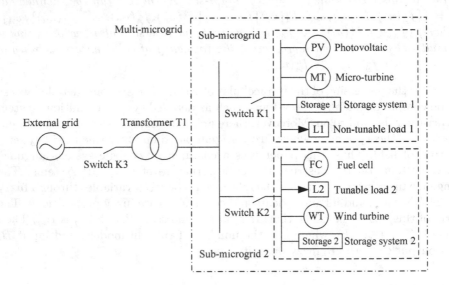

Fig. 1. A sketch map of a simple multi-microgrid.

In this study, PFdP systems are used to fulfill stable operation and power balance of multi-microgrids when the multi-microgrids contain more uncertain and inaccurate information than a single microgrid. In order to better describe a large amount of uncertain and inaccurate information contained in the multi-microgrids, the promoters and fuzzy theory are integrated into dP systems, then PFdP systems and PCF P systems are defined. Besides, the proposed PFdP systems and PCF P systems are applied to the multi-microgrids power balance. And the experiments are implemented to achieve the internal power balance of multi-microgrids and the power balance when multi-microgrids are accessed to the grid.

3   PFdP Systems

In this paper, PFdP system is an improved dP system through the introduction of promoters and fuzzy theory on the basis of dP system, it can better describe the information contained a lot of uncertainty and inaccuracy. Similarly, the dP system contains cell-like P systems as subsystems, the PFdP system contains PCF P systems as itself subsystems.

3.1   Distributed P Systems

Distributed P systems, proposed by Gh. Păun in 2010, aim at solving the problem in a distributed way in membrane computing framework. This proposed distributed structure is based on cell-like P systems whose skin membranes can complete communication according to the designated rules of the antiport type through channels as in tissue-like P systems, where parts of a problem can be introduced as inputs to various components, and then processed in parallel [4]. The respective devices are called dP systems.

Definition 2. [4] *A dP system (of degree $n \geq 1$) is a construct*

$$\Delta = (O, \Pi_1, \ldots, \Pi_n, R) \tag{1}$$

where:

(1) O is an alphabet of objects;

(2) $\Pi_1, \ldots, \Pi_n$ are cell-like P systems with O as the alphabet of objects and the skin membranes labeled with $s_1, \ldots, s_n$, respectively;

(3) R is a finite set of the form $(s_i, u/v, s_j)$, where $1 \leq i, j \leq n, i \neq j$, and $u, v \in V^*$, with $uv \neq \lambda$; $|uv|$ is called the weight of the rule $(s_i, u/v, s_j)$.

The systems $\Pi_1, \ldots, \Pi_n$ are called components of the system Δ and the rules in R are called inter-components communication rules. Each component can take an input, handle it, communicate with other components through the rules, and provide the answer to the problem at the end of the calculation.

Furthermore, the promoters [17–19] combining with fuzzy theory [13,14] are introduced into dP systems and cell-like P systems, then PFdP systems and PCF P systems are proposed.

3.2   PFdP Systems

Definition 3. *A PFdP system is as following.*

$$\Delta = (V, \Pi_1, \ldots, \Pi_n, A_1, \ldots, A_n, R_1, \ldots, R_n) \tag{2}$$

where:

(1) V is a finite nonempty alphabet, whose objects are fuzzy multi-sets and represent the fuzzy quantity of the system inputs;

(2) $\Pi_1, \ldots, \Pi_n$ *are PCF P systems with V as the alphabet of objects and the skin membranes labeled with $s_1, \ldots, s_n$, respectively;*

(3) $A_1, \ldots, A_n$ *are promoters in membranes, each value is fuzzy number between $[0, 1]$. In this paper, the position of the promoter in the system pattern is unaltered, so that it is not necessary to redefine the promoter for each calculation, and its value can be automatically evolved according to the rules in the initial pattern. Once the system has been built, the promoter will evolve repeatedly;*

(4) R *is a finite set of rules with the form $(s_i, ua_i/va_j, s_j)$, where $1 \leq i, j \leq n, i \neq j$, and $u, v \in V^*$, with $uv \neq \lambda$; a_i, a_j are promoters in the membranes. Here, $(s_i, ua_i/va_j, s_j)$ indicates the antiport rule, when the rule is running, the object u in the membrane s_i is exchanged with the object v in the membrane s_j. Moreover, the rules in R are also called the communication rules among the PCF P systems.*

The structure of a PFdP system is shown in Fig. 2. In the model Δ, the initial elements of each subsystem model are similar, only the numbers and types of elements have some difference. In Fig. 3, there are two classes: component class and scheme class. The highest level pattern is scheme class, and the component class which is the lowest level pattern is transitional level. Moreover, among the component classes, they can carry out communication and exchange their objects through communication rules. Scheme class and component class both can be multiple levels, which is conducive to the expansion of system scale.

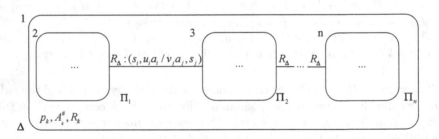

Fig. 2. A PFdP system.

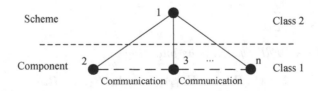

Fig. 3. Tree structure of the PFdP system.

In the PFdP systems, two classes of rules are defined for two levels, in which the membrane of component class is represented by s, the membrane of scheme class is represented by k.

(a) In the skin membrane of component class s, a class rule R_A (also called communication rule) can be used: $(s_i, u_i a_i / v_j a_j, s_j); a_i > a_j$. u_i, v_j represent the objects in two skin membranes, i, j represent the labels of the two skin membranes. The rule indicates that when the promoters a_i, a_j and the objects u_i, v_j exist in the two skin membranes and meet excitation condition $a_i > a_j$, R_A will be activated, and the object u_i in membrane s_i and the object v_j in membrane s_j will be exchanged.

(b) In the scheme class membrane k, a class rule R_B can be used: $p_k a_{k1} a_{k2} \rightarrow (c_k a_{k1} a_{k2}, out); a_{k1} > a_{k2}$. p_k represents the object, and k represents the number of the corresponding promoters and rules. The rule indicates that when the promoters a_{k1}, a_{k2} and the object p_k exist and meet excitation condition $a_{k1} > a_{k2}$, R_B will be activated, and the object p_k will be transformed into c_k which is the output of the system and transported from scheme class membrane k to external environment.

3.3 PCF P Systems

Definition 4. *A PCF P system is as following.*

$$\Pi = (V, \mu, n, \omega_1, \ldots, \omega_m, A_1, \ldots, A_m, R_1, \ldots, R_m, i_0, o_0) \tag{3}$$

where:

(1) V is a finite nonempty alphabet of objects, its definition is consistent with the objects within PFdP systems;

(2) μ represents the membrane structure which composed by m membranes;

(3) n indicates the stages of the PCF P system. Stage contains the import level, central level and export level. As is shown in Fig. 4, membranes 3, 4, 5, 6 are the import levels, membrane 2 is the central level and membrane 1 is the export level. Among them, the export level is the highest stage pattern, the import level is the lowest stage pattern, and the central level which attached to the next stage and the upper stage can do the transition operation. Moreover, the central stage can be multiple levels, the import and export stages only have one;

(4) $\omega_i (1 \le i \le m)$ represents the fuzzy multi-set existing in the areas i of μ;

(5) $A_i (1 \le i \le m)$ is promoter contained in each membrane, its value is fuzzy number between $[0, 1]$. And its definition is also consistent with the promoters within PFdP systems;

(6) $R_i (1 \le i \le m)$ is a finite set of evolution rules existing in the areas i of μ;

(7) i_0 is the input area of whole system;

(8) o_0 is the output area of whole system.

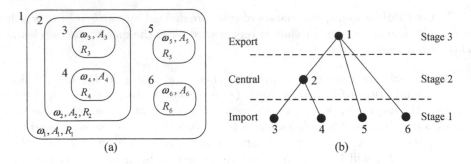

Fig. 4. A PCF P system. (a) Membrane structure; (b) Tree structure.

In addition, a class rule is defined for the import stage and central stage membranes of PCF P systems, in which the membranes of import stage and central stage are represented by n. The rule of the output stage membrane is similar to rule R_B of PFdP systems. In the import stage and central stage membranes n, a class rule R_C can be used: (a) $d_j a_j \rightarrow (c_j a_j, in_{n+1}); d_j > a_j;$ (b) $d_j a_j \rightarrow (c_j a_j); d_j \le a_j$. d_j represents the object, and represents the number of the corresponding promoters and rules. The former indicates that when the promoter a_j and the object d_j exist and meet excitation condition $d_j > a_j$, $R_C(a)$ will be activated, and the object d_j will be transformed into c_j and transported from membrane n to the next stage membrane $n + 1$. In contrast, when the promoter a_j and the object d_j exist and meet excitation condition $d_j \le a_j$, $R_C(b)$ will be activated, and the object d_j will be transformed into c_j and stay in membrane n.

Furthermore, according to Ref. [20], the emergence of a chemical substance makes the occurrence of biochemical reactions possible. This chemical substance (also called promoter) is different from catalysts, it can evolve alone, and the evolution process can be carried out in parallel with the reaction. In this paper, the following two types promoters are defined for the membranes in PFdP systems and PCF P systems. The values of the promoters all are between $[0, 1]$.

(a) Native promoter $A_i^*(1 \le i \le m)$, with the form $A^*[a_1, a_2, \dots, a_m]$, is included in the import membrane and central membrane without import membrane. The position of the native promoter in the model does not change, and its value is automatically evolved by the rules in the initial pattern of the import membrane and central membrane without import membrane.

(b) Derivative promoter $A_i^\#(1 \le i \le m)$ is included in the central membrane, export membrane, the component class membrane and the scheme class membrane. The position of the derivative promoter in the model is unaltered, and its value is automatically evolved according to the rules in the initial pattern of the central membrane, export membrane, the component class membrane and the scheme class membrane. Its form is $A^\#[a_{n-(n+1)}, a_{n-(n+1)-(n+2)}, \dots, a_{n-(n+1)-\dots-(k-1)-k}]$, where $1 < n < k$, $1 < k < m$. $a_{n-(n+1)}, a_{n-(n+1)-(n+2)}, \dots, a_{n-(n+1)-\dots-(k-1)-k}$ are generated accompanying the cell movement between membrane n and the last stage membrane. $A^{\#}$ is a set of promoters from membrane n to membrane k through the membranes $n + 1, \ldots, k - 1$. For instance, when the object d_j in the last stage membrane x meets the corresponding excitation condition, and the relative derivative promoter exists and meets the condition, then the object d_j will be changed by the rule R_x from membrane x to the next stage membrane y. Here, the derivative promoter a_{x-y} is generated with this movement, the subscripts x, y represent the two membranes that carry out the relevant motion.

4 Application of PFdP Systems to Power Balance in Multi-microgrids

Corresponding to the definition of PFdP systems, it is necessary to complete the fuzzification of inputs in PFdP systems. And the simple multi-microgrid system in Sect. 2.2 is used as an example to demonstrate the correctness and feasibility of the proposed theory, three case studies are implemented to realize the internal power balance of multi-microgrids and the power balance when multi-microgrids are connected to the grid.

4.1 Fuzzification of Inputs in PFdP Systems

The values of inputs are between $[0, 1]$ after the fuzzy processing, and represent the deviation degree of the input electrical quantity. Similarly, when data is outputted from the system, it also needs to be processed by defuzzification to be the actual data. The detailed processing is as follows:

For the non-tunable micro-source and non-tunable load, due to their output power are constants, the states of them always are remained. Polarity "±0" is used to express maintaining, the "±0" can be omitted in the calculation in this paper. There are three states of the tunable micro-source and tunable load: increase state, decrease state and maintaining state. Polarity "+" means increase and "−" means decrease, polarity "±0" means maintaining. The range of adjustable power is converted to the value of $[0, 1]$ to complete the fuzzification process. For storage systems, the state of charge (SOC) indicates the charge state of battery, there are three states of storage systems: charge state, discharge state and maintaining state. Polarity "+" means charge and "−" means discharge, polarity "±0" means maintaining. The percentage of electricity is converted to the number of $[0, 1]$ to complete the fuzzification process. In addition, there are two state of each sub-microgrid and each multi-microgrid: selling state and buying state. Polarity "+" means buying and "−" means selling. The power difference is converted to the number of $[0, 1]$ to complete the fuzzification process. In this paper, it is not mathematical in the sense of positive or negative. Promoter also has a polarity, the corresponding promoter also be with "+" and "−".

4.2   Reasoning Calculation

In order to test the correctness and feasibility of the constructed multi-microgrid model based on PFdP system, the reasoning calculation is implemented by using the data which meets the system input object requirements and reflects the multi-microgrid operating status. Taking the multi-microgrid parallel structure studied in this paper as an example, so the model has one PFdP system and two PCF P systems, and the grid acts as an external environment in the PFdP system. A multi-microgrid system model based on PFdP system is established, as shown in Figs. 5 and 6.

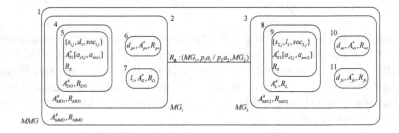

Fig. 5. A multi-microgrid model based on PFdP systems.

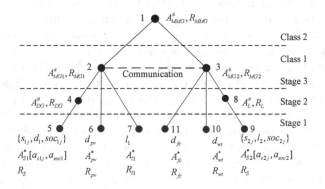

Fig. 6. The tree structure.

Three kinds of operation states data for multi-microgrid are used to carry out the reasoning calculation, namely: (1) the power generations of two sub-microgrids within the multi-microgid are both greater than the power consumptions; (2) the power generations of the two sub-microgrids within the multi-microgrid are both less than the power consumptions; (3) one sub-microgrid power generation is more than power consumption and another sub-microgrid power generation is less than power consumption. The reasoning results are shown in Table 1.

Table 1. Reasoning results of three operation states.

States	The input of system	The output of system
1	$(s_1, 0.2), (d_1, 0.2), (soc_1, 0.55),$ $(d_{pv}, 0.8), (l_1, 0.1), (s_2, 0.1), (l_2, 0.2),$ $(soc_2, 0.7), (d_{wt}, 0.8), (d_{fc}, 0.2)$	$\omega_{out} = -\{(s_1, +0.2), (d_1, -0.2),$ $(soc_1, +0.75), (s_2, +0.1),$ $(l_2, +0.2), (soc_2, +0.7)\}$
2	$(s_1, 0.06), (d_1, 0.1), (soc_1, 0.3),$ $(d_{pv}, 0.1), (l_1, 0.9), (s_2, 0.1), (l_2, 0.2),$ $(soc_2, 0.45), (d_{wt}, 0.1), (d_{fc}, 0.2)$	$\omega_{out} = +\{(s_1, -0.06), (d_1, +0.1),$ $(soc_1, -0.24), (s_2, -0.1),$ $(l_2, -0.2), (soc_2, -0.35)\}$
3	$(s_1, 0.1), (d_1, 0.3), (soc_1, 0.6),$ $(d_{pv}, 0.9), (l_1, 0.1), (s_2, 0.1), (l_2, 0.2),$ $(soc_2, 0.4), (d_{fc}, 0.15), (d_{wt}, 0.2)$	$\omega_1 = \{(s_1, +0.1), (d_1, -0.3),$ $(soc_1, +0.7), (s_2, -0.1),$ $(l_2, -0.2), (soc_2, -0.3)\}$

To make the reasoning process intelligible, a detailed example reasoning process is introduced with case one as an example. When the power generations of two sub-microgrids within the multi-microgid are both greater than the power consumptions, the formula is described as following.

$$\Delta_1 = (V, \mu, \omega_1, \ldots, \omega_{11}, A_1, \ldots, A_{11}, R_1, \ldots, R_{11}, i_0, o_0) \tag{4}$$

where:

(1) $V = \{s_1, s_2, soc_1, soc_2, d_1, d_{pv}, d_{wt}, d_{fc}, l_1, l_2\}$;

(2) $\mu = [[[[]_5]_4[]_6[]_7]_2[[]_9]_8[]_{10}[]_{11}]_3]_1$;

(3) $\omega_1 = \omega_2 = \omega_3 = \omega_4 = \omega_8 = \lambda, \ \omega_5 = \{(s_1, 0.2), (d_1, 0.2), (soc_1, 0.55)\},$ $\omega_6 = (d_{pv}, 0.8), \ \omega_7 = (l_1, 0.1), \ \omega_9 = \{(s_2, 0.1), (l_2, 0.2), (soc_2, 0.6)\}, \ \omega_{10} = (d_{wt}, 0.8), \ \omega_{11} = (d_{fc}, 0.2)$;

(4) $A_1 = A_2 = A_3 = A_4 = A^\#, \ A_5 = [a_{s1} = 0.9, a_{soc1} = 0.8], \ A_6 = A_7 = A_{10} = A_{11} = \lambda, \ A_8 = A^\#, \ A_9 = [a_{s2} = 0.8, a_{soc2} = 0.8]$;

(5) $R_1 = R_2 = R_3 = R_B, \ R_4 = R_5 = R_8 = R_9 = R_C, \ R_6 = R_7 = R_{10} = R_{11} = \lambda, \ R_{1-2} = R_A$;

(6) $i_0 = \{5, 6, 7, 9, 10, 11\}, \ o_0 = \{1, 2, 3, 4, 5, 8, 9\}$.

The detailed reasoning process is described as follows.

Step 1. Objects are included in membranes 5, 6, 7, 9, 10, 11, so the parallel operations start in 5, 6, 7, 9, 10, 11. In membranes 5, there are $s_1 = 0.2, soc_1 = 0.55$, and $s_1 < a_{s1} \& soc_1 < a_{soc1}$. Rule R_5 meets the excitation conditions, hence ω_5 moves into membrane 4. In membranes 9, there are $s_2 = 0.1, soc_2 = 0.6$, and $s_2 < a_{s2} \& soc_2 < a_{soc2}$. Rule R_9 meets the excitation conditions, hence ω_9 moves into membrane 8. In addition, the objects in membranes 6, 7, 10, 11 only have maintaining state, so they are the constants and always stay in the membranes.

Step 2. Membrane 4 gets the object $\omega_5 = \{(s_1, +0.2), (d_1, 0.2), (soc_1, +0.75)\}$ from membrane 5, then $d_1 = 0.2, a_{d1} = a_{s1} - s_1 = 0.7, d_1 < a_{d1}$. Rule R_4 meets the excitation conditions, hence ω_4 moves into membrane 2. Similarly, membrane 8 gets the object $\omega_9 = \{(s_2, +0.1), (l_2, 0.2), (soc_2, +0.7)\}$ from membrane 9, then $l_2 = 0.2$, $a_{l2} = a_{s2} - s_2 = 0.7$, $l_2 < a_{l2}$. Rule R_8 meets the excitation conditions, hence ω_8 moves into membrane 3.

Step 3. Membrane 2 gets the object $\omega_4 = \{(s_1, +0.2), (d_1, -0.2), (soc_1, +0.75)\}$ from membrane 4, then $a_{MG1} = a_{d1} - |d_1| = 0.5 > 0 \& a_{MG2} > 0$. Rule R_2 meets the excitation conditions, hence ω_2 moves into membrane 1. Similarly, membrane 3 gets the object $\omega_8 = \{(s_2, +0.1), (l_2, +0.2), (soc_2, +0.7)\}$ from membrane 8, then $a_{MG2} = a_{l2} - l_2 = 0.5 > 0 \& a_{MG1} > 0$. Rule R_3 meets the excitation conditions, hence ω_3 moves into membrane 1.

Step 4. Membrane 1 gets the objects $\omega_2 = -\{(s_1, +0.2), (d_1, -0.2), (soc_1, +0.75)\}$ from membrane 2 and $\omega_3 = -\{(s_2, +0.1), (l_2, +0.2), (soc_2, +0.7)\}$ from membrane 3. Thus, $a_{MMG} = a_{MG1} + a_{MG2} = 1 > 0$, Rule R_1 meets the excitation conditions, then the object $\omega_{out} = -\{(s_1, +0.2), (d_1, -0.2), (soc_1, +0.75), (s_2, +0.1), (l_2, +0.2), (soc_2, +0.7)\}$ which is the output of the system will be transported to the external environment. This is the end of operation.

The meaning of output result is as follows: $s_1 = +0.2$ and $soc_1 = +0.75$ represent that the storage system 1 is charged to $75\% SOC$; $d_1 = -0.2$ represents that the tunable micro-source reduces power generation; $s_2 = +0.1$ and $soc_2 = +0.7$ represent that the storage system 2 is charged to $70\% SOC$; $l_2 = +0.2$ represents that the tunable load increases power demand. Besides, the polarity "−" included in objects ω_2 and ω_3 indicates that the power generations of the sub-microgrid 1 and the sub-microgrid 2 are both larger than the power consumptions. After the internal control of multi-microgrid system, the system power still cannot maintain balance, so the polarity "−" included in object ω_{out} indicates that multi-microgrid system should sell the power to the grid to maintain itself power balance.

Similarly, in the second case, the reasoning result shows that the multi-microgrid system still cannot maintain its own power balance after its internal control, the system needs to buy the power from the grid to achieve its own power balance, the output reflects the adjustment measure at the next moment. In the third case, the reasoning result shows that the internal balance of the system is maintained through the communication and power exchange between the subsystems. The output object ω_1 indicates that the internal adjustment measure has completed and the internal power balance of the system has been maintained without the need of grid-connection. It can be seen that the correctness and feasibility of the proposed theory are verified through the reasoning results.

5   Conclusions

This paper proposes distributed fuzzy P systems with promoters for multi-microgrids power balance, which provides a new feasible way for solving the problem of multi-microgrids power balance. On the basis of dP systems, the promoters and fuzzy theory are integrated into the dP system so that it can better characterize a lot of uncertain and inaccurate information and makes itself more suitable for control field. In addition, the proposed method is applied to the multi-microgrids power balance, and the correctness and feasibility of the proposed method can be verified through a simple multi-microgrid system. Moreover, three case studies are implemented to achieve the internal power balance of multi-microgrids and the power balance when multi-microgrids are accessed to the grid.

This study focuses on the correctness and feasibility of the proposed method and the results of application examples are obtained by manual computation. To test the superiority of PFdP systems for multi-microgrids energy management and control, our future work will construct the multi-microgrids energy management and control model based on PFdP systems, simulate them on MATLAB, and compare with the traditional control method of multi-microgrids.

Acknowledgment. This work was partially supported by the National Natural Science Foundation of China (No. 61472328), Chunhui Project Foundation of the Education Department of China (No. Z2016143), Research Fund of Sichuan Science and Technology Project (No. 2015HH0057) and Innovation Fund for Graduate Students of Xihua University (No. ycjj2017059).

References

1. Păun, G.: Computing with membranes. J. Comput. Syst. Sci. **61**(1), 108–143 (2000)
2. Păun, G., Rozenberg, G., Salomaa, A.: The Oxford Handbook of Membrane Computing. Oxford University Press, New York (2010)
3. Wang, T., Zhang, G., Pérez-Jiménez, M.J.: Fuzzy membrane computing: theory and applications. Int. J. Comput. Commun. **10**(6), 904–935 (2015)
4. Păun, G., Pérez-Jiménez, M.J.: Solving problems in a distributed way in membrane computing: dP systems. Int. J. Comput. Commun. **2**, 238–250 (2010)
5. Reina-Molina, R., Díaz-Pernil, D., Real, P., et al.: Membrane parallelism for discrete morse theory applied to digital images. Appl. Algebra Eng. Commun. Comput. **26**(1), 49–71 (2015)
6. Elias, S., Rjalakshmi, V., Sivaranjani, S.: Representation of smart environments using distributed P systems. In: Das, V.V., Stephen, J. (eds.) CNC 2012. LNICSSITE, vol. 108, pp. 159–164. Springer, Heidelberg (2012). https://doi.org/10.1007/978-3-642-35615-5_23
7. Elias, S., Gokul, V., Krithivasan, K., et al.: A variant of distributed P systems for real time cross layer optimization. J. Univers. Comput. Sci. **18**(13), 1760–1781 (2012)
8. Bompard, E., Estebsari, A., Huang, T., et al.: A framework for analyzing cascading failure in large interconnected power systems: a post-contingency evolution simulator. Int. J. Elec. Power. **81**, 12–21 (2016)
9. Estebsari, A., Pons, E., Huang, T., Bompard, E.: Techno-economic impacts of automatic undervoltage load shedding under emergency. Electr. Pow. Syst. Res. **131**, 168–177 (2016)
10. Wang, J., Chen, K., Li, M., et al.: Cell-like fuzzy p system and its application in energy management of micro-grid. J. Comput. Theor. Nanos. **13**(6), 3643–3651 (2016)

11. Luo, J., Wang, J., Shi, P., et al.: Micro-grid economic operation using genetic algorithm based on P systems. ICIC Express Letters **9**(2), 609–618 (2015)
12. Liu, T., Wang, J., Sun, Z., Luo, J., He, T., Chen, K.: An improved particle swarm optimization and its application for micro-grid economic operation optimization. In: Pan, L., Păun, G., Pérez-Jiménez, M.J., Song, T. (eds.) BIC-TA 2014. CCIS, vol. 472, pp. 276–280. Springer, Heidelberg (2014). https://doi.org/10.1007/978-3-662-45049-9_44
13. Miyamoto, S.: Multisets and Fuzzy Multisets. Soft Computing and Human-centered Machines. Springer, Japan (2000)
14. Shen, V.R.L.: Knowledge representation using high-level Fuzzy petri nets. IEEE Trans. Syst. Man Cybern. Part A Syst. Hum. **36**(6), 1220–1227 (2006)
15. Hatziargyriou, N., Asano, H., Iravani, R., et al.: Microgrids. IEEE Power Energy **5**(4), 78–94 (2007)
16. Luo, F.J., Chen, Y.Y., Xu, Z., et al.: Multi-agent based cooperative control framework for microgrids' energy imbalance. IEEE Trans. Ind. Inform. **13**(3), 1046–1056 (2017)
17. Pan, L.Q., Păun, G., Song, B.S.: Flat maximal parallelism in P systems with promoters. Theor. Comput. Sci. **623**, 83–91 (2016)
18. Song, B.S., Pan, L.Q.: The computational power of tissue-like P systems with promoters. Theor. Comput. Sci. **641**, 43–52 (2016)
19. Pan, L.Q., Wang, Y.F., Jiang, S.X., Song, B.S.: Flat maximal parallelism in tissue P systems with promoters. Rom. J. Inf. Sci. Tech. **20**(1), 42–56 (2017)
20. Păun, G.: Membrane computing: an introduction. Theor. Comput. Sci. **287**(1), 73–100 (2002)

Cell-Like P Systems with Symport/Antiport Rules and Promoters

Suxia Jiang[1], Yanfeng Wang[1], Jinbang Xu[2], and Fei Xu[2($\boxtimes$)]

[1] School of Electric and Information Engineering,
Zhengzhou University of Light Industry, Zhengzhou 450002, Henan, China
[2] Key Laboratory of Image Information Processing and Intelligent Control,
School of Automation, Huazhong University of Science and Technology,
Wuhan 430074, Hubei, China
fei_xu@hust.edu.cn

Abstract. Cell-like P systems with symport/antiport rules (CSA P systems, for short) are a class of computational models in membrane computing, inspired by the way of transmembrane transport of substances through membrane channels between neighboring regions in a cell. In this work, we propose a variant of CSA P systems called cell-like P systems with symport/antiport rules and promoters (CSAp P systems, for short), where symport/antiport rules are regulated by multisets of promoters, and the computation power of CSAp P systems is investigated. Specifically, it is proved that CSAp P systems working in the maximally parallel mode, having any large number of membranes and promoters and using only symport rules of length 1 or antiport rules of length 2, are able to compute only finite sets of non-negative integers. Furthermore, we show that CSAp P systems with two membranes working in a sequential mode when having at most two promoters and using only symport rules of length 2, or having at most one promoter and using symport rules of length 1 and antiport rules of length 2, are Turing universal.

Keywords: Bio-inspired computing · Membrane computing · Cell-like P system · Symport/antiport rule · Promoter · Computation power

1 Introduction

Membrane computing is a computing paradigm inspired by the architecture and functioning of biological membranes in living cells [18], which is a branch of nature computing and an active research area of bio-inspired computing. Since then membrane computing has been continuously and rapidly developed [19,21]. *Membrane systems* (or *P systems*) are a framework of computational models of membrane computing, which are distributed parallel computing devices. According to the membrane structure of P systems, many classes of P systems were proposed, there exist two main types: *cell-like P systems* [18] and *tissue-like P systems* [15] or *neural-like P systems* [11]. With the motivation of real-life biological processes and theoretical computer science, several variants of P systems have

© Springer Nature Singapore Pte Ltd. 2017
C. He et al. (Eds.): BIC-TA 2017, CCIS 791, pp. 343–358, 2017.
https://doi.org/10.1007/978-981-10-7179-9_26

been proposed [14,30,37,41], and the computation power of various P systems was investigated [6,17,38]. Meanwhile, various P systems combined with some applications were surveyed widely, for instance, with respect to biology systems and synthetic biology [4], the improvement of individual intelligence algorithm [22,23], and electronic circuit design or ecosystems [36,39,40]. For comprehensive details and the most up-to-date resources of membrane computing, we can refer to the P systems web address http://ppage.psystems.eu.

Cell-like P systems are a class of basic computational models based on a hierarchical arrangements of membranes, the nested structure of membranes is called membrane structure, each membrane in the structure is encoded by different digital labels. A membrane present in the skin membrane is called elementary if there are no any other membranes within it, otherwise, it is non-elementary. A compartment (or region) is an closed place delimited by each membrane, in which multisets of symbols or objects and sets of operating rules are stored (corresponding to the abstraction of biochemical substances and reaction processes in cells).

Cell-like P systems with symport/antiport rules (CSA P systems, for short) as a variant of cell-like P systems were initially proposed in [17], which are a class of computational models inspired by the biological phenomena of transmembrane transport of chemicals stored in cells. In CSA P systems, the processes of using rules can be formalized by considering symport rules of the form (x, in) and (x, out) (representing that two molecules pass across a membrane together), and antiport rule of the form $(x, out; y, in)$ (meaning that two molecules pass simultaneously through a membrane in opposite directions). The computation power and efficiency of CSA P systems have been investigated widely [1,20,32].

It is known that a P system can work in several different modes: *maximally parallel* way [29,31]; *minimally parallel* use of rules [5] and *asynchronous* mode [8]. Recently, a *flat maximally parallel* mode formally defined in [24] is an attractive strategy of using rules, in this way, the computation power of tissue P systems with promoters was investigated in [25], where a maximal set of applicable rules associated with each region is chosen in each step, but each rule in the set is applied exactly once at that step). In this paper, the *sequential* mode proposed in [9,12] is considered, that is only one rule can be applied at the level of each membrane in each transition step, and in parallelism at the level of the system [27].

We remark that several variants of cell-like P systems were considered when using rules depending on some specifical contexts, for example, cell-like P systems with catalytic [20], P systems with antimatter [2] and membrane systems with promoters/inhibitors [3] where promoters are used to formalize the reaction enhancing roles of various substances present in cells. Recently, promoters were introduced into cell-like P systems, a variant of cell-like P systems with promoters was proposed in [24], where the computation power and efficiency of P systems with promoters working in the flat maximally parallel way were investigated. Moreover, tissue P systems with promoters were also investigated in [28]. Therefore, it is of interest to construct cell-like P systems with symport/antiport rules and promoters. With the motivation of the open problem, in what follows, we consider a variant of CSA P systems with promoters, where symport and antiport rules may be regulated by multisets of promoter objects.

In this paper, a variant of CSA P systems called cell-like P systems with symport/antiport rules and promoters (CSAp P systems, for short) is proposed, we investigate the computation power of CSAp P systems working in the sequential mode. The main contributions of the current work are summarized as the following two points:

(1) Promoters are considered by cell-like P systems with symport/antiport rules, we construct a variant of CSA P systems, called cell-like P systems with symport/antiport rules and promoters (CSAp P systems). In CSAp P systems, the symport rules and antiport rules may be regulated by promoters regarded as the specified objects of permitting contexts.
(2) The computation power of CSAp P systems is investigated. Specifically, in the case of maximal parallelism of using rules, it is proved that CSAp P systems with any number of membranes and arbitrary number of promoters, by using only symport rules of length 1 or using only antiport rules of length 2, are able to only generate finite sets of non-negative integers. Moreover, we further proved that CSAp P systems of degree two working in a sequential way when having at most two promoters and using only symport rules of length 2, or having at most one promoter and using symport rules of length 1 and antiport rules of length 2, are Turing universal.

2   Cell-Like P Systems with Symport/Antiport Rules and Promoters

In this section, we first recall some basic concepts and notations of formal language theory [26] and membrane computing [21], for further details and comprehensive information of them, the reader can refer to [7]. Subsequently, we elucidate the definition of communication P systems with promoters and illustrate a CSAp P system with a given example.

An *alphabet* Γ is a finite non-empty set, in which there are many different *symbols* as its elements, an ordered sequence of symbols is defined as a *string*, the empty string is represented by λ, and the set of all strings over Γ is represented by Γ^*, we denote the set of non-empty strings by $\Gamma^+ = \Gamma^* \setminus \{\lambda\}$. A *multiset* $\mathcal{M}$ over the alphabet Γ is defined as a two-tuples (Γ, f), where $f : \Gamma \to \mathbb{N}$ is a mapping, $\mathbb{N}$ is the set of natural numbers. We denote by $M_f(\Gamma)$ the set of all finite non-empty multisets over Γ.

Definition 1. *A cell-like P system with symport/antiport rules and promoters, of degree $q \geq 1$, is a tuple*

$$\Pi = (\Gamma, \mathcal{E}, \mu, \mathcal{M}_1, \ldots, \mathcal{M}_q, \mathcal{R}_1, \ldots, \mathcal{R}_q, i_{out}),$$

where

- Γ is an alphabet of objects (corresponding to a finite non-empty set);
- $\mathcal{E} \subseteq \Gamma$ is the set of objects initially presented in the environment;
- μ is a rooted tree with q nodes labeled by $1, \ldots, q$ (in other words, represents the membrane structure of Π including q nested membranes labeled with $1, \ldots, q$, respectively);
- $\mathcal{M}_i, 1 \leq i \leq q$, are finite multisets of objects over Γ associated with the region i;
- $\mathcal{R}_i, 1 \leq i \leq q$, are finite sets of communication rules associated with the corresponding region i, of the following forms:
  - Symport rules: (u, out) or $(u, out)|_P$, and (u, in) or $(u, in)|_P$, where $u \in M_f(\Gamma)$, $|u| > 0$, and $P \subseteq \Gamma$ is a non-empty set of promoters (also called promoter objects);
  - Antiport rules: $(u, out; v, in)$ or $(u, out; v, in)|_P$, where $u, v \in M_f(\Gamma)$, $|u| > 0$, $|v| > 0$, and P is also a non-empty set of promoters;
- $i_{out} \in \{0, 1, \ldots, q\}$ is the output region.

Several notations of the system Π are explained as follows: (1) $\mathcal{E}$ as a subset of Γ may be empty, it means that there does not exist the exchange of substances between the system Π and the environment; (2) $\mathcal{M}_1, \ldots, \mathcal{M}_q$ respectively represents the finite multiset of objects initially located in the system corresponding to each region or membrane with label $i \in \{1, \ldots, q\}$; (3) $\mathcal{R}_1, \ldots, \mathcal{R}_q$ denote finite sets of communication rules associated with each membrane with label i ($1 \leq i \leq q$), with or without multiset of promoters; (4) for each membrane with label $i \in \{1, \ldots, q\}$, the case of $i = 1$ (resp., $i = 0$) denotes the skin membrane (resp., the environment), and $p(i)$ is defined as the *parent membrane* of membrane with label i, thus the environment is the "parent" of the skin membrane, we have $p(1) = 0$; (5) the length of communication rules are defined in the usual way described for the basic cell-like P systems with symport/antiport rules as follows: a symport rule $(u, in/out)$ or $(u, in/out)|_P$ (resp., an antiport rule $(u, out; v, in)$ or $(u, out; v, in)|_P$) is defined as $|u|$ (resp., $|u| + |v|$); (6) i_{out} is a distinguished region encoded as the output of the system.

In this paper, we assume a global clock for all regions of the system Π, a *configuration* of such a P system in each time is transformed into another one by using symport/antiport rules in a chosen modes, which is described by the multisets of objects over Γ present in each region of this system at that time, and the multiset of objects over $\Gamma \setminus \mathcal{E}$ associated with the environment at that moment (also, we have an arbitrary large number of copies of objects from $\mathcal{E}$). The *initial configuration* is $(\mathcal{M}_1, \ldots, \mathcal{M}_q; \emptyset)$.

Starting from the initial configuration, we get a *transition* between two adjacent configurations of the system, and a sequence of transitions is called a *computation*. After a period of time, if a computation halts when the system reaches a configuration when no rules are applicable at that moment, we call the current configuration as the *halting configuration*. Only a halting computation gives a result which refers to the number of copies of objects present in the output region i_{out}.

A general symport rule denoted by $(u, out) \in \mathcal{R}_i$ (resp., $(u, in) \in \mathcal{R}_i$) is used to a configuration at a moment if only the multiset u present in membrane

i (resp., in the parent membrane $p(i)$). A symport rule associated with a set of promoters P is denoted by $(u, out)|_P \in \mathcal{R}_i$ (resp., $(u, in)|_P \in \mathcal{R}_i$), which is applicable to a configuration only if a multiset of promoter objects from P is present in the same region with u (resp., only if a multiset of promoter objects from P is present in membrane i and the multiset u is present in its parent membrane $p(i)$). When a symport rule $(u, out)|_P$ (resp., $(u, in)|_P$) is applied at one step, the multiset u is sent out of membrane i (resp., brought into membrane i). However, we note that a symport rule of form $(u, in)|_P$ (here $u \in \mathcal{E}$ and P is a multiset of objects in the skin membrane) is not allowed when CSAp P systems working in the maximally parallel mode, because the application of such rules would lead to an infinite iteration of introducing u into a region.

An antiport rule is denoted by $(u, out; v, in) \in \mathcal{R}_i$ (resp., $(u, out; v, in)|_P \in \mathcal{R}_i$), which is applicable to a configuration at some point if only the multiset u appears in membrane i and the multiset v presents in the parent membrane $p(i)$ (resp., only if both the multiset u and the multiset of promoter objects from P are placed in membrane i, as well as the multiset v present in the parent membrane $p(i)$). In this way, u are sent to the parent membrane $p(i)$ from membrane i, and v are brought into membrane i.

For CSAp P systems working in a maximally parallel way, the presence of promoter objects associated with a set of rules makes it possible to use rules in the set as many times as possible without any restriction. Specifically, rules with multisets of promoter objects from a set $\mathcal{R}_i$ can be used only if the multiset of promoters represented by P is also placed in region i. However, the promoter objects are not necessarily directly participating in the rules at one step, that is, the promoters are not modified by the application of the associated rule, but they may be regarded as general objects to participate in other use of rules, and then may be exchanged at the same step.

In what follows, rules of CSAp P systems are applied in sequential way at the level of membranes: in each step, for each region of the system, at most one rule can be used once (if there are more than one rule are applicable to the current configuration, one of them is nondeterministically chosen and applied); the rules are used in parallelism at the level of system: in each step, all regions which have one applicable rule must do it. Note that this sequential way of applying rules has one restriction: if certain specified objects as promoters participate in a enabled rule at one step, the rule is the only one which is applied for those objects at that step, then at the next step, as general objects, they could participate in the interaction by means of the corresponding rules.

We denote by $N(\Pi)$ a set of natural numbers computed by this system Π, and by $NOcP_m(pro_k; sym_t, anti_q; X)$, $X \in \{max, sequ\}$ the family of all sets of natural numbers computed by Π, where m refers to the number of membranes in the system, k denotes the number of promoter objects associated with each rule, using symport rules of length at most t and antiport rules of length at most q, and working in the transition mode X. If any one of parameters in the set $\{m, k, t, q\}$ is not bounded, it is replaced by $*$.

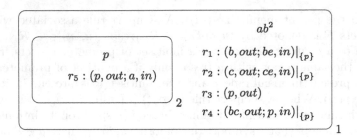

Fig. 1. The example system Π_{exam}

In what follows, we illustrate a CSAp P system with a given example.

Example 1. We consider a CSAp P system Π_{exam} shown in Fig. 1, having one membrane labeled with 2 placed in the skin membrane labeled with 1. The multisets of objects ab^2c^2 are initially placed in membrane with label 1, one copy of object p is located in membrane with label 2, any large number of copies of objects b, c and e are stored in the environment. The membrane 1 is the output region, where the number of copies of object e corresponds to the result of computation of the system. Let us describe the system as

$$\Pi_{exam} = (\{a, b, c, p\}, \{b, c, e\}, [\, [\ ]_2\,]_1, ab^2, p, \mathcal{R}_1, \mathcal{R}_2, 1),$$

and the following sets of rules

$$\mathcal{R}_1 = \{r_1 : (b, out; be, in)|_{\{p\}}, r_2 : (c, out; ce, in)|_{\{p\}}, r_3 : (p, out), r_4 : (bc, out; p, in)|_{\{e\}}\},$$
$$\mathcal{R}_2 = \{r_5 : (p, out; a, in)\}.$$

We now see how the system Π_{exam} works in the modes of maximal parallelism. At step 1, only rule r_5 from $\mathcal{R}_2$ is enabled and used, one copy of object p is sent to membrane with label 1 and one copy of object a is brought into membrane with label 2. Then, at step 2, with the presence of a promoter object p inside membrane 1, a maximal multiset of applicable rules $\{r_1, r_2, r_3\}$ is chosen and enabled. Two copies of object b (resp., c) are sent to the environment and the multiset of objects be (resp., ce) are brought into membrane 1 by using rule r_1 (resp., r_2) two times, and the number of object e in membrane 1 is increased by two at each time as long as rules r_1, r_2 keep being applied; synchronously, the promoter object p is also sent the environment at the same step by using rule r_3. At the next step, rule r_4 is applied, one copy of object b together with one copy of object c are sent to the environment, and the object p is brought back into membrane 1. At step 4, the maximal set of rules $\{r_1, r_2, r_3\}$ is applied again, but each rule in the set is used only one time, respectively, and then one copy of each object b, c and six copies of object e are present in membrane 1 at that moment. At step 5, by using rule r_4 again, objects b and c are together sent to the environment, and one copy of object p is brought into membrane 1, then the computation halts. Thus, the number generated by Π_{exam} working in the mode of maximal parallelism is 6.

It is well-known that $NFIN$ is referred to a family of all finite sets of positive integers and NRE represents a family of recursively enumerable sets of natural numbers [10].

The following fundamental results Theorem 1 can be inferred from some existing results (see Theorems 5.3 and 5.4 in Sect. 5 in [28]), because tissue P systems with one cell and cell-like P systems with one membrane are equivalent.

Theorem 1. $NOcP_1(pro_1; sym_2; max) = NOcP_1(pro_1; sym_1, anti_2; max) = NRE$.

3   Computation Power of Cell-Like P Systems with Symport/Antiport Rules and Promoters

In this section, the computation power of CSAp P systems are investigated. Specifically, we prove that CSAp P systems with any number of membranes and promoters working in the maximally parallel mode, and using only symport rules or antiport rules are able to compute only finite sets of non-negative integers. Simultaneously, the computational completeness of CSAp P systems with using rules in the sequential mode is investigated by simulating register machine [13]: a CSAp P system, having two membranes and two promoters associated with rules, by using only symport rules of length 2, as well as having two membranes and one promoter, by using symport rules of length 1 and antiport rules of length 2, are Turing universality.

A *register machine* is denoted by $M = (m, H, l_0, l_h, I)$, where m is the number of registers; H is the set of instruction labels; the initial instruction is labeled with $l_0 \in H$, and the halting instruction is labeled with $l_h \in H$ (corresponding to instruction HALT); I is the set of program instructions, of which any one instruction is labeled by only one label from H, that is, there exists the one-to-one correspondence between labels and instructions.

Concretely, each program instruction from I is one of three types: ADD instruction $l_i : (\text{ADD}(r), l_j, l_k)$ shows that the corresponding register r is added 1, and then the previous instruction label l_i is replaced by the next instruction label l_j or l_k (being chosen non-deterministically); SUB instruction $l_i : (\text{SUB}(r), l_j, l_k)$ expresses that register r is subtracted 1 (if it is non-zero) and replaced by the instruction labeled with l_j, otherwise (namely the register r is zero), the present instruction directly go to the next instruction labeled with l_k; $l_h : \text{HALT}$ is the halting instruction, with the appearance of l_h, there are no instructions can be used, so the computation halts.

It is known that the set of all natural numbers computed by a register machine M is denoted by $N(M)$, and a computation of M is described as follows: with all registers empty, the machine starts from the initial instruction label l_0, then proceeds to apply various program instructions with respect to labels indicated by ADD instructions or SUB instructions. When the register machine reaches the halt instruction l_h at some point, the computation halts, we define the number n stored in the first register at that time as the computational result by M. A non-deterministic register machine can precisely generate a family of sets of recursively enumerable natural numbers, it follows that the machine can characterize NRE [16].

Theorem 2. $NOcP_*(pro_*; sym_1; max) \subseteq NFIN$.

Proof. Obviously, for a CSAp P system with only symport rules of length 1 and working in the maximally parallel mode, in order to increase the number of objects of this system, if and only if such symport rules as (u, in) or $(u, in)|_p$ ($u \in \mathcal{E}$, P is a multiset of objects in the skin membrane) are applied. However, these applications would lead to an infinite iteration of introducing object u into the system, and the computation can not stop. Therefore, the number of finite objects initially present in the system can only be reduced or remain the same, that is, a set of numbers generated by such a system is included in $NFIN$.

Theorem 3. $NOcP_*(pro_*; anti_2; max) \subseteq NFIN$.

Proof. For a CSAp P systems working in the maximally parallel manner, and using only antiport rules of length 2 $(u, out; v, in)$ or $(u, out; v, in)|_p$ ($u, v \in \Gamma$, and $|u| = |v| = 1$), the number of objects (including promoter objects) in any one region of the system cannot be changed. Hence, the number of objects initially stored in the system remain the same during the computational process. Hence, only finite sets of natural numbers can be generated by communication P systems with promoters.

In what follows, two computationally universal results are obtained by communication P systems when the suitable combination between promoter objects and the symport/antiport rules is considered.

Theorem 4. $NOcP_2(pro_2; sym_2; sequ) = NRE$.

Proof. We only need to prove the inclusion $NRE \subseteq NOcP_2(pro_2; sym_2; sequ)$ in the sense that the reverse inclusion can be obtained from the Church-Turing thesis.

A communication P system with promoters Π, consisting of two membranes and symport/antiport rules associated with one promoter, is constructed to simulate a register machine $M = (m, H, l_0, l_h, I)$, where only symport rules of length 2 are applied in a sequential manner.

$$\Pi = (\Gamma, \mathcal{E}, \mathcal{M}_1, \mathcal{M}_2, \mathcal{R}_1, \mathcal{R}_2, 1),$$

where

- $\Gamma = \{a_i \mid 1 \le i \le m\} \cup \{l, l', l'', l''' \mid l \in H\} \cup \{e, p\}$,
- $\mathcal{E} = \{a_i \mid 1 \le i \le m\} \cup \{l \mid l \in H\}$,
- $\mu = [\,[\ ]_2\,]_1$,

- $\mathcal{M}_1 = \{l_0, e\} \cup \{l', l''' \mid l \in H\}$, $\mathcal{M}_2 = \{p\} \cup \{l'' \mid l \in H\}$, and each set of rules $\mathcal{R}_i$ associated with membrane i is constructed as follows:
- For each ADD instruction $l_i : (\text{ADD}(r), l_j, l_k)$ of M,
  - the rules in $\mathcal{R}_1$ are considered as follows:
    $r_1 : (l_i l_i', out) \mid_{\{l_i'' l_i'''\}}$,
    $r_2 : (l_i' l_j, in)$,
    $r_3 : (l_i' l_k, in)$,
    $r_4 : (p, out) \mid_{\{l_i'\}}$,
    $r_5 : (p a_r, in)$;
  - the rules in $\mathcal{R}_2$ are considered as follows:
    $r_6 : (e l_i, in) \mid_{\{l_i''\}}$,
    $r_7 : (l_i l_i'', out)$,
    $r_8 : (l_i'' l_i''', in) \mid_{\{p\}}$,
    $r_9 : (p, out) \mid_{\{l_i'''\}}$,
    $r_{10} : (l_i', in) \mid_{\{l_i'''\}}$,
    $r_{11} : (l_i'' l_i''', out) \mid_{\{l_i'\}}$,
    $r_{12} : (p l_i'', in) \mid_{\{l_i'\}}$,
    $r_{13} : (e l_i', out) \mid_{\{p\}}$.

An ADD instruction l_i is simulated by Π with the following processes: At step 1, with the presence of promoter object l_i'' in membrane 2, rule r_6 is enabled, objects l_i and e are both brought into membrane 2, then the object l_i will be sent back to membrane 1 together with object l_i'' at the next step by using rule r_7. At step 3, in the influence of promoter objects $l_i'' l_i'''$ present in membrane 1, two objects l_i, l_i' are sent to the environment by applying rule r_1, in simultaneously parallel way, l_i'' and l_i''' as general objects, with the presence of promoter object p in membrane 2, are again brought into membrane 2 by applying rule r_8. At step 4, due to one copy of object l_i' presenting in the environment, it carries one copy of object l_j or l_k into membrane 1 by applying rule r_2 or r_3 (non-deterministically chosen), meanwhile, object p is moved from membrane 2 to membrane 1 by applying rule r_9 in the influence of a promoter object l_i'''. Then, by using rule r_4 associated with a promoter object l_i', object p will be sent to the environment at the next step, as well as the object l_i' will be brought into membrane 2 at the next step by applying rule r_{10}. At step 6, because of one copy of object p appearing in the environment, rule r_5 is applicable, one copy of object a_r is brought into membrane 1 together with the object p, synchronously, two objects l_i'', l_i''' are sent out of membrane 2 under the motivation of promoter object l_i' by applying rule r_{11}. At step 7, rule r_{12} is enabled and used, objects p and l_i'' are gotten back to membrane 2. At step 8, with the presence of p as a promoter in membrane 2, by applying rule r_{13}, objects e and l_i' are sent back to membrane 1. Hence, the system starts to simulate an instruction with label l_j or l_k.

Therefore, ADD instruction l_i can be correctly simulated by such P system Π.

- For each SUB instruction $l_i : (\text{SUB}(r), l_j, l_k)$ of M,
  - the rules in $\mathcal{R}_1$ are considered as follows:

$r_{14} : (l_i l'_i, out) \mid_{\{l''_i l'''_i\}},$

$r_{15} : (l'_i l_k, in),$

$r_{16} : (pa_r, out) \mid_{\{l'_i\}},$

$r_{17} : (pl_j, in);$

$r_{18} : (l_k, out) \mid_{\{l_j\}},$

- the rules in $\mathcal{R}_2$ are considered as follows:

$r_{19} : (el_i, in) \mid_{\{l''_i\}},$

$r_{20} : (l_i l''_i, out),$

$r_{21} : (l''_i l'''_i, in) \mid_{\{p\}},$

$r_{22} : (p, out) \mid_{\{l'''_i\}},$

$r_{23} : (l'_i, in) \mid_{\{l'''_i\}},$

$r_{24} : (l''_i l'''_i, out) \mid_{\{l'_i\}},$

$r_{25} : (pl''_i, in) \mid_{\{l'_i\}},$

$r_{26} : (el'_i, out) \mid_{\{p\}}.$

A SUB instruction l_i is simulated by Π constructed above in the following way: In the first four steps, by using each of rules $r_{19}, r_{20}, r_{21}, r_{14}, r_{15}, r_{22}$ from $\mathcal{R}_\in$ for SUB instruction (respectively corresponding to rules $r_6, r_7, r_8, r_1, r_3, r_9$ from $\mathcal{R}_\in$ for ADD instruction), the simulation process of a SUB instruction is similar as that of a ADD instruction. From step 5 on, we have two cases.

- If there exists at least one copy of object a_r in membrane 1 (meaning that the number stored in register r is non-empty). In this case, at step 5, rule r_{16} can be applied, and then in the influence of promoter object l'_i, object p together with one copy of object a_r are sent to the environment (the number of object a_r is reduced, representing that the number stored in register r is decreased by one), at the same step, l'_i as a general object is also brought into membrane 2 by applying rule r_{23}. At the next step, object p located in the environment carries one copy of object l_j into membrane 1 by applying rule r_{17}, meanwhile, under the motivation of promoter object l'_i, two objects l''_i, l'''_i are sent from membrane 2 to membrane 1 by applying rule r_{24}. At step 7, in the influence of object l_j (here it is regarded as a promoter object), rule r_{18} is enabled, object l_k is sent to the environment (corresponding to the system starts to simulate the instruction l_j), as well as objects p and l''_i are gotten back to membrane 2 by using rule r_{25} at the same step. At the last step, with the appearance of a promoter object p in membrane 2, rule r_{26} is applicable, two objects e, l'_i are sent back to membrane 1. Thus, the system starts to simulate an instruction with label l_j.

- If there is no object a_r in membrane 1 (corresponding to the number stored in the currently simulated register r is 0). At step 5, only rule r_{23} is applicable, and object l'_i is brought into membrane 2, and it is regarded as a promoter object at the next step, rule r_{24} is enabled and applied, two objects l''_i, l'''_i are sent from membrane 2 to membrane 1. At step 7, under the motivation of promoter object l'_i, objects p and l''_i are gotten back to membrane 2 by using rule r_{25}. At step 8, with the appearance of object p in membrane 2, rule r_{26} is applicable, objects e and l'_i are sent back to membrane 1. Hence, the system starts to simulate an instruction with label l_k.

Thus, the SUB instruction of M can be exactly simulated by this system Π.

During the simulation of M, when the object l_h appears in membrane 1 at a certain step, no rule can be applied in this system, then the computation halts. At that time, the number of copies of objects a_1 remaining in membrane 1 corresponds to the result computed by system Π, thus $N(M) = N(\Pi)$.

Theorem 5. $NOcP_2(pro_1; sym_1, anti_2; sequ) = NRE$.

Proof. It is a must to prove the inclusion $NRE \subseteq NOcP_2(pro_1; sym_1, anti_2; sequ)$, and then the reverse inclusion can be obtained from the Church-Turing thesis.

A communication P system with promoters Π, of degree two, by using symport/antiport rules associated with one promoter, is constructed to simulate a register machine $M = (m, H, l_0, l_h, I)$, where symport rules of length 1 and antiport rules of length 2 are applied in a sequential manner.

$$\Pi = (\Gamma, \mathcal{E}, \mathcal{M}_1, \mathcal{M}_2, \mathcal{R}_1, \mathcal{R}_2, 1),$$

where

- $\Gamma = \{a_i \mid 1 \leq i \leq m\} \cup \{l, l', l'', l''', l^{iv} \mid l \in H\} \cup \{b, b'\}$,
- $\mathcal{E} = \{a_i \mid 1 \leq i \leq m\} \cup \{l'', l^{iv} \mid l \in H\}$,
- $\mu = [\, [\ ]_2\,]_1$,
- $\mathcal{M}_1 = \{l_0, b\}$, $\mathcal{M}_2 = \{b'\} \cup \{l', l''' \mid l \in H\}$, each set of rules $\mathcal{R}_i$ associated with membrane i is constructed as follows:
- For each ADD instruction $l_i : (\text{ADD}(r), l_j, l_k)$ of M,
  - The set $\mathcal{R}_1$ consists of the following rules:
    - $r_1 : (l_i, out; l''_i, in)$,
    - $r_2 : (b, out; a_r, in) \mid_{\{l''_i\}}$,
    - $r_3 : (b, in)$,
    - $r_4 : (l''_i, out; l_j, in) \mid_{\{l'''_i\}}$,
    - $r_5 : (l''_i, out; l_k, in) \mid_{\{l'''_i\}}$,
  - The set $\mathcal{R}_2$ consists of the following rules:
    - $r_6 : (l'''_i, out; l''_i, in)$,
    - $r_7 : (l''_i, out; b, in)$,
    - $r_8 : (b, out; l'''_i, in)$;

An ADD instruction l_i is simulated by Π as follows: At step 1, because of the presence of object l_i (here $l_i \neq l_h$) in membrane 1, rule r_1 is enabled, object l_i is sent to the environment and one copy of object l''_i initial located in the environment is brought into membrane 1. At step 2, in the influence of l''_i as a promoter object, object b is sent to the environment and one copy of object a_r is sent into membrane 1 by applying r_2; synchronously, object l''_i is sent into membrane 2 and object l'''_i is sent out of membrane 2 by using r_6. Subsequently, object b is gotten back by using rule r_3. At step 4, object l''_i (resp., b) is sent out of (resp., sent to) membrane 2 by applying rule r_7, then object l''_i is sent to the environment and one copy of object l_j or l_k (we remark that $l_j \neq l_k$) is brought into membrane 1 by using rule r_4 or r_5 (non-deterministic chosen) associated with a promoter object l_i'''' at the next step, meanwhile, object l_i'''' (resp., object b) is sent back to membrane 2 (resp., membrane 1). Thereupon the system starts to simulate an instruction with label l_j or l_k.

Hence, ADD instruction l_i can be correctly simulated by such P system Π.

- For each SUB instruction $l_i : (\text{SUB}(r), l_j, l_k)$ of M,
  - The set $\mathcal{R}_1$ consists of the following rules:
    $r_9 : (l_i, out; l_i'', in) \mid_{\{l_i''''\}}$,
    $r_{10} : (a_r, out; l_i^{iv}, in) \mid_{\{l_i'\}}$,
    $r_{11} : (l_i'', out; l_j, in) \mid_{\{l_i^{iv}\}}$,
    $r_{12} : (l_i^{iv}, out) \mid_{\{l_j\}}$,
    $r_{13} : (l_i'', out; l_k, in) \mid_{\{b'\}}$,
  - The set $\mathcal{R}_2$ consists of the following rules:
    $r_{14} : (l_i''', out; l_i, in) \mid_{\{b'\}}$,
    $r_{15} : (l_i, out)$,
    $r_{16} : (l_i', out; l_i'', in)$,
    $r_{17} : (l_i'', out; l_i''', in)$,
    $r_{18} : (b', out; l_i', in) \mid_{\{l_i''''\}}$,
    $r_{19} : (b', in)$.

A SUB instruction l_i is simulated by Π constructed above in the following way: At the first step, with the presence of a promoter object b' in membrane 2, rule r_{14} is enabled and applied, object l_i''' is sent out of membrane 2, and object l_i is sent to the same membrane which will get back at the next step by using rule r_{15} and proceed to be sent to the environment at step 3 by using rule r_9, as well as one copy of object l_i'' is brought into membrane 1. At step 4, rule r_{16} is applicable, object l_i'' (resp., object l_i') is sent to (resp., out of) membrane 2. In the following work, there exist two cases.

- If there is at least one copy of object a_r in membrane 1 (corresponding to one case that the number stored in register r is non-empty). In this case, at step 5, rule r_{10} associated with a promoter object l_i' is applied, one copy of object l_i^{iv} initial present in the environment is brought into membrane 1 and one copy of object a_r is sent to the environment (representing that the number stored in the register r is reduced by one); in synchronous parallel way, rule r_{17} from $\mathcal{R}_2$ is applicable, object l_i''' (resp., object l_i'') is sent to (resp., out of) membrane 2. At the next step, due to object l_i^{iv} appearing in membrane 1, by using rule r_{11}, one copy of object l_j is sent from the environment to membrane 1 and object l_i'' is gotten back to the environment, as well as rule r_{18} associated with a promoter l_i'''' is used concurrently, object l_i' (resp., object b') is sent to (resp., out of) membrane 2. At step 7, object l_i^{iv} is sent back to the environment and object b' is sent back to membrane 2 by applying rule r_{12} and r_{19}, respectively. Hence, the system starts to simulate an instruction with label l_j.
- If there is no object a_r in membrane 1 (corresponding to another case that the number stored in the currently simulated register r is 0). At step 5, only

rule r_{17} from $\mathcal{R}_2$ is applicable, object l_i'''' (resp., object l_i'') is sent to (resp., out of) membrane 2. At the next step, with the appearance of promoter object l_i'''' in membrane 2, object l_i' (resp., object b') is sent to (resp., out of) this membrane by using rule r_{18}. At step 7, by applying rule r_{13}, one copy of object l_k is brought into membrane 1, object l_i'' is gotten back to the environment; simultaneously, by applying rule r_{19}, object b' is sent back to membrane 2. Thus, the system starts to simulate an instruction with label l_k.

Thus, the SUB instruction of M can be exactly simulated by this system Π.

During the simulation of M, when the object l_h appears in membrane 1 at any moment, no rule can be applied, and then the computation halts. At that time, the number of copies of objects a_1 stored in membrane 1 corresponds to the result computed by system Π, thus $N(M) = N(\Pi)$.

4   Conclusions and Discussions

In this paper, we mainly investigate the computation power of CSAp P systems working in the maximal parallel manner and sequential manner. It is proved that only finite sets of non-negative integers can be generated by such P systems with any number of membranes and arbitrary number of promoter objects, when using only symport rules of length 1 or using only antiport rules of length 2 working in the maximally parallel manner. Furthermore, we prove that the computational completeness of CSAp P systems working in the sequential manner, with two membranes and two promoters, by using only symport rules of length 2, or with two membranes and one promoter, by using symport rules of length 1 and antiport rules of length 2, are Turing universality.

It is known that a flat maximally parallel manner as an attractive strategy of using rules was formally defined in [24], then the computation power of several variants of tissue P systems were investigated in [25,35]. Therefore, it is worth investigating the computation power of CSAp P systems when working in the flat maximally parallel manner.

Membrane division as an interesting biological phenomenons is incorporated in P systems to generate an exponential workspace in polynomial time. The SAT problem can be efficiently solved by P systems with promoters and membrane division [24] and by tissue P systems with promoters and membrane division [28]. In order to investigate whether CSAp P system with membrane division can solve the NP-complete problems, it is of interest to construct a CSAp P system with membrane division.

The NP-complete and PSPACE problems can be solved by several variants of cell-like P systems in the context of time-freeness [33,34]. It remains open whether a time-free solution to NP-complete or PSPACE problems can be obtained by CSAp P systems and membrane division.

Acknowledgments. The work of S. Jiang and Y. Wang was supported by National Natural Science Foundation of China (61632002 and 61472372), Science and Technology Innovation Talents of Henan Province (174200510012), and the Innovation Scientists and Technicians Troop Construction Projects of Henan Province (154200510012). The work of F. Xu was supported by National Natural Science Foundation of China (61502186) and China Postdoctoral Science Foundation (2016M592335).

References

1. Alhazov, A., Rogozhin, Y.: Minimal cooperation in symport/antiport P systems with one membrane. In: Proceedings of the Third Brainstorming Week on Membrane Computing, pp. 29–34. Sevilla (2005)
2. Alhazov, A., Aman, B., Freund, R.: P systems with anti-matter. In: Gheorghe, M., Rozenberg, G., Salomaa, A., Sosík, P., Zandron, C. (eds.) CMC 2014. LNCS, vol. 8961, pp. 66–85. Springer, Cham (2014). https://doi.org/10.1007/978-3-319-14370-5_5
3. Bottoni, P., Martín-Vide, C., Păun, G., Rozenberg, G.: Membrane systems with promoters/inhibitors. Act. Inform. **38**, 695–720 (2002)
4. Ciobanu, G., Păun, G., Pérez-Jiménez, M.J.: Applications of Membrane Computing. Springer, Berlin (2005)
5. Ciobanu, G., Pan, L., Păun, G.: P systems with minimal parallelism. Theor. Comput. Sci. **378**(1), 117–130 (2007)
6. Díaz-Pernil, D., Gutiérrez-Naranjo, M.A., Pérez-Jiménez, M.J., Riscos-Núñez, A.: Solving the Independent set problem by using tissue-like P systems with cell division. In: Mira, J., Ferrández, J.M., Álvarez, J.R., Paz, F., Toledo, F.J. (eds.) IWINAC 2009. LNCS, vol. 5601, pp. 213–222. Springer, Heidelberg (2009). https://doi.org/10.1007/978-3-642-02264-7_23
7. Dassow, J., Păun, G.: On the power of membrane computing. J. Univ. Comput. Sci. **5**(2), 33–49 (1999)
8. Frisco, P., Govan, G., Leporati, A.: Asynchronous P systems with active membranes. Theor. Comput. Sci. **429**, 74–86 (2012)
9. Freund, R., Oswald, M.: Modelling grammar systems by tissue P systems working in the sequential mode. Fund. Inform. **76**, 305–323 (2007)
10. Freund, R., Ibarra, O.H., Păun, G. (eds.): Matrix languages, register machines, vector addition systems. In: The 3rd Brainstorming Week Membrane Computing, pp. 155–168 (2005)
11. Ionescu, M., Păun, G., Yokomori, T.: Spiking neural P systems. Fund. Inform. **71**(2–3), 279–308 (2006)
12. Jiang, K., Pan, L.: Spiking neural P systems with anti-spikes working in sequential mode induced by maximum spike number. Neurocomputing **171**, 1674–1683 (2016)
13. Korec, I.: Small universal register machines. Theor. Comput. Sci. **168**(2), 267–301 (1996)
14. Leporati, A., Manzoni, L., Mauri, G., Porreca, A.E., Zandron, C.: Shallow Nonconfluent P systems. In: Leporati, A., Rozenberg, G., Salomaa, A., Zandron, C. (eds.) CMC 2016. LNCS, vol. 10105, pp. 307–316. Springer, Cham (2017). https://doi.org/10.1007/978-3-319-54072-6_19
15. Martín-Vide, C., Pazos, J., Păun, G., Rodríguez-Patón, A.: Tissue P systems. Theor. Comput. Sci. **296**(2), 295–326 (2003)
16. Minsky, M.L.: Computation: Finite and Infinite Machines. Prentice-Hall, Englewood-Cliffs (1967)

17. Păun, A., Păun, G.: The power of communication: P systems with symport/antiport. New Gener. Comput. **20**(3), 295–305 (2002)
18. Păun, G.: Computing with membranes. J. Comput. Syst. Sci. **61**(1), 108–143 (2000). Also in Turku Center for Computer Science-TUCS, Report 208, November 1998
19. Păun, G., Păun, R.: Membrane computing and economics: numerical P systems. Fund. Inform. **72**(1–2), 213–227 (2006)
20. Păun, G., Rozenberg, G., Salomaa, A.: The Oxford Handbook of Membrane Computing. Oxford University Press, New York (2010)
21. Păun, G.: Membrane Computing: An Introduction. Springer Science & Business Media, Berlin (2002)
22. Peng, H., Wang, J., Pérez-Jiménez, M.J., Riscos-Núñez, A.: An unsupervised learning algorithm for membrane computing. Inf. Sci. **304**, 80–91 (2015)
23. Peng, H., Wang, J., Shi, P., Riscos-Núñez, A., Pérez-Jiménez, M.J.: An automatic clustering algorithm inspired by membrane computing. Pattern Recogn. Lett. **68**, 34–40 (2015)
24. Pan, L., Păun, G., Song, B.: Flat maximal parallelism in P systems with promoters. Theor. Comput. Sci. **623**, 83–91 (2016)
25. Pan, L., Wang, Y., Jiang, S., Song, B.: Flat maximal parallelism in tissue P systems with promoters. Rom. J. Inf. Sci. Technol. **20**(1), 42–56 (2017)
26. Rozenberg, G., Salomaa, A. (eds.): Handbook of Formal Languages, vol. 1. Springer, Berlin (1997)
27. Song, B., Pan, L., Pérez-Jiménez, M.J.: Cell-like P systems with channel states and symport/antiport rules. IEEE Trans. Nanobiosci. **15**(6), 555–566 (2016)
28. Song, B., Pan, L.: The computational power of tissue-like P systems with promoters. Theor. Comput. Sci. **641**, 43–52 (2016)
29. Song, T., Pan, L.: Spiking neural P systems with rules on synapses working in maximum spiking strategy. IEEE Trans. Nanobiosci. **14**(4), 465–477 (2015)
30. Song, T., Pan, L.: Spiking neural P systems with request rules. Neurocomputing **193**, 193–200 (2016)
31. Song, T., Pan, L.: Spiking neural P systems with rules on synapses working in maximum spikes consumption strategy. IEEE Trans. Nanobios. **14**(1), 38–44 (2016)
32. Song, B., Pérez-Jiménez, M.J., Pan, L.: Efficient solutions to hard computational problems by P systems with symport/antiport rules and membrane division. BioSystems **130**, 51–58 (2015)
33. Song, B., Pérez-Jiménez, M.J., Pan, L.: An efficient time-free solution to SAT problem by P systems with proteins on membranes. J. Comput. Syst. Sci. **82**, 1090–1099 (2016)
34. Song, B., Pérez-Jiménez, M.J., Pan, L.: An efficient time-free solution to QSAT problem using P systems with proteins on membranes. Inf. Comput. Sci. **529**, 61–68 (2014). https://doi.org/10.1016/j.ic.2017.06.005
35. Song, B., Zhang, C., Pan, L.: Tissue-like P systems with evolutional symport/antiport rules. Inf. Sci. **378**, 177–193 (2017)
36. Wang, J., Shi, P., Peng, H.: Membrane computing model for IIR filter design. Inf. Sci. **329**, 164–176 (2016)
37. Wu, T., Zhang, Z., Păun, G., Pan, L.: Cell-like spiking neural P systems. Theor. Comput. Sci. **623**, 180–189 (2016)
38. Zandron, C., Leporati, A., Ferretti, C.: On the computational efficiency of polarizationless recognizer P systems with strong division and dissolution. Fund. Inform. **87**(1), 79–91 (2008)

39. Zhang, G., Gheorghe, M., Pérez-Jiménez, M.J.: Real-Life Applications with Membrane Computing. Springer, Berlin (2016)
40. Zhang, G., Pérez-Jiménez, M.J., Gheorghe, M.: Data modeling with membrane systems: applications to real ecosystems. Real-life Appl. Membr. Comput. **25**, 259–355 (2017)
41. Zhang, X., Pan, L., Păun, A.: On the universality of axon P systems. IEEE Trans. Neural Netw. Learn. Syst. **26**(11), 2816–2829 (2015)

Dynamical Analysis of a Novel Chaotic Circuit

Junwei Sun[1,2], Nan Li[1,2], and Yanfeng Wang[1,2(✉)]

[1] Henan Key Lab of Information-Based Electrical Appliances,
Zhengzhou University of Light Industry, Zhengzhou 450002, China
[2] College of Electrical and Electronic Engineering,
Zhengzhou University of Light Industry, Zhengzhou 450002, China
{junweisun,yanfengwang}@yeah.net

Abstract. Chaotic circuit is an effective tool to observe and analyze chaotic phenomena, to verify chaos theory and to promote its application. The recent research work focuses on how to better analyze the basic circuit characteristics and to design application circuits. In this paper, a new chaotic system is proposed, whose dynamical behaviors are discussed with the change of the parameters in detail. The specific effects of different parameters on the system are also discussed. By adjusting these parameters of the proposed circuit, this nonlinear circuit can produce the different dynamical behaviors, such as, hyper chaotic behavior, periodic behavior, transient behavior, etc. In addition, the simulation results of Matlab can further prove the feasibility of this circuit.

Keywords: Chaotic system · Dynamical analysis · Lyapunov exponent · Bifurcation diagrams · Unknown parameters

1 Introduction

With the development of the control area, the control and application of chaotic system [1,2] have become an important research direction in nonlinear science. It is known that, the nonlinear functions [3–5] lead to chaos in nonlinear dynamical system. If the nonlinear circuit of the system is different, the dynamical behavior and characteristics of chaotic systems are different in general. An important tool in modeling and analyzing these phenomena is the study of dynamical systems and chaos. By introducing nonlinear devices [6,7] and establishing nonlinear mathematical models to the chaotic circuit [8–10], a large number of application circuits have been proposed and rich achievements have been obtained. Also, the emergence and manufacturing success of memristor have greatly promoted the development of nonlinear systems [11]. It motivates many researchers to develop different nonlinear circuits and utilizes these circuits in studying nonlinear phenomena and chaos. For example, a known circuit as the Modified Vander Pol oscillator (MVPO) was introduced by Shinrikiet [12]. Gaito derived a nonlinear chaotic circuit from the MVPO, which is called the Autonomous Van der Pol-Duffing (ADVP) oscillator [13,14]. Many of the existing chaotic circuit systems or mathematical models are based on the typical circuit systems of the

© Springer Nature Singapore Pte Ltd. 2017
C. He et al. (Eds.): BIC-TA 2017, CCIS 791, pp. 359–368, 2017.
https://doi.org/10.1007/978-981-10-7179-9_27

past, such as well-known systems Lorenz system [15], Rössler system [16], Chen system [17], and so on. Also, some complicated dynamical behaviors including period doubling bifurcation [18], self-excited oscillations [19,20], transient chaos [21,22]and hyper chaos [23,24] and so on are observed in these systems.

Nowadays, some new chaotic systems are found and constructed constantly, and it can make people have a deeper understanding of the chaotic phenomenon, enrich and improve the research content of chaos theory. Moreover, it is the case not only in deeper and wider theoretical studies but also in many newly found real-world applications, such as, the encryption of information, chaotic synchronization of signals and processing of images, etc. However, these systems [15–17] always have the special features from the perspective of circuit design, so it is of practical significance to study the ordinary two-order autonomous circuit [25–27] system which is easy to implement.

Obviously, more and more chaotic systems [28–30] are found to be very necessary. In this work, a new chaotic circuit system is designed and implemented, which expands the traditional chaotic system. Various nonlinear analysis tools such as phase portraits, time series, bifurcation diagrams band the spectrum of Lyapunov exponents are exploited to characterize different scenarios to chaos in the novel circuit. What's more, by changing the parameter values of the equation, the circuit will produce the different behaviors such as hyper chaos, transient chaos, period doubling and so on.

The rest of paper is organized as follows. In Sect. 2, a novel chaotic system is proposed. In Sect. 3, the corresponding effects of the system parameters are analyzed in detail. Finally, some conclusions and suggestions for future work are given in Sect. 4.

2   Chaotic System and Its Basic Characteristics

In this part, a new dynamical equation is given. On this basis, a simple global observation of the system is carried out by using Lyapunov exponents diagrams and Matlab phase diagrams.

2.1   Chaotic System Model

The chaotic circuit is given by

$$\begin{cases} \dot{x} = a * y, \\ \dot{y} = b * (-x + y) + y * z, \\ \dot{z} = c - y^2, \end{cases} \tag{1}$$

where x, y and z are three state variables of the chaotic system (1). a, b, and c are three parameters of the chaotic system (1). If the three parameters of the system (1) are chosen as $a = 1$, $b = 1$, $c = 1$, then the system (1) is chaotic.

Through the Matlab simulation, the Lyapunov exponent graph of the chaotic system (1) is plotted as the following in Fig. 1. It can be concluded that the

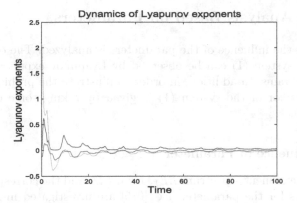

Fig. 1. Lyapunov exponents of chaotic system (1) versus parameter t

Lyapunov exponents are $L_1 > 0$, $L_2 > 0$ and $L_3 < 0$ in Fig. 1, which implies that the chaotic system (1) is hyper chaotic.

Corresponding the attractor of the chaotic system (1) in different directions with initial conditions: $x(0) = 1$, $y(0) = 1$, $z(0) = 1$ are shown in Fig. 2(a)–(d).

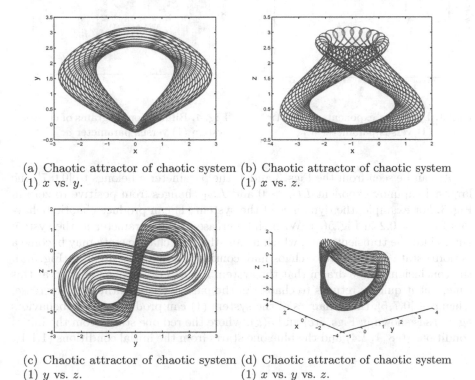

(a) Chaotic attractor of chaotic system (1) x vs. y.

(b) Chaotic attractor of chaotic system (1) x vs. z.

(c) Chaotic attractor of chaotic system (1) y vs. z.

(d) Chaotic attractor of chaotic system (1) x vs. y vs. z.

Fig. 2. Chaotic attractor.

3   Kinetic Analysis Based on Parameters

In this section, the influence of the parameters is analyzed. The overall characteristics of the system (1) can be observed by Lyapunov exponent graphs and Bifurcation diagrams. In addition, in order to illustrate the problem better, the dynamical behavior of the system (1) is given by taking some corresponding parameters values.

3.1   The Influence of Parameter a

The Lyapunov exponents spectrum LE_1, LE_2, LE_3 and the corresponding bifurcation diagrams for the parameter $a \in [0, 5]$ are investigated in Figs. 3 and 4, respectively. The parameters are chosen as $b = 1$, $c = 1$ and the initial conditions of the system (1) are $x_0 = 1$, $y_0 = 1$, $z_0 = 1$.

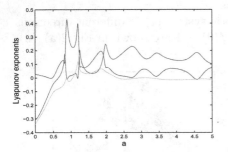

Fig. 3. Lyapunov exponents of chaotic system (1) versus parameter a.

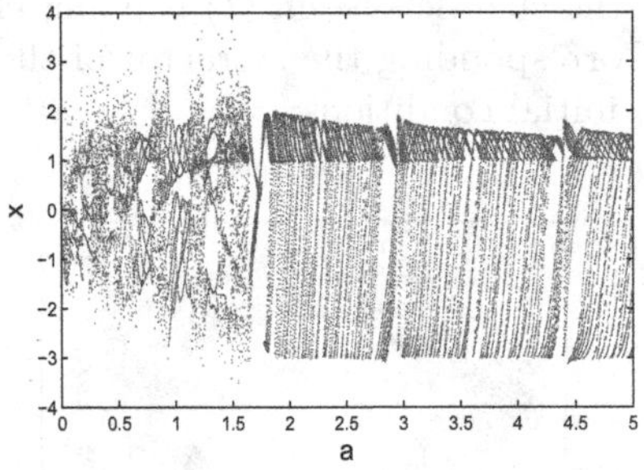

Fig. 4. Bifurcation diagrams of chaotic system (1) versus parameter a.

As can be seen from the Figs. 3 and 4, the parameter a belongs to [0,0.7], the largest Lyapunov exponent $LE_1 > 0$ and LE_1 changes from positive to zero in Fig. 3. For example, the dynamics of the system (1) can produce chaotic behaviors for $a = 0.2$ in Fig. 5(a). With the increase of the parameter a, the system enters into the transient state, which means that the chaotic state may become a periodic state or the state of chaos may continue to be maintained. In Fig. 5(b), the conclusion can be drawn that the system has a periodic phenomenon at this time, but it quickly returns to chaos. As the parameter a continues to increase, when $a \in [0.7, 5]$, the dynamics of the system (1) can produce chaotic behaviors again as is shown in Figs. 5(c) and 5(d), where the red one starts from the initial conditions (0.8, 1, 1.4) and the blue one starts from the initial conditions (1,1,1).

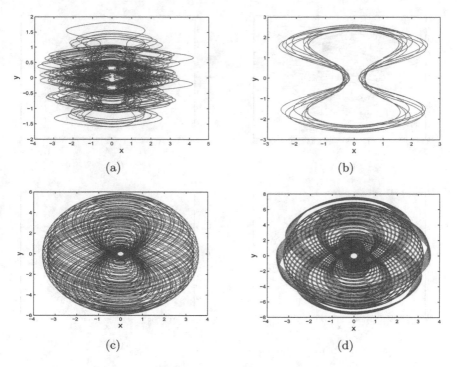

(a)   (b)

(c)   (d)

Fig. 5. The phase diagrams of the system with the change of the parameter a: (a) a = 0.2, (b) a = 0.7, (c) a = 3, (d) a = 5, (the red one starts from the initial condition (0.8, 1, 1.4), the blue one starts from (1,1,1). (Color figure online)

3.2   The Influence of Parameter b

The Lyapunov exponents spectrum LE_1, LE_2, LE_3 and the corresponding bifurcation diagrams versus $b \in [0,5]$ are investigated in Figs. 6 and 7 for the system (1), respectively. The values of parameters are $a = 1$, $c = 1$ and the initial conditions of the system (1) are $x_0 = 1$, $y_0 = 1$, $z_0 = 1$.

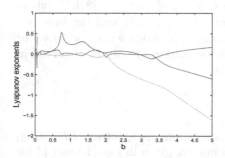

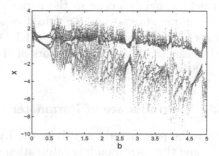

Fig. 6. Lyapunov exponents of chaotic system (1) versus parameter b.

Fig. 7. Bifurcation diagrams of chaotic system (1) versus parameter b.

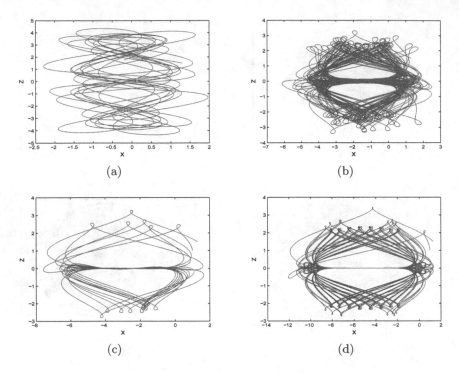

Fig. 8. The phase diagrams of the system with the change of the parameter b: (a) $b =$ 0.15, (b) $b = 1.5$, (c) $b = 2.75$, (d) $b = 5$, (the red one starts from the initial condition (1.5, 2.1, 1.3), the blue one starts from (1,1,1). (Color figure online)

With the increase of the parameter $b \in [0, 0.1]$, the maximum Lyapunov exponent LE_1 changes from positive to zero in Fig. 6. When b belongs to $[0.1, 0.2]$ and $[2.6, 2.9]$, the dynamics of the system (1) can produce the period-doubling bifurcations behaviors in Figs. 8(a) and 8(c). The main chaotic dynamics of the system (1) can be produced in the regions of $b \in [0.2, 2.6]$ and $b \in [2.9, 5]$, so the dynamical behaviors of the coexisting bifurcation modes and the coexisting attractors mainly occur in the regions of $b \in [0.2, 2.6]$ and $b \in [2.9, 5]$, where the red one starts from the initial conditions (1.5, 2.1, 1.3) and the blue one starts from the initial conditions (1,1,1). For example, when b is equal to 1.5 or 4, the chaotic dynamics behaviors of the chaotic system (1) can be observed in Figs. 8(b) and 8(d).

3.3   The Influence of Parameter c

When the parameter $c \in [0.7, 5]$, the Lyapunov exponents spectrum LE_1, LE_2, LE_3 and the corresponding bifurcation diagrams are given in Figs. 10 and 11 for the system (1), respectively. The parameters are $a = 1$ and $b = 1$, the initial conditions of the chaotic system (1) are $x_0 = 1, y_0 = 1, z_0 = 1$.

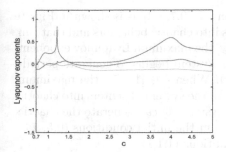

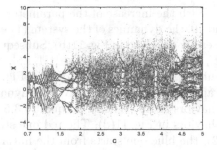

Fig. 9. Lyapunov exponents of chaotic system (1) versus parameter c.

Fig. 10. Bifurcation diagrams of chaotic system (1) versus parameter c.

By observing the Figs. 9 and 10, it is gained that the largest Lyapunov exponent is from 0 to positive for the parameter c, so this periodic behavior indicates that the system is transient. From Fig. 11(a), it can be easily seen that the system (1) can generate the chaotic dynamical behaviors.

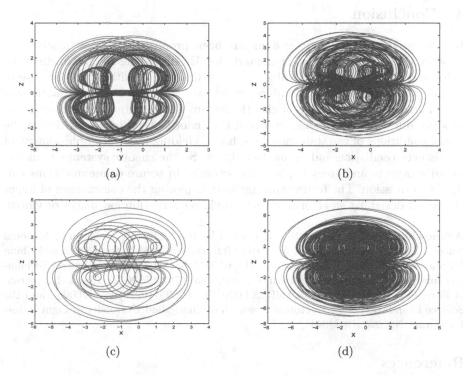

Fig. 11. The phase diagrams of the system with the change of the parameter c: (a) $c = 0.7$, (b) $c = 1.2$, (c) $c = 1.5$, (d) $c = 3.5$, (the red one starts from the initial condition (0.5, 1.3, 2.2), the blue one starts from (1,1,1).

With the increase of the parameter, when $c \in [0.7, 1.4]$ as is shown in Figs. 9 and 10, the dynamics of the system (1) enters into chaotic behaviors and that can be easily observed in Fig. 11(b). Subsequently, the maximum Lyapunov exponent LE_1 equals to zero when $c \in [1.4, 1.9]$, so the system begins to generate period-doubling behaviors as is shown in Fig. 11(c). When $c \in [1.9, 5]$, the maximum Lyapunov exponent is positive, the dynamics of the system (1) enters into chaotic behaviors again. When c is equal to 3.5, the system (1) can generate the chaotic behaviors in Fig. 11(d). The red one starts from the initial conditions (0.5, 1.3, 2.2), the blue one starts from the initial conditions (1,1,1).

Remark: Compared the new system with the classical systems [15–17], it can be concluded that the new system is more sensitive to the parameters and initial conditions, and the dynamic behaviors of the system are more abundant. By observing the variables phase graphics, it can be seen clearly that the system have abundant dynamical behaviors under different variables with the same initial conditions or same variables with different initial conditions. Obviously, the different variable values can improve the characteristics of the system and produce more complex trajectory of behaviors.

4   Conclusion

In this work, a new chaotic system has been proposed. The new system can produce these rich dynamical characteristics. By discussing the parameter variables and the system initial values, we can find the sensitivity of the system to the parameter and initial values, which are the values of the chaotic system. Furthermore, the value of chaotic system can be adjusted or changed to produce different phenomena. States of the chaotic system are sensitive to the initial conditions of the state variables, hence yielding the special phenomena of coexistence oscillation and its multi-stability. So the chaotic system circuit has broad prospects and great application potential in secure communications and data transmission. The future work includes exploring the convenience of hyper chaos and designing an algorithm that provides encryption for images or videos.

Acknowledgments. The work is supported by the State Key Program of National Natural Science of China (Grant No. 61632002), the National Natural Science of China (Grant Nos. 61572446, 61472372, 61603347, 61603348, 61602424), Science and Technology Innovation Talents Henan Province (Grant No. 174200510012), Research Program of Henan Province (Grant Nos. 15IRTSTHN012, 162300410220, 17A120005), and the Science Foundation of for Doctorate Research of Zhengzhou University of Light Industry (Grant No. 2014BSJJ044).

References

1. Lü, J.G.: Chaotic dynamics of the fractional-order Lü system and its synchronization. Phys. Lett. A **354**, 483–489 (2006)
2. Lü, J.H., Chen, G.R., Cheng, D.Z.: A new chaotic system and beyond: the generalized Lorenz-like system. Int. J. Bifurc. Chaos **14**, 1507–1537 (2004)

3. Lü, J.G.: Generating chaos via decentralized linear state feedback and a class of nonlinear functions. Chaos Solitons Frac. **25**, 403–413 (2005)
4. Feki, M.: Observer-based synchronization of chaotic systems with unknown nonlinear function. Chaos Solitons Frac. **39**, 981–990 (2009)
5. Wan, Z.C.: Synchronization between two different chaotic systems using nonlinear control function. Microelectr. Comput. **25**, 52–55 (2008)
6. Chua, L.O., Kang, S.M.: Memristive device and systems. IEEE Proc. **64**, 209–223 (1976)
7. Lorenz, E.N.: Deterministic nonperiodic flow. J. Atmosph. Sci. **20**, 130–141 (1963)
8. Li, Q., Hu, S., Tang, S., Zeng, G.: Hyperchaos and horseshoe in a 4D memristive system with a line of equilibria and its implementation. Int. J. Circ. Theor. Appl. **42**, 1172–1188 (2013)
9. Iu, H.H.C., Yu, D.S., Fitch, A.L., Sreeram, V., Chen, H.: Controlling chaos in a memristor based circuit using a twint notch filter. IEEE Trans. Circ. Syst. **58**, 1337–1344 (2011)
10. Bao, B.C., Ma, Z.H., Xu, J.P., Liu, Z., Xu, Q.: A simple memristor chaotic circuit with complex dynamics. Int. J. Bifurc. Chaos **21**, 2629–2645 (2011)
11. Buscarino, A., Fortuna, L., Frasca, M., Gambuzza, L.: A chaotic circuit based on Hewlett-Packard memristor. Chaos **22**, 23–36 (2012)
12. Diaz, G., Coimbra, C.F.M.: Nonlinear dynamics and control of a variable order oscillator with application to the Van der Pol equation. Nonlinear Dyn. **56**, 145–157 (2009)
13. Vincent, U.E., Nbendjo, B.R.N., Ajayi, A.A., Njah, A.N., Mcclintock, P.V.E.: Hyperchaos and bifurcations in a driven Van der Pol-duffing oscillator circuit. Int. J. Dyn. Control **3**, 363–370 (2015)
14. Matouk, A.E.: Chaos, feedback control and synchronization of a fractional-order modified autonomous Van der Pol-Duffing circuit. Chaos Soliton Fract **16**, 975–986 (2011)
15. Jia, Q.: Hyperchaos generated from the Lorenz chaotic system and its control. Phys. Lett. A **336**, 217–222 (2007)
16. Rössler, O.E.: An equation for continuous chaos. Phys. Lett. A **57**, 397–398 (1976)
17. Li, C., Chen, G.: Chaos in the fractional order Chen system and its control. Commun. Nonlinear Sci. **22**, 549–554 (2004)
18. Bi, Q.S., Ma, R., Zhang, Z.D.: Bifurcation mechanism of the bursting oscillations in periodically excited dynamical system with two time scales. Nonlinear Dyn. **79**, 101–110 (2015)
19. Radwan, A.G., Soliman, A.M., El-Sedeek, A.L.: An inductorless CMOS realization of Chua's circuit. Chaos Solitons Frac. **18**, 149–158 (2003)
20. Radwan, A.G., Soliman, A.M., El-Sedeek, A.L.: MOS realization of the conjectured simplest chaotic equation. Circ. Syst. Signal Proc. **22**, 277–285 (2003)
21. Bao, B.C., Liu, Z., Xu, J.P.: Steady periodic memristor oscillator with transient chaotic behaviors. Electr. Lett. **46**, 237–238 (2010)
22. Bao, B.C., Ma, Z.H., Xu, J.P., Liu, Z., Xu, Q.: A simple memristor chaotic circuit with complex dynamics. Int. J. Bifurc. Chaos **21**, 2629–2645 (2011)
23. Fitch, A.L., Yu, D., Iu, H., Sreeram, V.: Hyperchaos in a memristor-based modified canonical Chua's circuit. Int. J. Bifurc. Chaos **22**, 125–133 (2015)
24. Liu, H., Kadir, A., Li, Y.: Asymmetric color pathological image encryption scheme based on complex hyper chaotic system. Int. J. Light Electr. Optics **127**, 5812–5819 (2016)
25. Tokida, C., Saito, T.: On a synchronization phenomena in third order autonomous chaotic circuit. Am. J. Phys. **72**, 379–385 (2012)

26. Kilic, R., Saracoglu, O.G., Yildirim, F.: Experimental observations of EMI effects in autonomous Chuas chaotic circuit. Chaos Solitons Frac. **32**, 1168–1177 (2007)
27. Koliopanos, C.L., Kyprianidis, I.M., Stouboulos, I.N., Anagnostopoulos, A.N., Magafas, L.: Chaotic behaviour of a fourth-order autonomous electric circuit. Chaos Solitons Fract. **16**, 173–182 (2003)
28. Sun, J.W., Wu, Y.Y., Cui, G.Z.: Finite-time Real combination synchronization of three complex-variable chaotic systems with unknown parameters via sliding mode control. Nonlinear Dyn. **88**, 1677–1690 (2017)
29. Sun, J.W., Wang, Y., Wang, Y.F., Shen, Y.: Finite-time synchronization between two complex-variable chaotic systems with unknown parameters via nonsingular tterminal sliding mode control. Nonlinear Dyn. **85**, 1105–1117 (2016)
30. Sun, J.W., Shen, Y.: Quasi-ideal Memory System. IEEE Trans. Cyber. **45**, 1353–1362 (2015)

The Logic Circuit Design of Fire Alarm System Device by DNA Strand Displacement

Yanfeng Wang[1,2], Jixiang Li[1,2], Chun Huang[1,2], and Junwei Sun[1,2(✉)]

[1] Henan Key Lab of Information-Based Electrical Appliances,
Zhengzhou University of Light Industry, Zhengzhou 450002, China
junweisun@yeah.net

[2] College of Electrical and Electronic Engineering,
Zhengzhou University of Light Industry, Zhengzhou 450002, China

Abstract. DNA strand displacement acted as a useful tool is most widely used in the majority computing system. In this paper, a four-input fire alarm system device based on DNA strand displacement is designed. The whole reaction course is programmed and simulated in the software visual DSD, which presenting the superb simulation results with inputs and outputs through compiling the procedure for computation device. According to the results of the Visual DSD software, the method of DNA strand displacement by dual-rail circuits is feasible to achieve more complex logic computation. This investigation on the basis of DNA strand displacement by dual-rail circuits may have a great prospect for the development and application in the biological information processing, molecular computing, and so on.

Keywords: DNA strand displacement · Fire alarm system device · Logic circuit · Visual DSD · Molecular computing

1 Introduction

DNA computing is a new field that combining computer science and molecular biology subject [1,2]. DNA is acted as the computing tool, utilizing its formidable parallel computing ability, solved lots of problems such as: Hamilton path, maximal clique problem, and so on [3,4]. DNA computing has coalesced a lot of molecule operation technology: self-assembly, fluorescence labeling, strand displacement and nano-power [5]. DNA strand displacement technology is a new method in the bio-computing recent years, and which has become a common method in DNA self-assembly [6–9]. DNA strand displacement technology is also a dynamic DNA nanotechnology, which has the spontaneity, sensitivity and veracity [10–12]. In recent years, DNA strand displacement technology has reached a tremendous development [13–16]. Through the strand displacement cascade reaction, the dynamical connection adjacent logic module has been achieved which makes it possible for the researchers to establish large-scale, complicated logic circuit [17]. Moreover, with the advantage of high-capacity information accumulation,

© Springer Nature Singapore Pte Ltd. 2017
C. He et al. (Eds.): BIC-TA 2017, CCIS 791, pp. 369–379, 2017.
https://doi.org/10.1007/978-981-10-7179-9_28

high performance parallel computing, programming and simulating, DNA strand displacement technology had acquired an in-depth study in the fields of molecular computing, nano-machine, diagnosis and remedy of the disease [18–20]. DNA-computing has the gigantic proficiency in solving some math problems, managing the nano-machine and discussing the life course. The biochemistry logic circuit is the basis of the DNA-computing [21]. So, by the way of mastering the design procedures to structure the biochemistry logic circuit is that based on DNA strand displacement has the significant research means [22]. In the real life, democracy has enjoyed for popular support, so we could encounter election everywhere, especially in entertainment program, the four-input fire alarm system device. The four-input fire alarm system device is the alarm device when there is an emergency. When there are some emergencies, smoke, temperature, fire, manual buttons will be induced changes, when the above four cases in the three, the fire alarm will be started immediately after the emergency rescue measures. Because when the fire occurs, the above four cases will generally occur at the same time. So far, the fire alarm system device has been divided into two types: wired and wireless. The wired fire alarm system device had retreated from the market, and the wireless had become the main stream. Compared with the existing work [23–25], there are some advantages, which can make our study more attractive and interesting than the previous logic circuit. First, improved the traditional unreliable fire accident alarm device [23], the strategy based on DNA strand displacement is applied to the logic circuit of four-input fire alarm system device firstly. Second, compared with scaling up digital circuit computation with DNA strand displacement cascades using DNA strand displacement reactions [24], the results of the logic circuit designed of four-input fire alarm system device are displayed and implemented through the use of the dual-rail method [25]. In addition, the use of dual-rail circuits model based on DNA strand displacement also reflects the nano-level logic circuit toward a large-scale direction [26]. In this paper, the content is given as follows: the introduction is shown in the Sect. 1, which includes the backgrounds and significance for the study. The reaction about the DNA strand displacement is shown in the Sect. 2. Section 3 is that the design of the logic circuit designed of four-input fire alarm system device is described, which could calculate the difference and conversion from logic circuit to seesaw circuit. The results of simulation are presented in the Sect. 4. Finally, the conclusion for the logic circuit of four-input fire alarm system device on the basis of DNA strand displacement by dual-rail circuits is given in the Sect. 5.

2   DNA Strand Displacement

DNA strand displacement technique is originated from DNA self-assembly technique, which multiple DNA single strand come into being the course of orderly multi-dimensional assembly spontaneously on account of base complementary pair rule [23–26]. DNA strand displacement reaction needs a single-strand and a double-strand. The single-strand is complementary pair with the one strand of the double-strand based on A, G, C, T (A is paired with T, G is paired with C). The one strand of double-strand has a toehold domain, which is an exposed single strand domain in the double-strand. The toehold domain can be reacted with the part of the signal-strand firstly, and conducted branch migration until the one strand of double-strand substituted by the single-strand in the next time, and forming a new single-strand finally. Compared with the combination synchronization [27,28], the method of DNA strand displacement by dual-rail circuits is feasible to achieve more complex logic computation. If a new toehold domain in the new double-strand is generated, it occurs similar reaction that we called reverse reaction. It will be reached a dynamic equilibrium. If there is no new toehold domain produced, the reaction is finished. Whereas, there are two kinds of reaction of DNA strand displacement (shown in Fig. 1), we usually called the single-strand as input strand, and the new single-strand is called as the output strand. DNA strand displacement is implemented at the natural temperature without enzymes or transcription machinery [29–31]. The reaction trends toward controlled the state what we hope only by changing the length and sequence of toehold domain.

Fig. 1. (a) The reversible reaction of the DNA strand displacement. T* is the toehold domain, T1* is the new toehold domain. R is the branch migration domain. (b) The irreversible reaction of the DNA strand displacement. T2* is the toehold domain, R1 is the branch migration domain.

3   Logic Circuit of Four-Input Fire Alarm System Device

3.1   Digital Logic Circuit

The logic operation adapts two kinds of state, which are "0" and "1". The "0" represents there is no inductive signal input and the "1" represents there are the inductive signal inputs. In the digital logic circuit, logic algorithm includes three fundamental logic operation, namely logic AND, logic OR, and logic NOT. In the logic circuit of four-input fire alarm system device which calculates the result of 4 inductive signals whether or not happened. If there are 3 inductive signal inputs select "1" at least, then the result will show "1", otherwise the result will show "0" (Fig. 2).

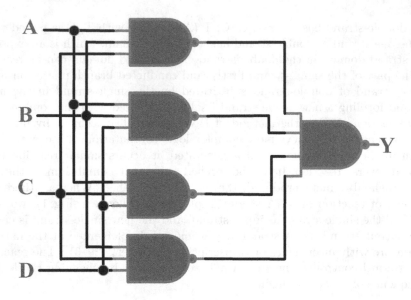

Fig. 2. The digital logic circuit of four-input fire alarm system device.

3.2   Dual-Rail Logic Circuit

In the DNA computing, the NOT gate is difficult to be implemented directly. Because the NOT gate must be operated in a low input signal reacted by an upstream gate in DNA strand displacement reaction, which should be released a high output signal, and a low input signal that can't be computed, so the NOT gate can't be reacted with others. To address this problem, the dual-rail logic circuit is used. Namely a circuit of AND, OR, NOT, NAND and NOR gates are transformed into an identical dual-rail circuit that only included AND and OR gates. In the new circuit, there will be contained roughly twice as many gates, each input X with X_0 and X_1 is represented the state "0" and "1", respectively, the ON and OFF can be used to command whose input state. If neither of them is ON, there is indicated that the logical value of X has not been computed yet; if the X_0 is ON, which is indicated that the logical value of X must be "0"; while if the X_1 is ON, which is indicated that the logical value of X must be "1". If both X_0 and X_1 are ON, then the circuit occur mistake. With this notation, each original AND, OR, NAND gate can be implemented by using one AND gate and one OR gate. In the Fig. 4, it is appeared that the four inputs were transformed into eight inputs (in Fig. 3) through the dual-rail circuit, which represents the state ON or OFF, respectively. And the AND, OR, NOT gate are transformed into five-pair AND gate and OR gate. Ultimately, the dual-rail circuit come into being output signal Y_0 and Y_1 represent OFF and ON, respectively.

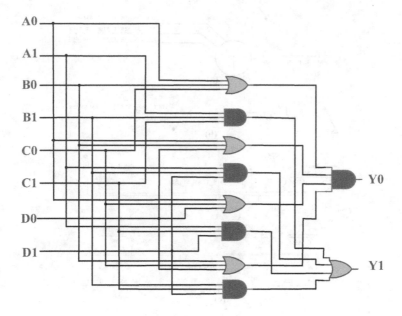

Fig. 3. The dual-rail logic circuit of the four-input fire alarm system device.

3.3   The Seesaw Cascade Circuit

In the designed of four-input fire alarm system device circuit based on DNA strand displacement, the seesaw circuits are presented by using a systematic abstraction. The first is amplifying gate which contains three signal strands, 'input', 'fuel', and 'output', which are all the single-stranded DNA molecules. They will be interacted with partially double-stranded DNA molecules we called gate: 'signal complexes' and 'threshold complexes' based on the underlying mechanism of 'toehold-mediated DNA strand displacement', in which another single-stranded DNA molecule is displaced another from the complex double strand with the help of a short 'toehold' domain, that is used to acquire a original input signal strand. The first amplifying gate can be used as an example, which has the one input and four output (shown in Fig. 4(a)) and one of the first amplifying gate reaction mechanism (shown in Fig. 4(c)).

The second is the integrate gate, which serving multiply inputs and one output (shown in Fig. 5(a)). There is no threshold and fuel in integrate gate. Another, there is a mechanism (shown in Fig. 5(b)). Following the integrate gate, the threshold gate is divided into two variants: AND gate and OR gate, that can differentiate them with the threshold value. If the input is two, then the AND gate's threshold value is 1.2, the OR gate is 0.6; If the input is three, then the AND gate's threshold value is 2.4, the OR gate is 0.6 (shown in Fig. 5(c)). The whole seesaw cascade circuit is shown in Fig. 6.

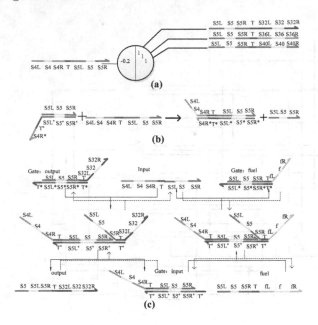

Fig. 4. (a) The amplifying gate of the seesaw cascade circuit. (b) The threshold reaction of the amplifying gate. (c) The reaction mechanism of the amplifying gate, solid arrow represent forward reaction, dotted arrow represent reverse reaction.

4   Simulation with Visual DSD

Visual DSD is an implementation of a programming language for constituent DNA circuits based on the DNA strand displacement. The language is included the basic elements of sequence domains, toeholds and branch migration. The interface is composed of setting section, coding section and display section. In the setting section, it is setting for simulation condition, condition results and molecular model visual effect. In the coding section, it is usually for devising DNA molecular structure through compile program; setting parameter. For instance: the reaction time, the information collecting times, the molecular combine, the separate time, and so on. In the display section, it is usually for preserving the data about simulation platform compile; simulating and analyzing. Including molecular computing simulation of the whole process, the changing curve graph of DNA molecular, the initial state and terminate state of molecular model. In this research, there are 16 conditions, the results of the four-input fire alarm system device is shown in Fig. 7. In the 16 simulation plots, the simulation time is 100000 s. We put the threshold value of OFF is "0.1x", so the threshold value of ON is "0.9x", and the initial concentration of the input strand is 90. In the process, the concentration of input strands almost the same. Roughly fall into two stage: in 0–4000 s, the molecular quantitative of input strands is reduced

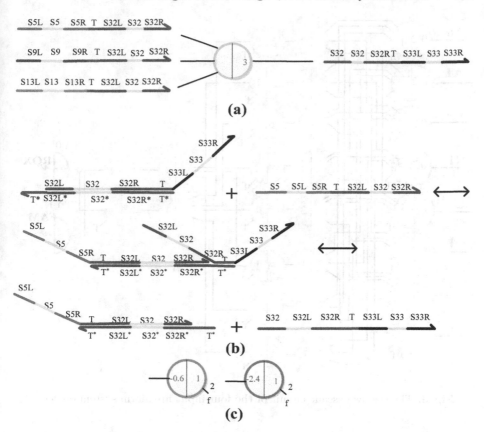

Fig. 5. (a) The integrate gate of the seesaw cascade circuit. (b) The reaction mechanism of the integrate gate. (c) The three-input threshold gate with the logic OR and AND.

sharply, that is because the higher concentration of input strands occurred strand displacement reaction with amplifying gate. But, the output strand is few. On account of seesaw circuit is cascade reaction, if the output strand of first stage is generated, then the cascade reaction will be turned into the input strand of the second stage. On this account, the cascade reaction needs some time for the produce of the output strand. After 4000 s, the density of the input strands is changed via undulating, and keeping essentially constant. The output strands will growth exponentially when the time reached to 40000 s, the reaction velocity will slow down with the concentration decrease of reactants. And the output strands are reached saturation. The gray line represents Y_1, the red line represents Y_0.

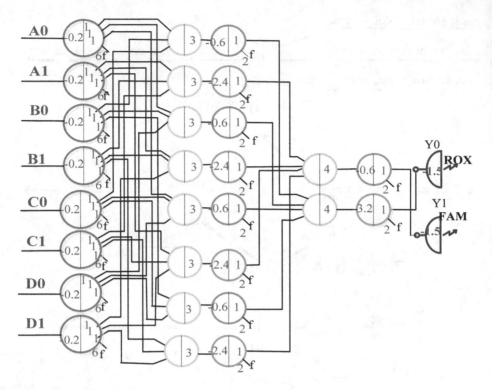

Fig. 6. The seesaw cascade circuit of the four-input fire alarm system device

5   Conclusion

In this paper, the structure of the reaction mechanism model of DNA strand displacement has been constructed firstly. Secondly, the logic circuit model of four-input fire alarm system device based on DNA strand displacement has been designed and implemented through the dual-rail circuits. Finally, the reaction process of DNA strand displacement has been simulated and the results of the logical operations can be displayed correctly through the specialized Visual DSD software. According to the results of the simulation, the compound displacement of DNA strands is an effective method for logic computation. The four-input fire alarm system device circuit can be generalized to the more inputs fire alarm system device. This investigation for the four-input fire alarm system device based on DNA strand displacement by dual-rail circuits designed may have a great prospect for the development and application in the biological informa-tion processing, molecular computing, and so on. Due to the limited experimen-tal conditions, the experiments of DNA strand displacement will be the future research directions.

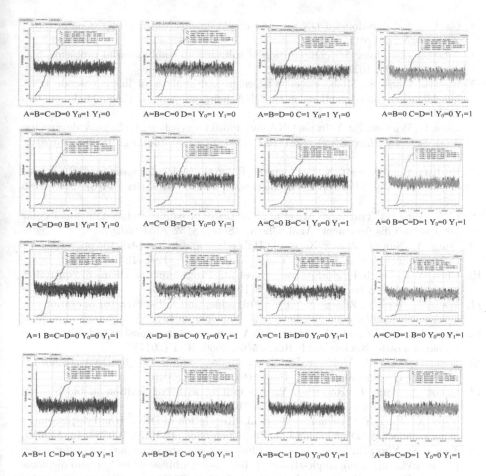

Fig. 7. The simulation result plots of the four-input fire alarm system device. (Color figure online)

Acknowledgments. The work is supported by the State Key Program of National Natural Science of China (Grant No. 61632002), the National Natural Science of China (Grant Nos. 61572446, 61472372, 61603348, 61602424), Science and Technology Innovation Talents Henan Province (Grant No. 174200510012), Research Program of Henan Province (Grant Nos. 15IRTSTHN012, 162300410220, 17A120005), and the Science Foundation of for Doctorate Research of Zhengzhou University of Light Industry (Grant No. 2014BSJJ044).

References

1. Winfree, E.: DNA computing by self-assembly. Bridge **33**(4), 31–38 (2003)
2. Wang, Z., Wu, Y., Tian, G., et al.: The application research on multi-digit logic operation based on DNA strand displacement. J. Comput. Theor. Nanosci. **12**(7), 1252–1257 (2015)

3. Cardelli, L.: Two-domain DNA strand displacement. Math. Struct. Comput. Sci. **23**(2), 247–271 (2013)
4. Adleman, L.: Molecular computation of solutions to combinatorial problems. Science **266**(5187), 1021–1024 (1994)
5. Bui, H., Garg, S., Miao, V., et al.: Design and analysis of linear cascade DNA hybridization chain reactions using DNA hairpins. New J. Phys. **19**(1), 015006 (2017)
6. Qian, L., Winfree, E.: A simple DNA gate motif for synthesizing large-scale circuits. J. R. Soc. Interface **8**(62), 1281–1297 (2011). https://doi.org/10.1098/rsif.2010.0729
7. Bartlett, E.J., Brissett, N.C., Plocinski, P., et al.: Molecular basis for DNA strand displacement by Nhej repair polymerases. Nucleic Acids Res. **44**(5), 2173–2186 (2016)
8. Li, F., Tang, Y., Traynor, S.M., et al.: Kinetics of proximity-induced intramolecular DNA strand displacement. Anal. Chem. **88**(16), 8152–8157 (2016)
9. Wang, Y., Sun, J., Zhang, X., et al.: Half adder and half subtractor operations by DNA self-assembly. J. Comput. Theor. Nanosci. **8**(7), 1288–1295 (2011)
10. Chen, Y.J., Dalchau, N., Srinivas, N., et al.: Programmable chemical controllers made from DNA. Nat. Nanotechnol. **8**(10), 755–762 (2013)
11. Wang, Y., Sun, J., Zhang, X., et al.: Full adder and full subtractor operations by DNA self-assembly. Adv. Sci. Lett. **4**(2), 383–390 (2011)
12. Yang, D., Tan, Z., Mi, Y., et al.: DNA nanostructures constructed with multi-stranded motifs. Nucleic Acids Res. **45**(6), 3606–3611 (2017)
13. Song, T., Garg, S., Mokhtar, R., et al.: Analog computation by DNA strand displacement circuits. ACS Synth. Biol. **5**(8), 898–912 (2016)
14. Genot, A., Fuji, T., Rondelez, Y.: Computing with competition in biochemical networks. Phys. Rev. Lett. **109**(20), 208102 (2012)
15. Yang, X., Tang, Y., Traynor, S.M., et al.: Regulation of DNA strand displacement using an allosteric DNA toehold. J. Am. Chem. Soc. **138**(42), 14076–14082 (2016)
16. Zhang, X., Ying, N., Shen, C., et al.: Fluorescence resonance energy transfer-based photonic circuits using single-stranded tile self-assembly and DNA strand displacement. J. Nanosci. Nanotechnol. **17**(2), 1053–1060 (2017)
17. Zhang, X., Zhang, W., Zhao, T., et al.: Design of logic circuits based on combinatorial displacement of DNA strands. J. Comput. Theor. Nanosci. **12**(7), 1161–1164 (2015)
18. Lakin, M., Stefanovic, D.: Supervised learning in adaptive DNA strand displacement networks. ACS Synth. Biol. **5**(8), 885–897 (2016)
19. Wang, Y., Cui, G., Zhang, X., et al.: Logical NAND and NOR operations using algorithmic self-assembly of DNA molecules. Phys. Procedia **33**, 954–961 (2012)
20. Qian, L., Winfree, E., Bruck, J.: Neural network computation with DNA strand displacement cascades. Nature **475**(7356), 368–372 (2011)
21. Wang, Y., Zhang, W., Li, X., et al.: Localized DNA circuits on DNA origami. J. Comput. Theor. Nanosci. **13**(6), 3942–3947 (2016)
22. Wang, Z., Cai, Z., Sun, Z., et al.: Research of molecule logic circuit based on DNA strand displacement reaction. J. Comput. Theor. Nanosci. **13**(10), 7684–7691 (2016)
23. Zhang, C., Yang, J., Xu, J.: Circular DNA logic gates with strand displacement. Langmuir **26**(3), 1416–1419 (2009)
24. Qian, L., Winfree, E.: Scaling up digital circuit computation with DNA strand displacement cascades. Science **332**(6034), 1196–1201 (2011)

25. Sawlekar, R., Montefusco, F., Kulkarni, V.V., et al.: Implementing nonlinear feedback controllers using DNA strand displacement reactions. IEEE Trans. Nanobiosci. **15**(5), 443–454 (2016)
26. Shi, X., Wang, Z., Deng, C., et al.: A novel bio-sensor based on DNA strand displacement. Plos One **9**(10), e108856 (2014)
27. Sun, J., Wang, Y., Wang, Y., et al.: Finite-time synchronization between two complex-variable chaotic systems with unknown parameters via nonsingular terminal sliding mode control. Nonlinear Dyn. **85**(2), 1105–1117 (2016)
28. Sun, J., Shen, Y.: Quasi-ideal memory system. IEEE Trans. Cybern. **45**(7), 1353–1362 (2015)
29. Shi, X., Lu, W., Wang, Z., et al.: Programmable DNA tile self-assembly using a hierarchical sub-tile strategy. Nanotechnology **25**(7), 075602 (2014)
30. Yang, J., Jiang, S., Liu, X., et al.: Aptamer-binding directed DNA origami pattern for logic gates. ACS Appl. Mater. Interfaces **8**(49), 34054–34060 (2016)
31. Yang, J., Dong, C., Dong, Y., et al.: Logic nanoparticle beacon triggered by the binding-induced effect of multiple inputs. ACS Appl. Mater. Interfaces **6**(16), 14486–14490 (2014)

An Improved Spiking Neural P Systems with Anti-Spikes for Fault Location of Distribution Networks with Distributed Generation

Chengyu Tao[1,2,3], Jun Wang[1,2,3]($\boxtimes$), Tao Wang[1,2,3], and Yanxiang Yang[1,2,3]

[1] School of Electrical Engineering and Electronic Information, Xihua University,
Chengdu 610039, People's Republic of China
745257101@qq.com

[2] Sichuan Province Key Laboratory of Power Electronics Energy-saving Technologies
and Equipment, Xihua University, Chengdu 610039, People's Republic of China

[3] Key Laboratory of Fluid and Power Machinery, Ministry of Education,
Xihua University, Chengdu 610039, People's Republic of China

Abstract. This paper proposes a method for fault location in distribution networks with distributed generation based on an improved spiking neural P system with anti-spikes (IASNP system). In the IASNP system, firing mechanism, fuzzy logic, new types of neurons and a matrix algorithm are introduced. The IASNP system is used to model the distribution networks while its matrix algorithm locates faults by considering the causality between regions and the associated nodes. Finally, two cases, including a multi source distribution network and distribution network with distributed generation, are used to verify the validity and accuracy of the proposed method.

Keywords: Spiking neural P system with anti-spikes · Distribution networks · Distributed generation · Fault location

1 Introduction

Spiking neural P systems (SNP systems) are the type of P systems [1] and distributed and parallel computing models inspired by the neurobiological behavior of neurons sending electrical impulses (spikes) along axons to other neurons [2–5]. ASNP systems are a variant of SNP systems consisting of two types of objects inspired by the functioning of inhibitory impulses among biological neurons [6,7]. Except for participating in spiking and forgetting rules, anti-spikes can also participate in the annihilating rule [8]. Peng mentioned that if anti-spikes and spikes are sent to the environment respectively, then it is separately marked with −1 and 1; otherwise, it is marked with 0 [9]. In this paper, spike trains of ASNP systems corresponds to fault current in distribution networks with distributed generation (DG), so ASNP systems are used to locate faults of distribution networks with DG.

© Springer Nature Singapore Pte Ltd. 2017
C. He et al. (Eds.): BIC-TA 2017, CCIS 791, pp. 380–395, 2017.
https://doi.org/10.1007/978-981-10-7179-9_29

DG is an emerging and small power supply which is connected to 35 kV and below distribution networks. When the lines fault in distribution networks with DG, it is important to locate and isolate the fault quickly and accurately for safe and stable operation of the distribution network [10]. The research methods of fault location for distribution networks with DG include: matrix algorithm [11], impedance based methods [12], artificial neural networks [13], wavelet analysis [14], optimization methods [15], Petri net [16], multi-agent system [17], support vector machines [18]. Each method has its own advantages and disadvantages.

Matrix algorithm is a simple method for fault location. Matrix algorithm is easy to realize in engineering and fast in calculation, but it is also a local search algorithm which is poor in fault tolerance. Impedance based method is widely researched in fault location of distribution networks with DG and has the advantages of less investment. But it is deeply affected by line impedance, loads and power parameters, and fault tolerance is poor. So, the power parameters and line impedance are not considered in recent study [12]. The research of neural network for fault location mainly focuses on multi-layer perceptron neural network, radial basis function neural network and back propagation neural network. Neural networks have strong learning ability, but numerous samples and long training time are needed. Wavelet analysis is used to locate the fault based on time of traveling wave arriving at the measuring point and has the problem of inaccurate location due to influence of the structure and noise in distribution networks. Ant colony algorithm, genetic algorithm, particle swarm optimization, hybrid differential evolution/particle swarm optimization algorithm, bacterial foraging algorithm, harmony algorithm are applied in fault location of distribution networks with DG. However, there are many shortcomings, such as enormous calculations, long search time, local optimization, and relatively complex models.

It has a great influence on the distribution network structure, the power flow direction and fault current after DG connection into distribution networks. When the line fails, the direction of fault current is changed from single direction to multiple direction [19]. Spike trains, described by 1, -1 and 0, of ASNP systems can be exactly used to distinguish the direction of fault current. Hence, fault location of distribution networks with DG is implemented based on IASNP systems. To solve inaccuracy of fault location in distribution networks with DG, a method, base on IASNP systems, is presented in this paper. IASNP systems are introduced to model distribution networks with DG and then the inference algorithm based on matrix is applied to locate faults. In order to make a better understanding of the process of establishing fault location model for distribution networks with DG based on IASNP systems, basic fault location units of two nodes and three nodes are proposed.

The remainder of this paper will be organized as follows. Section 2 states problems. Section 3 describes IASNP systems. In Sect. 4, a method of fault location in distribution network with DG is presented. Two cases are given in Sect. 5. Conclusions are finally drawn in Sect. 6.

2   Problem Description

A collection of feeders enclosed by a set of adjacent switches (circuit breakers(CBs), tie switches, and sectionalizing switches) is called a region where all adjacent switches are associated nodes. As shown in Fig. 1, CB_1, CB_2 and CB_3 are associated nodes of region (1), where S is a main power source and DG is a primary distributed power supply with power rating below 250kVA. The associated node CB_1 of region (1) in the distribution network with DG flows through fault current and if fault current flows from the associated node CB_1, but does not severally flow out from the CB_2 and CB_3, the region (1) faults [20]. When DG is connected to distribution networks, the structure of distribution networks is transformed from single power supply to multiple power supply. If the lines fail, the direction and magnitude of short circuit current will be affected by the type, position and capacity of DG. Moreover, if permeability of DG and stiffness ratio are respectively greater than 10% and 20%, the impact of DG connected to distribution networks will not be ignored and current protection is not applicable [21]. Therefore, it is of great value to locate faults accurately and realize the protection in distribution networks with DG.

Protection of multiple power distribution networks is achieved by the directional over-current protection (the directional protection and the current protection) where fault current amplitude is only determined by the current protection and current direction is judged by power direction relay of the direction protection. In Fig. 1, when the k faults, DG generates fault current. And if the direction of relay is assumed to be from the main power source to the end of DG, sensitivity of direction detection will not be affected by DG. Meanwhile, fault current may not be detected for small DG capacity and the advantage of the positive direction indicated by the arrow in Fig. 1 is that sensitivity and reliability of the positive component can always be guaranteed due to the large main power capacity wherever the faults occur [22]. Thus, the direction from main power supply to load or DG is specified as positive in this article.

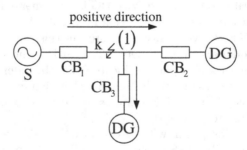

Fig. 1. Fault location principle of distribution networks with DG.

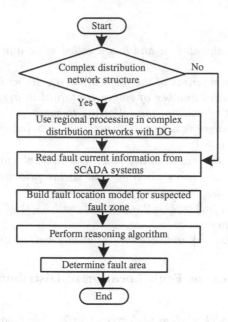

Fig. 2. Flow chart of fault location in distribution networks with DG.

In this paper, IASNP systems are used to locate faults in distribution networks with DG when fault information is complete or missing from CBs. The flow chart of the fault location of distribution networks with DG is shown in Fig. 2, First of all, complex distribution networks with DG are properly partitioned. Secondly, the fault current information of CBs is read from the SCADA system. Next, corresponding fault location model is established for the suspected fault region. Then, reasoning algorithm is developed to locate faults. Finally, fault regions can be located accurately through the fault judgment condition.

3 IASNP Systems for Fault Location of Distribution Networks with DG

In this part, we first give the definition of the original ASNP systems and then introduce the definition of IASNP systems. Finally, we make a comparison between ASNP systems and IASNP systems.

3.1 ASNP Systems

Definition 1. *An ASNP system of degree $m(m \geq 1)$ is a construct of the form*

$$\Pi = (O, \sigma_1, \ldots, \sigma_m, syn, in, out) \tag{1}$$

where

(1) $O = \{a, \bar{a}\}$ is the alphabet (a and $\bar{a}$ are called spike and anti-spike, respectively);

(2) $\sigma_1, \sigma_2, \ldots, \sigma_m$ are neurons of the form $\sigma_i = (n_i, R)$ with $1 \le i \le m$, where
   - $n_i \ge 0$ is the initial number of spikes contained in σ_i;
   - R is a finite set of rules of the following forms:
      (a) $E/b^c \to b'$ where is a regular expression over $\{a\}$ or $\{\bar{a}\}$, while $b, b' \subseteq \{a, \bar{a}\}$ and $c \ge 1$;
      (b) $a\bar{a} \to \lambda$ is the annihilating rule. The mutual annihilation of spikes and anti-spikes takes no time and it has priority over spiking and forgetting rules;

(3) $syn \subseteq \{1, 2, \ldots, m\} \times \{1, 2, \ldots, m\}$ with $(i,i) \notin syn$, is the set of synapses between neurons;

(4) $in, out \in \{1, 2, \ldots, m\}$ indicate the input and output neuron, respectively.

3.2   IASNP Systems for Fault Location of Distribution Networks with DG

Definition 2. *An IASNP system of degree $m(m \ge 1)$ is a construct of the form*

$$\Pi = (O, \sigma_1, \ldots, \sigma_m, syn, in, out) \qquad (2)$$

where

(1) $O = \{a, \bar{a}\}$ is the alphabet (a and $\bar{a}$ are called spike and anti-spike, respectively);

(2) $\sigma_1, \sigma_2, \ldots, \sigma_m$ are neurons of the form $\sigma_i = (\theta_i, r_i)$ with $1 \le i \le m$, where
   - $\theta_i \in \{1, -1, 0\}$ is the potential value of the spike contained in neuron σ_i;
   - r_i is a finite set of rules of the following forms:
      (a) $E/b^\theta \to b'^\beta, k$, where is a regular expression over $\{a\}$ or $\{\bar{a}\}$. If only a included in σ_i, $\theta_i \in \{1, 0\}$ and if only $\bar{a}$ contained in σ_i, $\theta_i \in \{-1, 0\}$. Where $k \in \{k_1, \bar{k}_1\}$, neuron σ_i sends pulses to neurons σ_j along the synapse is indicated by k_1 and neuron σ_j sends pulses to neurons σ_i along the synapse is indicated by $\bar{k}_1$; Otherwise, k is $\emptyset$;
      (b) $a\bar{a} \to \lambda$ is the annihilating rule. The mutual annihilation of spikes and anti-spikes takes no time and it has priority over spiking and forgetting rules;

(3) $syn \subseteq \{1, 2, \ldots, m\} \times \{1, 2, \ldots, m\}$ with $(i,i) \notin syn$, is the set of synapses between neurons;

(4) $in \in \{1, 2, \ldots, m\}$ indicate the input neuron;

(5) $out \in \{1, 2, \ldots, m\}$ indicate a set of the output neuron which is spiking trains consisted of neuron $\{\sigma_1, \ldots, \sigma_j\}$ in turn, $1 \le j \le m$.

Content of neuron σ_i is denoted by discrete values instead of the number of spikes in IASNP systems, which can be interpreted as the potential spike value of neuron σ_i. There are two types of synapses indicated by k_1 and $\bar{k}_1$. Besides, output of system Π is a spike train consisted of neuron $\{\sigma_1, \ldots, \sigma_j\}$ in turn.

In IASNP systems, neurons are divided into two categories: node neurons and region neurons. As shown in Fig. 3(a) and (b), node neurons contain two types: node neurons with positive spikes and node neurons with anti-spikes. If a node neuron receives a spikes, it will fire and emit a spike. The parameter β of the firing rule contained in a node neuron is equal to θ. The region neuron is shown in Fig. 4. If the number of spikes received by a region neuron is identical to the number of pre synapses, it will fire and emit a spike. The parameter β of the firing rule contained in a region neuron is also equal to θ.

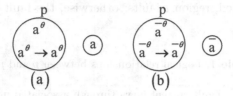

Fig. 3. Node neuron. (a) Node neuron with positive spikes and its simplified form; (b) Node neuron with anti-spikes and its simplified form.

Fig. 4. (a) Region neuron; (b) Region neuron simplified form.

4   Fault Location Method for Distribution Networks with DG Based on IASNP Systems

The method of establishing fault location model for distribution networks with DG based on IASNP systems and the inference algorithm will be given in this region.

4.1   The Principle of Modeling

There are three kinds of fault currents flowing through the associated node j of region i. The p_1 indicates that fault current flows through the associated node j of region i and the direction of fault current is the same as the positive direction. The p_2 indicates that fault current flows through the associated node j of region i and the direction of fault current is opposite to the positive direction. The p_3 indicates that fault current does not flow through the associated node j of region i. There are three connections between the associated node j and region i. The q_1 indicates that fault current flows into region i from the associated node j. The q_2 indicates that fault current flows out of the associated node j from region i. The q_3 indicates that the associated node j is not connected to region i. The specific relationship between fault location and topology of the distribution network with DG and direction of fault current is shown in Table 1. And operator is expressed by $\wedge$.

In Table 1, if p_1 and q_1 are simultaneously satisfied, region i faults. As p_1 and q_1 are simultaneously satisfied, fault current flows into region i from CB_j and does not flow out from region i. According to the principle of fault location in Sect. 2, region i can be judged to be faulty. Similarly, if p_2 and q_2 are also simultaneously satisfied, region i faults; otherwise, the fault cannot be located properly.

Table 1. Logical relationships between p and p.

$p \wedge q$		Fault current flows through associated node j with region i		
		p_1	p_2	p_3
Connection between region i and associated node j	q_1	Region i faults	No fault	No fault
	q_2	No fault	Region i faults	No fault
	q_3	No fault	No fault	Region i faults

As shown in Fig. 5, the structure of distribution networks with DG consists of two types of branch nodes: Fig. 5(a), three nodes with DG and Fig. 5(b), two nodes with DG where positive direction is indicated by the arrow. Region (1) is enclosed by CB_1, CB_2 and CB_3 and region (2) is enclosed by CB_1 and CB_2.

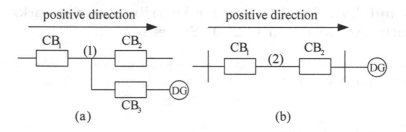

Fig. 5. (a) Three nodes with DG; (b) Two nodes with DG.

According to the principle of fault location in distribution networks with DG and the connection between nodes and feeder region, the basic units of fault location model are established, as shown in Fig. 6. CB_1 to CB_3 are denoted by node neurons σ_{i1} to σ_{i3} and region is expressed by region neuron σ_j in Fig. 6(a). The synapses k_1 and $\bar{k}_1$ between node neuron and region neuron indicate that

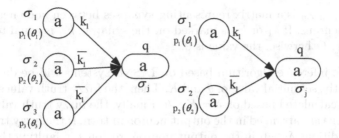

Fig. 6. Fault location models with DG based on IASNP systems. (a) Three nodes; (b) Two nodes.

CBs are respectively located at upstream and downstream of the region. As shown in Fig. 5(a), CB_1 is located at upstream of the region while CB_2 and CB_3 are located at downstream of the region. In the same way, CB_1 is located at upstream of the region while CB_2 is located at downstream of the region, as shown in Fig. 5(b).

4.2   Reasoning Algorithm

The fuzzy truth values of node neurons and the connections between node neurons and region neurons are described as follows. If fault current flows through the associated node j of region i and the direction of fault current is the same as the positive direction, θ_i will be equal to 1. Also, θ_i will be equal to -1, if fault current flows through the associated node j of region i and the direction of fault current is the opposite to the positive direction. When fault current does not flow through the associated node j of region i, θ_i is equal to 0. If CBs connected to region are located at upstream of region, k_1 will be equal to 1 and if CBs connected to region are located at downstream of region, $\overline{k}_1$ will be equal to -1; Otherwise, the value is equal to 0.

The reasoning algorithm based on IASNP systems for distribution networks with DG will be described in this part. If fuzzy truth value of node neuron is given, fuzzy truth values of other unknown neurons will be reasoned out by the algorithm. Let's assume that m node neurons, n region neurons, 1 output neuron are contained in the process of reasoning where m, n are respectively the number of CBs and regions in distribution networks with DG. To better illustrate the reasoning algorithm, we introduce some matrices as follows.

(1) $\theta_i = \{1, -1, 0\}$ is a vector of fuzzy truth values in the node neurons, where $\theta = (\theta_1, \theta_2, \ldots, \theta_m)^T$ denotes fuzzy truth value in the node neuron, $1 \le i \le m$.
(2) $\delta = (\delta_1, \delta_2, \ldots, \delta_m)$ is a vector of fuzzy truth values in the region neurons, where $\delta_i = \{1, -1, 0\}$ denotes fuzzy truth value in the i region neuron, $1 \le i \le n$.
(3) $out = \{\delta_1, \delta_2 \ldots, \delta_n\}$ is a output neuron, where the fuzzy truth values of region neurons are arranged sequentially.

(4) $K = (k_{ij})_{m \times n}$ is a matrix representing synapses between node neurons and region neurons. If k_1 or $\bar{k}_1$ is marked on the synapse, k_{ij} is equal to -1 or 1 severally; Otherwise, the value is 0.

Next, the inference algorithm based on IASNP systems will be described as follows. Firstly, set initial value of θ and K. Then, the fuzzy truth values of region neurons are calculated based on $\delta = K \times \theta$. Finally, the fuzzy truth values of the region neurons are arranged in the output neuron in turn. If the fuzzy truth value satisfies conditions $\delta_i > 0$ in the output neuron, region i is faulty; otherwise, If the fuzzy truth value satisfies conditions $\delta_i < 0$ in the output neuron, region is not faulty.

5   Case Studies

Several cases of distribution networks with DG are proposed to verify the validity and accuracy of IASNP systems. Each case contains single fault, multiple fault and incomplete information acquired from SCADA systems.

5.1   Fault Location of Simple Distribution Networks with DG

The system is a multi-power ring network with closed-loop operation, which includes three power supplies, CB_1 to CB_{10} and feeder regions (1) to (8), as shown in Fig. 7. The fault location model of distribution networks with DG based on IASNP systems is shown in Fig. 8.

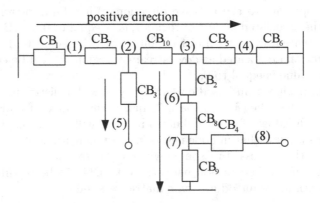

Fig. 7. Multi-power distribution networks.

Single fault: when region (3) faults, we read fault current direction of CB_1 to CB_{10} from the SCADA systems and get initial value θ which is a matrix of dimension 19. Meanwhile, matrix K obtained by synaptic connections between node neurons and region neurons consists of 8 rows and 10 columns.

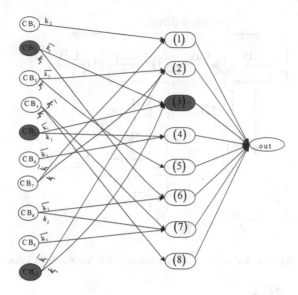

Fig. 8. Fault location model of multi-power distribution networks.

$$\theta = \begin{pmatrix} 1 & -1 & 0 & 0 & -1 & -1 & 1 & -1 & -1 & 1 \end{pmatrix}^T$$

$$K = \begin{pmatrix} 1 & 0 & 0 & 0 & 0 & 0 & -1 & 0 & 0 & 0 \\ 0 & 0 & -1 & 0 & 0 & 0 & 1 & 0 & 0 & -1 \\ 0 & -1 & 0 & 0 & -1 & 0 & 0 & 0 & 0 & 1 \\ 0 & 0 & 0 & 0 & 1 & -1 & 0 & 0 & 0 & 0 \\ 0 & 0 & 1 & 0 & 0 & 0 & 0 & 0 & 0 & 0 \\ 0 & 1 & 0 & 0 & 0 & 0 & 0 & -1 & 0 & 0 \\ 0 & 0 & 0 & -1 & 0 & 0 & 0 & 1 & -1 & 0 \\ 0 & 0 & 0 & 1 & 0 & 0 & 0 & 0 & 0 & 0 \end{pmatrix}$$

The fuzzy truth values of δ obtained by the algorithm are sequentially arranged in output neuron *out*.

$$out = \begin{pmatrix} 0 & 0 & 3 & 0 & 0 & 0 & 0 & 0 \end{pmatrix}^T$$

Multiple fault: from the condition of fault location, region is judged to be faulty which verifies the practicability and accuracy of fault location in distribution networks with DG based on IASNP systems. When region (3) and (5) fault, the reasoning results are as follows. From the condition of fault location, region (3) and (5) is judged to be faulty.

$$\theta = \begin{pmatrix} 1 & -1 & 1 & 0 & -1 & -1 & 1 & -1 & -1 & 0 \end{pmatrix}^T$$

$$out = \begin{pmatrix} 0 & 0 & 2 & 0 & 1 & 0 & 0 & 0 \end{pmatrix}^T$$

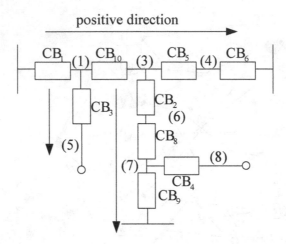

Fig. 9. Multi-power distribution networks with incomplete information.

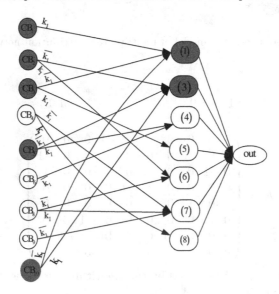

Fig. 10. Fault location model of multi-power distribution networks with incomplete information.

Incomplete information is acquired from SCADA systems: When the fault current information of CB_7 cannot be read from the SCADA system for faulted region, CB_7 is removed from the diagram to form the new multi-power distribution networks, as shown in Fig. 9. The initial values of θ and K are given again respectively. A model of fault location in distribution networks with DG based on IASNP systems is shown in Fig. 10. According to the inference algorithm in Sect. 4.2, we can get results.

$$\theta = \begin{pmatrix} 1 & -1 & 0 & 0 & -1 & -1 & -1 & -1 & -1 \end{pmatrix}^T$$

$$out = \begin{pmatrix} 2 & 1 & 0 & 0 & 0 & 0 & 0 \end{pmatrix}^T$$

From the result of reasoning, we can make a conclusion that region (1) and (3) fault. But, the fuzzy truth value of θ_1, θ_3, θ_{10} connected with δ_1 are respectively 1, 0 and -1 and the synaptic relationship of node neurons θ_1, θ_3, θ_{10} and region neuron δ_1 are severally 1, -1 and -1. From the equation $1 \times 1 + 0 \times (-1) + (-1) \times (-1) = 2$, we can see that fault current flows only from region (1). Therefore, according to the principle of fault location, region (1) is faulty. Similarly, according to the equation $(-1) \times (-1) + (-1) \times (-1) + (-1) \times 1 = 1$, we can see that fault current flows from region (3) and flows out of region (3). So, region (3) is not faulty.

5.2   Fault Location of Complex Distribution Network with DG

CB_{32} and CB_{35} are normally open tie switches that divide the distribution network with DG into separate open loop networks A, B and C in Fig. 11 [24]. Actually, distribution networks are usually designed by closed loop and operated by open loop. When the fault has little or no influence on other regions, it can be properly partitioned. For example, the distribution network is divided into four regions I, II, III, IV in Fig. 11, where the red dotted line represents the parting line between regions. Due to the limited space, the model of fault location in complex distribution networks with DG is omitted and we only give the initial values and inference results of case 2.

Single fault: When region (2) faults in region I, we read fault current direction of CB_1 to CB_7 from SCADA systems and get initial value θ. At the same time, matrix K is obtained according to the synaptic connection between node neurons and region neurons and the reasoning results are as follows.

$$\theta = \begin{pmatrix} 1 & 1 & -1 & 0 & 0 & 0 & -1 \end{pmatrix}^T$$

$$K = \begin{pmatrix} 1 & -1 & 0 & 0 & 0 & 0 & 0 \\ 0 & 1 & -1 & 0 & 0 & 0 & 0 \\ 0 & 0 & 1 & -1 & 0 & 0 & -1 \\ 0 & 0 & 0 & 1 & -1 & 0 & 0 \\ 0 & 0 & 0 & 0 & 1 & -1 & 0 \\ 0 & 0 & 0 & 0 & 0 & 1 & 0 \\ 0 & 0 & 0 & 0 & 0 & 0 & 1 \end{pmatrix}$$

$$out = \begin{pmatrix} 0 & 2 & -1 & 0 & 0 & 0 & -1 \end{pmatrix}^T$$

According to the spiking trains of the output neuron and the criterion of fault location, the fault can be located in region (2).

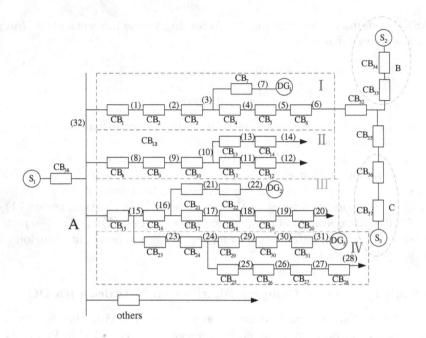

Fig. 11. Schematic diagram of complex distribution networks with DG.

Multiple fault: When region (28) and (29) fault in region IV, we read fault current direction of CB_{23} to CB_{31} from the SCADA systems and get initial value θ. The inference results are as follows.

$$\theta = \begin{pmatrix} 1\ 1\ 1\ 1\ 1\ 1\ 1 & -1 & -1 \end{pmatrix}^{T}$$

$$out = \begin{pmatrix} 0 & -1\ 0\ 0\ 0\ 1\ 2\ 0 & -1 \end{pmatrix}^{T}$$

According to the spiking trains of the output neuron and the criterion of fault location, fault can be located in region (28) and (29).

Incomplete information is acquired from SCADA systems: When the fault current information of CB_{25} cannot be read from the SCADA system for faulted region (28), CB_{25} is removed from the diagram to form the new distribution networks with DG.

$$\theta = \begin{pmatrix} 1\ 1\ 1\ 1\ 1 & -1 & -1 & -1 \end{pmatrix}^{T}$$

$$out = \begin{pmatrix} 0\ 1\ 0\ 0\ 0\ 1\ 0\ 0 & -1 \end{pmatrix}^{T}$$

From the reasoning results, we can see that (24) and (28) fault. On the basis of the principle of eliminating fault in case 1, region (24) is not faulty.

5.3   Comparison Analysis

Recently, case 1 and case 2 have been studied by several methods, such as matrix algorithm [24], ant colony algorithm [23], memetic algorithms [26]. Ma [24] locates faults in multi-power distribution networks based on improved matrix algorithm. Tao [23, 26] combines complex switching functions to locate faults by iterating constantly using improved memetic algorithm and improved ant colony algorithm. In this paper, an IASNP systems are used to locate faults in a distribution network with DG. Moreover, the problem of fault location in distribution networks with DG is described by the two basic units composed of node neurons and region neurons.

The comparison results of IASNP systems and other methods on case 2 are showed in Table 2. When multiple faults occur, there is a 1% possibility that fault cannot be accurately located by using the memetic algorithm. At the same time, when the fault information is inaccurate obtained from the SCADA system, there is a 2% possibility of inaccurate location for multiple faults. Also, if multiple faults occur at the two regions along a feeder without DG, such as (25) and (27), region (27) cannot be properly located [23]. Comparison results show that IASNP system is not only applicable to all distribution network with DG but also can locate all faults more accurately.

Table 2. Comparison between IASNP systems and other methods.

Algorithm	Type		
	Multiple faults	Inaccurate fault information	Related to fault location
Ant colony algorithm	100%	100%	Yes
Memetic algorithm	99%	98%	No
IASNP systems	100%	100%	No

6   Conclusion

Faults are accurately located based on IASNP systems for distribution networks with DG. By combining the characteristics of spikes and electrical quantities effectively, the electrical quantities are introduced into research of fault location based on ASNP systems. Also, compared with the fault diagnosis model for a component, it is easier to model for topology of whole distribution networks with DG [27]. The graphical model of fault location is convenient to express the logical relation so that the process of fault location can be well understood. What's more, owing to the ability of processing information in parallel, models of fault location can locate faults more quickly, which is beneficial to the safe and stable operation of distribution networks.

The spikes in fuzzy spiking neural P systems (FSNP systems) represent the confidence of the protection device and component fault while the spikes in IASNP systems indicate current direction. The fault diagnosis model based on FSNP systems is set up on the relay protection principle while the model based on IASNP systems is built according to topology and current relation. Also, fuzzy spiking neural P system is used for fault component identification and IASNP system can be applied to locate faults.

When the fault occurs, the structure of distribution networks is divided into several regions and then the fault location model is established for each region. Therefore, whether the structure of distribution networks is complex or not, the proposed modeling method based on IASNP systems are applicable. The reasoning results in two cases show that the proposed method can accurately locate single faults, multiple faults and the situation of incomplete information. In addition, the cases of incomplete information are only considered in this paper but there exists information distortion in distribution networks. Future work will focus on studying fault information distortion in distribution networks with DG and application of this method to power system fault diagnosis.

Acknowledgments. This work was partially supported by the National Natural Science Foundation of China (No. 61472328), Chunhui Project Foundation of the Education Department of China (No.Z2016143), Research Fund of Sichuan Science and Technology Project (No. 2015HH0057) and Innovation Fund for Graduate Students of Xihua University (No. ycjj2017058).

References

1. Păun, G.: Computing with membranes. Int. J. Comput. Syst. Sci. **61**, 108–143 (2000)
2. Ionescu, M., Păun, G., Yokomori, T.: Spiking neural P systems. Fundam. Inform. **71**, 279–308 (2006)
3. Păun, G., Pérez-Jiménez, M.J., Rozenberg, G.: Spike trains in spiking neural P systems. Int. J. Found. Comput. **17**, 975–1002 (2006)
4. Peng, H., Wang, J., Prez-Jimnez, M.J., Wang, H., Shao, J., Wang, T.: Fuzzy reasoning spiking neural P system for fault diagnosis. Inform. Sci. **235**, 106–116 (2013)
5. Wang, J., Peng, H.: Adaptive fuzzy spiking neural P systems for fuzzy inference and learning. Int. J. Comput. Math. **90**, 857–868 (2013)
6. Pan, L.Q., Păun, G.: Spiking neural P systems with anti-spikes. Int. J. Comput. Commun. **4**, 273–283 (2009)
7. Jiang, K.Q., Pan, L.Q.: Spiking neural P systems with anti-spikes working in sequential mode induced by maximum spike number. Neurocomputing **171**, 1674–1683 (2016)
8. Song, T., Pan, L.Q., Wang, J., Venkat, I., Subramanian, K.G., Abdullah, R.: Normal forms of spiking neural P systems with anti-spikes. IEEE Trans. Nanobiosci. **11**, 352–359 (2012)
9. Peng, X.W., Fan, X.P., Liu, J.X.: Performing balanced ternary logic and arithmetic operations with spiking neural P systems with anti-spikes. Adv. Mater. Res. **505**, 378–385 (2012)
10. Cai, Y., Cao, Y., Li, Y., Huang, T., Zhou, B.: Cascading failure analysis considering interaction between power grids and communication networks. IEEE Trans. Smart Grid **7**, 530–538 (2016)
11. Teng, J.H., Huang, W.H., Luan, S.H.: Automatic and fast faulted line-region location method for distribution systems based on fault indicators. IEEE Trans. Power Syst. **29**, 1653–1662 (2014)

12. Jia, K., Bi, T.S., Ren, Z.F., Thomas, D., Sumner, M.: High frequency impedance based fault location in distribution system with DGs. IEEE Trans. Smart Grid **10**, 1–10 (2016)
13. Zayandehroodi, H., Mohamed, A., Shareef, H., Farhoodnea, M.: A novel neural network and backtracking based protection coordination scheme for distribution system with distributed generation. Int. J. Electr. Power Energy Syst. **43**, 868–879 (2012)
14. Goudarzi, M., Vahidi, B., Naghizadeh, R.A., Hosseinian, S.H.: Improved fault location algorithm for radial distribution systems with discrete and continuous wavelet analysis. Int. J. Electr. Power Energy Syst. **67**, 423–430 (2015)
15. Pradhan, A.K., Routray, A., Gudipalli, S.M.: Fault direction estimation in radial distribution system using phase change in sequence current. IEEE Trans. Power Deliv. **22**, 2065–2071 (2007)
16. Zhou, Q., Zheng, B.L., Wang, C.S., Zhao, J.H., Wang, Y.: Fault location for distribution networks with distributed generation sources using a hybrid DE/PSO algorithm. In: Power and Energy Society General Meeting, pp. 1–6. IEEE Press, Canada (2013)
17. Calderaro, V., Piccolo, A., Galdi, V., Siano, P.: Identifying fault location in distribution systems with high distributed generation penetration. In: AFRICON, pp. 1–6. IEEE Press, Kenya (2009)
18. El-Zonkoly, A.M.: Fault diagnosis in distribution networks with distributed generation. Electr. Power Syst. Res. **81**, 1482–1490 (2011)
19. Huang, T., Voronca, S.L., Purcarea, A.A., Estebsari, A., Bompard, E.: Analysis of chain of events in major historic power outages. Adv. Electr. Comput. **14**, 63–70 (2014)
20. Liu, P.C., Li, X.L.: Fault location algorithm of distribution network with distributed generation based on multi population genetic algorithm. Power Syst. Prot. Control **44**, 36–41 (2016)
21. Liu, J., Yun, B.J., Cui, Q., He, L.T., Zheng, J.M.: A fast self healing distributed intelligent feeder automation system. Autom. Electr. Power Syst. **34**, 62–66 (2010)
22. Cong, W., Pan, Z.C., Wang, C.S., Yu, G.C., Wang, W., Gou, T.S., Song, Z.M.: Regional Longitudinal Protection Scheme for Power Distribution System with High Permeability DG. vol. 33, pp. 81–85 (2009)
23. Tao, W.Q., Yang, G., Zhang, J.Y.: Fault section locating for distribution network with DG based on improved ant colony algorithm. In: 8th International Power Electronics and Motion Control Conference, pp. 1–4. IEEE Press, China (2016)
24. Ma, Y., Mao, Y., Li, H.J.: An improved matrix algorithm for fault location in distribution network. In: 3rd International Conference on Intelligent System Design and Engineering Applications, pp. 289–293. IEEE Press, China (2013)
25. Yang, G.: Fault Location of Distribution Network with DG. HeFei University of technology, China (2014)
26. Tao, W.Q., Yang, G., Ding, M., Lu, S.Q., He, Q.: Application of improved memetic algorithm for fault location in distribution network with DG. J. Electron. Meas. Instrum. **30**, 265–273 (2016)
27. Wang, T., Zhang, G.X., Zhao, J.B., He, Z.Y., Wang, J., Perez-Jimenez, M.J.: Fault diagnosis of electric power systems based on fuzzy reasoning spiking neural P systems. IEEE Trans. Power Syst. **30**, 1182–1194 (2015)

Five-Input Square Root Logical Operation Based on DNA Strand Displacement

Yanfeng Wang[1,2], Panru Wang[1,2], and Junwei Sun[1,2(✉)]

[1] Henan Key Lab of Information-Based Electrical Appliances,
Zhengzhou University of Light Industry, Zhengzhou 450002, China
junweisun@yeah.net
[2] College of Electrical and Electronic Engineering,
Zhengzhou University of Light Industry, Zhengzhou 450002, China

Abstract. In recent years, DNA strand displacement technology has played a significant role in DNA computing. In this paper, a five-bit square-root digital logic circuit based on DNA strand displacement is designed by using a simple DNA reaction mechanism. The whole reaction process of logic circuit operations can be programmed and simulated through using the Visual DSD simulation software. According to the simulation results, the square-root logic circuit is feasible to achieve the desired logical computations. Through analyzing the simulation results, the feasibility of the designed circuit is demonstrated. And it is proves that DNA strand displacement may have a great potential and bright prospect in the construction of large-scale logic circuits.

Keywords: DNA strand displacement · DNA computing · Square-root · Visual DSD

1 Introduction

DNA computing is a new field in which includes computer science and molecular biology subject [1,2]. DNA is a palmary nanoscale engineering material for biochemical circuits, which has been used as a computing substrate and the first demonstration of solving a seven-city Hamiltonian path problem in 1994 [3]. In recent years, DNA is served as a computing tool, which has been used widely in logic circuit, nano-medicine, molecular device, nano-network, and so on [4–8]. DNA computing comprises some of molecular operation technologies, for instance DNA self-assembly [9–11], probe machine [12] and DNA strand displacement [13–16]. DNA strand displacement has become a new method in the bio-computing, and which is also a common method in DNA self-assembly. DNA strand displacement has a series of advantages, such as which can be taken place

---

Please note that the LNCS Editorial assumes that all authors have used the western naming convention, with given names preceding surnames. This determines the structure of the names in the running heads and the author index.

© Springer Nature Singapore Pte Ltd. 2017
C. He et al. (Eds.): BIC-TA 2017, CCIS 791, pp. 396–404, 2017.
https://doi.org/10.1007/978-981-10-7179-9_30

at room temperature and do not require any enzymes; which may apply that simplicity, scalability, and modularity for large-scale applications [17].

On the basis of DNA strand displacement cascade reaction [18,19], DNA strand displacement technology played an important role in solving some math problems [20,21] and managing nano-machines. In 2006, the largest digital circuit was built based on DNA strand displacement cascade reaction, which was involved 12 initial DNA species [22]. Lots of biochemistry logic circuits have been constructed on the basis of the DNA strand displacement, which can be used to achieve our desired purpose.

In this paper, we firstly introduce the reaction mechanism of DNA strand displacement. Then, according to the rules of the logical operations, the five-digit square-root logic circuit is designed, and which can be translated into the corresponding dual-rail circuit and seesaw logic circuit. The seesaw logic circuit can be simulated by using the Visual DSD simulation software. The DSD programming language is used to design and analysis for DNA circuit.

Compared with the previous work [23–25], there are some advantages, which can make our research more significative and attractive. First, the molecular logic computing model [23] based on DNA self-assembly has existed; and now the strategy on the basis of DNA strand displacement is applied to design the five-input-three-output square-root logic circuit. Second, the square-root of a four-bit binary number operation is a special case of the five-digit square-root logic operation [24]; the five-input-three-output square-root logic circuit is the further extension of the four-bit binary number. In addition, the dual-rail circuit model based on DNA strand displacement also makes the nano-level logic circuits toward a large-scale logic circuit direction [25]. This logic circuit can be used to construct the more complex logic circuit in the future.

The paper is organized as follows. In the Sect. 1, the introduction is described. And then, in the Sect. 2, the DSD and the seesaw motifs of basic gates are given. In the Sect. 3, the binary five-digit square-root circuit and the dual-rail circuit are depicted. In the Sect. 4, the seesaw circuit and the simulation results are represented. Finally, the conclusion of the five-bit square-root circuit is presented in the Sect. 5.

2 DSD and Seesaw Motif of Basic Gates

DNA strand displacement is a dynamic process, which means a single strand can be displaced through another single strand from the complex double-strand. The process of DNA strand displacement is shown in the Fig. 1. Firstly, the domain T with a short toehold usually is consisted of 4–6 base sequences [26,27] and the domain T^* is the Watson-Crick complement pair of T. The strand $< S1\,T\,S2 >$ and the strand $< S2\,T\,S3 >$ represent the input strand and the output strand, respectively. The domain $< S2\,T >$ is recognition domain. If the input strand and the output strand have the same toehold domain, then the previous output signal could be acted as the input signal of the next logical operation. Based on the particular condition, the DNA logic gates can be constructed by using DNA strand displacement technology.

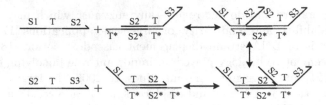

Fig. 1. The DNA strand displacement reaction mechanism. The strand $< S1\,T\,S2 >$ is the input strand. The T represents the toehold domain. The $< S2\,T >$ is the recognition domain. And the strand $< S2\,T\,S3 >$ is the output strand.

The basic logic gates include AND, OR and NOT, which can be translated into the corresponding DNA seesaw logic gates [28,29], as shown in Fig. 2. The two states of the logical operation are defined the digit "0" and the digit "1" in which represent the event false and true, respectively. In the DNA seesaw logic gates, the low concentration and the high concentration represent the digit "0" and digit "1", respectively. The DNA seesaw logic circuit can be simulated by using the Visual DSD software [30,31].

In Fig. 2, there are amplifying gates, integration gates, AND gates and OR gates, and which are all used to construct the DNA seesaw logic circuit in the Sect. 4. The red digit -0.6 and -1.2 are both the threshold value. The value of the fuel is the two times of the total output value.

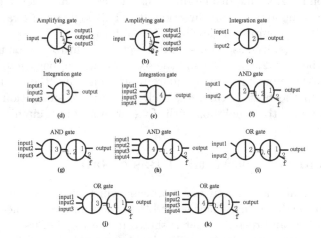

Fig. 2. The seesaw motifs of basic logic gates. (a) One-input-three-output amplifying gate. (b)One-input-four-output amplifying gate. (c) Two-input-one-output integrating gate. (d)Three-input-one-output integrating gate. (e) Four-input-one-output integrating gate. (f)–(h) Abstract diagrams of seesaw AND gates. (i)–(k) Abstract diagrams of seesaw OR gates.

3 Binary Square-Root Circuit and Dual-Rail Circuit

In this paper, a five-digit square-root logic circuit is designed, which is a combinational logic circuit. The truth table of the five-bit square-root logic circuit is shown in Table 1, in which there are five kinds of logical operation cases. According to the function of the truth table, the corresponding five-input-three-output square-root digital logic circuit is designed, as shown in Fig. 3. In Fig. 3, the logic circuit has been processed from the left to the right. Five inputs are contained in the left side of the square-root logic circuit, which are X_1, X_2, X_3, X_4 and X_5, three outputs are included in the right side of the logic circuit, which are Y_1, Y_2 and Y_3. AND, OR and NOT logic gates are used to constructed the Boolean functions of logic circuit. In Fig. 3, there are five NOT gates, seven AND gates and one OR gate, which are included in the square-root digit logic circuit.

Table 1. Truth table of the five-digit square root circuit

Binary input $X_5X_4X_3X_2X_1$	Decimal input	Binary output $Y_3Y_2Y_1$	Decimal output
00000	0	000	0
00001	1	001	1
00100	4	010	2
01001	9	011	3
10000	16	100	4

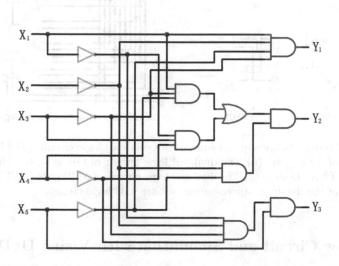

Fig. 3. Digital logic circuit of the five-input-three-output square-root. X_1, X_2, X_3, X_4 and X_5 are five input signals; Y_1, Y_2 and Y_3 are three output signals, respectively. The NOT logic gate is labeled by green color. The AND logic gate is labeled by blue color. The OR logic gate is labeled through red color. (Color figure online)

If the inputs are absent in the response, the false outputs will be generated. To avoid this situation, the five-bit square-root combinational logic circuit can be turned to the corresponding dual-rail logic circuit, which is consisted of a series of AND gates and OR gates. Among which, the OR gate is labeled by blue color, and the AND gate is labeled by green color. The basic AND, OR, NAND and NOR logic gates all can be translated into the corresponding dual-rail logic circuit, as shown in Fig. 4 (a)–(d), respectively. In the dual-rail logic circuit, the initial input is presented by a pair of inputs which can be represented by logic "ON" and "OFF". In the square-root dual-rail logic circuit, taking the input X_1 as an example, the input X_1 is divided into X_{10} and X_{11}. If the input X_1 is taken part in the reaction, the input X_{10} is shown as the logic "OFF" state, and then the input X_{11} is expressed through the logic "ON" state. In this paper, the dual-rail logic circuit of the five-input-three-output square-root is shown in Fig. 4 (e).

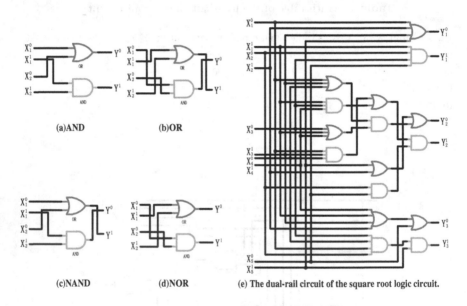

Fig. 4. The five-input-three-output square-root dual-rail logic circuit. (a) The dual-rail logic circuit of AND gate. (b) The dual-rail logic circuit of OR gate. (c) The dual-rail logic circuit of NAND gate. (d) The dual-rail logic circuit of NOR gate. (e) The dual-rail logic circuit of the five-input-three-output square-root logic circuit.

4   Seesaw Circuit and Simulation with Visual DSD

In terms of the seesaw basic logic gates and the dual-rail logic circuit of the five-input-three-output square-root, the seesaw circuit of the square-root logic circuit is given in Fig. 5, which could be simulated through using the Visual DSD simulation software.

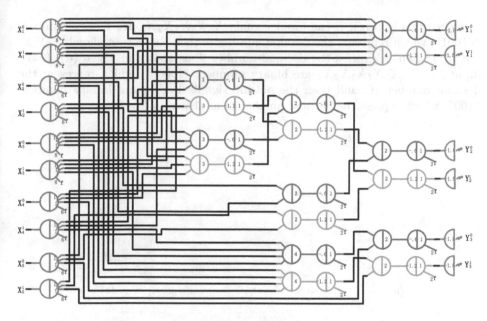

Fig. 5. The seesaw logic circuit of the five-bit square root logic circuit. The amplifying gate is labeled by orange color. The OR gate is labeled by blue color. The AND gate is labeled by light green. The report gate is labeled by gray green. (Color figure online)

Visual DSD is a design and analysis tool for DNA strand displacement systems. In this article, the reaction process of the five-bit square-root logic operation based on DNA strand displacement is simulated through using the Visual DSD software, and the five square-root operations are completed through the designed logic circuit. The simulation results of the five-input-three-output square-root logic circuit are displayed in Fig. 6 (a)–(e). In Fig. 6 (a)–(e), the output value Y_{10} and the output value Y_{11} are expressed by using the red curve line and green curve line, respectively; the output value Y_{20} and the output value Y_{21} are represented by using the blue curve line and the yellow curve line, respectively; the output value Y_{30} and the output value Y_{31} are depicted by using the orange curve line and the purple curve line, respectively. In this paper, the total concentration of the response is 100 nM. The concentration range of the output result is 0–10 nM, which represents the logic "OFF", and the output result concentration range is 90–100 nM, which represents the logic "ON". In Fig. 6, if the input signals $X_5X_4X_3X_2X_1$ are binary numbers "00000", which represent the decimal number 0; then the output signals $Y_3Y_2Y_1$ are binary numbers "000", which express the decimal number 0, as shown in Fig. 6 (a). If the input signals $X_5X_4X_3X_2X_1$ are binary numbers "00001", which represent the decimal number 1; and the output signals $Y_3Y_2Y_1$ are binary numbers "001" which express the decimal number 1, as shown in Fig. 6 (b). If the input signals $X_5X_4X_3X_2X_1$ are binary numbers "00100", which represent the decimal number 4; then the output signals $Y_3Y_2Y_1$ are binary numbers "010", which express the decimal number 2, as shown in Fig. 6 (c). If the input signals $X_5X_4X_3X_2X_1$ are binary numbers "01001"; which represent the decimal number 9, then the output signals $Y_3Y_2Y_1$ are "011", which express the decimal number 3, as shown in Fig. 6 (d). If the input signals $X_5X_4X_3X_2X_1$ are binary numbers "10000", which represent the decimal number 16; and then the output signals $Y_3Y_2Y_1$ are binary numbers "100", which express the decimal number 4, as shown in Fig. 6 (e).

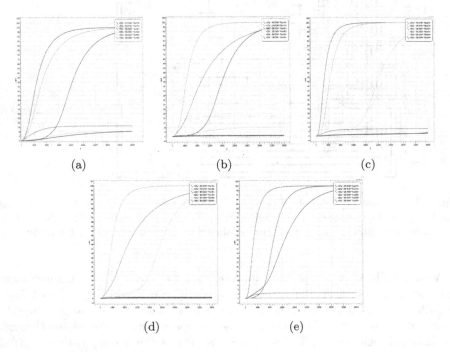

(a)   (b)   (c)

(d)   (e)

Fig. 6. The simulation results with Visual DSD. (Color figure online)

According to the simulation results, the following conclusions can be obtained. The logic "ON" curve and logic "OF" curve both enter into the stable area, which correctly express the logic "1" and logic "0", respectively. Although the simulation results have a high availability and the desired purpose is completed as we expected, which is still needed to be demonstrated by actual experiment.

5   Conclusion

In this paper, the truth table of the desired circuit had been drawn, and then the square-root digital logic circuit had been designed. The digital logic circuit can be transformed into the dual rail logic circuit on the basis of the method of dual rail. Then, the dual rail logic can be translated into the biochemical seesaw logic circuit based on the method of the seesaw logic gates. Ultimately, the reaction process of the five-input-three-output square-root logic circuit had been simulated by using the specialized Visual DSD software. The specific binary input signals include "00000", "00001", "00100", "01001" and "10000", which can be transformed into the corresponding decimal numbers "0", "1", "4", "9" and "16". The final binary output signals contain "000", "001", "010", "011" and "100", which can be transformed into the corresponding decimal numbers "0", "1", "2", "3" and "4". From the simulation results, the logic circuit achieves the square-root logical operations. DNA strand displacement is an effective theory for biological computation, the investigation of the square-root logic circuit may have a light prospect for the development and application in the biological information processing, molecular computing, and so on. Owing to the limited experimental conditions, the experiments of self-assembly will be the further research directions in the future.

Acknowledgments. The work is supported by the State Key Program of National Natural Science of China (Grant No. 61632002), the National Natural Science of China (Grant Nos. 61572446, 61472372, 61603348, 61602424), Science and Technology Innovation Talents Henan Province (Grant No. 174200510012), Research Program of Henan Province (Grant Nos. 15IRTSTHN012, 162300410220, 17A120005), and the Science Foundation of for Doctorate Research of Zhengzhou University of Light Industry (Grant No. 2014BSJJ044).

References

1. Winfree, E.: DNA computing by self-assembly. Bridge **33**, 31–38 (2003)
2. Cardelli, L.: Two-domain DNA strand displacement. Math. Struct. Comp. Sci. **23**, 247–271 (2013)
3. Adleman, L.M.: Molecular computation of solutions to combinatorial problems. Science **266**, 1021–1024 (1994)
4. Mao, C., LaBean, T.H., Reif, J.H., Seeman, N.C.: Logical computation using algorithmic self-assembly of DNA triple-crossover molecules. Nature **407**, 493–496 (2000)
5. Song, X., Eshra, A., Dwyer, C., Reif, J.: Renewable DNA seesaw logic circuits enabled by photoregulation of toehold-mediated strand displacement. RSC Adv. **7**, 28130–28144 (2017)
6. Chhabra, R., Sharma, J., Liu, Y., Rinker, S., Yan, H.: DNA self-assembly for nanomedicine. Adv. Drug. Deliver. Rev. **62**, 617–625 (2010)
7. DelRosso, N.V., Hews, S., Spector, L., Derr, N.D.: A molecular circuit regenerator to implement iterative strand displacement operations. Angewandte Chem. **129**, 4514–4517 (2017)
8. Santini, C.C., Bath, J., Turberfield, A.J., Tyrrell, A.M.: A DNA network as an information processing system. Int. J. Mol. Sci. **13**, 5125–5137 (2012)
9. Iyer, A.S., Paul, K.: Self-assembly: a review of scope and applications. IET Nanobiotechnol. **9**, 122–135 (2014)
10. Shi, X.L., Lu, W., Wang, Z.Y., Pan, L.Q., Cui, G.Z., Xu, J., LeBean, T.H.: Programmable DNA tile self-assembly using a hierarchical sub-tile strategy. Nanotechnol. **25**, 075602 (2014)

11. Yin, P., Choi, H.M.T., Calvert, C.R., Pierce, N.A.: Programming biomolecular self-assembly pathways. Nature **451**, 318–322 (2008)
12. Xu, J.: Probe machine. IEEE Trans. Neural Netw. Learn. Syst. **27**, 1405–1416 (2016)
13. Song, T.Q., Garg, S., Mokhtar, R., Bui, H., Reif, J.: Analog computation by DNA strand displacement circuits. ACS Synth. Biol. **5**, 898–912 (2016)
14. Zhu, J.B., Zhang, L.B., Dong, S.J., Wang, E.K.: Four-way junction-driven DNA strand displacement and its application in building majority logic circuit. ACS Nano **7**, 10211–10217 (2013)
15. Srinivas, N., Ouldridge, T.E., Sulc, P., Schaeffer, J.M., Yurke, B., Louis, A.A., Doye, J.P.K., Winfree, E.: On the biophysics and kinetics of toehold-mediated DNA strand displacement. Nucleic Acids Res. **41**, 10641–10658 (2013)
16. Yang, J., Dong, C., Dong, Y.F., Liu, S., Pan, L.Q., Zhang, C.: Logic nanoparticle beacon triggered by the binding-induced effect of multiple inputs. ACS Appl. Mater. Inter. **6**, 14486–14492 (2014)
17. Wang, Y.F., Sun, J.W., Zhang, X.C., Cui, G.Z.: Half adder and half subtractor operations by DNA self-assembly. J. Comput. Theor. Nanos. **8**, 1288–1295 (2011)
18. Eckhoff, G., Codrea, V., Ellington, A.D., Chen, X.: Beyond allostery: catalytic regulation of a deoxyribozyme through an entropy-driven DNA amplifier. Syst. Chem. **1**, 1–6 (2010)
19. Farhadtoosky, S., Jahanian, A.: Customized placement algorithm of nanoscale DNA logic circuits. J. Circuit. Syst. Comp. **26**, 1750150 (2017)
20. Zhang, X.Y., Liu, Y.I., Luo, B., Pan, L.Q.: Computational power of tissue P systems for generating control languages. Inf. Sci. **278**, 285–297 (2014)
21. Sawlekar, R., Montefusco, F., Kulkarni, V.V., Bates, D.G.: Implementing nonlinear feedback controllers Using DNA strand displacement reactions. IEEE T. Nanobiosci. **15**, 443–454 (2016)
22. Seelig, G., Soloveichik, D., Zhang, D.Y., Winfree, E.: Enzyme-free nucleic acid logic circuits. Science **314**, 1585–1588 (2006)
23. Zhang, C., Ma, L.N., Dong, Y.F., Yang, J., Xu, J.: Molecular logic computing model based on DNA self-assembly strand branch migration. Chin. Sci. Bull. **58**, 32–38 (2013)
24. Qian, L.L., Winfree, E.: Scaling up digital circuit computation with DNA strand displacement cascades. Science **332**, 1196–1201 (2011)
25. Shi, X.L., Wang, Z.Y., Deng, C.Y., Song, T., Pan, L.Q., Chen, Z.H.: A novel biosensor based on DNA strand displacement. PLoS One **9**, e108856 (2014)
26. Zhang, D.Y., Winfree, E.: Control of DNA strand displacement kinetics using toehold exchange. J. Am. Chem. Soc. **131**, 17303–17314 (2009)
27. Yurke, B., Mills, A.P.: Using DNA to power nanostructures. Genet. Program. Evol. M. **4**, 111–122 (2003)
28. Qian, L.L., Winfree, E.: A simple DNA gate motif for synthesizing large-scale circuits. J. R. Soc. Interface **8**, 1281–1297 (2011)
29. Yang, J., Jiang, S.X., Liu, X.R., Pan, L.Q., Zhang, C.: Aptamer-binding directed DNA origami pattern for logic gates. ACS Appl. Mater. Inter. **8**, 34054–34060 (2016)
30. Lakin, M.R., Youssef, S., Polo, F., Emmott, S., Phillips, A.: Visual DSD: a design and analysis tool for DNA strand displacement systems. Bioinformatics **27**, 3211–3213 (2011)
31. Lakin, M.R., Parker, D., Cardelli, L., Kwiatkowska, M., Phillips, A.: Design and analysis of DNA strand displacement devices using probabilistic model checking. J. R. Soc. **9**, 1470–1485 (2012)

Design and Analysis of Complement Circuit by Using DNA Strand Displacement Reaction

Guangzhao Cui[1], Yangyang Jiao[1(✉)], Jianxia Liu[2(✉)], Jixiang Li[1], Xuncai Zhang[1], and Zhonghua Sun[1]

[1] School of Electrical and Information Engineering,
Zhengzhou University of Light Industry, Zhengzhou 450002, China
jiaoyyvip@163.com
[2] School of information management, Zhengzhou University,
Zhengzhou 450001, China
jianxialiuedu@163.com

Abstract. In recent years, DNA strand displacement technology has been become an integral part of DNA computing, which is proved that the complement circuit is played an important role in computer circuits. In this paper, a four-bit complement logic circuit based on DNA strand displacement is designed and simulated. Through the analysis about the simulation results, which is proved that the designed circuit is reliable, and the four-bit complement logic circuit based on DNA strand displacement design is also shown that the DNA strand displacement has a bright future in the construction of large-scale logic circuits.

Keywords: DNA strand displacement · Complement circuit · Visual DSD · DNA computing

1 Introduction

Many scientists have demonstrated that superior capabilities are obtained by DNA computing for processing and delivering information [1]. Therefore, a new difference is made by dynamic DNA nanotechnology with the progress of DNA nanotechnology, which can be taken the place of traditional silicon materials, and some simple logic computing functions have been realized, but there is still a large gap in practical application [2,3]. Because of the more stringent conditions of biochemical reaction are required, biochemical reaction such as temperature, rate of combination, and so on, which lead the reaction process is difficult to be controlled, so the success rate is not high [4,5]. So only these problems are solved, a real leap in DNA computing can be produced. With the appearance of DNA strand displacement, this situation has been greatly changed [6–8]. Because the DNA strand displacement was happening at room temperature and does not require any enzymes, which uses its simplicity, scalability, and modularity for large-scale applications [9]. In traditional computer computing, the data processing is executed by CPU which is the main task to complete [10].

© Springer Nature Singapore Pte Ltd. 2017
C. He et al. (Eds.): BIC-TA 2017, CCIS 791, pp. 405–419, 2017.
https://doi.org/10.1007/978-981-10-7179-9_31

When the arithmetic operation and logic operation are performed by arithmetic unit, the full adder is regarded as the main computing device. The full adder is needed to convert the data that involved in the operation into the complement form through the complement circuit, so that the adder and subtraction operation can be accomplished only by using the full adder. The complement circuit is played a very important role in this process [11,12]. In biological computing, we should also achieve the data processing and calculation, so the design of complement circuit based on DNA strand displacement is of great value. In this paper, a complementary logic circuit is designed and simulated through the tool of visual DSD. The paper is organized as follows. In Sect. 2, the basic principles of DNA strand displacement which are used in the following sections are recalled. In Sect. 3, which is about the logic circuit, the definition of double track circuit and biochemical cascade circuit is given. The simulation and the analysis of the complementary circuits are investigated respectively in Sects. 4 and 5.

2   DNA Strand Displacement

DNA strand displacement technology is originated from DNA self-assembly technology. DNA self assembly technology is a process that based on the DNA base complementary pairing principle, and the spontaneous assembly of multiple DNA single chains [13]. A DNA double strand and a single strand are required of the DNA strand displacement reaction, and one of the single strand or double strand based on base A, G, C, T complementary pairing (A is paired to T, C is paired to G). The strand of double stranded has a small toehold field, which has two states: active and inactive state. When it is exposed, which is in an active state, i.e., The domain a* and c* in Fig. 1. When it is covered, which is in the inactive state [14]. When it is in the active state, complementary area on a single strand binding reaction, the rest of the single strand and one of the double strand begin to be branched, migrated and will gradually be replaced (b is branch migration area) to form a new double stranded structure and a new single strand. If there are some small fulcrums becoming active state as Fig. 1(a) a* in the double strand area, the reaction will be produced to a opposite direction until the reaction is reached dynamic balance. This reaction is called the reversible reaction, which can be produced more output signals by adding fuel [15,16]. It plays a major role in the design of a cascade of logic circuits even if there is no fulcrums to become active, the reaction will be finished [17,18]. This is the two forms of strand displacement, the single strand before reaction is called input chain by us, the double strands is called gate complex, after the reaction the single chain was called output chain. The reaction rate is determined by the number of the small fulcrums, generally in 6–10 h, the reaction rate is saturated. The Fig. 1 is the displacement reaction with two forms of strand [19]. DNA strand applied in this logic circuit can be divided into three kinds strand: invading strand, output strand and double-stranded complex [20]. The invading strand and double-stranded complex may be reacted once mingled together and there are some new species strand will be produced in this process. As shown in the

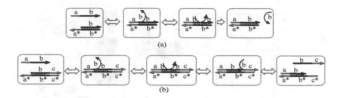

Fig. 1. (a) DNA chain substitution irreversible reaction. (b) Reversible reaction of DNA chain substitution.

Fig. 1, the toehold a located in the invading strand (namely the single-strand) first binds to the exposed toehold a* which is located in the double-stranded complex. A new double-stranded complex is produced in this reaction process which is adhered with an overhanging single strand [21]. Since the domain b in the overhanging strand has the same sequence with the bound one, which is performed complementary pairs with domain b* until completely displaced the bound one, that is called branch migration. The bound strand will be fallen off and be free when it is attached to the double-stranded complex only by the short toehold a domain [22]. Through the computational system completely, the input signals are translated into output signals.

3   Complement Circuit

3.1   Digital Logic Circuit

The logic operation is adopted two kinds of state "0" and "1". In digital electronic circuit, three basic logical operations are included in logic algorithm, which are named logic AND, logic OR and logic NOT. The value of logic AND is "1", when two input numbers both are "1", while it is "0" if alternative of two numbers are "0". The value of logic OR is "0" when both of two inputs are "0", otherwise it is "1". The logic NOT is achieved that output state is opposite. In the four-digit complement logic circuits, the complement of four-digit binary number is computed, which is added a symbol digit F, when it is "0" on behalf of the positive binary number is, when it is "1", on behalf of the negative binary number in the opposite. At the same time, a carried input signal C_0 is defined and it is always set to "0". The positive numbers complement is itself, the complement of negative number is started from the right end of the X_0 until find the first "1" number from right to left, the "1" is set in the X_i site, including the X_i and then right position, the number remains unchanged, the number on the left side of it is reversed, F remains the same. The logic circuit diagram is shown in Fig. 2. The circuit is included in seven AND gates, twelve OR gates, eight NOT gates.

3.2   Dual-Rail Logic Circuit

In order to perform the four-digit complement digital logic circuit, a six-layer circuit for complement digital logic circuit is designed, which is contained six

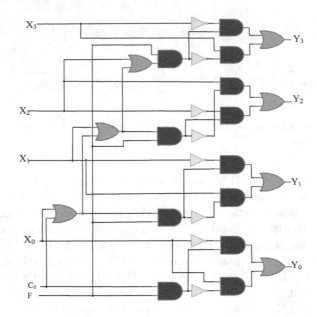

Fig. 2. The logic circuit of the 4-digit complement digital logic circuit.

AND logic gates and three OR logic gates. In the DNA computing, there are some difficulties in the implementation of NOT gate, because in the DNA strand displacement reaction, the NOT logical operation is converted to the low concentration input signals into a high concentration output signals, conversely, that can also be converted a high concentration input signals into a low concentration output signals. In order to avoid the false output which makes computation result uncertain due to the absence of inputs, the dual-rail logic algorithm is adopted [15, 16]. In the dual-rail logic circuit, each original input is transformed into a pair of inputs of which alternative can be represented by logic ON or OFF. Taking one input X_1 as an example, when input X_1 is absence from taking part in the reaction, then the X_1^0 in the dual-rail logic circuit is shown logic ON, at the same time, the X_1^1 shows logic OFF. Each AND, OR or NOT logic function should be achieved through a pair of AND and OR logic gates in the dual-rail logic circuit. The output signal Y is also converted into Y_0 and Y_1. If the final output Y_0 is reached 1, which indicating that the output signal is 0, on the contrary, If the Y_1 is reached 1, which indicating that the output signal is 1. The dual-rail logic circuit is shown in Fig. 3.

3.3   Seesaw Cascade Circuit

The dual-rail logic circuit should be transformed into a seesaw circuit which located in the first stage of reaction [17–19]. In the seesaw cascade circuit, the forward gates are set as two kinds, named amplifying gate (shown in Fig. 4) which can be produced the multiple outputs and integrating gates (shown in Fig. 5)

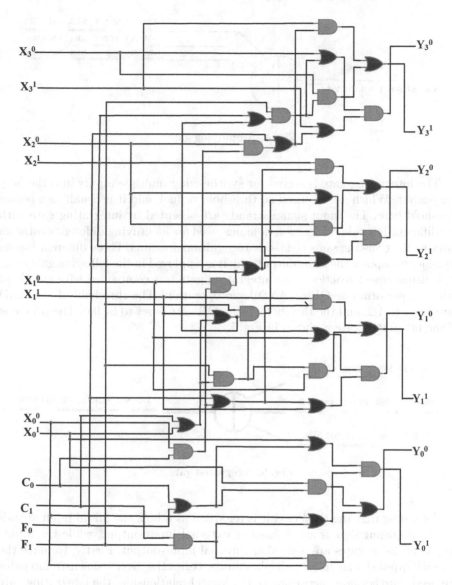

Fig. 3. The dual-rail logic circuit of complement circuit.

which can be used to receive the multiple inputs. Four kinds of signal strands are contained in amplifying gate: input strand, threshold strand, fuel strand and output strand. The amplifying gate can be translated one single-strand input into multiple outputs which has the same gate base strand recognition on the left of toehold but different right-side recognition for combining with the different downstream gates. More than enough free fuel is needed to facilitate sufficient reaction for producing abundant outputs. The principle of the gate is shown in Fig. 4.

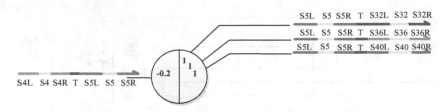

Fig. 4. Amplifying gate.

The integrating gate is served for synthesizing multiple inputs into the only one output. Which are required no threshold or fuel, and it is usually set before threshold gate. The input signal strands are accepted by integrating gate with the different left-side recognition domains used for identifying different upstream gates while it has the same right-side recognition domains. Those different inputs are able to displace the same output which is employed in the following gate complex displacement reaction. One integrating gate is accompanied with threshold gate can perform one OR or AND logic operation. The threshold of the AND gate is set to 1.2, and the threshold of the OR gate is set to be 0.6. The principle of the integrated gate is shown in Fig. 5.

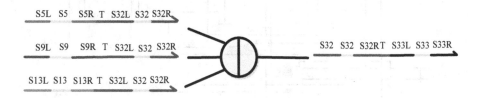

Fig. 5. Integrated gate.

Assuming that the total circuit is regarded as a box, the initial input signals and final output signals are defined as external input-output, while the input-output of inside gates are defined as internal input-output. Firstly, to make the external input signals to be multiple shunt satisfies the diverse downstream gates are need. Furthermore, according to the logical relationship, the integrating gate is converted two different internal input into the same internal output, which is subsequently participated in performing AND or OR logic through threshold gate judgment. Then, more sophisticated logic computation can be implemented by building multilayer composite structure for integration gate and threshold gate. Finally, the ultimate output are reported by the fluorescence signals. The whole seesaw circuits of calculation is shown in Fig. 6.

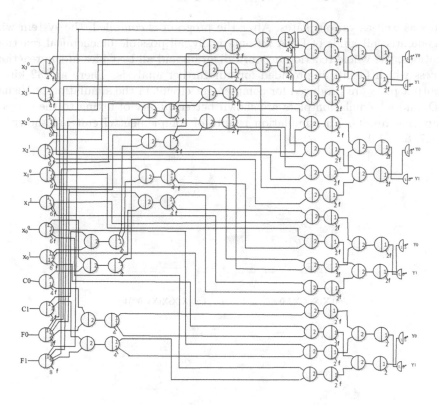

Fig. 6. The biochemical logic circuit of 6:4 complement circuit.

4   Simulation with Visual DSD

Visual DSD is a kind of design for DNA strand displacement process, which is also a kind of simulation and analyze software. In addition, the software of Visual DSD can be used to build the DNA strand displacement computational model and the analysis about the model is produced. Coding region, setting section and display section are included in the Visual DSD, which is designed by Matthew Lakin etc. The setting region is mainly used to set the simulation condition, simulation visual results or the visual effects of the molecular model. The compiler has a drop-down menu, four kinds of compiler: limited, unlimited, default, complex are included to choose from. In the limited, unlimited, default condition it is thought that the DNA molecule will be migrated exactly, but only in a complex condition is changed uncertain. In addition, the special attention needs is that the limited approach is not applied to unproductive responses. When the program is running, the initial mode of the system is the default. The reaction process of logic circuit based on DNA strand displacement using DSD simulation is investigated. In the software of the Visual DSD, the logic circuit of complement circuit is implemented by the compiling program code. The definition is described for DNA species by the code, reaction rate, graph points as well as various gates. After the program is compiled, the system will be generated all kinds of DNA automatically, all possible biochemical reaction equations, the whole reaction network diagram and all text files in the reaction process which facility is provided for our further analysis. There are 32 kinds of output plots are produced for complement circuit in the simulation of Visual DSD, and all simulation plots are shown better quality of fitting to the correct computing results. The simulation results of complement circuit are shown in Figs. 7, 8 and 9.

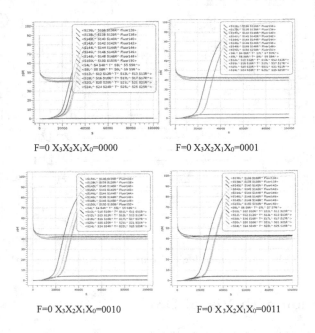

$$F=0 \quad X_3X_2X_1X_0=0000 \qquad F=0 \quad X_3X_2X_1X_0=0001$$

$$F=0 \quad X_3X_2X_1X_0=0010 \qquad F=0 \quad X_3X_2X_1X_0=0011$$

Fig. 7. The four bit complement circuit simulation diagram. (Color figure online)

In the 32 simulation diagrams, the positive number "0"–"15" is represented through the first 16, the last 16 diagrams are represented for the negative number "15"–"0", the simulation time is 100000 s, we define "0.9X" threshold is set to ON, the "0.1X" threshold is set to OFF, the initial concentration of input chain is 90, each case is concluded in six inputs in 0–4000 s. The concentration of the input chain is dropped sharply, because at this point the concentration of the input chain is relatively higher, then the output chain is very few, which is because the seesaw circuit is a cascade circuit, output chain is needed some time. After 4000 s, the reactants are fully reacted began to stabilize until the end of the reaction. But after a period of time, the concentration of the output strand is increased in the exponent until 60000 s the reaction rate begins to decline and the output strand tends to saturation. In the simulation, some lines are indicated that their reaction rate is the same coincidentally. In the simulation diagrams, red is represented Y_0^0, green is represented Y_0^1, blue is on behalf of

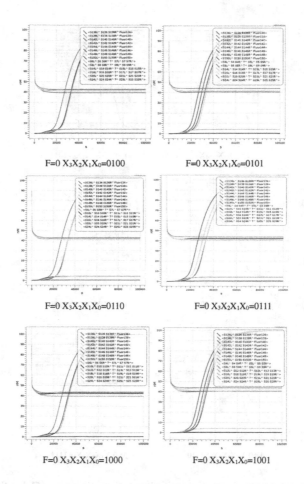

Fig. 8. The four bit complement circuit simulation diagram. (Color figure online)

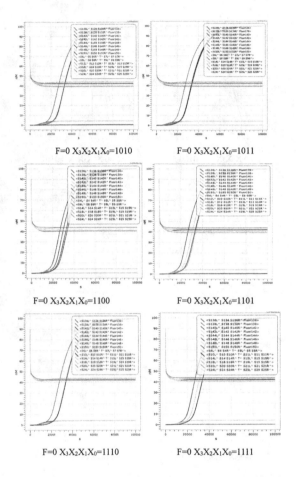

Fig. 9. The four bit complement circuit simulation diagram. (Color figure online)

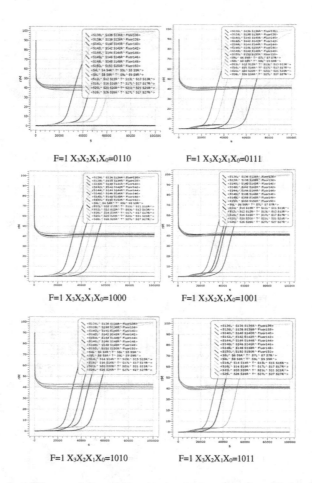

F=1 $X_3X_2X_1X_0$=0110

F=1 $X_3X_2X_1X_0$=0111

F=1 $X_3X_2X_1X_0$=1000

F=1 $X_3X_2X_1X_0$=1001

F=1 $X_3X_2X_1X_0$=1010

F=1 $X_3X_2X_1X_0$=1011

Fig. 10. The four bit complement circuit simulation diagram. (Color figure online)

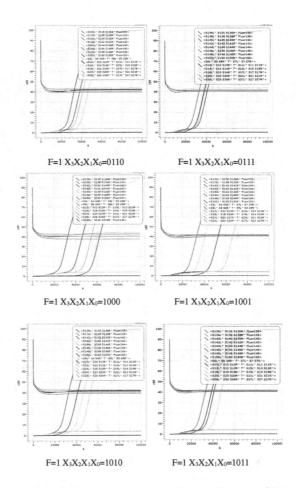

F=1 $X_3X_2X_1X_0$=0110   F=1 $X_3X_2X_1X_0$=0111

F=1 $X_3X_2X_1X_0$=1000   F=1 $X_3X_2X_1X_0$=1001

F=1 $X_3X_2X_1X_0$=1010   F=1 $X_3X_2X_1X_0$=1011

Fig. 11. The four bit complement circuit simulation diagram. (Color figure online)

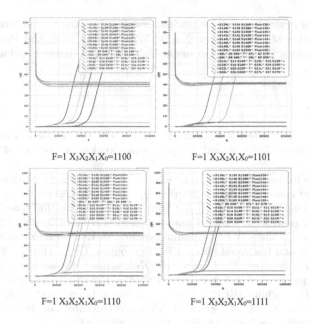

$F=1\ X_3X_2X_1X_0=1100$ $F=1\ X_3X_2X_1X_0=1101$

$F=1\ X_3X_2X_1X_0=1110$ $F=1\ X_3X_2X_1X_0=1111$

Fig. 12. The four bit complement circuit simulation diagram. (Color figure online)

Y_1^0, light yellow is represented Y_1^1, deep yellow is on behalf of Y_2^0, purple is on behalf of Y_2^1, cyan is represented Y_3^0, brown is represented Y_3^1. As is shown in the diagrams, the desired results and the simulation results are quite ideal (Figs. 10, 11 and 12).

5   Conclusion

In this paper, the reaction mechanism of DNA strand displacement is presented firstly. Subsequently, the logic circuit is designed and translated equivalently into seesaw circuit which is implemented in DNA strand. Furthermore, the process of strand displacement reaction is simulated in the specialized software Visual DSD. The simulation results are reached our expected requirement. From the diagrams, the output results Y_0, Y_1, Y_2 and Y_3 are generated need more and more layers. In the simulation diagrams we can see clearly is that the generation required more and more time, the number of layers of the circuit is proportional to the time of the reaction. According to the simulation results, this method of the complement circuit by using DNA strand displacement reaction is feasible and the results are reliable. Through the design and simulation of the complement circuit by using DNA strand displacement reaction, DNA strand displacement technology has a great potential in the construction of a large-scale logic circuit. With further research, DNA strand displacement technology may be combined with other techniques, such as nano-meter circuit, transport characteristic of nanometer structure, and so on.

Acknowledgments. The work for this paper was supported by the National Natural Science Foundation of China (Grant Nos. 61572446, 61472372), and Program for Science and Technology Innovation Talents in Universities of Henan Province (Grant No. 15HASTIT019).

References

1. Srinivas, N., Ouldridge, T.E., Sulc, P., et al.: On the biophysics and kinetics of toehold-mediated DNA strand displacement. Nucleic Acids Res. **41**(22), 10641–10658 (2013)
2. Qian, L., Winfree, E.: Scaling up digital circuit computation with DNA strand displacement cascades. Science **332**(6034), 1196–1201 (2011)
3. Wang, Y., Tian, G., Hou, H., et al.: Simple logic computation based on the DNA strand displacement. J. Theor. Comput. Chem. **11**(9), 1975–1982 (2014)
4. Sun, J., Yin, Q., Shen, Y.: Compound synchronization for four chaotic systems of integer order and fractional order. EPL (Europhys. Lett.) **106**(4), 40005 (2014)
5. Zhang, D.Y., Winfree, E.: Control of DNA strand displacement kinetics using toehold exchange. J. Am. Chem. Soc. **131**(47), 17303–17314 (2009)
6. Xu, J.: Probe machine. IEEE Trans. Neural Netw. Learn. **27**(7), 1405–1416 (2016)
7. Yang, D., Tan, Z., Mi, Y., et al.: DNA nanostructures constructed with multi-stranded motifs. Nucleic Acids Res. **45**(6), 3606–3611 (2017)
8. Chen, Y.J., Dalchau, N., Srinivas, N., et al.: Programmable chemical controllers made from DNA. Nat. Nanotechnol. **8**(10), 755–762 (2013)
9. Li, F., Tang, Y., Traynor, S.M., et al.: Kinetics of proximity-induced intramolecular DNA strand displacement. Anal. Chem. **88**(16), 8152–8157 (2016)
10. Cai, Y.H.: Computer complement the design of circuit implementation and application research. Hebei Norm. Univ. Natl. Newsp. **34**(2), 2095–3763 (2014)
11. Matthew, R., David, P., et al.: Design and analysis of DNA strand displacement devices using probabilistic model checking. R. Soc. Interface **7**(72), 1470–1485 (2012)
12. Gaber, R., Lebar, T., Majerle, A., et al.: Designable DNA-binding domain enable construction of logic circuit in mammalian cells. Nat. Chem. Biol. **10**(3), 203–208 (2014)
13. Phillips, A., Cardelli, L.: A programming language for composable DNA circuits. J. R. Soc. Interface **6**(Suppl. 4), S419–S436 (2009)
14. Eckhoff, G., Codrea, V., Ellington, A.D., et al.: Beyond allostery: catalytic regulation of a deoxyribozyme through an entropy-driven DNA amplifier. J. Syst. Chem. **1**(1), 13 (2010)
15. Qian, L., Winfree, E.: A simple DNA gate motif for synthesizing large-scale circuits. In: Goel, A., Simmel, F.C., Sosík, P. (eds.) DNA 2008. LNCS, vol. 5347, pp. 70–89. Springer, Heidelberg (2009). https://doi.org/10.1007/978-3-642-03076-5_7
16. Bui, H., Garg, S., Miao, V., et al.: Design and analysis of linear cascade DNA hybridization chain reactions using DNA hairpins. New J. Phys. **19**(1), 015006 (2017)
17. Qian, L., Soloveichik, D., Winfree, E.: Efficient turing-universal computation with DNA polymers. In: Sakakibara, Y., Mi, Y. (eds.) DNA 2010. LNCS, vol. 6518, pp. 123–140. Springer, Heidelberg (2011). https://doi.org/10.1007/978-3-642-18305-8_12
18. Sakakibara, Y., Mi, Y. (eds.): DNA 2010. LNCS, vol. 6518. Springer, Heidelberg (2011). https://doi.org/10.1007/978-3-642-18305-8

19. Lebar, T., Majerle, A., Ster, B., et al.: Designable DNA-binding domains enable construction of logic circuits in mammalian cells. Nat. Chem. Biol. **10**(3), 203–208 (2014)
20. Yang, X., Tang, Y., Traynor, S.M., et al.: Regulation of DNA strand displacement using an allosteric DNA toehold. J. Am. Chem. Soc. **138**(42), 14076–14082 (2016)
21. Zhang, X., Ying, N., Shen, C., et al.: Fluorescence resonance energy transfer-based photonic circuits using single-stranded tile self-assembly and DNA strand displacement. J. Nanosci. Nanotech. **17**(2), 1053–1060 (2017)
22. Zhang, X., Zhang, W., Zhao, T., et al.: Design of logic circuits based on combinatorial displacement of DNA strands. J. Comput. Theor. Nanosci. **12**(7), 1161–1164 (2015)

Extreme Learning Machine Based on Evolutionary Multi-objective Optimization

Yaoming Cai[1], Xiaobo Liu[2(✉)], Yu Wu[1], Peng Hu[1], Ruilin Wang[1], Bi Wu[1], and Zhihua Cai[1]

[1] School of Computer Science, China University of Geosciences (Wuhan), Wuhan, Hubei 430074, China
[2] Hubei Key Laboratory of Advanced Control and Intelligent Automation for Complex Systems, School of Automation, China University of Geosciences (Wuhan), Wuhan, Hubei 430074, China
xbliu@cug.edu.cn

Abstract. Extreme learning machine (ELM), which proposed for generalized single-hidden layer feedforward neural networks, has become a popular research topic due to its fast learning speed, good generalization ability, and ease of implementation. However, ELM faces redundancy and randomness in the hidden layer which caused by random mapping of features. In ELM, although evolutionary algorithms have archived impressive improvement, they have not considered the sparsity of the hidden layers. In this paper, a hybrid learning algorithm is proposed, termed EMO-ELM, which adopts evolutionary multi-objective algorithm to optimise two conflict objectives simultaneously. Furthermore, the proposed method can be used for supervised classification and unsupervised sparse feature extraction tasks. Simulations on many UCI datasets have demonstrated that EMO-ELM generally outperforms the original ELM algorithm as well as several ELM variants in classification tasks, moreover, EMO-ELM achieves a competitive performance to PCA in sparse feature extraction tasks.

Keywords: Extreme learning machine · Evolutionary multi-objective optimization · Feature extraction · Classification

1 Introduction

Extreme learning machine (ELM) is a generalized single-hidden layer feedforward neural networks (SLFNs), which has unique characteristics, i.e., fast training speed, good generalization, and universal approximation or classification capability [1]. In contrast to the traditional gradient-based methods which require great effort in hyper parameter tuning, ELM randomly generates the parameters of hidden layers during training stage and mathematically calculates the least squares minimum norm solution of the parameters of the output layers [2,3]. As its popularity, ELM has been widely applied in image recognition [4–6], remote sensing image classification [7–9], and protein structure prediction [10].

© Springer Nature Singapore Pte Ltd. 2017
C. He et al. (Eds.): BIC-TA 2017, CCIS 791, pp. 420–435, 2017.
https://doi.org/10.1007/978-981-10-7179-9_32

However, the random mapping layer adopted by ELM result in three short-comings: (1) a large number of hidden nodes is required, (2) unstable performance, and (3) dense outputs of hidden layers. Focus on these problems, on the one hand, Huang et al. [11,12] proposed kernel-based ELM (KELM), which assumes the feature mapping of ELM is unknown to users, to avoid the random mapping and obtained competitive performance to SVM. As the ELM has good diversity, other alternatives combined the ensemble learning with ELM, such as voting-based ELM (V-ELM) [13] and ensemble based ELM (EN-ELM) [14].

On the other hand, evolutionary algorithms (EAs) have obtained great success in ELM optimization. The main idea of evolutionary ELM is to encode the parameters of hidden layers as individuals then evolve them to update generations to minimize model error. It benefits from the global search ability of EAs, the randomness caused by the random mapping can be reduced. The first work involved evolutionary ELM is E-ELM [15], which adopt differential evolution algorithm (DE) to search optimal hidden parameters. Since then, many evolutionary ELM variants have been gradually proposed, including SaE-ELM [16], Evo-ELM [17] and M-ELM [18].

From the point of view of objective optimization, the aforementioned evolutionary ELMs are single-objective optimization. However many real-world optimization problems have to simultaneously optimize multiple conflicting measures of performance, or objectives [19]. Actually, multi-objective optimization also reflects the essence of optimization problems. Furthermore, evolutionary multi-objective optimization (EMO) has shown great power in kinds of optimization problems [20,21], such as structure optimization of deep learning model [22] and sparse feature learning [23]. In [24], the authors proposed a model selection method for ELM using multi-objective optimization, but, the sparsity of hidden layers has not taken into account.

Motivated by the fact that the random mapping layer of ELM could be further improved in aspects of veracity and sparsity, this paper propose a novel ELM based on evolutionary multi-objective optimization, called EMO-ELM, which is applied in classification and feature extraction problems. The main contributions of this paper are as follows:

(1) Unlike the evolutionary single-objective ELM, EMO-ELM simultaneously considers the ELM model error and the sparsity constraint of the hidden layer into optimization.
(2) EMO-ELM provide an alternative for feature extraction, moreover, it guarantees good sparsity for transformed features.
(3) In fact, our proposed method can be regarded as an evolutionary multi-objective ELM framework for classification or feature extraction. In this framework, various kinds of EMO algorithms can be used.

The rest of this paper is organized as follows. Section 2 reviews the basic ELM, and some improved ELMs, such as E-ELM. Section 3 describes the proposed method in details for classification and feature extraction. Experimental results of classification on 13 UCI data sets and feature extraction on 6 UCI data sets are analyzed in Sect. 4.

2 Related Works

2.1 Extreme Learning Machine (ELM)

ELM is a single-hidden-layer neural network, its parameters between the input layer and the hidden layer are random generated, and the output parameters can be determined via a closed-form solution. Hence ELM has very fast training speed. Actually, ELM is consist of a nonlinear random feature mapping and a linear regression classifier.

Consider a data set with training samples $\mathbf{X} = \{x_i\}_{i=1}^{N}$ in $\mathbb{R}^m$ (m-dimensional feature space) and class labels $\mathbf{T} = \{t_i\}_{i=1}^{N}$, where $t_i \in \mathbb{R}^C$ is the vector label encoded using one-hot. N is the total number of training samples. Let $\mathbf{W}_{ij}$ be the weight for the connection from the j-th neuron in the hidden layer to the i-th neuron in the input layer, using b_j for the bias of the j-th neuron in the hidden layer. Suppose the number of hidden nodes is L, then the weights matrix and bias vector can represent as $\mathbf{W} \in \mathbb{R}^{m \times L}$ and $b \in \mathbb{R}^L$ respectively.

In general, the training of ELM consists of two stages. In the first stage, the parameters $\mathbf{W}$ and b are random generated, then the input data are mapped into an L-dimensional space via a nonlinear activation function $g(\cdot)$, such as Sigmoid function. This process can write as:

$$h_i = g\left(\mathbf{W}^T x_i + b\right) \tag{1}$$

Here, $h_i \in \mathbb{R}^{1 \times L}$ is the output the hidden layer of input x_i. The final output of x_i is indicated as:

$$f(x_i) = h_i \beta \tag{2}$$

Where $\beta \in \mathbb{R}^{L \times C}$ is the output weight matrix connects the hidden layer and the output layer.

The second stage is well-known ridge regression or regularized least squares, which aims to solve the output weight by minimizing the following learning problem.

$$Minimize : \|\beta\|_p^{\sigma_1} + \lambda \|\mathbf{H}\beta - \mathbf{T}\|_q^{\sigma_2} \tag{3}$$

Where $\sigma_1 > 0$, $\sigma_2 > 0$, $p, q = 0, \frac{1}{2}, 1, 2, \cdots, +\infty$, and $\mathbf{H} = [h_1, h_2, \cdots, h_N]^T$. When the penalty coefficient λ is infinitely large in (3), the output weight β can be calculated as:

$$\beta = \mathbf{H}^{\dagger}\mathbf{T} \tag{4}$$

where $\mathbf{H}^{\dagger}$ indicates the Moore-Penrose generalized inverse of $\mathbf{H}$. According to ELM learning theory, ELM with minimum norm of output weights has better generalization performance and a more robust solution [12, 25]. Now, the output weight can be expressed as:

$$\beta = \left(\mathbf{H}^T\mathbf{H} + \frac{\mathbf{I}}{\lambda}\right)^{-1} \mathbf{H}^T\mathbf{T} \tag{5}$$

or

$$\beta = \mathbf{H}^T \left(\mathbf{H}\mathbf{H}^T + \frac{\mathbf{I}}{\lambda}\right)^{-1} \mathbf{T} \tag{6}$$

Finally, given a set of new samples $\mathbf{X}_{ts}$, its prediction is given below:

$$y\left(\mathbf{X}_{ts}\right) = \arg\max_{c=1,\cdots,C} g\left(\mathbf{X}_{ts}\mathbf{W} + b\right)\beta \qquad (7)$$

The overall algorithm procedure of ELM is given in Algorithm 1.

Algorithm 1. ELM

Input: training set $\{\mathbf{X}_{tr}, \mathbf{T}_{tr}\}$, testing set $\mathbf{X}_{ts}$, hidden node number L,
    activition function $g\left(\cdot\right)$
Output: prediced class lables
1 Random generate hidden-layer parameters $\mathbf{W}, b$;
2 Calculate the hidden layer activations $\mathbf{H}$ accoding to (1);
3 Calculate output weights β according to (4);
4 Predict testing lables according to (7);

2.2 Evolutionay ELM

Recent years, many evolutionary ELMs were proposed aim to address the issues caused by the random mapping layer of ELMs. One of the most successful is the adoption of differential evolution (DE) which consists of three major operators: mutation, crossover, and selection. The mutation operation maintains the diversity of the population, the crossover operation passes outstanding individuals to the next generation, and the selection operation selects good individuals with hightness [18]. The earlier improvements only focus on minimizing RMSE or classification error, such as E-ELM [15] and Evo-ELM [17]. However, the sparsity of the outputs of the hidden layer has not taken into consideration simultaneously. In fact, the optimization of ELM essentially is a multi-objective optimization problem. Mao et al. [24] proposed to use multi-objective optimization method to do model selection for ELM, but, the multi-objective optimization method has not drawn much attention in ELM.

2.3 ELM for Feature Extraction

Only a few existing research studies on ELMs have dealt with the problem of feature extraction. In [26], the linear and nonlinear ELM based autoencoder (ELM-AE) and sparse autoencoder (SELM-AE) were investigated to reduce feature dimension. Unlike the ELM, ELM-AE, and SELM-AE claim the hidden layer parameters are orthogonal or sparse, and an identity function is learned using ELM. This feature extraction procedure can be formalized as:

$$\widetilde{\mathbf{X}} = \mathbf{X}\mathbf{W}^T \qquad (8)$$

However, this procedure is still linear transformation with respect to the input data. Therefore, both algorithms are only effective when the original data are linearly separable. Unfortunately, this condition is usually violated in most classification problems. Moreover, the non-optimized random mapping will lead to an unstable performance.

The proposed EMO-ELM is related to the sparse autoencoder neural networks (SAE) [27,28] which learn feature representation nonlinearly by imposing a sparsity constraint. However, there are two main differences between SAE and EMO-ELM. First, the learning mechanisms are very different. For EMO-ELM, rather than train networks using the gradient-based method, we train networks via EA which bases on population. Second, in SAE, the constraint must be incorporated in the loss function, on the contrary, EMO-ELM directly represents loss function using multi-objective problem.

3   EMO-ELM

In this section, we introduce EMO-ELM for classification and EMO-ELM for feature extraction respectively. In order to construct our multi-objective model, two conflict objectives function f_1 and f_2 with respect to the decision variable $[\mathbf{W}, \boldsymbol{b}]$ are defined. It has slightly different for different tasks, but the unified representation can be written as:

$$\min_{\mathbf{W},\boldsymbol{b}} \boldsymbol{F}\left(\mathbf{W}, \boldsymbol{b}\right) = \min_{\mathbf{W},\boldsymbol{b}} \left\{f_1, f_2\right\} \tag{9}$$

The detailed descriptions are given as follows.

3.1   EMO-ELM for Classification

In supervised classification scenario, our objective functions are defined as crossover validation error and hidden layer sparsity. For the first objective, we directly use classification error, rather than squared loss of training data, because EMO excel at those problems that are hard to modeling or dispersed. It can be wtitten as:

$$f_1 = \frac{1}{s} \sum_{k=1}^{s} \left(1 - \frac{1}{n} \sum_{i=1}^{n} I\left(\boldsymbol{t}_i, y\left(\boldsymbol{x}_i\right)\right)\right) \tag{10}$$

Where s denotes s-folds crossover validation is used, $n = \frac{N}{s}$ indicates the number of validation samples. I is a sign function, defined as following.

$$I\left(\boldsymbol{t}_i, y\left(\boldsymbol{x}_i\right)\right) = \begin{cases} 1 & \arg\max \boldsymbol{t}_i = \arg\max \boldsymbol{y}\left(\boldsymbol{x}_i\right) \\ 0 & otherwise \end{cases} \tag{11}$$

Consider that the outputs of hidden layer lack of sparsity and interpretability, thus a sparsity constraint is taken into account in the second objective. This procedure is similar to the SAE. Assume the activation function is sigmoid, therefore the activation value limited in range of $(0, 1)$. Informally, we think of a hidden neuron as being active (or as ring) if its output value is close to 1, or as being inactive if its output value is close to 0. We would like to constrain the hidden neurons to be inactive most of the time. We first define average activation of j-th hidden neuron as

$$\hat{\rho}_j = \frac{1}{n} \sum_{i=1}^{n} g_{ij}(\boldsymbol{x}_i) \tag{12}$$

Further let ρ be the desired activation, our goal is to enforce $\rho = \hat{\rho}_j$. In order to measure the difference between ρ and $\hat{\rho}_j$, the KL-divergence is adopted, it is expressed as:

$$KL(\rho \parallel \hat{\rho}_j) = \rho \log \frac{\rho}{\hat{\rho}_j} + (1 - \rho) \log \frac{1 - \rho}{1 - \hat{\rho}_j} \tag{13}$$

Consider all hidden neurons, the second objective is expressed as:

$$f_2 = \sum_{j=1}^{L} KL(\rho \parallel \hat{\rho}_j) \tag{14}$$

Note that f_1 aims to eliminate randomness by obtaining minimum classification error and f_2 will guarantee the outputs of the hidden layer are sparse.

By performing EMO, we obtain a set of solutions denote as $S = \{(\mathbf{W}_i, \boldsymbol{b}_i)\}_{i=1}^{NP}$ and its corresponding objective vector $U = \left\{[u_1, u_2]^T\right\}_{i=1}^{NP}$, where NP is the size of population. In general, these solutions provide good diversity and can be viewed as equal optimum. Therefore, it is possible to construct an ensemble of ELM use S, such that avoid making a decision from a series of solutions. Firstly, we generate a group of ELM classifiers use S, denote as $M = \{M_1, \cdots, M_{NP}\}$. Then we assign a weight to each ELM via the following equation.

$$\omega_i = \mu \frac{1}{u_1^i} + (1 - \mu) \frac{1}{u_2^i} \tag{15}$$

Here μ is a weight parameter which balance two objective values. Finally, new samples are predicted through weighted voting. The complete process of EMO-ELM for classification is given in Algorithm 2.

3.2   EMO-ELM for Feature Extraction

Contrast to the traditional ELM-AE which transform data linearly we extract features by a optimized nonlinear random mapping. In order to guarantee the sparsity and separability of extracted features, we retain objective function f_2

Algorithm 2. EMO-ELM for classification

Input: $\{\mathbf{X}_{tr}, \mathbf{T}_{tr}\}$, $\mathbf{X}_{ts}$, ρ, L, NP, gen, μ, optional EMO parameters
Output: prediced lables
1 Initialize population of size NP;
2 Evaluate f_1, f_2;
3 Rank population;
4 **for** $iter = 1$ *to gen* **do**
5   Selection;
6   Crossover;
7   Mutation;
8   Evaluate f_1, f_2;
9 **end**
10 Obtain non-dominated solutions S;
11 $\hat{y} \leftarrow \emptyset$;
12 **for** $i = 1$ *to size* (S) **do**
13   Calculate ω_i according to (15);
14   Train ELM_j using $\{\mathbf{X}_{tr}, \mathbf{T}_{tr}\}$ under parameters $\mathbf{W}_i, \boldsymbol{b}_i$;
15     $\hat{y} \leftarrow \boldsymbol{y}(\mathbf{X}_{test})$;
16 **end**
17 Weighted voting for $\hat{y}$;
18 Return labels;

---

as (14) and modify objective function f_1 as root mean squared error (RMSE) with cross-validation for f_1, which is defined as follows:

$$f_1 = \frac{1}{s} \sum_{k=1}^{s} \left(\sqrt{\frac{\sum_{i=1}^{n} \|\boldsymbol{x}_i - \boldsymbol{y}(\boldsymbol{x}_i)\|_2^2}{n \times m}} \right) \tag{16}$$

Moreover, to carry out feature extraction task, the best solution needs to be selected from Pareto-optimal set to build the feature mapping layer of ELM. In this paper, we choose the solution that has the smallest value for f_1. Different methods can use for this selection, such as knee region based methods [29].

Similar to the autoencoder neural networks, we use the output of the hidden layer of ELM as the extracted features. This procedure expresses as follows:

$$\hat{\mathbf{X}} = g(\mathbf{X}\mathbf{W}_{best} + \boldsymbol{b}_{best}) \tag{17}$$

Where $\hat{\mathbf{X}}$ is the transformed feature from raw data $\mathbf{X}$, $[\mathbf{W}_{best}, \boldsymbol{b}_{best}]$ indicates the best solution. The pseudocode of EMO-ELM for feature extraction is given in Algorithm 3.

Algorithm 3. EMO-ELM for feature extraction

Input: X, ρ, L, NP, gen, optional EMO parameters
Output: extracted feature
1 Initialize population of size NP;
2 Evaluate f_1, f_2;
3 Rank population;
4 **for** $iter = 1$ to gen **do**
5 | Selection;
6 | Crossover;
7 | Mutation;
8 | Evaluate f_1, f_2;
9 **end**
10 Obtain non-dominated solutions S;
11 Sort solutions according to f_2;
12 Use the best solution to generate hidden layer;
13 Extract features according to (17);
14 Return extrated features $\hat{\mathbf{X}}$;

---

4   Experimental Evaluation

This section is divided into two subsections. Subsection 4.1 gives an analysis of classification tasks using EMO-ELM, including the convergence of the proposed method and the comparison of classification accuracy. Subsection 4.2 shows the experimental results for feature extraction tasks, including the convergence analysis, sparsity analysis, and separability comparison.

Our experiments are carried out by the well-known NSGA-II [30], its parameters NP, pc, and pm are set to 50, 0.7, and 0.3 respectively, and 3-fold cross-validation is used in objective function f_1. The reported data sets are widely used benchmarks that taken from UCI repository[1], and all samples are normalized in prepossessing. For classification, we uniformly randomly select 60% of the labeled samples for training and the rest for testing. Also, all the experiments are conducted in the Python 2.7 computational environment running on a computer with a 3.20 GHZ i5 CPU.

4.1   Experiment on Classification Task

Convergence analysis is an important part of evolutionary computing. In order to observe the convergence of the proposed EMO-ELM, we performed our method on 6 real data sets with parameters $gen = \{100, 500, 1000, 2000, 5000\}$, $L = 50$ and $\rho = 0.05$, The results indicated in Fig. 1, the horizontal axis is sparsity constraint, and the vertical axis is 3-fold cross-validation training error. From the Fig. 1, we get the conclusions that the objective functions will converge to the

---

[1] https://archive.ics.uci.edu/ml/datasets.html.

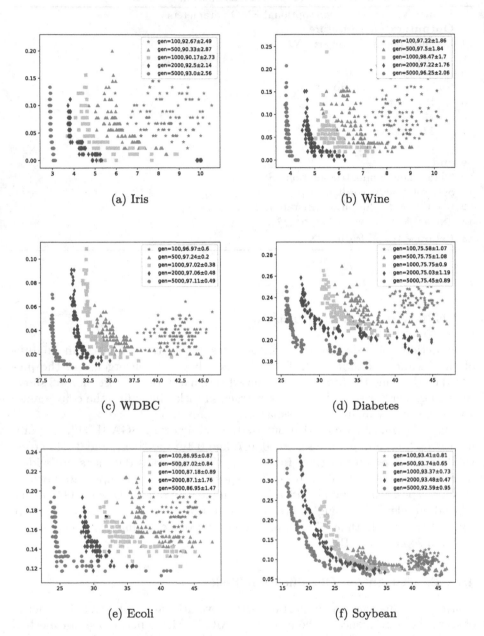

Fig. 1. Convergence and accuracy comparison using different generations. (a) Iris, (b) Wine, (c) Cotton, (d) Diabetes, (e) Ecoli, and (f) Soybean

Table 1. Comparison w.r.t. mean classification accuracy and standard deviation (%).

Data description					ELM	KELM	Ada-ELM	E-ELM	EMO-ELM
Data set	#train	#test	#fea.	#class					
Iris	90	60	4	3	90.92 ± 4.74	83.33 ± 2.98•	90.50 ± 4.22•	91.50 ± 3.69	**92.00 ± 2.45**
Cotton	213	143	21	6	86.15 ± 1.32•	88.04 ± 3.17	88.74 ± 2.51	85.52 ± 1.85•	**89.09 ± 2.01**
WDBC	341	227	30	6	95.92 ± 1.09•	94.45 ± 1.24•	96.51 ± 1.48•	96.49 ± 1.12•	**97.08 ± 0.93**
Ecoli	196	131	7	5	85.99 ± 2.87	73.13 ± 3.99•	75.34 ± 3.18•	84.66 ± 2.83•	**86.03 ± 2.84**
Chart	360	240	60	5	84.96 ± 2.29•	**97.54 ± 0.84**○	97.48 ± 0.87○	89.08 ± 1.80•	93.38 ± 1.94
Glass	123	82	10	5	83.05 ± 3.95•	72.44 ± 3.28•	85.00 ± 3.45•	**90.85 ± 3.75**○	87.44 ± 2.73
Soybean	405	270	35	18	91.50 ± 1.63 •	89.43 ± 2.01•	91.76 ± 1.43•	91.81 ± 1.69•	**93.02 ± 1.23**
Wine	106	71	13	3	94.44 ± 2.20•	97.29 ± 1.49	95.42 ± 3.11•	95.00 ± 3.24•	**97.29 ± 1.28**
SPECTF	160	107	44	2	76.36 ± 2.42•	76.36 ± 3.04•	78.18 ± 3.25	74.21 ± 4.66•	**78.22 ± 3.47**
Diabetes	460	308	8	2	75.15 ± 2.04•	64.19 ± 2.61•	71.06 ± 1.95•	74.85 ± 1.73•	**76.51 ± 2.02**
Car	1036	692	6	4	86.37 ± 1.71•	96.42 ± 0.82○	**97.05 ± 0.61**○	89.82 ± 1.07○	88.16 ± 0.96
Dermatology	219	147	34	6	95.68 ± 1.68•	96.22 ± 1.40•	95.99 ± 1.82•	95.24 ± 1.34•	**96.77 ± 1.18**
Libras	216	144	90	15	68.30 ± 4.78•	**83.65 ± 2.82**○	82.47 ± 3.44○	68.58 ± 3.56•	74.72 ± 2.99

• Statistically significant degradation
○ Statistically significant upgradation

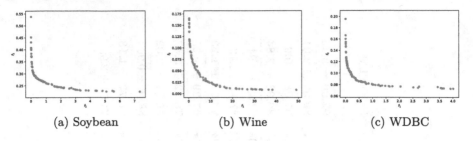

(a) Soybean   (b) Wine   (c) WDBC

Fig. 2. Convergence of feature extraction with 50 neurons and 5000 generations. (a) Soybean, (b) Wine, (c) WDBC

Pareto front with the increase of evolving generations. Furthermore, too much iteration could not obtain a better accuracy because EMO seeks to a group of compromise solutions.

Furthermore, we compare EMO-ELM with four ELM variants, including basic ELM, E-ELM, AdaBoost ELM, and KELM. For all methods, the number of hidden neurons and maximal iteration is set to be 50 and 1000, and the penalty coefficient of KELM determined by grid search in the range of $[1, 10, 100, 1000, 10000]$. Each method repeatedly executed 20 times, and the average testing accuracy and standard deviation are computed. The results are given in Table 1. From the Table 1, EMO-ELM are superior to the basic ELM in both aspects of average accuracy and standard deviation on all data sets. The performance of basic ELM is greatly influenced by the random mapping layer, while our method show effectiveness in respects of parameters optimization and alleviating randomness. The KELM only got three successes v.s EMO-ELM. And comparing with Ada-ELM, EMO-ELM is superior to Ada-ELM on eight data sets. Moreover, comparing with the single objective based evolutionary ELM our method achieved better performance in most of data sets.

4.2   Experiment on Feature Extraction Task

In order to evaluate the effectiveness of feature extraction using EMO-ELM, we carry out experiments in three aspects. Firstly, we analyze the convergence of the proposed method. Secondly, we plot the sparsity of the extracted feature. Finally, we compare classification accuracy for three feature extraction methods.

Figure 2 shows the convergence of feature extraction EMO-ELM on (a) Soybean, (b) Wine, (c) WDBC, where $L = 50$, $gen = 5000$, $\rho = 0.05$. Unlike classification task which evaluates classification error, in feature extraction task the RMSE is used. Therefore the Pareto fronts are smoother than classification tasks.

In order to illustrate the sparsity of extracted features, histogram is employed. In Fig. 3, we show the histograms of extracted features for each feature dimensions for three real data sets Soybean, Wine, and WDBC. Observe (a), (c), and (e), the activation of the hidden neurons are restricted to a small value after

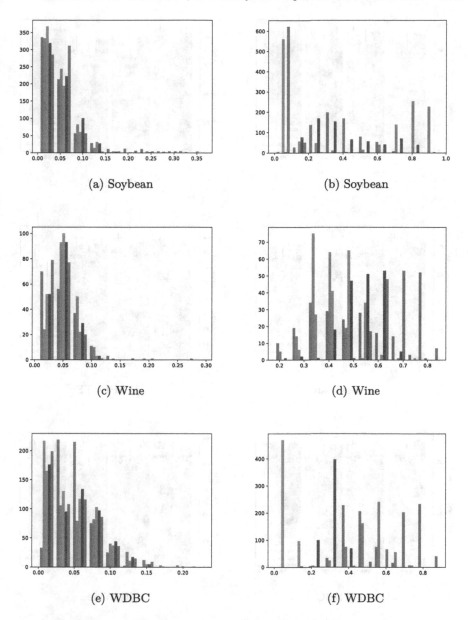

(a) Soybean

(b) Soybean

(c) Wine

(d) Wine

(e) WDBC

(f) WDBC

Fig. 3. Histogram of features. (a), (c), and (e) show the histograms of extracted features on of Soybean, Wine, and WDBC using EMO-ELM with $\rho = 0.05$; (b), (d), and (f) represent the histograms of random mapping of Soybean, Wine and WDBC.

optimizing, i.e., 0.05. These neurons have a big activations are viewed as active, in other words, EMO-ELM restrains most of the hidden neurons. Furthermore, those neurons which have small activations can be deemed to be unnecessary

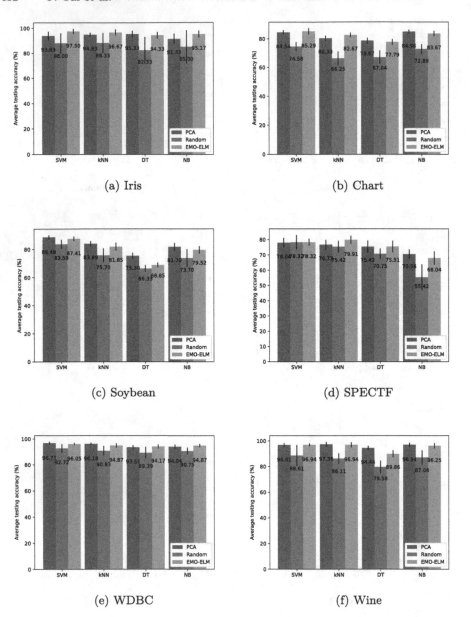

Fig. 4. Comparison of classification accuracy of PCA, random mapping and EMO-ELM. (a) Iris, $L = 2$, (b) Chart, $L = 5$, (c) Soybean, $L = 10$, (d) SPECTF, $L = 5$, (e) WDBC, $L = 5$, (f) Wine, $L = 5$

and redundant. On the contrary, the random mapping, which is showed in the second row, are chaotic and random. Thus, the features extracted by EMO-ELM are sparser than the random mapping of ELM.

The separability is an important indicator for feature extraction tasks. We compare three feature extraction methods in term of classification accuracy on 6 data sets by four frequently-used classifiers Support Vector Machine (SVM), k-Nearest Neighbors (kNN), Decision Tree (DT) and Naive Bayes (NB). The results are visualized as bar plots in Fig. 4. By comparison, EMO-ELM is competitive to PCA with respect to classification accuracy. In contrast to random mapping, the accuracy has been significantly enhanced by EMO-ELM. Moreover, observe the standard deviation, EMO-ELM eliminate the randomness caused by the random mapping.

5   Conclusions

In this paper, we proposed a novel ELM algorithm based on evolutionary multi-objective optimization, named EMO-ELM, to optimize the hidden layer of ELM. The EMO-ELM can use for classification and feature extraction tasks by modifying objective functions. In fact, the multi-objectives optimization involved in ELM has reflected the intrinsic nature of optimization problems. For classification, the cross-validation classification error and the sparsity of hidden layer are adopted. For feature extraction, the RMSE and the sparsity of feature mapping are adopted. Actually, the proposed EMO-ELM can be viewed as a general EMO-based ELM framework in which kinds of evolutionary multi-objective algorithms are applicable.

Our experiments show that EMO-ELM improves the classification accuracy and can extract sparse features. However, there are also some valuable problems should be further study in future works, such as how to construct a deep model with EMO-ELM to learn deep features. Additionally, we also note that if other classifiers replace the output layer of ELM, it still works well in most situations. Thus we think it is necessary to develop alternatives for ELMs and perfect its theory.

Acknowledgment. We thank the reviewers for their valuable comments and suggestions. This work was partially supported by the National Natural Science Foundation of China under grant No. 61603355 and No. 61403351, and the Fundamental Research Funds for National University, China University of Geosciences (Wuhan) under grant No. G1323541717.

References

1. Tang, J., Deng, C., Huang, G.B.: Extreme learning machine for multilayer perceptron. IEEE Trans. Neural Netw. Learn. Syst. **27**(4), 809–821 (2016)
2. Huang, G.B., Chen, L., Siew, C.K., et al.: Universal approximation using incremental constructive feedforward networks with random hidden nodes. IEEE Trans. Neural Networks **17**(4), 879–892 (2006)
3. Huang, G.B., Zhu, Q.Y., Siew, C.K.: Extreme learning machine: theory and applications. Neurocomputing **70**(1), 489–501 (2006)

4. Minhas, R., Baradarani, A., Seifzadeh, S., Wu, Q.J.: Human action recognition using extreme learning machine based on visual vocabularies. Neurocomputing **73**(10), 1906–1917 (2010)

5. Zong, W., Huang, G.B.: Face recognition based on extreme learning machine. Neurocomputing **74**(16), 2541–2551 (2011)

6. Zeng, Y., Xu, X., Shen, D., Fang, Y., Xiao, Z.: Traffic sign recognition using kernel extreme learning machines with deep perceptual features. IEEE Trans. Intell. Transp. Syst. (2016)

7. Chen, C., Li, W., Su, H., Liu, K.: Spectral-spatial classification of hyperspectral image based on kernel extreme learning machine. Remote Sens. **6**(6), 5795–5814 (2014)

8. Pal, M., Maxwell, A.E., Warner, T.A.: Kernel-based extreme learning machine for remote-sensing image classification. Remote Sens. Lett. **4**(9), 853–862 (2013)

9. Lv, Q., Niu, X., Dou, Y., Xu, J., Lei, Y.: Classification of hyperspectral remote sensing image using hierarchical local-receptive-field-based extreme learning machine. IEEE Geosci. Remote Sens. Lett. **13**(3), 434–438 (2016)

10. Savojardo, C., Fariselli, P., Casadio, R.: Betaware: a machine-learning tool to detect and predict transmembrane beta barrel proteins in prokaryotes. Bioinformatics, bts728 (2013)

11. Huang, G.B., Zhou, H., Ding, X., Zhang, R.: Extreme learning machine for regression and multiclass classification. IEEE Trans. Syst. Man Cybern. Part B (Cybern.) **42**(2), 513–529 (2012)

12. Huang, G.B.: An insight into extreme learning machines: random neurons, random features and kernels. Cogn. Comput. **6**(3), 376–390 (2014)

13. Cao, J., Lin, Z., Huang, G.B., Liu, N.: Voting based extreme learning machine. Inf. Sci. **185**(1), 66–77 (2012)

14. Liu, N., Wang, H.: Ensemble based extreme learning machine. IEEE Signal Process. Lett. **17**(8), 754–757 (2010)

15. Zhu, Q.Y., Qin, A.K., Suganthan, P.N., Huang, G.B.: Evolutionary extreme learning machine. Pattern Recogn. **38**(10), 1759–1763 (2005)

16. Cao, J., Lin, Z., Huang, G.B.: Self-adaptive evolutionary extreme learning machine. Neural Process. Lett. **36**, 1–21 (2012)

17. Li, K.E., Wang, R.A.N., Kwong, S.A.M., Cao, J.: Evolving extreme learning machine paradigm with adaptive operator selection and parameter control. Int. J. Uncert. Fuzz. Knowl.-Based Syst. **21**(Suppl. 02), 143–154 (2013)

18. Zhang, Y., Wu, J., Cai, Z., Zhang, P., Chen, L.: Memetic extreme learning machine. Pattern Recogn. **58**, 135–148 (2016)

19. Mukhopadhyay, A., Maulik, U., Bandyopadhyay, S., Coello, C.A.C.: A survey of multiobjective evolutionary algorithms for data mining: Part I. IEEE Trans. Evol. Comput. **18**(1), 4–19 (2014)

20. Pan, L., He, C., Tian, Y., Su, Y., Zhang, X.: A region division based diversity maintaining approach for many-objective optimization. Integr. Comput.-Aided Eng. (Preprint), 1–18 (2017)

21. Gu, S., Cheng, R., Jin, Y.: Multi-objective ensemble generation. Wiley Interdisc. Rev. Data Mining Knowl. Discov. **5**(5), 234–245 (2015)

22. Liu, J., Gong, M., Miao, Q., Wang, X., Li, H.: Structure learning for deep neural networks based on multiobjective optimization. IEEE Trans. Neural Netw. Learn. Syst. (2017)

23. Gong, M., Liu, J., Li, H., Cai, Q., Su, L.: A multiobjective sparse feature learning model for deep neural networks. IEEE Trans. Neural Netw. Learn. Syst. **26**(12), 3263–77 (2015)

24. Mao, W., Tian, M., Cao, X., Xu, J.: Model selection of extreme learning machine based on multi-objective optimization. Neural Comput. Appl. **22**(3–4), 521–529 (2013)
25. Huang, G.B.: What are extreme learning machines? filling the gap between frank Rosenblatt's dream and John von Neumann's puzzle. Cogn. Comput. **7**(3), 263–278 (2015)
26. Kasun, L.L.C., Yang, Y., Huang, G.B., Zhang, Z.: Dimension reduction with extreme learning machine. IEEE Trans. Image Process. **25**(8), 3906–3918 (2016)
27. Hinton, G.E., Salakhutdinov, R.R.: Reducing the dimensionality of data with neural networks. Science **313**(5786), 504–507 (2006)
28. Chao, T., Hongbo, P., Yansheng, L., Zhengrou, Z.: Unsupervised spectral-spatial feature learning with stacked sparse autoencoder for hyperspectral imagery classification. IEEE Geosci. Remote Sens. Lett. **12**(12), 2438–2442 (2015)
29. Rachmawati, L., Srinivasan, D.: Multiobjective evolutionary algorithm with controllable focus on the knees of the pareto front. IEEE Trans. Evol. Comput. **13**(4), 810–824 (2009)
30. Deb, K., Pratap, A., Agarwal, S., Meyarivan, T.: A fast and elitist multiobjective genetic algorithm: NSGA-II. IEEE Trans. Evol. Comput. **6**(2), 182–197 (2002)

An Ions-Medicated Single Molecular Multi-functional DNA Cascade Logic Circuit and Signal Amplifier Model

Bingjie Guo[1], Xiangxiang Chen[3], Tao Wu[2], and Yafei Dong[1,2(✉)]

[1] College of life sciences, Shannxi Normal university, Xi'an 710119, China
{GuoBingjie,dongyf}@snnu.edu.cn
[2] College of computer sciences, Shannxi Normal university, Xi'an 710119, China
1871091542@163.com
[3] Software Institute, ShaanXi Electronic Technical College, Xi'an 710125, China

Abstract. In this paper, a single molecular multi-functional DNA cascade logic circuit and signal amplifier model was demonstrated by two single molecular multi-functional ions DNA probe(SMIP) to detect environment mercury and silver ion pollution, these two SMIP random coil structures turned into different hairpin-like structures with T-Hg^{2+}-T or C-Ag$^+$-C via inputting mercury and silver ions, then, use the SMIP structure "OR" and "AND" logic gate and unimolecular mulfunctional DNA logic amplifier model (UMDA). Finally, we proved the feasibility of our model by PAGE and fluorescence alteration.

Keywords: Molecular · Multi-functional · Ions-medicated · DNA computing

1 Introduction

Environment pollution, especially heavy ions pollution, is attracted a great number of attention from the public because of the serious social consequence and resulting adverse effect on living organism [1,2]. Among them, silver and mercury ions are two of the most toxic metallic pollutants and damage to the human health in different structures and ways. The most serious harm of Ag$^+$ and Hg^{2+} is that they can direct pollution water resource, accumulate to agricultural products and aquatic products and enter the human food chain [3,4]. It will finally cause degenerative diseases of motor center and neurological due to intracellular protein denaturation [5,6]. Therefore, It is urgent for us to study the detection method of silver and mercury ions in the fields of environmental monitoring, food safety, pharmaceutical analysis and clinical diagnosis [7].

Over the past decades, a variety of environment detection schemes have already been proposed. Including atomic absorption spectrometry(AAS)[8], inductive coupled plasma mass spectrometry(ICP-MS)[9], colorimetry [10], fluorescent techniques [11] and electrochemical methods [12], etc. Whereas, these

© Springer Nature Singapore Pte Ltd. 2017
C. He et al. (Eds.): BIC-TA 2017, CCIS 791, pp. 436–445, 2017.
https://doi.org/10.1007/978-981-10-7179-9_33

analytical methods always have several shortcoming, including sophisticated instrument, high cost, low-specificity and so on. In the circumustances, with low cost, high efficiency, time-saving, simple operation, high sensitivity and specificity, DNA molecule has became a new force of the environmental monitoring industry and occupied more and more important position [13].

Because of the high diversity, sensitivity and accuracy of their structure, DNA molecular have provided new ideas for numerous fields [14]. Among them, utilize the high specificity binding of metal ions with the functional DNA to achieve different logic functions has attracted widely attention. Since the discovery of Hg^{2+} can interact with thymine-thymine(T-T) mismatch with high affinity, cytosine-cytosine(C-C)pairs can capture Ag^+ efficiently and specifically [15–17]. A large number of ion detectors, sensors and DNA nano devices are designed and presented. These devices usually depend on the change of the DNA structure cause by Hg^{2+} and Ag^+, then achieve certain functions or certain logic relations. For instance, in 2012, a unimolecular multifunctional DNA probe was designed based on ions-medicated molecular structure change to artificially detect Ag^+ and Hg^{2+} in water samples [18]. In 2016, Yun Lv et al. have reported an electrochemical detection of glutathione based on Hg^{2+} mediated strand displacement reaction [19]. Although ion-medicated DNA molecule has been used in many aspects, its application in signal amplification field is far from rich imagination, one structure to achieve two or more functions are more rarer. so, it's badly in need of designing and putting forward more types of unimolecular multifunctional DNA logic circuit models that be used to constrict more complex logic circuit and signal amplifier.

With the emergence and development of molecular biology, DNA computing has emerged and developed into a new and potential interdisciplinary subject on the basis of computational science and molecular biology [20]. It makes full use of the massive storage capacity of DNA molecular and massive parallelism of biochemical reaction, molecular computer or information processing on the molecular scale, that be given breathtaking speed and massive storage facilities development on the base of DNA computing, is a promising substitute of the traditional silicon-based computer technologies [21]. Thus, design and construct efficiency and economic logic component are of great significant for the development of this research area.

Motivated by the above arguments, we have designed and proposed a unimolecular mulfunctional DNA logic amplifier model (UMDA)(Fig. 1) by marking use of logic gates, strand displacement and ion-mediated molecular structural modification. We use Hg^{2+} and Ag^+ ions as a foreign aid stimuli to control the stabilities of DNA structures. This UMDA, which include two ion detection (D1 and D2 show in Table 1) and one logic signal amplifier model, not only can realize direct and rapid detect both of Hg^{2+} and Ag^+ ions, but also can implement further logic amplifier calculate, we did so by controlling Hg^{2+} and Ag^+ ions input thus leading to the change in the structure of D1 and D2. Then, we use the output of D1 and D2 ultimately triggers a DNA-based "AND" logic fluorescence amplifier nanodevice in solution.

2   Experiment

2.1   Materials

All DNA were purchased from Sangon Biotechnology Co., Ltd(Shanghai, China) and purified by PAGE and ULTRAPAGE, their sequences are listed in Table 1. All DNA sequence ($100 \mu M$)were obtained in ultrapure water as stock solution. $Cl_2HgO_8 \cdot 3H_2O$, NAOH, $Na_2EDTA \cdot 2H_2O$, $AgNO_3$, $(HOCH_2)_3CNH_2$, Tris, CH_3COOH, $C_4H_6O_4Mg \cdot 4H_2O$, $CH_2 = CHCONH_2$, $(H_2C = CHCONH)_2CH_2$, NaCl, $(NH_4)_2S_2O_8$, HCONH$_2$, TEMED, $MgCl_2 \cdot 6H_2O$, $(CH_3)_2NCH_2CH_2N(CH_3)_2$, 6*loading buffer were bought from Xi'an JingBo Bio-Technique Co. ammonium persulfate and stain all were bought from Sigma-Aldrich Co. LLC. 10 * TAE/Mg^{2+} buffer (48.4 g Tris base, 26.75 g Mg(CH_3COOH)$_2$, 20 ml 0.5 mol/L EDTA, 1L, pH 8.0) and the 500 mL mother liquor of acrylamide at the concentration of 40% (217 gacrylamide and 8 g N, N'-Methylenebisacrylamide), Stain-All were purchased from AAT Bioquest inc.

2.2   DNA Sequence

Table 1. The DNA strand-sequences in the experiment

Single-strand	Strand-sequence(5'-3')
D1	FAM-GTACACTGTAAAAAAAAAAAAAAAAACACTGTG-BHQ
D2	BHQ-CACTCTGAAAAAAAAAAAAAAAAAACAGTGTAC-FAM

2.3   Experiment Methods

Native PAGE. Computing models are formed by the DNA strands'hybrization under slow annealing. In the course of constructing DNA logic computing models, various equimolar DNA strands are added to a final concentration of $2 \mu M$ in 20 mM Tris-acetate buffer after dissolved by pure water. The mixture hybridized under the reaction condition of 95 °C for 4 min, 55 °C for 30 min, 45 °C for 30 min, 35 °C for 25 min, 15 °C for 30 min, and 4 °C for permanent thermal insulation. Then a few of microliters of Hg^{2+} and Ag^+ stock solution(100 μM) was added to achieve $2 \mu M$ concentration while the black without ions and incubated for 30 min at room temperature. Then, the obtaining products are detected by native PAGE. Reactions are initiated by the addition of the input DNA. In addition, the input DNA strands and DNA logic modules are mixed and react for over 2 h at room temperature.

Fluorescent Signal Detection. In this study, we choose to label substrates with fluorophore FAM and quencher BHQ. And the fluorescent results are obtained using a fluorescent scanning spectrometer for FAM at 492 nm excitation and 518 nm emission by EnSpire ELIASA from PerkinElmer USA.

3   Results and Discussion

Here, a single molecular multi-functional DNA cascade logic circuit and signal amplifier model was construct, which are mediated by Hg^{2+} and Ag^+, and the fluorescent intensity and native PAGE are regarded as the output signal.

3.1   Establishment of Ion Detection

As shown in Fig. 1, we put forward two SMIP, named as D1(31nt) and D2(31nt) respectively, for the analysis of Hg^{2+} and Ag^+ by taking advantage of ions-medicated DNA molecular conformation transformation. In normal conditions, D1 and D2 are random coil structure, In the presence of Hg^{2+} and Ag^{2+}. D1, which are labeled with fluorophore (FAM) and quencher moiety (BHQ) at the 5'- and 3'-termini respectively, can transform from random coil structure to hairpin structure because of T-Hg^{2+}-T or C-Ag^+-C mismatch can be formed in the stem. If Ag+ is added, a 7 base pair-long stem will be builded at the two ends of D1 with one C-Ag^+-C mismatch. If Hg^{2+} is added, a 6 base pair-long stem will be structured with one T-Hg^{2+}-T mismatch. Similarly, D2, which are labeled with fluorophore (FAM) and quencher moiety (BHQ) at the 3'-and 5'-termini respectively, can produce structure change similar with D1. In the presence of Ag^+, a 6 base pair-long stem will be built at the two ends of D2 with one C-Ag^+-C mismatch. If Hg^{2+} is added, a 6 base pair-long stem will be structured with one T-Hg^{2+}-T mismatch. When D1 and D2 form stable hairpin structure, the tail end of the fluorophore (FAM) and the quencher moiety (BHQ) were close enough to produce fluorescence resonance energy transfer (FRET) in four cases. So, we can regard the fluorescence change as the detection mark to achieve the rapid detection of mercury and silver ions.

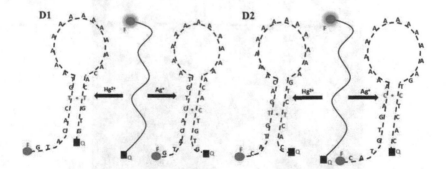

Fig. 1. the schematic diagram of ions detect and "OR" logic gate

Table 2. The true value table of "OR" logic gate

Input1(Ag^+)	Input2(Hg^{2+})	Output	Output
0	0	0	0
0	1	1	1
1	0	1	1
1	1	1	1

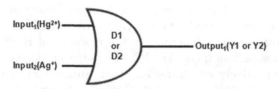

3.2 Establishment of Cascaded Logic Circuit and Signal Amplifier

"OR" logic gate based on Hg^{2+} and Ag^+. From the concept of SIMP, we built two "OR" logic gates based on the particular characteristics of Hg^{2+} and Ag^+. Two metal-ions (Hg^{2+} and Ag^+) act as inputs in this gate. The route is expressed in Fig. 1. We design special base at the two end of D1 and D2, that can form stable hairpin structure under the function of ions. The "OR" gate gets its name from the fact that it behaves after the fashion of the logical inclusive "or", The output is "true" (or 1), if either or both of the inputs are "true" (or 1). If both inputs are "false" (or 0), then the output is "false" (or 0). Single strand D1 is labeled with

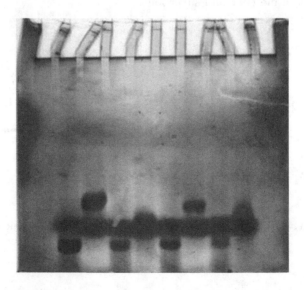

Fig. 2. The PAGE analysis of strand displacing operations

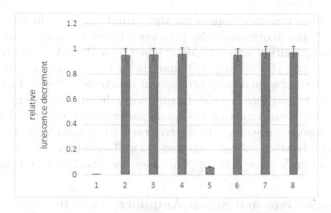

Fig. 3. Relative variations of fluorescent intensity of "OR" logic gate

fluorophore and biotin at two terminals. In the initial state $(0,0)$, D1 is in the structure of the random coil structure, and both ends of the fluorescent groups and quenching groups are not close to each other, so the system of fluorescence without variation, outing a low signal(0), D1 has faster gel running speed than other displaced products because of its smaller molecular weight (Fig. 2, lane 1). When Hg^{2+} or Ag^+ is input, the two end of D1 is partially complementary to each other and cleverly folded into a stem loop structure with $T-Hg^{2+}-T$ or $C-Ag^+-C$ base pairs to form a molecular beacon, that make the two ends of the fluorescent group and the quenching group are close enough to produce the fluorescence resonance energy transfer (FRET), which makes the system produce large fluorescence signal changes and outing a high signal(1), the product Y1 will gradually form with a slow gel running speed (Fig. 2, lane 2,3). When Hg^{2+} and Ag^+ are added at the same concentration, D1 selectively interacts with two kinds of ions, resulting in a large variation and outing a high signal(1) (Fig. 2, lane 4). Similarly, without adding anything, D2 has faster gel running speed than other displaced products because of its smaller molecular weight (Fig. 2, lane 5). When input Ag^+ or Hg^{2+}, D2 changed their construction and has a relative slower gel running speed (Fig. 2, lane 6,7). When input Ag^+ and Hg^{2+}, D2 changed more complex construction (Fig. 2, lane 8).

The relative fluorescence variation is normalized as $\Delta I = (F-F0)/F0$, where F0 is the fluorescent intensity before adding input ions; F is the fluorescent intensity after adding input ions and incubating for 2 h, and average values of each set of data is obtained by repeating the experiments three times. As shown in Fig. 1c, in the absence of Hg^{2+} or Ag^+, almost the fluorescence significantly variation was observed as $\Delta I1 = 0.01$ (Fig. 3. lane 1), $\Delta I5 = 0.07$ (Fig. 3. lane 5), its value is far below the threshold value 0.4. However, adding anyone of the inputs, the fluorescence decrease was much more, $\Delta I2 = 0.95$ (D1 adding Ag+, Fig. 3, lane 2), $\Delta I3 = 0.96$ (D1 adding Hg2+, Fig 3, lane 3), $\Delta I6 = 0.96$ (D2 adding Ag^+, Fig. 3, lane 6) and $\Delta I7 = 0.97$ (D2 adding Hg^{2+}, Fig. 3, lane 7). And fluorescent decrease reaching threshold represents the output signal 1. In the presence of Hg^{2+} and Ag^+, the fluorescence also presents a larger variation reaching threshold represents the output signal 1. $\Delta I4 = 0.96$ (D1 adding Ag^+ and Hg^{2+}, Fig. 3, lane 4) $\Delta I8 = 0.98$ (D2 adding Ag^+ and Hg^{2+}, Fig. 3, lane 8). In fluorescent experiments part, the final concentration of substrate DNA is $2\,\mu M$, the final concentration of input ions is $2\,\mu M$. In summary, the absence of any one or both of Hg^{2+} and Ag^+ can triggering DNA hairpin structure generated and accompanied fluorescence quenching. On the contrary, when neither of Hg^{2+} and Ag^+ are exist in the reaction solution, D1 and D2 still maintain their inherent linear structure. The truth value table of "OR" logic gate is shown in Table 2.

"AND" Logic Gate and Signal Amplifier. From the above content, we know that both of D1 and D2 have three forms. The three different forms of D1 had been named Y11, Y12 and Y13 respective, and the three different forms of D2 had been named Y21, Y22 and Y23 respectively. Thereinto, the Y11 and Y21 respectively represent the single strand D1 and D2, Y1 and Y22 respectively represent hairpin structure of D1 and D2 that binding Ag^+ form C-Ag^+-C base pairs. Y13 and Y23 respectively represent hairpin structures of D1 and D2 that binding Hg^{2+} form T-Hg^{2+}-T base pairs. Here, a double input cascade AND logic calculation model that on the basis of ions-mediated and the principle of strand displacement, had been established, the reaction mechanism is shown in Fig. 4. In this model, as long as one of three kinds of structure forms of D1 and D2 exist at the same time, both of them will form D1D2 double helix structure with a period of not matching area by strand displacement. Furthermore, because of the fluorescent groups of D1 and D2 are close to each other and make the fluorescence intensity of the system increases greatly, we record the output results(Y) to "1". However, when there is only one of D1 and D2, D1 and D2 do not react, the fluorescence intensity remains constant, the output (Y) is recorded as '0', and if the D1 and D2 are not present, there is no fluorescence resonance energy transfer, and the output (Y) is recorded as '0'.

As is shown in Fig. 2(c), the fluorescent results were used to detect the feasibility and validity of apparatus for signal recovery mediated by DNA strand-displacement. Owning to 5' fluorescence and 3'quencher of D1 hybridized for initially stable substrate Y12 and Y13,3' fluorescence and 5' quencher of D1 hybridized for initially stable substrate Y22 and Y23, the fluorescence intensity is very low and even can be ignored. Mixing one of Y11, Y12 and Y13 with one of Y21, Y22 and Y23, fluorescence increased 83%,63%,77%,66%,82%,71%,68%,79% and 81% relative to the initially state respectively after 8h, reaching the presupposed value (Fig. 5). which powerfully demonstrated the feasibility and validity the recovery of fluorescence for the signal recovery apparatus mediated by DNA strand-displacement. The concentration of substrates and DNA are $2\,\mu M$. The truth table was shown in Table 3.

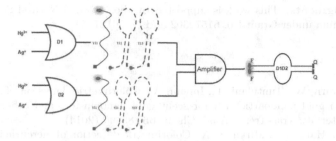

Fig. 4. The schematic diagram of ions detect and "AND" logic gate

Table 3. The true value table of "AND" logic gate

Y1	Y2	Y
0	0	0
0	1	0
1	0	0
1	1	1

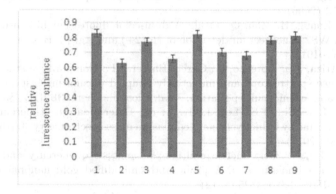

Fig. 5. Relative variations of fluorescent intensity of "AND" logic gate

4 Conclusion

In summary, a single molecular multi-functional DNA cascade logic circuit and signal amplifier model has been developed based on the ions-medicated strand-displacement reaction. Firstly, we designed two SMIP to effectively detect Ag^+ and Hg^{2+}. Second, we made use of the $C-Ag^+-C$ and $T-Hg^{2+}-T$ special construction to build a "OR" logic gate. To the base of our knowledge, this is the first time that using the special structure of Ag^+ and Hg^{2+} ions mediated to construct Boolean logic gate. Finally, we have built a cascading "AND" logic gate on the previous basis. This novel strategy may provide a new pathway for molecular logic gates, DNA computing, and ions detection research.

Acknowledgments. This work is supported by the National Natural Science Foundation of China under Grant No. 61572302 and No. 61272246.

References

1. Chansuvarn, W., Tuntulani, T., Imyim, A.: Colorimetric detection of mercury(II) based on gold nanoparticles, fluorescent gold nanoclusters and other gold-based nanomaterials. Trac-Trend. Anal. Chem. **65**, 83–96 (2014)
2. Lee, J.S., Han, M.S., Mirkin, C.A.: Colorimetric detection of mercuric ion (Hg 2+) in aqueous media using DNA-functionalized gold nanoparticles. Angew. Chem. **46**(22), 4093 (2007)
3. Wang, S., Xu, H., Yang, Q., et al.: A triphenylamine-based colorimetric and turn-on fluorescent probe for detection of cyanide anions in live cells. RSC Adv. **5**(59), 47990–47996 (2015)
4. Li, L., Li, B., Di, C., et al.: Visual detection of melamine in raw milk using gold nanoparticles as colorimetric probe. Food Chem. **122**(3), 895–900 (2010)
5. Li, L., Li, B., Qi, Y., et al.: Label-free aptamer-based colorimetric detection of mercury ions in aqueous media using unmodified gold nanoparticles as colorimetric probe. Anal. Bioanal. Chem. **393**(8), 2051–7 (2009)
6. Miyake, Y., Togashi, H., Tashiro, M., et al.: Mercury II-mediated formation of thymine-Hg II-thymine base pairs in DNA duplexes. J. Am. Chem. Soc. **128**, 2172–2173 (2006)
7. Zuo, X., Zhang, H., Zhu, Q., et al.: A dual-color fluorescent biosensing platform based on WS2 nanosheet for detection of Hg(2+) and Ag(+). Biosens. Bioelectron. **85**, 464 (2016)
8. Gómez-Ariza, J.L., Lorenzo, F., Garcia-Barrera, T.: Comparative study of atomic fluorescence spectroscopy and inductively coupled plasma mass spectrometry for mercury and arsenic multispeciation. Anal. Bioanal. Chem. **382**(2), 485–492 (2005)
9. Fong, B.M.W., Siu, T.S., Lee, J.S.K., et al.: Determination of mercury in whole blood and urine by inductively coupled plasma mass spectrometry. J. Anal. Toxicol. **31**(5), 281 (2017)
10. Qing, Z., He, X.: Colorimetric multiplexed analysis of mercury and silver ions by using a unimolecular DNA probe and unmodified gold nanoparticles. Anal. Methods **4**(10), 3320–3325 (2012)
11. Deng, W., Tan, Y., Li, Y., et al.: Square wave voltammetric determination of Hg(II) using thiol functionalized chitosan-multiwalled carbon nanotubes nanocomposite film electrode. Microchim. Acta **169**(3–4), 367–373 (2010)
12. Zhao, J., Zhu, L., Guo, C., et al.: A new electrochemical method for the detection of cancer cells based on small molecule-linked DNA. Biosens. Bioelectron. **49**(11), 329–333 (2013)
13. Wang, F., Liu, X., Willner, I.: DNA Switches: from Principles to Applications. Angew. Chem. Int. Edit. **54**(4), 1098–129 (2015)
14. Miyake, Y., Togashi, H., Tashiro, M., et al.: MercuryII-mediated formation of Thymine-HgII-Thymine base pairs in DNA duplexes. J. Am. Chem. Soc. **128**(7), 2172–3 (2006)
15. Tanaka, Y., Oda, S., Yamaguchi, H., et al.: 15N–15N J-coupling across Hg(II): direct observation of Hg(II)-mediated T-T base pairs in a DNA Duplex. J. Am. Chem. Soc. **129**(2), 244–5 (2007)
16. Ono, A., Cao, S., Togashi, H., et al.: Specific interactions between silver(I) ions and cytosine-cytosine pairs in DNA duplexes. Chem. Commun. **39**(39), 4825 (2008)

17. Feng, W., Xue, X., Liu, X.: One-step, room-temperature, colorimetric detection of mercury (Hg(2+)) using DNA/nanoparticle conjugates. J. Am. Chem. Soc. **130**(11), 3244–3245 (2008)

18. He, X., Qing, Z., Wang, K., et al.: Engineering a unimolecular multifunctional DNA probe for analysis of Hg2+ and Ag+. Anal. Methods. **4**(2), 345–347 (2012)

19. Yun, L., Yang, L., Mao, X., et al.: Electrochemical detection of glutathione based on Hg 2+ -mediated strand displacement reaction strategy. Biosens. Bioelectron. **85**, 664–668 (2016)

20. Farhadtoosky, S., Jahanian, A.: Customized placement algorithm of nanoscale DNA logic circuits. J. Circuit. Syst. Comp. **26**(10), 1750150 (2017)

21. Yang, J., Dong, C., Dong, Y., et al.: Logic nanoparticle beacon triggered by the binding-induced effect of multiple inputs. Acs Appl. Mater. Inter. **6**(16), 14486–14492 (2014)

A Recommendation Approach Based on Latent Factors Prediction of Recurrent Neural Network

Ruihong Li[1,2(✉)], Xingquan Zuo[1,2], Pan Wang[1,2], and Xinchao Zhao[3]

[1] School of Computer Science, Beijing University of Posts and Telecommunications,
Beijing, China
liruihongbob@qq.com, zuoxq@bupt.edu.cn
[2] Key Laboratory of Trustworthy Distributed Computing and Service,
Ministry of Education, Beijing University of Posts and Telecommunications,
Beijing, China
[3] School of Science, Beijing University of Posts and Telecommunications,
Beijing, China

Abstract. Recommender systems have received much attention due to their wide applications. Current recommender approaches typically recommend items to user based on the rating prediction. However, the predicted ratings cannot truly reflect users interests on items because the rating prediction is usually based on history data and does not consider the effect of time factor on uses interests (behaviors). In this paper, we propose a recommendation approach combining the matrix factorization and a recurrent neural network. In this approach, all the items rated by a user are considered as time series data. The matrix factorization is used to obtain latent vectors of those items. The recurrent neural network is taken as a time series prediction model and trained by the latent vectors of historical items, and then the trained model is used to predict the latent vector of the item to be recommended. Finally, a recommendation list is formed by mapping the latent vector into a set of items. Experimental results show that the proposed approach is able to produce an effective recommend list and outperforms those comparative approaches.

Keywords: Recommender systems · Matrix factorization · Recurrent neural network · Latent factor

1 Introduction

Recommender systems are received much attention in recent years [1]. They help users find information or goods that interest them and make enterprises get more profits by recommending suitable items to users. Recommender systems have been applied to a variety of areas, such as movies, music, books, news and services recommendation.

Numerous recommender approaches have been proposed over the years [2]. Among those approaches, content-based approaches and collaborative filtering (CF) approaches are two typical categories of recommend approaches.

© Springer Nature Singapore Pte Ltd. 2017
C. He et al. (Eds.): BIC-TA 2017, CCIS 791, pp. 446–455, 2017.
https://doi.org/10.1007/978-981-10-7179-9_34

CF approaches are probably the most successfully and widely used techniques in recommender systems and includes neighbor-based CF [1–4] and model-based CF.

As a representative of the model-based CF, the matrix factorization (MF) approach [5,6] represents the interaction between users and items with a rating matrix. It assumes that users and items are in the same latent space, and that each user or item can be represented by a latent vector in the latent space. It predicts unknown ratings in the matrix through a matrix factorization model, which decomposes the rating matrix into users and items latent vectors.

Many researchers proposed improved matrix factorization approaches to get better predicting results. Koren [7] proposed an approach combining the matrix factorization with a neighbor-based approach, and integrated implicit feedback in the modeling process. Salakhutdinov [8] proposed a probabilistic matrix factorization model which greatly reduce the overfitting of the traditional matrix factorization model. In [9], Salakhutdinov et al. further used the Markov Chain Monte Carlo model to optimize the parameters to reduce the overfitting and improve predicting accuracy of the probabilistic matrix factorization. In [10], the item factors between the matrix factorization and item embedding parts are shared, and the rating matrix and item co occurrence matrix are factorized at the same time. Some approaches are proposed to improve predicting results through adding supplementary information to MF [11–14]. For example, Gopalan et al. used Poisson factorization to model both user ratings and document content. Rather than modeling the two types of data as independent factorization problems, they connected the two latent factorizations using a correction term [11]. Mcauley et al. developed statistical models that combine latent dimensions in rating data with topics in review text, taking the corpus likelihood acts as a regularizer for the rating prediction model [12].

In practice, the predicted rating of a user on an item may not truly reflect the users interest on the item. For example, the rating of a user on an item is usually predicted based on all history data, and the predicted rating is not very high. That does not mean that the user does not have interest in the item all the time. The user may be interested in the item at some particular time because the interest of a user usually changes over time. Therefore, time is an import factor that has an effect on recommendation results.

In this paper, we propose a recommendation approach combining the matrix factorization approach with a recurrent neural network (RNN). Instead of predicting ratings of a user on items directly, our approach considers the items rated by a user as a time series data, and then use the RNN as a time series prediction model to predict a recommend list to the user. First, all items rated by a user are sorted according to the time when the user rates those items. Then, the matrix factorization approach is used to get latent factor vectors of those items. Subsequently, the RNN uses latent vectors of historical items to predict the latent vector of the item that may interest the user. Finally, a number of items with latent vectors closest to the predicted one forms the final recommendation list.

The main contributions of this paper include: (1) propose a recommendation approach combining the matrix factorization and the recurrent neural network; (2) latent factors of items are introduced into the prediction of a recommend list. To the best of our knowledge, our approach is the first work on applying latent factors to the time series prediction model for items recommendation.

This paper is organized as follows. Section 2 presents the proposed recommendation approach. Section 3 gives experimental results and the analysis. Section 4 concludes this paper.

2 Proposed Recommendation Approach

Given the time series of items rated by a user, our approach is to predict a set of items that the user will consume next.

Take the movie recommendation for example, suppose that there are n users $\{U_1, U_2, ..., U_n\}$ and m movies $\{I_1, I_2, ..., I_n\}$. All the movies watched by a user can be sorted by the time when the user watches movies, thereby getting a sequence of movies, denoted by S. Let $\{I_{t_k}, I_{t_k+1}, ...I_{t_k+T}\}$ be $(T+1)$ consecutive items in S, where t_k is the index of the kth item in S.

In our approach, items $\{I_{t_k}, I_{t_k+1}, ...I_{t_k+T-1}\}$ are used to predict item I_{t_k+T}. The key issue is how to express an item in the sequence S. A straight forward method is to adopt the one-hot encoder to represent an item [21]. However, the one-hot encoder would consume too many memory resources because there may be millions of items for some recommendation problems. In this paper, we use the matrix factorization approach to get a low-rank latent vector for an item. Each item is represented by a latent vector. The number of dimensions of the latent vector is much smaller than that of one-hot encoder of items.

Our approach is shown in Fig. 1. First, the matrix factorization approach is used to decompose the rating matrix into latent vectors of items, such that each item corresponds to a unique latent vector. Let κ be the number of dimensions of a latent vectors. In the example shown in Fig. 1, $\kappa = 5$. For the consecutive items $\{I_{t_k}, I_{t_k+1}, ...I_{t_k+T}\}$ in S, latent vectors of items $\{I_{t_k}, I_{t_k+1}, ...I_{t_k+T-1}\}$ are taken as the inputs of the RNN to predict the latent vector of item I_{t_k+T}. Finally, the recommend list is constructed by s items whose latent vectors are closest to the predicted latent vector. Suppose that n_j is the index of the jth item in the s sequence items. The recommendation list is expressed by $\{I_{n_1}, I_{n_2}, ..., I_{n_s}\}$. This approach integrates the time factor into the RNN model to emphasize the change of users interests and behaviors with time.

2.1 Generating Latent Vectors by Matrix Factorization

Matrix factorization is one of the most popular and useful CF models in recommender systems. Users interaction with items, especially explicit feedback, are typically represented by a rating matrix. Take a movie recommendation for example, a user rates a movie after watching it. The rating is from 1 to 5, representing the users evaluation on the movie. Figure 2 is a rating matrix with m

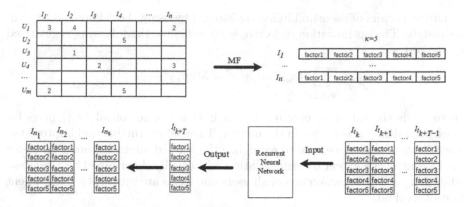

Fig. 1. The proposed recommendation approach

users and n items. Each row is a users watching history, and each column represents the history of one movie being watched. There are many missing ratings in the matrix. The goal of matrix factorization approach is to predict those missing ratings in the matrix, and then recommend those movies with high predicted ratings to users.

	I_1	I_2	I_3	I_4	$\cdots$	I_n
U_1	3	4				2
U_2				5		
U_3			1			
U_4			2			3
$\cdots$						
U_m	2			5		

Fig. 2. An example of rating matrix

Instead of predicting items ratings, in this paper we use the matrix factorization to get items latent vectors. Matrix factorization is based on the assumption that latent vectors of users and items are in the same latent space, and that each user and item can be expressed by a latent vector. Given a rating matrix, matrix factorization decomposes the matrix into the product of users and items latent factors, denoted by $p_u \in \Re^\kappa (u = 1, ..., m)$ and $q_i \in \Re^\kappa (i = 1, ..., n)$, respectively, where κ is the number of dimensions of latent vectors. The rating of user u on item i is predicted by

$$\widehat{r_{ui}} = p_u q_i^T \tag{1}$$

Latent vectors of users and items are learned by using those known ratings in the matrix. The optimization objective is to minimize the following regularized squared error.

$$\min_{p^*,q^*} \sum_{(u,i)\in D} (r_{ui} - p_u q_i^T)^2 + \lambda(\|p_u\|^2 + \|q_i\|^2)^2 \tag{2}$$

where r_{ui} is the rating of user u on item i; D is the set of all (u,i) pairs for which the rating r_{ui} is known in the matrix. To avoid overfitting and improve the generalization ability, we need to regularize the learned latent factors. Parameter λ is to control the extent of regularization and usually determined by the cross-validation [5]. The latent vectors of all users and items are learned by the gradient descent method.

2.2   Recurrent Neural Network for Latent Vectors Prediction

Neural networks have been applied to recommender systems in recent years [15,17,21]. Literatures [15,16] used a shallow Restricted Boltzmann Machines neural network to predict the ratings. In literatures [17,18], unknown ratings are predicted by auto-encoder neural networks trained by an unsupervised learn algorithm. Paul et al. [19] devised a recommender system which is comprised of two neural networks, one for candidate generation and the other for ranking.

Instead of using a neural network to predict the ratings, this paper uses a recurrent neural network to predict the list of items that interests a user. Recurrent neural networks have been proved to be effective for time series prediction, and as such, we adopt a recurrent neural network to predict the latent vectors of items.

The recurrent network is shown in Fig. 3. Recurrent neural networks all loops with themselves, allowing information to persist. In this process, each step every unit takes previous outputs as one part of inputs. So the process is much like a chain, and naturally fit to model the sequence data.

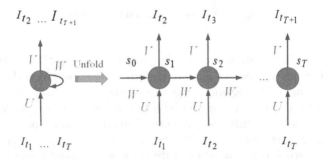

Fig. 3. Predicting latent vectors by RNN.

In Fig. 3, s_t is the state of the RNN at time step t. $U(V)$ is the input(output) weight of the RNN. W is the state weight of the RNN. Inputs of the RNN are items latent vectors. The number of RNN unfolded back steps is denoted by T, which is also the window size of the items sequence.

In this paper, we adopt a popular RNN named Long Short-Term Memory (LSTM). The parameter W is learned by the Backpropagation Through Time algorithm [22], and other parameters are learned by the Backpropagation learning algorithm. We use the following square loss function, which is to be minimized by the learning algorithms.

$$\widehat{r_{ui}} = E_{t_k}(I_{t_k}, \widehat{I_{t_k}}) = \frac{1}{2}(I_{t_k} - \widehat{I_{t_k}})^2 \tag{3}$$

$$E = \sum_{t_k} E_{t_k}(I_{t_k}, \widehat{I_{t_k}}) = \frac{1}{2}\sum_{t_k}(I_{t_k} - \widehat{I_{t_k}})^2 \tag{4}$$

where I_{t_k} is the kth item in the sequence S, and $\widehat{I_{t_k}}$ is the corresponding predicted item. The loss function value is the sum of errors between predicted latent vectors and actual ones. In the item sequence S, each set of $(T+1)$ consecutive items is regarded as a training example. As shown in Fig. 3, latent vectors of the first (last) T items are inputs (outputs) of the RNN.

2.3 Generate a Recommendation List by Predicted Latent Vectors

The output of the RNN is a predicted latent vector. Recall that we have the latent vectors of all items. The n items whose latent vectors are closest to the predicted one are chosen to form the recommendation list.

Euclidean distance is used to calculate the distance of any two latten vectors.

$$dist(q_i, q_j) = \sqrt{\sum_x (q_{ix} - q_j)^2} \tag{5}$$

where q_i and q_j are any two latent vectors.

3 Experiments

To verify the proposed approach, it is applied to a real life dataset, MovieLens (1M), which is a popular dataset to test recommendation approaches. The dataset has total 6040 users and 3952 movies. A user rates a movie after watching it. There are 1000209 ratings, each of which is an integer from 1 to 5. Every user watched at least 20 movies in the dataset.

3.1 Performance Metrics

The commonly used matrix of recall rate is used to evaluate the proposed approach and those comparative approaches. For user i, the recall rate is expressed by

$$recall_i = |recom\_list_i \bigcap target\_list_i|/|target\_list_i| \tag{6}$$

For user i, the last n items in the sequence S are used as test data, and other items are used to train the RNN. As stated in Sect. 2.3, the recommendation list predicted by the RNN, $recom\_list_i$, contains n items. $target\_list_i$ consists of the last n items, that is, the last n movies actually watched by the user.

The average recall rate is defined as follows.

$$avg\_recall = \sum_{i \in Users} recall_i / |Users| \tag{7}$$

where $Users$ represents the set of all users. In the following experiments, the matrix of recall rate refers to the average recall rate.

3.2 Experiment Settings

As stated in Sect. 2, for a user, a movies sequence S can be obtained. In the sequence S, the last 10 movies are chosen as test data, and other movies as training data to train the RNN. In the training data, the size of time window, T, is set as 10. It means that every 10 consecutive movies in the sequence are treated as a training example. The number of items in the recommendation list, s, is given by 10.

The number of dimensions of latent vectors, κ, is set to be 10. The matrix factorization in our approach is realized by the open source software LIBMF. The MF models learning rate is set as 0.05 and the training epoch as 800.

We implement the RNN (LSTM) in the tensorflow framework of version 0.12. The learning rate is given by 0.1 and the training epoch by 6. The parameter of hidden size of the LSTM is set to be 10 and the number of RNN unfolded back steps is set as 9.

3.3 Experiment Results

The proposed approach is compared against the following typical recommendation approaches.

- Item-based KNN [3,4]: item-based k-nearest neighbor collaborative filtering.
- User-based KNN [1,2]: user-based k-nearest neighbor collaborative filtering.
- MF: basic Matrix Factorization recommender.
- Biased MF: biased Matrix Factorization recommender.
- BPMF [9]: Bayesian Probabilistic Matrix Factorization using Markov Chain Monte Carlo.
- PMF [8]: Probabilistic Matrix Factorization.

All above comparative approaches are implemented using the open source platform librec [20]. They use the same training and test data as our approach.

Experiment results are presented in Table 1. Table 1 shows that the proposed approach outperforms all of the matrix factorization approaches and the two neighbor-based CF approaches. Average recall rates obtained by all matrix factorization approaches are smaller than 0.08, and are much smaller than that of

Table 1. Comparison results on MovieLens (1M) dataset.

Methods	Item-based-KNN	User-based-KNN	MF
Recall rate	0.003	0.019	0.004
Methods	BPMF	PMF	Biased MF
Recall rate	0.002	0.008	0.007
Methods	Our approach		
Recall rate	0.024		

Table 2. The produced recommendation list for a user.

Recommendation list of movies	
Movies	Movie types
Regret to Inform(1998)	Documentary
It's a Wonderful Life(1963)	Drama
Charade(1963)	Comedy,Mystery,Romance,Thriller
Toy Story(1995)	Animation,Childrens,Comedy
Run Silent,Run Deep(1958)	War
Beauty and the Beast (1991)	Animation,Childrens,Musical
Day the Earth Stood Still(1951)	Drama,War
Sting(1973)	Comedy,Crime
Great Escape(1963)	Adventure,War
Running Free(2000)	Drama
Actually watched list of movies	
Movies	Movie types
Beauty and the Beast(1991)	Animation,Childrens,Musical
Toy Story(1995)	Animation,Childrens,Comedy
Aladdin(1992)	Animation,Childrens,Comedy
Close Shave(1995)	Animation,Comedy,Thriller
Antz(1998)	Animation,Childrens
Hunchback of Notre Dame(1996)	Animation,Childrens,Musical
Bugs Life(1998)	Animation,Childrens,Comedy
Mulan(1998)	Animation,Childrens
Hercules(1997)	Animation,Childrens,Comedy
Pocahontas(1995)	Animation,Childrens,Musical

our approach. Among all comparative approaches, the user-based KNN obtains the best average recall rate 0.019, which is also lower than that of our approach. For the movie recommendation problem, interests and behaviors of users may change over time and the problem is actually a time series prediction problem.

RNN is a powerful tool for the time series prediction, such that it is more suitable for such problem than matrix factorization approaches, which recommend movies based on predicted ratings and do not consider the effect of time factor on recommendation results.

To observe recommendation results intuitively, Table 2 gives the recommended list produced by our approach for a user. The actually watched movies by the user are also given in the Table. We can see that many movies in the recommendation list belong to the types of animations and comedies. Most of actually watched movies also belong to the two types. It indicates that our approach is able to recommend appropriate movies to the user and those movies reflect the users interests.

4   Conclusions

In this paper, a recommendation approach combining a matrix factorization and a recurrent neural network is proposed. Different from the traditional recommendation approaches based on ratings prediction, this approach considers the items rated by a user as a set of time series data. First, the matrix factorization is used to obtain latent vectors of all items, such that the time series items are transformed into time series latent vectors. Then, the recurrent neural network is taken as a time series prediction mode to predict a latent vector. Finally, a recommendation list is produced by the predicted latent vector. Experiments show that the proposed approach outperforms those comparative approaches and can produce appropriate recommend lists for users.

Acknowledgement. This work was supported in part by National Natural Science Foundation of China (61374204; 61375066)

References

1. Breese, J.S., Heckerman, D., Kadie, C.: Empirical analysis of predictive algorithms for collaborative filtering. In: Proceedings of the Fourteenth conference on Uncertainty in artificial intelligence, pp. 43–52. Morgan Kaufmann Publishers Inc., Madison (1998)
2. Resnick, P., Iacovou, N., Suchak, M., Bergstrom, P., Riedl, J.: GroupLens: an open architecture for collaborative filtering of netnews. In: Proceedings of the ACM Conference on Computer Supported Cooperative Work, pp. 175–186. ACM, Chapel Hill (1994)
3. Sarwar, B., Karypis, G., Konstan, J., Riedl, J.: Item-based collaborative filtering recommendation algorithms. In: Proceedings of the 10th International Conference on World Wide Web, pp. 285–295. ACM, Hong Kong (2001)
4. Deshpande, M., Karypis, G.: Item-based top-N recommendation algorithms. ACM Trans. Inf. Syst. **22**(1), 143–177 (2004)
5. Koren, Y., Bell, R., Volinsky, C.: Matrix factorization techniques for recommender systems. Computer **42**(8), 30–37 (2009)

6. Paterek, A.: Improving regularized singular value decomposition for collaborative filtering. In: Proceedings of KDD Cup and Workshop, pp. 5–8. ACM, California (2007)
7. Koren, Y.: Factorization meets the neighborhood: a multifaceted collaborative filtering model. In: Proceedings of the 14th ACM SIGKDD International Conference on Knowledge Discovery and Data Mining, pp. 426–434. ACM, New York (2008)
8. Salakhutdinov, R., Mnih, A.: Probabilistic matrix factorization. In: International Conference on Neural Information Processing Systems, pp. 1257–1264. Curran Associates Inc., Vancouver (2007)
9. Salakhutdinov, R., Mnih, A.: Bayesian probabilistic matrix factorization using Markov chain Monte Carlo. In: International Conference on Machine Learning, pp. 880–887. ACM, Helsinki (2008)
10. Liang, D., Altosaar, J., Charlin, L., Blei, D.M.: Factorization meets the item embedding: regularizing matrix factorization with item co-occurrence. In: ACM Conference on Recommender Systems, pp. 59–66. ACM, Boston (2016)
11. Gopalan, P., Charlin, L., Blei, D.M.: Content-based recommendations with poisson factorization. In: International Conference on Neural Information Processing Systems, pp. 3176–3184. MIT Press, Montreal (2014)
12. Mcauley, J., Leskovec, J.: Hidden factors and hidden topics: understanding rating dimensions with review text. In: ACM Conference on Recommender Systems, pp. 165–172. ACM, Hong Kong (2013)
13. Shan, H., Banerjee, A.: Generalized probabilistic matrix factorizations for collaborative filtering. In: IEEE International Conference on Data Mining, pp. 1025–1030. IEEE Computer Society, Sydney (2010)
14. Wang, C., Blei, D.M.: Collaborative topic modeling for recommending scientific articles. In: ACM SIGKDD International Conference on Knowledge Discovery and Data Mining, pp. 448–456. ACM, San Diego (2011)
15. Salakhutdinov, R., Mnih, A., Hinton, G.: Restricted boltzmann machines for collaborative filtering. In: International Conference on Machine Learning, pp. 791–789. ACM, Corvallis (2007)
16. Georgiev, K., Nakov, P.: A non-IID framework for collaborative filtering with restricted boltzmann machines. In: International Conference on Machine Learning, pp. 1148–1156. Atlanta (2013)
17. Sedhain, S., Menon, A.K., Sanner, S., Xie, L.: AutoRec: autoencoders meet collaborative filtering. In: Proceedings of the 24th International Conference on World Wide Web, pp. 111–112. ACM, Florence (2015)
18. Wu, Y., DuBois, C., Zheng, A.X., Ester, M.: Collaborative denoising auto-encoders for top-N recommender systems. In: Proceedings of the Ninth ACM International Conference on Web Search and Data Mining, pp. 153–162. ACM, San Francisco (2016)
19. Covington, P., Jay, A., Emre, S.: Deep neural networks For Youtube recommendations. In: ACM Conference on Recommender Systems, pp. 191–198. ACM, Boston (2016)
20. Guo, G., Zhang, J., Sun, Z., Yorke-Smith, N.: LibRec: a Java library for recommender systems. In: UMAP Workshops (2015)
21. Wu, C., Wang, J., Liu, J., Liu, W.: Recurrent neural network based recommendation for time heterogeneous feedback. Knowl. Based Syst. **109**, 90–103 (2016)
22. Gers, F.A., Schmidhuber, J., Cummins, F.: Learning to forget: continual prediction with LSTM. In: International Conference on Artificial Neural Networks, pp. 850–855. Edinburgh (1999)

Hypervolume-Based Multi-level Algorithm for the Bi-criteria Max-Cut Problem

Li-Yuan Xue[1], Rong-Qiang Zeng[2,3]([✉]), Hai-Yun Xu[3], Zheng-Yin Hu[3], and Yi Wen[3]

[1] EHF Key Laboratory of Science, School of Electronic Engineering, University of Electronic Science and Technology of China, Chengdu, China
xuely2013@gmail.com
[2] School of Mathematics, Southwest Jiaotong University, Chengdu, China
zrq@swjtu.edu.cn
[3] Chengdu Documentation and Information Center, Chinese Academy of Sciences, Chengdu, China
{xuhy,huzy,wenyi}@clas.ac.cn

Abstract. The multi-level approach is known to be a highly effective metaheuristic framework for tackling several types of combinatorial optimization problems, which is one of the best performing approaches for the graph partitioning problems. In this paper, we integrate the multi-level approach into the hypervolume-based multi-objective local search algorithm, in order to solve the bi-criteria max-cut problem. The experimental results indicate that the proposed algorithm is very competitive, and the performance analysis sheds lights on the ways to further improvements.

Keywords: Multi-objective optimization · Hypervolume contribution · Multi-level approach · Local search · Max-cut problem

1 Introduction

The multi-level paradigm is a simple and useful approach to tackling a number of combinatorial optimization problems. Generally, this approach allows one to approximate the initial problem by solving successively smaller and easier sub-problems, which is one of the best performing approaches for the graph partitioning problems [5].

The basic idea of multi-level approaches is to first coarsen the original graph down to the smaller one with a certain number of vertices, continue this process until there is no improvements of the whole population, and project the subgraphs back toward the original one [6]. In our situation, we apply the multi-level approaches to solve the bi-criteria max-cut problem.

Given an undirected graph $G = (V, E)$ with the vertex set $V = \{1, \ldots, n\}$ and the edge set $E \subset V \times V$. Each edge $(i, j) \in E$ is associated with two weights

© Springer Nature Singapore Pte Ltd. 2017
C. He et al. (Eds.): BIC-TA 2017, CCIS 791, pp. 456–465, 2017.
https://doi.org/10.1007/978-981-10-7179-9_35

w_{ij}^1 and w_{ij}^2. The max-cut problem is to seek a partition of the vertex set V into two disjoint subsets V_1 and V_2, which is mathematically formulated as follows [1]:

$$f_k(V_1, V_2) = max \sum_{i \in V_1, j \in V_2} w_{ij}^k \qquad (1)$$

where w_{ij}^k is the weight of the kth ($k \in \{1, 2\}$) graph.

As one of Karps 21 NP-complete problems with numerous practical applications [7], a large number of metaheuristics have been proposed to tackle this problem, including tabu search [2], breakout local search [7], variable neighborhood search [9], scatter search [11], global equilibrium search [13], hybrid approaches [14], etc.

In this paper, we integrate the multi-level approaches into the hypervolume-based multi-objective local search algorithm, which employs a dedicated multi-level operator based on the entire population. In order to evaluate the efficacy of the proposed algorithm, we carry out the experiments on the benchmark instance of max-cut problem. The computational results and the performance analysis provide an explanation to the behavior of the proposed algorithm and shed lights on the ways to further improvements.

The rest of the paper is organized as follows. In the next section, we present the brief introduction to the basic notations and definitions of multi-objective optimization. In Sect. 3, we describe the details of the proposed hypervolume-based multi-level algorithm, which is used to deal with the bi-criteria max-cut problem. In Sect. 4, we present the computational results and comparisons on the benchmark instances of max-cut problem. Finally, the conclusions are provided in Sect. 5.

2 Multi-objective Optimization

In this section, we briefly introduce the basic notations and definitions of multi-objective optimization. Without loss of generality, we assume that X denotes the search space of the optimization problem under consideration and $Z = \Re^n$ denotes the corresponding objective space with a maximizing vector function $Z = f(X)$, which defines the evaluation of a solution $x \in X$ [8]. Specifically, the dominance relations between any two solutions x_1 and x_2 are presented below [10,12,18]:

Definition 1 *(Pareto Dominance). A decision vector x_1 is said to dominate another decision vector x_2 (written as $x_1 \succ x_2$), if $f_i(x_1) \geq f_i(x_2)$ for all $i \in \{1, 2, \ldots, n\}$ and $f_j(x_1) > f_j(x_2)$ for at least one $j \in \{1, 2, \ldots, n\}$.*

Definition 2 *(Pareto Optimal Solution). $x \in X$ is said to be Pareto optimal if and only if there does not exist another solution $x' \in X$ such that $x' \succ x$.*

Definition 3 *(Non-dominated Solution). $x \in S$ ($S \subset X$) is said to be non-dominated if and only if there does not exist another solution $x' \in S$ such that $x' \succ x$.*

Definition 4 *(Pareto Optimal Set). S is said to be a Pareto optimal set if and only if S is composed of all the Pareto optimal solutions.*

Definition 5 *(Non-dominated Set). S is said to be a non-dominated set if and only if any two solutions $x_1 \in S$ and $x_2 \in S$ such that $x_1 \nsucc x_2$ and $x_2 \nsucc x_1$.*

Actually, we are interested in finding the Pareto optimal set, which keeps the best compromise among all the objectives. However, it is very difficult or even impossible to generate the Pareto optimal set in a reasonable time for the NP-hard problems.

Therefore, we aim to obtain a non-dominated set which is as close to the Pareto optimal set as possible. That's to say, the whole goal is to identify a Pareto approximation set with high quality. Actually, there are some state-of-the-art algorithms for multi-objective optimization, such as ENS [15], LMEA [16] and KnEA [17], etc.

3   Hypervolume-Based Multi-level Algorithm

In our work, we integrate the multi-level approaches into the hypervolume-based multi-objective local search algorithm, in order to deal with the bi-criteria max-cut problem. The general scheme of Hypervolume-Based Multi-Level Algorithm (HBMLA) is presented in Algorithm 1, and the main steps of the proposed algorithm are presented in the following subsections.

Algorithm 1. Hypervolume-Based Multi-Level Algorithm

    Input: N (Population size)
    Output: A: (Pareto approximation set)
    Step 1 - Initialization: $P \leftarrow N$ randomly generated individuals
    Step 2: $A \leftarrow \Phi$
    Step 3 - Fitness Assignment: Assign a fitness value to each individual $x \in P$
    Step 4:
    while Running time is not reached **do**
      repeat
        1) Hypervolume-Based Local Search: $x \in P$
      until all neighbors of $x \in P$ are explored
        2) Multi-Level Approach: P
        3) $A \leftarrow$ Non-dominated individuals of $A \bigcup P$
    end while
    Step 5: Return A

In HBMLA, each individual in an initial population is generated by randomly assigning the vertices of the graph to two vertex subsets V_1 and V_2 with equal number. Then, we use the Hypervolume Contribution (HC) indicator defined in [4] to realize the fitness assignment for each individual.

After the fitness assignment, we optimize the initial population with the hypervolume-based local search procedure, in order to improve the entire quality of the initial population. Then, we apply the multi-level approach to further improve this population so as to obtain a high quality Pareto approximation set.

3.1   Hypervolume-Based Local Search

In [4], based on the dominance relation, the HC indicator divides the whole population into two sets: non-dominated set and dominated set, and calculates the hypervolume contribution of each individual in the objective space, according to two objective function values.

In fact, the individual belonging to the non-dominated set is assigned a positive value, while the individual belonging to dominated set is assigned to a negative value. Afterwards, each individual is optimized by the hypervolume-based local search procedure, which is presented in Algorithm 2 below.

Algorithm 2. Hypervolume-Based Local Search

Steps:

1) $x^* \leftarrow$ an unexplored neighbor of x by randomly changing the values of the variables of x
2) $P \leftarrow P \bigcup x^*$
3) calculate two objective function values of x^*
4) calculate the fitness value of x^* in P with the HC indicator
5) update all the fitness values of $z \in P$ $(z \neq x^*)$
6) $\omega \leftarrow$ the worst individual in P
7) $P \leftarrow P \backslash \{\omega\}$
8) update all the fitness values of $z \in P$
9) if $\omega \neq x^*$, Progress $\leftarrow$ True

In the hypervolume-based local search procedure, we implement the one-flip move based neighborhood, which is realized by moving a randomly selected vertex to the opposite set. The corresponding move gain value is calculated as follows:

$$\Delta_i = \sum_{x \in V_1, x \neq v_1} w_{v_i x} - \sum_{y \in V_2} w_{v_i y}, \; v_i \in V_1 \tag{2}$$

$$\Delta_i = \sum_{x \in V_2, y \neq v_1} w_{v_i y} - \sum_{y \in V_1} w_{v_i x}, \; v_i \in V_2 \tag{3}$$

Let Δ_i be the move gain of representing the change in the fitness function, and Δ_i can be calculated in linear time by the formula above, more details about this formula can be found in [14]. Then, we can calculate the objective function values high efficiently with the streamlined incremental technique.

More Specifically, we randomly select two vertices from two sets and put them into the opposite set, so as to obtain an unexplored neighbor x^* of the individual x. According to the HC indicator, a fitness value is assigned to this new individual. the individual ω with the worst fitness value will be deleted from the population P. The whole population is optimized by the hypervolume-based local search procedure.

3.2   Multi-level Approach

The multi-level approach is known to be very effective to tackle graph partitioning problems, especially handling the instances with large size [5,6]. In this work, we apply the multi-level approach to improve the quality of the population optimized by the hypervolume-based local search procedure, the pseudo-code of which is presented in Algorithm 3 below.

Algorithm 3. Multi-level Approach

while $D_i > D * m$ do
   repeat
      1) $D_i \leftarrow D$
      2) $Num \leftarrow 0$
      3) for $i \leftarrow 1, \ldots, D_i$ do
         a) $Num \leftarrow Num+1$ if and only if the ith variable of $x_k = 0$ (or 1) $k = 1, \cdots, N$
         b) $D_i \leftarrow D - Num$
         c) Coarsening level (G)
         d) Hypervolume-Based Local Search: $x'_k \in P$, $k = 1, \cdots, N$
      end for
   end while

In the multi-level approach, we aim to further optimize the whole population by simplifying the original graph. Actually, the individual x_i can be represented as "0's" and "1's". Specifically, one variable is equal to 0, which refers to that the corresponding vertex belongs to the set V_1, while one variable being equal to 1 means that the corresponding vertex belongs to the set V_2.

Then, we count the exact number Num of the variables with same value for all the individuals in the population, and coarsen the current graph down to a smaller one by deleting all the variables with same value. Afterwards, we obtain a sub-graph from the original one.

Assuming that the number of vertices in the original graph is equal to D, the dimension of generated sub-graph is $D - Num$, and each individual x_i is represented as x'_i, which is applied to hypervolume-based local search for further improvements.

The whole procedure will repeat until the dimension D_i of the current graph is no bigger than $D * m$, where m is a pre-defined number used to control the levels in Algorithm 3. In our case, we set this number m to 0.2, which means the dimension of the last sub-graph is less than 20 percent of the original graph.

4 Experiments

In this section, we present the computational results of three multi-objective optimization algorithms on 9 groups of benchmark instances of max-cut problem. All the algorithms are programmed in C++ and compiled using Dev-C++ 5.0 compiler on a PC running Windows 7 with Core 2.50 GHz CPU and 4 GB RAM.

4.1 Parameters Settings

In order to conduct the experiments on the bi-objective max-cut problem, we use two single-objective benchmark instances of max-cut problem with the same dimension provided in [7][1] to generate one bi-objective max-cut problem instance. All the instances used for experiments are presented in Table 1 below.

Table 1. Single-objective benchmark instances of max-cut problem used for generating bi-objective max-cut problem instances.

	Dimension	Instance 1	Instance 2
bo_mcp_800_01	800	g1.rud	g2.rud
bo_mcp_800_02	800	g11.rud	g12.rud
bo_mcp_800_03	800	g15.rud	g19.rud
bo_mcp_800_04	800	g17.rud	g21.rud
bo_mcp_2000_01	2000	g22.rud	g23.rud
bo_mcp_2000_02	2000	g32.rud	g33.rud
bo_mcp_2000_03	2000	g35.rud	g39.rud
bo_mcp_1000_01	1000	g43.rud	g44.rud
bo_mcp_3000_01	3000	g49.rud	g50.rud

In addition, the algorithms need to set a few parameters, we only discuss two important ones: the running time and the population size, more details about the parameter settings for multi-objective optimization algorithms can be found in [3,14]. The exact information about the parameter settings in our work is presented in the following Table 2.

4.2 Performance Assessment Protocol

In this paper, we evaluate the efficacy of 3 different neighborhood combination strategies with the performance assessment package provided by Zitzler et al.[2]. The quality assessment protocol works as follows: First, we create a set of 20 runs

---

[1] More information about the benchmark instances of max-cut problem can be found on this website: http://www.stanford.edu/~yyye/yyye/Gset/.

[2] More information about the performance assessment package can be found on this website: http://www.tik.ee.ethz.ch/pisa/assessment.html.

Table 2. Parameter settings used for bi-objective max-cut problem instances: instance dimension (D), vertices (V), edges(E), population size (P) and running time (T).

	Dimension (D)	Vertices (V)	Edges (E)	Population (P)	Time (T)
bo_mcp_800_01	800	800	19176	20	40''
bo_mcp_800_02	800	800	1600	20	40''
bo_mcp_800_03	800	800	4661	20	40''
bo_mcp_800_04	800	800	4667	20	40''
bo_mcp_2000_01	2000	2000	19990	50	100''
bo_mcp_2000_02	2000	2000	4000	50	100''
bo_mcp_2000_03	2000	2000	11778	50	100''
bo_mcp_1000_01	1000	1000	9990	25	50''
bo_mcp_3000_01	3000	3000	6000	75	150''

with different initial populations for each strategy and each benchmark instance of bi-objective max-cut problem. Then, we generate the reference set RS^* based on the 60 different sets $A_0, \ldots, A_{59}$ of non-dominated solutions.

According to two objective function values, we define a reference point $z = [r_1, r_2]$, where r_1 and r_2 represent the worst values for each objective function in the reference set RS^*. Afterwards, we assign a fitness value to each non-dominated set A_i by calculating the hypervolume difference between A_i and RS^*. Actually, this hypervolume difference between these two sets should be as close as possible to zero [19].

4.3 Computational Results

In this subsection, we present the computational results on 9 groups of bi-objective max-cut problem instances, which are obtained by three different neighborhood combination strategies. The information about these algorithms are described in the following table:

Table 3. The abbreviation for three algorithms.

	Algorithm Description
IBMOLS	Indicator-Based Multi-Objective Local Search
HBMOLS	Hypervolume-Based Multi-Objective Local Search
HBMLA	Hypervolume-Based Multi-Level Algorithm

In Table 3, IBMOLS [3] refers to the indicator-based multi-objective local search algorithm, HBMOLS [4] refers to the hypervolume-based multi-objective local seach algorithm, and HBMLA is our proposed algorithm in this paper.

The computational results are summarized in Table 4. In this table, there is a value both **in bold** and **in grey box** at each line, which is the best result obtained on the considered instance. The values both **in italic** and **bold** at each line refer to the corresponding algorithms which are **not** statistically outperformed by the algorithm obtaining the best result (with a confidence level greater than 95%).

From Table 4, we can observe that all the best results are obtained by the HBMLA algorithm, which statistically outperforms the other two algorithms on all the instances except for two instances (bo_mcp_2000_01 and bo_mcp_2000_03). Moreover, the results on some instances obtain by HBMOLS is close to the results obtained by HBMLA. Especially, the most significant result is achieved on the instance bo_mcp_800_01, where the average hypervolume difference value obtained by HBMLA is much smaller than the values obtained by the other two algorithms.

Table 4. The computational results on bi-objective max-cut problem obtained by the algorithms IBMOLS, HBMOLS and HBMLA.

Instance	Algorithm		
	IBMOLS	HBMOLS	HBMLA
bo_mcp_800_01	0.254434	0.256161	**0.176608**
bo_mcp_800_02	0.249072	0.228909	**0.215991**
bo_mcp_800_03	0.184891	0.187312	**0.144510**
bo_mcp_800_04	0.268977	0.231876	**0.227784**
bo_mcp_2000_01	0.653541	*0.646400*	**0.615655**
bo_mcp_2000_02	0.592027	0.576449	**0.525756**
bo_mcp_2000_03	0.488837	*0.484398*	**0.453584**
bo_mcp_1000_01	0.235171	0.213016	**0.195599**
bo_mcp_3000_01	0.267231	0.260312	**0.217708**

Obviously, IBMOLS and HBMOLS do not perform as well as HBMLA, in which the multi-level approach has the distinct contribution. We suppose that there exists some key vertices in the representation of the individuals, which means these vertices should be fixed in one of these two sets in order to search the local optima effectively. IBMOLS and HBMOLS can fix a number of vertices during the local search process, nevertheless, these two algorithms will be trapped in the local optima without any strategy so that there are no more vertices to be fixed.

On the other hand, HBMLA has a chance to jump out of the local optima with the multi-level approach. Actually, this strategy allows one to coarsen the original graph down to a smaller sub-graph by extracting the fixed vertices during the local search process. More vertices can be effectively fixed by optimizing the sub-graph with the hypervolume-based local search procedure. Thus, HBMLA has a better performance on all the instances.

5 Conclusion

In this paper, we have presented an effective hypervolume-based multi-level algorithm to deal with the bi-criteria max-cut problem. The proposed algorithm has integrated the multi-level approach into the hypervolume-based optimization, in order to further improve the entire quality of the Pareto approximation set. For this purpose, we have carried out the experiments on 9 groups of the benchmark instances of max-cut problem. The computational results indicate that the HBMLA algorithm are very competitive, which has a good performance on all the tested instances.

Acknowledgments. The work in this paper was supported by the Fundamental Research Funds for the Central Universities (Grant No. A0920502051722-53) and supported by the West Light Foundation of Chinese Academy of Science (Grant No: Y4C0011001).

References

1. Angel, E., Gourves, E.: Approximation algorithms for the bi-criteria weighted max-cut problem. Discrete Appl. Math. **154**, 1685–1692 (2006)
2. Arraiz, E., Olivo, O.: Competitive simulated annealing and tabu search algorithms for the max-cut problem. In: Genetic and Evolutionary Computation Conference (GECCO 2009), pp. 1797–1798. Springer (2009)
3. Basseur, M., Liefooghe, A., Le, K., Burke, E.: The efficiency of indicator-based local search for multi-objective combinatorial optimisation problems. J. Heuristics **18**(2), 263–296 (2012)
4. Basseur, M., Zeng, R.-Q., Hao, J.-K.: Hypervolume-based multi-objective local search. Neural Comput. Appl. **21**(8), 1917–1929 (2012)
5. Benlic, U., Hao, J.-K.: An effective multilevel tabu search approach for balanced graph partitioning. Comput. Oper. Res. **38**, 1066–1075 (2011)
6. Benlic, U., Hao, J.-K.: A multilevel memetic approach for improving graph k-partitions. IEEE Trans. Evol. Comput. **15**(2), 624–642 (2011)
7. Benlic, U., Hao, J.-K.: Breakout local search for the max-cut problem. Eng. Appl. Artif. Intell. **26**, 1162–1173 (2013)
8. Coello, C.A., Lamont, G.B., Van Veldhuizen, D.A.: Evolutionary Algorithms for Solving Multi-Objective Problems (Genetic and Evolutionary Computation). Springer-Verlag New York Inc., Secaucus (2007)
9. Festa, P., Pardalos, P.M., Resende, M.G.C., Ribeiro, C.C.: Randomized heuristics for the max-cut problem. Optim. Methods Softw. **17**, 1033–1058 (2002)
10. He, C., Tian, Y., Jin, Y., Zhang, X., Pan, L.: A radial space division based evolutionary algorithm for many-objective optimization. Appl. Soft Comput. **61**, 603–621 (2017)
11. Marti, R., Duarte, A., Laguna, M.: Advanced scatter search for the max-cut problem. INFORMS J. Comput. **21**(1), 26–38 (2009)

12. Pan, L., He, C., Tian, Y., Su, Y., Zhang, X.: A region division based diversity maintaining approach for many-objective optimization. Integr. Comput. Aided Eng. pp. 1–18 (2017)
13. Shylo, V.P., Shylo, O.V.: Solving the maxcut problem by the global equilibrium search. Cybern. Syst. Anal. **46**(5), 744–754 (2010)
14. Wu, Q., Wang, Y., Lü, Z.: A tabu search based hybrid evolutionary algorithm for the max-cut problem. Appl. Soft Comput. **34**, 827–837 (2015)
15. Zhang, X., Tian, Y., Cheng, R., Jin, Y.: An efficient approach to non-dominated sorting for evolutionary multi-objective optimization. IEEE Trans. Evol. Comput. **19**(2), 201–213 (2015)
16. Zhang, X., Tian, Y., Cheng, R., Jin, Y.: A decision variable clustering-based evolutionary algorithm for large-scale many-objective optimization. IEEE Trans. Evol. Comput. **99**(1), 1–17 (2016)
17. Zhang, X., Tian, Y., Jin, Y.: A knee point-driven evolutionary algorithm for many-objective optimization. IEEE Trans. Evol. Comput. **19**(6), 761–776 (2015)
18. Zitzler, E., Künzli, S.: Indicator-based selection in multiobjective search. In: Yao, X., Burke, E.K., Lozano, J.A., Smith, J., Merelo-Guervós, J.J., Bullinaria, J.A., Rowe, J.E., Tiňo, P., Kabán, A., Schwefel, H.-P. (eds.) PPSN 2004. LNCS, vol. 3242, pp. 832–842. Springer, Heidelberg (2004). https://doi.org/10.1007/978-3-540-30217-9_84
19. Zitzler, E., Thiele, L.: Multiobjective evolutionary algorithms: a comparative case study and the strength pareto approach. Evol. Comput. **3**, 257–271 (1999)

Comparator Logic Circuits Based on DNA Strand Displacement by DNA Hairpin

Zicheng Wang$^{(\boxtimes)}$ and Hongbo Meng

College of Electrical and Electronic Engineering,
Zhengzhou University of Light Industry, Zhengzhou 450002, China
wzch@zzuli.edu.cn, msymccg@163.com

Abstract. DNA computing is a hot research topic in recent years, molecular logic gate is an important foundation of DNA computer architecture and implementation. Local hairpin DNA chain substitution reaction can increase the reliability of molecular logic gates, Make the reaction more efficient and more thoroughly. In this paper, using local hairpin DNA strand displacement, the comparator circuit is coded and simulated base on the double logic circuit. The simulation results further confirmed the feasibility and effectiveness of the DNA strand displacement reaction in the study of biochemical logic circuits, The comparator circuit can be used for biological computer and building large-scale molecular logic circuits in the future.

Keywords: DNA strand displacement · Comparator · Visual DSD · DNA hairpin

1 Introduction

Demand for high-performance scientific computing keep rising, while the traditional electronic computer components production is near limit, the scientific community is looking for a new computing model to break through the limit of traditional computer systems [1–4]. DNA computing has been got attention for its high parallelism, low energy consumption and large information storage capacity [5–7]. Since the end of the 20th century, DNA computing has made great progress in theory and technology. In 2006, Seelig based on chain substitution reaction principle, design and gate, or gate, not gate logic module, and use of these modules into logic circuit [8]. In 2011, Winfree and Lulu Qian design improved the DNA of a single gate - seesaw gate, join a new concept called "fuel", for the groundwork of large-scale circuits [9–11]. Paving the way for the composition of large-scale circuits in the future [12–15].

As a new type of calculation method, DNA strand displacement technology has prominent advantages and powerful functions [16–19]. In this paper, based on the structure of DNA strand displacement by DNA hairpin, the comparator logic circuit is coded and simulated on the basis of the double logic circuit. As the overall DNA molecular strand displacement reaction has slow diffusion speed

© Springer Nature Singapore Pte Ltd. 2017
C. He et al. (Eds.): BIC-TA 2017, CCIS 791, pp. 466–475, 2017.
https://doi.org/10.1007/978-981-10-7179-9_36

and wrong molecular collision problems, to solve this problem, Muscat proposed the basic module construction mechanism based on locality DNA hairpin strand displacement reaction [20–22], and combined with the dual logic thought, we successfully constructed the local half-adder logic circuit and the local full adder logic circuit on the DNA origami substrate. The experimental data demonstrate that there is excellent transmission performance among the three bound DNA cards. So we use the locality replacement of the molecular chain to increase its stability in this article. The simulation results show that the model has the advantages of fast reaction speed, high reliability and more thoroughly, it is more easy to combine the current biochip technology for large-scale integrated circuits on account of DNA.

2 DNA Hairpin Strand Displacement

DNA molecules are an ideal material for molecular computing, provide a great potential for construction of molecular logic circuits [23,24]. Because of the relatively slow molecular diffusion and the wrong molecular collision in the DNA molecular strand displacement, more and more researchers have preferred to application of locality DNA strand displacement. Based on the principle of non-linear system [25–27], in the locality DNA molecular circuit, part of the DNA molecules are bounded to one DNA substrate, then the DNA molecules only be react to DNA molecules that get close enough, which effectively avoid the problems of slow diffusion speed and wrong molecular collision in overall DNA molecular strand displacement reaction [28–30].

DNA hairpin is a DNA structure that form by self complementary and joined by single-stranded loop. Locality DNA strand displacement reaction is shown in Fig. 1. We fix DNA hairpin on the origami, and each card defines a coordinate, to facilitate our experiments and simulation. In the DSD simulation [31], only one chain with the same coordinates can react. In Fig. 1, we add an input single chain $<a_0, s>$, a_0 in this single strand is paired with the small point a_0* of the hairpin, Then, the s chain in $<a_0, s>$ is paired with the card's s^*, single chain $<a_0, s>$ and $<a_0^*, s^*>$ pair into double chain at this time. While y and s in the card are opened, y and s are in single stranded forms at the other end of the complementary chain s^* and a_0^*. At this point, the single ring of the hairpin is opened, the y which was not involved in the reaction is activated, and then it can conduct pairing reaction with other DNA chain. The DNA card is fixed (A_0, Y) and can't move. This will avoid the collision problem between wrong molecular.

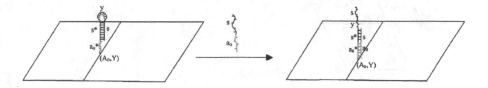

Fig. 1. Locality DNA hairpin strand displacement reaction

3   Construct Comparator Circuits by Locality DNA Hairpin

3.1   Construct Basic Gates by Locality DNA Hairpin

The molecular circuit is composed of different logic gates, basic logic gates include AND gates, OR gates, and NOT gates. But for Biochemical circuit, there are many difficult in constructing NOT gate. So we adopt the thought of double logic circuit, it is all made of AND gate and OR gate, has dynamic binding between AND gate and OR gate, then comparator's logic circuit is finished. Before this, we should design AND gate and NOT gate's locality DNA hairpin logic circuit.

Locality DNA hairpin strand displacement AND gate reaction has shown in Fig. 2, We fix four DNA hairpin on the origami, define coordinates as (A_0, Y), $(B_0, Y), (A_0, B_0), (X, Y)$. At same time, we define the distance between (A_0, Y), (B_0, Y) to (A_0, B_0) less than the distance to (X, Y), $<a_0, s>$ and $<b_0, s>$ as input, $<z, s>$ as output what we need.

1. When we add a single chain a_0, the fulcrum a_0 will complementary pair the DNA hairpin a_0* in (A_0, Y) firstly, then open (A_0, Y) fulcrum y, y will complementary pair fuel $y*$, open fulcrum x, it will react with nearest DNA

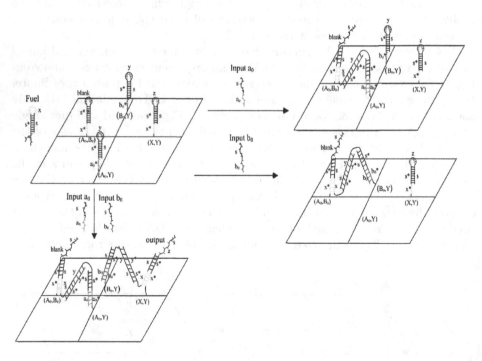

Fig. 2. AND gate construction of locality DNA hairpin strand displacement reaction

because of the feature of locality DNA hairpin strand displacement. So fulcrum x will complementary pair $x*$ in (A_0, B_0), open blank, the reaction finish. No output.

2. When we add a single chain b_0, the fulcrum b_0 will complementary pair the DNA hairpin b_0* in (B_0, Y) firstly, then open (B_0, Y) fulcrum y, y will complementary pair fuel $y*$, open fulcrum x, x will firstly complementary pair $x*$ in (A_0, B_0) at this time, open blank, the reaction finish. As we can see, we couldn't get output we need when add chain $<a_0, s>$ or $<b_0, s>$ singly.

3. We add input chain $<a_0, s>$ and $<b_0, s>$, $<a_0, s>$ will complementary pair the DNA hairpin a_0^* in (A_0, Y), it conduct the reaction progress that only has chain $<a_0, s>$, open blank. But meanwhile $<b_0, s>$ will complementary pair the DNA hairpin b_0^* in (B_0, Y), open fulcrum y in (B_0, Y), y will complementary pair fuel y^*, open fulcrum x, so x will react with DNA hairpin in (X, Y), and will complementary pair x^*, then open hairpin structure, get output $<z, s>$ that we need.

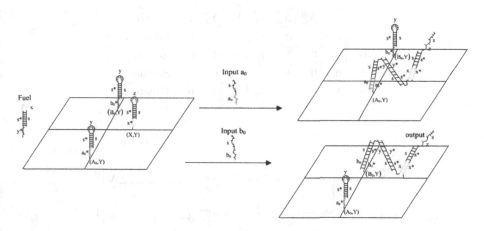

Fig. 3. OR gate construction of locality DNA hairpin strand displacement reaction

Then we conduct locality DNA hairpin strand displacement OR gate reaction. As shown in Fig. 3, OR gate only fixes three DNA hairpin on the origami, $(A_0, Y), (B_0, Y), (X, Y)$. We define chain $<a_0, s>$ and $<b_0, s>$ as input, $<z, s>$ as output what we need.

1. When we add a single chain a_0, the fulcrum a_0 will complementary pair the DNA hairpin a_0^* in (A_0, Y) firstly, then open (A_0, Y) is fulcrum y, y will complementary pair fuel y^*, open fulcrum x, it will react with DNA hairpin in (X, Y) and will complementary pair x^*, open hairpin structure, we can get output $<z, s>$ that we need.

2. When we add single chain b_0, the reaction progress is same as when add a_0, we can get output $<z, s>$ which we need.

3.2   Construct Comparator Circuits by Locality DNA Hairpin

A digital comparator compares binary that has same figure, judge numeric value of logic circuit. Compare two n-bit binary, need judge from high to low, if the altitude is same, we can be re-judged next, result are greater, equal or smaller respectively. The two outputs of the comparator circuit represent a state respectively. The input of circuit are two binary numbers x_1 and x_2, output are y_1, y_2, Respectively indicate $x_1 > x_2$ and $x_1 < x_2$.

In this article, we use the idea of dual logic circuits, dual logic circuits uses two different DNA chain for logic 0 and 1. When $x^0 x^1 = 01$, x^0 and x^1 are stand for logic 1, logic 0 is $x^0 x^1 = 10$. The truth table is shown in Table 1. In dual logic circuit, circuit initial state only happen when x^0 and x^1 are 0 at same time. When x^0 and x^1 are 1 at same time, which stand for circuit error. Considering these above, we design comparator logical circuits in Fig. 4.

Table 1. Digital comparator true table

X_1^0	X_1^1	X_2^0	X_2^1	Y_1^0	Y_1^1	Y_2^0	Y_2^1	Result
1	0	1	0	1	0	1	0	Equal
0	1	0	1	1	0	1	0	Equal
1	0	0	1	1	0	0	1	Smaller
0	1	1	0	0	1	1	0	Greater

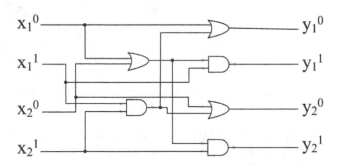

Fig. 4. The logic circuit of the digital comparator

Through the digital comparator logic circuit and true table, we can make dynamic binding between DNA hairpin strand displacement AND gate and OR gate, design locality DNA hairpin strand displacement reaction circuit Figure on DNA origami, as shown in Fig. 5. We also design biochemical experimental logic circuit Figure accordingly, as shown in Fig. 6.

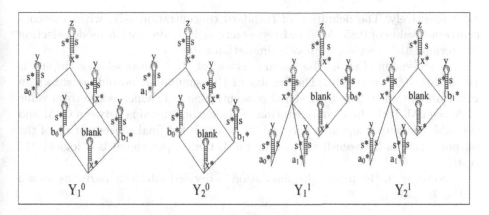

Fig. 5. The design of digital comparator for locality DNA hairpin strand displacement

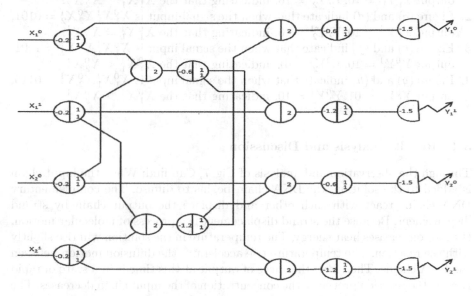

Fig. 6. Experimental logic circuit Figure of digital comparator

3.3 Simulation in Visual DSD

Visual DSD is a kind of simulation test based on DNA strand displacement reaction of biochemical circuit software. This software is designed by Matthew Lakin et al. In this paper, Visual DSD software platform is used to simulate the operation process of molecular logic circuits, The feasibility and accuracy of the data selector logic circuit are verified.

In order to fully and completely biochemical reaction, set the reaction time is 50000 s. Define 2 kinds of fluorescence signals in Fig. 7(a)–(d), said Y_1^0 and Y_2^0 respectively. Define 2 kinds of fluorescence signals in Fig. 7(e)–(h), said Y_1^1 and

Y_2^1 respectively. The definition of standard concentration is 1, when the concentration value of 0.85 nM–1 nM represents logic 1, simulation mode selection "Deterministic", can get a smooth simulation curve.

As shown in Fig. 4, the binary state of the data selector input is $1010, 0101, 1001$ and 0110. The results of the simulation output as shown in Fig. 7 are obtained. The total signal concentration is 1, which is the total value of $N = 1$ nM, If the final concentration of the output signal is between 0 nM and 0.15 nM, the output signal is a logical "0" state; If the final concentration of the output signal is between 0.85 nM and 1 nM, the output signal is a logical "1" state.

According to the input, the simulation is divided into four parts, as shown in Fig. 7:

1. Figure (a) and (b) indicate that when the signal input is $X_1^0 X_1^1 X_2^0 X_2^1 = 1010$, output $Y_1^0 Y_1^1 = 10, Y_2^0 Y_2^1 = 10$, indicating that the $X_1^0 X_1^1 = X_2^0 X_2^1$.
2. Figure (c) and (d) indicate that when the signal input is $X_1^0 X_1^1 X_2^0 X_2^1 = 0101$, output $Y_1^0 Y_1^1 = 10, Y_2^0 Y_2^1 = 10$, indicating that the $X_1^0 X_1^1 = X_2^0 X_2^1$.
3. Figure (e) and (f) indicate that when the signal input is $X_1^0 X_1^1 X_2^0 X_2^1 = 1001$, output $Y_1^0 Y_1^1 = 10, Y_2^0 Y_2^1 = 01$, indicating that the $X_1^0 X_1^1 < X_2^0 X_2^1$.
4. Figure (g) and (h) indicate that when the signal input is $X_1^0 X_1^1 X_2^0 X_2^1 = 0110$, output $Y_1^0 Y_1^1 = 01, Y_2^0 Y_2^1 = 10$, indicating that the $X_1^0 X_1^1 > X_2^0 X_2^1$.

3.4   Result Analysis and Discussion

Through the observation and analysis of Fig. 7, Can find: When the input chain is added to the solution, the DNA chain begins to diffuse, The complementary DNA chains react with each other and displace the output chain by strand displacement, Because the strand displacement is a process of molecular motion, the motion releases heat energy, The temperature in the solution will rise slightly with the reaction. The temperature rise accelerates the diffusion motion between the DNA chains, Therefore, the curve of output at this time is in a state of rapid rise; As the reaction proceeds, the concentration of the input chain decreases. The curve gradually leveled off, The concentration of output will gradually stabilize between 0.85 nM and 1 nM.

Simulation show that: When the simulation time arrives at 50000 s, When the simulation time arrives at 50000 s, the curve representing logic 1 is stable within the reasonable range of 0.85 nM–1 nM, This curve represents the "ON". Curve that represents the logical "0", close to the X axis, Although some of the curves have slight shocks, they are still within the bounds of the "OFF" range of 0 nM–0.15 nM.

Through the simulation, we can see that the molecular circuit can achieve the function of the comparator better, and the speed is fast, the effect is accurate, and the implementation is simple, Moreover, the circuit has good expansibility, It creates the foundation for the realization of large-scale cascaded circuits in the future.

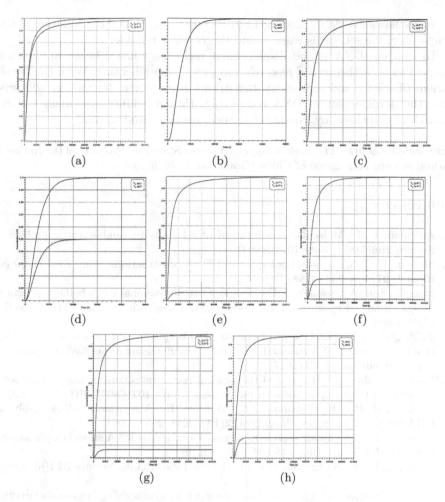

(a)   (b)   (c)

(d)   (e)   (f)

(g)   (h)

Fig. 7. The simulation in Visual DSD

4   Conclusion

In this paper, based on the special information storage mode of DNA computing and its ability of parallel computing, we introduce the DNA replacement reaction into the molecular circuit model of comparator.

The model has the following characteristics: (1) the molecular components are simple in structure, stable in operation, and can plug and play. (2) the biochemical reaction is carried out at room temperature without external force and catalyst, the cost is low, the operation is simple, the experimental conditions are low, and the error is small. (3) the ability of information hiding and logical judgment. Finally, based on the DSD simulation platform, this paper has carried on the simulation to this molecular logic circuit model. The results show that the molecular logic circuit designed in this paper can realize the function of the comparator, the scheme is feasible and the result is reliable.

To sum up, DNA strand displacement technology has a broad application prospect in both theoretical research and practical application. With the development of science and technology, the strand displacement technology will promote the development of DNA computing, thus providing new ideas for the research of cryptography, computer science, medicine and so on.

Acknowledgments. The work is supported by the State Key Program of the National Natural Science Foundation of China (Grant No. U1304620)

References

1. Adleman, L.M.: Molecular computation of solutions to combinatorial problems. Science **266**(5187), 1021–1024 (1994)
2. Seeman, C.: DNA nanotechnology: novel DNA constructions. Ann. Rev. Biophys. Biomol. **27**, 225–248 (1998)
3. Mao, C., Sun, W., Seeman, N.C.: Designed two dimensional DNA holliday junction arrays visualized by atomic force microscopy. J. Am. Chem. Soc. **121**(23), 5437–5443 (1999)
4. Thubagere, A.J., Thachuk, C., Berleant, J.: Compiler-aided systematic construction of large-scale DNA strand displacement circuits using unpurified components. Nat. Commun. **8**, 14373 (2017)
5. Mao, C., Labean, T.H., Reif, J.H.: Logical computation using algorithmic self-assembly of DNA triple-crossover molecules. Nature **407**(6803), 493–496 (2000)
6. Rothemund, P.W.K., Papadakis, N., Winfree, E.: Algorithmic self-assembly of DNA Sierpinski triangles. PLoS Biol. **2**(12), 2041–2053 (2004)
7. Song, T., Garg, S., Mokhtar, R.: Analog computation by DNA strand displacement circuits. ACS Synth. Biol. **5**(8), 898–912 (2016)
8. Georg, S., David, S.: Enzyme-free nucleic acid logic circuits. Science **314**(8), 1585–1588 (2006)
9. Qian, L., Winfree, E.: A simple DNA gate motif for synthesizing large-scale circuits. In: Goel, A., Simmel, F.C., Sosík, P. (eds.) DNA 2008. LNCS, vol. 5347, pp. 70–89. Springer, Heidelberg (2009). https://doi.org/10.1007/978-3-642-03076-5_7
10. Qian, L.L., Winfree, E.: Scaling up digital circuit computation with DNA strand displacement cascades. Science **332**(6034), 1196–1201 (2011)
11. Qian, L.L., Winfree, E., Bruck, J.: Neural network computation with DNA strand displacement cascades. Nature **475**(7356), 368–372 (2011)
12. Brun, Y.: Arithmetic computation in the tile assembly model: addition and multiplication. Theor. Comput. Sci. **378**(1), 17–31 (2006)
13. Bartlett, E.J., Brissett, N.C., Plocinski, P.: Molecular basis for DNA strand displacement by NHEJ repair polymerases. Nucleic Acids Res. **44**(5), 2173–2186 (2016)
14. Zhang, Z., Fan, T.W., Hsing, I.M.: Integrating DNA strand displacement circuitry to nonlinear hybridization chain reaction. Nanoscale **9**(8), 2748–2754 (2007)
15. David, Y., Erik, W.: Control of DNA strand displacement kinetics using toehold exchange. J. Am. Chem. Soc. **131**(47), 17303–17314 (2009)
16. Yuan, J., Nell, D.: Programmable chemical controllers made from DNA. Nat. Nanotechnol. **8**, 755–762 (2013)

17. Matthew, R., Simon, Y., Luca, C., Andrew, P.: Abstractions for DNA circuit design. R. Soc. Interface 470–486 (2011)
18. Yurke, B., Mills, A.P.: Using DNA to power nanostructures. Genet. J. Program. Evolvable Mach. **4**, 111–122 (2003)
19. Phillips, A., Cardelli, L.: A programming language for composable DNA circuits. Interface **6**(4), 419–436 (2009)
20. Yang, X., Tang, Y., Traynor, S.M.: Regulation of DNA strand displacement using an allosteric DNA toehold. J. Am. Chem. Soc. **138**(42), 14076–14082 (2016)
21. Lakin, M.R., Youssef, S., Cardrlli, L.: Abstractions for DNA circuit design. J. R. Soc. Interface **9**(68), 470–486 (2012)
22. Matthew, R., David, P.: Design and analysis of DNA strand displacement devices using probabilistic model checking. J. R. Soc. Interface **7**(72), 1470–1485 (2012)
23. Thachuk, C., Winfree, E., Soloveichik, D.: Leakless DNA strand displacement systems. In: Phillips, A., Yin, P. (eds.) DNA 2015. LNCS, vol. 9211, pp. 133–153. Springer, Cham (2015). https://doi.org/10.1007/978-3-319-21999-8_9
24. Shi, X.L., Lu, W., Wang, Z.Y., Pan, L.Q., Cui, G.Z., Xu, J., Thomas, H.L.: Programmable DNA tile self-assembly using a hierarchical sub-tile strategy. Nanotechnology **25**(7), 075602 (2014)
25. Sun, J., Wu, Y., Cui, G.: Finite-time real combination synchronization of three complex-variable chaotic systems with unknown parameters via sliding mode control. Nonlinear Dynam. **88**(3), 1677–1690 (2014)
26. Sun, J., Wang, Y., Wang, Y.: Finite-time synchronization between two complex-variable chaotic systems with unknown parameters via nonsingular terminal sliding mode control. Nonlinear Dynam. **85**, 1105–1117 (2016)
27. Sun, J., Shen, Y.: Quasi-ideal memory system. IEEE Trans. Cybern. **45**(7), 1353–1362 (2015)
28. Yang, J., Jiang, S.X., Liu, X.R., Pan, L.Q., Zhang, Q.: Aptamer-binding directed DNA origami pattern for logic gates. ACS Appl. Mater. Inter. **8**, 34054–34060 (2016)
29. Yang, J., Dong, C., Dong, Y.F., Liu, S., Pan, L.Q., Zhang, C.: Logic nanoparticle beacon triggered by the binding-induced effect of multiple inputs. ACS Appl. Mater. Inter. **6**(16), 14486–14492 (2014)
30. Shi, X.L., Wang, Z.Y., Deng, C.Y., Song, T., Pan, L.Q., Chen, Z.H.: A novel biosensor based on DNA strand displacement. PLoS ONE **9**(10), e108856 (2014)
31. Matthew, L., Simon, Y.: Visual DSD: a design and analysis tool for DNA strand displacement systems. Bioinformatics **27**(22), 3211–3213 (2011)

Experimental Study of Distributed Differential Evolution Based on Different Platforms

Lin Shi, Zhi-Hui Zhan$^{(\boxtimes)}$, Zi-Jia Wang, and Jun Zhang

School of Computer Science and Engineering,
South China University of Technology, Guangzhou 510006, China
cszhanzhh@scut.edu.cn

Abstract. With the increasing complexity of real-world optimization problems, many challenges appear to evolutionary algorithms (EAs). When solving these time-consuming or high-complexity problems, although EAs can guarantee the high quality of solutions, the intolerable time costs will influence their availabilities drastically. Thus, many attempts have been made to overcome that problem. With the rapid development of the distributed computing paradigm and platforms, such as the Message Passing Interface (MPI) and Open Multi-Processing (OpenMP), distributed computing has become readily available and affordable for realizing more powerful EAs. In order to find out whether these platforms have any particular difficulties or preference, whether one of them would be more suitable for EAs, we analyze the performance of different distributed EAs (DEAs) based on different distributed computing platforms, using differential evolution (DE) as an example. Finally, we find out that both MPI and OpenMP have their own superiorities and they can improve the speedup obviously. However, MPI is more suitable for computationally expensive problems and can achieve higher speedup than OpenMP.

Keywords: Message Passing Interface (MPI) · Open Multi-processing (OpenMP) · Distributed · Differential Evolution (DE)

1 Introduction

Evolutionary algorithms (EAs), which maintain multiple candidate solutions, have the potential advantages for solving hard optimization problems, and have been applied into many real-world applications [1–3]. However, based on the

L. Shi—Student Member, IEEE; Z-H. Zhan, Member, IEEE; Z-J. Wang, Student Member, IEEE; J. Zhang, Fellow, IEEE.

This work was partially supported by the National Natural Science Foundations of China (NSFC) with Nos. 61772207, 61402545, and 61332002, the Natural Science Foundations of Guangdong Province for Distinguished Young Scholars with No. 2014A030306038, the Project for Pearl River New Star in Science and Technology with No. 201506010047, the GDUPS (2016), and the Fundamental Research Funds for the Central Universities.

© Springer Nature Singapore Pte Ltd. 2017
C. He et al. (Eds.): BIC-TA 2017, CCIS 791, pp. 476–486, 2017.
https://doi.org/10.1007/978-981-10-7179-9_37

mechanism of iterative evaluations and mutual learning, EAs are criticized for their requirements of high computational resources and heavy time expenses to obtain the final optimized-enough solutions. With the rapid development of information technique and the arrival of the era of the big data, the increasing complexity of the problems brought new challenges to EAs. The high-complexity problems bring a huge number of local optima which are hard to solve, while dealing with these problems is often time-consuming since their computational cost of fitness evolution is extremely high. Since we own huge idle resources but limited time, when a traditional sequential EA cannot provide satisfactory results within a required time, a distributed EA (DEA) may be effective to reduce the execution time and improve the qualities of solutions. That is due to the DEA often divides the update and evaluation of different individuals into different processes in parallel to reduce the time, while keep the communication between different processes can improve the population diversity and avoid getting trapped in the local optima [4].

Many EAs, including genetic algorithm (GA) [5,6], ant colony optimization (ACO) [7,8], particle swarm optimization (PSO) [9–13] and differential evolution (DE) [14–16] are all extended and applied in the distributed environment to parallelize the processing of EAs. However, when design a DEA, two things are necessarily addressed. One is the distribution of the evolution tasks, the other is the communication among processors. In many literatures, three famous distributed model called master-slave (i.e. global parallelization) [17–19], island (i.e. coarse-grained model) [20,21], and cellular (i.e. ne-grained model) [22,23] models are frequently used to build DEAs. After choosing a distributed model, different programming platforms can be selected to accomplish the algorithm, such as the Message-Passing Interface (MPI) [24,25] and Open Multi-Processing (OpenMP) [26,27].

According to the results reported in these literatures mentioned above, these DEAs have enhanced the performance of the traditional EAs, in terms of execution time, diversity maintenance, and solution accuracy. In order to further analyze these developments and find out the difficulties or preference in different platforms, this paper develops two different DEA based on different platforms. DE is a widely used EA whose performance is greatly promising in many optimization problems and real-world applications, which is adopted in this paper. Besides, the master-slave distributed model, due to its simple mechanism, is also applied in this paper. Therefore, we presented two distributed DE (DDE) variants using master-slave distributed model based on two different platforms, MPI and OpenMP, to further analyze and discuss strengths and weaknesses in different platforms. The experimental results show that both MPI and OpenMP have their own superiorities and they can improve the speedup obviously, while MPI is more suitable for high-complexity problems and can achieve higher speedup than OpenMP.

The rest of the paper is organized as follows. In Sect. 2, DE and the basic master-slave distributed model are reviewed. Section 3 develops two DDE variants using MPI and OpenMP, respectively. Experiments are conducted in Sect. 4 for in-depth comparisons. Finally, conclusions are drawn in Sect. 5.

2   Related Work

2.1   DE

Differential evolution (DE) is an effective global optimization algorithm which evolves according to the difference between two individuals. Given a problem with dimension of D, assume that the population size is NP, the initial population $\{x_{i,0}=(x_{i1}, x_{i2}, ..., x_{iD})—i=1, 2, , NP\}$ is randomly generated according to a uniform distribution in the search space as (1).

$$x_{i,j,0} = x_{i,min} + rand \times (x_{i,max} - x_{i,min}) \tag{1}$$

where $x_{i,min}$ and $x_{i,max}$ are the predefined lower and upper bounds of the jth dimension, and rand is a random number in range [0,1].

After initialization, DE performs the mutation, crossover, and selection operations for each individual to update the population at each generation. The algorithm terminates until the terminal conditions are met. The three operations are described in detail as follows.

Mutation: At each generation g, each individual $x_{i,g}$ generates a mutant vector $v_{i,g}$ by the mutation operation. Three frequently used mutation strategies are listed as follows:
   DE/rand/1

$$v_{i,g} = x_{r1,g} + F \times (x_{r2,g} - x_{r3,g}) \tag{2}$$

   DE/best/1

$$v_{i,g} = x_{best,g} + F \times (x_{r1,g} - x_{r2,g}) \tag{3}$$

   DE/current-to-best/1

$$v_{i,g} = x_{i,g} + F \times (x_{best,g} - x_{i,g}) + F \times (x_{r1,g} - x_{r2,g}) \tag{4}$$

where the indexes $r1$, $r2$, and $r3$ are distinct random integers selected from $\{1, 2, NP\}$ and different from i. The $x_{best,g}$ is the best individual in generation g. F is a positive parameter called amplification factor to control the scale of the differential vectors.

Crossover: In order to inherit the advantages from the parent, a binary crossover is commonly performed on the parent and the mutant vector to form a trial vector $u_{i,g} = (u_{i1,g}, u_{i2,g}, u_{iD,g})$, shown as:

$$u_{i,j,g} = \begin{cases} v_{i,j,g}, & \text{if } rand(0, 1) \leq CR \text{ or } j = j_{rand} \\ x_{i,j,g}, & \text{otherwise .} \end{cases} \tag{5}$$

In (5), j_{rand} is randomly selected from 1 to D for each individual to ensure that trial vector has at least one component different from $x_{i,g}$. The crossover rate CR within [0,1] is another parameter which controls the proportion of trial vector components inherited from mutant vector.

Selection: After the crossover, the trial vector $u_{i,g}$ is compared with target vector $x_{i,g}$ to determine which individual survives in the next generation $g + 1$ according to their fitness values. For example, for a maximization problem, the selected vector is given by:

$$x_{i,g+1} = \begin{cases} u_{i,g}, & \text{if } f(u_{i,g}) \geq f(x_{i,g}) \\ x_{i,g}, & \text{otherwise} \end{cases} \qquad (6)$$

where f is the fitness function.

2.2   Master-Slave Model in de

The master-slave model is illustrated as Fig. 1. Considering the high computational cost in fitness evaluation, when applied in DE, the master generally performs mutation, crossover, selection operations, and sends individuals to slaves for fitness evaluations. After the evaluation, each slave sends the fitness value of individual back to master. Until now, we have finished a loop sequent. The process will be repeated until the termination criterion is met.

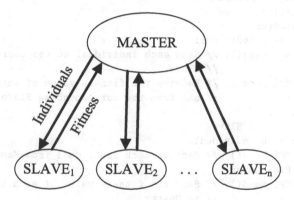

Fig. 1. The distributed framework of the master-slave model

As we can see, the communications only exist between master and slaves where the master sends individuals to slaves and the slaves return their fitness values back to the master, and there is no communication among slaves. Such a model is synchronous that the master has to wait to receive the information from all slaves before proceeding to the next generation.

The speedup of such a model can be computed as:

$$speedup = \frac{T_s}{T_p} \qquad (7)$$

where T_s is the time needed to finish the whole evolutionary process on a serial computer, while T_p is the time needed to finish the same evolutionary process on the parallel computer (with p processors).

3   DDE Based on Different Platforms

3.1   DDE Based on MPI

The MPI is a relatively complete library of message-passing routines. The MPI functions support process-to-process communication, group communication, setting up and managing communication groups, and interacting with the environment.

The overall DDE algorithm based on MPI is shown in Fig. 2, where the numprocs means the number of threads, while the myid indicates the current thread.

```
Begin
1.     //MPI Initialize
2.     MPI_Init(&argc, &argv);
3.     MPI_Comm_rank(MPI_COMM_WORLD, &myid);
4.     MPI_Comm_size(MPI_COMM_WORLD, &numprocs);
5.     Initialize the population.
6.     If myid==0  //Master
7.        Mutation.
8.        Crossover.
9.        For each individual
10.           MPI_Send(); // Send each individual to the corresponding
                          // Slave.
11.           MPI_Recv(); // Receive the fitness value of each individ-
                          // ual from the corresponding Slave.
12.        End For
13.     Else        //Slaves
14.        For each individual
15.           MPI_Recv(); // Receive each individual from Master.
16.           Evaluation.
17.           MPI_Send(); // Send the fitness value of each individual
                          // to Master.
18.        End For
19.     End If
20.     Stop if the terminal criteria is satisfied, otherwise go to
        Step 6.
End.
```

Fig. 2. The algorithm of DDE based on MPI

There are several advantages when using MPI. First, it shows good scalability and could be implemented efficiently on the multi-machine, as a result, it can handle computationally expensive and high-complexity problems. Second, due to its specific communication mechanism, users can allocate individuals to any designated processor. Last, each thread has its own memory and variables, so there's no need to worry about conflicts.

However, some disadvantages are also brought by MPI. First, it is relatively hard to use because users have to make major modifications on the original serial algorithm, such as building communications. Second, the properties of MPI will be seriously affected by the communication time.

3.2 DDE Based on OpenMP

OpenMP is a set of compiler directives and library routines that are used to express shared-memory parallelism. The majority of the OpenMP interface is a set of compiler directives. The programmer adds these to a sequential program to tell the compiler what parts of the program to execute concurrently, and to specify synchronization points.

When combined OpenMP with DDE, the pseudo-code is shown in Fig. 3, where n is the number of threads predefined by users.

```
Begin
1.    Initialize.
2.    Mutation.
3.    Crossover.
4.    #pragma omp parallel num_threads(n)
5.    #pragma omp parallel for
6.       Evaluation.
7.    End For
8.    Stop if the terminal criteria is satisfied, otherwise go to
      Step 2.
End
```

Fig. 3. The algorithm of DDE based on OpenMP

Compared with MPI, OpenMP has the following superiorities. First, it is easier to use where users only make minor changes on the original serial algorithm. Second, the shared-memory mechanism simplifies the communication between individuals. However, it can only be used on the shared-memory hardware, which is not universal. Besides, it cannot be implemented on the multi-machine system, which further restricts its widely application. Meanwhile, the allocation between task and thread is automatic, users cannot intervene.

4 Experimental Results

After the qualitative analysis of the merits and demerits between MPI and OpenMP, in this part, we conduct the experiments to make the quantitative comparisons.

4.1   Experimental Setup

In our experiments, DE/rand/1 mutation strategy is used, and the amplification factor F and crossover rate CR are set as 0.5 and 0.9, respectively. Sphere function is used here to test the performance of these two DDE algorithms, shown in (8).

$$f(x) = \sum_{i=1}^{D} x_i^2; \tag{8}$$

The population size is set as 50, while the dimension of problem is set as 30. We set the maximum of fitness evaluations (FEs) as 3000. All experiments are conducted on the PC with 8 Intel Core i7 CPUs. To avoid the phenomenon of hyper-threading, the number of threads used in our experiments is 1–8. Besides, all algorithms run 30 times independently and the mean results are reported.

4.2   Results and Discussion

In this subsection, we compare the speedup of these two DDE algorithms. Considering that it is too fast to evaluate such a Sphere function, we add a delay function to simulate the time-consuming problem. The delay function delays the evaluation function by 1 s, 2 s, 5 s, and 10 s, respectively. Under these four circumstances, we test the speedup and draw the speedup curve with the increasing threads of these two algorithms, shown in Figs. 4 and 5.

From the figures presented above, we can see that:

(1) With the increasing of the threads, the speedup of both MPI and OpenMP are rising steadily.
(2) With the increasing of the delay time, the speedup of both MPI and OpenMP are rising steadily.
(3) Both of MPI and OpenMP cannot achieve the linear speedup or the superlinear speedup. That may be due to the communication cost in MPI and OpenMP.
(4) There is no significant difference between 1 thread and 2 threads in MPI. That is because in MPI, these must be a thread called Master to control the process of evolution, as a result, the threads used in the evaluation is actually the $n-1$. Therefore, if we have 2 threads, only 1 thread is used for evaluation, which is similar to sequential DE.
(5) The superiority of MPI becomes increasingly obvious with the growing threads, it outperforms OpenMP significantly when the number of threads is larger than 4. However, when the number of threads is smaller than 4, the performance of OpenMP is slightly better than MPI. That means when dealing with computationally expensive or high-complexity problems, we prefer to use MPI rather than OpenMP, while if we solve the relatively simple problems, OpenMP seems to be a good choice.

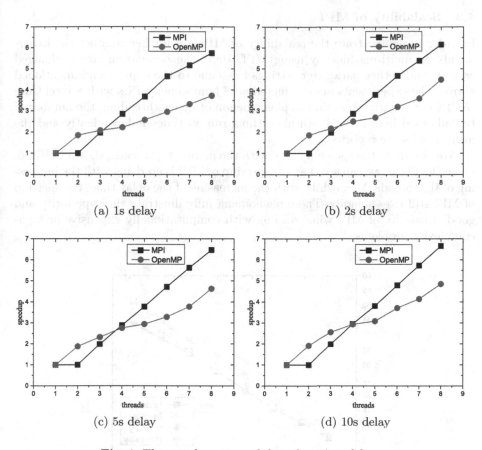

(a) 1s delay

(b) 2s delay

(c) 5s delay

(d) 10s delay

Fig. 4. The speedup curve of these four time delays

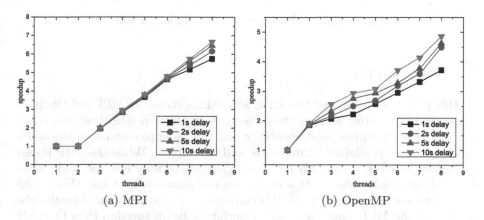

(a) MPI

(b) OpenMP

Fig. 5. The speedup curve of these two algorithms

4.3   Scalability of MPI

In order to demonstrate the scalability of MPI, we further conduct the experiments on multi-machine by using MPI. Here, the population size is changed as 400, while other parameter settings are same to the experiments mentioned above. The experiments are conducted on 8 homogeneity PCs with 8 Intel Core i7 CPUs. Similarly, to avoid the phenomenon of hyper-threading, the number of threads used here is 8–64. All algorithms run 30 times independently and the mean results are reported.

We also draw the speedup curve with the increasing threads, shown in Fig. 6. From the Fig. 6, we can see that the speedup of MPI keep rising with the increasing of the threads. Meanwhile, with the increasing of the delay time, the speedup of MPI still rises steadily. These phenomena fully illustrate the superiority and good scalability of MPI when dealing with computationally expensive or high-complexity problems.

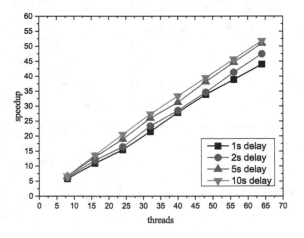

Fig. 6. The speedup curve of MPI on multi-machine

5   Conclusion

In this paper, we compared two DDE algorithms based on MPI and OpenMP respectively to further analyze the difficulties or preference in these two different platforms. MPI has good scalability and can be implemented on the multi-machine, but it is relatively hard to use and accomplish. While OpenMP is easy to realize, however, it can only be used on shared-memory machine and cannot be used on multi-machine. As a result, we can conclude that the MPI is universal and scalable, while OpenMP is convenient. Our experimental results also show that the MPI can achieve better performance on speedup than OpenMP when the number of threads is large, while OpenMP can outperform MPI if the number of threads is small. As a result, we can conclude that if we tackle the relatively simple problems, OpenMP is a good choice due to its convenience and good performance on small threads. When dealing with high-complexity problems, MPI is better than OpenMP because of its good scalability and good performance on large threads.

Acknowledgments. This work was partially supported by the National Natural Science Foundations of China (NSFC) with Nos. 61772207, 61402545, and 61332002, the Natural Science Foundations of Guangdong Province for Distinguished Young Scholars with No. 2014A030306038, the Project for Pearl River New Star in Science and Technology with No. 201506010047, the GDUPS (2016), and the Fundamental Research Funds for the Central Universities.

References

1. Wang, Z.Y., Xing, H.L., Li, T.R., Yang, Y., Qu, R., Pan, Y.: A modified ant colony optimization algorithm for network coding resource minimization. IEEE Trans. Evol. Comput. **20**(3), 325–342 (2016)
2. Yoon, Y., Kim, Y.H.: An efficient genetic algorithm for maximum coverage deployment in wireless sensor networks. IEEE Trans. Cybern. **43**(5), 1473–1483 (2013)
3. Hu, X.M., Zhang, J., Chung, H.S.H., Li, Y., Liu, O.: SamACO: variable sampling ant colony optimization algorithm for continuous optimization. IEEE Trans. Cybern. **40**(6), 1555–1566 (2010)
4. Zhan, Z.H., Liu, X.F., Zhang, H.X., Yu, Z.T., Weng, J., Li, Y., Gu, T.L., Zhang, J.: Cloudde: a heterogeneous differential evolution algorithm and its distributed cloud version. IEEE Trans. Parallel Distrib. Syst. **28**(3), 704–716 (2017)
5. Zhang, X.Y., Zhang, J., Gong, Y.J., Zhan, Z.H., Chen, W.N., Li, Y.: Kuhn-Munkres parallel genetic algorithm for the set cover problem and its application to large-scale wireless sensor networks. IEEE Trans. Evol. Comput. **20**(5), 695–710 (2016)
6. Roberge, V., Tarbouchi, M., Okou, F.: Strategies to accelerate harmonic minimization in multilevel inverters using a parallel genetic algorithm on graphical processing unit. IEEE Trans. Power Electron. **29**(10), 5087–5090 (2014)
7. Huang, H.C.: SoPC-based parallel ACO algorithm and its application to optimal motion controller design for intelligent omnidirectional mobile robots. IEEE Trans. Ind. Inform. **9**(4), 1828–1835 (2013)
8. Huang, H.C.: A Taguchi-based heterogeneous parallel metaheuristic ACO-PSO and its FPGA realization to optimal polar-space locomotion control of four-wheeled redundant mobile robots. IEEE Trans. Ind. Inform. **11**(4), 915–922 (2015)
9. Hossain, M.S., Moniruzzaman, M., Muhammad, G., Ghoneim, A., Alamri, A.: Big data-driven service composition using parallel clustered particle swarm optimization in mobile environment. IEEE Trans. Serv. Comput. **9**(5), 806–817 (2016)
10. Wang, Z.J., Zhan, Z.H., Zhang, J.: An improved method for comprehensive learning particle swarm optimization. In: Proceedings of IEEE Symposium Series on Computational Intelligence, pp. 218–225 (2015)
11. Zhan, Z.H., Wang, Z.J., Lin, Y., Zhang, J.: Adaptive radius species-based particle swarm optimization for multimodal optimization problems. In: Proceedings of IEEE Congress on Evolutionary Computation, pp. 2043–2048 (2016)
12. Wang, Z.J., Zhan, Z.H., Du, K.J., Yu, Z.W., Zhang, J.: Orthogonal learning particle swarm optimization with variable relocation for dynamic optimization. In: Proceedings of IEEE Congress on Evolutionary Computation, pp. 594–600 (2016)

13. Kusetogullari, H., Yavariabdi, A., Celik, T.: Unsupervised change detection in multitemporal multispectral satellite images using parallel particle swarm optimization. IEEE J. Sel. Top. Appl. Earth Obs. Remote Sens. **8**(5), 2151–2164 (2015)

14. Weber, M., Neri, F., Tirronen, V.: Shuffle or update parallel differential evolution for large-scale optimization. Soft Comput. **15**(11), 2089–2107 (2011)

15. Li, Y.L., Zhan, Z.H., Gong, Y.J., Chen, W.N., Zhang, J., Li, Y.: Differential evolution with an evolution path: a DEEP evolutionary algorithm. IEEE Trans. Cybern. **45**(9), 1798–1810 (2015)

16. Chen, Z.H., Jiang, X.W., Li, J.B., Li, S.S., Wang, L.W.: PDECO: parallel differential evolution for clusters optimization. J. Comput. Chem. **34**(12), 1046–1059 (2013)

17. Dubreuil, M., Gagn, C., Parizeau, M.: Analysis of a master-slave architecture for distributed evolutionary computations. IEEE Trans. Cybern. **36**(1), 229–235 (2006)

18. Wang, Z.J., Zhan, Z.H., Zhang, J.: Parallel multi-strategy evolutionary algorithm using message passing interface for many-objective optimization. In: Proceedings of IEEE Symposium Series on Computational Intelligence, pp. 1–8 (2016)

19. Mendiburu, A., Lozano, J.A., Alonso, J.M.: Parallel implementation of EDAs based on probabilistic graphical models. IEEE Trans. Evol. Comput. **9**(4), 406–423 (2005)

20. Weber, M., Neri, F., Tirronen, V.: A study on scale factor in distributed differential evolution. Inf. Sci. **181**, 2488–2511 (2011)

21. Weber, M., Neri, F., Tirronen, V.: A study on scale factor/crossover interaction in distributed differential evolution. Artif. Intell. Rev. **39**(3), 195–224 (2013)

22. Alba, E., Dorronsoro, B.: The exploration/exploitation tradeoff in dynamic cellular genetic algorithms. IEEE Trans. Evol. Comput. **9**(2), 126–142 (2005)

23. Giacobini, M., Tomassini, M., Tettamanzi, A.G., Alba, E.: Selection intensity in cellular evolutionary algorithms for regular lattices. IEEE Trans. Evol. Comput. **9**(5), 489–505 (2005)

24. Ismail, M.A.: Parallel genetic algorithms (PGAs): master-slave paradigm approach using MPI. In: E-Tech, pp. 83–87 (2004)

25. Zhang, G.-W., Zhan, Z.-H., Du, K.-J., Lin, Y., Chen, W.-N., Li, J.-J., Zhang, J.: Parallel particle swarm optimization using message passing interface. In: Handa, H., Ishibuchi, H., Ong, Y.-S., Tan, K.C. (eds.) Proceedings of the 18th Asia Pacific Symposium on Intelligent and Evolutionary Systems, Volume 1. PALO, vol. 1, pp. 55–64. Springer, Cham (2015). https://doi.org/10.1007/978-3-319-13359-1_5

26. Herda, M.: Parallel genetic algorithm for capacitated p-median problem using OpenMP protocol. In: Proceedings of IEEE International Symposium on Computational Intelligence and Informatics, pp. 347–352 (2016)

27. Wang, D.Z., Wang, D.W., Yan, Y., Wang, H.F.: An adaptive version of parallel MPSO with OpenMP for uncapacitated facility location problem. In: Proceedings of IEEE Chinese Control and Decision Conference, pp. 2387–2391 (2008)

Derivation Languages of Splicing P Systems

Kalpana Mahalingam[1], Prithwineel Paul[1], Bosheng Song[2], Linqiang Pan[2,3(✉)], and K.G. Subramanian[4]

[1] Department of Mathematics, Indian Institute of Technology,
Madras, Chennai 600036, India
kmahalingam@iitm.ac.in, prithwineelpaul@gmail.com
[2] Key Laboratory of Image Information Processing and Intelligent Control
of Education Ministry of China, School of Automation,
Huazhong University of Science and Technology, Wuhan 430074, Hubei, China
boshengsong@hust.edu.cn, lqpan@mail.hust.edu.cn
[3] School of Electric and Information Engineering,
Zhengzhou University of Light Industry, Zhengzhou 450002, Henan, China
[4] Faculty of Science, Liverpool Hope University, Liverpool L16 9JD, UK
kgsmani1948@gmail.com

Abstract. Labelled splicing P systems are distributed parallel computing models, where sets of strings that evolve by splicing rules are labelled. In this work, we consider labelled splicing systems with the following modifications: (i) The strings in the membranes are present in arbitrary number of copies; (ii) the rules in the regions are finite in number. Results on the language family generated by the labelled splicing system in comparison with the language families of the Chomsky hierarchy, including recursively enumerable languages, are obtained, by involving only either one or two membranes in the P systems considered.

Keywords: Splicing operation · P system · Labelled splicing P system · Chomsky hierarchy

1 Introduction

In the area of DNA computing, Head [5,6] proposed a mathematical model known as splicing system while studying the recombination behaviour of DNA molecules in the presence of appropriate restriction enzymes and a ligase. This system involves an operation called splicing on strings of symbols, which, informally expressed, is a "cut" and "paste" operation. In the standard model of a splicing system, a splicing rule of the form $r : u\#v\$x\#y$ ($\#, \$$ are two special symbols) can be applied to two strings $\alpha = puvq$ and $\beta = rxys$, for strings p, q, u, v, x, y over an alphabet so that the string α is cut between u and v while β is cut between x and y and the result of an application of the rule r yields a string $puys$. With a finite number of axiom strings and a finite number of splicing

K.G. Subramanian—Honorary visiting professor at Liverpool Hope University.

rules, it has been shown (see, for example, [6]) that only regular languages can be generated. In subsequent studies of splicing systems additional ingredients [1,3,4,9,12,16] have been introduced and investigated yielding results characterizing recursively enumerable languages.

The field of membrane computing was born when Păun [11,13] proposed a novel computing model taking motivation from the membrane structure and the functioning of living cells. This computing model with a generic name of P system has some minimal features in its basic version, such as (i) a hierarchical arrangement of membranes, one within another and all the membranes enclosed in a single membrane, called skin membrane; (ii) the regions delimited by the membranes can have objects which can evolve by using specified evolution rules; (iii) the evolved objects can remain in the same membrane or move to adjacent membranes; (iv) all the objects in all the regions evolve in parallel, if rules in the regions are applicable. Based on the operation of splicing on strings, Păun [11] linked the two areas of DNA computing and membrane computing by defining splicing P systems and established results characterizing recursively enumerable languages.

Controlled computations in different types of P systems have been considered (see, for example, [7,14,20]), by associating labels with the rules in the regions of the respective P system and considering sequences of labels of rules used in the steps of a computation. In such studies, several results pertaining to the language computing power of these P systems have been established. In [8], a variant of splicing P system, called labelled spicing system, has been considered by assigning labels to the splicing rules and the family of languages generated by these systems is compared with the language families of the Chomsky hierarchy.

In this work, we continue the study of labelled splicing systems relaxing certain restrictions in the definition formulated in [8] with the following modifications: (i) The strings in the membranes are present in arbitrary number of copies unlike in [8] wherein certain strings were required to be present only in a finite number; (ii) the rules in the regions are finite in number unlike in [8] where the rule set can be a regular set. We obtain comparison results on the language family generated by the labelled splicing system in comparison with the language families of the Chomsky hierarchy. Specifically, the control languages of splicing P systems with one or two membranes, consisting of the strings of labels of rules used during a computation, are considered here and characterization results for the family of recursively enumerable languages are obtained.

2   Preliminaries

In this section, we first recall the definition of splicing P systems [13,16]. For unexplained notions and results relating to formal grammars and languages we refer to [15] and relating to P systems, to [11,13].

Definition 1. *A splicing P system of degree* m (≥ 1) *is a construct* $\Pi = (V_1, T_1, \mu, A_1, \ldots, A_m, R_1, \ldots, R_m)$, *where:*

(i) V_1 is an alphabet;

(ii) $T_1 \subseteq V_1$ is the terminal alphabet;

(iii) μ is a membrane structure with m membranes;

(iv) $A_i \subseteq V_1^*$, $(1 \leq i \leq m)$ is a finite language associated with the membrane i, $(1 \leq i \leq m)$;

(v) R_i, $(1 \leq i \leq m)$ is a set of splicing rules r associated with the membrane i, $(1 \leq i \leq m)$, where r is a splicing rule over V_1 of the form $r = (u_1 \# u_2 \$ u_3 \# u_4; tar_1, tar_2)$ with $u_1, u_2, u_3, u_4 \in V_1^*$, $\#, \$ \notin V_1$ and $tar_1, tar_2 \in \{here, in, out, in_j\}$ are target indicators.

A configuration of Π is an m-tuple $(M_1, \cdots, M_m)$ of languages over V_1. The m-tuple $(A_1, \cdots, A_m)$ is the initial configuration. Let $(M_1, \cdots, M_m), (M_1', \cdots, M_m')$ be two consecutive configurations of Π. We denote by $(M_1, \ldots, M_m) \Rightarrow (M_1', \ldots, M_m')$, a transition from $(M_1, \cdots, M_m)$ to $(M_1', \cdots, M_m')$, i.e., $(M_1', \cdots, M_m')$ can be reached by an application of splicing rules of Π to all possible strings that are in the corresponding membranes of the configuration $(M_1, \ldots, M_m)$. After the application of the rules, the result of each splicing is distributed to other membranes according to the target indicators. Formally, for $i \in \{1, \cdots, m\}$, if $x = x_1 u_1 u_2 x_2$, $y = y_1 u_3 u_4 y_2 \in M_i$ and $r = (u_1 \# u_2 \$ u_3 \# u_4; tar_1, tar_2) \in R_i$, $x_1, x_2, y_1, y_2, u_1, u_2, u_3, u_4 \in V_1^*$, the splicing $(x, y) \vdash_r (z, w), z, w \in V_1^*$, i.e., $(x_1 u_1 | u_2 x_2, y_1 u_3 | u_4 y_2) \vdash_r (x_1 u_1 u_4 y_2, y_1 u_3 u_2 x_2)$ can take place in membrane i. The strings $z(= x_1 u_1 u_4 y_2)$ and $w(= y_1 u_3 u_2 x_2)$ pass to the membranes indicated by tar_1 and tar_2, respectively.

The splicing rule $(u_1 \# u_2 \$ u_3 \# u_4; tar_1, tar_2)$ is also written as:

$$
(\,\frac{u_1 \quad\;\; u_2}{u_3 \quad\;\; u_4}\; ; tar_1, tar_2\,)
$$

A computation in a splicing P system Π is a sequence of transitions between configurations of Π which starts from the initial configuration $(A_1, \cdots, A_m)$. The result of the computation consists of all strings over terminal alphabet T_1 which are sent outside the system at some moment of the computation. The result of the computation is denoted as $L(\Pi)$ (i.e., the language generated by system Π).

In splicing P systems the strings present in the membranes are considered to be available in arbitrary number of copies. Hence, after application of any rule r to any two strings x and y, the strings x and y still will be present in the system.

When the system has only one membrane, a sequence of transitions is denoted as $M_1 \Rightarrow M_2 \Rightarrow \ldots \Rightarrow M_k$ $(M_1 = A_1)$ as in [16].

The possibilities that can happen in a splicing P system with one membrane as discussed in [16] are now recalled.

Let a string w be present in a membrane. At the same time the same string w be produced by a rule r and sent out of the current membrane. There exist two possibilities: One possibility is to keep the original string w in the membrane and send the newly produced w outside the membrane. The second possibility is to send the string w out of the membrane and keep no copy of it in the membrane.

Also, there can be situations where two splicing rules produce the same w where one of the rules has target indicator *here* and other has target indicator *in* or *out*. Also both the situations with both kinds of rules can happen at the same time.

The possible cases discussed in detail in [16] are as follows: Let w be a string produced in membrane i by a rule r and at the same time w is sent out of the membrane by the targets *in* or *out*. Then the possibilities are given by the following:

(1) the string w is sent out of the membrane and no copy of it remains inside the membrane;

(2) the string w is sent out of the membrane but still copies of w can be present in the system, provided any of the following conditions is satisfied: (a) the string w is present in the membrane where the rule is applied; (b) the membrane contains another splicing rule r' which produces w with target indicator *here*; (c) both the conditions 2a and 2b are satisfied; (d) one of the conditions 2a or 2b is satisfied.

A splicing P system is said to be of type x if the ways the strings evolve are as mentioned in the variant $x \in \{1, 2a, 2b, 2c, 2d\}$ [16]. The family of languages generated by splicing P systems with one membrane where the strings evolve according to the variant x is denoted as $ELSP_m(spl, in, x)$.

Computational power of the different variants of splicing P systems has been investigated in [16] and the following theorems in [16] describe the computation power of the variants. The family of recursively enumerable languages is denoted by RE while the family of regular languages is denoted by REG.

Theorem 1. $ELSP_1(spl, in, 1) = RE$.

Theorem 2. $ELSP_1(spl, in, 2d) = REG$.

Theorem 3. $ELSP_1(spl, in, 2a) = REG$.

Note that in the cases mentioned above, splicing at any step occurs between any two strings present in the system. But, here we will consider another variant of splicing P systems, where splicing at any step occurs between strings generated in the previous step and the axioms.

3   Labelled Splicing P Systems

Labelled splicing systems were considered in [8]. We here restate the definition with certain modifications as pointed out in the introduction.

Definition 2. *A labelled splicing P system of degree m (≥ 1) is a construct of the form*
$$\Pi = (V_1, T_1, \mu, A_1, A_2, \ldots, A_m, R_1, R_2, \ldots, R_m, Lab),$$
where:

- $V_1, T_1, \mu, A_1, A_2, \ldots, A_m, R_1, R_2, \ldots, R_m$ *are as in Definition 1.*
- *A label is associated with each rule in* $R_1 \cup R_2 \cup \ldots \cup R_m$ *and Lab is the alphabet of the labels of the rules with* $V_1 \cap Lab = \emptyset$.

The same label can be assigned to different rules but a rule cannot have multiple labels. The rules of labelled splicing P system are written in the form $(a : x_1 \# x_2 \$ y_1 \# y_2; tar_1, tar_2)$, where $a \in Lab$, $x_1, x_2, y_1, y_2 \in V_1^*$, $tar_1, tar_2 \in \{here, out, in\}$. We will discuss mainly two variants given by the following:

(1) All the rules present in the membranes have distinct labels.
(2) The rules in the membranes may not have distinct labels. But, at a time only the rules with the same label are applied, i.e., if a rule labelled r is applied in a membrane i, then at the same time other rules labelled only r and λ (empty) in membrane "i" as well as in all other membranes, can be applied.

A computation in a labelled splicing P system Π is called *label restricted* if in each step of a computation only rules with same label and λ (empty) label are applied.

Let C and C' be two successive configurations and by $C \overset{b}{\Rightarrow} C'$, we mean that only "$b$" labelled and λ labelled rules are applied in all the membranes to reach the configuration C' derived from C.

Splicing rules present in the membranes are applied in parallel to pass from one configuration to another configuration. The strings in the membranes are present in arbitrary number of copies. So after the application of any rule labelled "r" to the strings x and y, the copies of the strings x and y will still remain inside the membrane. The different cases of splicing P systems are discussed in [16]. As in [16], there exist mainly two cases: if there exists a word w and at the same time this word is produced by any rule in the membrane and also sent to an outer or inner membrane, then there are two possibilities. The first one is to keep the original w and send away the newly produced w; Secondly, send the w away from the membrane and also remove all copies of it from the membrane.

Here, we consider both the possibilities and define derivation languages for both the cases. In the first case, if a string is present inside the system, it will remain there forever and in the other case, if a string is sent outside a membrane, all copies of it are sent outside and no copy of it remains inside.

CASE (A'):

(1) Let $x_0, y_0 \in A_i$.
(2) $(x_0, y_0) \vdash^{a_1} (x_0', y_0')$ (the strings x_0' and y_0' can stay in membrane i or can be sent to any membrane inside the membrane i chosen non-deterministically or can be sent to the membrane outside the membrane i depending on the target indications in the a_1 labelled rule.
(3) $(x_1, y_1) \vdash^{a_2} (x_1', y_1')$ where one of x_1 or y_1 is chosen from $\{x_0', y_0'\}$; assuming that x_1 has been chosen, the other string y_1 is chosen from the axioms present in the membrane to which the string x_1 belongs, depending on the target indication of the rule applied in the previous step.

(4) $(x_2, y_2) \vdash^{a_3} (x_2', y_2')$ where x_2 and y_2 are chosen in the same manner as in the previous step.
This computation ends when a step which is given below, is reached:

(5) $(x_{n-1}, y_{n-1}) \vdash^{a_n} (x_n', y_n')$ where any one of the x_n' and y_n' is over the terminal set T_1 and also it is sent outside the skin membrane using the a_n labelled rule.

Then the string $a_1 a_2 \ldots a_n$ is called a *regulated* word or *control* word generated by the system Π. The set of all regulated words or control words generated by the system Π is denoted as $RLSPS(\Pi)$. The family of regulated languages generated by the splicing P systems with atleast m membranes is denoted as $RLSPS_m$. Also, if each rule of the splicing P system is labelled in a unique manner, then the language associated with the terminal derivations is called the *Szilard language generated by the splicing P systems*. The family of Szilard languages generated by the splicing P systems of degree m is denoted as $SZLSPS_m$. When the number of membranes is unbounded, m is replaced by $*$. Also, when λ labelled rules are used the systems are denoted as $RLSPS_{m,\lambda}$ and $SZLSPS_{m,\lambda}$. In this case system will never halt, since the reaction inside the membranes will never stop.

CASE (B'): If the labels of the label restricted transitions starting from an initial configuration and ending in a terminal configuration (i.e., a configuration is reached where a terminal strings is generated and is sent outside the membranes), are sequentially concatenated, a string over Lab is generated. It is called *regulated* string or *control* string. The set of all strings generated by all label restricted computations in Π with m membranes is denoted by $RLSPS_{ter,m}(\Pi)$ and when λ labelled rules are allowed it is denoted as $RLSPS_{ter,m,\lambda}(\Pi)$. The family of languages $RLSPS_{ter}(\Pi)$ associated with Π with at most m membranes, is denoted by $RLSPS_{ter,m}$ and $RLSPS_{ter,m,\lambda}$ respectively. If the number of membranes is unbounded, then the subscript m is replaced with $*$. Similarly, when the labeling is done in one to one manner, the family of languages generated by the system is denoted as $SZLSPS_{ter,m}$ and $SZLSPS_{ter,*}$, respectively.

4   Comparison Results

Theorem 4. *Labelled splicing P systems with two membranes can generate recursively enumerable languages as control languages, i.e., $RLSPS_{2,\lambda} = RE$.*

Proof. Given a grammar (N, T, P, S) (with the number of symbols in $N \cup T$ being n) in Kuroda normal form, generating a recursively enumerable language, a labelled P system $(V_1, T_1, \mu, A_1, A_2, R_1, R_2, Lab)$ is constructed as described below.

Let $N \cup T \cup \{B\} = \{\alpha_1, \alpha_2, \ldots, \alpha_n\}, B \notin N \cup T$ and the rules of P are written in the form $u_i \rightarrow v_i, 1 \leq i \leq m$. Also, $u_{m+j} = v_{m+j} = \alpha_j, 1 \leq j \leq n$.

Note that, when $1 \leq i \leq m$, the rules $u_i \rightarrow v_i \in P$ are simulated; and when rotation step is performed, the index $(n+1), (n+2), \ldots, (n+m)$ is used to avoid any confusion with the indexes used during simulation.

- $V_1 = \{Y_n \mid n \in N\} \cup \{Y_t \mid t \in T\} \cup \{Y_B, X, X', Y, Y', Z, Z'\} \cup \{X_i \mid 0 \leq i \leq (n+m)\} \cup \{Y_i \mid 0 \leq i \leq (n+m)\}$; where $V_1 \cap Lab = \emptyset$.
- $T_1 = \{Y_t \mid t \in T\} \cup \{Y_\lambda\}$.
- $A_1 = \{XY_BY_SY, X_iY_{v_i'}Y_{v_i''}Z, X_iY_{v_i}Z, ZY_{i-1}, Z', ZY' \mid 1 \leq i \leq (n+m), v_i', v_i'' \in N, v_i \in N \cup T \cup \{B\} \cup \{\lambda\}\}$.
- R_1 contains the following rules:
  $(\lambda : X_iY_{v_i'}Y_{v_i''}\#Z\$X\#; in, out)$; if $|v_i| = 2$ and $v_i = v_i'v_i'', |v_i'| = 1, |v_i''| = 1, 1 \leq i \leq m$,
  $(\lambda : X_iY_\lambda\#Z\$X\#; in, out)$; if $|v_i| = 1$ and $u_i \rightarrow v_i \in P, 1 \leq i \leq m$,
  $(\lambda : X_iY_{v_i}\#Z\$X\#; in, out)$; if $|v_i| = 0$ and $u_i \rightarrow \lambda \in P, 1 \leq i \leq m$,
  $(\lambda : X_iY_{v_i}\#Z\$X\#; in, out)$; if $m+1 \leq i \leq m+n$,
  $(\lambda : \#Y_i\$Z\#Y_{i-1}; in, out); 1 \leq i \leq (m+n)$,
  $(\lambda : \#Y_0\$Z\#Y'; in, out), (\lambda : X_0\#\$X'\#Z; out, here)$,
  $(\lambda : \#BY\$Z'\#; here, out), (\lambda : X\#\$\#Z'; out, out)$.
- $A_2 = \{ZY_i, X_{i-1}Z, XZ, ZY \mid 1 \leq i \leq (n+m)\}$.
- R_2 contains the following rules:
  $(\lambda : \#Y_{u_i}'Y_{u_i}''Y\$Z\#Y_i; out, here)$ if $|u_i| = 2$ and $u_i = u_i'u_i'', |u_i| = 1, |u_i''| = 1, 1 \leq i \leq m$,
  $(v_i : \theta\#Y_{u_i}Y\$Z\#Y_i; out, here)$ if $\theta \in \{Y_B\} \cup \{Y_t \mid t \in T\}, |u_i| = 1, u_i \rightarrow v_i \in P, 1 \leq i \leq m$,
  $(\lambda : \#Y_{u_i}Y\$Z\#Y_i; out, here), (m+1) \leq i \leq (m+n)$,
  $(\lambda : X_i\#\$X_{i-1}\#Z; here, out), 1 \leq i \leq n+m$,
  $(\lambda : X'\#\$X\#Z; here, out), (\lambda : \#Y'\$Z\#Y; out, here)$.
- $Lab = T \cup \{\lambda\}$.

The rules in the grammar G are in Kuroda normal form. Every element of $L(G)$ can be generated by the application of the recursive rules $A \rightarrow BC, AB \rightarrow CD, A, B, C, D \in N$ in any manner and then by the application of the terminal rules $A \rightarrow a, A \rightarrow \lambda, A \in N, a \in T$ in leftmost manner. Let $x \in L(G)$, if the splicing rules are applied in the same manner in which the rules of the grammar G are applied, then a string over the terminal alphabet of Π is generated and it is sent outside the membrane. If the labels of the applied splicing rules are concatenated, then the string x is generated. Hence, $x \in RLSPS_{2,\lambda}(\Pi)$. This implies that, $L(G) \subseteq RLSPS_{2,\lambda}(\Pi)$. Also, if the rules in a grammar G are applied in the same sequence as in any terminal derivation of the splicing P system Π, then $RLSPS_{2,\lambda}(\Pi) \subseteq L(G)$. Hence, $L(G) = RLSPS_{2,\lambda}(\Pi)$. So, we can conclude that each recursively enumerable language can be generated as control language of a splicing P system of degree 2.

Theorem 5. *Every recursively enumerable language can be written as a homomorphic image of the Szilard language generated by the splicing P system with two membranes.*

Proof. Let $G = (N, T, P, S)$ be a type-0-grammar in Kuroda normal form. We construct a splicing P system Π with two membranes such that $L(G) = h(SZLSPS_2(\Pi))$.

Let $N \cup T \cup \{B\} = \{\alpha_1, \alpha_2, \ldots, \alpha_n\}$, $B \notin N \cup T$ and the rules of P are written in the form $u_i \rightarrow v_i, 1 \leq i \leq m$. Also, $u_{m+j} = v_{m+j} = \alpha_j, 1 \leq j \leq n$.

Note that, when $1 \leq i \leq m$, the rules $u_i \rightarrow v_i \in P$ are simulated; and when rotation step is performed, the index $(n+1), (n+2), \ldots, (n+m)$ is used to avoid any confusion with the indexes used during simulation.

Let $\Pi = (V_1, T_1, \mu, A_1, A_2, R_1, R_2, Lab)$ be a labelled splicing P system, where

- $V_1 = Y_N \cup Y_T \cup \{Y_B, X, X^{'}, Y, Y^{'}, Z, Z^{'}\} \cup \{X_i \mid 0 \leq i \leq (n+m)\} \cup \{Y_i \mid 0 \leq i \leq (n+m)\}$;
- $T_1 = \{Y_t \mid t \in T\} \cup \{Y_\lambda\}$;
- $\mu = [_1[_2]_2]_1$;
- $A_1 = \{XY_BY_SY, X_iY_{v_i^{'}}Y_{v_i^{''}}Z, X_iY_{v_i}Z, X_iY_{v_i}Z, ZY_{i-1}, Z^{'}, ZY^{'} \mid 1 \leq i \leq (n+m)\}$;
- R_1 contains the following rules:
  $(d_{v_i} : X_iY_{v_i^{'}}Y_{v_i^{''}}\#Z\$X\#; in, out)$; if $|v_i| = 2$ and $v_i = v_i^{'}v_i^{''}, |v_i^{'}| = 1, |v_i^{''}| = 1, 1 \leq i \leq m$,
  $(d_{v_i^{'''}} : X_iY_\lambda\#Z\$X\#; in, out)$; if $|v_i| = 1$ and $u_i \rightarrow v_i \in P, 1 \leq i \leq m$,
  $(d_{v_i^{'}} : X_iY_{v_i}\#Z\$X\#; in, out)$; if $|v_i| = 0$ and $u_i \rightarrow \lambda \in P, 1 \leq i \leq m$,
  $(d_{v_i^{''}} : X_iY_{v_i}\#Z\$X\#; in, out)$; if $m+1 \leq i \leq m+n$,
  $(d_{Y_i} : \#Y_i\$Z\#Y_{i-1}; in, out); 1 \leq i \leq (m+n)$,
  $(d_{Y_0} : \#Y_0\$Z\#Y^{'}; in, out)$, $(d_{X_0} : X_0\#\$X^{'}\#Z; out, here)$,
  $(d_B : \#Y_BY\$Z^{'}\#; here, out)$, $(d_1 : X\#\$\#Z^{'}; out, out)$.
- $A_2 = \{ZY_i, X_{i-1}Z, XZ, ZY \mid 1 \leq i \leq (n+m)\}$;
- R_2 contains the following rules:
  $(d_{u_i^{'''}} : \#Y_{u_i^{'}}^{'}Y_{u_i^{''}}^{''}Y\$Z\#Y_i; out, here)$ if $|u_i| = 2$ and $u_i = u_i^{'}u_i^{''}, |u_i^{'}| = 1, |u_i^{''}| = 1, 1 \leq i \leq m$.
  $(d_{u_i^{''}} : \theta\#Y_{u_i}Y\$Z\#Y_i; out, here)$ if $\theta \in \{B\} \cup \{Y_t \mid t \in T\}, |u_i| = 1, 1 \leq i \leq m$.
  $(d_{u_i^{'}} : \#Y_{u_i}Y\$Z\#Y_i; out, here), (m+1) \leq i \leq (m+n)$,
  $(d_{X_i} : X_i\#\$X_{i-1}\#Z; here, out), 1 \leq i \leq n+m$.
  $(d_{X^{'}} : X^{'}\#\$X\#Z; here, out), (d_{Y^{'}} : \#Y^{'}\$Z\#Y; out, here)$.
- $Lab = \{d_{v_i} \mid |v_i| = 2, u_i \rightarrow v_i \in P\} \cup \{d_{v_i^{'''}} \mid |v_i| = 1, u_i \rightarrow v_i \in P\} \cup \{d_{v_i^{'}} \mid |v_i| = 0, u_i \rightarrow v_i \in P\} \cup \{d_{v_i^{''}} \mid (m+1) \leq i \leq (m+n)\} \cup \{d_{u_i^{'''}} \mid |u_i| = 2, u_i \rightarrow v_i \in P\} \cup \{d_{u_i^{''}} \mid |u_i| = 2, u_i \rightarrow v_i \in P\} \cup \{d_{u_i} \mid (m+1) \leq i \leq (m+n)\} \cup \{d_{Y_i} \mid 1 \leq i \leq (m+n)\} \cup \{d_{Y_0}, d_B, d_1\} \cup \{d_{X_i} \mid 1 \leq i \leq n+m\} \cup \{d_{X^{'}}, d_{Y^{'}}\}$.

Now, we construct the morphism $h : (Lab)^* \rightarrow T^*$ such that

$h(d_{v_i}) = \lambda$, if $|v_i| = 2, u_i \rightarrow v_i \in P, 1 \leq i \leq m$;
$h(d_{v_i^{'''}}) = \lambda$, if $|v_i| = 1, u_i \rightarrow v_i \in P, 1 \leq i \leq m$;
$h(d_{v_i^{'}}) = \lambda$, if $|v_i| = 0, u_i \rightarrow v_i \in P, 1 \leq i \leq m$;
$h(d_{v_i^{''}}) = \lambda$, if $(m+1) \leq i \leq (m+n)$;
$h(d_{Y_i}) = \lambda, (m+1) \leq i \leq (m+n)$; $h(d_B) = \lambda$; $h(d_1) = \lambda$;
$h(d_{u_i^{'''}}) = \lambda$, if $|u_i| = 2, u_i \rightarrow v_i \in P, 1 \leq i \leq m$;
$h(d_{u_i^{''}}) = v_i$, if $|u_i| = 1, u_i \rightarrow v_i \in P, 1 \leq i \leq m$;
$h(d_{u_i^{'}}) = \lambda$, if $(m+1) \leq i \leq (m+n)$;

$h(d_{v_i''}) = \lambda$, if $(m+1) \leq i \leq (m+n)$;
$h(d_{X_i}) = \lambda, (m+1) \leq i \leq (m+n); h(d_{X'}) = \lambda; h(d_{Y'}) = \lambda$.

The rules in the grammar G are in Kuroda normal form. Every element of $L(G)$ can be generated by application of the recursive rules $A \to BC, AB \to CD, A, B, C, D \in N$ in any manner and then by application of the terminal rules $A \to a, A \to \lambda, A \in N, a \in T$ in leftmost manner. Let $x \in L(G)$, if the splicing rules are applied in the same manner in which the rules of the grammar G are applied, then a string over the terminal alphabet of Π is generated and it is sent outside the membrane. If the labels of the applied splicing rules are concatenated, then homomorphic image of the string becomes x. Hence, $x \in h(SZLSPS_2(\Pi))$. This implies that, $L(G) \subseteq h(SZLSPS_2(\Pi))$. Also, if the rules in a grammar G are applied in the same sequence as in any terminal derivation of the splicing P system Π, then $h(SZLSPS_2(\Pi)) \subseteq L(G)$. Hence, $L(G) = h(SZLSPS_2(\Pi))$. So, we can conclude that each recursively enumerable language can be written as a homomorphic image of the Szilard language generated by a splicing P system of degree 2.

In a subsequent result, we show that if the rules in the membrane are applied in label restricted manner (i.e., CASE (B')), then recursively enumerable languages can be generated as control languages by the labelled splicing P systems with one membrane when λ labelled rules are allowed.

When the definition of labelled splicing system of CASE (A') is considered, then any context-free language can be written as a control language generated by a labelled splicing P system with one membrane and without λ labelled rules.

Theorem 6. $CF \subseteq RLSPS_1$.

Proof. Let L be any non-empty context-free language and $G = (N, T, P, S)$ be a context-free grammar in Greibach normal form such that $L = L(G)$. We construct a labelled splicing P system with one membrane, $\Pi = (V_1, T_1, [_1]_1, A_1, R_1, Lab)$, such that $L = L(G) = RLSPS_1(\Pi)$.

Let $\Pi = (V_1, T_1, [_1]_1, A_1, R_1, Lab)$ be a labelled splicing P system, where

- $V_1 = \{X, Y, Y_1\} \cup N \cup \Delta_1$, for $\Delta_1 = \{Y_a \mid A \to a\alpha, \alpha \in N^+, a \in T\} \cup \{Y_a \mid A \to a \in P, a \in T, , A \in N\}$;
- $T_1 = \{Y\} \cup \Delta_1$;
- $A_1 = \{XSY\} \cup \Delta_2 \cup \Delta_3$, where
  $\Delta_2 = \{Y_a \alpha Y_a \mid A \to a\alpha \in P, a \in T, \alpha \in N^+, A \in N\}$,
  $\Delta_3 = \{YY_a, Y_a Y_1 \mid A \to a \in P, a \in T, A \in N\}$,
- R_1 contains the following rules:

$$
\begin{array}{ll}
(a : Y\alpha\#Y_a\$XA\#Y; here, out), \quad \} & \\
(a : Y\alpha\#Y_a\$YA\#Y; here, out), \quad \} & \text{for } A \to a\alpha \in P \\
(a : Y\alpha\#Y_a\$YA\#\beta_1\beta_2\ldots\beta_iY; here, out) \} \ \beta_i \in N, 1 \leq i \leq (n-1) & \\
(a : Y\alpha\#Y_a\$YA\#\beta_1\beta_2\ldots\beta_n; here, out), \} & \beta_n \in N.
\end{array}
$$

$$(a : Y_a \# Y_1 \$ X A \# Y; out, out), \qquad \} \qquad \text{for } A \to a \in P$$
$$(a : Y \# Y_a \$ Y A \# \beta_1 \beta_2 \ldots \beta_i Y; here, out), \} \; \beta_i \in N, 1 \le i \le (n-1).$$
$$(a : Y \# Y_a \$ Y A \# \beta_1 \beta_2 \ldots \beta_n; here, out), \; \} \qquad \beta_n \in N;$$
$$(a : Y_a \# Y_1 \$ Y A \# Y; out, out), \qquad \}$$

where $n = Max\{|\alpha| \mid A \to a\alpha \in P\}$.

- $Lab = T$.

For each rule of the form $D \to a\alpha \in P$, the labelled splicing system Π contains "a" labelled rules, $(a : Y\alpha \# Y_a \$ X A \# Y; here, out)$, $(a : Y\alpha \# Y_a \$ Y A \# \beta_1 Y; here, out)$, $(a : Y\alpha \# Y_a \$ Y A \# \beta_1 \beta_2 Y; here, out)$, $(a : Y\alpha \# Y_a \$ Y A \# \beta_1 \beta_2 \beta_3 Y; here, out)$, $\ldots$, $(a : Y\alpha \# Y_a \$ Y A \# \beta_1 \beta_2 \ldots \beta_n; here, out)$. These labelled splicing rules can be applied to the pair of strings XAY, $Y\alpha Y_a$ and $YAQY$, $Y\alpha Y_a$, where $Q \in N^*, \alpha \in N^+$, respectively. At first $Y\alpha Y_a$ and XSY are spliced and $Y\alpha Y$ and XSY_a are produced and XSY_a is sent outside the membrane but $Y\alpha Y$ stays inside the membrane and can be spliced further with the rules present in the system.

If XSY and $Y_a Y_1$ are spliced together, it will produce XSY_1 and $Y_a Y$ and send outside the membrane. Strings of the form $YAQY$, $Q \in N^*, A \in N$ can be spliced with the strings $Y\alpha Y_a$ and YY_a to obtain YAY_a and $Y\alpha QY$ or YQY. After the application of the rule $(a : Y_a \# Y_1 \$ Y A \# Y)$ to YAY and $Y_a Y_1$, the strings YDY_1 and $Y_a Y$ are produced, which is a terminal string. Both the strings are sent outside the membrane and the labels of the applied rules are collected as output.

In the above construction, the labelled splicing P system Π simulates the rules of P in R. If the splicing rules in Π are applied in the same sequence as the rules are applied in the derivation $S \Rightarrow^* x$ for $x \in L(G)$, then a terminal string is sent outside the membrane at the same time when a terminal string is generated in G. Thus $x \in L(G)$ if and only if there exists a terminal derivation in Π such that the concatenation of the labels of the applied rules will generate x. Whenever the rules $A \to a\alpha, A \to a$ are applied to in G, the corresponding "a" labelled splicing rules are applied in the system Π and vice-versa. Thus $L(G) = RLSPS_1(\Pi)$.

Theorem 7. $RLSPS_{ter,1,\lambda} = RE$.

Proof. The inclusion $RLSPS_{ter,1,\lambda} \subseteq RE$ follows from the Church-Turing thesis. So, we prove the inclusion $RE \subseteq RLSPS_{ter,1,\lambda}$. Let $G = (N, T, P, S)$ be a grammar in Kuroda normal form. We construct a splicing P system $\Pi = (V_1, T_1, \mu, A_1, R_1, Lab)$ in the such a way that $RLSPS_{ter,1,\lambda}(\Pi) = L(G)$.

Let $\{Y_n \mid n \in N\} \cup \{Y_t \mid t \in T\} \cup \{Y_B\} = \{a_1, a_2, \ldots, a_n\}$, where $a_n = Y_B$ and $Y_B \notin \{Y_n \mid n \in N\} \cup \{Y_t \mid t \in T\}$.

- $V_1 = \{Y_n \mid n \in N\} \cup \{Y_t \mid t \in T\} \cup \{Y_B\} \cup \{X, Y, Y_\lambda, Z, Z_\lambda, Z', Z'', X_i, Y_i, X_j', Y_j', X_j'', Y_j'', X', Y', X'', Y''\}$, where $1 \le i \le n, 1 \le j \le (n-1), 2 \le k \le n$.
- $T_1 = \{Y_t \mid t \in T\} \cup \{X, Y\}$.
- $\mu = [_1]_1$.

- $A_1 = \{XY_BY_SY\}\cup\{ZY_i, ZY_j', ZY_j'', X'Z, X''Z, ZY, X_ia_iZ, X_j'Z, X_j''Z, ZY'',$
  $ZY', XZ\}\cup\{ZY_vY_j \mid u \to va_j \in P\}\cup\{Z'Y_\lambda, X'Z_\lambda, Z_\lambda Y_\lambda, Y_\lambda Z_\lambda, X_jZ_\lambda\}.$
- R_1 will contain the following rules:

For $a_i, a_i', \mathbf{a} \in \{Y_n \mid n \in N\}\cup\{Y_t \mid t \in T\}\cup\{Y_B\}$,

1. $(\lambda : \dfrac{\mathbf{a} \quad\mid\quad Y_uY}{Z \quad\mid\quad Y_vY_j}$; here, out$)(u \to va_j \in P)$

2. $(\lambda : \dfrac{\beta \quad\mid\quad a_iY_uY}{Z \quad\mid\quad Y_i}$; here, out$)(u \to \lambda \in P)$, $\beta \in X \cup Y_B$

3. $(a : \dfrac{\beta_1 \quad\mid\quad a_iY_uY}{Z \quad\mid\quad Y_i}$; here, out$)(u \to a \in P)$, $\beta_1 \in X \cup Y_B$

4. $(\lambda : \dfrac{a_i' \quad\mid\quad a_iY}{Z \quad\mid\quad Y_i}$; here, out$)$

5. (i) $(\lambda : \dfrac{\mathbf{a} \quad\mid\quad Y_k}{Z \quad\mid\quad Y_{k-1}'}$; here, out$)$ 5. (ii) $(\lambda : \dfrac{\mathbf{a} \quad\mid\quad Y_j'}{Z \quad\mid\quad Y_j''}$; here, out$)$

6. (i) $(\lambda : \dfrac{X_1 \quad\mid\quad \mathbf{a}}{X' \quad\mid\quad Z}$; out, here$)$ 6. (ii) $(\lambda : \dfrac{\mathbf{a} \quad\mid\quad Y_j''}{Z \quad\mid\quad Y}$; here, out$)$

7. (i) $(\lambda : \dfrac{\epsilon \quad\mid\quad Y_BY''}{Z'' \quad\mid\quad \epsilon}$; here, out$)$ 7. (ii) $(\lambda : \dfrac{\mathbf{a} \quad\mid\quad Y_j''}{Z \quad\mid\quad Y_j}$; here, out$)$

8. (i) $(\lambda : \dfrac{X \quad\mid\quad \mathbf{a}}{X_ia_i \quad\mid\quad Z}$; out, here$)$ 8. (ii) $(\lambda : \dfrac{X_k \quad\mid\quad \mathbf{a}}{X_{k-1}' \quad\mid\quad Z}$; out, here$)$

9. (i) $(\lambda : \dfrac{X_j' \quad\mid\quad \mathbf{a}}{X_j'' \quad\mid\quad Z}$; out, here$)$ 9. (ii) $(\lambda : \dfrac{\mathbf{a} \quad\mid\quad Y_1}{Z \quad\mid\quad Y'}$; here, out$)$

10. (i) $(\lambda : \dfrac{\mathbf{a} \quad\mid\quad Y'}{Z \quad\mid\quad Y''}$; here, out$)$ 10. (ii) $(\lambda : \dfrac{X'' \quad\mid\quad \mathbf{a}}{X \quad\mid\quad Z}$; out, here$)$

11. (i) $(\lambda : \dfrac{X'' \quad\mid\quad \mathbf{a}}{\epsilon \quad\mid\quad Z'}$; out, out$)$ 11. (ii) $(\lambda : \dfrac{X_j'' \quad\mid\quad \mathbf{a}}{X_j \quad\mid\quad Z}$; out, here$)$

12. (i) $(\lambda : \dfrac{\mathbf{a} \quad\mid\quad Y_uY}{\mathbf{a} \quad\mid\quad Y_uY}$; out, out$)$ 12. (ii) $(\lambda : \dfrac{\epsilon \quad\mid\quad a_iY_uY}{\epsilon \quad\mid\quad a_iY_uY}$; out, out$)$

13. (i) $(\lambda : \dfrac{\epsilon \quad\mid\quad a_iY}{\epsilon \quad\mid\quad a_iY}$; out, out$)$ 13. (ii) $(\lambda : \dfrac{\mathbf{a} \quad\mid\quad Y_j'}{Z \quad\mid\quad Y_j''}$; out, out$)$

14. (i) $\left(\lambda : \dfrac{X_1 \mid a}{X_1 \mid a} ; \text{out, out}\right)$ 14. (ii) $\left(\lambda : \dfrac{X' \mid a}{X' \mid a} ; \text{out, out}\right)$

15. (i) $\left(\lambda : \dfrac{a \mid Y''}{a \mid Y''} ; \text{out, out}\right)$ 15. (ii) $\left(\lambda : \dfrac{a \mid Y_B Y''}{a \mid Y_B Y_{''}} ; \text{out, out}\right)$

16. (i) $\left(\lambda : \dfrac{a \mid Y''_j}{a \mid Y''_j} ; \text{out, out}\right)$ 16. (ii) $\left(\lambda : \dfrac{X \mid a}{X \mid a} ; \text{out, out}\right)$

17. (i) $\left(\lambda : \dfrac{X_k \mid a}{X_k \mid a} ; \text{out, out}\right)$ 17. (ii) $\left(\lambda : \dfrac{X'_j \mid a}{X'_j \mid a} ; \text{out, out}\right)$

18. (i) $\left(\lambda : \dfrac{a \mid Y_1}{a \mid Y_1} ; \text{out, out}\right)$ 18. (ii) $\left(\lambda : \dfrac{a \mid Y'}{a \mid Y'} ; \text{out, out}\right)$

19. (i) $\left(\lambda : \dfrac{X'' \mid a}{X'' \mid a} ; \text{out, out}\right)$ 19. (ii) $\left(\lambda : \dfrac{X''_j \mid a}{X''_j \mid a} ; \text{out, out}\right)$

20. (i) $\left(\lambda : \dfrac{\alpha \mid \epsilon}{\alpha \mid \epsilon} ; \text{out, out}\right)$ for all $\alpha \in A_1$

21. (i) $\left(\lambda : \dfrac{Z \mid vY_j}{Z' \mid Y_\lambda} ; \text{here, here}\right)$ 21. (ii) $\left(\lambda : \dfrac{Z \mid Y_i}{Z' \mid Y_\lambda} ; \text{here, here}\right)$

22. (i) $\left(\lambda : \dfrac{Z \mid Y'_{k-1}}{Z' \mid Y_\lambda} ; \text{here, here}\right)$ 22. (ii) $\left(\lambda : \dfrac{Z \mid Y''_j}{Z' \mid Y_\lambda} ; \text{here, here}\right)$

23. (i) $\left(\lambda : \dfrac{X' \mid Z}{X' \mid Z_\lambda} ; \text{here, here}\right)$ 23. (iii) $\left(\lambda : \dfrac{X'' \mid Z}{X' \mid Z_\lambda} ; \text{here, here}\right)$

24. (i) $\left(\lambda : \dfrac{Z \mid Y}{Z' \mid Y_\lambda} ; \text{here, here}\right)$ 24. (ii) $\left(\lambda : \dfrac{Z'' \mid \epsilon}{Z^\lambda \mid Y_\lambda} ; \text{here, here}\right)$

25. (i) $\left(\lambda : \dfrac{Z \mid Y_j}{Z' \mid Y_\lambda} ; \text{here, here}\right)$

26. (i) $\left(\lambda : \dfrac{X_i a_i \mid Z}{X' \mid Z_\lambda} ; \text{here, here}\right)$ 26. (ii) $\left(\lambda : \dfrac{X'_{k-1} \mid Z}{X' \mid Z_\lambda} ; \text{here, here}\right)$

27. (i) $\left(\lambda : \dfrac{X''_j \mid Z}{X' \mid Z_\lambda} ; \text{here, here}\right)$ 27. (ii) $\left(\lambda : \dfrac{Z \mid Y'}{Z' \mid Y_\lambda} ; \text{here, here}\right)$

$28.\ (i)\ \left(\lambda : \dfrac{Z \mid Y''}{Z' \mid Y_\lambda} ;\ \text{here, here}\right)$ $28.\ (ii)\ \left(\lambda : \dfrac{X' \mid Z}{X' \mid Z_\lambda} ;\ \text{here, here}\right)$

$29.\ (i)\ \left(\lambda : \dfrac{\epsilon \mid Z'}{Y_\lambda \mid Z_\lambda} ;\ \text{here, here}\right)$ $29.\ (ii)\ \left(\lambda : \dfrac{X_j \mid Z}{X_j \mid Z_\lambda} ;\ \text{here, here}\right)$

$30.\ (i)\ \left(\lambda : \dfrac{D_2 \mid \lambda}{Z_\lambda \mid Y_\lambda} ;\ \text{here, here}\right)$

$31.\ (i)\ \left(\lambda : \dfrac{X_i a_i \mid Z_\lambda}{X' \mid Z} ;\ \text{here, here}\right)$ $31.\ (ii)\ \left(\lambda : \dfrac{X'_{k-1} \mid Z_\lambda}{X' \mid Z} ;\ \text{here, here}\right)$

$32.\ (i)\ \left(\lambda : \dfrac{X''_j \mid Z_\lambda}{X' \mid Z} ;\ \text{here, here}\right)$ $32.\ (ii)\ \left(\lambda : \dfrac{Z \mid Y_\lambda}{Z' \mid Y'} ;\ \text{here, here}\right)$

$33.\ (i)\ \left(\lambda : \dfrac{Z \mid Y_\lambda}{Z' \mid Y''} ;\ \text{here, here}\right)$ $33.\ (ii)\ \left(\lambda : \dfrac{X \mid Z_\lambda}{X' \mid Z} ;\ \text{here, here}\right)$

$34.\ (i)\ \left(\lambda : \dfrac{\epsilon \mid Z_\lambda}{Y_\lambda \mid Z_l} ;\ \text{here, here}\right)$ $34.\ (ii)\ \left(\lambda : \dfrac{X_j \mid Z_\lambda}{X_j \mid Z} ;\ \text{here, here}\right)$

$35.\ (i)\ \left(\lambda : \dfrac{D_2 \mid Y_\lambda}{Z_\lambda \mid \lambda} ;\ \text{here, here}\right)$

$36.\ (i)\ \left(\lambda : \dfrac{Z \mid Y_\lambda}{Z' \mid vY_j} ;\ \text{here, here}\right)$ $36.\ (ii)\ \left(\lambda : \dfrac{Z \mid Y_\lambda}{Z' \mid Y'_{k-1}} ;\ \text{here, here}\right)$

$37.\ (i)\ \left(\lambda : \dfrac{Z \mid Y_\lambda}{Z' \mid Y''_j} ;\ \text{here, here}\right)$ $37.\ (ii)\ \left(\lambda : \dfrac{X' \mid Z_\lambda}{X' \mid Z} ;\ \text{here, here}\right)$

$38.\ (i)\ \left(\lambda : \dfrac{X'' \mid Z_\lambda}{X' \mid Z} ;\ \text{here, here}\right)$ $38.\ (ii)\ \left(\lambda : \dfrac{Z \mid Y_\lambda}{Z' \mid Y} ;\ \text{here, here}\right)$

$39.\ (i)\ \left(\lambda : \dfrac{Z'' \mid Y_\lambda}{Z_\lambda \mid \epsilon} ;\ \text{here, here}\right)$ $39.\ (ii)\ \left(\lambda : \dfrac{Z \mid Y_\lambda}{Z' \mid Y_j} ;\ \text{here, here}\right)$

At any time only the same labelled rules and λ labelled rules are applicable. When the λ labelled rule in (1) is applied, the rule (12)(i) and rule (20) also splice in parallel the strings which are spliced using the rule (1). Both the strings are sent outside the membrane using the rules in (12)(i) and (20). Also, other strings in the axiom is sent outside the membrane using the λ labelled rules in (20) at the same time. Again, at the same time the strings present in the axiom is transformed into different molecules using the λ labelled rules from (21) to (30). So, after application of λ labelled rule in (1), only a string of the form XwY where $w \in (\{Y_n \mid n \in N\} \cup \{Y_B\})^*$ and the transformed strings produced after application of the rules from (21) to (30) are present in the system. Other strings are sent outside the membrane and no copies of those strings remain inside the membrane. Hence, only the rules from (31) to (39) are applicable. The produced strings are the elements of the axiom A_1.

The same process happens when any of the rules from (2) to (11) are applied. When a terminal string is sent outside the system, the labels of the applied rules are concatenated and it belongs to $RLSPS_{ter,1,\lambda}(\Pi)$.

Since the rules of the grammar G is in Kuroda normal form, any element of G can be generated first by application of the recursive rules and then by applying the terminal rules in the left most manner. The labelled splicing P system with one membrane is constructed in such a way that, if the label of the transitions of a terminal derivation (i.e., when a terminal string is sent outside the system) is concatenated, then the generated string belongs to $L(G)$. Hence, $RLSPS_{ter,1,\lambda}(\Pi) \subseteq L(G)$.

If the labelled splicing rules simulating the rules in G are applied in the same sequence, then a terminal string is sent outside by the splicing P system at the same time when a terminal string is generated in G. Also, the concatenation of the labels of the transition generates the terminal string generated by the grammar G. Hence, $L(G) \subseteq RLSPS_{ter,1,\lambda}(\Pi)$.

5   Conclusions and Future Work

In this work we have generated the context-free and recursively enumerable language families using labelled splicing P systems with a small number (one or two) of membranes, improving a number of results in [8]. It will be interesting to look at controlled splicing P systems generating other families of languages such as the languages obtained by Lindenmayer systems [15] or the language families described by other control devices [2]. Circular words, capturing the feature of DNA molecules occurring in circular form, have been considered and circular splicing systems have been studied (see, for example, [6]). It will be of interest to consider splicing on circular words in the framework of P systems and make a corresponding study as done here. It will also be interesting to consider the idea of control languages in other kinds of P systems studied recently [10, 17–19, 21].

Acknowledgments. The authors are grateful to the reviewers for their very useful comments which helped to improve the presentation. The second author acknowledges University Grants Commission for the financial support. The work was supported by National Natural Science Foundation of China (61320106005, 61602192, and 61772214), China Postdoctoral Science Foundation (2016M600592, 2017T100554), and the Innovating Scientists and Technicians Troop Construction Projects of Henan Province (154200510012).

References

1. Alhazov, A., Rogozhin, Y., Verlan, S.: On small universal splicing systems. Int. J. Found. Comput. Sci. **23**(7), 1423–1438 (2012)
2. Dassow, J., Păun, G.: Regulated Rewriting in Formal Language Theory. Springer, Heidelberg (1989)
3. Freund, F., Freund, R., Oswald, M.: Splicing test tube systems and their relation to splicing membrane systems. In: Jonoska, N., Păun, G., Rozenberg, G. (eds.) Aspects of Molecular Computing. LNCS, vol. 2950, pp. 139–151. Springer, Heidelberg (2003). https://doi.org/10.1007/978-3-540-24635-0_10
4. Freund, R., Kari, L., Păun, G.: DNA computing based on splicing: the existence of universal computers. Theor. Comput. Syst. **32**, 69–112 (1999)
5. Head, T.: Formal language theory and DNA: an analysis of the generative capacity of specific recombinant behaviours. B. Math. Biol. **49**, 737–759 (1987)
6. Head, T., Păun, G., Pixton, D.: Language theory and molecular genetics: generative mechanisms suggested by DNA recombination. In: Rozenberg, G., Salomaa, A. (eds.) Handbook of Formal Languages, vol. 2, pp. 295–360. Springer, Heidelberg (1996). https://doi.org/10.1007/978-3-662-07675-0_7
7. Krithivasan, K., Păun, G., Ramanujan, A.: On controlled P systems. Fundam. Inf. **131**(3–4), 451–464 (2014)
8. Mahalingam, K., Paul, P., Rama, R.: Chomsky control on splicing P system. In: Proceedings of the 4th Asian Conference on Membrane Computing, Hefei, China (2015)
9. Mitrana, V., Petre, I., Rogojin, V.: Accepting splicing systems. Theor. Comput. Sci. **411**, 2414–2422 (2010)
10. Pan, L., Păun, G., Zhang, G., Neri, F.: Spiking neural P systems with communication on request. Int. J. Neural Syst. https://doi.org/10.1142/S0129065717500423
11. Păun, G.: Computing with membranes. J. Comput. Syst. Sci. **61**(1), 108–143 (2000)
12. Păun, G., Rozenberg, G., Salomaa, A.: DNA Computing: New Computing Paradigms. Springer, Heidelberg (1998)
13. Păun, G., Rozenberg, G., Salomaa, A. (eds.): The Oxford Handbook of Membrane Computing. Oxford University Press, New York (2010)
14. Ramanujan, A., Krithivasan, K.: Control words of transition P systems. In: Bansal, J.C., Singh, P.K., Deep, K., Pant, M., Nagar, A.K. (eds.) BIC-TA 2012. AISC, vol. 201, pp. 145–155. Springer, Heidelberg (2013). https://doi.org/10.1007/978-81-322-1038-2_13
15. Rozenberg, G., Salomaa, A. (eds.): Handbook of Formal Languages (3 Volumes). Springer, Heidelberg (1997)
16. Verlan, S., Margenstern, M.: About splicing P systems with one membrane. Fundam. Inf. **65**(3), 279–290 (2005)
17. Wu, T., Zhang, Z., Păun, G., Pan, L.: Cell-like spiking neural P systems. Theor. Comput. Sci. **623**, 180–189 (2016)
18. Song, T., Gong, F., Liu, X., Zhao, Y., Zhang, X.: Spiking neural P systems with white hole neurons. IEEE Trans. NanoBiosci. **15**(7), 666–673 (2016)
19. Song, T., Pan, L.: Spiking neural P systems with rules on synapses working in maximum spikes consumption strategy. IEEE Trans. NanoBiosci. **14**(1), 37–43 (2015)
20. Zhang, X., Liu, Y., Luo, B., Pan, L.: Computational power of tissue P systems for generating control languages. Inf. Sci. **278**, 285–297 (2014)
21. Zhang, X., Pan, L., Păun, A.: On universality of axon P systems. IEEE Trans. Neural. Netw. Learn. **26**(11), 2816–2829 (2015)

Adaptive Cauchy Differential Evolution with Strategy Adaptation and Its Application to Training Large-Scale Artificial Neural Networks

Tae Jong Choi[1] and Chang Wook Ahn[2(✉)]

[1] Department of Computer Engineering, Sungkyunkwan University,
2066, Seobu-ro, Jangan-gu, Suwon-si, Gyeonggi-do, Republic of Korea
gry17@skku.edu
[2] School of Electrical Engineering and Computer Science,
Gwangju Institute of Science and Technology (GIST),
123 Cheomdangwagi-ro, Buk-gu, Gwangju 61005, Republic of Korea
cwan@gist.ac.kr

Abstract. Artificial neural networks are a computational system, and usually, backpropagation algorithm is used for learning a task, because of its simplicity. However, backpropagation algorithm is likely to converge to a local minimum or saddle point, so that a global minimum may not be found. Differential Evolution (DE) is a simple yet powerful global optimization algorithm for solving multi-dimensional continuous functions. In this paper, we propose a new DE algorithm by combining two excellent DE algorithms, Adaptive Cauchy DE (ACDE) and Self-adaptive DE (SaDE). ACDE shows promising performance by using the Cauchy distribution based on control parameter adaptation. However, ACDE uses only one mutation strategy. SaDE adapts mutation strategies automatically, which shows its effectiveness. Therefore, we extend ACDE with the strategy adaptation of SaDE for enhancing the global optimization performance. The result indicates that the extended ACDE performs better than standard DE not only on conventional benchmark problems but also for training neural networks.

Keywords: Differential evolution algorithm · Adaptive strategy control · Adaptive parameter control · Artificial neural networks

1 Introduction

Artificial neural networks are a computational system, which is inspired by the process of human brain. This computational system has a learning ability, that is, it can master a task by given training data. For example, a neural network that learned human voice can classify sound whether it is human voice or not. Also, artificial neural networks have been applied to a verity of practical problems such as image classification, text translation, and time series forecasting.

© Springer Nature Singapore Pte Ltd. 2017
C. He et al. (Eds.): BIC-TA 2017, CCIS 791, pp. 502–510, 2017.
https://doi.org/10.1007/978-981-10-7179-9_39

A multilayer neural network has more than one hidden layers, and it uses backpropagation algorithm for learning a task. Backpropagation algorithm tunes the weights of each neuron by propagating error from the output layer to the hidden layers. In other words, the weights of each neuron are adjusted based on how much the neuron contributes the total error of the neural network. And usually, a gradient descent method is used for this purpose, because of its simplicity. However, a gradient descent method is likely to converge to a local minimum or saddle point, so that a global minimum may not be found.

Differential Evolution (DE) is a simple yet powerful global optimization algorithm for solving multi-dimensional continuous functions [1,2]. Recently, researches related to neural network training using DE algorithm are increasing [3–7]. In this paper, we propose a new DE algorithm by combining two excellent DE algorithms, Adaptive Cauchy DE (ACDE) [8] and Self-adaptive DE (SaDE) [9]. ACDE shows promising performance by using the Cauchy distribution based control parameter adaptation. However, ACDE uses only one mutation strategy, DE/rand/1/bin, there is, therefore, room for improvement. Similar to ACDE, SaDE shows promising performance by adapting mutation strategies. We extend ACDE with the strategy adaptation of SADE, called ACDEwSA, for enhancing the global optimization performance. We compared ACDEwSA with standard DE on conventional benchmark problems. The result indicates that ACDEwSA performs better than standard DE on not only unimodal benchmark problems but also multimodal benchmark problems. Also, we applied ACDEwSA to train neural networks and compared it with standard DE. In view of numerical optimization, some state-of-the-art evolutionary algorithms can be found in [10–14]. Also, in view of large-scale optimization, some state-of-the-art training artificial neural networks can be found in [15–17].

This paper is organized as follows. In Sect. 2, we introduce the evolutionary procedures of standard DE. In Sect. 3, we explain ACDEwSA in detail. In Sect. 4, we present and discuss the experimental results. In Sect. 5, we conclude this paper.

2   Differential Evolution

In this section, we explain the evolutionary procedures of standard DE (DE/rand/1/bin). The population of standard DE is composed of NP individuals, and each individual is consisted of D-dimensional vector. An ith individual is represented by $X_{i,G} = \{x_{i,1,G}, \ldots, x_{i,D,G}\}$. In initialization phase, the minimum bound ($X_{min} = \{x_{min,1}, \ldots, x_{min,D}\}$) and maximum bound ($X_{max} = \{x_{max,1}, \ldots, x_{max,D}\}$) of a problem are initialized. After that, each individual is initialized as follow:

$$x_{i,j,0} = x_{min,j} + rand_{i,j} \cdot (x_{max,j} - x_{min,j}) \tag{1}$$

Standard DE has three evolutionary operators, mutation, crossover, and selection. The mutation operator is the first phase for generating a child individual. In this operator, a mutant vector is created based on three donor individuals.

A mutant vector that is represented by $V_{i,G} = \{v_{i,1,G}, \ldots, v_{i,D,G}\}$ is calculated as follow:

$$V_{i,G} = X_{r_1,G} + F \cdot (X_{r_2,G} - X_{r_3,G}) \qquad (2)$$

Here, $X_{r_1,G}$, $X_{r_2,G}$, and $X_{r_3,G}$ represent the donor individuals, which are randomly selected from the population, and F represents the scaling factor. The crossover operator is the second phase for generating a child individual. A trial vector that is represented by $U_{i,G} = \{u_{i,1,G}, \ldots, u_{i,D,G}\}$ is calculated as follow:

$$u_{i,j,G} = \begin{cases} v_{i,j,G} & \text{if } rand_{i,j} \leq CR \text{ or } j = j_{rand} \\ x_{i,j,G} & \text{otherwise} \end{cases} \qquad (3)$$

Here, CR represents the crossover rate. The selection operator is the last operator. This operation determines which of the two individuals, the parent and child individuals, to include as the next generation individual. Selection is based on comparing two individuals, the parent individual and the child individual. If the value of the target vector's fitness is better than the value of the trial vector's fitness, the parent individual will be maintained in the population at next generation and the child individual will be eliminated. Otherwise, the parent individual will be replaced with the child individual. The next generation individual is selected as follow:

$$X_{i,G+1} = \begin{cases} U_{i,G} & \text{if } f(U_{i,G}) \leq f(X_{i,G}) \\ X_{i,G} & \text{otherwise.} \end{cases} \qquad (4)$$

Standard DE executes these three operators until satisfying one of the termination conditions.

3   The Proposed Algorithm

DE algorithm has three control parameters, scaling factor, crossover rate, and population size, and it also has many mutation strategies. Applying a proper mutation strategy and control parameter values result in a significant impact on the performance. Thus, to achieve a better result, it is required to find an appropriate strategy and parameter values. However, the trial-and-error method is ineffective because it requires plenty of computational resources.

To replace the trial-and-error method, adaptive and self-adaptive methods are devised. Self-adaptive DE (SaDE) is one of them. To find a proper mutation strategy, SaDE maintains the success and failure memories. SaDE monitors the results of the selection operator in every generation and stores them in the memories. After that, in every predefined generation, SaDE adapts the strategy probability based on the accumulated information of the memories. SaDE shows not only the effectiveness of the strategy adaptation but also performs better than the compared DE algorithms.

In this section, we explain the extended ACDE, called ACDEwSA. First, we present which mutation strategies are used in ACDEwSA. We selected two mutation strategies, DE/rand/1/bin and DE/target-to-best/2/bin, for the strategy pool. The reason that we applied these mutation strategies was maintaining a balance between the exploration and the exploitation properties. DE/rand/1/bin has good properties in solving multimodal problems, and DE/target-to-best/2/bin well solve unimodal problems. It is possible that to accelerate the exploitation property, we could apply DE/best/1/bin or DE/current-to-best/1/bin instead of DE/target-to-best/2/bin. However, DE/best/1/bin or DE/current-to-best/1/bin likely to converge to a local minimum. Therefore, to prevent the premature convergence, we used DE/target-to-best/2/bin.

Second, we present how to perform the strategy adaptation in ACDEwSA. Similar to SaDE, ACDEwSA maintains the success and failure memories, and monitors the results of the selection operator in every generation and stores them in the memories. After that, in every predefined generation, ACDEwSA adapts the strategy probability based on the accumulated information of the memories. Therefore, we simply applied the strategy adaptation of SaDE to ACDE as follow:

$$p_{k,G} = \frac{s_{k,G}}{\sum_{i=1}^{K} s_{k,G}} \tag{5}$$

$$s_{k,G} = \frac{\sum_{g=G-LP}^{G-1} ns_{k,G}}{\sum_{g=G-LP}^{G-1} ns_{k,G} + \sum_{g=G-LP}^{G-1} nf_{k,G}} \tag{6}$$

Here, in Eq. 5, $p_{k,G}$ represents the probability of choosing the Kth strategy, and $S_{k,G}$ represents the success rate when Kth strategy is chosen. In Eq. 6, $ns_{k,G}$ represents the number of successfully evolved child individuals generated by the Kth strategy, and $nf_{k,G}$ represents the number of unsuccessfully evolved individuals generated by the Kth strategy. Thus, the strategy adaptation in ACDEwSA is same with the strategy adaptation in SaDE.

Third, we present how to perform the control parameter adaptation in ACDE wSA. In [8], it is verified that applying a long-tailed distribution to the arithmetic mean of a set of successfully evolved individuals' control parameter values at last generation performs better than applying a short-tailed distribution through several experiments. The control parameter adaptation of ACDE performs as follow:

$$F_{i,G} = F_{avg,G-1} + randc_i(0, 0.1) \tag{7}$$

$$CR_{i,G} = CR_{avg,G-1} + randc_i(0, 0.1) \tag{8}$$

Here, $F_{i,G}$ and $CR_{i,G}$ represent the control parameter values of ith individual at generation G and $F_{avg,G-1}$ and $CR_{avg,G-1}$ represent the arithmetic mean of a set of successfully evolved individual's control parameter values. $randc_i(0, 0.1)$ represents the Cauchy distribution with the scale parameter 0.1. To update $F_{i,G}$ and $CR_{i,G}$, ACDE uses the success and the failure memories of control parameters. In ACDEwSA, we applied two mutation strategies. We assumed that each mutation strategy is differently affected by the same value. Therefore, we modified the control parameter adaptation of ACDE by augmenting the control parameters and the success and the failure memories. The control parameter adaptation of ACDEwSA performs as follow:

$$F_{i,k,G} = F_{avg,k,G-1} + randc_{i,k}(0, 0.1) \tag{9}$$

$$CR_{i,k,G} = CR_{avg,k,G-1} + randc_{i,k}(0, 0.1) \tag{10}$$

Here, $F_{i,k,G}$ and $CR_{i,k,G}$ represent the control parameter values of Kth strategy of ith individual at generation G and $F_{avg,k,G-1}$ and $CR_{avg,k,G-1}$ represent the arithmetic mean of a set of successfully evolved individuals' control parameter values of Kth strategy. This extension allows to allocate appropriate control parameter values for each mutation strategy, thus effectively combining ACDE and SaDE.

4   Performance Evaluation

4.1   Conventional Benchmark Problems

We compared ACDEwSA with standard DE on conventional benchmark problems [18]. The conventional benchmark problems are listed in Table 1. In this table, search spaces represent the minimum and maximum bounds of a problem. The compared DE algorithms are described as follows:

Table 1. Conventional Benchmark Problems

F	D	S	F_{min}
$F_1(x) = \sum_{i=1}^{D} x_i^2$	30, 100	$[-100, 100]^D$	0
$F_2(x) = \sum_{i=1}^{D} |x_i| + \prod_{i=1}^{D} |x_i|$	30, 100	$[-10, 10]^D$	0
$F_3(x) = \sum_{i=1}^{D} (\sum_{j=1}^{i} x_j)^2$	30, 100	$[-100, 100]^D$	0
$F_4(x) = max_i(|x_i|, 1 \leq i \leq D)$	30, 100	$[-100, 100]^D$	0
$F_5(x) = \sum_{i=1}^{D-1} [100(x_{i+1} - x_i^2)^2 + (x_i - 1)^2]$	30, 100	$[-30, 30]^D$	0
$F_6(x) = \sum_{i=1}^{D} (\lfloor x_i + 0.5 \rfloor)^2$	30, 100	$[-100, 100]^D$	0
$F_7(x) = \sum_{i=1}^{D} ix_i^4 + random[0, 1)$	30, 100	$[-1.28, 1.28]^D$	0
$F_8(x) = \sum_{i=1}^{D} -x_i sin(\sqrt{|x_i|}) + 4.1898288727243369 \cdot D$	30, 100	$[-500, 500]^D$	0
$F_9(x) = \sum_{i=1}^{D} [x_i^2 - 10cos(2\pi x_i) + 10]$	30, 100	$[-5.12, 5.12]^D$	0
$F_{10}(x) = -20exp(-0.2\sqrt{\frac{1}{D} \sum_{i=1}^{D} x_i^2}) - exp(\frac{1}{D} \sum_{i=1}^{D} cos2\pi x_i)$ $+ 20 + exp(1)$	30, 100	$[-32, 32]^D$	0
$F_{11}(x) = \frac{1}{4000} \sum_{i=1}^{D} x_i^2 - \prod_{i=1}^{D} cos(\frac{x_i}{\sqrt{i}}) + 1$	30, 100	$[-600, 600]^D$	0
$F_{12}(x) = \frac{\pi}{D} \{10sin^2(\pi y_1) + \sum_{i=1}^{D-1} (y_i - 1)^2[1 + 10sin^2(\pi y_{i+1})]$ $+ (y_D - 1)^2\} + \sum_{i=1}^{D} u(x_i, 10, 100, 4)$ $y_i = 1 + \frac{1}{4}(x_i + 1)$ $u(x_i, a, k, m) = \begin{cases} k(x_i - a)^m & , x_i > a \\ 0 & , -a \leq x_i \leq a \\ k(-x_i - a)^m & , x_i < -a \end{cases}$	30, 100	$[-50, 50]^D$	0
$F_{13}(x) = 0.1\{sin^2(3\pi x_1) + \sum_{i=1}^{D-1} (x_i - 1)^2[1 + sin^2(3\pi x_{i+1})]$ $+ (x_D - 1)^2[1 + sin^2(2\pi x_D)]\} + \sum_{i=1}^{D} u(x_i, 5, 100, 4)$	30, 100	$[-50, 50]^D$	0

(1) ACDEwSA;
(2) Standard DE with F = 0.5 and CR = 0.9;

In the experiments, the population size NP was set by 100 in $D = 30$ and 400 in $D = 100$. The every control parameter values used in the experiments were the recommend control parameter values in their papers. The maximum number of generations in $D = 30$ was assigned by 1500 for F_1, F_6, F_{10}, F_{12}, and F_{13}, 2000 for F_2 and F_{11}, 5000 for F_3, F_4, and F_9, 20000 for F_5, 3000 for F_7, 9000 for F_8. The maximum number of generations in $D = 100$ was assigned by 2000 for F_1, 3000 for F_2, F_{10}, F_{11}, F_{12}, and F_{13}, 8000 for F_3, 15000 for F_4, 20000 for F_5, 1500 for F_6, 6000 for F_7, 9000 for F_8 and F_9. All experiment results were gathered by independently running 50 times. To be clear, the best result on each problem was marked in boldface.

The average error (Mean) and its standard deviation (Std. Dev.) of the experiments collected by ACDEwSA and standard DE for F_1–F_{13} for $D = 30$ and $D = 100$ are described in Tables 2 and 3. In D = 30 experiments, ACDEwSA performed better than standard DE in not only the unimodal benchmark problems but also the multimodal problems except F_5 and F_{11} benchmark problems. Standard DE showed the best performance in F_5 and F_{11} benchmark problem. Although ACDEwSA used not only the control parameter adaptation but also the strategy adaptation, standard DE showed better results than ACDEwSA in some benchmark problems. This implies that the best configuration is better than adaptive and self-adaptive methods. We can observe similar results in D = 100 experiments. In D = 100 experiments, ACDEwSA performed better than standard DE in all the benchmark problems.

Table 2. The experimental results, $D = 30$

		F_1	F_2	F_3	F_4	F_5	F_6	F_7
ACDEwSA	Mean	**2.73E-45**	**3.62E-33**	**1.88E-16**	**1.67E-03**	7.98E-01	0.00E+00	**2.02E-03**
	Std. Dev.	**7.70E-45**	**2.09E-33**	**3.88E-16**	**9.17E-03**	1.60E+00	0.00E+00	**6.68E-04**
Standard DE	Mean	7.59E-14	2.18E-10	3.85E-11	1.26E-01	**7.98E-02**	0.00E+00	4.58E-03
	Std. Dev.	5.56E-14	1.18E-10	4.25E-11	3.16E-01	**5.59E-01**	0.00E+00	1.06E-03

		F_8	F_9	F_{10}	F_{11}	F_{12}	F_{13}
ACDEwSA	Mean	**2.36E-11**	0.00E+00	**3.11E-15**	3.45E-04	**1.57E-32**	**1.35E-32**
	Std. Dev.	**0.00E+00**	0.00E+00	**7.89E-31**	1.71E-03	**1.64E-47**	**8.21E-48**
Standard DE	Mean	1.51E+03	6.76E+01	9.94E-11	**0.00E+00**	9.15E-15	4.00E-14
	Std. Dev.	5.47E+02	2.52E+01	5.06E-11	**0.00E+00**	8.37E-15	3.10E-14

4.2 Training Multilayer Perceptron

We compared ACDEwSA with standard DE on training neural networks. The compared DE algorithms are described as follows:

(1) ACDEwSA;
(2) Standard DE with F = 0.5 and CR = 0.9;

Table 3. The experimental results, $D = 100$

		F_1	F_2	F_3	F_4	F_5	F_6	F_7
ACDEwSA	Mean	**3.26E-21**	**7.26E-25**	**2.88E-05**	**3.42E+00**	**9.58E-01**	**2.00E-02**	**6.18E-03**
	Std. Dev.	2.79E-21	6.88E-25	3.35E-05	7.56E-01	1.70E+00	1.40E-01	1.32E-03
Standard DE	Mean	1.99E+01	4.78E-01	1.25E+05	9.36E+01	4.03E+01	2.13E+02	2.78E-02
	Std. Dev.	4.86E+00	7.65E-02	1.65E+04	1.70E+00	9.98E+00	4.31E+01	5.77E-03

		F_8	F_9	F_{10}	F_{11}	F_{12}	F_{13}
ACDEwSA	Mean	**2.91E-11**	**3.56E-17**	**5.88E-02**	**3.15E-03**	**6.22E-04**	**6.60E-04**
	Std. Dev.	1.94E-26	2.49E-16	2.33E-01	6.21E-03	4.35E-03	2.61E-03
Standard DE	Mean	2.91E+04	8.07E+02	1.99E+00	1.24E-01	3.27E-02	4.83E-01
	Std. Dev.	1.09E+03	2.25E+01	5.65E+00	4.12E-02	1.99E-02	1.84E-01

The datasets we used is Breast Cancer, Breast Cancer Wisconsin Diagnostic (WDBC), and Breast Cancer Wisconsin Prognostic (WPBC) [19]. The WDBC and WPBC datasets are divided into a total of 32 input features and two classes. And, the Breast-Cancer dataset is divided into a total of 9 input features and two classes. In WDBC dataset, there are 569 instances, of which 75% is used as training data and the remaining 25% is used as test data. In WPBC dataset, there are 198 instances, of which 75% is used as training data and the remaining 25% is used as test data. And, in Breast-Cancer dataset, there are 286 instances, of which 75% is used as training data and the remaining 25% is used as test data. In the experiments, the population size NP was set by 100. The every control parameter values used in the experiments were the recommend control parameter values in their papers. All experiment results were gathered by independently running 50 times. We used the following settings.

(1) Neural Network for WDBC and WPBC: [50, 50, 40, 40, 30, 30, 20, 20, 10, 10, 2]
(2) Neural Network for Breast-Cancer: [50, 50, 40, 40, 30, 30, 2]
(3) Maximum number of generations: 100

In the network structure of [50, 50, 40, 40, 30, 30, 20, 20, 10, 10, 2], each individual has approximately 11300 chromosomes including bias. In the network structure of [50, 50, 40, 40, 30, 30, 2], each individual has approximately 10000 chromosomes including bias. Therefore, the training multilayer perceptron problem can be considered as a large-scale optimization problem. Table 4 shows the experimental results. To be clear, the best result on each problem was marked in boldface. As we can see from the table, ACDEwSA performs better than standard DE in WDBC and Breast-Cancer. However, as can be seen from this result, the performance difference between ACDEwSA and standard DE is not huge compared to the conventional benchmark problems. Therefore, new models suitable for neural networks training are needed.

Table 4. The experimental results of the training of the multilayer perceptron

		Network Structure	Experimental Results	
			Mean	Std. Dev.
WDBC	ACDEwSA	[50, 50, 40, 40, 30, 30, 20, 20, 10, 10, 2]	**3.78.E-01**	**7.10.E-02**
	Standard DE		4.08.E-01	5.26.E-02
WPBC	ACDEwSA	[50, 50, 40, 40, 30, 30, 20, 20, 10, 10, 2]	3.47.E-01	3.67.E-05
	Standard DE		**2.04.E-01**	**6.30.E-05**
Breast-Cancer	ACDEwSA	[50, 50, 40, 40, 30, 30, 2]	**7.91.E-02**	**1.09.E-03**
	Standard DE		1.30.E-01	1.81.E-01

5   Conclusion

In this paper, we propose a new DE algorithm, called ACDEwSA, for training neural networks. ACDEwSA is a combination of ACDE and SaDE and has
proven to perform well in conventional benchmark problems. We conducted an
experiment to train neural networks using ACDEwSA. In our experiments we
used WDBC, WPBC, and Breast-Cancer datasets. Experimental results confirmed that ACDEwSA showed slightly better training performance compared
to standard DE, but confirmed that performance was not significantly different
from standard DE. We will consider a special type of DE algorithm for training
neural networks for future work.

Acknowledgement. This work was supported by the National Research Foundation of Korea (NRF) grant funded by the Korea government (MSIT) (No. NRF-
2017R1C1B2012752). In addition, this work was supported by the NRF grant funded
by MSIT (No. NRF-2015R1D1A1A02062017). Correspondence should be addressed to
Dr. Chang Wook Ahn; cwan@gist.ac.kr.

References

1. Storn, R., Price, K.: Differential evolution-a simple and efficient heuristic for global
   optimization over continuous spaces. J. Global Optim. **11**(4), 341–359 (1997)
2. Price, K., Storn, R.M., Lampinen, J.A.: Differential Evolution: A Practical Approach to Global Optimization. Springer Science & Business Media, New York
   (2006)
3. Ilonen, J., Kamarainen, J.-K., Lampinen, J.: Differential evolution training algorithm for feed-forward neural networks. Neural Process. Lett. **17**(1), 93–105 (2003)
4. Slowik, A., Bialko, M.: Training of artificial neural networks using differential evolution algorithm. In: 2008 Conference on Human System Interactions, pp. 60–65.
   IEEE (2008)
5. Wang, L., Zeng, Y., Chen, T.: Back propagation neural network with adaptive differential evolution algorithm for time series forecasting. Expert Syst. Appl. **42**(2),
   855–863 (2015)
6. Donate, J.P., Li, X., Sánchez, G.G., de Miguel, A.S.: Time series forecasting by
   evolving artificial neural networks with genetic algorithms, differential evolution
   and estimation of distribution algorithm. Neural Comput. Appl. **22**(1), 11–20
   (2013)

7. Piotrowski, A.P.: Differential evolution algorithms applied to neural network training suffer from stagnation. Appl. Soft Comput. **21**, 382–406 (2014)
8. Choi, T.J., Ahn, C.W., An, J.: An adaptive cauchy differential evolution algorithm for global numerical optimization. Sci. World J. **2013**, 1–12 (2013). https://doi.org/10.1155/2013/969734. Article no. 969734
9. Qin, A.K., Huang, V.L., Suganthan, P.N.: Differential evolution algorithm with strategy adaptation for global numerical optimization. IEEE Trans. Evol. Comput. **13**(2), 398–417 (2009)
10. Zhang, X., Tian, Y., Cheng, R., Jin, Y.: A decision variable clustering-based evolutionary algorithm for large-scale many-objective optimization. IEEE Trans. Evol. Comput. **PP**(99), 1 (2016)
11. Cheng, R., Jin, Y., Narukawa, K., Sendhoff, B.: A multiobjective evolutionary algorithm using gaussian process-based inverse modeling. IEEE Trans. Evol. Comput. **19**(6), 838–856 (2015)
12. Zhang, L., Pan, H., Su, Y., Zhang, X., Niu, Y.: A mixed representation-based multiobjective evolutionary algorithm for overlapping community detection. IEEE Trans. Cybern. **47**, 2703–2716 (2017)
13. Pan, L., He, C., Tian, Y., Su, Y., Zhang, X.: A region division based diversity maintaining approach for many-objective optimization. Integr. Comput. Aided Eng. **24**, 279–296 (2017)
14. He, C., Tian, Y., Jin, Y., Zhang, X., Pan, L.: A radial space division based evolutionary algorithm for many-objective optimization. Appl. Soft Comput. **61**, 603–621 (2017)
15. Ma, X., Liu, F., Qi, Y., Wang, X., Li, L., Jiao, L., Yin, M., Gong, M.: A multiobjective evolutionary algorithm based on decision variable analyses for multiobjective optimization problems with large-scale variables. IEEE Trans. Evol. Comput. **20**(2), 275–298 (2016)
16. Gong, M., Liu, J., Li, H., Cai, Q., Su, L.: A multiobjective sparse feature learning model for deep neural networks. IEEE Trans. Neural Netw. Learn. Syst. **26**(12), 3263–3277 (2015)
17. Cheng, R., Jin, Y.: A competitive swarm optimizer for large scale optimization. IEEE Trans. Cybern. **45**(2), 191–204 (2015)
18. Yao, X., Liu, Y., Lin, G.: Evolutionary programming made faster. IEEE Trans. Evol. Comput. **3**(2), 82–102 (1999)
19. Lichman, M.: UCI Machine Learning Repository. University of California, School of Information and Computer Science, Irvine, CA (2013). http://archive.ics.uci.edu/ml

Effect of Transfer Functions in Deep Belief Network for Short-Term Load Forecasting

Xiaoyu Zhang, Rui Wang(✉), Tao Zhang, Yajie Liu, and Yabin Zha

College of Information Systems and Management,
National University of Defense Technology,
Changsha 410073, People's Republic of China
ruiwangnudt@gmail.com

Abstract. Deep belief network (DBN) has become one of the most popular techniques for short-term load forecasting. The transfer functions play a vital role on the effective of DBN. In this study, different combinations of three commonly used transfer functions, i.e., logsig, purelin and tansig, in a DBN are examined. Experimental results show that a combination of purelin and tansig transfer functions produces the best load forecasting, and is therefore recommended to use.

Keywords: Short-term load forecast · Deep belief network · Logsig function · Tansig function · Purelin function

1 Introduction

Short-term load forecasting is an important part of load prediction, which plays a crucial role in operation of both traditional and deregulated power systems. Particularly in deregulated electricity market, short-term load forecasting is a useful tool for economic and reliable operation of power system. Many operating decisions are based on the load forecasting, such as dispatch scheduling of generating production, reliability and security analysis and maintenance plan for generators [1]. Therefore, short-term load forecasting is vital for the market players in competitive electricity market [2]. Improving the accuracy of short-term load forecasting can increase the appropriateness of planning and scheduling, and simultaneously, reduce operational costs of power systems.

In literature, there have been a variety of methods proposed for load forecasting [3]. The traditional forecasting methods include, for example, regression analysis method [4], Kalman filtering method [5], autoregressive integrated moving average method (ARIMA) [6], state space model [7], exponential soothing [8]. These methods are well-established. However, they are often criticized for

Y. Zha—This work was supported by the National Natural Science Foundation of China (Nos. 61403404, 61773390, 715711871371181) and the Distinguished Natural Science Foundation of Hunan Province (No. 2017JJ1001).

C. He et al. (Eds.): BIC-TA 2017, CCIS 791, pp. 511–522, 2017.
https://doi.org/10.1007/978-981-10-7179-9_40

their incapability of handling non-linear load time series. To overcome such draw-backs, intelligent algorithms, e.g., artificial neural network (ANN), Knowledge based expert system (KBES), have been proposed for load forecasting. These methods do not require any complex mathematical formulations or quantitative correlations between inputs and outputs. Effective utilization of intelligent algo-rithms in the context of illdefined processes (such as load time series), have led to their wide applications in Short-term sort of limitations. For example, the ANN learns well the load forecasting [9,10]. However, these methods also encounter training data, but it sometimes produces great forecast error in the test phase. Especially, it requires effective feature selection and input/output mapping pro-cedure. Also, the training procedure of a KBES model is often time-consuming [13,14].

Recently, deep learning has become increasingly popular in both academia and industry. Deep belief network (DBN) is one of the most popular deep learn-ing models. The deep belief network is a probabilistic generative model, the bottom layer is observable, and the multiple hidden layers are created by stack-ing multiple restricted Boltzmann machines (RBMs) on top of each other. Deep belief network has already been applied successfully to solve many problems [15]. Facts proved that deep belief network performs significantly better than feed-forward neural networks [16,17].

In this paper, several different transfer functions are examined. The best one is applied in the DBN model to perform short-term lad forecasting in a city of Britain. The remainder of the paper is organized as follows. In Sect. 2, Deep belief networks are introduced, and the improved methods of deep belief network model is proposed. In Sect. 3, a case is studied, and discussions are arranged. Finally in Sect. 4, the main conclusions and a discussion for future work are given.

2   Deep Belief Network

Deep belief network is a probabilistic generative model. The network structure of classical DBN is a deep neural network, which is composed of several layers of RBM and a layer of BP. As is known to all, the whole training of DBN contains two stages: pretraining and fine tuning. Figure 1 shows an example of a DBN structure with L hidden layers.

2.1   Pretraining

Pretraining is the process of initialization of network parameters, that is, the connection weights and bias between two layers. This process is obtained through an unsupervised greedy optimization algorithm of RBM.

A restricted Boltzmann machine (RBM) is composed of two different layers of units, with weighted connection between them. It consists of one layer of visi-ble nodes and one layer of hidden units. Figure 2 shows a typical RBM structure. Nodes in each layer have no connections between them, which are connected to all other units in another layer. Connections between nodes are bidirectional and

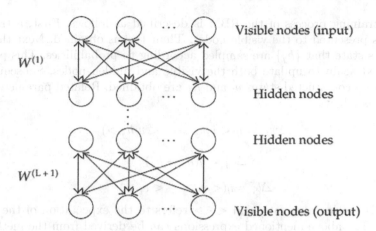

Fig. 1. A DBN structure with L hidden layers

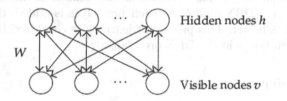

Fig. 2. Illustration of a typical RBM

symmetric. Restricted Boltzmann machines (RBMs) have been used as generative models of many different types of data [18]. Next take a one layer RBM as
an example: The RBM is an energy model. The energy function of the visible
layer and hidden layer is defined as:

$$E(v, h; \theta) = -\sum_{ij} w_{ij} v_i h_j - \sum_{i} b_i v_i - \sum_{j} w_j v_j \qquad (1)$$

where v_i and h_j represent the states of visible node i and hidden node j, respectively. w_{ij} is the connection weight between the visible layer and hidden layer.
a_j and b_i are the bias of node j and i, respectively. θ is a model parameter
$\theta = \{w, a, b\}$. For binary state nodes, that is, v_i and $h_j \in \{0, 1\}$, the state of h_j
is set to 1 under certain probability:

$$p_{h_j} = p(h_j = 1|v) = \sigma(b_i + \sum_{i} w_{ij} v_i) \qquad (2)$$

where $\sigma(x)$ is the logistic sigmoid function $1/(1 + exp(-x))$. After the binary
states are set for the hidden units, the state of v_i is set to 1 with a certain
probability:

$$p_{v_i} = p(v_i = 1|h) = \sigma(a_j + \sum_{j} w_{ij} h_j) \qquad (3)$$

The training process of the RBM is described as follows. First, a training sample is presented to the visible nodes. Than $\{v_i\}$ is obtained. Next the hidden nodes state that $\{h_j\}$ are sampled according to probabilities. This process is repeated again to update both the visible and hidden nodes. Subsequently, the one-step constructed states v_i' and h_j' are obtained. Related parameters are updated as follows:

$$\Delta w_{ij} = \eta(< v_i h_j > - < v_i' h_j' >) \tag{4}$$

$$\Delta a_j = \eta(h_j - h_j') \tag{5}$$

$$\Delta b_i = \eta(< v_i > - < v_i' >) \tag{6}$$

where η is the learning rate, and $< \cdot >$ refers to the expectation of the training data. The above-mentioned expressions can be derived from the method of Contrastive Divergence (CD) which has been demonstrated as effective.

We train sequentially as many RBMs as the number of hidden layers in the DBN to construct a DBN model. As each new layer is added, the overall generative model gets better. This process of learning is continued till a prescribed number of hidden layers in the DBN are trained.

2.2   Fine Tuning

After pretraining, each layer of DBN obtains their initial parameters. Then the DBN starts fine tune the whole structure. Based on the loss function of the actual data and predicted data, the gradient descent (GD) algorithm is applied to adjust the network parameters. The loss function is defined as follows:

$$L(x, x') = \|x - x'\|_2^2 \tag{7}$$

where x is denoted as the actual data, and x' is the predicted data.

2.3   The Transfer Functions

A variety of transfer functions are available for BP networks. The input values of the log-sigmoid function can be any value between 0 and 1; The input values of the tan-sigmoid function may take any value, and its output values range from -1 to 1; The input and output values of the linear transfer function may take any value. The BP network usually has one or more of the hidden layers; the input layer of neurons usually takes sigmoid transfer function. The output layer of neurons usually adopts purelin transfer function. The above transfer functions are illustrated in Fig. 3.

However, it is observed that an individual use of the transfer function does not always produces satisfied predication results. This study proposes to examine several different combinations of the above transfer functions. Specifically, the considered combinations of transfer functions are logsig-logsig; logsig-purelin; logsig-tansig; tansig-purelin; tansig-logsig; tansig-tansig; purelin-purelin; purelin-logsig; purelin-tansig.

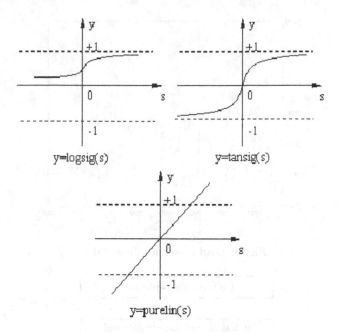

Fig. 3. Three different transfer functions

3   Case Study

The hourly load data of a region in the UK is employed to examine the forecasting effect of the models. The historical load data from June to September 2014 is selected as the training sample. The load output for the next seven days is chosen as test samples. After a preliminary experimental study, a good setting of the training sample is obtained, that is, load data of every three days is used as the inputs. The load data of the fourth day is set as the target data. Figure 4 shows an example of load power for June 2014.

3.1   Experiment Description

After several tests, the DBN model with one hidden layer is selected in this paper. The main steps of load prediction are shown in Fig. 5.

The forecast accuracy is measured by the mean squared error (MSE), which is defined as follows:

$$MSE = \frac{1}{N} \sum_{i=1}^{N} (X(i) - X'(i))^2 \tag{8}$$

where N is the forecast horizon, $X(i)$ is the actual load of day, and $X'(i)$ is the load forecast of day i.

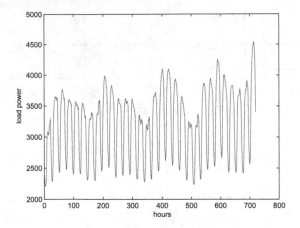

Fig. 4. Load power for June 2014

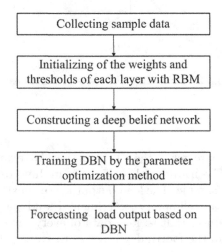

Fig. 5. Illustration of the load forecast steps

3.2   Results

Different combinations of transfer functions are applied to train the DBN model. All experimental results (load forecast) are shown in Tables 1 and 2. Furthermore Figs. 6, 7, 8, 9, 10, 11, 12, 13 and 14 intuitively provide the true load as well as the predicated load using different combinations of transfer functions.

Tables 1 and 2 shows the comparison result of the seven days. Among them, the MSE of DBN with the purelin-tansig function combination is the minimum, i.e., 8.221e-04. The mean absolute error with logsig-logsig function combination is 0.006.

Table 1. Comparison of testing performance

Method	log-log	log-pure	log-tan	tan-pure	tan-log
Epochs	112	79	152	135	163
MSE	0.0060	0.0058	0.0018	8.4634e-04	0.0015

Table 2. Comparison of testing performance

Method	tan-tan	pure-pure	pure-log	pure-tan
Epochs	137	130	152	131
MSE	0.0010	9.0869e-04	0.0022	8.2210e-04

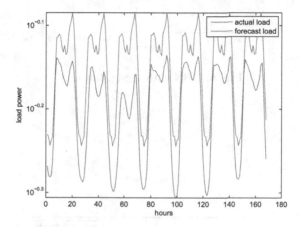

Fig. 6. DBN with logsig, logsig

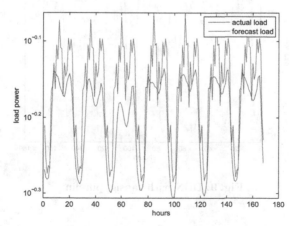

Fig. 7. DBN with logsig, purelin

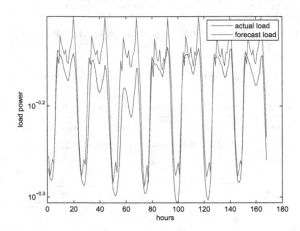

Fig. 8. DBN with logsig, tansig

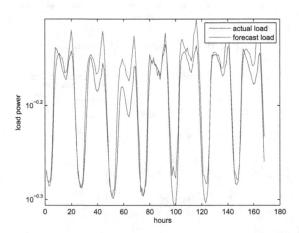

Fig. 9. DBN with tansig, purelin

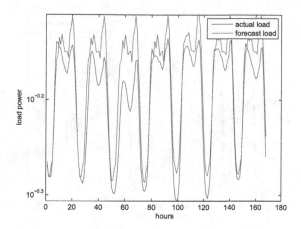

Fig. 10. DBN with tansig, logsig

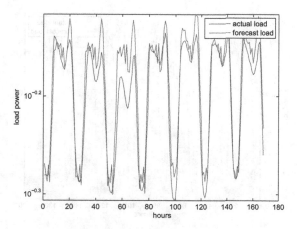

Fig. 11. DBN with tansig, tansig

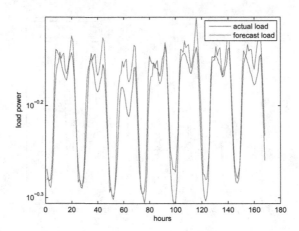

Fig. 12. DBN with purelin, purelin

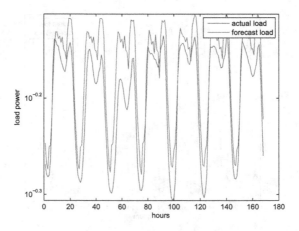

Fig. 13. DBN with purelin, logsig

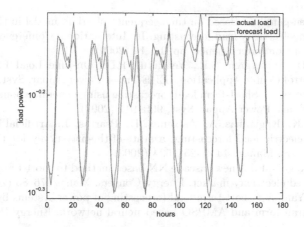

Fig. 14. DBN with purelin, tansig

According to the experimental results, we can tentatively conclude that the DBN with purelin-tansig transfer function provides the best prediction accuracy on medium scale data.

4   Conclusions

The environment of competitive electricity market necessitates an accurate load prediction. This paper has made a first attempt to examine the effect of different combinations of transfer functions used in a DBN model for load forecasting. Our preliminary results have clearly shown that the combination of purelin-tansig transfer function produces the best result, which is therefore recommended to use.

In future, we would like to study the effect of other factors of the deep believe network for load forecasting so as to improve the predication accuracy even further.

References

1. Amjady, N.: Short-term hourly load forecasting using time-series modeling with peak load estimation capability. IEEE Trans. Power. Syst. 49805 (2001)
2. Fan, S., Chen, L.: Short-term load forecasting based on an adaptive hybrid method. IEEE Trans. Power. Syst. 798–805 (2006)
3. Nie, H., Liu, G., Liu, X., Wang, Y.: Hybrid of ARIMA and SVMs for short-term load forecasting. Energy Procedia **16**, 1455–1460 (2012)
4. Amral, N., Ozveren, C.S., King, D.: Short term load forecasting using multiple linear regression. In: 42nd International Universities Power Engineering Conference 2007, pp. 1192–1198. IEEE (2007)
5. Zhang, M., Bao, H., Yan, L., Cao, J., Du, J.: Research on processing of short-term historical data of daily load based on Kalman filter. Power Syst. Tech. 39–42 (2003)

6. Wei, L., Zhen-gang, Z.: Based on time sequence of arima model in the application of short-term electricity load forecasting. In: International Conference on Research Challenges in Computer Science, pp. 11–14 (2009)

7. Irisarri, G.D., Widergren, S.E., Yehsakul, P.D.: On-Line Load Forecasting for Energy Control Center Application. IEEE Trans. Power Appar. Syst. 71–78 (1982)

8. Christiaanse, W.R.: Short-term load forecasting using general exponential smoothing. IEEE Trans. Power Appar. Syst. 900–911 (2007)

9. Metaxiotis, K., Kagiannas, A., Askounis, D., Psarras, J.: Artificial intelligence in short term electric load forecasting: a state-of-the-art survey for the researcher. Energy Convers. Manag. **44**, 1525–1534 (2003)

10. Kouhi, S., Keynia, F.: A new cascade NN based method to short-term load forecast in deregulated electricity market. Energy Convers. Manag. 76–83 (2013)

11. Zhang, X., Yan, W.: Short-term load forecasting of power systems by combination of wavelet transform and AMPSO based neural network, Energy Procedia 46–57 (2011)

12. Lauret, P., Fock, E., Randrianarivony, R.N., Manicom-Ramsamy, J.F.: Bayesian neural network approach to short time load forecasting. Energy Convers. Manag. **49**, 1156–1166 (2008)

13. Ho, K.L., Hsu, Y.Y., Chen, C.F., Lee, T.E., Liang, C.C., Lai, T.S.: Short term load forecasting of Taiwan power system using a knowledge-based expert system. IEEE Trans. Power. Syst. **5**, 1214–1221 (1990)

14. Kandil, M.S., El-Debeiky, S.M., Hasanien, N.E.: Long-term load forecasting for fast developing utility using a knowledge-based expert system. IEEE Trans. Power. Syst. 1558–1573 (2002)

15. Hinton, G.E., Salakhutdinov, R.R.: Reducing the dimensionality of data with neural networks. Science **313**, 504–507 (2006)

16. Chao, J., Shen, F., Zhao, J.: Forecasting exchange rate with deep belief networks. In: Proceedings of the International Joint Conference on Neural Networks (IJCNN 2011), San Jose, California, USA, pp. 1259–1266 (2011)

17. Zhang, X., Wang, R., Zhang, T., et al.: Short-term load forecasting based on a improved deep belief network. In: International Conference on Smart Grid and Clean Energy Technologies, pp. 339–342 (2016)

18. Hinton, G.E., Osindero, S., Teh, Y.W.: A fast learning algorithm for deep belief nets. Neural. Comput. **18**, 1527–1554 (2000)

Cloud Service Resource Allocation with Particle Swarm Optimization Algorithm

Shi Cheng[1(✉)], Lantian Guo[2], Tao Yang[3], Jiqiang Feng[4], Yifei Sun[5],
Chang Shao[6], and Qiqi Duan[6]

[1] School of Computer Science, Shaanxi Normal University, Xi'an, China
cheng@snnu.edu.cn
[2] Shenzhen Research Institute, Northwestern Polytechnical University,
Shenzhen, China
guolt0211@gmail.com
[3] School of Automation, Northwestern Polytechnical University, Xi'an, China
[4] Institute of Intelligent Computing Science, Shenzhen University, Shenzhen, China
[5] School of Physics and Information Technology,
Shaanxi Normal University, Xi'an, China
[6] Shenzhen Key Lab of Computational Intelligence,
Department of Computer Science and Engineering,
Southern University of Science and Technology, Shenzhen, China

Abstract. Cloud service resource allocation is an essential task in cloud computing. The cloud service resource allocation problem is modeled as an optimization problem, and is solved via different particle swarm optimization (PSO) variants in this paper. The aim of our method is to minimize the delay and the price at the same time. Based on the experimental results, it could be conducted that the good performance could be achieved via PSO algorithms. The future research is to utilize PSO algorithms on solving more real-world problems, especially with other quality of service problems.

Keywords: Cloud service resource allocation · Swarm intelligence · Particle swarm optimization

1 Introduction

Cloud computing is an attractive paradigm which provides computing, storage and networking resources as services [10,11,15–18]. IT providers (e.g., Google, Microsoft, Amazon, etc.) strive to offer powerful and reliable cloud services to their customers in an on-demand pay-as-you-go model. At the same time, both individual and enterprise customers apply cloud services to their commercial information systems or personal applications. Simultaneously, we have seen a phenomenal increase in the usage and deployment of mobile platforms and applications worldwide.

As the increasing number of cloud services deployed for mobile platforms, and applications provide the same or similar functionalities, it is not easy for

© Springer Nature Singapore Pte Ltd. 2017
C. He et al. (Eds.): BIC-TA 2017, CCIS 791, pp. 523–532, 2017.
https://doi.org/10.1007/978-981-10-7179-9_41

mobile users to find a suitable cloud service among various providers or servers immediately. In order to differentiate them, Quality of Service (QoS) which are non-functional attributes (e.g., response time, throughput, reliability, availability, security) is widely used to evaluate services. However, with the explosive growth in mobile applications, platforms and end user demands, limitations at the mobile devices end (e.g., computation and storage capacity, energy, shared wireless medium) significantly impede further improvements in application quality of service (QoS).

To overcome these limitations, effective cloud service resource allocation strategies are proposed to enable mobile users and mobile application providers for elastically utilizing resources in an on-demand fashion by allocation strategies that bridge available cloud services and the mobile environment. For a mobile application solution, three types of cloud services that have different functions cooperate to complete a task. The effective cloud service resource allocation strategies can be able to choose appropriate services that meet users' requirement and preferences to achieve a optimized services combination. Distinguish from web services, one of the main issues in cloud computing is that it is a few approaches consider the price of the service. Therefore, a highlight work for cloud service resource allocation is required to explore the trade-off between the benefits of uploading tasks and the price that mobile users must pay for the same.

Particle swarm optimization (PSO) algorithm is a population-based stochastic algorithm modeled on social behaviors observed in flocking birds [7]. A particle flies through the search space with a velocity that is dynamically adjusted according to its own and its companion's historical behaviors [13]. Each particle's position represents a solution to the problem. Particles tend to fly toward better and better search areas over the course of the search process [4,8].

In order to solve the cloud service resource allocation problem, the corresponding mathematical model was established at first, i.e., the solved problem was modeled to an optimization problem with several constraints. There are too many solutions for the services combination problems, thus, it is very difficult or impossible to solve that problem manually and it may be very slow to find the solution by the traditional algorithms. An intelligent algorithm, particle swarm optimization algorithm, was chosen to find optimized solution of the established mathematical model. The contributions of the paper are as follows:

1. modeling the cloud service resource allocation problem to an optimization problem;
2. utilizing different variants of particle swarm optimization algorithms to solve the cloud service resource allocation problem;
3. collecting real world cloud service QoS data for experiment, and setup a demo for cloud service resource allocation task.

The remaining of the paper is organized as follows. Section 2 introduces the cloud service resource allocation problem. Section 3 reviews the basic concepts of a particle swarm optimization algorithm. Experiments on variants of PSO algorithms with different population size are conducted in Sect. 4. Finally, Sect. 5 concludes with some remarks and future research directions.

2   Cloud Service Resource Allocation

Cloud computing refers to a large pool of virtualized resources that can be dynamically configured to provide elastic services that meet the needs of its users. With the explosive growth in mobile applications, platforms and end user demands, limitations at the mobile device end (e.g., computation and storage capacity, energy, shared wireless medium) significantly impede further improvements in application quality of service (QoS).

2.1   Problem Description

Cloud services provide scalable access to applications and resources. The effective cloud service resource allocation strategies could be able to choose appropriate services that meet users' requirement and preferences to achieve a optimized services combination. It aims to overcome these limitations by integrating cloud computing into the mobile environment. The mobile users and mobile application providers is able to elastically utilize resources in an on-demand fashion via this strategy. An illustration of cloud service resource allocation is given in Fig. 1.

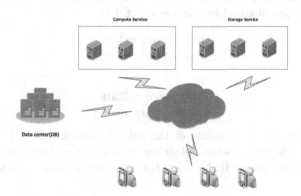

Fig. 1. Illustration of cloud service resource allocation

In mobile cloud computing task, cloud data centers play a role that bridges available cloud services (computing, storage and networking resources) and the mobile environment (mobile users, mobile application developers and so on). The cloud data centers are responsible for forwarding the date among them and integrating cloud computing into the mobile environment. There are many factors influence the cloud service resource allocation strategies. In our study, we consider the physical location of cloud services and service price of them.

Firstly, since some data centers are far apart and we know that the physical distance is one of the most important factors leading to network latency, thus, if the users tend to deploy the service to different cloud service platforms, our system must consider the delay for them. Note that, the data center is given the corresponding physical location including latitude and longitude coordinates, so that we can calculate the distance of the latitude and longitude coordinates of the city where the service center is combined, and then work out a simulated time delay based on the distance. And that, we can get the physical distance of any two data centers, and simulate a random delay based on this distance.

Secondly, another important factor influencing the service resource allocation is the service price. Our study employs storage cloud services and compute cloud services, so the price calculation is mainly for these two types of cloud services to calculate. Thus, the total price is the sum of prices for these two services.

2.2 Objective Function

Corresponding the aforementioned two factors, there are two objectives in our cloud service resource allocation problems, i.e., the delay and the price. The aim of the problem solving can be seen as an optimization of the price and delay, that is, to find a set of delayed and lowest-cost combinations of services in all the service portfolios we have previously obtained. The multi-objective optimization problem is defined as a vector of decision variables in the feasible region, so that a set of conflicting objective functions are minimized at the same time as possible. The problem could be modeled in Eq. (1):

$$\begin{cases} \text{minimum } delay \\ \text{minimum } price \end{cases} \tag{1}$$

subject to

$$\begin{cases} 0 \leq price \leq 200\$ \\ delay \leq 100\,\text{ms} \end{cases} \tag{2}$$

The Eq. (2) gives two constraints of the solved problem. 200\$ is upper bound of $price$. 100 ms is upper bound of $delay$, which means the system thinks the service is failed to connect if the delay time is greater than 100 ms.

2.3 Delay Calculation

The calculation of delay is based on the distance between the server and the user. The distance calculation equation proposed by Google was utilized in the experimental study. The distance is calculated based on Eq. (3).

$$distance = 2 \times 6378.137$$
$$\times \arcsin \sqrt{\sin^2(a/2) + \cos(lat_1) \times \cos(lat_2) \times \sin^2(b/2)} \tag{3}$$
$$a = lat_1 - lat_2 \tag{4}$$
$$b = long_1 - long_2 \tag{5}$$

where the lat_1 and lat_2 are latitudes of two candidate locations respectively. a is the difference value between latitudes of two candidate locations. The $long_1$ and $long_2$ are longitudes of two candidate locations respectively. b is the difference value between longitudes of two candidate locations. The distance values are in kilometers (km). 6378.137 km is the radius of the earth.

$$delay = distance/600 + random(-5,5) \qquad (6)$$

The delay is calculated via Eq. (6), where the value 600 is an empirical number and the delay values (in milliseconds, or ms) are associated with a random noise in $[-5, 5]$ ms.

2.4 Price Calculation

Different service providers have different strategies on the prices. Some providers have a constant prices for different kinds of storages, while the others take a linear decreasing price with the increasing of storages. The Fig. 2 gives an examples of five kinds of storage pricing.

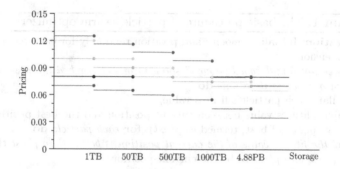

Fig. 2. An examples of five kinds of storage pricing.

3 Particle Swarm Optimization

Particle swarm optimization emulates the swarm behavior and the individuals represent points in the n-dimensional search space [9,12]. A particle represents a potential solution. Each particle is associated with two vectors, $i.e.$, the velocity vector and the position vector. For the purpose of generality and clarity, i is used to index the particles or solutions (from 1 to m), j is used to index the dimensions (from 1 to n), m represents the number of particles and n the number of dimensions. The position of a particle is represented as $\mathbf{x}_i$, and $\mathbf{x}_i = [x_{i1}, x_{i2}, \ldots, x_{ij}, \ldots, x_{in}]^T$. The velocity of a particle is represented as $\mathbf{v}_i = [v_{i1}, v_{i2}, \ldots, v_{ij}, \ldots, v_{in}]^T$, i represents the ith particle, $i = 1, \cdots, m$, and j

is the jth dimension, $j = 1, \cdots, n$. The velocity and position update equations in canonical PSO algorithm are as follow [9,12]:

$$\mathbf{v}_i \leftarrow w\mathbf{v_i} + c_1 \text{rand}()(\mathbf{p}_i - \mathbf{x}_i) + c_2 \text{rand}()(\mathbf{p}_n - \mathbf{x}_i) \qquad (7)$$

$$\mathbf{x}_i \leftarrow \mathbf{x}_i + \mathbf{v}_i \qquad (8)$$

where w denotes the inertia weight, c_1 and c_2 are two positive acceleration constants, rand() is a random function to generate uniformly distributed random numbers in the range $[0, 1]$ and are different for each dimension and each particle, $\mathbf{x}_i$ represents the ith particle's position, $\mathbf{v}_i$ represents the ith particle's velocity, $\mathbf{p}_i$ is termed as personal best, which refers to the best position found by the ith particle, and $\mathbf{p}_n$ is termed as local best, which refers to the position found by the members in the ith particle's neighborhood that has the best fitness evaluation value so far.

The basic procedure of PSO is shown as Algorithm 1. A particle updates its velocity according to Eq. (7), and updates its position according to Eq. (8). The $c_1 \text{rand}()(\mathbf{p}_i - \mathbf{x}_i)$ part can be seen as a cognitive behavior, while $c_2 \text{rand}()(\mathbf{p}_n - \mathbf{x}_i)$ part can be seen as a social behavior.

Algorithm 1. The basic procedure of particle swarm optimizer

---

1 **Initialization**: Initialize velocity and position randomly for each particle in every dimension;

2 **while** *have not found "good enough" solution or not reached the pre-determined maximum number of iterations* **do**

3   Calculate each particle's fitness value;

4   Compare fitness value between current position and the best position in history (personal best, termed as *pbest*); **for** *each particle* **do**

5   **if** *the fitness value of the current position is better than pbest* **then**

6   update *pbest* to be the current position;

7   Select the particle which has the best fitness value among current particle's neighborhood, this particle is called the neighborhood best (termed as *nbest*); Update each particle's velocity and position, respectively;

Different topology structure can be utilized in PSO, which will have different strategy to share search information for every particle [4]. Different topologies have different number of neighbors for each particle. The particle swarm's convergence speed and population diversity are affected by the topology structure of particles, *i.e.*, by the size of the neighborhoods. Take star and ring structures, which are two typical topology structures in particles, as examples. For PSO with a star structure, each particle has a large neighborhoods, the global best solution found is used by all particles to update their positions. In other words, the star structure has the smallest diameter and average distance which means that search information has the fastest propagation speed. For PSO with a ring structure, each particle has a small neighborhoods, the neighborhood best solution found is used by a few particles to update their positions. The ring structure has a large diameter and average distance which means that search information has a slow propagation speed [4, 14]. Particle swarm optimization algorithm has been utilized in solving different kinds of problems [2, 6] and numerous real world applications, such as text mining [3], and so on.

4 Experimental Study

4.1 Experimental Data

CloudHarmony is a cloud service QoS testing website. CloudHarmony tracks the service providers by monitoring the times and duration of downtime failures for many cloud service providers. We employ CloudHarmony API to obtain the basic information of each cloud service provider and the provision of cloud services QoS attributes. In CloudHarmony's official website, we could get cloud service provider monitoring data through API interface. Firstly, API is invoked to get a JSON format file including cloud service provider ID monitored by CloudHarmony. Secondly, the provider Id is accessed as a query to get the details information of the service provider. Finally, we stored these data utilizing MongoDB.

4.2 Parameter Settings

In all experiments, the population in PSO algorithms has 50 individuals. Each algorithm runs 40 times, 500 iterations in every run. All other parameters of PSO are taken from [1]. The parameters' setting for three algorithms is as follows:

1. Particle swarm optimization algorithm:
   - $w = 0.72984$; $c_1 = c_2 = 1.496172$.

4.3 Experimental Results

The mobile environment is dynamic and rapidly changing. A large number of services are offered by various service providers with different quality of service (QoS) attributes and price. Especially, in the mobile environment, these QoS parameters frequently change values. The cloud service resource allocation process handles a large amount of data and services, computation time is an important attribute to consider for the fulfillment of users' tasks.

Figure 3 gives an illustration of the locations of storage and computing services. The computing and storage service providers have different locations. There are 284 locations for computing services and 107 locations for storage service in the system. The same provider offers different pricing for different services. There are 653 kinds computing services and 45 kinds storage services. The cloud service resource allocation problem is modeled as an optimization problem. The aim of optimization is to find the optimal computing and storage

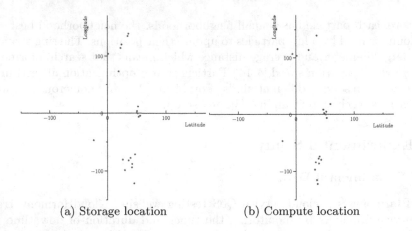

(a) Storage location   (b) Compute location

Fig. 3. The locations of storage and computing services

services. The service has two constraints, the price and the time delay, which are related to the kinds of services and location of services providers. Based on the results, the PSO algorithm could obtain good performance on this problem.

The PSO algorithm with different structures are utilized to solve the cloud service resource allocation problems. A problem has been utilized as an example to show the effective of PSO algorithms. The requirements for the computing services are as follows:

- Computing times: 200;
- CPU core: 8;
- Hard disk type: SSD;
- Operation System: Linux.centos.

The requirements for the storage service are as follows:

- Storage: 300 G;
- Hard disk type: Sata.

After the optimization, the optimized result is as follows:

- Storage: azure: storage city: Shanghai;
- Computing: azure: compute city: Beijing;
- Delay: 15 ms;
- Price: 65.60$.

5   Conclusions

Cloud service resource allocation is a critical issue in cloud computing. In this paper, the cloud service resource allocation problem is modeled as an optimization problem, and is solved via different particle swarm optimization (PSO) variants. Based on the experimental results, it could be conducted that the good performance could be achieved via PSO algorithms. The future research is to utilize PSO algorithms on solving more real-world problems, especially with big data analytics problems [5] and quality of service problems.

Acknowledgement. This work was supported in part by the National Natural Science Foundation of China under Grant 61672433, 61672334, 61401283, and 61402373; in part by the Shenzhen Science and Technology Innovation Committee under grant number ZDSYS201703031748284 and Shenzhen Science and Technology Innovation Committee Basic Research Project under Grant 201703063000511, in part by the Fundamental Research Funds for the Central Universities under Grant GK201703062 and GK201603014, and in part by Natural Science Basic Research Plan in Shaanxi Province of China under Grant 2017JQ6070.

References

1. Bratton, D., Kennedy, J.: Defining a standard for particle swarm optimization. In: Proceedings of the 2007 IEEE Swarm Intelligence Symposium (SIS 2007), pp. 120–127, April 2007
2. Cheng, S.: Population diversity in particle swarm optimization: definition, observation, control, and application. Ph.D. thesis, Department of Electrical Engineering and Electronics, University of Liverpool (2013)
3. Cheng, S., Shi, Y., Qin, Q.: Particle swarm optimization based semi-supervised learning on Chinese text categorization. In: Proceedings of 2012 IEEE Congress on Evolutionary Computation (CEC 2012), pp. 3131–3198. IEEE, Brisbane, Australia (2012)
4. Cheng, S., Shi, Y., Qin, Q.: Population diversity based study on search information propagation in particle swarm optimization. In: Proceedings of 2012 IEEE Congress on Evolutionary Computation (CEC 2012), pp. 1272–1279. IEEE, Brisbane, Australia (2012)
5. Cheng, S., Zhang, Q., Qin, Q.: Big data analytics with swarm intelligence. Ind. Manag. Data Syst. **116**(4), 646–666 (2016)
6. Coello, C.A.C., Pulido, G.T., Lechuga, M.S.: Handling multiple objectives with particle swarm optimization. IEEE Trans. Evol. Comput. **8**(3), 256–279 (2004)
7. Eberhart, R., Kennedy, J.: A new optimizer using particle swarm theory. In: Proceedings of the Sixth International Symposium on Micro Machine and Human Science, pp. 39–43 (1995)
8. Eberhart, R., Shi, Y.: Particle swarm optimization: Developments, applications and resources. In: Proceedings of the 2001 Congress on Evolutionary Computation (CEC 2001), Seoul, pp. 81–86 (2001)
9. Eberhart, R., Shi, Y.: Computational Intelligence: Concepts to Implementations, 1st edn. Morgan Kaufmann Publishers, San Francisco (2007)
10. Hossain, M.S., Moniruzzaman, M., Muhammad, G., Ghoneim, A., Alamri, A.: Big data-driven service composition using parallel clustered particle swarm optimization in mobile environment. IEEE Trans. Serv. Comput. **9**(5), 806–817 (2016)
11. Huang, J., Liu, G., Duan, Q.: On modeling and optimization for composite network-cloud service provisioning. J. Netw. Comput. Appl. **45**, 35–43 (2014)
12. Kennedy, J., Eberhart, R., Shi, Y.: Swarm Intelligence. Morgan Kaufmann Publishers, San Francisco (2001)

13. Qin, Q., Cheng, S., Zhang, Q., Li, L., Shi, Y.: Particle swarm optimization with interswarm interactive learning strategy. IEEE Trans. Cybern. **46**(10), 2238–2251 (2016)
14. Rada-Vilela, J., Zhang, M., Seah, W.: A performance study on synchronicity and neighborhood size in particle swarm optimization. Appl. Soft Comput. **17**(6), 1019–1030 (2013)
15. Rahimi, M.R., Ren, J., Liu, C.H., Vasilakos, A.V., Venkatasubramanian, N.: Mobile cloud computing: A survey, state of art and future directions. Mob. Netw. Appl. **19**(2), 133–143 (2014)
16. Wang, S., Liu, Z., Zheng, Z., Sun, Q., Yang, F.: Particle swarm optimization for energy-aware virtual machine placement optimization in virtualized data centers. In: Proceedings of the 2013 International Conference on Parallel and Distributed Systems (ICPADS 2013), pp. 102–109. IEEE Computer Society, Washington, DC, USA (2013)
17. Wang, S., Sun, Q., Zou, H., Yang, F.: Particle swarm optimization with skyline operator for fast cloud-based web service composition. Mob. Netw. Appl. **18**(1), 116–121 (2013)
18. Wang, S., Zhou, A., Hsu, C.H., Xiao, X., Yang, F.: Provision of data-intensive services through energy- and QoS-aware virtual machine placement in national cloud data centers. IEEE Trans. Emerg. Top. Comput. **4**(2), 290–300 (2016)

Markov-Potts Prior Model and Fuzzy Membership Based Nonparametric SAR Image Change Detection

Ronghua Shang[✉], Weitong Zhang, Yijing Yuan, and Licheng Jiao

Key Laboratory of Intelligent Perception and Image Understanding
of Ministry of Education, International Research Center for Intelligent Perception
and Computation, Joint International Research Laboratory of Intelligent Perception
and Computation, Xidian University, Xi'an 710071, Shanxi, China
rhshang@mail.xidian.edu.cn

Abstract. In order to improve the accuracy of synthetic aperture radar (SAR) image change detection, a novel unsupervised non-parametric method for change detection is described. The method treats the prior data and the observed data as two independent events and adopts a simple algorithm to realize and validate the effectiveness of the proposed method. Firstly, the prior distribution is obtained by MRF with Potts model of the initial classification result by k-means with the prior data. Secondly, the fuzzy probability is obtained through fusing gray value and texture feature fuzzy membership of the observed data. Meanwhile, the fuzzy probability is regarded as the data likelihood probability. Finally, by using the Bayesian formula and the independent distribution criteria to calculate the maximum a posteriori (MAP) probability, change detection can be regarded as the product of two probabilities of two independent events. Simulation results show that the proposed method effectively combines the gray and texture information of difference image, overcomes the shortcomings of using probability statistic model and parameter estimation, reduces the influence of speckle noise of SAR image and improves the accuracy of image change detection.

Keywords: Synthetic aperture radar (SAR) · Change detection · Independent events · Maximum a posteriori (MAP) probability

1 Introduction

The goal of image detection is to detect changed regions in multiple images which are taken from the same place in different times. SAR system is not sensitive to atmospheric and illumination conditions, so SAR images change detection played a more and more important role in remote sensing community. Therefore, remote sensing image change detection has made a significant development. In recent years a lot of novel and effective methods have been proposed and used to improve the performance of SAR image change detection.

© Springer Nature Singapore Pte Ltd. 2017
C. He et al. (Eds.): BIC-TA 2017, CCIS 791, pp. 533–543, 2017.
https://doi.org/10.1007/978-981-10-7179-9_42

The process of a nonparametric change detection method can be divided into three steps: (1) image preprocessing; (2) difference image calculating; (3) change areas identification. These three steps all impact on the accuracy of change detection. In this paper, we adopt the SAR images which have been preprocessed. Therefore, the performance of SAR image change detection mainly relies on the latter two steps. Therefore, good methods which are used to forming and classifying the difference image are very important. Especially in the third step, identifying the change area is a very important process. And these methods mainly can be divided into classification methods and statistical methods.

In the classification methods, Celik [1] presented unsupervised change detection in satellite images by using principal component analysis and k-means clustering. Patra et al. [2] proposed histogram thresholding for unsupervised change detection, and change detection is viewed as an unsupervised classification problem with two classes. Gong et al. [3] employed fuzzy C-means (FCM) algorithm to detect change areas in synthetic aperture radar images. In the statistical methods, an early paper introduced the use of the hidden Markov chain (HMC) model [4] to detect multi-temporal SAR images and introduced the use of the Markov random field (MRF) [5] model with maximum a posteriori (MAP) probability to detect change area in SAR images. And Xiong et al. [6] proposed a threshold selection method by using two SAR change detection measures based on the Markov random field model.

As mentioned above, the statistical methods require to select a proper probability statistical model for the changed and unchanged pixels in the difference image. Moreover, they need to deduce some parameter estimation. Meanwhile, it will bring some drawbacks: (1) It cannot guarantee to choose a proper probability statistical model for difference image; (2) The accuracy of parameter estimation will affect probability statistical model. (3) It cannot make full use of the information of difference image.

In order to overcome the weakness mentioned above, we propose a method which treats the prior data and the observed data as two independent events. The prior data is the initial classification results by k-means and the observed data is the difference image. Thus we use the fuzzy probability by fusing gray value and texture feature fuzzy membership of FCM method [7] for the observed data to replace the data likelihood probability of Bayesian formula. Change detection can be regarded as the product of two probabilities of two independent events. Fuzzy membership matrices of the observed data is used to replace model, so there will be no probability statistical model needed. Besides, we do not need parameter estimation. And the most important thing is that the fuzzy probability of the observed data is independent and unrelated with the prior data. Therefore, the MAP can be regarded as the product of two probabilities of two independent events. The gray value based membership matrix ensures the preservation of image details, but d the results will have a lot of spots due to the speckle noise. The texture feature based membership matrix can reduce the influence of speckle noise, but cannot preserve the details of the image. Hence, fusing the gray and texture features can acquire better information.

2   Proposed Method

This section focuses on describing the process of the proposed method. Firstly, image fusion based on wavelet transform is used to generate the difference image. Then, the prior distribution of initial classification is calculated and the data likelihood distribution is obtained by fusing the gray and texture features. Finally, the rules of MAP probability and Bayes formula are used to image classification.

2.1   Generate the Difference Image

The quality of the difference image is very important for SAR image change detection. The subtraction and the ratio operator are usually used to generate the difference images, but the ratio operator is more suitable for SAR images due to the speckle noise [8]. And the ratio difference image usually comprises log-ratio and mean-ratio difference images. The multiplicative speckle noise can be transformed into an additive one by the log-ratio operator. And the log-ratio operator can enhance the low-intensity pixels and weaken the high-intensity pixels of difference image. With the mean-ratio operator, the local mean value of each pixel of the image is modified. And the mean-ratio operator may emphasize the differences in the low intensities of the temporal images. Gong et al. [3] illustrated the advantages and disadvantages of these two methods and presented a new method which adopts a fusion scheme based on wavelet transform to fuse log-ratio image and mean-ratio image. This approach can get better information than the mean-ratio image or log-ratio image. Here, the proposed method adopts this method to generate the difference image.

In this paper, the proposed method regards the prior data and the observed data as independent event with each other and uses these two probabilities of two independent events to get the result of change detection.

2.2   Prior Distribution

In order to describe the mathematical model of multi-objective CARP more concisely, we first assume that there are T routes in a feasible solution. We use a decision variable M_e^t to denote whether the edge e in the t-th route ($t \in T$) is served. Secondly, k-means is used to classify the difference image and get the initial detection result x. The result x is regarded as the prior data and MRF with Potts model is used to dispose the prior data and to get the prior distribution. Gibbs distribution [9] provides a model method which depends on entity to contact context correlation. It can be defined as follows:

$$p(\mathbf{x}) = Z^{-1} \exp(-U(\mathbf{x})) \tag{1}$$

where $U(\mathbf{x})$ is the total energy function and $U(\mathbf{x}) = \sum_{c \in C} V_c(\mathbf{x})$, Z denotes the normalizating constant and $Z = \sum_x \exp^{-U(\mathbf{x})}$, $\mathbf{x}$ represents the initial detection result. $V_c(\mathbf{x})$ is the potential function associated with class c.

According to the theory of Hammersley-Clifford [10], Besag ensures the relation-ship between the MRF and Gaussian random field (GRF). Therefore, the prior probability of initial detection result x can be expressed as follows:

$$p(x_i) = \frac{\exp(-u(x_i))}{\sum_{x_i \in \mathcal{L}} \exp(-u(x_i)}$$ (2)

And $V_c(x_i) = \delta(x_i, x_j) - 1$, $j \in N_i$ and $\delta(x_i, x_j) = \begin{cases} 0 & x_i = x_j \\ 1 & x_i \neq x_j \end{cases}$ by the

Potts model [11,12], x_i is the class label of the i-th pixel. N_i is the neighbor set of a position i. The energy function is $u(x_i) = -\beta_i \sum_{c \in C} V_c(x_i) = -\beta_i \sum_{j \in N_i} [\delta(x_i, x_j) - 1]$, where β is the smoothing parameter and its value is usually between 0.8 and 1.4, and $\beta = 1$.

2.3   Data Likelihood

The difference image is regarded as the observed data. And the fuzzy membership of the gray value and texture features of the difference image are fused. Firstly, it utilizes the gray value to calculate the fuzzy membership matrix U_1 of the difference image. The calculation of the fuzzy membership matrix is performed as follows:

$$u_{ij} = \frac{1}{\sum_{r=1}^{k} (\frac{d(z_i, v_j)}{d(z_i, v_r)})^2}$$ (3)

where $u_{ij} \in [0, 1]$ represents the fuzzy membership of the i-th pixel to class j, and $\sum_{j=1}^{k} u_{ij} = 1, (i = 1, 2, \cdots, N)$. N denotes the total number of pixels of the difference image. k is the number of classes. z_i is the gray value and texture features of the i-th pixel of the difference image. v_j is the clustering center of class j. $d(z_i, v_j)$ is the Euclidean distance between object z_i and the clustering center v_j.

Secondly, in order to improve the accuracy of change detection, feature vectors are extracted and used to calculate the fuzzy membership matrix U_2 by Eq. (3). In Eq. (3), feature vectors are regard as the clustering centers.

Furthermore, the key operations are feature selection and extraction. In order to extract multi-scale image information and make full use of local time-frequency characteristics, multi-scale variation characteristics, direction features and translation invariance, nonsubsampled wavelet transform [13] is adopted to extract textural information of SAR images.

Figure 1 shows four sub-images by wavelet decomposition of the image. H and L represent the high-pass and low-pass filters. LL sub-image is obtained by the transverse and longitudinal low-pass filter. The sub-images of LH, HL and HH contain high frequency component. Based on Fig. 1, utilizing the energy of each sub-image as the measure of texture feature, norm l_1 is used to calculate the energy of each pixel.

$$E = \frac{1}{MN} \sum_{m=1}^{M} \sum_{n=1}^{N} |\omega(m, n)|$$ (4)

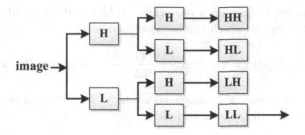

Fig. 1. Nonsubsampled wavelet transform

where $M \times N$ is the size of image. m and n represent the row and column of the image respectively, and ω is wavelet coefficient. The dimension of feature vector is $D = 3 \times L + 1$. L is the selection of decomposition level of wavelet. In experiments, three-level wavelet decomposition and 15×15 sliding window is used to get feature vectors.

Thirdly, the key issue to generate the second independent event is the realization of fusion rule which merges the membership partition matrices U_1 and U_2 to produce fuzzy probability matrix U. Both the gray value and texture feature membership matrices have obtained effective results for SAR image change detection respectively but they still have some disadvantages. For the fusion rule, we expect it can combine the advantages of the gray and texture membership partition matrices, so that it can enhance the information of changed regions in the greatest extent. The fusion regulation can be described as follows£Q

$$P(\mathbf{y}) = U(m, n, k) = \begin{cases} \max(U_1(m, n, k), U_2(m, n, k)) & if \ k = 2 \\ \min(U_1(m, n, k), U_2(m, n, k)) & if \ k = 1 \end{cases} \tag{5}$$

where m and n represent the row number and column number of the difference image $\mathbf{y}$ respectively, and $k = 1$ or 2 is the number of classes. U_1 and U_2 are the fuzzy membership matrix of gray value and texture features respectively. This fusion rule aims at guaranteeing noise insensitiveness and image details preservation simultaneously.

2.4   The MAP Probability

Based on the theory of Bayes formula [14], given the observed data $\mathbf{y}$, i.e. the difference image, the posterior distribution of $\mathbf{x}$ can be described as follows:

$$P(\mathbf{x}|\mathbf{y}) = \frac{P(\mathbf{y}|\mathbf{x})P(\mathbf{x})}{P(\mathbf{Y})} \propto P(\mathbf{y}|\mathbf{x})P(\mathbf{x}) \tag{6}$$

where $P(\mathbf{x})$ is the prior distribution of classes. $P(\mathbf{y}|\mathbf{x})$ is the conditional likelihood probability of the difference image $\mathbf{y}$ when given the label image $\mathbf{x}$. $P(\mathbf{Y})$ is a normalizing constant. In order to get the best result $\hat{\mathbf{x}}$ of change detection,

538   R. Shang et al.

its necessary to get maximum a posteriori (MAP) probability of $P(\mathbf{x}|\mathbf{y})$ based on the difference image, which can be described as

$$\hat{\mathbf{x}} = \arg \max P(\mathbf{x}|\mathbf{y}) = \arg \max \frac{P(\mathbf{y}|\mathbf{x})P(\mathbf{x})}{P(\mathbf{Y})} = \arg \max P(\mathbf{y}|\mathbf{x})P(\mathbf{x}) \qquad (7)$$

As mentioned above, $\mathbf{x}$ is independent to $\mathbf{y}$, so the conditional likelihood probability $P(\mathbf{y}|\mathbf{x})$ can be described as

$$P(\mathbf{y}|\mathbf{x}) = \frac{P(\mathbf{xy})}{P(\mathbf{x})} = \frac{P(\mathbf{x})P(\mathbf{y})}{P(\mathbf{x})} = P(\mathbf{y}) \qquad (8)$$

And Eq. (7) can be described as

$$\hat{\mathbf{x}} = \arg \max P(\mathbf{y})P(\mathbf{x}) \qquad (9)$$

The flowchart of the proposed method for SAR images is shown in Fig. 2.

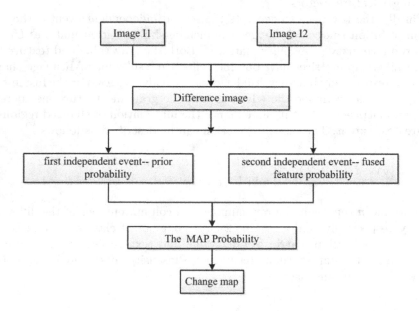

Fig. 2. The flowchart of the proposed SAR image change detection method.

3   Simulation Results

3.1   Description of Experimental Data Sets

In order to show the effectiveness of the proposed method for SAR image change detection, we utilized two data sets to test. The first data set (301×301) is named as Bern data set and is taken by the ERS-2 satellite SAR sensor over an area near the city of Bern in April and May 1999. And the flood hit this area during that time. The second data set (7666 × 7692) is named as HuangHe dataset which is acquired at the Yellow River Estuary of China in June 2008 and June 2009. This data set is too huge to show the detail information of change areas, so an image (257 × 289) is selected to test [1].

3.2   Evaluating Indicators

Besides, in order to evaluate the effectiveness of the proposed method, five indicators [15] are used to evaluate the quality of the results. (1) False alarm (FA). (2) Missed alarm (MA). (3) Overall error (OE). (4) Kappa coefficient. (5) Percentage of correct classification (PCC). And the smaller value of FA, MA and OE is, the better result is, the higher value of kappa and PCC is, the better result is.

3.3   Contrast Methods

Five contrast methods are used in the experiments, which are: (1) Change detection uses two-threshold EM and MRF algorithms (MRF) [16]. (2) Change detection uses Gaussian Mixture model and Genetic Algorithm (GMGA) [17]. (3) Change detection based on images fusion and fuzzy clustering (RFLICM) [3]. (4) In the proposed method, the data likelihood probability is changed into the fuzzy probability only with the gray value (TIE-G). (5) In the proposed method, the data likelihood probability is changed into the fuzzy probability only with the texture feature (TIE-T).

3.4   Experimental Results and Analysis

The experiments were conducted in the software of Matlab R2010a by the computer of Intel(R) Core(TM) 2 Duo CPU. And all methods based on the same method to deal the difference image.

Results on the Bern Data Set. On Bern data set, a comparison analysis is carried out on six different methods. The change detection results are shown in Fig. 3. From Fig. 3, the results of MRF and RFLICM have more missing information. And the result of GMGA has much false change information. The proposed method does not to use any distribution model, but adopts the gray value and texture feature of the difference image to get results which are shown in Figs. 3(g) and (h). In Fig. 3(g), it reduces much false change information, but also increases the missing information. In Fig. 3(f), the result reduces the spots, but the detailed change information cannot be detected. In contrast, by fusing the gray and texture features of the difference image, the result generated by the proposed method gets the best result which is illustrated in Fig. 3(i).

The quantitative analysis on Bern data set are shown in Table 1. From Table 1, TIE-T gets the highest value of FA but the lowest value of MA. Compared with TIE-T,MRF, GMGA, and RFLICM, TIE-G has a lower value of FA

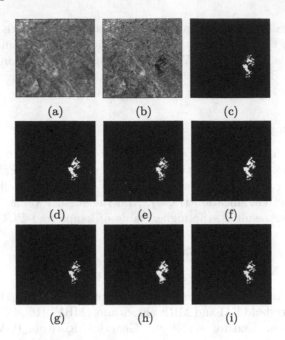

Fig. 3. Experiment results of the Bern data set. Images acquired (a) before and (b) after the flood. (c) Ground truth. (d) MRF. (e) GMGA. (f) RFLICM. (g) TIE-G. (h) TIE-T. (i) TIE.

Table 1. Results on Bern data set

Method	FA	MA	OE	PCC	Kappa
MRF	226	111	337	0.9963	0.8592
GMGA	269	90	359	0.9960	0.8438
RFLICM	303	85	388	0.9957	0.8444
TIE-G	146	179	325	0.9964	0.8555
TIE-T	516	29	545	0.9940	0.8022
TIE	**132**	151	**283**	**0.9969**	**0.8769**

but increase the value of MA. The result of the proposed method has the lowest value of FA. The change detection result of TIE-T is the worst, and the proposed method has the highest PCC and Kappa and the lowest OE.

Results on the HuangHe Data Set. In the second data set experiment, it uses a more complicated data where the speckle noise on Fig. 4(b) is much greater than Fig. 4(a). In Fig. 4(d), (e) and (g), the results of change detection acquired by MRF, GMGA and TIE-G have lots of spots, which are sensitive to noise. This phenomenon can be explained that the MRF, GMGA and TIE-G fail to consider the image speckle noise and the features context information and the distribution of difference image. However, in Fig. 4(h), the result of TIE-T which adopts the texture feature reduces much spots and gets a good result. And in Fig. 4(f), the RFLICM which only uses the gray value of the difference image is also affected by speckle noise. By contrast, the proposed algorithm fusing the gray value and the texture feature of difference image can resist the speckle noise, thereby it can reduce the error rate and preserve the detail information of the change detection result. It can be seen that the proposed method can obtain a higher accurate rate at different levels of noise of multi-temporal SAR images. The numerical results on HuangHe data set are shown in Table 2. In Table 2, the result of GMGA is the worst. And the results of RFLICM and TIE-T are much higher in kappa and PCC. The maximum Kappa and PCC are acquired by the proposed method. These quantitative results on the HuangHe data set confirm the ability of the proposed method to restrain speckle noise.

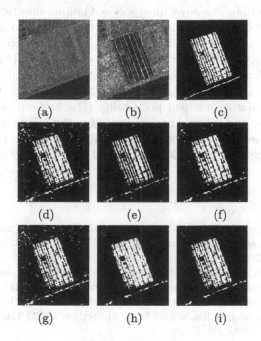

Fig. 4. Results of the HuangHe data set. Images acquired (a) before and (b) after the lands reclamation. (c) Ground truth. (d) MRF. (e) GMGA. (f) RFLICM. (g) TIE-G. (h) TIE-T. (i) TIE.

It can be seen from the simulation results above that the proposed method can effectively obtain the changed area and improve the accuracy of change detection result for multi-temporal SAR images.

Table 2. Results on HuangHe data set

Method	FA	MA	OE	PCC	Kappa
MRF	3082	1394	4476	0.9397	0.8017
GMGA	3943	683	4642	0.9305	0.7610
RFLICM	1585	2016	3601	0.9515	0.8301
TIE-G	2440	1696	4136	0.9443	0.8116
TIE-T	2514	1279	3793	0.9489	0.8297
TIE	1105	1970	**3075**	**0.9586**	**0.8530**

4   Conclusion

In this paper, we proposed a novel unsupervised nonparametric method for SAR images change detection. This method treats the prior data and the observed data as two independent events and regards the change detection problem as the MAP probability problem for the product of two probabilities of two independent events. The key idea is to fuse the fuzzy membership of gray value and texture characteristics of the difference image. Meanwhile, the fuzzy probability is regarded as the data likelihood probability. The method of this paper realized the automation and reduced parameter estimation with simple information. The experimental results on two groups of SAR images show that the proposed method can effectively improve the accuracy of image change detection results.

References

1. Celik, T.: Unsupervised change detection in satellite images using principal component analysis and k-means clustering. IEEE Trans. Geosci. Remote Sens. Lett. **6**(4), 772–776 (2009)
2. Patra, S., Ghosh, S., Ghosh, A.: Histogram thresholding for unsupervised change detection of remote sensing images. Int. J. Remote Sens. **32**(21), 6071–6089 (2011)
3. Gong, M.G., Zhou, Z.Q., Ma, J.J.: Change detection in synthetic aperture radar images based on images fusion and fuzzy clustering. IEEE Trans. Image Process. **21**(4), 2141–2151 (2012)
4. Derrode, S., Mercier, G., Pieczynski, W.: Unsupervised change detection in SAR images using a multicomponent HMC model. In: 2nd International Workshop Analysis of Multi-temporal Remote Sensing Images, pp. 195–203 (2003)
5. Cheung, Y., Li, M., Cao, X.C.: Lip segmentation and tracking under MAP-MRF framework with unknown segment number. Neurocomputing **104**(15), 155–169 (2013)
6. Xiong, B.L., Chen, Q., Jiang, Y.M., Kuang, G.Y.: A threshold selection method using two SAR change detection measures based on the Markov random field model. IEEE Trans. Geosci. Remote Sens. Lett. **9**(2), 287–291 (2012)
7. Zhao, F.: Fuzzy clustering algorithms with self-tuning non-local spatial information for image segmentation. Neurocomputing **106**(15), 115–125 (2013)

8. Rignot, E.J.M., van Zyle, J.J.: Change detection techniques for ERS-1 SAR data. IEEE Trans. Geosci. Remote Sens. **31**(4), 896–906 (1993)
9. Geman, S., Geman, D.: Stochastic relaxation, gibbs distributions, and the bayesian restoration of images. IEEE Trans. Pattern Anal. Mach. Intell. **6**(11), 721–741 (1984)
10. Besag, J.: Spatial interaction and the statistical analysis of lattice systems. J. R. Stat. Soc. **36**(2), 192–236 (1974)
11. Hacheme, A., Ali, M.D.: Joint NDT image restoration and segmentation using Gauss-Markov-Potts prior models and variational bayesian computation. IEEE Trans. Image Process. **19**(9), 2265–2277 (2010)
12. Krinidis, S., Chatzis, V.: A robust fuzzy local information C-means custering algorithm. IEEE Trans. Image Process. **19**(5), 1328–1337 (2010)
13. Fukuda, S., Hirosawa, H.: A wavelet-based texture feature set applied to classification of multifrequency polarimetric SAR images. IEEE Trans. Geosci. Remote Sens. **37**(5), 2282–2286 (1999)
14. Carincotte, C., Derrode, S., Boutennance, S.: Unsupervised change detection on SAR images using fuzzy hidden Markov chains. IEEE Trans. Geosci. Remote Sens. **44**(2), 432–441 (2006)
15. Jia, L., Li, M., Zhang, P., Wu, Y., Zhu, H.: SAR image change detection based on multiple kernel K-means clustering with local-neighborhood information. IEEE Trans. Geosci. Remote Sens. Lett. **13**(6), 856–860 (2016)
16. Bazi, Y., Bruzzone, L., Melgani, L.: Image thresholding based on the EM algorithm and generalized Gaussian distribution. Pattern Recognit. **40**(2), 619–634 (2007)
17. Celik, T.: Image change detection using Gaussian mixture model and genetic algorithm. J. Vis. Commun. Image Reprent. **21**(8), 965–974 (2000)

Computing Stability of Products of Grassmannians with Fixed Total Dimension Using MAXIMA

Dun Liang[✉]

Yau Mathematical Sciences Center, Tsinghua Univeristy,
Haidian, Beiing 10084, China
dliang@math.tsinghua.edu.cn
http://www.ymsc.tsinghua.edu.cn

Abstract. We realize the Hilbert-Mumford stability of products of Grassmannians with fixed total dimension base on Mumford's computation in [8] in the computer algebra system Maxima. The problem is reduced to be a discrete algorithm and by some techniques of strings in Maxima, the coding is universal and effective. This code can prove the classical results for point sets and lines in projective spaces in Geometric Invariant Theory.

Keywords: Geometric Invariant Theory · Numerical criterion of stableness · Maxima · Grassmannian

1   Introduction

Geometric Invariant Theory (GIT in short) was founded by Mumford in [8] to answer the question that whether quotients exist in the category of algebraic varieties. Given an algebraic variety X with an action of a reductive group G on it, one chooses a linearization L (See Definition 1), then there exists a subset $X^{\mathrm{ss}}(L)$ of X which contains the so called semi-stable points (See Definition 2). GIT says that the quotient $X^{\mathrm{ss}}(L)//G$ is a categorical quotient of X. Furthermore, one has so called the set of stable points $X^{\mathrm{s}}(L) \subset X^{\mathrm{ss}}(L)$ such that the $X^{\mathrm{s}}(L)/G$ is a geometric quotient (See [8]). In order to compute these sets, we have

Theorem 1 (Hilbert-Mumford Numerical Criterion, See [8]). *Let $\mathcal{X}(G)^*$ be the set of one-parameter subgroups of G. There exists a real valued function $\mu^L(x, \lambda)$ such that*

- *A point $x \in X^{\mathrm{ss}}(L)$* $\Leftrightarrow$ *$\mu^L(x, \lambda) \leq 0$ for all $\lambda \in \mathcal{X}(G)^*$.*
- *A point $x \in X^{\mathrm{s}}(L)$* $\Leftrightarrow$ *$\mu^L(x, \lambda) < 0$ for all $\lambda \in \mathcal{X}(G)^*$.*

© Springer Nature Singapore Pte Ltd. 2017
C. He et al. (Eds.): BIC-TA 2017, CCIS 791, pp. 544–556, 2017.
https://doi.org/10.1007/978-981-10-7179-9_43

In this paper all varieties and algebraic groups are over the complex numbers unless the ground field is pointed out. Grassmannian is a fundamental construction in algebraic geometry. As a set the Grassmannian $\mathbf{Gr}_{n,r}$ contains all linear subspaces of a fixed dimension r of a vector space or a projective space. The local coordinates of Grassmannians are called the Plücker coordinates (See [14]). Fix a projective space $\mathbb{P}^n$ of dimension n. For $r_1, \ldots, r_m$ where $0 \leq r_i \leq n$ for each $i = 1, \ldots, m$, consider the product

$$X_{\mathbf{r},n} = \prod_{i=1}^{m} \mathbf{Gr}_{r_i,n}.$$

The special linear group $\mathrm{SL}(n+1, \mathbb{C})$ acts diagonally on this product. Mumford computed the function $\mu^L(x, \lambda)$ (See [8] and also Theorem 2) for this action. In this paper, we realize this formula in the computer algebra system Maxima. We will see that Mumford's formula in Theorem 2 could be reduced to a discrete algorithm (See Algorithm 1). By this algorithm, the inputs of the program are not subspaces but points in the product set $\mathcal{P}_{n+1}^{r_1+1} \times \cdots \times \mathcal{P}_{n+1}^{r_m+1}$ where we denote $\mathcal{P}_l^r$ to be the set of subsets of $\{0, 1, \ldots n\}$ whose cardinalities are r.

The coding requires some string techniques in Maxima. This technique is wildly used in programming, and will give a big extension of function defining in Maxima, making the program flow easier to be controlled.

This construction has many applications. The most classical example are point sets in projective spaces. They are on one hand models of moduli spaces of curves (See [7,14]), and on the other hand related to theta functions (See [12]). In order to check that our coding is correct, we prove two classical theorems of points on the plane and lines in the 3 space. Due to classical geometry, 7 points on the plane is related to the non-hyperelliptic curves of genus 3 (See [15]) and lines in 3 space is related to cubic surfaces (See [14]).

This paper is organized by the following. Section 2 introduces Mumford's formula in [8]. The basic concepts of Grassmannians, their products, linearizations and stability will be listed in order to give this formula. Section 3 shows that this problem is essentially a discrete problem for programming, and summarizes this conclusion to Algorithm 1. Then we introduce the general string technique in Sect. 4 in order to proceed the coding. In Sect. 5 we use a general example to illustrate the coding of our algorithm. This coding is general in the sense that any other case could be computed by simply changing the data at the beginning claiming part of the notebook. We list two applications of this coding, the stability of point sets and lines in the projective spaces, and they are in Sect. 6.

2 Linearizations and Stability of Products of Grassmannians with Fixed Total Dimension

In general, let G be a reductive affine algebraic group, that means any finite dimensional representation is reducible (See [17]), and X be a quasi-projective variety. Denote the action of G on X by $g.x$ for $g \in G$ and $x \in X$.

Definition 1 (See [9]). *Let* $\pi : L \to X$ *be a line bundle on* X. *Suppose* L *admits a* G-*action* $g.l$ *for* $g \in G$ *and* $l \in L$. *If* $\pi(g.l) = g.\pi(l)$ *for all* $g \in G$ *and* $l \in L$, *we say this action is a* G-**linearization** *of* L *and* L *is a* **linearized** G-*bundle.*

For any line bundle L, there exists a number n such that $L^{\otimes n}$ admits a G-linearization (See [9]).

Definition 2 (See [8]). *Let* L *be a* G-*linearized line bundle on* X *and* $x \in X$.

- *The point* x *is called* **semi-stable** *with respect to* L *if there exists* $m > 0$ *and* $s \in \Gamma(X, L^m)^G$ *(the* G-*invariant sections) such that* $X_s = \{\, y \in X \mid s(y) \neq 0 \,\}$ *is affine and contains* x.
- *The point* x *is called* **stable** *with respect to* L *if* x *is semi-stable and additionally the isotropy group* G_x *is finite and all orbits of* G *in* X_s *are closed where* X_s *is defined in the definition above.*
- *The point* x *is called* **unstable** *with respect to* L *if it is not semi-stable.*

We shall denote the set of semi-stable (respectively stable, unstable) points by

$$X^{\mathrm{ss}}(L), \quad X^{\mathrm{s}}(L), \quad X^{\mathrm{us}}(L).$$

In this paper we consider the stability problem of Grassmannian manifolds. As a set, the Grassmannian $\mathbf{Gr}_{r,n} = \mathbf{Gr}(r+1, n+1)$ is the set of r-dimensional projective subspaces of the projective space $\overline{V} = \mathbb{P}^n(\mathbb{C})$. In fact it is a complex manifold, we will skip this material and for details see [14]. Let V be the affine cone of $\overline{V}$, we fix a standard basis $\{e_0, \ldots, e_n\}$ of V. Let W be an $r + 1$-dimensional linear subspace of V and let $\overline{W}$ be the corresponding linear subspace of W. Suppose W is spanned by a basis $\{u_0, \ldots, u_r\}$, then the frame $u_0 \wedge \cdots \wedge u_r \in \bigwedge^{r+1}(V)$ determines W. The linear space $\bigwedge^{r+1}(V)$ is of dimension $\binom{n+1}{r+1}$ with a basis

$$\{e_{i_0} \wedge \cdots \wedge e_{i_r} \mid 0 \leq i_0 < i_1 < \cdots < i_r \leq n\}.$$

Fix the lex order of this basis, the coordinates of the frame $u_0 \wedge \cdots \wedge u_r$ expanded with respect of this basis in the projective space $\mathbb{P}\left(\bigwedge^{r+1}(V)\right)$ is called the Plücker coordinates of $\overline{W}$. Note that different frames of the same subspace are only differ up to a scalar (the determinant of the matrix of base change), the Plücker coordinates is independent of the choice of the frame. In fact, if $A = (a_{ij})_{(n+1)\times(n+1)}$ is the matrix of $\{u_0, \ldots, u_n\}$ relative to $\{e_0, \ldots, e_n\}$, that is, $u_i = \sum_{j=0}^{n} a_{ij} e_j$ for $i = 0, \ldots, n$, then

$$u_1 \wedge \cdots \wedge u_r = \sum_{0 \leq i_0 < \cdots i_r \leq n} A_{i_0 \ldots i_r} e_{i_0} \wedge \cdots \wedge e_{i_r}$$

where $A_{i_0 \ldots i_r}$ is the determinant of the submatrix of A constructed by the $i_1, \ldots, i_r$-th columns of A. Let $N = \binom{n+1}{r+1} - 1$, we have the Plücker map

$$\begin{aligned} p : \mathbf{Gr}_{r,n} &\longrightarrow & \mathbb{P}^N(\mathbb{C}) \\ W &\longmapsto & (A_{i_0, \ldots, i_r})_{0 \leq i_0 < \cdots i_r \leq n} \end{aligned}$$

From this embedding one sees that $\mathbf{Gr}_{r,n}$ is projective.

Fix a projective space $\mathbb{P}^n(\mathbb{C})$, for $0 \le r \le n$, the special linear group $SL(n+1,\mathbb{C})$ acts on $\mathbf{Gr}_{r,n}$ by changing the frames linearly. Let $\mathscr{I} = \{1,2,\ldots,n\}$. For $\mathbf{r} = (r_1,\ldots,r_m) \in \mathscr{I}^m$, let

$$X_{\mathbf{r},n} = \prod_{i=1}^{m} \mathbf{Gr}_{r_i,n}.$$

Then $SL(n+1,\mathbb{C})$ acts diagonally on $X_{\mathbf{r},n}$.

Lemma 1 (See [9]). *Any line bundle on $X_{\mathbf{r},n}$ is isomorphic to $L_{\mathbf{k}}$ for some $\mathbf{k} = (k_1,\ldots,k_m) \in \mathbb{Z}^m$ where*

$$L_{\mathbf{k}} = \bigotimes_{i=1}^{m} \mathrm{pr}_i^* \left(\mathcal{O}_{\mathbf{Gr}_{r_i,n}}(1)^{\otimes k_i} \right)$$

where $\mathrm{pr}_i : X_{\mathbf{r},n} \to \mathbf{Gr}_{r_i,n}$ *is the i-th projection. The line bundle $L_{\mathbf{k}}$ is very ample if and only if $\mathbf{k} = (k_1,\ldots,k_m) \in \mathbb{Z}_+^m$, that is, all the k_i's are positive.*

Theorem 2 (See [8]). *Let $\mathcal{W} = (W_1,\ldots,W_m) \in X_{\mathbf{r},n}$. Then $\mathcal{W} \in X_{\mathbf{r},n}^{\mathrm{ss}}(L_{\mathbf{k}})$ if and only if for any proper linear subspace W of $\mathbb{P}^n$*

$$(n+1)\sum_{j=1}^{m} k_j[\dim(W_j \cap W) + 1] \le (\dim W + 1)\sum_{i=1}^{m} k_i(r_i + 1). \tag{1}$$

Furthermore, $\mathcal{W} \in X_{\mathbf{r},n}^{\mathrm{s}}(L_{\mathbf{k}})$ if and only if (1) strictly holds.

3 Discrete Problem

Theorem 2 gives a clear description of stableness of products of Grassmannians. However, the randomness of the testing space W in the theorem still makes the computation inexplicit. On the other hand, testing the general Plücker coordinates involves so many cases to be considered. In fact, the proof of the theorem gives a narrow restriction of the form of the matrix of W.

Notation as the previous section, let $\{e_0,\ldots,e_n\}$ be the standard basis of V. For each $0 \le s \le n$, let $\overline{E}_s$ be the linear space of V spanned by $\{e_0,\ldots,e_s\}$, and let E_s be the projective subspace determined by $\overline{E}_s$.

Theorem 3 (See [9]). *The inequality (1) in Theorem 2 can be replaced by a system of inequalities*

$$-\sum_{i=1}^{m} k_i(r_i+1)(s+1) + (n+1)\left(\sum_{i=1}^{m} k_i(\dim(W_i \cap E_s) + 1)\right) \le 0 \tag{2}$$

for all $0 \le s \le n$.

Now consider one Grassmannian $\mathbf{Gr}_{r,n}$. Let $W \in \mathbf{Gr}_{r,n}$ be a projective subspace. For any j such that $0 \le j \le r$, there exists a unique ν_j such that

$$\dim(W \cap E_{\nu_j}) = j, \quad \dim(W \cap E_{\nu_j-1}) = j-1.$$

Let A be the matrix of W, then A will be of the form

$$\begin{pmatrix} a_{00} \cdots a_{0\nu_0} & 0 & \cdots & \cdots & \cdots & \cdots & 0 \\ a_{10} \cdots & \cdots & \cdots & a_{1\nu_1} & 0 & \cdots & \cdots & 0 \\ \vdots & \cdots & \cdots & \vdots & \cdots & \cdots & \cdots & \vdots & 0 \\ a_{r0} \cdots & \cdots & \cdots & \cdots & \cdots & a_{r\nu_r} & 0 & \cdots 0 \end{pmatrix}$$

where for all j, we have $a_{j\nu_j} \ne 0$. If $i_j > \nu_j$ for some j, then the Plücker coordinate $p_{i_0 \ldots i_r} = 0$, and $p_{\nu_0 \ldots \nu_r} \ne 0$. Obviously we have $\nu_j > \nu_{j-1}$ because or else we have $\nu_j = \nu_{j-1}$ then one can use a line transformation to make $a_{(j-1),\nu_{j-1}} = 0$, a contradiction.

Let us come back to the products of Grassmannians, notations as the previous section, consider $\mathcal{W} = (W_1, \ldots, W_m) \in X_{\mathbf{r},n}$. For each W_i, define $(\nu_1^{(i)}, \ldots, \nu_{r_i}^{(i)})$ as above. That is, for each $0 \le j \le r_i$, we have

$$\dim(W_i \cap E_{\nu_j^{(i)}}) = j \quad \text{and} \quad \dim(W_i \cap E_{\nu_j^{(i)}-1}) = j-1.$$

Then for each $0 \le s \le n$, we have

$$\dim(W_i \cap E_s) = \begin{cases} j & \text{if } \nu_j^{(i)} \le s < \nu_{j+1}^{(i)} \\ r_i & \text{if } \quad s \ge \nu_{r_i}^{(i)} \end{cases} \tag{3}$$

for $0 \le j < r_i$.

For each W_i we have $0 \le \nu_0^{(i)} < \ldots < \nu_{r_i}^{(i)} \le n$, so $\nu_0^{(i)}, \ldots, \nu_{r_i}^{(i)}$ are distinct positive integers. Thus, the vector $(\nu_1^{(i)}, \ldots, \nu_{r_i}^{(i)}) \in \mathbb{Z}_+^{r_i}$ is uniquely determined by the subset $\{\nu_0^{(i)}, \ldots, \nu_{r_i}^{(i)}\} \subset \{0, 1, \ldots, n\}$. The condition (2) in Theorem 3 only restricts the numbers $\dim(W_i \cap E_s)$ for all $0 \le i \le m$ and $0 \le s \le n$, but these numbers are determined by (3). If we denote $\mathcal{P}_l^r$ to be the set of subsets of $\{0, 1, \ldots n\}$ whose cardinalities are r, then one can regard the condition (2) as a system of inequalities whose variables are

$$\left(\{\nu_0^{(1)}, \ldots, \nu_{r_1}^{(1)}\}, \ldots, \{\nu_0^{(m)}, \ldots, \nu_{r_m}^{(m)}\} \right) \in \mathcal{P}_{n+1}^{r_1+1} \times \cdots \times \mathcal{P}_{n+1}^{r_m+1}.$$

We will compute the unstable points because not only they are easier to be computed but also they have special geometrical considerations.

Algorithm 1. Input: positive integers: $n, r, m, (r_1, \ldots, r_m), (k_1, \ldots, k_m)$. Output:

1. for $i = 1$ thru m return $\mathcal{P}_{n+1}^{r_i+1}$;
   end{for}
2. define the lex order on $\mathcal{P}_{n+1}^{r_1+1} \times \cdots \times \mathcal{P}_{n+1}^{r_m+1}$;

3. for $i = 1$ thru m,
   for $\{v_0^{(i)}, \ldots, v_{r_i}^{(i)}\} \in \mathcal{P}_{n+1}^{r_i+1}$,
   for $j = 0$ thru r_i, for $s = 0$ thru n,
   if $s < v_{r_i}^{(i)}$ then

   define $D(\{v_0^{(i)}, \ldots, v_{r_i}^{(i)}\}, s) = j$ if $v_j^{(i)} \leq s$ and $v_{j+1}^{(i)} < s$;
   else define $D(\{v_0^{(i)}, \ldots, v_{r_i}^{(i)}\}, s) = r_i$;
   end{if}
   end{for} end{for} end{for} end{for}
4. for $v = (\ \{v_0^{(1)}, \ldots, v_{r_1}^{(1)}\}, \ldots, \{v_0^{(m)}, \ldots, v_{r_m}^{(m)}\}\ ) \in \mathcal{P}_{n+1}^{r_1+1} \times \cdots \times \mathcal{P}_{n+1}^{r_m+1}$
   if

$$-\sum_{i=1}^{m} k_i(r_i + 1)(s + 1) + (n + 1) \left(\sum_{i=1}^{m} k_i(D(\{v_0^{(i)}, \ldots, v_{r_i}^{(i)}\}, s) + 1) \right) > 0$$

   then return v, next v;
   else next v, next s;
   end{if}
   end{for}

4   Strings in Maxima

Here we introduce three useful functions for strings in Maxima (See [16]). These functions give a big extension of the programming and library of Maxima. They are, the function "`sconcat()`", the function "`simplode()`" and the function "`eval_string()`". The idea of the usage is that we let Maxima to "write a sentence as a string" and then "read it in Maxima".

The Function `sconcat()`. This function combines strings together. A string in Maxima could be represented as words in between the double quotation marks.

Example 1

```
sconcat("map","of","the world");
```

   mapofthe world

Note that the output will combine the strings without spaces, but the spaces in the strings are preserved.

The Function `simplode()`. This function will combine the members of a list as a string. This time the members of the list may not necessarily be strings, but the output is a string.

Example 2

```
simplode([1,2,a,b,x+y]);
```

12aby+x

One could separate the members with another string, this time input the string after the list with a comma in front of the double quotient marks.

Example 3

```
simplode([a,b,c],"+");
```

a+b+c

Note that this a+b+c is a string, not an expression in Maxima.

The Function `eval_string()`. This function evaluates the string if it is an expression in Maxima.

Example 4

```
eval_string("sin(%pi/6)");
```

$$\frac{1}{2}$$

Here we have and example to combine these functions together.

Example 5

```
A:[5,3];
```

$$[5, 3]$$

```
B:simplode(A,",");
```

5,3

```
C:sconcat("binomial(",B,")");
```

binomial(5,3)

```
eval_string(C);
```

10

5 A General Construction via MAXIMA

We realize the Algorithm 1 in Maxima. As a general example, we take $n = 5$, $m = 3$, $\mathbf{k} = (1, 2, 3)$ and $\mathbf{r} = (1, 2, 3)$. To claim this, we input

```
block(n:5, m:3, k:[1,2,3], r:[1,2,3],display(n,m,k,r));
```

First, we construct the list of the set $\mathcal{P}_n^p$. Let

```
L:create_list(i,i,1,n+1);
```

$$[1, 2, 3, 4, 5, 6]$$

Then the function

```
W(L,p):= full_listify(subset(
        powerset(setify(L)),lambda([x],is(cardinality(x)=p+1))));
```

defines the list of elements of $\mathcal{P}_n^p$ for any $0 \le p \le n + 1$.

Let $X = (\nu_0, \ldots, \nu_r)$ be the list of integers $0 \le \nu_0 < \ldots < \nu_r \le n$ which is defined for a subspace W as above. Then then function

```
Dimension(X,m):=length(sublist(X,lambda([x],is(x<=m))))-1;
```

outputs the number $\dim(W \cap E_m)$ in (3). With these definitions, we can construct the numerical criterion, and that is

Theorem 4. *Definitions as above, for each* r_i, *we give* $\mathcal{P}_n^{r_i}$ *a lex order. Let* $w = (w_1, \ldots, w_m)$, $0 \le w_i \le \binom{n+1}{r_i+1}$ *be an index that points out an element in* $\mathcal{P}_{n+1}^{r_1+1} \times \cdots \times \mathcal{P}_{n+1}^{r_m+1}$ *such that the i-th entry is the* w_i*-th element in the set* $\mathcal{P}_{n+1}^{r_i+1}$. *Then the function*

```
f(w,s):=(n+1)*sum(k[i]*(Dimension(W(L,r[i])[w[i]],s)+1),i,1,length(r))
        -sum(k[i]*(r[i]+1)*(s+1),i,1,length(r));
```

represents the condition (2) in Theorem 3.

Here we introduce a computer technique problem of cartesian products in Maxima. In Maxima, if A and B are two sets, then one computes the cartesian product by

```
cartesian_product(A,B);
```

and this input also works for finitely many sets. But for a given list L of sets, there is no function that represents the cartesian product of all elements in the list in Maxima. This problem can be solved by the technique we introduced in Sect. 4.

Lemma 2. *Let* L *be a list of sets, then*

```
Cart(L):=
  eval_string(sconcat("cartesian_product(",simplode( L,", "),")"));
```

defines the function that outputs the cartesian product of all entries of the list L.

Using the function W(L, p) we construct the list of all possible vectors $(\nu_0^{(i)}, \ldots, \nu_{r_i}^{(i)})$ by

```
create_list(W(L,r[i]),i,1,length(r));
```

$[[[1, 2], [1, 3], [1, 4], [1, 5], [1, 6], [2, 3], [2, 4], [2, 5], [2, 6], [3, 4], [3, 5], [3, 6], [4, 5], [4, 6], [5, 6]],$
$[[1, 2, 3], [1, 2, 4], [1, 2, 5], [1, 2, 6], [1, 3, 4], [1, 3, 5], [1, 3, 6], [1, 4, 5], [1, 4, 6], [1, 5, 6], [2, 3, 4],$
$[2, 3, 5], [2, 3, 6], [2, 4, 5], [2, 4, 6], [2, 5, 6], [3, 4, 5], [3, 4, 6], [3, 5, 6], [4, 5, 6]],$
$[[1, 2, 3, 4], [1, 2, 3, 5], [1, 2, 3, 6], [1, 2, 4, 5], [1, 2, 4, 6], [1, 2, 5, 6], [1, 3, 4, 5], [1, 3, 4, 6],$
$[1, 3, 5, 6], [1, 4, 5, 6], [2, 3, 4, 5], [2, 3, 4, 6], [2, 3, 5, 6], [2, 4, 5, 6], [3, 4, 5, 6]]]$

This information is read by the following. The element $W(L, r[1])[6] = [2, 3]$ means the 2×6 matrix that represents the subspace in the first entry is of the form

$$\begin{pmatrix} * \, a \, 0 \, 0 \, 0 \, 0 \\ * \, * \, b \, 0 \, 0 \, 0 \end{pmatrix}$$

where a and $b \neq 0$.

Thus, if we give an index for each $W(L, r[i])$ by the lex order, an element

$$\nu = (\; \{\nu_0^{(1)}, v_1^{(1)}\}, \; \{\nu_0^{(2)}, v_1^{(2)}, v_2^{(2)}\}, \; \{\nu_0^{(3)}, v_1^{(3)}, v_2^{(3)}, v_3^{(3)}\} \;) \in \mathcal{P}_6^2 \times \mathcal{P}_6^3 \times \mathcal{P}_6^4$$

could be determined by

$$A : \mathtt{Cart(P)}$$

where P is the list of the sets of index created as

```
P:create_list(setify(
   create_list(i,i,1,length(W(L,r[j]))))),j,1,length(r));
```

$$[\{1, 2, 3, 4, 5, 6, 7, 8, 9, 10, 11, 12, 13, 14, 15\},$$
$$\{1, 2, 3, 4, 5, 6, 7, 8, 9, 10, 11, 12, 13, 14, 15, 16, 17, 18, 19, 20\},$$
$$\{1, 2, 3, 4, 5, 6, 7, 8, 9, 10, 11, 12, 13, 14, 15\}]$$

For each element in A, we check the semistability condition. We look for the points that satisfies $f(x, i) \leq 0$ for $i = 0, 1, 2, 3, 4, 5$ at the same time. For universal purpose, we use the same "spelling trick" as we did in the construction of cartesian products. This time let

```
SS:eval_string(sconcat("subset(AA,lambda([x],is(",simplode(create_list(
   sconcat("f(x,",i,")<=0"), i,0,n)," and "),")))"));
```

where the output of

```
simplode(create_list(sconcat("f(x,",i,")<=0"), i,0,n)," and ");
```

is

```
f(x,0)<=0 and f(x,1)<=0 and f(x,2)<=0 and  f(x,3)<=0 and
f(x,4)<=0 and f(x,5)<=0
```

The output is too big to be presented here. On the other hand, this is just an example which general enough to explain the formula, so we will not exhibit it here.

6   More Examples

In order to check the correctness of our coding, let us prove some classical theorems for stableness. The most well-known examples for Grassmannians are point sets and lines of projective spaces, they are, subspaces of dimension 0 and 1.

6.1   7 Points in $\mathbb{P}^2$

In [9], the situation when all r_i's are equal and all k_i are equal is called **democratic**. We wish to check the following theorem.

Theorem 5 (See [9]). *For m points on the plane, they are semistable if and only if no point is repeated more than $m/3$ times and no more than $2m/3$ points are on a line.*

Here we take seven points on $\mathbb{P}^2$ as an example, this is the situation when $n = 2, m = 7, r_i = 0$ and $k_i = 1$ for all $i = 1, \ldots, 7$. We have to claim these data at the beginning of the code.

```
n:2; m:7; r:create_list(0,i,1,m);
k:create_list(1,i,1,m);
```

Then we define the function f(x,i) and Cart(P) the same as the previous section. The difference is that for the lists W(L,j)'s, since they are democratic, the stability is unchanged in an $\mathfrak{S}_m$ orbit where $\mathfrak{S}_m = \mathfrak{S}_7$ is the symmetric group that permutes the values in the vector $(\nu^{(1)}, \ldots, \nu^{(m)})$. Thus one only needs to check the stability condition for representatives for each orbit. The function "**permute**" in MAXIMA gives all permutes of a list. Now let ff be the equivalence relation

```
ff(x,y):=elementp(x,permutations(y));
```

that $x \sim y$ if and only if x is a permutation of y. In order to get the representatives, one first define a lex order for the vector of the values and then take the first one in each orbit. That is

```
P:create_list(setify(
  create_list(i,i,1,length(W(L,r[j]))))
  ,j,1,length(r))

AA:setify(create_list(t[1],t,sort(
  full_listify(equiv_classes(Cart(P),ff)))));
```

The output is the list

$$[[1,1,1,1,1,1,1], [1,1,1,1,1,1,2], [1,1,1,1,1,1,3], [1,1,1,1,1,2,2],$$
$$[1,1,1,1,1,2,3], [1,1,1,1,1,3,3], [1,1,1,1,2,2,2], [1,1,1,1,2,2,3],$$
$$[1,1,1,1,2,3,3], [1,1,1,1,3,3,3], [1,1,1,2,2,2,2], [1,1,1,2,2,2,3],$$
$$[1,1,1,2,2,3,3], [1,1,1,2,3,3,3], [1,1,1,3,3,3,3], [1,1,2,2,2,2,2],$$
$$[1,1,2,2,2,2,3], [1,1,2,2,2,3,3], [1,1,2,2,3,3,3], [1,1,2,3,3,3,3],$$
$$[1,1,3,3,3,3,3], [1,2,2,2,2,2,2], [1,2,2,2,2,2,3], [1,2,2,2,2,3,3],$$
$$[1,2,2,2,3,3,3], [1,2,2,3,3,3,3], [1,2,3,3,3,3,3], [1,3,3,3,3,3,3],$$
$$[2,2,2,2,2,2,2], [2,2,2,2,2,2,3], [2,2,2,2,2,3,3], [2,2,2,2,3,3,3],$$
$$[2,2,2,3,3,3,3], [2,2,3,3,3,3,3], [2,3,3,3,3,3,3], [3,3,3,3,3,3,3]]$$

Consider the semistable points, computed by

```
SS:eval_string(
  sconcat(
   "subset(AA,lambda([x],is(",
     simplode(create_list(
   sconcat("f(x,",i,")<=0"), i,0,n)," and
   "),")))"));
```

We have

$$[1,1,2,2,3,3,3], [1,1,2,3,3,3,3], [1,1,3,3,3,3,3], [1,2,2,2,3,3,3],$$
$$[1,2,2,3,3,3,3], [1,2,3,3,3,3,3], [1,3,3,3,3,3,3], [2,2,2,2,3,3,3],$$
$$[2,2,2,3,3,3,3], [2,2,3,3,3,3,3], [2,3,3,3,3,3,3], [3,3,3,3,3,3,3]$$

The "1"'s are those points that equal to $[1,0,0]$, thus we checked Theorem 5 for $m = 7$.

6.2   Lines in $\mathbb{P}^3$

This time let

```
n:3; r:1; k:1; L:create_list(i,i,1,n+1);
```

The functions $W(L, r)$ and $Dimension(X, m)$ defined as above. Let Y be the set

```
Y:setify(create_list(i,i,1,length(W(L,r))));
```

$$\{ 1, 2, 3, 4, 5, 6 \}$$

that gives an index for $W(L, r)$. For any set Y, we can define the cartesian power of Y by

```
Cart(L,n):=eval_string(sconcat(
        "cartesian_product(",
        simplode(
        create_list("L,",i,1,n-1)),"L",")"));
```

For democratic case, the function $f(x, i)$ has an easier representation given by

```
f(w,s):=(n+1)*sum(
        (Dimension(W(L,r)[w[i]],s)+1),i,1,length(w))
        -(s+1)*length(w)*(r+1);
```

The relation `ff` is the same one in the previous section, we define

```
AA(m):= setify(create_list(t[1],t,sort(
        full_listify(
        equiv_classes(Cart(Y,m),ff)))));
```

which is the list of indices of the vectors

$$(\nu_0^{(1)}, \nu_1^{(1)}, \nu_0^{(2)}, \nu_1^{(2)}, \ldots, \nu_0^{(m)}, \nu_1^{(m)})$$

where m is the number of the lines we wish to compute.

Proposition 1. *There are no stable points when $m = 4$.*

Proof. Input the condition $f(x, i) < 0$ for $i = 0, 1, \ldots n$ as

```
SS:eval_string(
   sconcat(
    "subset(AA(4),lambda([x],is(",
      simplode(
        create_list(
        sconcat("f(x,",i,")<0"), i,0,n),
      " and "),")))"));
```

   Output

$$\{\,\}$$

∎

Using the proof of Proposition 1, we can also proof that there are no stable points for $m \leq 4$ and there are no semistable points for $m = 1, 2$ (See [9]).

7   Conclusion and Further Questions

We have computed the stability problem for Grassmannians. This is just a starting programming for the computations of stabilities. For the computational aspects of GIT, the book [10] has a systematic introduction on problems of a fixed action and linearization for finite groups and reductive matrix groups. But there is an issue of the choice of linearization before we use the algorithms in this book. And in fact the construction of moduli space is depended on this choice. The goal of this whole project aims to construct classical moduli spaces in Maxima. We can compute the stability not only for the products of Grassmannians, but also for hypersurfaces.

The choices of the linearizations form the space of linearization with a convex structure similar to birational geometry. This is so called the variation of GIT (See [11,13]). The VGIT of the situation in this paper is explicit by the construction of weight polytopes, and this inform us to the mission of coding convex theory in Maxima.

References

1. Smith, T.F., Waterman, M.S.: Identification of common molecular subsequences. J. Mol. Biol. **147**, 195–197 (1981)
2. May, P., Ehrlich, H.-C., Steinke, T.: ZIB structure prediction pipeline: composing a complex biological workflow through web services. In: Nagel, W.E., Walter, W.V., Lehner, W. (eds.) Euro-Par 2006. LNCS, vol. 4128, pp. 1148–1158. Springer, Heidelberg (2006). https://doi.org/10.1007/11823285_121
3. Foster, I., Kesselman, C.: The Grid: Blueprint for a New Computing Infrastructure. Morgan Kaufmann, San Francisco (1999)
4. Czajkowski, K., Fitzgerald, S., Foster, I., Kesselman, C.: Grid information services for distributed resource sharing. In: 10th IEEE International Symposium on High Performance Distributed Computing, pp. 181–184. IEEE Press, New York (2001)
5. Foster, I., Kesselman, C., Nick, J., Tuecke, S.: The Physiology of the Grid: an Open Grid Services Architecture for Distributed Systems Integration. Technical report, Global Grid Forum (2002)
6. National Center for Biotechnology Information. http://www.ncbi.nlm.nih.gov
7. Igusa, J.: Arithmetic varieties and moduli of genus two. Ann. Math., Second Ser. **72**(3), 612–649 (1960)
8. Mumford, D., Fogarty, J., Kirwan, F.: Geometric Invariant Theory. Ergebnisse der Mathematik und ihrer Grenzgebiete (2) (Results in Mathematics and Related Areas (2)), vol. 34, 3rd edn. Springer, Berlin (1994)
9. Dolgachev, I.: Lectures on Invariant Theory. Cambridge University Press, Cambridge (2010)
10. Derksen, H., Kemper, G.: Computational Invariant Theory. Springer, Berlin (2002)
11. Dolgachev, I., Hu, Y.: Variation of geometric invariant theory quotients. Publications Math. Inst. Hautes Études Sci. **87**(1), 5–51 (1998)
12. Dolgachev, I., Ortland, D.: Point sets in projective spaces and theta functions. Asterique **165** (1988)
13. Thaddeus, M.: Geometric Invariant Theory and Flips. J. Am. Math. Soc. **9**(3), 691–723 (1996)
14. Griffiths, P., Harris, J.: Principles of Algebraic Geometry. Springer, New York (1978)
15. Ren, Q., Sam, S., Schrader, G., Sturmfels, B.: The universal kummer threefold. Exp. Math. **22**(3), 327–362 (2013)
16. Maxima Reference Manual. http://maxima.sourceforge.net/docs/manual/maxima.html
17. Borel, A.: Linear Algebraic Groups. GTM, vol. 126. Springer, New York (1991)

Predictive Controller Design Using Ant Colony Optimization Algorithm for Unmanned Surface Vessel

Dongming Zhao[1(✉)], Tiantian Yang[1], Wen Ou[2], and Hao Zhou[1]

[1] School of Automation, Wuhan University of Technology, Wuhan 430070, China
dmzhao@whut.edu.cn
[2] School of Automation, Huazhong University
of Science and Technology, Wuhan 430070, China

Abstract. This paper presents a predictive control approach based on ant colony optimization algorithm for critical maneuvering of unmanned surface vehicle in high sea environment. The algorithm uses the generalized predictive control to get the predictive course value. In the process of the algorithm, the ant colony algorithm is used to obtain the optimal control sequence of the rudder angle. The obtained simulation results show that the algorithm solves the problem of overshoot of course controller, and realizes the precise control of USV course in the case of large disturbance of wind and wave, then solves the saturation nonlinear problem of unmanned surface vessel in extreme sea condition.

Keywords: Unmanned surface vessel · Ant colony algorithm · Predictive control · Course control

1 Introduction

The unmanned surface vessel (USV) show a wide range of applications in military and civilian areas with the advantages of operating in harsh sea conditions and high-risk environments. In the process of carrying out the task, unmanned surface vessel is supposed to have a reliable performance to achieve the high-precision cruise according to the specified task line. The precise control of unmanned surface vessel course is the core technology to realize its high precision tracing, especially when the unmanned surface vessel is operating above the design sea condition, the disturbance torque like the wind and waves is obviously enhanced, and the control system is in a saturated non-linear state. In recent years, a lot of control algorithm have been proposed for the course control of the USV [2–10]. Li et al. proposed an adaptive Radial Basis Function neural network controller for the nonlinear course control of unmanned surface vessel with modeling errors and unknown bounded environment disturbances [4]. An optimizing sliding mode cascade control structure is proposed to determine the optimal sliding surface parameters for sliding mode control of

© Springer Nature Singapore Pte Ltd. 2017
C. He et al. (Eds.): BIC-TA 2017, CCIS 791, pp. 557–566, 2017.
https://doi.org/10.1007/978-981-10-7179-9_44

underactuated unmanned surface vessel systems [5]. Further, nonlinear course controller is designed by backstepping method [6,7]. The fuzzy control approach is also applied to the course control of unmanned surface vessel [8–10]. None of the above algorithms consider high precision tracking and non-linear saturation problem in harsh sea condition. So how to develop an effective approach for course control of unmanned surface vessel is still an open question.

In this paper, an approach of course predictive control based on ant colony algorithm is proposed to solve the problem of unmanned surface vessel course control in extreme sea condition. The CARIMA model is used to predict the next course output of the unmanned surface vehicle, and to correct it with the feedback value of actual course. Ant colony optimization algorithm has the characteristics of distributed computing, easy to find the global optimal solution, strong robustness. Based on the above characteristics, the ant colony algorithm can improve the computational power and optimization efficiency of the objective function in the predictive control model. So in the process of the predictive control algorithm, the ant colony algorithm is used to rolling optimize the objective function, which makes the optimal steering angle control be obtained quickly.

This paper is organized as follows: Sect. 2 describes the basic parameters of the unmanned surface vessel and presents the maneuvering model. Section 3 elaborates the proposed predictive control algorithm. Section 4 provides the simulation results and lake test results. Section 5 gives the conclusion of this paper.

2 Background

The unmanned surface vessel used in the paper is shown in Fig. 1, with the main parameters shown in Table 1.

Fig. 1. Photos of the unmanned surface vessel

Considering the disturbance of the wind, wave and current, the maneuvering motion model of unmanned surface vessel is expressed as:

$$T_1 T_2 \ddot{\Psi} + (T_1 + T_2)\dot{\Psi} + \Psi + a\Psi^3 = K\delta + KT_3\dot{\delta} + f_a + f_\omega + f_l \qquad (1)$$

Table 1. Main parameters of unmanned surface vessel

Parameter	Value
Length /m	8.075
Vertical length /m	8
Draft depth /m	0.6
Moulded depth/m	1.15
Full loaded displacement/T	3.2
Maximum speed /kn	12
Cruising speed /kn	6
Propulsion mode	Water jet propulsion

$$T_1T_2 = (m + \lambda_{22})(I_z + \lambda_{66})/C \qquad (2)$$

$$T = T_1 + T_2 - T_3 \qquad (3)$$

where Ψ is the course angle, δ is the rudder angle, T is the rudder index, K is the rotational index, the other parameters is the unmanned surface vessel maneuverability parameters. f_a is equivalent disturbance rudder angle of the wind, f_w is equivalent disturbance rudder angle of the disturbances due to waves, f_l is equivalent disturbance rudder angle of the disturbances due to currents (Fig. 2).

According to the calculation method in the literature [15] and the z-type test data of $\Psi/\delta = 15°/15°$ for the draft state in the Taihu, the K, T parameters of the unmanned surface vessel are obtained as follows:

$$K = 2.9097, \ T = 55.8855 \qquad (4)$$

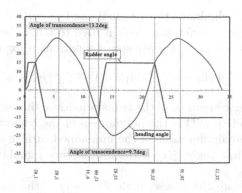

Fig. 2. Fitting result of 15°/15° Z test data of the unmanned surface vessel

3   Design of Predictive Controller

The structure of the predictive control system for the unmanned surface vessel is as follows:

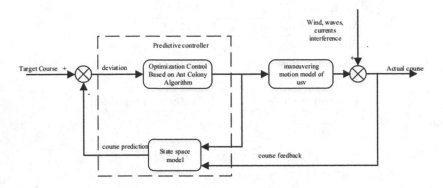

Fig. 3. System structure of predictive control

The predictive controller adopts the generalized predictive control algorithm based on ant colony algorithm. Firstly, the future course output state is predicted according to the state space model. Secondly, the output error is used to evaluate the predicted value. Thirdly, the ant colony algorithm is used to obtain the optimal control sequence of the rudder angle. Finally, the control action of the current time should be added to the system. At this point the control loop is completed (Fig. 3).

3.1   State Space Model

CARIMA model can eliminate the residuals and is suitable for systems with non-stationary random interference. So it is used to build the state space model of unmanned surface vessel. The state space equations is expressed as:

$$A(z^{-1})\Psi(k) = B(z^{-1})\delta(k-1) + \xi(k)/(1-z^{-1}) \tag{5}$$

where z^{-1} is the inverse operator of the transformation, that is the backward time operator. $A(z^{-1})$ and $B(z^{-1})$ is the polynomial of the backward time operator. $\Psi(k)$ is the output prediction value of the unmanned surface vessel course angle, $\delta(k)$ is the input course angle, $\xi(k)$ is the interference signal of the wind, waves, and currents.

In order to calculate the course angle $\Psi(k+j)$ of the forward j step of the system's course angle $\Psi(k)$, two sets of Diophantine equations is introduced by:

$$\begin{cases} 1 = E_j A(1-z^{-1}) + z^{-j}F_j \\ \quad E_j B = G_j + z^{-j}H_j \end{cases} \tag{6}$$

Both sides of the Eq. (4) multiply $E_j(z^{-1})z^j$, and then substitute the Diophantine Eq. (5) into the Eq. (4), the result is the prediction value of course angle:

$$\Psi(k+j) = G_j\delta(k+j-1) + H_j(1-z^{-1})\delta(k-1) + F_j\Psi(k) + E_j\xi(k+j) \quad (7)$$

Further on the above reduction, the prediction value of course angle is calculated by the equation:

$$\Psi(k+j) = G_j\delta(k+j-1) + \Psi_0(k+j) \quad (8)$$

where

$$\Psi_0(k+j) = H_j(1-z^{-1})\delta(k-1) + F_j\Psi(k) + E_j\xi(k+j) \quad (9)$$

3.2 Feedback Correction

The error calculation formula of the prediction value and the actual value at k time is as follows:

$$e(k) = \Psi(k) - \Psi_a(k) \quad (10)$$

where $\Psi_a(k)$ is the actual output value of the course angle.

At k time, the prediction value of the course angle in the prediction time domain is corrected as follows:

$$\Psi(k+j) = G_j(1-z^{-1})\delta(k+j-1) + \Psi_0(k+j) + e(k) \quad (11)$$

The purpose of the predictive controller is to reduce the deviation between the predicted course value and the preset course value, so the objective function used in this system for optimizing control is:

$$J = \sum_{j=1}^{N_\Psi}[\Psi(k+j) - \Psi_p(k+j)]^2 + \lambda\sum_{j=1}^{N_\delta}[\triangle\delta(k+j-1)]^2 \quad (12)$$

where $\Psi_p(k+j)$ is the setting course, $N_\Psi = 20$ is the prediction horizon, $N_\delta = 2$ is the control time domain, and $\lambda = 1$ is the control weighted coefficient.

3.3 Ant Colony Algorithm

The system uses ant colony algorithm to optimize the control objective function. Ant colony algorithm has good robustness in solving performance, and can be implemented in parallel. The ant colony algorithm is used to minimize the objective function within the range of the rudder angle to obtain the optimal control sequence. The implementation steps of the algorithm are as follows:

(1) **The ant pheromone distribution initialization, set the number of iterations;**

(2) **10 Ants are to be initialized in the neighborhood, moving according to the following transfer probability. For each ant, the objective function is defined, the probability of the transfer of the ant at the moment is as follows:**

$$p_{ij}(k) = \frac{[\tau_j(k)]^{1.2}[\triangle J_{ij}(k)]^2}{\sum_r [\tau_r(k)]^{1.2}[\triangle J_{ir}(k)]^2} \tag{13}$$

where $\tau_j(k)$ is the j-neighborhood attracting intensity of the ants at k time; $\triangle J_{ij} = J_i - J_j$ is the difference value of the target function;

(3) **Calculate the objective function value of each ant, and record the optimal control sequence in the current ant colony;**

(4) **Revise the intensity of pheromone according to the pheromone update equation, and the equation is as follows:**

$$\begin{cases} \tau_j(k+1) = 0.7\tau_j(k) + \sum \triangle \tau_j \\ \triangle \tau_j = 1/J_j \end{cases} \tag{14}$$

(5) **Number of iterations $N = N + 1$**

(6) **If the number of iterations does not reach the end iteration number 100, the second step is returned, otherwise, the loop is terminated and the optimal control sequence is outputted.**

Optimization of control object function by Ant Colony Algorithm, the optimal control law of the system output can be obtained, and then the optimal control rudder angle of unmanned surface vessel is obtained. Finally, the rudder angle of unmanned surface vessel is obtained as follows:

$$\delta = (G^T G + \lambda I)^{-1} G^T [\Psi_p - F\Psi(k) - H\triangle\delta(k-1)] \tag{15}$$

4   Test Analysis

4.1   Simulation Results

The disturbance of wind and waves on unmanned surface vessel are simulated using white noise and a second-order wave transfer function [11]. The disturbance of ocean current simulates with a constant value.

$$y(s) = K_c\omega(s)\frac{K_\omega s}{s^2 + 2\zeta\omega_0 s + \omega_0^2} \tag{16}$$

where $\omega(s)$ is a Gaussian white noise with a mean of zero, the power spectrum density is 0.1, and $K_c = 5$ is a constant disturbance coefficient, $\zeta = 0.3, K_\omega = 0.42, \omega_0 = 0.606$. Simulation of wind power level 4, the sea state of the big wave.

In the case of wind, wave and current interference, when the setting course is 15°, the effect of PID control and predictive control is shown in the following figure.

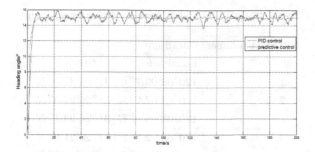

Fig. 4. Contrast diagram of course angle

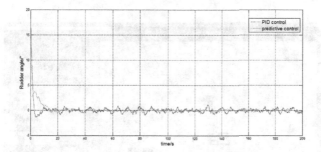

Fig. 5. Contrast diagram of rudder angle

Figures 4 and 5 shows that the control stability of traditional PID has become worse with external disturbances. Compared with the predictive controller, steering range of PID is larger and steering frequency of PID is faster. The predictive controller can realize the stable course control, and has the characteristics of strong anti-interference.

4.2 Unmanned Surface Vessel Test

The designed predictive controller is applied to unmanned surface vessel, and the course control experiment was carried out in Taihu, Wuxi, Jiangsu province. The test time was 21 June 2017, the weather conditions were as follows: cloudy day, the wind direction was southeast wind, the wind speed was 4 stages, and the wave height was 1 m.

Six target points are selected for the course control experiment in Taihu, the latitude and longitude of the target point as shown in Table 2. The speed of the unmanned surface vessel was 2.09497 m/s during the test. The photo of the monitoring software interface is shown in Fig. 6.

It can be seen from Figs. 6, 7 and Table 3 that the unmanned surface vessel can pass through the target points when disturbed by wind and waves. The maximum tracking error is 19.9193 m.

Table 2. Latitude and longitude of the target point

Target number	Coordinate	
	Longitude	Latitude
1	$120°08'03.7''E$	$31°26'31.4''N$
2	$120°08'07.7''E$	$31°26'27.9''N$
3	$120°08'06.5''E$	$31°26'23.1''N$
4	$120°08'02.3''E$	$31°26'21.0''N$
5	$120°07'57.4''E$	$31°26'24.3''N$
6	$120°07'59.0''E$	$31°26'29.4''N$

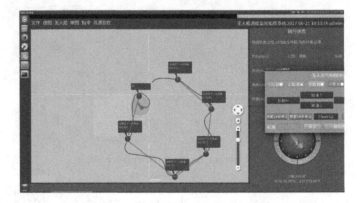

Fig. 6. Contrast diagram of rudder angle

Table 3. Average performance measures of predictive control

Number of target points arriving	Total distance (m)	Frechet distance (m)
6	993.573	19.9193

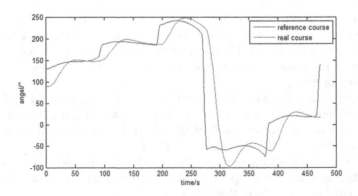

Fig. 7. Contrast diagram of rudder angle

5 Conclusion

In this paper, the predictive controller based on ant colony optimization algorithm is designed for the course control of unmanned surface vessel. The experimental results show that the predictive controller has good robustness and anti - jamming. The predictive controller solves the problem caused by large disturbances and the overshoot of the steering controller. Finally, the feasibility of the designed controller is verified by the results of the actual unmanned surface vessel test.

References

1. Liu, C., Chu, X., Wu, Q., Wang, G.: USV Development Status and Prospects. China Shipbuilding, pp. 194–205 (2014)
2. Mcninch, L.C., Muske, K.R., Ashrafiuon, H.: Model-based predictive control of an unmanned surface vessel. In: 11th IASTED International Conference on Intelligent Systems and Control, pp. 385–390 (2008)
3. Wang, C.S., Xiao, H.R., Han, Y.Z.: Applications of ADRC in unmanned surface vessel course tracking. J. Appl. Biomat. Bio. **427–429**, 897–900 (2013)
4. Li, C., Zhao, Y., Wang, G., Fan, Y., Bai, Y.: Adaptive RBF neural network control for unmanned surface vessel course tracking. In: International Conference on Information Science and Technology, pp. 285–290. IEEE (2016)
5. Mcninch, L.C., Ashrafiuon, H.: Predictive and sliding mode cascade control for unmanned surface vessels. In: American Control Conference, pp. 184–189. IEEE (2011)
6. Jiang, L., Mu, D., Fan, Y., Wang, G.: Study on USV model identification and nonlinear course control. Comput. Meas. Control **24**, 133–136 (2016)
7. Mu, D., Zhao, Y., Wang, G., Fan, Y., Bai, Y.: USV model identification and course control. In: Sixth International Conference on Information Science and Technology, pp. 263-267. IEEE (2016)
8. Mu, D., Zhao, Y., Wang, G., Fan, Y., Bai, Y.: Course control of USV based on fuzzy adaptive guide control. In: Control and Decision Conference, pp. 6433–6437. IEEE (2016)
9. Larrazabal, J.M., Penas, M.S.: Intelligent rudder control of an unmanned surface vessel. Exper. Syst. Appl. **55**, 106–117 (2016)
10. Abdolmalaki, R.Y., Mahjoob, M.J., Abbasi, E.: Fuzzy LQR controller for heading control of an unmanned surface vessel. In: International Workshops in Electrical-Electronics Engineering. ACE (2013)
11. Wang, Y.: Based on auto disturbance rejection control algorithm for course autopilot of unmanned surface vessel design. Dalian Maritime University (2014)
12. Annamalai, A.S.K.: An adaptive autopilot design for an uninhabited surface vehicle. University Of Plymouth (2014)
13. Ruirui, L.: Research And Application On Generalized Predictive Control Based on Particle Swarm Optimization Algorithm. LanZhou JiaoTong University (2012)
14. Yang, J.: Ant Colony Algorithm and Its Application Research. Zhejiang University (2007)

15. Shangyong, F.: Ship Maneuverability. National Defense Industry Press, Beijing (1988)
16. Moe, S., Pettersen, K.Y.: Set-based Line-of-Sight (LOS) path following with collision avoidance for underactuated unmanned surface vessel. In: 24th Mediterranean Conference Control and Automation, pp. 402–409. IEEE (2016)

Two-Dimensional DOA Estimation of Multipath Signals Using Compressive Sensing

Lin Zhao, Jian Xu$^{(\boxtimes)}$, and Jicheng Ding

College of Automation, Harbin Engineering University, Harbin, Heilongjiang, China
{zhaolin,xu}@hrbeu.edu.cn, aaron.heu@163.com

Abstract. Multipath signal is often considered an interference that must be removed. The coherence between multipath and direct component makes it difficult to use conventional direction-of-arrival (DOA) estimation methods in a smart antenna system. This study demonstrates a new multipath signal DOA estimation technique of the L-shaped array. The proposed algorithm first converts the two-dimensional DOA estimation to the DOA estimation of uniform linear array, and apply the independent component analysis algorithm to obtain the steering vectors with multipath information. Then, based on the special structure of the obtained steering vectors and spatial sparsity of the multipath signals, the algorithm uses the solution of the sparse signal reconstruction problem in the compressive sensing theory, and search the space spectrums to acquire the synthesis angles for each direct component and multipath component. Finally according to the geometric relationship to obtained the azimuth and elevation angles. Comparative simulation tests and analysis prove the effectiveness of the proposed algorithm in estimation accuracy.

Keywords: Multipath signal · L-shaped array · Independent component analysis · Compressive sensing

1 Introduction

The direction of arrival (DOA) estimation is an important research direction in the field of array signal processing. It uses the positional relationship between different elements in the sensor array to estimate the incident direction of the spatial signal. At present, the one-dimensional (1D) DOA estimation algorithms has been widely developed, especially the most classic subspace algorithm: multiple signal classification (MUSIC) [1] and estimating signal parameters via rotational invariance techniques (ESPRIT) [2]. However, in many fields such as radar, sonar, wireless communication and other practical applications, two-dimensional (2D) DOA estimation has a wider range of research value.

In recent years, due to the good performance [3], L-shaped array has attracted the attention of researchers because of its good performance, and many high-resolution algorithms have been proposed. 2D MUSIC algorithm is a kind of

© Springer Nature Singapore Pte Ltd. 2017
C. He et al. (Eds.): BIC-TA 2017, CCIS 791, pp. 567–579, 2017.
https://doi.org/10.1007/978-981-10-7179-9_45

typical representative algorithm in 2D DOA estimation, but it requires 2D scanning, computationally large. [4] proposes a reduced-dimension MUSIC algorithm, which transforms the 2D search problem into 1D search problem, and then uses the least squares method to obtain the 2D angle. The estimator of [5] applies the singular value decomposition (SVD) algorithm to a cross-correlation matrix that is constructed from both arrays of the L-shaped structure so as to avoid the computational burden of the complex pair-matching procedure. The algorithm in [6] proposes a DOA estimation technique based on linear operations applied to partial data matrix with L-shaped array configuration for uncorrelated sources.

In real environment, multipath effect is common, which is caused by the signal arriving at the receiver after reflection of obstacle. The multipath may cause the signal received by the array antenna to have a direct component and several multipath components, which are coherent to one another. These components will be merged into a source signal and make the signal subspace rank deficient when general DOA estimation methods are used. The estimated performance will decline and may fail.

For the DOA estimation of multipath signals, most researchers preprocess the coherent signals to achieve decoherence and then estimate the DOAs. Currently, coherent signal-preprocessing methods mainly include spatial smoothing algorithm [7], Toeplitz algorithm [8] and subspace fitting algorithm [9].

In recent years, the 2D DOA estimation of coherent sources has been studied [10,11], but few are based on L-shaped array, and the DOA of multipath components are not estimated. The new method defines the synthesis angles according to the spatial structural of the L-shaped array, convert the 2D DOA estimation to the 1D DOA estimation, then uses the independent component analysis (ICA) algorithm to obtain the steering vectors, and the compressive sensing (CS) theory is used to estimate the synthesis angles of the direct component and each multipath component of the array signals. Finally according to the geometric relationship to obtained the azimuth and elevation angles. This method is significant to suppress the multipath interference in the beamforming process. In addition, without decoherent preprocessing and 2D search, the calculation process is simplified.

2   Data Model

L-shaped array consists of two vertical uniform linear arrays (ULA) with the same structure. The array elements are located along x and y axes. Each ULA consists of M isotropic sensors. As shown in Fig. 1.

Assume N narrowband farfield plane signals from various directions impinging on an L-shaped array and two groups of mixed signals with M parallel channels are obtained. Let θ_n and ϕ_n be the azimuth and elevation angles of the n-th signal. The result is expressed as:

$$\begin{aligned} X(t) &= A_X(\theta, \phi) S(t) + n_X(t) \\ Y(t) &= A_Y(\theta, \phi) S(t) + n_Y(t) \end{aligned} \tag{1}$$

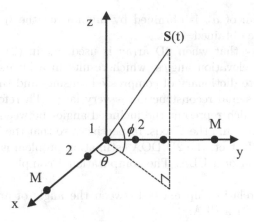

Fig. 1. The geometrical configuration of the L-shaped array for 2-D direction estimation

Where $S(t) = [s_1(t), s_2(t), \cdots, s_N(t)]^T$ is the source signals; $X(t) = [x_1(t), x_2(t), \cdots, x_M(t)]^T$ and $Y(t) = [y_1(t), y_2(t), \cdots, y_M(t)]^T$ are the received signals of each subarray; $A_X(\theta, \phi) = [a_x(\theta_1, \phi_1), a_x(\theta_2, \phi_2), \cdots, a_x(\theta_N, \phi_N)]$ and $A_Y(\theta, \phi) = [a_y(\theta_1, \phi_1), a_y(\theta_2, \phi_2), \cdots, a_y(\theta_N, \phi_N)]$ are the array manifolds; $a_x(\theta_n, \phi_n)$ or $a_y(\theta_n, \phi_n)$ (when the array shape is not specified, use a_n instead) is the steering vector of the n-th channel; and $n_X(t)$ and $n_Y(t)$ denote added white Gaussian noise (AWGN) vectors.

For every source signal, if P multipath components are also received, since the multipath components are attenuated relative to the direct component without waveform changing, a_n is rewritten as

$$\hat{a}_n = a_n + \sum_{p=2}^{P} c_n(p) \, al_n(p) \tag{2}$$

Where $al_n(p)$ is the steering vector of the p-th multipath component in the n-th channel; and $c_n(p)$ is the propagation attenuation coefficient of the p-th multipath component in the n-th channel.

3 Proposed Algorithm

Many studies have verified that the mixed signal can be separated into source signals using the ICA algorithm [12]. Hence, the linear mixed array, which is array manifold, $\hat{A}$ can be obtained.

In the multipath receipt environments, the steering vector $\hat{a}_n$ in the array manifold contains the multipath components, as shown in Eq. (2). If the expected DOAs are expended to the entire spacing spectrum, the DOA spacing distribution is sparse and satisfies the important assumption of the CS theory. Thus, the sparse spectrum of $\hat{a}_n$ is obtained by minimizing the l_1 norm. Then, the expected DOAs are obtained.

It is noteworthy that when 2D array is used, a_n in (2) is determined by both azimuth and elevation angles, which results in a huge number of atoms in the over-complete dictionary of compressed sensing, and the computation of subsequent sparse signal reconstruction is very large. Therefore, we define the synthesis angles, which represent the included angles between the directions of arrival and the X axis and the Y axis, respectively, so that the 2D dictionary can be reduced to 1D. In fact, the 2D DOA estimation problem is transformed into the DOA estimation of a ULA. The computational complexity can be greatly reduced.

The following relationship exists between the angle of arrival α_n and the steering vector a_n for a ULA:

$$a_n = \left[1, e^{j2\pi d \cos \alpha_n/\lambda}, \cdots, e^{j2\pi d(M-1)\cos \alpha_n/\lambda}\right]^{\mathrm{T}}, (n = 1, 2, \cdots, N) \quad (3)$$

Where d is the array element spacing, and λ is the wavelength of the received signal. The DOA estimation process can be divided into 3 steps: (1) separation of the signal using ICA to estimate the array manifolds $\hat{A}_X$ and $\hat{A}_Y$; (2) obtaining the synthesis angless of the direct and multipath components using CS; (3) obtained the azimuth and elevation angles from the estimated synthesis angles according to the geometric relationship.

3.1   Separating Signals Using the ICA Algorithm

The signals from different sources are typically statistically independent from one another. The ICA algorithm uses this characteristic to estimate the source signals from the observed mixed signals.

Because noise can be used as sources and separated from the mixed signals, a noisy signal model can be considered a promotion of a noise-free mode [13]. Therefore, a noise-free linear instantaneous mixture ICA model is discussed. The received signal of 1D mode can be simply expressed as

$$X(t) = AS(t) \quad (4)$$

A matrix W should be obtained when ICA is used to process the received mixed signal to estimate the source signal:

$$Y(t) = WX(t) = WAS(t) = GS(t) \quad (5)$$

Where the ICA output $Y(t) = [y_1(t), y_2(t), \cdots, y_N(t)]^{\mathrm{T}}$ is the estimation of unknown source signals $S(t) = [s_1(t), s_2(t), \cdots, s_N(t)]^{\mathrm{T}}$, W is the de-mixing matrix (or weighted matrix), and G is the global matrix. If the global matrix $G = \hat{W}\hat{A}$ has only one element that is approximately 1 in each row and each column and the other elements are approximately 0, the mixed signal will be successfully separated. Therefore, the inverse matrix (or pseudoinverse matrix when the number of sources N is not equal to the number of sensors M) $\hat{A}$ of the de-mixing matrix estimation $\hat{W}$ can be considered the estimation of array manifold A. There are some differences in amplitude, phase and sort order between $\hat{A}$ and A due to the inherent uncertainty of the ICA algorithm [12]. Fortunately, these differences do not affect the final DOA estimation results because the DOA depends on the ratio between the elements in a steering vector.

Since complex calculations must be solved in this study, we apply the complex fast independent component analysis (cFastICA) algorithm [14] to solve the ICA problem. In addition, the ICA algorithm should pre-process the received data, which includes centering and whitening the received data. These operations can improve the convergence properties, relieve the ill-posed problem, eliminate the information redundancy or reduce the effect of noise.

3.2   Estimating the DOA Using the Compressive Sensing Theory

CS theory [15] is a new signal sampling, encoding and decoding theory that fully uses the signal sparsity or compressibility. It can be used to accurately restore the original signal or estimate the signal parameters by using much less required measurement data than the classic Nyquist sampling theory. In the CS theory, using the sparsity priori conditions of the signal, the original signal can be reconstructed by the optimization theory algorithm with a high probability.

In Sect. 3.1, we describe how to obtain the estimated array manifold $\hat{A} = [\hat{a}_1, \hat{a}_2, \cdots, \hat{a}_N]$, $\hat{a}_n$ is the estimated steering vector with multipath component information and corresponds to each source signal. Equation (2) can be rewritten as

$$\hat{a}_n = \left[\tilde{a}_n, \tilde{a}l_n\left(2\right), \cdots, \tilde{a}l_n\left(P\right)\right]\left[\tilde{c}_n\left(1\right), \tilde{c}_n\left(2\right), \cdots \tilde{c}_n\left(P\right)\right]^{\mathrm{T}} + \dot{n} = BC + \dot{n} \quad (6)$$

Where $B = \left[\tilde{a}_n, \tilde{a}l_n\left(2\right), \cdots, \tilde{a}l_n\left(P\right)\right]$ is a set of steering vectors, which describe the direct component and multipath components, which are received from the same source and enter the array antenna. $C = [\tilde{c}_n\left(1\right), \tilde{c}_n\left(2\right), \cdots \tilde{c}_n\left(P\right)]^{\mathrm{T}}$ is a set of propagation attenuation coefficients of the multipath components relative to the direct components. In particular, $\tilde{c}_n\left(1\right)$ is the attenuation coefficient of the direct component, and its value is equal to 1. $\dot{n}$ is the discrepancy between the estimated steering vector (after adjusting the amplitude and sequence) and the actual steering vector caused by additive noise in (1).

According to the CS theory, the steering vector can be configured as the atoms of an over-complete dictionary. The specific method samples the angular space or uniformly discretizes the angle space. As a result, the angle space is divided into uniform grids. Suppose the indices of Q grids are $[\varphi_1, \varphi_2, \cdots \varphi_Q]$, these Q grids will be the candidate direction of the arrival vectors, and $P \ll Q$. According to Eq. (3), the over-complete dictionary is $B = [b\left(\varphi_1\right), b\left(\varphi_2\right), \cdots, b\left(\varphi_Q\right)]$, and $b\left(\varphi_q\right) = \left[1, e^{j2\pi d \cos\varphi_q/\lambda}, \cdots, e^{j2\pi d(M-1)\cos\varphi_q/\lambda}\right]^{\mathrm{T}}$, $(q = 1, 2, \cdots, Q)$.

Equation (6) is an underdetermined equation, and the solution obtained using traditional methods is not unique. However, its most sparse solution can be found by solving the optimization problem

$$\min \quad \|C\|_{l_0} \quad \text{s.t.} \quad \hat{a}_n = BC + \dot{n} \tag{7}$$

Where $\|C\|_{l_0}$ is the l_0 norm of C or the number of non-zero elements of C. This is a non-deterministic polynomial-time hard problem (NP-Hard) [16]. There are C_M^P possible linear combinations that satisfy Eq. (7). A simpler l_1 norm optimization can be used to solve this problem [17]. Furthermore, it can be converted to solve the second-order cone programming (SOCP) [18]:

$$\min \quad \|C\|_{l_1} \quad \text{s.t.} \quad \|\hat{a}_n - BC\|_{l_2}^2 \leq \beta^2 \tag{8}$$

Where β is the variance of $\dot{n}$. In practice, after acquiring and tracking the GNSS signal, the discrepancy between the local generated signal and the practical received signal separated by ICA can be obtained. Meanwhile, the discrepancy between the estimated steering vector (after adjusting the amplitude and sequence) and the actual steering vector can be obtained.

In this study, the interior point method (IPM) [19] is applied to solve Eq. (8) and achieve the sparse spectrum of C.

With reference to Eq. (6), the following conclusion can be made. For a signal source with a direct component and multipath components, if φ_q is equal to the DOA of the direct component, the attenuation coefficient c_q is approximately equal to 1. If φ_q is equal to the multipath component DOA, the attenuation coefficient c_q is approximately equal to the attenuation coefficient of this component. If φ_q is not equal to the direct component or multipath component DOA, the corresponding c_q is approximately equal to 0. Therefore, expected results can be obtained through the sparse spectrum peak. Additionally, the incident signal can be determined from the direct or multipath component based on the value of c_q.

3.3   Obtained the Azimuth and Elevation Angles

As mentioned in the previous section, we define the synthesis angles α and β to represent the included angles between the directions of arrival and the X axis and the Y axis, respectively. According to Fig. 1, there is obviously: $\cos \alpha = \cos \theta \cos \phi$, $\cos \beta = \sin \theta \cos \phi$.

After using ICA algorithm combined with CS theory, we obtain the α and β of direct component and multipath components, respectively. The general DOA estimation algorithm, such as MUSIC, need the eigenvalue decomposition of the covariance matrix of each subarray received data respectively, which leads to the feature vector sequence may be different, so the azimuth and elevation angles can not be calculated directly matched. The algorithm proposed in this paper can not only obtain the value of the space synthesis angle but also obtain the amplitude of the signal by using the sparse decomposition. The azimuth and pitch angles are solved by these two information, and the pairing is very simple.

The azimuths θ and elevations ϕ are obtained by using backstepping according to geometric relation:

$$\theta = \arctan\left(\frac{\cos\beta}{\cos\alpha}\right)$$
$$\phi = \arccos\left[\sqrt{(\cos\alpha)^2 + (\cos\beta)^2}\right]$$

(9)

The proposed DOA estimation algorithm is summarized as follows:

(1) Pre-process received subarray signals $X(t)$ of the L-shaped array, including the centering and whitening processes.
(2) Use ICA algorithm to estimate the de-mixing matrix $\hat{W}$.
(3) Calculate the inverse (or pseudoinverse) of the de-mixing matrix to obtain the array manifold estimation $\hat{A}$.
(4) Create an over-complete dictionary B according to the grid indices of the synthesis angle α space.
(5) Solve the SOCP problem and obtain the sparse spectrum of the propagation attenuation coefficient set $\hat{C}$ for a source signal.
(6) Find the peak values of the sparse spectrum and obtain the synthesis angles α of the direct and multipath components that correspond to $\hat{a}_n$.
(7) Obtain all the synthesis angles α of the direct and multipath components one-by-one.
(8) Repeat the steps from (1) to (7) for the received subarray signals $Y(t)$ of the L-shaped array to obtain the synthesis angles β.
(9) Calculate the azimuths θ and elevations ϕ from the obtained synthesis angles according to the Eq. (9).

4 Simulation

To verify the effectiveness and computational accuracy of the proposed algorithm, we compare it with the space smoothing combined (SS) with MUSIC algorithm [20] in the following aspects: spatial resolution, accuracy at different SNRs and snapshots.

Simulation conditions were set up based on assumptions of the actual GNSS signal transmission environment. To study the adaptability of the simulation, for the source signals, we set the existence of a multipath component and no multipath component. The following general simulation conditions are shown in Table 1. The GNSS navigation signals from 3 satellites are incident to an L-shaped array composed of two uniform linear arrays of 12 elements from different angles, the incident azimuths are 25°, 30° and 35°; the elevations are 85°, 75° and 60°. Each of the first two signals has a multipath component, and the incident azimuths are 40° and 45°; the elevations are 40° and 15°; and the third signal does not have multipath components. The propagation attenuation coefficients of the 2 multipath components are −6 dB, −7 dB.

Table 1. The general simulation conditions

Signal type		GNSS navigation signals		
Number of satellites		3		
Incident angles of direct components	Azimuth	25°	30°	35°
	Elevation	85°	75°	60°
Incident angles of multipath components	Azimuth	40°	45°	NA
	Elevation	40°	15°	NA
Propagation attenuation coefficients		−6 dB	−7 dB	NA

4.1   Spatial Resolution

For the Simulation 1, the signal-to-noise ratio (SNR) of the signals was 20 dB, and the sampling number was 2000. To verify the spatial resolution of the proposed algorithm clearly, we only show the spatial spectrum of synthesis angles α using SS-MUSIC and the proposed algorithm as Fig. 2. It can reflect the estimation contrast of azimuths and elevation angles.

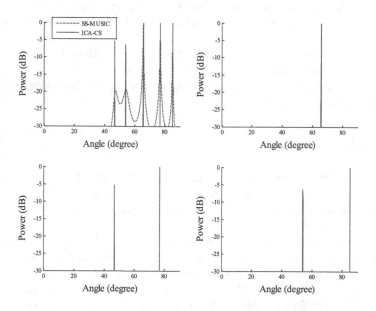

Fig. 2. Contrast diagram of spatial spectrum of the independent component analysis-compressive sensing and spatial smoothing-multiple signal classification algorithm

From the simulation results of the first subgraph, the ICA-CS algorithm has sharper peaks than SS-MUSIC. This means that the DOA estimation results from the ICA-CS algorithm have a higher resolution in the spatial spectrum. This is because the spatial spectrum of the MUSIC algorithm reflects the distance between the steering vector and noise subspace, and the performance of the algorithm depends on the orthogonality between them. In the coherent signal reception environment, a distorted covariance matrix causes the orthogonality to worsen. Correspondingly, the resolution of the MUSIC algorithm deteriorated. The spatial spectrum of the ICA-CS reflects the signal energy from a certain angle in the space domain, and the spatial spectrum amplitude is zero at the angle of no signal arrival; therefore, needle-shaped curves are observed in Fig. 2.

In addition, the synthesis angles of all the components can be achieved from the spatial spectrum of the array signal using the SS-MUSIC algorithm, but it is difficult to distinguish direct and multipath components received from the same source signal. The ICA-CS algorithm solves the steering vector corresponding to each source signal to calculate the synthesis angles of its direct and multipath components. It is shown in other three subgraphs in Fig. 2. Different multipath components and their attenuation can also be observed.

4.2   DOA Estimation Error at Various SNRs

The conditions of the Simulation 1, except for the SNR, were used to assess the 2D DOA estimation error at various SNRs. The range of tested SNR is 10–30 dB with an interval of 2 dB. The estimated DOA errors were obtained using 100 independent trials of the experiment. A different computer realization of the noise was rendered for each trial. For the first source signal, the root-mean-square error (RMSE) of the DOA estimation of the direct and multipath components changes with the SNR for different algorithms, as shown in Fig. 3. (The two graphs show the estimation results of the direct component and a multipath component).

Figure 3 shows that the error of the two algorithms gradually decreases to zero with increasing SNR. A larger SNR results in a smaller DOA RMSE. Whether it is a direct component or a multipath component, the introduced ICA-CS outperforms the SS-MUSIC algorithm. In particular, an expected DOA estimation is obtained using the ICA-CS at low SNR.

4.3   DOA Estimation Error in Various Snapshots

In the following, the conditions of Simulation 1, except the snapshot, were used to assess the 2D DOA estimation error in various snapshots. In this test, the snapshot changes from 400 to 2000. In total, 100 independent trials of the experiment were conducted. The RMSEs of the DOA estimation versus the number of snapshots are plotted in Fig. 4. (The two graphs show the direct component and a multipath component).

Figure 4 shows the DOA estimation RMSEs gradually decrease when the number of snapshots increases. The DOA estimation errors of the direct and a multipath component are less than 0.15° for the lowest number of snapshots using the ICA-CS algorithm. For the SS-MUSIC algorithm, whether for a direct

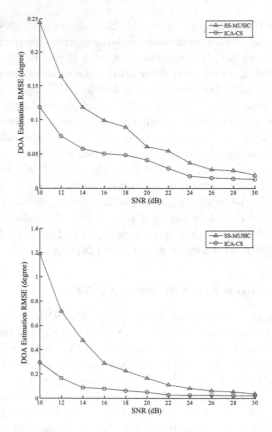

Fig. 3. DOA estimation root-mean-square errors of all components at various signal-to-noise ratios

component or two multipath components, its performance is significantly worse than the ICA-CS algorithm.

In Simulations 2 and 3, since the DOA estimation performance of the SS-MUSIC algorithm depends on the covariance matrix, and the low SNR and low snapshot conditions lead to covariance, a larger error occurs and creates a large distance error between the steering vector and the noise subspace. Additionally, the spatial smoothing algorithm reduces the array aperture and further decreases the estimation accuracy for the same number of antenna array elements.

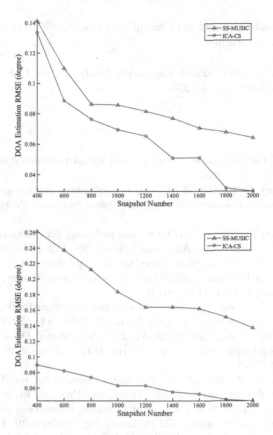

Fig. 4. DOA estimation root-mean-square errors of all components in various snapshots

5   Conclusion

In this paper, we proposed a multipath 2D DOA estimation method of L-shaped array, which combines the complex fast independent component analysis with the compressed sensing theory without decoherence processing. By defining the synthesis angles, the dimension of over-complete dictionary is reduced, and the computational complexity is greatly reduced. The simulation results illustrate the effectiveness of the proposed method. When the SNR is 10 dB, the RMSE is maintained below 0.3°, which is obviously better than the classic SS-MUSIC algorithm. When the SNR is 20 dB and the sampling number is only 400, the estimated DOA RMSE can be maintained below 0.15°, which is also applicable in the absence of sufficient data.

Because of the experimental conditions are relatively complex, for example, to satisfy the test requirements, we require many GNSS antennas and set them as a uniform linear array while ensuring that specified number of direct components and its corresponding multipath components are received by the antenna array.

Thus, we only make the software simulations and will perform the practical experiment in future studies.

Acknowledgments. This research was jointly funded by the China Natural Science Foundation (No. 61633008, 61304234).

References

1. Schmidt, R.: Multiple emitter location and signal parameter estimation. Int. J. Eng Res. **2**, 276–280 (1986)
2. Roy, R., Paulraj, A., Kailath, T.: ESPRIT-a subspace rotation approach to estimation of parameters of cisoids in noise. IEEE Trans. Antennas Propag. **34**, 1340–1342 (1986)
3. Hua, Y., Sarkar, T., Weiner, D.D.: An L-shaped array for estimating 2-D directions of wave arrival. IEEE Trans. Antennas Propag. **39**, 143–146 (1991)
4. Zhang, X., Xu, L., Xu, L., et al.: Direction of Departure (DOD) and Direction of Arrival (DOA) estimation in MIMO radar with reduced-dimension MUSIC. IEEE Commun. Lett. **14**, 1161–1163 (2010)
5. Liang, J., Liu, D.: Joint elevation and azimuth direction finding using L-shaped array. IEEE Antennas Wirel. Propag. Lett. **58**, 2136–2141 (2010)
6. Tayem, N., Majeed, K., Hussain, A.A.: Two-dimensional DOA estimation using cross-correlation matrix with L-shaped array. IEEE Antennas Wirel. Propag. Lett. **15**, 1077–1080 (2016)
7. Shan, T.J., Wax, M., Kailath, T.: On spatial smoothing for direction-of-arrival estimation of coherent signals. IEEE. Trans. Sig. Process. **33**, 806–811 (1985)
8. Chen, Y.M., Lee, J.H., Yeh, C.C., et al.: Bearing estimation without calibration for randomly perturbed arrays. IEEE. Trans. Sig. Process. **39**, 194–197 (1991)
9. Hamza, R., Buckley, K.: Second-order statistical analysis of totally weighted subspace fitting methods. IEEE. Trans. Sig. Process. **42**, 2520–2524 (1994)
10. Xie, J., He, Z., Li, H., et al.: 2D DOA estimation with sparse uniform circular arrays in the presence of mutual coupling. EURASIP. J. Adv. Sig. Process. **2011**(1), 127 (2011)
11. Liu, Z., Ruan, X., He, J.: Efficient 2-D DOA estimation for coherent sources with a sparse acoustic vector-sensor array. Multidimens. Syst. Sig. **24**(1), 105–120 (2013)
12. Hyvrinen, A., Oja, E.: Independent component analysis: algorithms and applications. Neural Netw. **13**, 411–430 (2000)
13. Zhao, L.: ICA algorithm and its application in array signal processing. Harbin Engineering University (2009)
14. Bingham, E., Hyvrinen, A.: A fast fixed-point algorithm for independent component analysis of complex valued signals. Int. J. Neural. Syst. **10**, 1–8 (2000)
15. Candes, E.J., Romberg, J.K., Tao, T.: Stable signal recovery from incomplete and inaccurate measurements. Commun. Pure Appl. Math. **59**, 1207–1223 (2006)
16. Candes, E.J., Wakin, M.B.: An introduction to compressive sampling. IEEE Trans. Sig. Process. **25**, 21–30 (2008)
17. Chen, S.S., Donoho, D.L., Saunders, M.A.: Atomic decomposition by basis pursuit. SIAM Rev. **43**, 129–159 (2001)
18. Malioutov, D., Cetin, M., Willsky, A.S.: A sparse signal reconstruction perspective for source localization with sensor arrays. IEEE Trans. Sig. Process. **53**, 3010–3022 (2005)

19. Candes, E., Romberg, J.: l1-MAGIC: recovery of sparse signals via convex programming, 14 April 2005. www.acm.caltech.edu/l1magic/downloads/l1magic.pdf
20. Al-Ardi, E.M., Shubair, R.M., Al-Mualla, M.E.: Computationally efficient DOA estimation in a multipath environment using covariance differencing and iterative spatial smoothing. In: IEEE International Symposium on Circuits, Systems and Signal Processing, ISCAS 2005, vol. 3804, pp. 3805–3808. IEEE (2005)

Enhanced Pairwise Learning for Personalized Ranking from Implicit Feedback

Yunzhou Zhang[1,2], Bo Yuan[1,2], and Ke Tang[1,2(✉)]

[1] Department of Computer Science and Technology, USTC-Birmingham Joint
Research Institute in Intelligent Computation and Its Applications,
University of Science and Technology of China, Hefei, China
zyunzhou@mail.ustc.edu.cn, ketang@ustc.edu.cn, yuanb@sustc.edu.cn
[2] Shenzhen Key Laboratory of Computational Intelligence,
Department of Computer Science and Engineering, Southern University of Science
and Technology, Shenzhen, China

Abstract. One-class collaborative filtering with implicit feedback has
attracted much attention, mainly due to the widespread of implicit data
in real world. Pairwise methods have been shown to be the state-of-the-
art methods for one-class collaborative filtering, but the assumption that
users prefer observed items to unobserved items may not always hold.
Besides, existing pairwise methods may not perform well in terms of Top-
N recommendation. In this paper, we propose a new approach called
EBPR, which relaxes the former simple pairwise preference assumption
by further exploiting the hidden connection in observed items and unobserved items. EBPR can also be used as a basic method and has the
extensive applicability, i.e., when combining our model with former pairwise methods, better performance can also be achieved. Empirical studies show that our algorithm outperforms the state-of-the-art methods on
four real-world datasets.

Keywords: Implicit feedback · Pairwise methods · Top-N recommendation

1 Introduction

Recently, *Collaborative Filtering* method has become one of the core technologies of recommendation systems. Most research on collaborative filtering focuses
on explicit feedbacks [1], like numerical ratings. However, in many real-world
scenarios, explicit feedbacks are not always available. On the contrary, there are
lots of data in "one-class" form, e.g., "clicks" on web pages, "views" on movies,
"plays" on music. Such data does not contain the scorings between users and
items, and is usually called implicit [2] or one-class [3] feedbacks. The one-class
problem is different from the explicit-feedback problem: the latter can obtain
users' positive and negative preferences through the rating scores, while the former only contains positive feedbacks, and the unobserved items cannot be simply
treated as negative, as the most possible is that users have not seen them.

© Springer Nature Singapore Pte Ltd. 2017
C. He et al. (Eds.): BIC-TA 2017, CCIS 791, pp. 580–595, 2017.
https://doi.org/10.1007/978-981-10-7179-9_46

As aforementioned, one-class problem usually poses the challenge of lacking negative feedbacks, especially in cases of data sparsity. A lot of negative examples and missing positive examples are mixed together and cannot be distinguished, which makes many existing classification algorithms not directly applicable to the problem. The previous algorithms designed for solving one-class collaborative filtering problem can be divided into two groups [4]: (1) pointwise regression methods, and (2) pairwise ranking methods. Pointwise methods take implicit feedback as absolute preference scores and minimize a pointwise square loss to approximate the absolute rating scores [3,5], while pairwise methods take pairs of items as basic units and try to maximize the likelihood of pairwise preferences over observed items and unobserved items [2]. Bayesian Personalized Ranking (BPR) [2] is the first approach that adopts such pairwise preference assumption.

Research shows that the pairwise methods are significantly preferable [6] to the pointwise ones, and have been the preferred solutions for one-class problem. This is mainly because that maximizing the likelihood of pairwise preferences is more suitable than approximating the absolute rating scores. The superiority of pairwise methods has been observed in various one-class collaborative filtering problems. A large number of new methods have also been proposed to further improve the BPR. However, the preference assumption of existing pairwise methods that users prefer observed items to unobserved items may not always hold. Besides, most of pairwise methods may not perform well in terms of Top-N recommendation, which is becoming more critical in personalized recommendation services. In this paper, we summarize and categorize the existing work on BPR, and discuss the shortcomings of current researches. Then we propose a more general method called EBPR (Enhanced Preference based Bayesian Personalized Ranking).

The remainder of this paper is organized as follows. In Sect. 2 we review the related work and discuss their limitations. Section 3 details our assumption and presents the proposed EBPR model. Our experimental evaluation is described in Sect. 4. Finally, Sect. 5 concludes the paper.

2 Related Work

2.1 Notations and Problem Definition

U is defined as the set of users and I as the set of items, $U = \{u\}_{u=1}^{n}$ and $I = \{i\}_{i=1}^{m}$, where n and m represent the number of users and items, respectively. Each of $u \in U$ has expressed their positive feedbacks on items $I_u^+ \subset I$. The goal of one-class problem is to recommend a personalized ranking list of items for a user from the unobserved item set, $I \setminus I_u^+$.

2.2 The BPR Algorithm

For an observed user-item interaction (u, i) and an unobserved user-item interaction (u, j), the relative preference of u is denoted by $i \succ_u j$, $i \in I_u^+$, $j \in I \setminus I_u^+$, which means that user u has a higher preference ranking for item i than j. BPR uses a binary random variable $\sigma\left(i \succ_u j\right)$ to denote whether user u prefers item i to item j or not, where σ is an indicator function.

In BPR, the likelihood of pairwise preference for a user u among all items is written as,

$$Pr\left(\succ_u\right) = \prod_{i,j \in I} Pr\left(r_{ui} > r_{uj}\right)^{\sigma\left(i \succ_u j\right)} \times \left[1 - Pr\left(r_{ui} > r_{uj}\right)\right]^{\left[1 - \sigma\left(i \succ_u j\right)\right]},$$

where $r_{ui} > r_{uj}$ indicates the latent preference configuration of user u over item i and item j. The two fundamental assumptions adopted by BPR are as follows:

(1) *Assumption of individual preference over items*: It assumes that user u prefers an item i over all the unobserved items if item i has been observed by user u.

(2) *Assumption of independence among users*: It assumes that the likelihood of pairwise preference of a user u is independent of the others.

Based on the above assumptions, the final objective function of BPR is as follows,

$$BPR = \prod_{u \in U} \prod_{i \in I_u^+} \prod_{j \in I \backslash I_u^+} Pr\left(r_{ui} > r_{uj}\right) \times \left[1 - Pr\left(r_{ui} < r_{uj}\right)\right].$$

2.3   Related Work on Pairwise Methods

Due to the advantages of pairwise methods, many new pairwise methods have been proposed to further improve the BPR algorithm. Overall, the existing algorithms can be categorized into 7 classes:

(1) *Relaxing the two fundamental assumptions in BPR.* The author puts forward two fundamental assumptions made in BPR, namely individual preference assumption over two items and independence assumption between two users, while some studies argue that the two fundamental assumptions are not always true in practice. CoFiSet [7] relaxes the individual pairwise assumption over items and proposes a new assumption that an individual user is likely to prefer a set of observed items to a set of unobserved items. GBPR [4] relaxes independence assumption between two users, considering that users' preferences are influenced by other users with the same interest. GBPR+ [8] goes one step beyond GBPR and adopts a set of items instead of one single item as used in GBPR, which is expected to relax the two fundamental assumptions and introduce richer interactions.

(2) *Improving the sampling strategies in BPR.* BPR randomly samples unobserved items with each positive item for every user. It is shown that sampling pairs randomly results in a biased solution and a prolonged training period, especially when the pool of items is large and the overall item-popularity is tailed. Zhang et al. proposes dynamic negative item sampling strategies

from the ranked list produced by the current prediction model, and to optimize the rank biased performance measures for Top-N recommendation [9]. Rendle et al. proposes a non-uniform sampling distribution which adapts both to the context and the current state of learning to speed up convergence [10]. Zhong et al. proposes a novel adaptive pairwise preference sampling algorithm that a triple (u, i, j) with larger difference between user u's preference on item i and item j will have a lower chance to be sampled [11]. Guo et al. considers that the unobserved items with the same class as the observed items have a greater chance of being the negative [12].

(3) *Improving the loss function in BPR.* In BPR algorithm, the author uses sigmoid function to define the individual probability that a user really prefers item i to item j. Some researchers improve the function and find that the performance of algorithm has been improved. Mao et al. proposes to control the trade-off between personalization and popularity tendency by adjusting the loss function with the generalized logistic loss function and the hinge loss function respectively [13]. Song et al. claims the AUC measure optimized by BPR is not suitable for quantifying such a ranking list including positive, negative, and unknown status, and introduces a generalized AUC (GAUC) which can measure both the head and tail of a ranking list to address this issue [14]. MR-BPR extends the BPR framework to the multi-relational case and derives a principled feature extraction scheme from the social data to extract prediction results on the target relation [15].

(4) *Mining implicit information between users and items.* If we obtain more interactive information, we can reduce the impact of data sparsity, relieve the cold-start problem, and finally improve the performance of the algorithm. SBPR [16] is based on the simple observation that a user's interest is influenced by his friends. PRIGP [17] thinks that users have their own preference on different items with different degrees modeled by the neighbors' implicit feedbacks, and then exploits this prior information to split items into different preference groups. HLBPR [18] proposes to construct additional item preference pairs from the unobserved items, and optimize the ranking object based on the extended pairs. UGPMF [6] combines the pairwise matrix factorization based on BPR and the user side contextual information in a unified model to find more appropriate representations for users and items.

(5) *Introducing transfer learning to BPR.* Most of the existing personalized ranking methods are limited by learning only from one domain of data source. Little work concerns how to model users' preferences information across distinct domains. CroRank [19] is the first model that utilizes users' inclinations transfered from the auxiliary domain to the target domain for obtaining better personalized ranking results.

(6) *Combining BPR with the practical application.* Due to the great success of pairwise methods for solving one-class collaborative filtering problem, some studies apply BPR to practical applications and find this can greatly increase productivity, e.g., pairwise interaction tensor factorization for personalized tag recommendation [20], supercharging recommender systems using taxonomies for learning user purchase behavior [21], relation extraction [22], etc.

(7) *Proposing listwise ranking instead of pairwise ranking.* Most of the past work on one-class recommendation problem has not focused on Top-N recommendation in designing recommendation models. As users usually only concern the first k items in the recommendation list, then there are also some work that generalize pairwise ranking methods to listwise. For example, TFMAP [23] learns a model by directly maximizing Mean Average Precision (MAP) in order to generate an optimally ranked list for individual users. CLiMF [24] is another listwise method where the model parameters are learned by directly maximizing the Mean Reciprocal Rank (MRR), a well-known information retrieval metric for measuring the performance of Top-N recommendations. However, due to their difficulty in modeling the inter-list loss and low efficiency on large-scale dataset, listwise approaches are not widely used, compared with pairwise ranking methods [9].

However, the main limitation of pairwise methods can be attributed to the pairwise preference assumption in BPR which maximize the likelihood of pairwise preferences over observed items and unobserved items. The reason is that some unobserved items which users did not have enough time to mark yet may be their preference. The core optimization idea of BPR that all the observed items should rank higher than all the unobserved items is too strict and unrealistic. Although most follow-up work try to relax it by incorporating auxiliary information, they do not refine the preference assumption, but just directly adopt the BPR criterion in their own applications.

With this problem in mind, we present a new algorithmic idea for attempting to solve the limitation to some extent. We refine the preference assumption in BPR, which is based on pairwise comparisons via maximizing the likelihood of preference difference instead of maximizing the likelihood of pairwise preference. Compared with the aforementioned work, the proposed Enhanced Preference based Bayesian Personalized Ranking (EBPR) is a novel basic algorithm for one-class collaborative filtering. In particular, EBPR inherits the merit of pairwise methods, and improves the preference assumption via comparing users' preference difference over the observed items and the unobserved items. By further exploring the implicit relationship over the observed items and the unobserved ones, we build a better model of users' preferences, which will seldom violate the ground-truth condition. Besides, our approach can be adopted to the aforementioned work to further improve their performance. We summarize EBPR and the aforementioned related works in Table 1.

Table 1. Summary of EBPR and other methods for one-class collaborative filtering w.r.t. different preference assumptions.

Preference assumption	Typical work
Absolute	WMF [3], PureSVD [5], etc.
Relative (pairwise preference)	BPR [2], GBPR [4], etc.
Relative (preference difference)	EBPR, EGBPR(our solution), etc.

3   The Proposed Algorithm EBPR

Although the BPR algorithm has achieved great success, from the previous analysis we can see that the pairwise preference assumption in BPR lacks generality. There are some unobserved items that users may be interested in. Even in the observed items, there may be some noisy data although users have clicked them. Therefore, the core optimization idea of BPR that all the observed items should rank higher than all the unobserved items is too strict and unrealistic.

In addition, one-class problem can be formulated as a special case of binary classification in recommended field, and Top-N recommendation has become the most common scenarios [9]. So the goal of recommending a satisfied sequential list for users becomes more important. However, the evaluation metric AUC used in BPR is unaffected by recommended list's length and preference threshold, not a rank biased measure [9]. Besides, AUC may not be adequate for accurate characterization of binary classification problem. As a result, this requires us to use evaluation metrics applicable to binary classification in recommended field, e.g., precision, recall, F1, and rank biased performance evaluation measures more sensitive to the sorted positions, e.g., NDCG, MAP.

In this section, we will detail our model assumption and describe the proposed personalized ranking algorithm EBPR.

3.1   Model Assumption

BPR method takes pairs of items as basic units and maximizes the likelihood of pairwise preference over observed item i and unobserved item j as $(u, i) \succ (u, j)$, which can be abbreviated as r_{uij}. Motived by this, we use $r_{uqq'}$ to denote the implicit preference relationship in the unobserved items, where $q, q' \in I \setminus I_u^+$. Simultaneously, $r_{upp'}$ is denoted the implicit preference relationship in the observed items, where $p, p' \in I_u^+$. The purpose of introducing $r_{uqq'}$ and $r_{upp'}$ is intended to propose our new algorithm for further exploring the implicit relationship over the observed items and the unobserved ones, and relax the limitation in BPR as previously mentioned.

We maximize the likelihood of preference difference values over observed items and unobserved items via optimizing the following partial ordering relation at the same time: $r_{uij} > r_{uqq'}, r_{uij} > r_{upp'}$. $r_{uij} = r_{ui} - r_{uj}$, $r_{uqq'} = r_{uq} - r_{uq'}$, $r_{upp'} = r_{up} - r_{up'}$, where $r_{ui}, r_{uj}, r_{uq}, r_{uq'}, r_{up}, r_{up'}$ denotes the preference of user u on item i, j, q, q', p, p', respectively, and all the items are sampled randomly. Here, the difference from all the aforementioned methods is that we consider the optimized triple (u, i, j) as a whole, and maximize preference difference values instead of maximizing preference values to relax the above limitation in BPR.

For the first inequality $r_{uij} > r_{uqq'}$, the difference value of user's preference between q, q' sampled from the unobserved items, namely $r_{uqq'}$, has the following three possible cases:

(1) Neither of the items does u like. Then the difference value between them will be small;
(2) User u likes q', doesn't like q. Then, the difference value between them will be negative;
(3) User u likes q, doesn't like q'. Then, the difference value between them will be positive.

For the first two cases of $r_{uqq'}$ described above, r_{uij} should be larger than it. For the third case, the previous researchers have found that the implied positive samples are comparative little in the unobserved items [3]. Based on this, the third case probability of $r_{uqq'}$ is even smaller. Besides, we also introduce parameter later to trade off the two inequalities. So the bad effects can be reduced to minimum. Therefore, when ignoring the third case, r_{uij} should always be larger than $r_{uqq'}$. From the latter experimental results, we can verify that such treatment is acceptable.

In fact, the first inequality has already introduced hidden preference information from the unobserved items and relaxes the simple pairwise preference assumption in BPR. Namely, we can not only introduce more opportunities for parameter learning, but also inject rich interactions in the unobserved items.

The followed is the second inequality $r_{uij} > r_{upp'}$. For p, p', sampled from the observed items, there is only one case: user u likes both of them, so the difference value of user's preference between them, namely $r_{upp'}$, will be small. So r_{uij} should always be larger than $r_{upp'}$.

Through the second inequality, we further explore the implicit information from the observed items and relax the simple pairwise preference assumption in BPR. Namely, we can not only introduce more opportunities for parameter learning, but also inject rich interactions in the observed items.

In general, the new model can solve the limitation in BPR as previously mentioned to some extent by refining the preference assumption via maximizing the likelihood of preference difference values instead of pairwise preference values. In particular, the proposed approach can further exploit the hidden richer preference interactions in the observed items and unobserved items.

3.2   Model Formulation

Based on the above explanation, we can represent the partial ordering pairs to be optimized for user u, $r_{uij} > r_{uqq'}, r_{uij} > r_{upp'}$, as follows,

$$\lambda \left(r_{uij} - r_{uqq'} \right) + (1 - \lambda) \left(r_{uij} - r_{upp'} \right) \tag{1}$$

where λ is a tradeoff parameter used to fuse their relation, which can be determined via empirically testing a validation set, and we abbreviate the above formula as $r_{\succ_u}$. Then, with this assumption, we have a new criterion called Enhanced Preference based Bayesian Personalized Ranking (EBPR) showing overall likelihood for all users and all items,

$$EBPR = \prod_{u \in U} \prod_{i,p,p' \in I_u^+} \prod_{j,q,q' \in I \backslash I_u^+} Pr\left(r_{uij} > r_{uqq'}, r_{uij} > r_{upp'}\right)$$
$$\times \left[1 - Pr\left(r_{uij} < r_{uqq'}, r_{uij} < r_{upp'}\right)\right] \tag{2}$$

Following BPR, we use $\sigma(x) = \frac{1}{1+e^{-x}}$ to approximate the probability $Pr(\cdot)$ so that the objective function is differentiable. Then we have $Pr\left(r_{\succ_u}\right)\left[1 - Pr\left(-\left(r_{\succ_u}\right)\right)\right] = \sigma\left(r_{\succ_u}\right)\left[1 - \sigma\left(-\left(r_{\succ_u}\right)\right)\right] = \sigma^2\left(r_{\succ_u}\right)$. Based on this trick, the objective function of EBPR can be represented as follows,

$$\min_{\Theta} -\frac{1}{2}lnEBPR + \frac{1}{2}R\left(\Theta\right) \tag{3}$$

where $\Theta = \{U_{u\cdot} \in R^{1 \times d}, V_{i\cdot} \in R^{1 \times d}, b_i \in R, u \in U, i \in I\}$ is a set of model parameters to be learned, $U_{u\cdot}$ is a latent feature vector describing user u, $V_{i\cdot}$ is a latent feature vector describing item i, b_i is the bias of item i, and d is the number of latent factors. $lnEBPR = \sum_{u \in U} \sum_{i,p,p' \in I_u^+} \sum_{j,q,q' \in I \backslash I_u^+} 2ln\sigma(\lambda(r_{uij} - r_{uqq'}) + (1 - \lambda)(r_{uij} - r_{upp'}))$ is the log-likelihood of EBPR, $R(\Theta) = \sum_{u \in U} \sum_{t \in S} \left[\alpha_u \|U_{u\cdot}\|^2 + \alpha_v \|V_{t\cdot}\|^2 + \beta_v \|b_t\|^2\right]$ is a regularization term to prevent overfitting in the learning process, and $S = \{i, p, p', j, q, q'\}$ is a group of items sampled randomly, where $i, p, p' \in I_u^+$, and $j, q, q' \in I \backslash I_u^+$. The individual preference is modeled by matrix factorization, for example $r_{ui} = U_{u\cdot}V_{i\cdot}^T + b_i$.

As a result, when we learned the model parameters Θ, we can predict the user u's preference on an unobserved item j via $r_{uj} = U_{u\cdot}V_{j\cdot}^T + b_j$. Then the personalized ranking list for user u can be obtained via picking up the top-k largest preference scores of items which are the most relevant to the user.

3.3 Model Learning

The optimization problem of the objective function in Eq. (3) can be solved by employing the widely used stochastic gradient descent (SGD) algorithm. The main process of SGD is to randomly select a record, which includes a user u, six items containing i, p, p', j, q, q', and iteratively update model parameters based on the sampled feedback records. The tentative objective function can be written as $f(u, S) = -ln\sigma(r_{\succ_u}) + \frac{\alpha_u}{2}\|U_{u\cdot}\|^2 + \frac{\alpha_v}{2}\sum_{t \in S}\|V_{t\cdot}\|^2 + \frac{\beta_v}{2}\sum_{t \in S}\|b_t\|^2 = ln\left[1 + exp\left(-r_{\succ_u}\right)\right] + \frac{\alpha_u}{2}\|U_{u\cdot}\|^2 + \frac{\alpha_v}{2}\sum_{t \in S}\|V_{t\cdot}\|^2 + \frac{\beta_v}{2}\sum_{t \in S}\|b_t\|^2$.

Then the gradients of the user-feature parameters w.r.t. the tentative objective function $f(u, S)$ can be reached as,

$$\frac{\partial f(u, S)}{\partial U_{u\cdot}} = \frac{\partial f(u, S)}{\partial r_{\succ_u}} \times \left(\lambda\left(V_{i\cdot} - V_{j\cdot} - V_{q\cdot} + V_{q'\cdot}\right)\right.$$
$$\left. + (1 - \lambda)\left(V_{i\cdot} - V_{j\cdot} - V_{p\cdot} + V_{p'\cdot}\right)\right) + \alpha_u U_{u\cdot},$$

and the gradients of the item-feature parameters,

$$\frac{\partial f(u, S)}{\partial V_{i\cdot}} = \frac{\partial f(u, S)}{\partial r_{\succ u}} \times U_{u\cdot} + \alpha_v V_{i\cdot},$$

$$\frac{\partial f(u, S)}{\partial V_{j\cdot}} = \frac{\partial f(u, S)}{\partial r_{\succ u}} \times (-U_{u\cdot}) + \alpha_v V_{j\cdot},$$

$$\frac{\partial f(u, S)}{\partial b_i} = \frac{\partial f(u, S)}{\partial r_{\succ u}} + \beta_v b_i,$$

$$\frac{\partial f(u, S)}{\partial b_j} = \frac{\partial f(u, S)}{\partial r_{\succ u}} \times (-1) + \beta_v b_j,$$

where $\frac{\partial f(u,S)}{\partial r_{\succ u}} = -\frac{exp(-(r_{\succ u}))}{1+exp(-(r_{\succ u}))} = -\frac{1}{1+exp(r_{\succ u})}$, and the similar gradients' solving process for items p, p', q, q'. With the above gradients, we can update the corresponding parameters Θ by walking along the descending gradient direction,

$$\Theta = \Theta - \gamma \frac{\partial f(u, S)}{\partial \Theta} \tag{4}$$

Θ can be $U_{u\cdot}, V_{t\cdot}, b_t$, where $t \in S = \{i, j, p, p', q, q'\}$, and $\gamma > 0$ is the learning rate. The algorithm to learn the model parameters is shown in Fig. 1.

Considering the computation complexity, the extra computational cost of new algorithm is mainly due to the calculation of gradient update for newly introduced four items p, p', q, q'. The time complexity of the update rule in Eq. (4) is $O(d)$, where d is the number of latent features. Then the total time complexity

---

Input: Training observed feedback $T_r = \{(u, i)\}$,

where $u \in U$ and $i \in I$.

Output: The learned model parameters

$\Theta = \{U_{u\cdot} \in R^{1 \times d}, V_{i\cdot} \in R^{1 \times d}, b_i \in R\}$.

For $t_1 = 1, ..., T$.

   For $t_2 = 1, ..., n$.

   Step 1. Randomly pick a user $u \in U$.

   Step 2. Randomly pick three items $i, p, p' \in I_u^+$.

   Step 3. Randomly pick three items $j, q, q' \in I \setminus I_u^+$.

   Step 4. Calculate $\frac{\partial f(u,S)}{\partial r_{\succ u}}$.

   Step 5. Update $U_{u\cdot}, V_{t\cdot}, b_t, t \in S$ via Eq.(4).

   End

End

Fig. 1. The algorithm of EBPR.

in Fig. 1 is $O(Tnd)$, where T is the number of iterations and n is the number of users. Complexity analysis shows that EBPR does not increase the time complexity much. Meanwhile, the time complexity for predicting a user's preference on an item is $O(d)$, the same as that of BPR. Thus, the complexity of our proposed approach EBPR and the seminal approach BPR are comparable in terms of efficiency. In the experiments, we mainly assess the accurateness of EBPR.

3.4 Adaptability of EBPR

As the proposed EBPR is a basic model of pairwise methods, then the new algorithm can also be migrated to the aforementioned modified work on BPR to further improve their performance.

Here we consider the GBPR algorithm, a state-of-the-art method for solving one-class collaborative filtering problem. The authors try to smooth the individual and independence assumptions as made in BPR via aggregating richer interactions among users. It has been found experimentally that by introducing other users who own the same interest with target user, the performance of BPR can be greatly improved. The overall likelihood for all users and all items of GBPR can be written as,

$$GBPR = \prod_{u \in U} \prod_{i \in I_u^+} \prod_{j \in I \setminus I_u^+} Pr\left(r_{Gui} > r_{uj}\right)\left[1 - Pr\left(r_{Gui} < r_{uj}\right)\right],$$

where G is a group of like-minded users who share the same positive feedback to item i, and $u \in G$. $r_{Gui} = \rho r_{Gi} + (1 - \rho) r_{ui}$ is the fused preference of group preference r_{Gi} and individual preference r_{ui}, where $r_{Gi} = \frac{1}{|G|} \sum_{w \in G} r_{wi}$. Note that $0 \leq \rho \leq 1$ is a tradeoff parameter used to fuse the two preferences.

Improving GBPR with our new approach model, we can obtain EGBPR (Enhanced GBPR), namely changing the original partial ordering relation $r_{uij} > r_{uqq'}, r_{uij} > r_{upp'}$ to the following: $r_{Gij} > r_{uqq'}, r_{Gij} > r_{upp'}$, where user group G is defined as before. Thus, the new likelihood is the following,

$$EGBPR = \prod_{u \in U} \prod_{i,p,p' \in I_u^+} \prod_{j,q,q' \in I \setminus I_u^+} Pr\left(r_{Gij} > r_{uqq'}, r_{Gij} > r_{upp'}\right)$$
$$\times \left[1 - Pr\left(r_{Gij} < r_{uqq'}, r_{Gij} < r_{upp'}\right)\right].$$

Following EBPR, we reach the objective function of our EGBPR,

$$\min_{\Theta} -\frac{1}{2}lnEGBPR + \frac{1}{2}R(\Theta) \tag{5}$$

where $\Theta = \left\{U_{u.} \in R^{1 \times d}, V_{i.} \in R^{1 \times d}, b_i \in R, u \in U, i \in I\right\}$ is a set of model parameters to be learned, and d is the number of latent factors,

$$lnEGBPR = \sum_{u \in U} \sum_{i,p,p' \in I_u^+} \sum_{j,q,q' \in I \setminus I_u^+} 2ln\sigma\left(\lambda\left(r_{Gij} - r_{uqq'}\right) + (1 - \lambda)\left(r_{Gij} - r_{upp'}\right)\right)$$

is the log-likelihood of EGBPR. $R(\Theta)$ is a regularization term to prevent over-fitting in the learning process, which is represented as follows,

$$R(\Theta) = \sum_{u \in U} \sum_{t \in S} \left[\alpha_w \sum_{w \in G} \|U_{w\cdot}\|^2 + \alpha_v \|V_{t\cdot}\|^2 + \beta_v \|b_t\|^2 \right],$$

and $S = \{i, p, p', j, q, q'\}$ is a group of items sampled randomly, where $i, p, p' \in I_u^+$, and $j, q, q' \in I \setminus I_u^+$.

We still use stochastic gradient descent (SGD) algorithm to optimize the objective function in Eq. (5). The only difference from EBPR is that we go one step and randomly sample a subset of like-minded users to construct the user group G. The algorithm's steps to learn the model parameters of EGBPR are similar to EBPR.

4   Experimental Evaluation

4.1   Datasets and Experimental Configuration

We use four real-world datasets for experiments, including MovieLens100K[1], MovieLens1M, UserTag [3] and NF5K5K [4]. MovieLens100K includes 100,000 ratings with 943 users and 1,682 movies, MovieLens1M includes 1,000,209 ratings with 6,040 users and 3,952 movies. UserTag dataset is from a social bookmarking site crawled from http://del.icio.us, containing 246,436 posts with 3,000 users and 2,000 tags. NF5K5K includes 282,474 ratings assigned by 5,000 users on 5,000 movies, which is randomly sampled 5,000 users from the user pool and 5,000 items from the item pool of the Netflix[2] dataset. We use "item" to denote movie (for MovieLens100K, MovieLens1M and NF5K5K) or tag (for UserTag).

Since we mainly study the one-class feedback, for MovieLens100K, Movie-Lens1M and NF5K5K, we take a pre-processing step mentioned in [25] to deal with the rating data, which only regards the ratings larger than 3 as the observed positive feedback. For all the four datasets, the observed user-item pairs are split into two halves randomly, one as training data, and the other as test data. Meanwhile, we randomly sample one user-item pair for each user from the training data to construct a validation set. We repeat the above procedure 20 times, so we have 20 copies of training data, test data, and validation data. The final experimental results are averaged over every evaluation metric on these 20 copies of test data.

4.2   Baselines and Parameter Settings

In order to demonstrate the advantages of our approach, we include comparisons with two state-of-the-art one-class recommendation methods, BPR and GBPR, as mentioned above. The two methods are very strong baselines, which are shown to be much better than other one-class methods [4].

---

[1] movielens: http://grouplens.org/datasets/movielens/.
[2] netflix: http://www.netflixprize.com/.

By exploiting the hidden richer preference interactions in the observed items and unobserved items, we extend BPR to our new model EBPR, and the same as GBPR and EGBPR. In order to realize a fair comparison, the same code framework as shown in Fig. 1 is applied for the four algorithms. Specifically, we search the regularization terms as $\alpha_u = \alpha_v = \beta_v \in \{0.001, 0.01, 0.1\}$ and the tradeoff parameters λ is searched around $\{0, 0.1, 0.2, \cdots, 1\}$, and the iteration number T is chosen in the range of $\{1000, 10000, 100000\}$. We select the best parameters $\alpha_u, \alpha_v, \beta_v$ and λ, and the best iteration number T for all algorithms according to the NDCG@5 performance on the validation data. For the learning rate γ, we fix it as 0.01. The number of latent dimensions in matrix factorization is fixed as $d = 20$, and the initialization value of U_u, V_i, b_i are configured the same as in [4]. For the user group G in GBPR and EGBPR, we fix the size as $|G| = 3$, and the other parameters remain the same as GBPR in the four datasets.

4.3   Evaluation Metrics

To evaluate the recommendation performance of models, several popular metrics are adopted in our experiment. As users usually only concern the first k items in the recommendation list, we adopt commonly used top-k evaluation metrics to measure the algorithm's performance, including top-k results of precision, recall, F1, 1-call, MAP, and NDCG, and we use $k = 5$ in our experiments.

4.4   Results and Analysis

The experimental results are shown in the Tables 2 and 3, which were designed to answer the following questions:

(1) How does our approach perform compared with BPR method for item recommendation?
(2) Compared with BPR, can the new algorithm recommend a more accurate rank biased list?
(3) Applied our proposed algorithm idea to other aforementioned modified work on BPR, can the recommendation performance be further improved?
(4) How does the time complexity of our approach in this paper?

The reasons for studying these questions:

(1) No matter what algorithm is proposed in recommended field, we are always concerned about the final recommendation results for users, which is embodied by the metrics such as precision, recall, F1, 1-call.
(2) As mentioned above, the rankings of the top items are more important than lower ones, so recommending a satisfied sequential list for users is more useful. Thus, we should pay attention to the algorithm's effect in this area, which is embodied by the metrics such as MAP, NDCG.

Table 2. Recommendation performance of BPR, EBPR, GBPR, EGBPR on Movie-Lens100K, MovieLens1M, UserTag and NF5K5K in the form of 'mean ± standard deviation'. Numbers in boldface are the best results, and marking * indicates EBPR or EGBPR is statistically superior to the corresponding BPR or GBPR algorithm significantly.

Data Set	Method	Prec@5	Rec@5	F1@5	1-call@5	MAP@5	NDCG@5
ML100K	BPR	$0.3649_{\pm0.0056}$	$0.0947_{\pm0.0022}$	$0.1300_{\pm0.0026}$	$0.8131_{\pm0.0099}$	$0.2475_{\pm0.0019}$	$0.3797_{\pm0.0065}$
	EBPR$_{(\lambda\,=\,0.9)}$	$\mathbf{0.3772*}_{\pm0.0053}$	$\mathbf{0.0959*}_{\pm0.0025}$	$\mathbf{0.1320*}_{\pm0.0026}$	$\mathbf{0.8153}_{\pm0.0097}$	$\mathbf{0.2508*}_{\pm0.0023}$	$\mathbf{0.3955*}_{\pm0.0067}$
	GBPR	$0.3900_{\pm0.0048}$	$0.1018_{\pm0.0024}$	$0.1402_{\pm0.0022}$	$0.8345_{\pm0.0093}$	$0.2644_{\pm0.0020}$	$0.4071_{\pm0.0041}$
	EGBPR$_{(\lambda\,=\,0.9)}$	$\mathbf{0.4024*}_{\pm0.0042}$	$\mathbf{0.1045*}_{\pm0.0022}$	$\mathbf{0.1441*}_{\pm0.0024}$	$\mathbf{0.8463*}_{\pm0.0096}$	$\mathbf{0.2683*}_{\pm0.0024}$	$\mathbf{0.4196*}_{\pm0.0044}$
ML1M	BPR	$0.4388_{\pm0.0019}$	$0.0738_{\pm0.0008}$	$0.1127_{\pm0.0009}$	$0.8508_{\pm0.0035}$	$0.2556_{\pm0.0007}$	$0.4517_{\pm0.0020}$
	EBPR$_{(\lambda\,=\,1.0)}$	$\mathbf{0.4536*}_{\pm0.0020}$	$\mathbf{0.0763*}_{\pm0.0006}$	$\mathbf{0.1164*}_{\pm0.0008}$	$\mathbf{0.8581*}_{\pm0.0032}$	$\mathbf{0.2612*}_{\pm0.0010}$	$\mathbf{0.4671*}_{\pm0.0024}$
	GBPR	$0.4454_{\pm0.0020}$	$0.0769_{\pm0.0007}$	$0.1173_{\pm0.0008}$	$0.8644_{\pm0.0039}$	$0.2602_{\pm0.0009}$	$0.4598_{\pm0.0020}$
	EGBPR$_{(\lambda\,=\,1.0)}$	$\mathbf{0.4497*}_{\pm0.0022}$	$\mathbf{0.0776*}_{\pm0.0007}$	$\mathbf{0.1185*}_{\pm0.0009}$	$\mathbf{0.8659}_{\pm0.0035}$	$\mathbf{0.2604}_{\pm0.0005}$	$\mathbf{0.4639*}_{\pm0.0023}$
UserTag	BPR	$0.2480_{\pm0.0029}$	$0.0377_{\pm0.0009}$	$0.0590_{\pm0.0011}$	$0.5468_{\pm0.0066}$	$0.1418_{\pm0.0008}$	$0.2550_{\pm0.0032}$
	EBPR$_{(\lambda\,=\,1.0)}$	$\mathbf{0.2826*}_{\pm0.0028}$	$\mathbf{0.0432*}_{\pm0.0007}$	$\mathbf{0.0673*}_{\pm0.0009}$	$\mathbf{0.5833*}_{\pm0.0046}$	$\mathbf{0.1515*}_{\pm0.0008}$	$\mathbf{0.2923*}_{\pm0.0028}$
	GBPR	$0.2915_{\pm0.0025}$	$0.0481_{\pm0.0008}$	$0.0744_{\pm0.0008}$	$0.6152_{\pm0.0058}$	$0.1631_{\pm0.0008}$	$0.2996_{\pm0.0025}$
	EGBPR$_{(\lambda\,=\,0.9)}$	$\mathbf{0.3100*}_{\pm0.0020}$	$\mathbf{0.0513*}_{\pm0.0006}$	$\mathbf{0.0795*}_{\pm0.0008}$	$\mathbf{0.6374*}_{\pm0.0064}$	$\mathbf{0.1676*}_{\pm0.0007}$	$\mathbf{0.3198*}_{\pm0.0025}$
NF5K5K	BPR	$0.2320_{\pm0.0021}$	$0.0943_{\pm0.0020}$	$0.1051_{\pm0.0016}$	$0.5699_{\pm0.0040}$	$0.1740_{\pm0.0014}$	$0.2509_{\pm0.0020}$
	EBPR$_{(\lambda\,=\,1.0)}$	$\mathbf{0.2397*}_{\pm0.0019}$	$\mathbf{0.0962*}_{\pm0.0012}$	$\mathbf{0.1071*}_{\pm0.0009}$	$\mathbf{0.5750*}_{\pm0.0034}$	$\mathbf{0.1761*}_{\pm0.0009}$	$\mathbf{0.2585*}_{\pm0.0023}$
	GBPR	$0.2412_{\pm0.0024}$	$0.0986_{\pm0.0021}$	$0.1102_{\pm0.0016}$	$0.5860_{\pm0.0046}$	$0.1808_{\pm0.0015}$	$0.2611_{\pm0.0029}$
	EGBPR$_{(\lambda\,=\,1.0)}$	$\mathbf{0.2439*}_{\pm0.0021}$	$\mathbf{0.1012*}_{\pm0.0019}$	$\mathbf{0.1117*}_{\pm0.0013}$	$\mathbf{0.5901*}_{\pm0.0043}$	$\mathbf{0.1813}_{\pm0.0013}$	$\mathbf{0.2640*}_{\pm0.0024}$

(3) Evaluating a good algorithm, not only its own performance, but also that whether the model can be applied to other algorithms, and leads to a better performance. That is to say, whether the proposed algorithm has a wider applicability.

(4) Finally, for all algorithms, the computational cost needs to be considered in the practical application.

First, we discuss the model's effectiveness. Table 2 details the average recommendation performance of different methods, and Wilcoxon rank-sum statistical tests have been used to check whether the difference between EBPR and the compared BPR algorithm, as well as EGBPR and the compared GBPR algorithm, are statistically significant (with a 0.05 significance level). As shown in this table, EBPR shows significant improvement compared with BPR on all evaluation metrics on all four datasets, which proves that our proposed algorithm does improve recommendation performance and can recommend a more accurate rank biased list for users. From the experimental results, we confirm a positive answer to our first two research questions.

Then, we discuss the model's adaptability. From Table 2, we find that EGBPR can further improve GBPR significantly on all evaluation metrics on all four datasets, which shows that the new approach assuredness can be used as a basic method and has the extensive applicability. Thus, we can give a positive answer to our third research question.

Finally, we discuss the model's time complexity. According to preceding analysis, the time complexity for predicting a user's preference on an item is the same as that of BPR, so we just make comparison on training time.

Table 3. Time complexity analysis

Data set	Method	Training time(s)
ML100K	BPR	271
	EBPR	308
	GBPR	317
	EGBPR	347
ML1M	BPR	5688
	EBPR	5928
	GBPR	6340
	EGBPR	6674
UserTag	BPR	1374
	EBPR	1605
	GBPR	1551
	EGBPR	1735
NF5K5K	BPR	2262
	EBPR	2461
	GBPR	2384
	EGBPR	2644

Table 3 details the average training time complexity of different methods in the four datasets, from which we can see that the new model does not increase the time complexity much. This finding also allows us to answer our last research question positively. All the analysis shows that exploiting the hidden richer preference interactions in the observed items and unobserved items via maximizing the likelihood of preference difference is indeed superior to that of simple pairwise preference assumption in BPR.

5   Conclusion and Future Work

In this paper, we first review recent work on one-class collaborative filtering and summarize the modified work on BPR, a seminal approach for processing such scene. Based on the problem of preference assumption in BPR, we propose an Enhanced Preference based Bayesian Personalized Ranking method to improve recommendation performance on one-class recommendation problem. Our model gives a more realistic preference assumption for each user that is able to capture the hidden richer interactions in the observed items and the unobserved items, which is more effective than that of simple pairwise preference assumed in BPR. In addition, our proposed model can be used as a basic method and has the extensive applicability combined with other methods to further improve the recommendation performance on one-class problem. We have conducted experiments on four real-world datasets. The result shows that our method outperforms state-of-the-art one-class recommendation methods, i.e., BPR and GBPR, and significantly improves the recommendation performance regarding various evaluation metrics.

For future work, we are interested in extending EBPR method in three ways: (1) introducing our model to other pairwise ranking methods to further improve their performance for personalized recommendation; (2) To deploy our method in real-world settings more applicably, we can incorporate side information into our approach, such as user social contexts [26] and reviews [27], etc.; (3) applying an active learning framework to sampling strategy for selecting training instances more effectively in the EBPR model.

Acknowledgments. This work was supported by the Ministry of Science and Technology of China (Grant No. 2017YFC0804003), the National Natural Science Foundation of China (Grant No. 61503357), and Science and Technology Innovation Committee Foundation of Shenzhen (Grant Nos. ZDSYS201703031748284, and JCYJ20170307105521943).

References

1. Bobadilla, J., Ortega, F., Hernando, A., et al.: Recommender systems survey. Knowl. Based Syst. **46**, 109–132 (2013)
2. Rendle, S., et al.: BPR: Bayesian personalized ranking from implicit feedback. In: Proceedings of the Twenty-Fifth Conference on Uncertainty in Artificial Intelligence. AUAI Press (2009)
3. Pan, R., et al.: One-class collaborative filtering. In: Eighth IEEE International Conference on Data Mining, ICDM 2008. IEEE (2008)
4. Pan, W., Li, C.: GBPR: group preference based Bayesian personalized ranking for one-class collaborative filtering. In: IJCAI 2013 (2013)
5. Cremonesi, P., Yehuda, K., Roberto, T.: Performance of recommender algorithms on Top-N recommendation tasks. In: Proceedings of the Fourth ACM Conference on Recommender Systems. ACM (2010)
6. Du, L., Li, X., Shen, Y.-D.: User graph regularized pairwise matrix factorization for item recommendation. In: Tang, J., King, I., Chen, L., Wang, J. (eds.) ADMA 2011. LNCS (LNAI), vol. 7121, pp. 372–385. Springer, Heidelberg (2011). https://doi.org/10.1007/978-3-642-25856-5_28
7. Pan, W., Chen, L.: CoFiSet: collaborative filtering via learning pairwise preferences over item-sets. In: Proceedings of the 2013 SIAM International Conference on Data Mining. Society for Industrial and Applied Mathematics (2013)
8. Pan, W., Chen, L.: Group Bayesian personalized ranking with rich interactions for one-class collaborative filtering. Neurocomputing **207**, 501–510 (2016)
9. Zhang, W., et al.: Optimizing Top-N collaborative filtering via dynamic negative item sampling. In: Proceedings of the 36th International ACM SIGIR Conference on Research and Development in Information Retrieval. ACM (2013)
10. Rendle, S., Freudenthaler, C.: Improving pairwise learning for item recommendation from implicit feedback. In: Proceedings of the 7th ACM International Conference on Web Search and Data Mining. ACM (2014)
11. Zhong, H., et al.: Adaptive pairwise preference learning for collaborative recommendation with implicit feedbacks. In: Proceedings of the 23rd ACM International Conference on Conference on Information and Knowledge Management. ACM (2014)

12. Guo, W., et al.: Personalized ranking with pairwise Factorization Machines. Neurocomputing **214**, 191–200 (2016)
13. Mao, X., Li, Q., Xie, H., Rao, Y.: Popularity tendency analysis of ranking-oriented collaborative filtering from the perspective of loss function. In: Bhowmick, S.S., Dyreson, C.E., Jensen, C.S., Lee, M.L., Muliantara, A., Thalheim, B. (eds.) DASFAA 2014. LNCS, vol. 8421, pp. 451–465. Springer, Cham (2014). https://doi.org/10.1007/978-3-319-05810-8_30
14. Song, D., Meyer, D.A., Tao, D.: Efficient latent link recommendation in signed networks. In: Proceedings of the 21st ACM SIGKDD International Conference on Knowledge Discovery and Data Mining. ACM (2015)
15. Krohn-Grimberghe, A., et al.: Multi-relational matrix factorization using Bayesian personalized ranking for social network data. In: Proceedings of the Fifth ACM International Conference on Web Search and Data Mining. ACM (2012)
16. Zhao, T., McAuley, J., King, I.: Leveraging social connections to improve personalized ranking for collaborative filtering. In: Proceedings of the 23rd ACM International Conference on Conference on Information and Knowledge Management. ACM (2014)
17. Qiu, S., et al.: Item group based pairwise preference learning for personalized ranking. In: Proceedings of the 37th International ACM SIGIR Conference on Research and Development in Information Retrieval. ACM (2014)
18. Chen, X., et al.: HLBPR: a hybrid local Bayesian personal ranking method. In: Proceedings of the 25th International Conference Companion on World Wide Web. International World Wide Web Conferences Steering Committee (2016)
19. Guo, Y., Wang, X., Xu, C.: CroRank: cross domain personalized transfer ranking for collaborative filtering. In: 2015 IEEE International Conference on Data Mining Workshop (ICDMW). IEEE (2015)
20. Rendle, S., Schmidt-Thieme, L.: Pairwise interaction tensor factorization for personalized tag recommendation. In: Proceedings of the Third ACM International Conference on Web Search and Data Mining. ACM (2010)
21. Kanagal, B., et al.: Supercharging recommender systems using taxonomies for learning user purchase behavior. Proc. VLDB Endow. **5**(10), 956–967 (2012)
22. Riedel, S., et al.: Relation extraction with matrix factorization and universal schemas. In: HLT-NAACL (2013)
23. Shi, Y., et al.: TFMAP: optimizing MAP for Top-N context-aware recommendation. In: Proceedings of the 35th International ACM SIGIR Conference on Research and Development in Information Retrieval. ACM (2012)
24. Shi, Y., et al.: CLiMF: learning to maximize reciprocal rank with collaborative less-is-more filtering. In: Proceedings of the Sixth ACM Conference on Recommender Systems. ACM (2012)
25. Sindhwani, V., et al.: One-class matrix completion with low-density factorizations. In: 2010 IEEE 10th International Conference on Data Mining (ICDM). IEEE (2010)
26. Geng, X., et al.: Learning image and user features for recommendation in social networks. In: Proceedings of the IEEE International Conference on Computer Vision (2015)
27. He, X., et al.: TriRank: review-aware explainable recommendation by modeling aspects. In: Proceedings of the 24th ACM International on Conference on Information and Knowledge Management. ACM (2015)

Improved OBS-NMF Algorithm
for Intrusion Detection

Wenping Ma[1], Yue Wu[2(✉)], Shanfeng Wang[1], and Maoguo Gong[1]

[1] Key Laboratory of Intelligent Perception and Image Understanding of Ministry
of Education, International Research Center for Intelligent Perception
and Computation, Xidian University, Xi'an, China
[2] School of Computer Science and Technology, Xidian University, Xi'an, China
ywu@xidian.edu.cn

Abstract. In this paper, the optimal brain surgeon (OBS) strategy is
introduced to improve the iterative rule of non-negative matrix factorization (NMF) algorithm for intrusion detection, which is called OBS-NMF
algorithm. A new convergence condition and criterion function are proposed to improve the performance of the OBS-NMF algorithm. Then
the proposed method is applied in the HIDS and NIDS, the experimental results show that our method can obtain higher accuracy and
better stability than the NMF algorithm, and achieves satisfying detection performance. The improved OBS-NMF algorithm is also suitable for
real-time intrusion detection.

Keywords: Intrusion detection · Feature extraction · Dimension
reduce · Non-negative matrix factorization · Optimal brain surgeon

1 Introduction

People began to focus on the research of computer security in the early 1970s,
now it has attracted broad attention. Being widely used, the computers are
attacked frequently by the virus and network invasion, which brings serious
threat to individual, even countries and regions. So it is quite necessary for us to
develop an active and effective measure to protect the security of the computing
system. The concept of the IDS was firstly elaborated in the report of Computer
Security Threat Monitoring and Surveillance by USAF in 1980s, and a new idea
about using the audit trail data to monitor intrusion activities was proposed.
Since then, kinds of methods based on the audit trail data are applied in IDS,
have become such an important detection means.

In intrusion detection methods, it assumes that the intrusion activities are
different from the normal activities, by which to judge intrusions. Anomaly detection can effectively detect the unknown attacks, so it has been a hotspot in the
intrusion detection field. There are many different classifications according to
the data source, in recent years, much research in anomaly detection focused
the profiling program behavior based on system call data [1–3]. Compared to

---

The corresponding author is Yue Wu (ywu@xidian.edu.cn).

C. He et al. (Eds.): BIC-TA 2017, CCIS 791, pp. 596–613, 2017.
https://doi.org/10.1007/978-981-10-7179-9_47

the other data, the species of system calls are more limited (the type of system calls are less than 221 in the kernel 2.7.10 Linux system only 80 types are frequently-used), and uneasy to be tampered by attacker. Therefore, the Anomaly Detection model based on system calls is more effective and simple and this attracts many researchers.

While there exist some problems in current intrusion detection system (IDS), such as poor detection performance, omission, false alarm and the ability to process high dimensional data is not strong. The computer data presents explosive growth nowadays, in the UNM daemon collection experiment, only 112 sendmail messages will produce more than 150 million system calls. So an effective method of intrusion detection must have the ability to process mass of real-time data [4].

In recent years, the Non-negative Matrix Factorization (NMF) [5] was introduced into the intrusion detection because of its efficient dimension Reduction ability. The NMF algorithm not only has the advantage of simple and good understandability, but consumes fewer resources. Now it has been successfully applied in face recognition, text classification and speech processing, etc. [6–8]. Wang uses the NMF to establish the intrusion detection model based on system call data. Using the NMF approach, the high-dimensional data was decomposed into low-dimensional space, where the intrusion activities are detected. This method can reduce the data effectually and consumes few resources. Though with high detection precision and real-time processing capacity, this method has poor stability and convergence, and it is hard to select proper thresholds. All of the above factors affect the detection results. In order to solve these problems, the optimal brain surgeon (OBS) [9] strategy is imported to improve the iterative mechanism of NMF and the stability. Meanwhile, the new convergence condition and judge function being used largely expand the range of threshold, the result shows that the proposed algorithm can obviously improves the performance of the intrusion detection system (Table 1).

The reminder of the paper is organized as follows. In Sect. 2, the Intrusion Detection System is described in detail that is based on the method of NMF, new improvement was adopted in each processing step to make the OBS-NMF algorithm more efficient. Sections 3 and 4 apply the OBS-NMF method to detect anomalous data in the system calls data and network intrusion data, and compares with several conventional methods. Section 5 gives our conclusions and describes the future work.

2   The Non-negative Matrix Factorization (NMF) Based on OBS

2.1   Preprocess

In program execution, the system will randomly assign an ID to a process, as a marking, it will have no meaning anymore in the course of carrying out. Meanwhile, the process invokes kinds of system calls, each of the system call is represented by a character, which can be used as the original analytical data to reflect

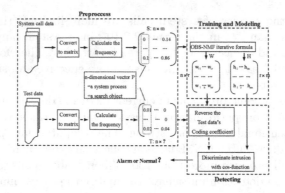

Fig. 1. Overall procedure of the OBS-NMF method

Table 1. Notation and terminology

S	The normal system call matrix being preprocessed with frequency characteristic
T	The test matrix after preprocessing
P	The unit process vector
n	Number of the element in P (big part of the system call)
m	Number of the training samples
W	Basis matrix after reduction of dimensionality
H	New feature of the original data learning based on W
r	Decomposition dimension

Table 2. The system calls format

Process ID	936	936	936	936	937	937	937	937
System call	1	100	100	104	1	1	100	101

the behavior of users and computers. Each system call is defined by only one single corresponding number, which is called System Call Number. The format is shown in Table 2.

The process numbers of the primary data extracted by UNM lab are discontinuous, as well as the system call numbers in each process. As the system call numbers are arranged according to its used sequence, the common IDS research methods considering the transition property of events often use sliding windows to divide sequences of system calls into short for modeling normal behaviors, then detect attacks by matching the data sequences [10]. As is known, the transition property has the advantage in detection precision. However, the size of the window need to be set factitiously. Detection performance is sensitive to window size. As the window size increases, detection performance improves, but the

Table 3. Common system calls

Number	Name	Description
1	exit	Terminate process execution
2	fork	Fork a child process
3	read	Read data from a file or socket
4	write	Write data to a file or socket
5	open	Open a file or socket
6	close	Close a file or socket
11	execve	Execute a program
37	kill	Send a kill signal
90	old mmap	Map memory
301	socket	Create a socket
303	connect	Connect a socket

computational expense increases greatly. When dealing with the huge high-dimension data, the short-sequences method consumes plenty of time, and cannot detect the intrusion quickly. In contrast, taking into account the frequency property, not only is suitable for real-time intrusion detection, also can achieve better performance. So the intrusion method in this paper is based on the system calls with frequency property (Fig. 1).

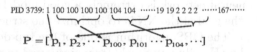

Fig. 2. Preprocessing of the system calls

The preprocessing of data as follows: firstly, put the system calls into corresponding process vector P, where each element p_i denote the number of times of the ith system call in this process, as shown in Fig. 2. The process 3739 totally uses 304 system calls of 39 species, the largest system call number being used is 167, that is the i_{max}. Next, calculate the probability of the system calls in each process and the maximal i_{max}. Select the maximal i_{max} as the row number of the matrix S to convert the original data into analyzable matrix. Finally, due to the system call invoked is very limited, it will be lots of 0 elements in the converted probability matrix, therefore, the row that including more than 95% zeros can be removed, as a result, most of useful information is preserved, as in Fig. 3. The reduction is helpful to improve the detection accuracy and efficiency of the algorithm. Likewise, other audit data can also be processed in the same way, which can keep the IDS adaptive and extendable (Table 3).

	Sp1	Sp2	Sp3	⋯⋯	⋯⋯	⋯⋯	⋯⋯	Sp m
Sc 1	1	1	0	⋯	⋯	⋯	⋯	3
Sc 2	0	2	2	⋯	⋯	⋯	⋯	0
Sc 3	2	0	1	⋯	⋯	⋯	⋯	1
Sc 4	10	0	1	⋯	⋯	⋯	⋯	5
⋯	0	0	0	⋯	⋯	⋯	⋯	0
⋯	0	0	0	⋯	⋯	⋯	⋯	0
⋯	0	0	1	⋯	⋯	⋯	⋯	0
Sc n	1	1	0	⋯	⋯	⋯	⋯	2

Fig. 3. Reduction of the "0" elements. Sc denotes the system call numbers, Sp denotes the system process. For simplicity, the elements in the matrix are the times of the system calls. The rows inside dashed frame are to removed.

2.2 Training and Modeling

The matrix pretreated characterizes the behavior of the original process, the rows of the matrix S can be regarded as the process dimension, and the S is the training sample matrix which is composed of m vectors. So the training and modeling of the intrusion detection simply operates on the matrix, that it simplifies the intrusion detection problem to judge whether the vector is normal. Yet being preprocessed, the dimension of the matrix is larger (the data dimension of CERT sendmail is still 41 after the pretreatment in Sect. 2.1), and a key system generally produces a large number of audit data, both are disadvantageous for the intrusion detection. A new OBS-NMF algorithm is presented for the IDS, the results show that it can effectively improve the detection performance and the real-time attribute with low occupancy rate.

The feedforward neural network is extremely a good model to solve the non-linear problems [11], the goal of the NN is to optimize the structure by minimizing connection weight. The OBS algorithm is one of the top-down optimization methods, put forward by Hassibi and Stork. Its mainly used to prune the weights of neural network, and reduce the complexity of the network. It has the advantage of rapid convergence and sensitive to the low initial conditions [12]. The OBS-NMF algorithm is improved based on the NMF algorithm which was proposed by Lee and Seung in 1999 [13]. The NMF was firstly imported the into IDS by Wang [14,16], and demonstrated a good performance. We integrate the OBS strategy and NMF algorithm to improve the iterative mechanism, and advance the convergence and robustness.

Improvement of the NMF Iterative Mechanism. The Eigen vectors in NMF algorithm are usually not close to the sample, only reflect the partial feature of the sample. While the OBS strategy assumes that the NN trained to a local minimum in error, modify weights according to the second derivative of error function. The goal of NMF algorithm is to produce the weight matrix W and coefficient matrix H that satisfies the formula $WH \approx V$, and minimize the reconstruction error.

$$\min_{W,H \geq 0} \|V - WH\|^2 \tag{1}$$

As an optimization problem, it is consistent with the OBS strategy. So, we can use the OBS method to solve the optimization problem and derive the weights increment. That is

$$\Delta W = -\frac{W_j e_j^T}{[Hess^{-1}]_{jj}} Hess^{-1} \qquad (2)$$

where the Hessian matrix $Hess = HH^T$, e_j is the jth column of the identity matrix, and $W_j = We_j$. So, the iterative formula of weight matrix W rewrites as follows.

$$W_{IN} \leftarrow ((H \cdot H^T)^{-1} \cdot H \cdot V^T)^T \qquad (3)$$

$$W = W + \Delta W \qquad (4)$$

Similarly, we can get the increment ΔH and H.

As the initial value of W and H are randomly selected in the formula, each weight is needed to be modulate according to the constraint condition. During the solution procedure, W and H are obtained alternately by means of iteration.

Improvement of the Convergence Conditions. In order to guarantee the convergence of decomposing matrix, let the sum of the elements in each column of H is a constant equal to 1 so that to make sure the consistency between the new feature and the primitive features.

$$\sum_{i=1}^{r} H_{ij} = \sum_{i=1}^{n} V_{ij} = 1, j = 1, 2, L, m \qquad (5)$$

For the sample $V = [v_1, v_2, ...v_m]$, after the data preprocess, our research is based on vectors. For that reason, it is better to use the Cosine-Angle as convergence condition.

$$Conv = \min_i (\frac{v_i^T (W h_i)}{\|v_i\|_2 \|W h_i\|_2}), i = 1, 2, ...m \qquad (6)$$

That is, chose the Minimum Cosine-Angle between the column vector of V and (WH) as the convergence condition, for a given value $\gamma (0.8 < \gamma < 1)$, if $Conv$ ge γ, then end the iteration. So far, the detection model is proposed.

2.3   Intrusion Detection

For sets of test data, using the preprocess method above, we can get a test matrix T. Using the basis W learned from normal training dataset, we obtain the coefficients h_t that correspond to the test vector t in T. Wang uses the iterative formula to get the h_t, which can introduce accumulative errors and increase the cost of time consuming. For simplicity and efficiency, we directly use the following formula to get the coefficients.

$$h_t = (W^T \cdot W)^{-1} \cdot W^T \cdot t \qquad (7)$$

Table 4. The procedure of the OBS-NMF algorithm

Step 1	Data preprocess, convert the system call data into suitable statistical matrix
Step 2	Choose suitable factorization factor r, the maximum iterating times and calculate the Hess matrix
Step 3	Calculate the decomposition matrix W and H according to the iterative formula, where the initial value of W and H are selected randomly
Step 4	Judge whether meet the convergence conditions, if meet, then jump to step 5, else go on with the iteration in step 3 until the maximum iterating times
Step 5	Calculate the characteristic coefficients h_t of the test data t, set the threshold φ, calculate the abnormality of h_t and h
Step 6	Output test results

Then, calculate the Sine distance between h_t and h, the abnormal behavior is distinguished if

$$e > \varphi$$

where φ is a predefined threshold, and the criterion function is defined as follows.

$$e = 1 - \max_i \left(\frac{h_t^T h_i}{\|h_t\|_2 \|h_i\|_2} \right), i = 1, 2 \dots m \tag{8}$$

The procedure of the OBS-NMF algorithm is shown in the Table 4.

3   Application of the OBS-NMF Method in the HIDS

3.1   Overview of the Experimental Data

The work capitalizes on the UNMs public System Call dataset [15] (CERTsendmail, UNMsendmail.Log), which are used to train and tested for the Intrusion Detection System. The CERTsendmail data include 147 normal processes and 36 abnormal processes, and only the syslog attack data (local, local2, remote1, remote2) are used in our experiment. The UNMsendmail.Log also includes 147 normal processes and two abnormal processes (UNMfwdloops and UNMsendmailsm), in order to test the performance of the method more effectively, the CERTsendmails intrusion data is added (Table 5).

3.2   Compared OBS-NMF with NMF Algorithm

In order to compare the performance of NMF algorithm with OBS-NMFs, we perform the experiment under the condition that equal to 8, the maximum iterating times is 2000. 47 processes are selected randomly as the training sample

Table 5. Experimental data set

Dataset		Process data	System call number	Process number
CERT Sendmail	Normal	Sendmail	19526	147
	Abnormal	Syslog-local1	1516	6
		Syslog-local2	1574	6
		Syslog-remote1	1861	7
		Syslog-remote2	1553	4
UNM sendmail.log	Normal	sendmail.log	31821	147
	Abnormal	UNMfwdloops	2569	10
		UNMsendmailsm	4186	15

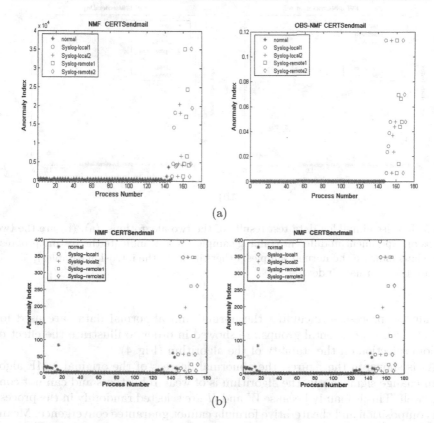

Fig. 4. CERTsendmail data test results of the two algorithms. (a), (b) are the two groups of experiment in different training samples, X-axis indicate the testing progress (Star signs indicate the normal samples, others indicate the intrusion samples), Y-axis indicate the anormaly index.

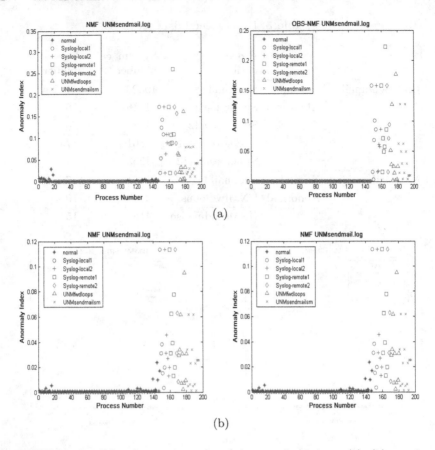

Fig. 5. UNMsendmail.log data test results of the two alogrothms. (a), (b) are the two groups of experiment in different training samples, X-axis indicate the testing progress (Star signs indicate the normal samples, others indicate the intrusion samples), Y-axis indicate the anormaly index.

and all the processes (including the normal and abnormal data) are used for testing. Two experimental groups are showed in order to illustrate the effect of random selection on the stability of the algorithm (Fig. 4).

As is shown in the figures, the abnormal degrees of the original NMF algorithm change significantly, the algorithm is of weak robustness and can not converge well. This is mainly because W and H are selected randomly in the process of decomposition and the iterative formula cannot guarantee convergence. Meanwhile, the stability of NMF algorithm is relevant to the random selecting of the samples (Fig. 5).

By contrast, the abnormal degree of the OBS-NMF algorithm reduces significantly, and is concentrated. It narrows the scope of abnormal degrees and easy to choose appropriate threshold to identify. Even we still chose the test samples and original value matrix randomly, it can also converge well. It greatly improves the robustness of the algorithm and can discriminant the intrusions better.

Although the stability of the OBS-NMF is improved, the detection performance is not obviously improved. So we propose the following improvement Strategy based on the OBS-NMF algorithm. For the sake of contrastive analysis. There are three improved algorithms based on different kinds of condition. Here the criterion function of the NMF algorithm is called difference method, and the convergence condition is called euclidean distance [12,13]. The new criterion function and convergence condition we proposed are respectively called Sine distance method and Cosine-Angle (Table 6).

Table 6. Three kinds of improved algorithms

Iterative algorithm	Criterion function	Convergence condition
OBS-NMF I	Difference method	Euclidean-distance
OBS-NMF II	Sine distance	Euclidean-distance
OBS-NMF III	Sine distance	Cosine-Angle

3.3 Improved OBS-NMF Algorithm

The experimental results show that the criterion function has great effect on the detection performance, with the same iterative principle, the performance of the algorithm II and III are obviously better than the algorithm I, as shown, the algorithm III is the best. We can conclude that the Sine distance method is superior to the criterion function used in NMF algorithm, meanwhile, influenced by the accumulated error, the convergence precision is unsatisfactory, and influence the accuracy and real-time performance of the system. While using the Cosine-Angle as the convergence condition, not only fits for the characteristic of training data, but also is corresponded to the thought of criterion function. It is more reasonable to deal with the system call data with angle, and can discriminant the intrusions better (Fig. 6).

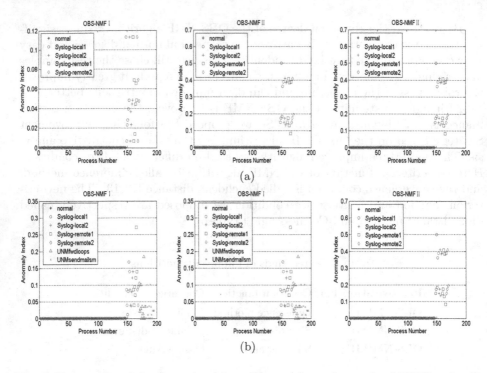

Fig. 6. Test results of the three algorithms. Figure (a) are the result of CERTsendmail data, Figure (b) are the result of UNMsendmail.log data.

3.4 Detection Rate Changing with the Threshold

Figure 7 shows that the detection performance of OBS-NMFI is obviously poor than the others, the abnormal detection rate of the OBS-NMFI algorithm reduced significantly, the range of the threshold is more narrow than the others. In the same threshold, the results of the algorithm using Sine distance as the criterion function are better than the OBS-NMFI algorithm. In the figure a(2) and a(3), As the detection rate firstly reduce to 95.65%, the range of the threshold expands from 0.094 to 0.146. Also in the figure b(2) and b(3), the range becomes larger in the high-level detection rate. So the Cosine-Angle can reflect the difference between the normal and abnormal samples to the most extend, and the data in mapping space can describe the primary data features as similar as possible. Maintaining the detection rate in high level, it is easier to select an appropriate threshold in the OBS-NMFIII algorithm.

3.5 Detection Rate Changing with Decomposition Factor

It is found that the detection performance is influenced by two parameters r and λ, the decomposition factor relates to the error of the reconstruction-matrix. In the basis matrix, the smaller r is, the greater the degree of data compression

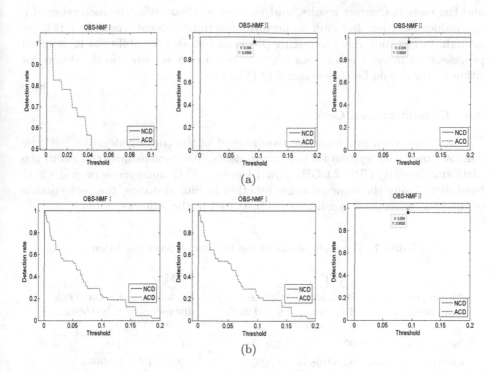

Fig. 7. The Relationship between Detection rate and the threshold of the three algorithms. Figure (a) are the result of CERTsendmail data, Figure (b) are the result of UNMsendmail.log data. The solid line indicates the Normal sample detection rate, and the dotted line indtcates the Abnormal sample detection rate.

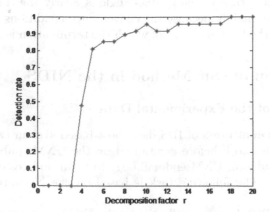

Fig. 8. The Relationship between Detection rate and decomposition-factor of the OBS-NMF III

and the more inaccurate results, and vice versa. Meanwhile, the increasing of r can reduce iteration, but gain no performance improvement when the r is large enough. In fact, not only the testing precision but also the ability of high speed processing of massive audit data must be taken into account. So the decomposition factor should be chosen suitably (Fig. 8).

3.6   Computational Cost

The new algorithm promotes the requirement of the convergence. We used the windows operating system for our experiments. We implemented the job in the platform: Intel(R) CPU 2.6 GHz (Dual Core), 1.75 G main memory and 120 G hard disk. Using the same criterion function of Sine distance, the performance of the two convergence conditions is illustrated in the following table.

Table 7. The performance of the two convergence conditions

	CERT		UNM	
Convergence conditions	Euclidean distance $\xi \leq 2*10^{-4}$	Cosine-Angle $\gamma \geq 0.9995$	Euclidean distance $\xi \leq 2*10^{-4}$	Cosine-Angle $\gamma \geq 0.9995$
Termination	90	230	40	110
Convergence value	0.00019834	0.99954	0.000184	0.99954
Training time	4.29 s	11.95 s	1.69 s	4.62 s
Detection time	0.51 s	0.51 s	0.58 s	0.59 s

The convergence conditions are selected artificially, which needed further studies. The training time of the Cosine-Angle is nearly the three times of the Euclidean distance, mainly because the convergence conditions based on Angle requires higher in the training error, of which the termination is larger (Table 7).

4   Application of Our Method in the NIDS

4.1   Overview of the Experimental Data

There are two different types of IDS data: host-based system call and Network Intrusion data. The work before capitalized on the UNMs public System Call dataset (CERTsendmail, UNMsendmail.Log) to train and tested the Intrusion Detection System. The following task is based on the Network data of KDD CUP99 [17].

The KDD CUP99 data was collected by the USAF in nine weeks which was used to simulated the LAN connection. It includes lots of Network intrusion and normal processes. There are 38 continuous variables, 3 Symbolic variables and one last Behavior ID in a complete data records, totally 42 dimensions. Test data and the training data were different in probability distribution. The test data contains some attack data which does not appear on the training data, and the experiment will be more realistic.

As our goal is not to classify the specific attack types, so the experiment can be simply regarded as a two-class problems, only to classify the normal data and abnormal date. Therefore, the normal data is used for training, and the mixing samples are used for testing. The training samples are 41 dimensions with no identifier, while there is one more dimensions in testing samples, 0 denotes the normal and 1 denotes the anomaly.

4.2 Compared OBS-NMF with NMF Algorithm

In order to simply contrast with the NMF algorithm, the improved OBS-NMF algorithm used a different criterion function, iterative mechanism and convergence conditions. We chose 39298 normal data as the training database and 30 data subsets as the testing databases, that each of the subset includes 39256 abnormal data and 9727 normal data. There we chose 10% of the samples in each databases as the experimental samples. The test results of the 1st, 3rd, 5th subset are shown as below.

The Evaluation Criterion are defined as following:

Detection rate = anomalous sample correctly classified/total anomalous samples

$$= \frac{TP}{(TP + FN)}$$

False alarm rate = normal sample incorrectly classified/total normal samples

$$= \frac{FP}{(FP + TN)}$$

Considering the similarity of data structure and the running time, we use 15 groups of the subsets as following table, the three pictorial diagram of them in Fig. 9 illustrate the detection results. In the Table 8, the result above in each subset is obtained by the method of the improved OBS-NMF, and the under one is obtained by the method of the NMF algorithm. In the experiment, there are 1178 training samples, 39256 abnormal data and 9727 normal data in the testing samples.

The decomposition factor is 8, and the maximum iteration is 1000. The threshold of the two methods are respectively 0.2 and 0.05.

4.3 Comparing of the Detection Performance

In order to illustrate the superiority of our method, we compare the detection rate on KDDCUP 99 data with other common method, shown as follows:

According to the table above, it is concluded that our method obtains higher detection rate than the other methods, also keeps low false positive rate. Comparing with other algorithms, it shows that our method can reach a better detection performance. The detection rate of NMF algorithm is poor mainly because of the lower normal sample detection rate (Table 9).

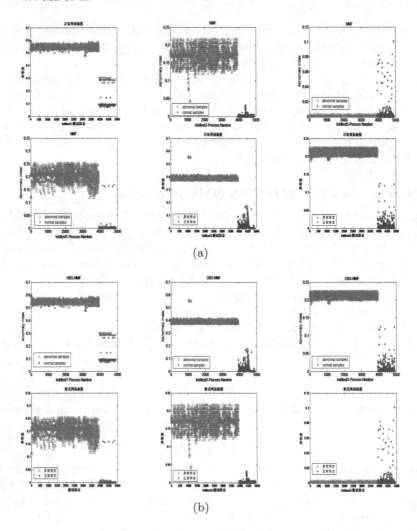

Fig. 9. The pictorial diagram result of the 1st, 3th, 5th subset of the KDDCUP99, figure (a) indicate the result of OBS-NMF method, figure (b) indicate the result of NMF method. The X-axis represents the anomaly index, the Y-axis represents the testing samples (triangle symbol indicates the intrusion samples, the Star signs indicates the normal samples).

4.4 Computational Cost

In order to show the computational cost, we run the OBS-NMF on a computer with 2.6 GHz 1.95 G DDR2 memory, we compare the computational cost of the two algorithms. The maximum iteration is 1000, and the decomposition factor is 8.

According to the table, the OBS-NMF algorithms takes longer time in training the samples than the NMF algorithms, that is mainly because the OBS

Table 8. The test results of the 15 groups subsets

Test subset	Detection rate (%)	False detection	Test subset	Detection rate (%)	False detection (%)	Test subset	Detection rate (%)	False detection (%)
1	94.85	0	11	100	2.8	21	100	0.42
	99.07	0		99.97	0.83		0	1.14
3	100	0	13	100	0	23	58.54	0.21
	97.32	0		100	0		5.78	0
5	97.78	0	15	99.97	0.21	25	100	0
	0	3.9		99.97	0		100	0
7	100	10.4	17	100	0	27	100	0
	100	82.41		100	0		100	0
9	100	4.94	19	100	0	29	97.81	3.5
	40.91	83.65		100	0		0	0.11

Table 9. The test results of types of algorithms in intrusion

Detction methods	OBS-NMF	NMF	K-means	PCA-SVM	K-NN	SVM	Cluster
Detection rate	99.3	89.2	71.4	96.4	91	98	93
False positive	2.6	5	1.12	4.2	8	10	10

iterative mechanism takes much more time, the Stopping Criterion based on the angle request higher training error precision, so it will execute more iterations. But in exchange, it can reach higher detection performance and be more stable.

The OBS-NMF algorithms can reach perfect detection performance in the Network intrusion data. The experiments results show that, comparing with the Euclidean distance criterion function used by Wang, our criterion function can not only reflect the difference between normal samples and abnormal samples but improve the detection precision. The results also demonstrate that, as the number of training is larger, it inevitably affect the detection result to select the samples randomly (Table 10).

Table 10. Computational Cost

	OBS-NMF	NMF
Number of training sample	1178	1178
Number of testing sample	4897	4897
Training time(s)	110.7	0.961
Testing time(s)	98.8	98.1

5   Conclusions

A new intrusion detection algorithm based on OBS-NMF is presented in this paper, we bring the new convergence condition and criterion rule to improve the OBS-NMF algorithm. Compared with the NMF algorithm, our method is more robust and stable, and can reach the same detection performance as NMF algorithm. While, because of the criterion rule the improvement of the detection performance is not obvious, so we propose the Sine distance as the criterion rule to improve the detection performance of abnormal samples.

The criterion function of our algorithm is different from the traditional judge function, that it uses the angle to measure the data diversity. The research object is the single process-vector after data preprocess, obviously that the criterion function fits for the structural characteristics of experimental data. The experiments show that, our method can reflect the difference better, and has effective detection performance.

In order to reduce the cumulative error and improve the detection performance, a new convergence condition is proposed based on the dot product of vectors, it not only extends the range of threshold, also is identical with the determine function. Although the OBS-NMFIII algorithm is more time consuming, it can converge well, and improves the detection precision. In conclusion, the OBS-NMFIII algorithm has obvious advantages in dealing with the high dimensional data, and is suitable for real-time intrusion detection.

Acknowledgment. This work was supported in part by the National Basic Research Program (973 Program) of China (No. 2013CB329402), the National Natural Science Foundation of China (No. 61573015 and 61702392) and the Fundamental Research Funds for the Central Universities under Grant JBX170311.

References

1. Alaeiyan, M.H., Parsa, S.: Automatic loop detection in the sequence of system calls. In: International Conference on Knowledge-Based Engineering and Innovation, pp. 720–723. IEEE (2015)
2. Canfora, G., Medvet, E., Mercaldo, F., Visaggio, C.A.: Detecting android malware using sequences of system calls. In: International Workshop on Software Development Lifecycle for Mobile, pp. 13–20. ACM (2015)
3. Cardona-Morrell, M., Chapman, A., Turner, R.M., Lewis, E., Gallego-Luxan, B., Parr, M., Hillman, K.: Pre-existing risk factors for in-hospital death among older patients could be used to initiate end-of-life discussions rather than rapid response system calls: a case-control study. Resuscitation, 76–80 (2016)
4. Ashfaq, R.A.R., Wang, X.Z., Huang, J.Z., Abbas, H., He, Y.L.: Fuzziness based semi-supervised learning approach for intrusion detection system. Inform. Sci. **378**, 484–497 (2017)
5. Hernando, A., Bobadilla, J., Ortega, F.: A non negative matrix factorization for collaborative filtering recommender systems based on a bayesian probabilistic model. Knowl-Based. Syst. **97**, 188–202 (2016)

6. Zafeiriou, S., Petrou, M.: Nonlinear non-negative component analysis algorithms. IEEE Trans. Image Process. **19**(4), 1050–1066 (2010)
7. Oza, N., Castle, J.P., Stutz, J.: Classification of aeronautics system health and safety documents. IEEE Trans. Power Syst. Man Cybern. Part C (Appl. Rev.) **39**(6), 670–680 (2009)
8. Grindlay, G., Ellis, D.: Multi-Voice polyphonic music transcription using eigen instruments. In: IEEE Workshop on Applications of Signal Processing to Audio and Acoustics, vol. 18(21), pp. 53–56 (2009)
9. Hassibi, B., Stork, D.G., Wolff, G.J.: Optimal Brain Surgeon and general network pruning. In: IEEE International Conference on Neural Networks, pp. 293–299 (1993)
10. Forrest, S., Hofmeyr, S. A., Somayaji, A., Longstaff, T, A.: A sense of self for unix processes. In: IEEE Symposium on Security and Privacy, pp. 120–128 (1996)
11. Tran, D., Tan, Y.K.: Sensorless illumination control of a networked led-lighting system using feedforward neural network. IEEE Trans. Ind. Electron. **61**(4), 2113–2121 (2014)
12. Attik, M., Bougrain, L., Alexandre, F.: Optimal brain surgeon variants for feature selection. In: IEEE International Joint Conference on Neural Networks, pp. 1371–1374. IEEE (2004)
13. Lee, D.D., Seung, H.S.: Algorithms for Nonegative Matrix Factorization. Adv. Neural Inf. Process. Syst. **13**, 556–562 (2001)
14. Wang, W., Guan, X.H., Zhang, X.L.: Profiling program and user behaviors for anomaly intrusion detection based on non-negative matrix factorization. In: IEEE Conference on Decision and Control, pp. 99–104 (2004)
15. Computer Immune Systems. http://www.cs.unm.edu/immsec/begin.html
16. Wang, W., Guan, X., Zhang, X.: Processing of massive audit data streams for real-time anomaly intrusion detection. IEICE Trans. Fund. Electron. **31**(1), 58–72 (2008)
17. KDDCUP 99 Data. http://www.kdd.ics.uci.edu.databases/kdd-cup99/kddcup99.html

Hand Target Extraction of Thermal Trace Image Using Feature and Manifold Inspired by Coordination of Immune

Tao Yang, Dongmei Fu[✉], Xiaogang Li, and Jintao Meng

Beijing Engineering Research Center of Industrial Spectrum Imaging,
School of Automation and Electrical Engineering and Institute for Advanced
Materials and Technology, University of Science and Technology Beijing,
Beijing, China
fdm_ustb@ustb.edu.cn

Abstract. In this paper, the immune mechanism is used to solve the problem of fuzzy target extraction in infrared thermal trace images. First, imitating the innate immunity, the maximum variance method was used to initially segment the image to obtain the decided target and background region and the undecided fuzzy region of the target. Then, inspired by the antigen-presenting mechanism, this paper constructed the feature set for each pixel in the image, which contained the gray information, the temperature information with their statistical values. Next, in order to express the characteristic changes of the antigen invading normal cells, the paper adopted the local preserving algorithm to do the mapping to obtain new feature states. Finally, in view of effector T-cell mechanism in adaptive immunity, the paper used the new feature states to measure the distances between fuzzy region and the target and background region, so as to decide the classification of the pixels of the fuzzy region. Through this process, the extraction of the fuzzy target in the thermal trace image is completed.

Keywords: Target extraction · Infrared image · Artificial immune · Manifold

1   Introduction

Infrared image, which can obtain an object surface temperature distribution information, is from the infrared imaging equipment. It is also known as the thermal image [1] for you can directly see the surface temperature distribution. Infrared image can be used as an important temperature measurement and diagnostic tool in industry or the night vision equipment in military [2,3]. There is one kind of infrared images, called thermal traces sequence images, which are a set of thermal images that are continuously shot over time on the same object surface by the infrared instrument. Since the temperature distribution of the object surface is constantly changing over time, the sequence images can observe

C. He et al. (Eds.): BIC-TA 2017, CCIS 791, pp. 614–622, 2017.
https://doi.org/10.1007/978-981-10-7179-9_48

the evolution of the thermal traces to infer the activity information of the object itself or the heat source that comes into contact with the object. It is important to use the temperature distribution variation information in the thermal traces sequence images to infer the historical activity state of the target in the image, since it will play an important role in the military and relevant analysis [4]. To this end, this paper takes the infrared images from AVIO-H2640 infrared device as our object. The shooting environment is of 27.2 Celsius, and the target in images is the hand thermal trace. We firstly let one hand put on a wood plank and then leave the hand to shoot the thermal trace on the plank. The examples of the thermal traces of the plank are shown in Fig. 1.

Fig. 1. The hand thermal trace sequence images, from left to right: (1) 1 s after hands leaving (2) 60 s after hands leaving (3) 180 s after hands leaving

The thermal diffusion phenomenon causes the thermal traces of the object surface become blurred over time. Observing 60 s and 180 s in Fig. 1, it is found that the hand target becomes increasingly difficult to recognize, especially the stronger ambiguity of the target edge, called the fuzzy target. In actual, we often only can get the thermal traces of the object surface after a heat source being away from a period of time. Extracting the target in this kind of image becomes a problem.

Among the existing main extraction methods, there are some shortcomings when to be used in the fuzzy target of thermal trace sequence images. The threshold segmentation method [5] is based on the difference of the gray information of the target and the background, but the regions in the fuzzy target has very low differences of the gray information resulting in poor performance of threshold method. The template method, like Prewitt [6], cannot guarantee the continuity of the target contour in the fuzzy region. The watershed method [7] is sensitive to noises. The fact that the more blurred the target is the lower SNR(Signal Noise Ratio) forces the watershed method is not suitable. Recently, some scholars have paid attention to the problem of this special fuzzy target extraction, such as artificial immune framework, which is combined with innate immunity and adaptive immunity, like Ref(reference) [8] proposed a coordinated immune template extraction algorithm. Further, Li Hui [9] also proposed an extended three-dimensional template to improve the extraction accuracy based on the coordination of immune framework. The Refs. [8,9] studies have achieved better results than the traditional methods, but the Ref. [8] did not take into account the sequence characteristics of the images, only used a single image and thus lost the information of time-varying thermal traces. While Ref. [9] considered the sequence characteristics, but it did not use the temperature and the location information of the target. Because of the better results based on the coordination of immune framework, this paper also further improves the work of Refs. [8,9] and puts forward an effective extraction method under the inspiration of coordination of immune.

The artificial immune system is a branch of intelligent computing. Inspired by immunological principles, researchers have constructed a number of concerned immune-based computing models. The use of artificial immune systems in pattern recognition, fault detection, computer security, and other applications is widespread [10]. The biological immune system includes innate immunity and adaptive immunity. The innate immunity identifies the original features of the antigen and those which cannot be recognized by the innate immunity will be processed and submitted by the antigen-presenting cell(APC), and thus they will be provided to adaptive immunological recognition [11]. The immune function of a human body complete through both innate and adaptive immune function and their interactions. Based on this fact, the researchers proposed coordinated immune models [12].

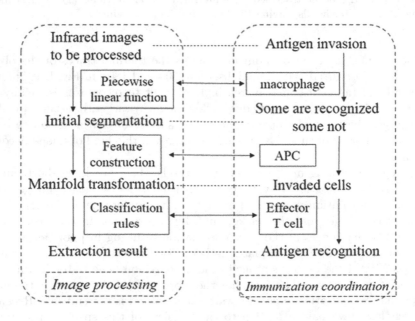

Fig. 2. The design flow chart of the proposed method

This paper, inspired by artificial immune system and based on the characteristics of hand thermal trace sequence image, firstly segments the image pixels into the decided pixel set and the undecided pixel set to be classified according

Table 1. The main symbols with their meanings in this paper.

Symbol	Meaning
f	An infrared image
T	Serial number of sequence images
f^T	T^{th} image of sequence images
(u, v)	One image pixel with its location
$f(u, v)$	Gray value of a pixel
$\tau(u, v)$	Temperature value of a pixel
$flag(u, v)$	Label of a pixel. Label +1: Target. Label -1 Background
$F(u, v)$	Features of MHC complex of a pixel
$S(u, v)$	Feature states: The variation of features after antigen invaded cell
$C_I : F \rightarrow S$	Invasion. Input: features of MHC complex. Output: feature states
$C_T : S \rightarrow flag$	Effetor T Cell. Input: feature states. Output: label
$C_B : (u, v) \mapsto flag(u, v)$	Macrophage. Input: pixel. Output: pixel label
$C_S : (u, v) \mapsto flag(u, v)$	APC. Input: pixel. Output: features of MHC complex
Other explanation	Pixels are antigens. Recognition of antigens is extraction of the target

to the antigen recognition process of innate immunity. Then, according to the mechanism of immune presentation of adaptive immune phase, the molecular characteristics of antigen peptide corresponding to image pixels, called MHC complexes, are defined. Then, the antigenic peptide complex molecule is characterized by the states in the invaded cells by the feature transformation based on the manifold method, so that the effector T cells can specifically recognize the invaded cells. Finally, the classification rules of the image pixels are designed to correspond to the antigen recognition process of the effector T cells. The design flow-chart of this paper is shown in Fig. 2.

The difference and improvement between this paper and Refs. [8,9] are: (1) we consider the sequence characteristics of the thermal trace, that is to say, we analyze the molecular characteristics of the MHC complex expressed by the pixel features over a period of time, and present the feature variation by manifold transformation after antigen invaded the cells. (2) We fully make use of the function of APC, that is, we not only take the gray-level information but also the temperature and position information with statistical values of the pixels neighborhood that maximizes the effect of the APC and the molecular characteristics of the antigen in order to let the immune cell recognize the antigens.

Here are the main symbols with meanings given in this paper, as shown in Table 1.

The following contents will be described in order of the process shown in Fig. 2.

2   Macrophages Recognize Antigens

When antigens just enter the human body, the innate immunity occurs. During this stage, macrophages can swallow the antigens that they recognize, but it probably will leave some antigens which cannot be recognized and those antigens will be processed by APC further. Inspired by this process, in this paper, the gray value is firstly used and design a piecewise linear function to mimic macrophages. The detailed process is:

Using OTSU method to obtain a segmentation threshold H and considering that the macrophage will not completely recognize all the antigens at once, we set a parameter H0 and have the following rules:

$$C_B(u,v) = flag(u,v) \quad \text{and} \quad flag(u,v) = \begin{cases} +1 & f(u,v) \geq H + H_0 \\ -1 & f(u,v) \leq H - H_0 \\ 0 & \text{otherwise} \end{cases} \quad (1)$$

when $flag(u,v) = 1$ means that the antigen has been recognized by macrophages, and correspondingly the current pixel (u,v) is the target pixel. When $flag(u,v) = -1$ means that there are not antigens that require immunity and correspondingly the current pixel (u,v) is the background pixel. When we have $flag(u,v) = 0$, it means that the macrophages that do not recognize and this part of the antigen will further invade other normal cells and those corresponding pixels are undecided belonging to the fuzzy region.

3   The Effect of Antigen-Presenting Cell to Antigen

When there are antigens not recognized by innate immune, human body will have adaptive immunity, in which the antigen-presenting cells(APC) will act on the antigen to express the surface antigenic peptide-MHC complex, exposing its molecular properties Inspired by this process, we need to expose richer feature information of each pixel.

Set the current pixel is (u,v), imitating the effect of APC we have the following:

$$C_S(u,v) = F(u,v) \quad \text{and}$$
$$F(u,v) = [f(u,v), \tau(u,v), u, v, f_{mean}^{u,v}, f_{var}^{u,v}, \tau_{mean}^{u,v}, \tau_{var}^{u,v}] \quad (2)$$

where $f_{mean}^{u,v}$ is the mean of gray values of 3×3 neighborhood of the pixel (u,v), $f_{var}^{u,v}$ represents the variance of gray values of 3×3 neighborhood of the pixel (u,v), and $\tau_{mean}^{u,v}$ and $\tau_{var}^{u,v}$ represent the mean and variance of gray values of 3×3 neighborhood of the pixel (u,v) respectively.

4   Feature States for Invaded Cell

When antigens further invade into the cell inside, the molecular characteristics of the antigens will be changed in order to be further identified by immune cells. We say that the antigens have new feature states. Inspired by this mechanism, for thermal trace images, it is necessary to do a mapping from features represented by APC to new feature states.

This paper adopted the linear local preserving algorithm based on manifold [13] to obtain the mapping transformation rule. The algorithm can keep the local position relationship with the features of the pixel.

First, take the pixel points in parts of the fuzzy pixel set, the target pixel set and background pixel set as data and suppose these data are $[x_1, x_2, \cdots, x_n]$. The mapping process is in the following:

(1) Use k nearest neighbor to get the local neighbor identification.
(2) The weight of two adjacent data.
   Giving a weight w_{ij} to two adjacent data x_i and x_j, like Gaussian relation. Calculate the weights for all the data and place those weights in a symmetric square matrix W.
(3) Optimization calculation
   The transformation result $y = Ax$ is obtained by solving the mathematical expression:

$$\min \sum_{ij} (y_i - y_j)^2 w_{ij} \tag{3}$$

(4) Representation of feature states after antigens invasion

$$C_I(u, v) = S(u, v) \quad \text{is completed by} \quad y_i = Ax_i$$

Through the transformation, the new feature states are represented after antigens invasion, and those new features will be specifically recognized by the immune cells.

5   Effector T Cells on Antigen Recognition

After antigen-presenting cell action and new feature states representation, the effector T cells can identify the antigens. This process corresponds to the classification of the blurred pixels in the fuzzy region of thermal trace images. The detailed recognition process is as follows:

$$C_T(u, v) = flag(u, v) \quad \text{and} \quad flag(u, v) =$$

$$\begin{cases} +1 & \min(S(u, v) - S_{target}(i, j)) \leq \min(S(u, v) - S_{background}(k, r)) \\ -1 & \min(S(u, v) - S_{target}(i, j)) > \min(S(u, v) - S_{background}(k, r)) \end{cases} \tag{4}$$

where $S_{target}(i, j)$ represents the feature state of the pixel (i, j) in the target pixel set, $S_{background}(k, r)$ represents the feature state of the pixel (k, r) in the background pixel set, $\min(S(u, v) - S_{target}(i, j))$ represents the minimum distance of the feature states between fuzzy region and target region, $\min(S(u, v) - S_{background}(k, r))$ represents the minimum distance of the feature states between fuzzy region and background region.

After the above-mentioned effector T cell immunization treatment, each pixel of fuzzy region in the image is assigned a label.

6   Experiment

The infrared sequence images in this paper record the hand trace within 200 s. This paper select 60 s, 120 s and 180 s as a set of sequence, and take the result of OTSU method for 1 s image as benchmark image, We test the segmentation result of the images for 180 s. All results are in Fig. 3.

The comparison methods include the OTSU method, prewitt operator, the watershed method, and Refs. [8,9]. In order to evaluate the accuracy of the target extraction, we select the false target extraction ratio(FPR)[14], Jaccard similarity index(J)[15], Dice similarity index(D)[16] and absolute error rate(ER)[17] as evaluation criteria. For proposed method, the parameter H_0 takes 0.03 and k takes 5. In Fig. 3, the left-to-right images are: the original infrared image, the benchmark image, prewitt operator, watershed method, OTSU method, Refs. [8,9] and the proposed method in this paper.

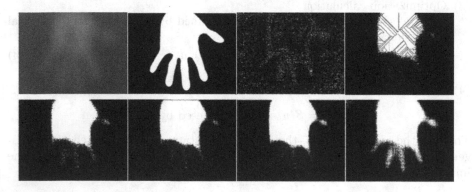

Fig. 3. The extraction results for 180 s after hands leaving.

The results of evaluation criteria are in the following:

Table 2. The evaluation criteria results for 180 s after hands leaving.

	FPR	J	D	ER
Prewitt	No continuous and closed target region			
watershed	**3.2**%	0.54	0.71	13.9%
OTSU	4.60%	0.62	0.77	11.60%
Ref. [8]	4.50%	0.62	0.77	11.50%
Ref. [9]	6.60%	0.64	0.78	11.30%
Our method	9.10%	**0.71**	**0.83**	**9.50**%

It can be seen from the above results that the method in this paper is effective in extracting fuzzy infrared target and is superior to other comparison methods.

The indexes of FPR in Table 2 are not the lowest for the proposed method, but FPR represents the false target extraction ratio, and only consider the low percentage of FPR can denote that the extracted target is real but not explain the integrity of the target. The proposed method is competent, because the indexes of J and D show that the proposed method can keep the original shape of the hand trace with the lowest error rate.

7 Conclusion

In this paper, the maximum variance method is used to realize the innate immune process to initially segment the target. Considering the effect of antigen presentation, the pixel feature set is constructed. The manifold method is used to map the original feature set and express the new feature states. Imitating the effector T cells for adaptive immune process, the target extraction is completed. The experimental results show that the proposed method has a more integral target extraction result and a lower extraction error rate than other methods.

8 The References Section

This paper is supported by National Natural Science Foundation of China (No. 61272358) and Fundamental Research Funds for the Central Universities (No. FRF-TP-16-082A1).

References

1. Romano, M., Ndiaye, C., Duphil, A., et al.: Fast infrared imaging spectroscopy technique. Infrared Phys. Technol. **68**, 152–158 (2015)
2. Taheri, G.A., Ahmadi, H., Omid, M., et al.: An intelligent approach for cooling radiator fault diagnosis based on infrared thermal image processing technique. Appl. Therm. Eng. **87**(3), 434–443 (2015)
3. Yang, Z.G., Liu, X.J., Zhang, Q.W.: Moving target recognition and tracking techniques based on infrared image. Appl. Mech. Mater. **608**, 473–477 (2014)
4. Yu, X., Fu, D.: Target extraction from blurred trace infrared images with a superstring galaxy template algorithm. Infrared Phys. Technol. **64**(3), 9–12 (2014)
5. Otsu, N.: A threshold selection method from gray-level histograms. IEEE Trans. Syst. Man Cybern. **9**(1), 62–66 (2007)
6. Yang, L., Zhao, D., Wu, X., et al.: An improved Prewitt algorithm for edge detection based on noised image. In: IEEE International Congress on Image and Signal Processing, pp. 1197–1200 (2011)
7. Tarabalka, Y., Chanussot, J., Benediktsson, J.A.: Segmentation and classification of hyper-spectral images using watershed transformation. Pattern Recogn. **43**(7), 2367–2379 (2010)
8. Fu, D.M., Yu, X., Tong, H.J.: Target extraction of blurred infrared image with an immune network template algorithm. Opt. Laser Technol. **56**(1), 102–106 (2014)
9. Li, H., Fu, D.M., Yang, T.: Hand target extraction from infrared images with descriptor based on pixel temporal characteristics. In: International Congress on Image & Signal Processing, Changchun, China, pp. 458–463 (2015)

10. Dasgupta, D., Yu, S., Nino, F.: Recent advances in artificial immune systems: models and applications. Appl. Soft Comput. **11**(2), 1574–1587 (2011)

11. Deretic, V., Saitoh, T., Akira, S.: Autophagy in infection, inflammation and immunity. Nat. Rev. Immunol. **13**(10), 722–737 (2013)

12. Weng, L., Liu, Q., Xia, M., et al.: Immune network-based swarm intelligence and its application to unmanned aerial vehicle swarm coordination. Neurocomputing **125**(125), 134–141 (2014)

13. He, X., Niyogi, P.: Locality preserving projections. Adv. Neural Inf. Process. Syst. **16**(1), 186–197 (2003)

14. Jadin, M.S., Taib, S.: Infrared image enhancement and segmentation for extracting the thermal anomalies in electrical equipment. Electron. Electr. Eng. **120**(4), 107–112 (2012)

15. Cárdenes, R., Bach, M., Chi, Y., Marras, I., de Luis, R., Anderson, M., Cashman, P., Bultelle, M.: Multimodal evaluation for medical image segmentation. In: Kropatsch, W.G., Kampel, M., Hanbury, A. (eds.) CAIP 2007. LNCS, vol. 4673, pp. 229–236. Springer, Heidelberg (2007). https://doi.org/10.1007/978-3-540-74272-2_29

16. Babalola, K.O., Patenaude, B., Aljabar, P., et al.: An evaluation of four automatic methods of segmenting the subcortical structures in the brain. Neuroimage **47**(4), 1435 (2009)

17. Tao, W.B., Jin, H., Liu, L.M.: Object segmentation using ant colony optimization algorithm and fuzzy entropy. Pattern Recogn. Lett. **28**(7), 788 (2007)

Motion Deblurring Based on Convolutional Neural Network

Yunfei Tan[1], Di Zhang[2], Fei Xu[2], and Danyang Zhang[2,3(✉)]

[1] Department of Physical Education,
Huazhong University of Science and Technology, Wuhan 430074, Hubei, China
276105832@qq.com

[2] Key Laboratory of Image Information Processing and Intelligent Control
of Education Ministry of China, School of Automation,
Huazhong University of Science and Technology, Wuhan 430074, Hubei, China
dizhang@hust.edu.cn, fei_xu@hust.edu.cn

[3] Department of Mathematics and Computer Science, York College,
City University of New York (CUNY), Jamaica, NY 11451, USA
dzhang@york.cuny.edu

Abstract. Object motion blur results when the object in the scene moves during the recording of a single exposure, either due to too rapid movement or long exposure, leaving streaks of the moving object in the image and thus degrading its quality. In this paper, we present a method to solve the object motion blur problem in images with clear static background. Specifically, we propose an object motion deblurring algorithm that uses a convolutional neural network with six convolutional layers to deblur the image. Taking advantages of the strong ability of feature learning in convolutional neural networks, our method can remove the blurring effect of fast-moving object while keeping the clear background untouched. It is well known that neural networks are best driven by large data sets and more data means more benefits for training convolutional neural networks; therefore, we generated training set of 144,000 images and test set of 32,400 images. Through carefully designed training process, our model learned the ability of deblurring the blurred object while keeping the clear background. The experiment results show that our approach can generate superior results to a representative image deblurring algorithm that treats the same blurred object and clear background.

Keywords: Convolutional neural network · Motion deblurring · Deep learning

1 Introduction

Image blur caused by relative motion between the camera and the object is called motion blur. There are primarily two types of motion blur, i.e., camera motion blur and object motion blur. Camera motion blur takes place when the camera moves (for any reason) during exposure process, making the whole image

© Springer Nature Singapore Pte Ltd. 2017
C. He et al. (Eds.): BIC-TA 2017, CCIS 791, pp. 623–635, 2017.
https://doi.org/10.1007/978-981-10-7179-9_49

blurred including both background and foreground objects. Object motion blur results when the object to be taken in the scene moves during the recording of a single exposure, either due to too rapid movement or long exposure, generating streaks of the moving object in the image. Note that object motion blur may not affect the background objects, i.e., the background is still clear, especially for static backgrounds. For example, in Fig. 1, a fast moving badminton creates blurring effect in the image with clear background either in lobby (Fig. 1(a)) or in kitchen (Fig. 1(b)).

(a) Blurred badminton I   (b) Blurred badminton II

Fig. 1. Blurred badminton with clear background

Motion blur can be modeled as convolution. Given a clear image $I(x, y)$ and a blur kernel $k(x, y)$, we can get blur image $f(x, y) = I(x, y) * k(x, y)$, where x is the height of the image, y is the width, and $*$ is a general convolution operator. We can obtain different kinds of motion blurred images by applying various blur kernels, e.g., Fig. 2 shows two types of motion blurred images generated by using two different blur kernels c and d, respectively.

If we assume that blur kernel is shift invariant (the same blur takes place regardless of the object location), this problem can be reduced to image deconvolution. Image deconvolution can be divided into non-blind deconvolution and blind deconvolution. If the blur kernel is known, the image blur problem can be solved by using non-blind deconvolution, e.g., we can use traditional methods to obtain the clear image, such as Weiner filter and Richardson-Lucy (RL) deconvolution [12,18]. In the case of blind deconvolution, i.e., the blur kernel is unknown and we reconstruct an image only by a single blurred image, this problem is more ill-posed than the non-blind deconvolution. Many researchers are concerned about this issue, and there are some methods proposed for the blind deconvolution [13,25].

If the blur kernel is not shift invariant, this problem is even more difficult than blind deconvolution [3,8]. For example, in Fig. 1, due to the rapid movement of the badminton, it is blurred in both images, but the backgrounds are still clear. Therefore, the blur kernel of the image changes with shifting. In order to detect and track the movement of badminton, the image needs to be deblurred. Dai and Wu proposed a two-layer model to remove partial blur from a single image

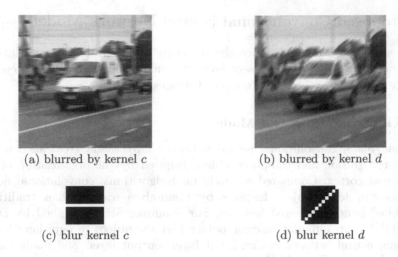

(a) blurred by kernel c (b) blurred by kernel d

(c) blur kernel c (d) blur kernel d

Fig. 2. Example of blurring image by different kernels.

by applying matting techniques [8], but their model requires a user assisted initialization step to start the whole process, thus it cannot deblur the image in a complete automatic manner.

Kim et al. investigated nonlinear camera response functions (CRFs) and showed how nonlinear CRFs can cause a shift invariant blur to behave as a shift variant blur [3]. They further introduced two methods to estimate the CRF directly from one or more blurred images to eventually deblur the images. Although their method is effective, it does not specifically handle the object motion blur with clear background problem. Pan et al. presented an algorithm to deblur images with outliers such as saturated pixels and non-Gaussian noise [14], which is opposite from the problem we are focusing on.

This paper mainly focuses on resolving object motion blur with clear background problem. Jia et al. presented a method to estimate the blur kernel and recover the clear image in 2008 and 2010, respectively [20,23]. Their paper is mainly based on the assumption that the blur kernel is shift-invariant, and their method is representative in effectively deblurring camera motion blurred images, but when it comes to reconstruct object motion blurred images with clear background, their method may not be effectual. We will show that our method outperforms Jia et al.'s method in Sect. 4.

This paper is organized as follows. In Sect. 2, we propose our convolutional neural network model and present how we generate blur kernels, training set, and test set. Section 3 shows how we train our neural network model such that it can learn how to deblur the blurred object and retain clear background. The experiment results are elaborated in Sect. 4, and the conclusion and future work are included in Sect. 5.

2   Proposed Convolutional Neural Network Model

In this section, we first introduce the structure of the proposed convolutional neural network model, then present how we generate different blur kernels, the training set of images, and the test set of images.

2.1   The Structure of Our Model

In recent years, convolutional neural networks have made great successes in pattern recognition and computer vision, inspired by the organization of primate visual cortex. Compared to traditional algorithms, convolutional neural networks can learn object features by themselves, rather than traditional algorithms' hand-engineered features. For example, SIFT designed by David Lowe [11] has to pinpoint interest points first for object recognition. A convolutional neural network has an input layer, output layer, and many hidden layers in between. These hidden layers may consist of convolutional layer, pooling layer, and/or fully connected layer.

The convolutional layer is the core of convolutional neural networks, which has the set of learnable kernels. In the forward pass, these kernels convolves with the input image, and will activate if detecting some specific features in the input image [10]. Unlike fully connected layer, convolutional layer can reduce the number of parameters, which allows convolutional neural networks to be deeper (in terms of number of layers) with fewer parameters and makes it easier for training a deep convolutional neural network.

The pooling layer consists of the neurons clustering at one layer into a single neuron in the next layer [1]. For example, max pooling only selects the maximum value from each cluster at the prior layer to be passed to the next layer; therefore, pooling will shrink the size of the input. In order to keep the image resolution, we do not use pooling layer in our model.

The structure of our convolutional neural network model contains six layers for image reconstruction purpose.

As shown in Fig. 3, the structure of our model is composed of feature extraction, non-linear mapping, and reconstruction parts. Input image size is 50 × 50 pixels. The layers Conv1, Conv2, Conv3 are used to extract features. In layer Conv1, there are 64 convolutional kernels. The size of each kernel is 7 × 7 pixels.

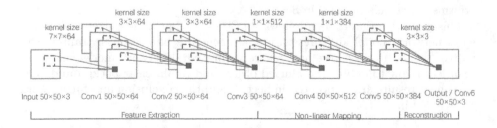

Fig. 3. The structure of our convolutional neural network model

In convolutional layers, we should note that if we have a 50×50 input image, and convolute with a 7×7 kernel, then there will be 44×44 neurons in the next hidden layer. To avoid the image resolution change, we apply a zero padding of size 3 as shown in Fig. 4. In other convolutional layers, we also use zero paddings to keep the spatial dimensions.

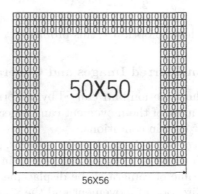

Fig. 4. Padding of size 3

The convolutional kernel size of Conv1, Conv2, Conv3 are $7 \times 7 \times 64$, $3 \times 3 \times 64$, $3 \times 3 \times 64$, respectively. The part of non-linear mapping includes two layers, i.e., Conv4 and Conv5, and their kernel sizes are $1 \times 1 \times 512$ and $1 \times 1 \times 384$, respectively. This part maps the blurred image to a clear image space. The layer of Conv6 reconstructs the image by $3 \times 3 \times 3$ convolutional kernel. Conv6 is like a mean filter that can sum up the images of Conv5, and then reconstruct the image. In order to keep image size the same, pooling layer is not applied. The stride of each layer in the model is set to 1.

The definition of our model is shown below. x_i represents the input image of the model, and y_i denotes label image. We choose the Euclidean loss as the loss function and $\sigma(x)$ as activate function. N is the batch size, which is set to 128. We assume that image deterioration model is $f(x)$, and our aim is to train a convolutional neural network $g(x_i; \theta) = f^{-1}$ to make $L(\theta)$ the smallest.

$$h_0 = x_i, h_l = \sigma(W_l \times h_{l-1} + b_l), l \in \{1, 2, 3, 4, 5, 6\},$$

$$L(\theta) = \frac{1}{2N} \sum_{i=1}^{N} \|g(x_i; \theta) - y_i\|_2^2,$$

where h_l means the intermediate result at the lth layer, b_l is the bias parameter, θ represents the weight parameter W and bias parameter b, and ELUS (Exponential Linear Units) [2] is used as the activate function, i.e.,

$$\sigma(x) = \begin{cases} x & \text{if } x > 0, \\ \alpha(exp(x) - 1) & \text{if } x \leq 0. \end{cases}$$

ELUS alleviates the vanishing gradient problem via the identity for positive values, and it leads not only to faster learning, but also to significantly better generalization performance than other activate functions [2].

In this way, the problem of motion deblurring can be modeled as optimizing:

$$\arg\min_{\theta} \frac{1}{2N} \sum_{i=1}^{N} ||g(x_i; \theta) - y_i||_2^2. \tag{1}$$

In Sect. 3, we will show how to optimize this problem.

2.2 Simulate Motion Blurred Images and Generate Blur Kernels

In all cases of motion blurs, motion blur caused by uniform rectilinear motion is more universal because most of the movement can be decomposed into uniform rectilinear motion under certain conditions.

We assume clear image $c(x, y)$ is moving along x-axis. $x(t_0)$ is the component in the horizontal direction and $y(t_0)$ is the component in the vertical direction. Let T be the exposure time of camera, L be displacement of images, and θ be the angle between the direction of movement and the x-axis. The blurred image can be written as

$$f(x, y) = \int_0^T c(x - x_0(t), y - y_0(t))dt.$$

If the image is only moving in x direction, the formula can be simplified as

$$f(x, y) = \int_0^T c(x - x_0(t), y)dt,$$

where

$$x_0(t) = \frac{S \times t}{T}.$$

The above equation is for continuous case, and the discrete case is

$$f(x, y) = \sum_{i=0}^{L} c(x - i, y)\Delta t,$$

where i is the distance of the image movement within Δt. On the other hand, motion blur is the superposition of the image after a series of moves. We can simulate motion blurred images by

$$f(x, y) = \frac{1}{L} \sum_{i=0}^{L-1} c(x - i, y).$$

If the direction of movement is not just horizontal. This formula is changed to

$$f(x, y) = \frac{1}{L} \sum_{i=0}^{L\cos(\theta)-1} \sum_{j=0}^{L\sin(\theta)-1} c(x - i, y - j).$$

Therefore, we can simulate motion blurred images by convolution

$$f(x, y) = c(x, y) * k(x, y),$$

where

$$k(x, y) = \begin{cases} \frac{1}{L} & \text{if } 0 \leqslant \sqrt{x^2 + y^2} \leqslant L, \frac{y}{x} = tan(\theta), \\ 0 & \text{otherwise.} \end{cases}$$

In our implementation, we discretize the range of motion orientation $[0, 180°]$ into 8 samples from $0°$ to $180°$ with interval of $22.5°$. The size of blur kernel is 11×11 pixels. We generate 8 kinds of blur kernels. In order to extend the blur kernel set, we resize the blur kernels from 8×8 to 15×15. This is equivalent to changing the motion length from 8 to 15. Longer the motion length is, the more blurred the image is, because in physics, the longer motion length represents the higher speed of object. Therefore, we obtain a blur kernel set S^k, which has 64 kinds of blur kernels that can represent most cases of motion (see Fig. 5).

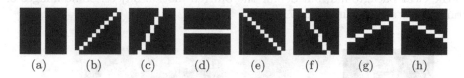

| (a) | (b) | (c) | (d) | (e) | (f) | (g) | (h) |

Fig. 5. The generated 8 kinds of blurred kernels

2.3   Generate Training Set and Test Set

Given the candidate motion kernel set S^k, we generate training set S^{train} and test set S^{test}. Our data set is from VOC2007 [5], which is used for object classification. Firstly, we randomly select 4000 images S^0 for our training set S^{train} and other 900 images S^1 for our test set S^{test} (all these are clear images). The size range of these images is from 300×300 to 500×500. In order to facilitate the processing of these pictures, we resize them all to 300×300. We divide S^0 evenly into two parts S^{0p} and S^{0q}, and each part has 2000 images. The operation for S^1 is the same as that to S^0, and we can get S^{0p} and S^{1p}. The next step is the most critical one, i.e., each image I in S^{0p} and S^{1p} convolves with a blur kernel k, which is randomly chosen from the above blur kernels, to generate blurred images S^{0b} and S^{1b}. That is, the blurred image $f = I * k$, where $f \in S^{0b}, S^{1b}$, $I \in S^{0p}, S^{1p}$, $k \in S^k$, and $*$ is the operation of convolution. The process of generating training set is shown in Fig. 6.

Now, S^{0b} has 2000 blurred images and S^{0q} has 2000 clear images. We combine S^{0b} and S^{0q} to become the input part of training set S^{train}, and the label part is the clear image set S^0. The same is applied to test set, i.e., the input part of test set consists of S^{1b} and S^{1q}, and the label part is S^1. Owing to the size of the input images of our model is 50×50, we have to decompose each image in training set S^{train} and test set S^{test} into patches of size 50×50.

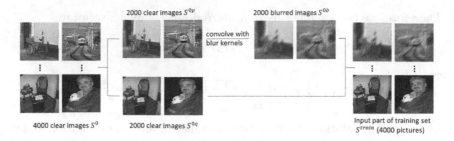

Fig. 6. The process of generating the input part of training set

Finally, the training set has 144,000 pictures, and test set has 32,400 pictures. The input images of both training set and test set are composed of blurred images and clear images. The purpose of using clear images in input part of training set and test set is to teach the proposed convolutional neural network to do nothing to the clear background, but deblur the blurred motion object. Some images of training set are shown in Fig. 7.

Fig. 7. Some images in training set before decomposed

3 Training Model

With the analysis in Sect. 2.1, our aim is to optimising the following problem:

$$\arg\min_{\theta} \frac{1}{2N} \sum_{i=1}^{N} ||g(x_i; \theta) - y_i||_2^2. \tag{2}$$

We use gradient descent algorithm [9] and backpropagation [19] to optimize our model. Backpropagation is an algorithm that is often used in artificial neural networks and can compute the gradient of each neuron after a batch of data. It can be written as the four formulae as below:

$$\delta^Q = \nabla_g L \odot \sigma'(z^Q),$$

$$\delta^q = ((\omega^{q+1})^T \delta^{q+1}) \odot \sigma'(z^q),$$

$$\frac{\partial L}{\partial b_j^q} = \delta_j^q,$$

$$\frac{\partial L}{\partial w_{jk}^q} = g_{q-1}^k \delta_j^q,$$

where δ^Q represents error in the output layer (the Qth layer), L denotes the loss function $\frac{1}{2N} \sum_{i=1}^N \|g(x_i; \theta) - y_i\|_2^2$, and g is output of the neural networks $g = \sigma(z^Q)$, $z = W \times x + b$, $\nabla_g L$ is defined as partial derivatives matrix $\frac{\partial L}{\partial g}$, $\odot$ means that the element-wise product of the two vectors, which is also called Hadamard product.

We can calculate the error contribution in each layer by

$$\delta^Q = \nabla_g L \odot \sigma'(z^Q),$$

$$\delta^q = ((\omega^{q+1})^T \delta^{q+1}) \odot \sigma'(z^q),$$

where q means qth layer. Then, we can compute $\frac{\partial L}{\partial b_j^q}$ and $\frac{\partial L}{\partial w_{jk}^q}$:

$$\frac{\partial L}{\partial b_j^q} = \delta_j^q,$$

$$\frac{\partial L}{\partial w_{jk}^q} = a_{q-1}^k \delta_j^q,$$

where w_{jk}^q is the weight between jth neuron in qth layer and kth neuron in $(q-1)$th layer. Finally, the parameters can be updated by

$$w^{new} = w - \eta \frac{\partial L}{\partial w},$$

$$b^{new} = b - \eta \frac{\partial L}{\partial b},$$

where η is the learning rate.

In our experiment, the learning rate is initialized to 0.003, and attenuates 0.96 per 100,000 iterations. Training results of convolutional neural network are influenced by initialization method, and we initialize parameters by Xavier [6]. The training loss curve shows (see Fig. 8) that the model converges after 300,000 iterations.

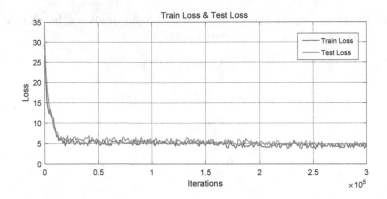

Fig. 8. Train and test loss curve

4   Experiment Results

The experiment results are shown in Fig. 9, where the left image is the blurred image, the middle image is the result that is generated by using Jia et al.'s method, and the right image is generated by using our method.

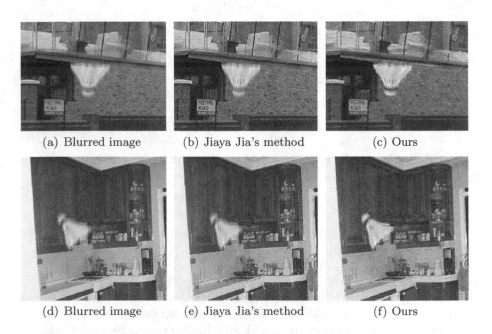

(a) Blurred image   (b) Jiaya Jia's method   (c) Ours

(d) Blurred image   (e) Jiaya Jia's method   (f) Ours

Fig. 9. Experiment results of deblurring

To evaluate the quality of image reconstruction, we use mean squared error (MSE):

$$MSE = \frac{1}{MN} \sum_{x=0}^{M-1} \sum_{y=0}^{N-1} [f(x,y) - \hat{f}(x,y)]^2,$$

where M is the height of the image and N is the width, $x \in M$, $y \in N$.

If the parts need not to be changed such as the clear background, then the smaller the MSE is, the better the algorithm performs in keeping the clear background untouched. We choose some patches of background in these pictures and calculate MSE to compare the ability of these two algorithms to retain the clear background. These patches are shown in Fig. 10, and the results of MSE are shown in Table 1.

From the results, we can draw a conclusion that the method proposed in [20,23] has no effect on the object motion blurred images because the blurred kernel of the image is not shift invariant, and our method can remove the object motion blur, and in the mean time keep the static background unchanged.

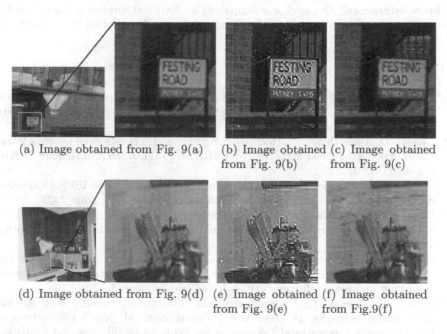

(a) Image obtained from Fig. 9(a)   (b) Image obtained from Fig. 9(b)   (c) Image obtained from Fig. 9(c)

(d) Image obtained from Fig. 9(d)   (e) Image obtained from Fig. 9(e)   (f) Image obtained from Fig.9(f)

Fig. 10. Comparison of the ability of retaining clear background

Table 1. Results of MSE

Fig. 10	(a) & (b)	(a) & (c)	(d) & (e)	(d) & (f)
MSE	386.662	62.1745	400.229	48.796

5   Conclusion and Future Work

This paper proposed a convolutional neural network model to deblur the object motion blurred images with clear background. Our convolutional neural network model contains six convolutional layers and has been demonstrated to be effective in learning the ability of deblurring the fast-moving object while retaining the clear background.

In the future, we will further improve our model and compare its performance with some deblurring algorithms that are based on shift variant blur kernels.

Recently, spiking neural P systems, as a member of spiking neural networks of the third generation, were proposed and investigated [7,15,22]. Spiking neural P systems have powerful computation power in the sense that they are Turing universal even consisting of a few neurons (or membranes) [16,21,24]. Spiking neural P systems have already been used for image processing [4,17]. As a future research line, it deserves to investigate the potential of spiking neural P systems used to deblur the object motion blurred images with clear background.

Acknowledgments. The work was supported by National Natural Science Foundation of China (61502186) and China Postdoctoral Science Foundation (2016M592335).

References

1. Ciregan, D., Meier, U., Schmidhuber, J.: Multi-column deep neural networks for image classification. In: 2012 IEEE Conference on Computer Vision and Pattern Recognition, pp. 3642–3649, June 2012
2. Clevert, D., Unterthiner, T., Hochreiter, S.: Fast and accurate deep network learning by exponential linear units (ELUs). CoRR abs/1511.07289 (2015). http://arxiv.org/abs/1511.07289
3. Dai, S., Wu, Y.: Removing partial blur in a single image. In: 2009 IEEE Conference on Computer Vision and Pattern Recognition, pp. 2544–2551, June 2009
4. Díaz-Pernil, D., Peña-Cantillana, F., Gutiérrez-Naranjo, M.A.: A parallel algorithm for skeletonizing images by using spiking neural P systems. Neurocomputing **115**, 81–91 (2013)
5. Everingham, M., Van Gool, L., Williams, C.K.I., Winn, J., Zisserman, A.: The PASCAL visual object classes challenge 2007 (VOC2007) results. http://www.pascal-network.org/challenges/VOC/voc2007/workshop/index.html
6. Glorot, X., Bengio, Y.: Understanding the difficulty of training deep feedforward neural networks. In: Teh, Y.W., Titterington, M. (eds.) Proceedings of the Thirteenth International Conference on Artificial Intelligence and Statistics. Proceedings of Machine Learning Research, vol. 9, pp. 249–256. PMLR, Chia Laguna Resort, Sardinia, Italy, 13–15 May 2010. http://proceedings.mlr.press/v9/glorot10a.html
7. Ionescu, M., Păun, G., Yokomori, T.: Spiking neural P systems. Fund. Inform. **71**(2–3), 279–308 (2006)
8. Kim, S., Tai, Y.W., Kim, S.J., Brown, M.S., Matsushita, Y.: Nonlinear camera response functions and image deblurring. In: 2012 IEEE Conference on Computer Vision and Pattern Recognition, pp. 25–32, June 2012

9. Kingma, D.P., Ba, J.: Adam: A method for stochastic optimization. CoRR abs/1412.6980 (2014). http://arxiv.org/abs/1412.6980

10. Lecun, Y., Bottou, L., Bengio, Y., Haffner, P.: Gradient-based learning applied to document recognition. Proc. IEEE **86**(11), 2278–2324 (1998)

11. Lindeberg, T.: Scale invariant feature transform. Scholarpedia **7**(5), 10491 (2012). revision # 153939

12. Lucy, L.B.: An iterative technique for the rectification of observed distributions. Astron. J. **79**, 745 (1974)

13. Moghaddam, M.E., Jamzad, M.: Linear motion blur parameter estimation in noisy images using fuzzy sets and power spectrum. EURASIP J. Adv. Sig. Process. **2007**(1), 068985 (2006). http://dx.doi.org/10.1155/2007/68985

14. Pan, J., Lin, Z., Su, Z., Yang, M.: Robust kernel estimation with outliers handling for image deblurring. In: 2016 IEEE Conference on Computer Vision and Pattern Recognition, pp. 2800–2808, June 2016

15. Pan, L., Păun, G., Zhang, G., Neri, F.: Spiking neural P systems with communication on request (2017). http://dx.doi.org/10.1142/S0129065717500423

16. Păun, A., Păun, G.: Small universal spiking neural P systems. BioSystems **90**(1), 48–60 (2007)

17. Peng, H., Wang, J., Pérez-Jiménez, M.J., Shi, P.: A novel image thresholding method based on membrane computing and fuzzy entropy. J. Intell. Fuzzy Syst. **24**(2), 229–237 (2013)

18. Richardson, W.H.: Bayesian-based iterative method of image restoration∗. J. Opt. Soc. Am. **62**(1), 55–59 (1972). http://www.osapublishing.org/abstract.cfm?URI=josa-62-1-55

19. Rumelhart, D.E., Hinton, G.E., Williams, R.J.: Learning representations by back-propagating errors. Nature **323**(6088), 533–536 (1986)

20. Shan, Q., Jia, J., Agarwala, A.: High-quality motion deblurring from a single image. ACM Trans. Graph. **27**(3), 73:1–73:10 (2008). http://doi.acm.org/10.1145/1360612.1360672

21. Wu, T., Păun, A., Zhang, Z., Pan, L.: Spiking neural P systems with polarizations. IEEE Trans. Neural Netw. Learn. Syst. (2017). http://dx.doi.org/10.1109/TNNLS.2017.2726119

22. Wu, T., Zhang, Z., Păun, G., Pan, L.: Cell-like spiking neural P systems. Theor. Comput. Sci. **623**, 180–189 (2016)

23. Xu, L., Jia, J.: Two-phase kernel estimation for robust motion deblurring. In: Daniilidis, K., Maragos, P., Paragios, N. (eds.) ECCV 2010. LNCS, vol. 6311, pp. 157–170. Springer, Heidelberg (2010). https://doi.org/10.1007/978-3-642-15549-9_12

24. Zhang, X., Pan, L., Păun, A.: On the universality of axon P systems. IEEE Trans. Neural Netw. Learn. Syst. **26**(11), 2816–2829 (2015)

25. Zhu, X., Šroubek, F., Milanfar, P.: Deconvolving PSFs for a better motion deblurring using multiple images. In: Fitzgibbon, A., Lazebnik, S., Perona, P., Sato, Y., Schmid, C. (eds.) ECCV 2012. LNCS, vol. 7576, pp. 636–647. Springer, Heidelberg (2012). https://doi.org/10.1007/978-3-642-33715-4_46

Author Index

Printed in the United States
By Bookmasters